CRIMINOLOGY
AND CRIME

CRIMINOLOGY AND CRIME

An Introduction

Harold J. Vetter
Ira J. Silverman
University of South Florida

HARPER & ROW, PUBLISHERS, New York
Cambridge, Philadelphia, San Francisco, London,
Mexico City, São Paulo, Singapore, Sydney

1817

PHOTO CREDITS

Chapter 1: From H. Gottesfeld, *Abnormal Psychology.* Chicago: Science Research Associates, 1979, p. 282. Reproduced by permission of SRA / *Chapter 2:* Rick Simonsen, Seattle / *Chapter 3:* Richard L. Roe (Publisher), *Society Today.* Del Mar, CA: CRM Books, 1971, p. 416 / *Chapter 4:* Doug Malin, *Spring 3100* Magazine / *Chapters 5 and 6:* U.S. Department of Justice, Federal Bureau of Investigation / *Chapter 7:* Daplan, DPI / *Chapter 8:* Jay Robert Nash, *Look for the Woman.* New York: M. Evans and Company, 1981, p. 41 / *Chapter 9: Crimes and Punishment: A Pictorial Encyclopedia of Aberrant Behavior.* New York: BPC Publishing Limited and Credit Sources, Inc., 1974, p. 106 / *Chapter 10:* Steve Eagle, Transaction / *Chapter 11:* Charles Gatewood, Magnum / *Chapter 12:* Stock, Boston / *Chapter 13:* National Council of Juvenile and Family Court Judges, Reno, NV / *Chapter 14:* Misha Erwitt, Magnum / *Chapter 15:* Benjamin Kleinmuntz, *Fundamentals of Abnormal Psychology,* Harper & Row, 1974, p. 101 / *Chapter 16:* Brody, Stock, Boston / *Chapter 17:* West, Photo Trends / *Chapter 18:* Drug Enforcement Agency News, Washington, D.C. / *Chapter 19:* South Carolina Department of Corrections, Columbia, SC

Sponsoring Editor: Alan McClare
Project Editor: Brigitte Pelner
Cover Design: Betty Sokol
Text Art: Reproduction Drawings, Ltd.
Production: Debra Forrest
Compositor: Donnelley/Rocappi, Inc.
Printer and Binder: R. R. Donnelley & Sons Company

CRIMINOLOGY AND CRIME: *An Introduction*

Library of Congress Cataloging in Publication Data

Vetter, Harold J., 1926-

    Criminology and crime.

    Includes bibliographies and index.
    1. Crime and criminals. 2. Crime and criminals—
United States. I. Silverman, Ira J. II. Title.
HV6025.V46 1986   364   85-27116
ISBN 0–06–046833–5

86 87 88 89 9 8 7 6 5 4 3 2 1

CONTENTS

part four: THE ADMINISTRATION OF JUSTICE   431

PREFACE

This book explores the fascinating field of contemporary criminology. It assumes no specialized knowledge or background; all that is taken for granted is an interest on the part of the reader in learning more about the ways in which criminologists study crime, criminals, criminal behavior, and the criminal justice system. It represents the shared convictions of a psychologist and a sociologist that pooling the insights of two disciplines provides a broader perspective on crime and criminology than is afforded by a single discipline.

The book consists of four parts:

Part One: Criminology and the Study of Crime
Part Two: Patterns of Criminal Behavior
Part Three: Theoretical Perspectives on Crime and Criminality
Part Four: The Administration of Justice

Part One offers a view of criminal behavior and its systematic study within contemporary criminology. The opening chapter explores some of the ways in which societies attempt to contain and control deviance by means of sanctions ranging from informal disapproval to the use of the police powers of the state. Antisocial attitudes, conduct norm violations, eccentricities, odd behavior—all of these are useful in shedding light on criminal conduct and its causes. Chapter 2 provides a critical examination of the raw materials on which criminological research is based: data which come from a variety of sources within the criminal justice system, including federal, state, and local crime reports, and from victimization surveys, cohort studies, and investigations of self-reported crime and delinquency. Chapter 3 focuses on the techniques and approaches used by criminologists in their work and introduces the student to the relationship between criminological theory and research.

Part Two outlines the major patterns of criminal behavior. Each of the chapters in this section supplies the latest empirical data on the extent of various crimes, as well as specific approaches by the criminal justice system toward the control, reduction, elimination, and prevention of these crimes.

In Part Three, beginning with the historical background of criminological theory, various approaches to the explanation of crime and criminality in contemporary criminology are examined in breadth and depth. Economic conditions and their relationship to criminality are dealt with in detail. Radical and critical criminology are discussed, along with the impact of economic factors on crime rates, and attention is given to the new and growing use of econometric models in criminological theory and research.

The contributions of sociology are covered in three chapters: sociological theories of criminality, sociopsychological theories, and the labeling perspective. We should like to emphasize that these chapters go beyond a mere description of the various approaches and make a real effort to discuss the interrelationships among theories and theorists and the strengths and weaknesses of the respective approaches.

In the chapter on psychiatric and psychological theories of criminality, we stress the point that basic differences exist between these approaches—differences which are often blurred or even ignored in many texts, leaving the reader with the erroneous impression that the two approaches are identical. The following chapter pursues the topic of biological factors in criminality and reviews recent research and theorizing in this area.

The agencies and institutions of the criminal justice system are described and analyzed in Part Four. Our concern here is not with the operational aspects of the administration of justice, which is a task for an introductory text in criminal justice, but rather with some of the topics that engage the interest of criminologists. Is there such an entity as a "police personality" and, if so, how can it be identified? How scientific are "scientific" jury selection methods? Are less-than-unanimous verdicts in felony trials consistent with due process and equal protection under the law? Is parole headed for extinction? These are some of the questions for which answers are sought in research by criminologists.

In the Epilogue which concludes this book, we have focused on a number of problems and issues that confront our society in its efforts to deal with the impact of crime. The costs of imprisoning offenders make it increasingly prohibitive to confine any but criminals with a history of violent offenses. However, the public perception that rehabilitating criminals is beyond the skills of correctional science and technology tends to provide grudging support for a return to punishment as the proper goal of the criminal justice system. Deeply embedded in this controversy over the disposition of criminals are fundamental differences in moral, religious, political, and philosophical beliefs which baffle the best-intentioned efforts to find simple answers for complex questions. We hope that our discussion helps to place some of these issues and problems in proper perspective.

The authors wish to acknowledge their indebtedness to Dr. Simon Dinitz and to Dr. Reed Adams for their comprehensive, critical, and helpful reviews. Ira Silverman would like to give special thanks to Dr. Dinitz—mentor, scholar, and friend—who contributed significantly to his graduate education and has continued to be a role model during his career. To Alan McClare, editor, and Brigitte Pelner, project editor, of Harper & Row we extend our warmest appreciation for their expertise, interest, and concern for the progress of the manuscript.

We are deeply grateful to Fran Hartl and Happy (Jane) Silverman for their love, support, and assistance throughout the preparation of the text. Without their extraordinary forbearance and unflagging support during the six years this book was in preparation, the project would never have reached completion. It is to them that we dedicate this book.

Harold J. Vetter
Ira J. Silverman

ONE

CRIMINOLOGY AND THE STUDY OF CRIME

When people read about crime in their daily newspapers or watch the television coverage of crimes on the evening news, their interest is likely to be rather general. They may be curious about what occurred, the identities of the criminal and the victim, whether or not a suspect was arrested, and what will happen to the person or persons accused of the crime. If the offense was unusual or shocking enough to arouse feelings of outrage and indignation, they may express concern over what society can do to reduce or prevent the occurrence of such crimes.

Criminologists are also interested in the details of crime events, in the characteristics of offenders and victims, and in the disposition of criminals and treatment of victims as part of the administration of justice. The concerns of the criminologist, however, go beyond description and disposition to deal with the *explanation* of criminal behavior. Criminologists study crime, criminals, and criminal behavior with the aim of achieving a scientific understanding of these phenomena. In recent years they have also devoted considerable attention to the criminal justice system and its operations as a potential contributor to the causes of crime.

The work done by criminologists has qualities which resemble those that characterize the efforts of other scientists: the precise statement and definition of terms; collection of systematic, objective observations under controlled conditions; the use of quantification in the description and analysis of results; and concern for the verification and reproducibility of findings. Like most scientists, criminologists hope their achievements will eventually prove to have useful applications. However, they feel the question of immediate practical application of results should not be allowed to dictate the direction of their research at the present time and at the current level of development in criminology. Some criminologists who teach believe the curricula they offer should serve as professional preparation for persons intending to work in the criminal justice system. Also, some see their discipline as having a clear responsibility to contribute to the improvement of the criminal justice system.

Laws are formal statements of some of the rules considered most fundamental to the continued existence and well-being of society and its members. Laws are enacted by the authority of legislative bodies and are codified in statutory form. Conformity is encouraged and deviation discouraged by the *penal sanction,* meaning the power of the state to invoke a variety of punitive actions, ranging from small fines and incarceration for a brief period of time to lengthy imprisonment and even capital punishment. In theory, laws apply equally to all members of our society; in practice, laws may exhibit many inequities in their application.

Crimes are considered offenses against the state; they are distinguished from *torts,* or private wrongs, for which redress may be sought through civil courts. Crimes are categorized by severity or seriousness into felonies and misdemeanors. Felonies are the more serious crimes, generally punishable by incarceration in a state prison for a term of one or more years; misdemeanors may be dealt with by fines or by sentences of up to one year in a county jail. Offenses may otherwise be classified into crimes against person, crimes against property, public order offenses, and political crimes. Criminologists have devised other *typologies* based on characteristics of the offender, rather than the crime, as part of the effort to seek underlying patterns of similarity and consistency that may be linked to causes of crime.

Conduct regarded as criminal varies considerably according to time and place, and it is nearly impossible to identify any type of behavior, no matter how extreme, that has been considered criminal in all societies and in every period for which we have an historical record. Cannibalism, incest, parricide, and infanticide have been positively sanctioned at various times within some cultures. At the present time in our own society, large numbers of people support the contention that such forms of behavior as gambling, prostitution, consensual adult homosexuality, and the consumption of marijuana should be exempt from legal sanctions (decriminalized) and left to individual discretion or, at worst, subjected to the disapproval and moral sanctions of the groups of which the individual is a member.

The actual amount of crime that occurs in our society—the *dark figure* of crime, as it is called—is unknown. Crime is exceedingly difficult to measure accurately because stealth and secrecy are among its basic characteristics. Offenders are not likely to identify themselves to a census taker or the Internal Revenue Service as robbers or burglars. Consensual crimes such as prostitution, where the "victim" is a satisfied customer, have little chance of appearing in the official crime statistics. Still other crimes such as embezzlement may never be reported to the police because the embezzler arranges to make restitution or the firm prefers to accept the loss rather than risk possible embarrassment or a steep increase in insurance rates.

Crime can be counted officially at the national level by means of documents like the *Uniform Crime Reports,* which are published annually by the U.S. Department of Justice, and by some states.

Although we depend upon the federal *UCR* as a principal source of criminal justice information, it is necessary when using this document to be aware of the shortcomings and limitations in the reporting procedures by which the *UCR* is compiled. These shortcomings impose constraints on the kinds of conclusions and generalizations that can be made from the information summarized in the *UCR.*

Official information on crime can be supplemented by unofficial data sources, such as cohort analysis, a research technique which involves following the members of a group who meet some common criterion (birth date, type of offense, parole release date) for a period of time usually measured in years in order to observe developmental changes in these individuals; victimization studies, in which selected persons are interviewed for purposes of determining whether they have been victims of crimes and, if so, the nature and extent of the crime and its consequences; and self-report studies, which ask selected groups of people to indicate offenses they may have committed, regardless of whether or not these crimes have been officially reported.

It should be noted that crime statistics serve many important purposes. They provide the public and the government with a perspective on the nature and extent of crime and its trends over time. Current statistics are essential for planning because they form the basis for future projections of crime. They affect the budgets of criminal justice agencies, and they have an impact on law and public policy decisions. For these and additional reasons, concern over accurate crime statistics is shared by criminal justice authorities and criminologists.

Scientific and technological accomplishments in the physical sciences have both enriched our lives and supplied the means for our self-destruction. Social and behavioral scientists believe the same methods of scientific inquiry that led to the discovery of antibiotics and the principles which underwrote the construction of the hydrogen bomb can help to solve social problems. Research is concerned with exploration, discovery, systematic observation, collection of data, and the testing of ideas in the real world. Theory is devoted to matters of explanation and interpretation, to ideas and hypotheses, and to the construction of a logical framework for fitting together the facts disclosed by research in order to determine what they mean. In addition, its task is to guide research into new and fruitful paths of exploration. Research and theory are inseparable partners: research without theory is like groping in the dark and theory without research is sterile.

Research in criminology consists largely of trying to find valid and reliable answers to questions about crime, criminals, criminal behavior, and the functioning of the criminal justice system through the application of systematic methods of inquiry. "What kinds of criminal offenses are committed most frequently by women?" "Do incarcerated felons show a higher incidence of psychiatric disorders than people of comparable age and personality characteristics in the general population?" "What are some of the major factors that affect sentencing decisions in cases of assaultive violence?" These questions are typical of those which engage the efforts of criminologists.

Specific research designs are dictated to a considerable extent by the kinds of information the investigator is seeking. *Archival research* uses documents, manuscripts, and records to help trace the influence of past events on present phenomena. *Descriptive research* uses such instruments as interviews, questionnaires, attitude scales, checklists, and inventories to gather meaningful data on crime-related topics in a variety of institutional settings. *Experimental* and *quasi-experimental* research involve attempts to assess the effect of a particular variable by subjecting it to manipulation under controlled conditions. This is the most exacting type of research in the scientific tradition, but its use in criminology is limited by ethical, as well as practical, considerations.

All research does not begin as an attempt to test some formal theory. Much valuable work of exploration and discovery in criminology has originated in the disciplined curiosity of investigators who sought to conduct a more precise measurement of some phenomenon or pursue an intriguing relationship between two variables. Nevertheless, the construction of theories and their continual reexamination and modification in the light of new information from research are two of the features which most clearly distinguish criminologists from other professionals in their approach to understanding crime.

chapter 1

CRIME, LAW, AND CRIMINOLOGY

Few social problems can stir up as much controversy as crime. From the nature of crime and its causes to how to deal with offenders, nearly every aspect of the crime problem arouses disagreement and contention. Crime is an emotionally charged topic, and public attitudes toward lawbreakers are deeply divided. An understandable desire for vengeance and concern for the prevention of further crimes are in conflict with humanitarian impulses and liberal social philosophies.

Fear of crime is widespread in American society. No one can be sure of the exact figures, but it has been estimated (Wright and Rossi, 1982) that there are approximately 120 million privately owned guns in this country and that someone has used a gun in self-defense at some time or other in about 15 percent of all gun-owning households. As public confidence in the ability of the criminal justice system to deal effectively with crime has diminished, a corresponding growth can be charted in the sales of police whistles, deadbolts, intricate locks and latches, attack dogs, and training courses in the martial arts. When viewed in relation to this level of fear and apprehension, the instant popularity of Bernhard Goetz (see "The Subway Vigilante" this chapter) is easy to understand. Private security has become a multibillion-dollar business that employs a larger work force than public law enforcement agencies (Bilek, 1977; LEAA, 1978; Cunningham and Taylor, 1984).

Is the public justified in this much concern over crime? This is a simple question to ask, but one that is exceedingly difficult to answer. Social reality is largely what a society believes about itself. If the members of a society believe themselves to be unsafe from crime in their homes, places of work or business, or in public areas, then those feelings of apprehensiveness and insecurity become an important part of the social reality that shapes their perceptions. By that standard, we are a society which sees itself as beleaguered by crime.

If crime in the United States is really as prevalent as these views seem to suggest, we ought to be among the world's best-informed people on the topic of crime. There are times when this appears to be true. When the cast of a popular television series kept referring to an obvious case of breaking and entering as a "robbery" on one of the episodes, thousands of indignant television viewers called or wrote to their local stations to point out the error. On the other hand, this might only prove that the public is better informed about crime than are some television script writers.

WHAT IS CRIME?

Legal authorities may find it sufficient to define a crime as "any social harm defined and made punishable by law" (Perkins, 1966), but criminologists are apt to find fault with definitions of this sort. For one thing, *crime is relative,* that is, the kinds of behavior covered by laws and statutes are not fixed and unchanging but vary according to time, place, and circumstances. For example, what the law says is illegal today may not be the same as what it said was illegal yesterday or may say is illegal tomorrow. Moreover, legal definitions prove unduly restrictive because they limit the study of criminal behavior to those persons who have been officially adjudicated criminal or delinquent; hence, a great deal of behavior potentially relevant to understanding and explaining criminality might never be examined.

The Subway Vigilante

Three days before Christmas in 1984. in a New York City subway car, a 37-year-old electronics technician named Bernhard Goetz shot four youths who had tried to shake him down for money. When they approached Goetz in a rowdy and intimidating manner (according to witnesses) and asked him for $5, he replied, "I have $5 for each of you," and fired five bullets from an unlicensed .38 caliber handgun, wounding all four, two of them in the back. One of the four, Darryl Cabey, aged 19, who was shot in the spine and is paralyzed from the waist down, lapsed into a coma and was listed in critical condition. Goetz fled Manhattan and drove to Concord, New Hampshire, where he turned himself in to the police a few days later. While the first New York grand jury that heard the case only indicted Goetz for illegal weapons possession, a second grand jury, after hearing new evidence, indicted him on four counts of attempted murder, four counts of assault, one count of reckless endangerment, and one count of possessing a weapon with the intent to use it.

Almost immediately—and perhaps inevitably—the media dubbed Goetz the "subway vigilante." Goetz is white and the youths he shot were black, but opinions about Goetz's actions did not split entirely along racial lines. Roy Innis, chairman of the Congress on Racial Equality, called Goetz "the avenger for all of us" and offered to raise money for his defense. On the other hand, Jimmy Breslin—a New York *Daily News* columnist who is white—attacked Goetz in print for racism.

People who ride the New York subway daily and can readily identify with Goetz's fear and frustration—he had been mugged four years earlier and had brooded ever since over the lenient treatment his attackers received in a New York court—were quick to applaud his actions. President Reagan sympathized with public frustration about crime but deplored their readiness to take the law into their own hands. But this is precisely the issue that Goetz's exercise in freelance law enforcement dramatizes: If the "state of nature" has returned to our big cities, can people be blamed for resorting to violence in order to spare themselves from becoming victims of violence?

It is unfortunate that Goetz should have been labeled a vigilante, because the choice of terms is especially inappropriate. The term *vigilante,* as Richard Maxwell Brown (1969) points out in his thoughtful study of vigilantism in American history, has referred to a member of a vigilance committee—a group of people organized without legal authority to keep order and punish criminals when conventional law enforcement agencies fail to do so. Vigilantism, says Brown, is "a violent sanctification of the deeply cherished values of life and property" (p. 139). Vigilantism is a collective response which has a mandate, of sorts, from those whom it purports to protect. Goetz's action as an avenger, however, has more in common with those portrayed by Charles Bronson in the movie *Death Wish.* Until more is known about Bernhard Goetz, many people are unwilling to stereotype him as either a folk hero or a pistol-packing psychopath.

While recognizing the necessity on legal grounds for dealing with crime as law-violating behavior, criminal justice professionals and criminologists find it worthwhile to consider criminal conduct as part of a much broader spectrum of **deviant behavior.** Deviance involves behavior that varies or diverges from social norms—the rules which help to regulate conduct within a group or society. Most people tend to be "socially invisible" within their communities. Deviance means, among other things, that an individual or group becomes visible to the majority when the deviant behavior elicits societal reactions.

NORMS AND SOCIALIZATION

People are born into an ongoing society that has rules to regulate the conduct of its members. These rules, or *norms,* may be simple or elaborate, but their purpose is the same: to protect the society against disruption and to safeguard its basic structure and values. We internalize these norms through the process of complex social learning which sociologists and psychologists refer to as **socialization.**

The principal agent of socialization, and the basic unit of society, is the family. Much of the culture is transmitted to the child by means of the informal learning that takes place within the family. Speech patterns, customs or folkways, and social values are acquired through communication between the generations. As the individual develops and matures, peer group associations tend to assume increasing importance in the socialization process. They may become a source of sharp conflict with parental norms, especially during the adolescent years.

Informal learning of the kind the individual receives in interactions with family and peer group members is supplemented by the formal learning the school provides. As an agency of socialization, the school ranks almost as high as the family and peer groups as the medium through which society perpetuates itself in the socialization process.

Social Sanctions

Norms are originally acquired and then maintained by means of rewards and punishments. When children do something of which their parents approve, they may be rewarded by a smile, caress, murmur of praise, or the tangible reward of candy, cookies, or even spending money. When children behave in ways disapproved of by the parents, they may incur some sort of punishment, ranging from a scolding to physical chastisement.

Rewards and punishments are incorporated into the normative structure as **social sanctions.** Sanctions may contain **proscriptive** or **prescriptive** elements. Proscriptions are statements of behavior that is forbidden (e.g., murder, rape, kidnapping, treason, and other forms of rebellion against group authority). Prescriptions are statements of behavior that is encouraged or reinforced (e.g., getting married, raising children, holding a steady job, paying taxes, and other forms of conduct that may foster the society's common welfare). Perhaps it will help us to understand how the operation of social sanctions promotes "proper" behavior if we conceive of social behavior as the kind of continuum depicted in Figure 1.1. Behavior toward the center of the continuum is controlled by social norms which the anthropologist or sociologist calls *folkways.* Enforcement of these customary ways of behaving is usually accomplished by *mild disapproval* (a cold stare, raised eyebrows, a reproving glance) or by *mild encouragement* (smile, applause, an approving glance). Behavior that threatens the existence of the group or is seen as necessary to the perpetuation of the group is controlled by a set of stronger norms called *mores,* which are enforced by more rigorous or severe expressions of social disapproval (verbal abuse, beatings, temporary ostracism) or by greater encouragement (monetary rewards, praise, testimonials, promotions).

Normative Variation

Norms do not supply a blueprint for behavior but only a rough sketch at best. As Williams (1970) has pointed out, "The institutionalized norms of social conduct never fully define concrete action. A norm is a standard (not necessarily explicit) for the course that action *should* follow, not a description of the action that actually occurs" (p. 413). Norms are general, while the situational contexts within which behavior occurs are specific; hence, considerable variability in behavior can occur around a standard.

It must also be noted that modern societies are composed of diverse subcultures with varying normative standards. Much of the behavior that deviates from presumably general or universal norms actually involves the conflict of subcultural norms.

SOCIAL VALUES AND LAW

In primitive or preliterate societies, rules governing normative behavior are perpetuated by word of mouth and passed from leader to leader. Eventually normative expectations can evolve into formal statements of proper behavior that are codified in written form as **laws.** These formal statements are likely to represent an expression of the most important values of a society at a given time. Things having social value include objects, conditions, or states which are considered desirable and good and for which people are willing to expend time and energy to own or achieve.

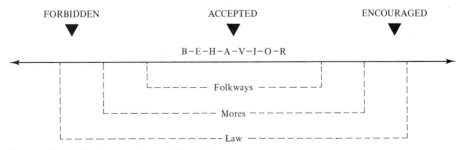

Figure 1.1 Continuum of social behavior.

Value-Consensus and Value-Conflict Models of Law

The nature of the relationship between social values and laws has been interpreted in sharply differing terms by the proponents of two positions that may be designated the **value-consensus** and **value-conflict** models. As Cole (1983) indicates, the basic premise of the value-consensus position is that the criminal law reflects societal values which "go beyond the immediate interests of particular groups and individuals and are thus an expression of the social consciousness of the whole society" (p. 92). According to this perspective, law develops through the efforts of a unified society to protect important social values from serious harm. To accomplish this purpose, it relies on the deliberations and rational decisions of governing bodies such as congresses or parliaments which incorporate the principal authority of the society (Hall, 1947).

In contrast, the value-conflict model views society as characterized by dissension rather than consensus, diversity rather than homogeneity, and perennial struggle for power. In the opinion of Chambliss (1973):

> Conventional myths notwithstanding, the history of criminal law is *not* a history of public opinion or public interest being reflected in criminal law legislation. On the contrary, the history of the criminal law is everywhere the history of legislation and appellate-court decisions which in effect (if not in intent) reflect the interests of the economic elites who control the production and distribution of the major resources of the society [p. 430].

Economic power bestows political power, a fact of life that has long been recognized in a wry twist on the Golden Rule: "Them that has the gold makes the rules." According to the conflict model, "the rules" (i.e., the law) become a tool of the dominant class in order to maintain and enhance its power over the weak. Law is used by the state "and its elitist government to promote and protect itself" (Quinney, 1974, p. 24). One of the ways this is done through the criminal law is by means of control over the processes of enforcement so that certain groups are singled out for labeling and stigmatization as "criminals" and "members of the dangerous classes."

It is difficult to accept either the consensus or conflict model as an exclusively accurate characterization of the social processes underlying the development of criminal law. Despite Quinney's assertion that the standards for what ought to be considered criminal conduct are a reflection of various group and class definitions, it seems probable that consensus on *crimes against the person* cuts across class lines in our society. Disagreement is more likely to be found with regard to laws that proscribe gambling, prostitution, and homosexual behavior between consenting adults—the kinds of offenses that are often designated "victimless crimes."

A Value-Divergence Model

An alternative position, which can be identified as a **value-divergence** model, recognizes the contributions of both the value-conflict and value-consensus models to an understanding of criminal law development. It emphasizes that the United States is not a cultural monolith but a mosaic composed of many diverse subcultures held together by certain shared beliefs and social values. These are stronger in the aggregate than are the forces of divisiveness. Seldom in this pluralistic society of ours can any body of statutes claim the support and allegiance of a majority of social groups.

Political scientist Stanley J. Makielski, in *Pressure Politics in America* (1980), deals with the processes by which an *interest group* ("a collection of more than two people who interact on the basis of a commonly shared concern," p. 17) is transformed into a *pressure group* that turns to the political system to press its demands. Interests "are the cement that binds a group together and the motivating power which impels a group into politics" (p. 21); and these interests—economic, social, or ideological—are the basis for structuring the kinds of policy concerns that characterize various groups. More importantly, the various ways by which pressure groups "gain access" through persuasion, mutual interest, established relationship, domination, or outright purchase provide the key to understanding how such groups exert influence upon the legislative activity that leads to statutory changes in the law like those illustrated in the boxed case on page 12.

DEVIANCE

Deviance is not a fundamental property of human behavior but is descriptive of certain kinds of conduct. Deviance can be ascribed to almost any behavior that departs from customary standards or expectations. However, the application of the term is a matter of discretion. Faculty members who attend their college's commencement ceremonies wearing warmup suits and jogging shoes are acting in a deviant manner as was the woman in the example on page 13.

Schur (1971) has stated that human behavior is deviant "to the extent that it comes to be viewed as involving a personally discreditable departure from a group's normative expectations and elicits interpersonal or collective reactions that serve to isolate, treat, correct, or punish individuals engaged in such behavior" (p. 24). This definition asserts that deviant behavior is regarded in negative terms by others and that their response to this behavior has the effect of either changing or suppressing the behavior itself or punishing the person who exhibits such behavior.

Deviance is also a matter of degree: cheating on an income tax return and committing armed robbery are both viewed as deviant behavior. But the person who perpetrates robbery is much more likely to be condemned and punished than is the tax violator. Schur's statement that behavior is deviant to the extent that it is personally discreditable emphasizes that normative violations do not have equally adverse effects on an individual's identity. Large sectors of our society are tolerant or even sympathetic toward tax violators, but robbery is universally condemned as a violent crime. People who commit such crimes and are convicted are apt to be scarred for the rest of their lives as a result of the stigma attached to individuals with a record of violent crime.

Schur's definition also identifies some of the possible reactions of individuals or groups toward those who engage in deviant behavior of various kinds. These reactions vary according to how seriously the deviance is perceived as a threat to basic social values, whether it is viewed as voluntary or something over which people have no control, and whether the deviant behavior ceases to be regarded as objectionable by a large minority or even majority of people in the society. During the 1960s and 1970s we saw movements to decriminalize various kinds of deviant behavior, including alcoholism, the consumption of certain drugs, and homosexuality between con-

Interest Groups and the Law of Prostitution

Interest group conflict is described in a study by Pamela Roby (1969) of the revision of the New York State penal law on prostitution. The new provisions made patronizing a prostitute an offense, restricted the police from using customers as witnesses in prosecutions, and prohibited plainclothes officers from obtaining solicitations from prostitutes. In addition, it reduced the penalty for prostitution from one year to fifteen days in jail. These changes were urged upon the Penal Law and Criminal Code Revision Commission by the American Social Health Association, defense attorneys, women's advocates, and some judges. The new sections of the penal code were passed in 1965 by the legislature, almost without notice. Only after they went into effect did New York City businessmen, politicians, and police, who viewed the revised statute as permissive, become alarmed that there would be a massive influx of prostitutes. In response to this pressure a "clean-up" of Times Square was instigated, thereby marking the start of a pitched battle with the police and the district attorney's office on the one side and the Civil Liberties Union, the Legal Aid Society, and certain judges on the other. The number of prostitutes arrested in the raids added fuel to the belief that the revisions had created an intolerable situation from the perspective of groups such as the New York City Hotel Association.

In response to this situation, amendments were submitted to the legislature by the Mayor's Committee on Prostitution. These recommendations would reclassify prostitution from a violation to a Class A misdemeanor (returning the sentence to one year) and would extend the loitering section in the penal code to include "loitering for the purpose of prostitution." Nearly ten months after the law had become effective the legislature rejected these proposed amendments and thus left it changed, at least temporarily.

Roby shows that during the different stages in the formulation and enforcement of the law, power shifted from one interest group to another:

> One group frequently exercised power with respect to one section of the law while another did so with respect to another section. In the final stage of the law's history, civil liberties and welfare groups dominated over businessmen and the police with respect to the clause making protitution a violation subject to a maximum fifteen-day sentence while the police and businessmen dominated over the civil liberties and welfare groups with respect to the nonenforcement of the "patron" clause.

Source: G. F. Cole, *The American System of Criminal Justice.* (Belmont, CA: Brooks/Cole, 1982.), pp. 53–54. Reproduced by permission of the author and publisher.

senting adults. Support for decriminalization was derived at least in part from the belief that these forms of behavior were outside the control of the persons involved. In effect, this removed them from the category of criminality and placed them in the category of mental illness or emotional disturbance, which allowed people to be treated rather than punished. Other acts such as participation in labor unions, di-

---

How Sweet It Is!

Santa Cruz, California (AP)—A 30-year-old woman, spurned in love, disguised herself as a chocolate Easter bunny Friday and tried to hop into her neighbor's heart, but wound up under psychiatric observation instead, police said.

A city police officer, who asked not to be identified, said he was investigating a complaint of a disturbance at a man's home when he spotted what looked like a tall, chocolate rabbit coming "hippity-hoppity" out of the yard.

After a closer look, the officer discovered it was a female neighbor who had covered her nude body with chocolate glaze.

The man told the officer he had called the police because of the woman's romantic advances over the last few months.

Source: Tampa Tribune, April 5, 1980, p. 6-A.

---

vorce, and doing business on Sunday have undergone a shift from condemnation, to tolerance, and finally to approval in terms of public reactions.

In summary, we can note that the deviance of an act or individual is relative, changeable, and a matter of degree, depending on the extent to which the behavior is perceived and responded to in certain ways. The analysis of social definitions of, and responses to, these types of behavior has come to be known as the "labeling perspective." We shall explore this approach in depth and detail in a later chapter.

LAW IN HISTORICAL PERSPECTIVE

Durant (1950) has identified four stages in the development of law: (1) personal revenge, (2) fines, (3) courts, and (4) assumption by the state of the obligation to prevent and punish wrongdoing.

The notion of revenge is embodied in the ancient principle of *lex talionis* or "law of equivalent retaliation." Talion law is often summarized—and misunderstood—by the expression "an eye for an eye, a tooth for a tooth." In its operation, talion law did not *demand* retaliatory justice by depriving the perpetrator of an eye for the one lost by the victim; rather, it limited the victim's legitimate claim to no more than an eye for the lost eye—not a tooth, an ear, or an arm, as well. Durant claims that the Abyssinians were so meticulous in measuring out this form of justice that when a boy fell from a tree on his companion and killed him, the judges decided that the requirements of justice could only be satisfied by allowing the bereaved mother to send another of her sons into the same tree to fall upon the offender's neck. This concept of equivalent retaliation has been retained in the notion of making penalties proportionate to the gravity or severity of the criminal offense, that is, "letting the punishment fit the crime." A modern revival of talion law is incorporated in the bill to provide "Q'sas," or the Law of Punishment, for the Islamic republic of Iran.

The Talion Law, Moslem Style

As part of their effort to rid Iranian society of undersirable foreign influences, the Islamic fundamentalist leaders called for a return to the kind of criminal sanctions advocated by the Koran, the holy book of Islam, and the sayings of the Prophet Mohammed. Known as the Law of Punishment, a 199-article bill was introduced in the Iranian parliament which established severe penalties for murder, assault, sodomy, adultery, and drunkenness. The bill went to great lengths to specify "fair retaliation." For example, Article 62 states: "The equality of body parts applies in the Law of Punishment. This means that for the punishment of someone who cuts the right hand off someone else, only the right hand of the offender should be cut off. If the offender does not have a right hand, then the left hand can be cut off, and if he has neither right not left hands, then one of his legs can be severed." For knife wounds and similar injuries, the bill specifies that punishment should be "in the same place, the same length and width and if possible the same depth." It empowers an Islamic court judge to order hair shaved to obtain "good implementation."

In Kerman, in southeastern Iran, two middle-aged women and two men—a young farmer and a worker with six children—were found guilty of prostitution, adultery, sodomy, and rape. First they were visited by Iranian clergymen, washed and clothed in white, and masked with ceremonial "hoods of the dead." Then workmen buried them in earth up to their chests, and rocks, ranging in size from nuts to baseballs, were assembled not far away. The presiding judge threw the first stone; then, five onlookers bombarded each of the condemned persons with rocks. Fifteen minutes later, all four were pronounced dead.

Source: Based on material reported in "Q'sas—The law of punishment," *Tampa Tribune,* November 12, 1982, p. 11-A, and "Death by stoning for sex crimes," *Newsweek,* July 14, 1980, p. 40.

In the second stage of law development, physical assault was replaced by fines or the award of appropriate damages as a means of securing equivalent retaliation. This ancient principle persists today in cases involving civil injuries as well as criminal offenses. The famous trial lawyer Melvin Belli once presented an artificial leg to a jury in a personal injury suit and asked the members how much money they would consider was an adequate payment for a lost limb.

The fines or settlements paid to avert personal revenge required some deliberation and adjudication of offenses and damages. In response to this need, a third natural development of the law was the establishment of courts. For many centuries, resort to the courts remained optional; should the offended party remain dissatisfied with the verdict, he or she was still free to seek personal revenge. These courts were not in all cases judgment seats as we know them today but more often were boards of voluntary conciliation. If offended parties were dissatisfied with the judgments rendered, they were still free to seek personal revenge.

In many cases, disputes were settled through *trial by ordeal,* a practice which persisted into the twentieth century in the form of the duel. Some of the practices involved in these "ordeals of God," as they were often called, are described in the box on page 16. Durant believes "the primitive mind resorted to an ordeal not so much on the medieval theory that a deity would reveal the culprit as in the hope that the ordeal, however unjust, would end a feud that might otherwise embroil the tribe for generations" (1950, p. 28).

The fourth advance in the development of law, according to Durant, was the assumption by the state of the obligation to punish wrongdoing and protect the citizen. Crimes came to be regarded as offenses against the state because their commission adversely affected the community. The state enlarged its domain of authority from merely settling disputes to making an effort to prevent them.

Common Law and Civil Law

When the Normans invaded England in the eleventh century, they found among the defeated Saxons a well-developed and workable system for the maintenance of public order and the administration of justice. This system had evolved over a lengthy period and was based on a body of **common law** which derived from the customs and collective experience of Saxon society. One of its principal features was its reliance on precedents in the process of continuously refining and developing suitable legal responses to meet the changing needs of a growing and dynamic society.

The Norman ruler, William the Conqueror, imposed his own chosen representatives on the existing system as a means of consolidating his power and authority. Under the royal justices appointed by William, state law became common law because it originated in the customary practices of the realm and was common to all England. Common law was thus firmly embedded in custom and tradition but continued to evolve through the process of judicial decision making.

Civil law derived from Roman antecedents and even earlier attempts by Sumerian and Babylonian societies to provide formal rules for the regulation of human conduct. Nearly two millenia before the birth of Christ, a Babylonian monarch named Hammurabi formulated a code which enunciated a series of stated offenses and their accompanying penalties. The historical significance of this Code of Hummurabi rests on its effort to standardize the relationship between crime and punishment. From these beginnings, civil law evolved as a system based on specific codes that are written and legislated.

American criminal law combines features of both civil and common law. One major source of criminal law in the United States is the statutes enacted by state legislatures and the Congress. These laws are usually compiled in codes which sort or classify statutes into separate headings. These state codes are usually subject to continual revision during the annual legislative sessions held at state capitals. The criminal laws for any state may be found in its penal code. Thus, if one wished to know how the state of Florida defined the crime of kidnapping or the crime of indecent exposure and the penalties imposed for committing these crimes, the place to find this information would be the latest or most up-to-date version of the Florida Penal Code, as provided in the Florida Statutes Annotated.

Trial by Ordeal

Trial by ordeal was a primitive means used to determine guilt or innocence by submitting the accused person to dangerous or painful tests believed to be under divine or supernatural control. That is, escape from death or injury was ordinarily taken to be a vindication of the innocence of the accused as reflected by the judgment of God (*judicium Dei*). The most common forms of ordeal were the wager of battle or trial by combat, in which the winner was held to be innocent; the ordeal of fire, in which the accused walked barefoot over hot coals or had to carry a red-hot iron in his hand; the trial by cold water (often applied to witches), which tested the accused by immersing him or her in water and accepting it as a sign of guilt if the person floated.

Other ordeals included the corsned trial, which involved placing hallowed bread into the mouth of the accused—if the individual swallowed the wafer (corsned), he was free from punishment; the trial of the cross, in which accuser and accused were placed before the cross with their arms extended, and the first who moved his hands or let his arms drop was considered guilty; and finally, the judgment of the bier, used in murder trials, in which the corpse of the murder victim was placed on a bier, the accused was required to touch the body, and if blood flowed or foam appeared at the mouth, the suspect was adjudged guilty.

Despite attempts to curb or abolish trial by ordeal in Europe, the practice continued into the fourteenth century. In England, forms of ordeal other than trial by combat were abolished by Henry III in the year 1219, following their condemnation by Pope Innocent III in 1216. The "ducking stool" for subjecting suspected witches to trial by water, however, was still used in colonial America as late as the seventeenth century.

As an offshoot of statutory law, *administrative law* comprises rulings made by government agencies at the federal, state, and local level. An official body such as a board of health is invested with the authority by the legislature or executive branch to sometimes establish regulations governing specific policy areas (e.g., social problems, safety and health standards, etc.), and violations of these administrative laws are handled by the criminal justice system.

The meaning and intent of criminal statutes are tested and interpreted within the context of specific cases. Therefore, criminal law is also "created" by judges in their rulings on various statutory laws. This resulting *case law* is heavily influenced by the principle of **stare decisis** ("let the decision stand"), which is the rule that requires judges to follow precedent in their judicial interpretations. Otherwise, as Eldefonso and Coffey (1981) observe, "the defendant in a civil or criminal case would never know whether or not his activities were lawful" (p. 36). Nevertheless, the time may come when prior decisions are overruled by the higher authority of a court of appeals and the existing case law is reversed or modified through this appellate process.

CHAPTER 787
KIDNAPPING; FALSE IMPRISONMENT; CUSTODY OFFENSES

Editorial Note

Laws 1974, c. 74–383, eff. Oct. 1, 1975, created this Chapter by transferring former Chapter 805 to this Chapter as §§ 787.02, 787.01, and 787.04, respectively, and adding § 787.03

787.01 Kidnapping

(1) (a) "Kidnapping" means forcibly, secretly, or by threat confining, abducting, or imprisoning another person against his will and without lawful authority, with intent to:

1. Hold for ransom or reward or as a shield or hostage.

2. Commit or facilitate commission of any felony.

3. Inflict bodily harm upon or to terrorize the victim or another person.

4. Interfere with the performance of any governmental or political function.

(b) Confinement of a child under the age of 13 is against his will within the meaning of subsection (1) if such confinement is without the consent of his parent or legal guardian.

(2) Whoever kidnaps a person is guilty of a felony of the first degree, punishable by imprisonment for a term of years not exceeding life or as provided in § 775.082, § 775.083, or § 775.084.

CHAPTER 800
CRIME AGAINST NATURE; INDECENT EXPOSURE

800.01 Repealed by Laws 1974, c. 74–121, § 1, eff. Oct. 1, 1974

800.02 Unnatural and lascivious act

Whoever commits any unnatural and lascivious act with another person shall be guilty of a misdemeanor of the second degree, punishable as provided in § 775.082 or § 775.083.

800.03 Exposure of sexual organs

It shall be unlawful for any person to expose or exhibit his sexual organs in any public place or on the private premises of another, or so near thereto as to be seen from such private premises, in a vulgar or indecent manner, or so to expose or exhibit his person in such place, or to go or be naked in such place. Provided, however, this section shall not be construed to prohibit the exposure of such organs or the person in any place provided or set apart for that purpose. Any person convicted of a violation hereof shall be guilty of a misdemeanor of the first degree, punishable as provided in § 775.082 or § 775.083.

SUBSTANTIVE CRIMINAL LAW AND CRIMINAL PROCEDURE

In our brief historical sketch of the antecedents of American criminal jurisprudence, we have referred rather informally to "criminal law." It is time to abandon this casual usage in favor of the more exact designation **substantive criminal law,** as distinguished from **criminal procedure.**

Substantive criminal law is concerned with acts, mental states, and the accompanying circumstances or consequences which constitute the necessary features of various crimes. It identifies particular kinds of behavior (acts or omissions) as wrongs against society or the state and prescribes the punishments to be imposed for such conduct. Whenever mention is made of criminal law throughout this book, it is substantive criminal law to which we shall be referring.

Criminal procedure sets forth the rules that direct the application and enforcement of the substantive criminal law. That is, criminal procedure lays down the steps that officials—police, prosecutors, judges, corrections personnel, and others—must follow in the administration of justice, from arrest to conviction and beyond.

Foundations of Criminal Law

Anglo-American criminal law is founded upon certain principles which have been traditionally observed by legislatures and the courts in the formulation and interpretation of the substantive law of crimes. They include: (1) legality, (2) *actus reus,* (3) *mens rea,* (4) concurrence of *actus reus* and *mens rea,* (5) harm, (6) causation, and (7) punishment.

Legality   A crime is defined legally as "an intentional act or omission in violation of a criminal law, committed without defense or justification and sanctioned by the state as a felony or misdemeanor" (Tappan, 1966, p. 10). The principle that there can be no crime unless a law exists which has been violated is embodied in the ancient Latin saying, *Nullum crimen sine lege*—"No crime without a law." This is one of the most venerated concepts in Anglo-American criminal law.

Actus Reus   Mere thoughts alone cannot constitute a crime. One can wish an enemy in the grave, fantasize the sexual violation of a woman, or harbor pleasant thoughts about evading the payment of income taxes—as long as these thoughts do not result in actions to bring about the desired results. However, it is necessary to distinguish mere thoughts from *speech,* because under our legal system *a crime can be committed by an act of speech.* For example, since we consider individuals who are acting in concert to represent a greater threat to society than does a lone offender, we regard an agreement by two or more persons to commit a crime an act of *criminal conspiracy.* Nevertheless, it is important to note that approximately half of the states have added by statute the additional requirement of *an act in furtherance of the conspiracy* (LaFave and Scott, 1972, pp. 476–78). Other crimes that can be committed by acts of speech include perjury, solicitation, and false pretenses.

Mens Rea   A further requirement for conduct to be considered criminal is the presence of a "guilty mind" (*mens rea*) in the actor. To demonstrate *mens rea,* it must be proven that an individual *intentionally* (purposefully), *knowingly, recklessly,* or *negligently* behaved in a given manner or caused a given result. A bus driver who fails to stop at an intersection and causes a collision with an automobile entering from a cross street would not be charged with a crime if it could be proved that he had been unaware his brakes were defective—that he had done everything he could to avert an accident. A crime has not been committed where an individual has not intentionally brought about a given result. Similarly, if someone buys goods from a local merchant not knowing that they are stolen merchandise, he is not guilty of the criminal offense of receiving stolen property. On the other hand, a man who drives his sports car 90 miles per hour through a residential area and kills a young child is likely to be convicted of manslaughter because his behavior constitutes a reckless disregard for the risks associated with this kind of behavior. A nightclub owner was found criminally negligent and convicted of manslaughter for failing to provide adequate fire-escapes, resulting in the death of many patrons during a fire. In affirming the owner's conviction, the court held that more than mere negligence was necessary, that is, that "a grave danger to others must have been apparent." As the court stated, "even if a particular defendant is so stupid (or) so heedless . . . that in fact he did not realize the grave danger," he is guilty of manslaughter "if an ordinary normal man under the same circumstances would have realized the gravity of the danger" (*Commonwealth* v. *Welansky,* 1944, cited by LaFave and Scott, pp. 212–13).

Offenses that involve no mental element but consist only of forbidden acts or omissions are classified as **strict liability offenses.** Thus, a statute may simply indicate that whoever does or omits doing a certain act, or whoever brings about a certain result is guilty of a crime. These statutes are justified on the grounds that there is a need to control the behavior in question, yet convictions would be difficult to obtain if the prosecution were required to prove fault. Examples of laws imposing liability without fault include liquor and narcotics laws, pure food laws, and traffic laws.

The law recognizes that there are certain groups of people who are not able to attain the requisite mental state. Children, mental defectives, and in some cases those diagnosed mentally ill are exempted from criminal responsibility because they are unable to appreciate the nature and quality of their behavior. In addition, *mens rea* is considered lacking when people are acting under coercion, defending themselves or others, or acting under statutory authority, such as the police officer acting in the line of duty.

Concurrence of *Actus Reus* and *Mens Rea*   Another basic premise of the criminal law is that the act and the mental state must concur in order for a crime to have been committed. If the act and the mental state are separated by a considerable gap in time, they cannot be said to be concurrent. As shown in the illustration on the facing page, the lack of concurrence between mental state and act is a strong argument for the proposition that the former did not activate or cause the latter.

Harm   There is the additional requirement in the criminal law that only conduct which is harmful in some way can be considered criminal. This idea is reflected in the substantive due process concept that a criminal statute is unconstitutional if it bears no reasonable relationship to the matter of injury to the public. It is important, however, to recognize that criminal harm is not restricted to *physical* injury. In cases of libel, perjury, and treason, no physical injury is inflicted. The criminal law must be seen as dealing with intangibles, such as harm to institutions, public safety, autonomy of women, reputation, and the like. In essence, criminal harm signifies loss of value because an individual who commits a crime does something that is contrary to community values (Hall, 1947).

Causation   Causation relates to those crimes which require that the defendant's conduct produce a given result. Some crimes such as perjury or forgery are defined in such a way that the crime comprises both the act itself and the intent to cause the harmful result, without regard to whether that result in fact occurs. On the other hand, offenses such as the intent-to-kill type of murder and the intent-to-injure type of battery require a given result. In these cases, it must be demonstrated that the defendant's conduct is the "but for" cause of the proscribed result and that the harm which actually occurred is similar enough to the intended result that the defendant can be held responsible for it.

In many instances, proving a causal connection poses few problems for the prosecution. If individual A, with intent to kill, drives a knife into the heart of individual B, the prosecutor would have no particular difficulty in demonstrating that A's action was the cause of B's death. In a small number of cases, however, the intended harm varies according to person, manner, and type. For example. Ms. A shoots Mr. B and, believing him dead, leaves the victim's body on an interstate highway. Mr. C fails to observe B, who is still alive, lying on the road and runs him over, killing him. Will Ms. A be convicted of the murder of Mr. B? Ms. A will be convicted if it can be demonstrated that her conduct was a substantial factor in bringing about Mr. B's death or if what happened to Mr. B was a foreseeable consequence of Ms. A's behavior.

The rule of causation has also been said to apply generally in cases of **felony murder.** At issue is the question of whether offenders can be held responsible for the unintended deaths that result from their perpetration of a crime. For example, individual A sets out to rob storeowner B and in the course of the robbery, B, in order to protect his property, fires at A and accidentally kills a customer. After the robbery has been foiled, a police officer shoots at A in order to stop him and kills a bystander.[1] Would A be held responsible for either or both of these deaths? In general,

---

[1]The behavior of the police officer in this case is consistent with the revision of the fleeing felon rule promulgated by the U.S. Supreme Court in 1985 in the case of *Tennessee* v. *Gardner* No. 83–1035 (*New York Times,* March 28, 1985, pp. 1, 14).

Concurrence of Mental State and Harmful Conduct

Alice is angry with Carol for having stolen the affections of her boyfriend, Bob. She plans to kill both of them with a pitcher of poisoned lemonade. But when she goes to Bob's apartment to invite them over for a picnic, she finds that they have eloped. Ten years later, at an intersection in Denver, Bob (who suffers from colorblindness) runs a traffic light. He and Carol are killed instantly when their motorcycle is totaled in a collision with a truck driven by none other than Alice.

Is Alice guilty of murder?

No, because there was no concurrence between the intent and the harmful conduct. Fate had delivered the couple into Alice's hands.

---

the courts have ruled that if the death is a natural and foreseeable consequence of the offense, the offender is liable (LaFave and Scott, 1972, pp. 263–64). Thus, A could be prosecuted for the murder of both the robber and the bystander.[2]

Punishment   Finally, the law must stipulate the sanctions to be applied for each crime. Under our legal system, citizens must not only be forewarned as to what conduct is forbidden, but must also be made aware of the consequences of such actions.

All of the above principles can be summarized in a single statement: "The harm forbidden in a penal law must be imputed to any normal adult who voluntarily commits it with criminal intent, and such a person must be subjected to the legally prescribed punishment" (Hall, 1947, p. 18).

Characteristics of Criminal Law

Sutherland and Cressey (1978) have identified four characteristics which distinguish the criminal law from other rules affecting human conduct: (1) politicality, (2) specificity, (3) uniformity, and (4) penal sanction.

Politicality   Criminal laws are enacted, modified, and repealed by duly constituted legislative bodies. As we have noted, in a pluralistic society such as ours with no system of universally shared social values, what is defined as criminal behavior during any given period depends to a considerable degree on what certain politically influential and powerful groups perceive as conduct that threatens their value system. Since the turn of the century, we have seen Prohibition enacted and repealed, the liberalization of abortion, gambling, and pornography laws, and the passage and subsequent modification of laws dealing with the possession and sale of marijuana and other drugs.

---

[2]According to the legal doctrine of transferred intent, "If a person intentionally directs force against one person wrongfully but, instead, hits another, his intent is said to be transferred from one to another and he is liable even though he did not intend it in the first instance" (*Black's Law Dictionary,* 1985, p. 778). LaFave and Scott (1972) have pointed out, however, that this doctrine is regarded by most lawyers as extremely controversial.

Specificity   If people are to obey the laws, then the laws must be stated in terms that clearly indicate what conduct is expected of them. A statute which specifies punishment for a commonly understood offense such as rape or robbery is likely to be reasonably clear. But a statute which prohibits "immoral acts" would be unclear and difficult to interpret. Any law which requires or prohibits the commission of an act in terms so vague that people of normal intelligence must guess at its meaning violates an essential requirement of due process, namely that the law as stated must be understandable to anyone who is not a legal expert. One of the longstanding objections to certain statutes that cover juvenile offenses is that they contain terms like "incorrigible" or "ungovernable" without indicating specific meanings.

Uniformity   Justice is usually portrayed as a blindfolded figure who weighs the evidence for the guilt or innocence of those who stand accused before her. The ideal in American criminal jurisprudence is that all persons who are adjudged by the law will be treated equally, regardless of their ethnic or national origins, religious convictions or affiliations, and social standing. This is a noble theory, but in practice "some people are more equal than others."

Penal Sanction   As we have already seen, criminal statutes must not only give people "fair warning" of what behavior to avoid; they must also convey some idea of the penalties that are incurred if laws are violated. The goal of punishment in the broadest terms is the protection of society, for the first duty of any government is to safeguard the lives and property of its citizens. A society which tolerates unrestrained theft and violence cannot endure for long. Given the propensities toward aggressive and predatory behavior which are widespread in many human societies, laws without penalties would be more honored in the breach than in the observance.

Criminal Procedure

The U.S. Constitution is the most authoritative source of criminal procedure in our country. Americans are introduced as children to the first ten amendments to the U.S. Constitution, known collectively as the Bill of Rights. They are instructed that the Bill of Rights provides certain safeguards to American citizens that are covered by such ringing phrases as "due process" and "equal protection under the law." They are less likely to be familiar with the historical fact that not until the passage of the Fourteenth Amendment in 1868 were these safeguards for the rights of the accused person made applicable to state courts. Prior to the Fourteenth Amendment, the Bill of Rights directly applied only to proceedings which took place in federal courts.

During the past two decades, the U.S. Supreme Court has made more changes in criminal procedure than had been made by the Court in the nearly two hundred years of its previous existence. Critics of the Court have complained that these changes have resulting in the "coddling of criminals" and have reflected a permissiveness that hurts law-abiding citizens. Any fair-minded review of what the Court has actually done will reveal the falsity of these charges. Since the Court has not created any new rights for criminals, it cannot have coddled criminals or been permissive of their evil ways. What the Court has done is to *equalize the rights of rich and*

Protecting the Rights of the Accused: The 14th Amendment

The 14th Amendment to the U.S. Constitution declares, in part, that "No State shall make or enforce any law which shall abridge the privileges or immunities of citizens of the United States, nor shall any State deprive any person of life, liberty, or property, without due process of law; nor deny to any person within its jurisdiction the equal protection of the law."

Ratification of the (14th Amendment), however, did not result in the overnight application of the Bill of Rights safeguards to persons accused of crimes in state. Nearly a century was to pass before the U.S. Supreme Court, under the leadership of Chief Justice Warren, in a series of landmark decisions involving such issues as search and seizure, self-incrimination, representation by counsel, etc., brought about the incorporation of most of the criminal justice provisions of the Bill of Rights and made them applicable to state courts.

---

poor suspects. The Court has not created any new rights, but it has extended to the poor, illiterate, and ignorant those rights which have long been known and enjoyed by the middle-class or upper-class defendant. In the following chapters of this book, we will try to document the direct and indirect impact of this "law revolution" on the administration of justice.

CLASSIFICATION OF CRIMES

Crimes are legally classified into **felonies** and **misdemeanors.** Felonies are the more serious crimes and are punishable by death or incarceration for a year or more in a state prison. Misdemeanors are less serious offenses which are punishable by a fine or a term of up to one year in a city or county jail. There are exceptions, as in the case of North Carolina, where misdemeanants are confined by the state Department of Corrections.

The felony-misdemeanor classification is extremely important for the criminal justice system and process. As Robin (1980) points out, whether a felony or misdemeanor was committed will affect:

- the conditions under which the police can make an arrest and the degree of force that will be authorized;
- the "charges" the prosecutor will ultimately press;
- the care exercised by the trial judge in accepting a guilty plea and admitting evidence into the record;
- the availability of procedural and constitutional safeguards;
- the quality of counsel and the conduct of the court;
- the determination of the court that will retain trial jurisdiction;
- the sentence that can be imposed;
- the type of institution to which an offender may be committed;
- the conditions of release from incarceration;

- the size of the jury; and
- whether a jury verdict must be unanimous [p. 10].

The factors cited above can have crucially significant consequences for the defendant; in some instances, they may be a matter of life or death.

Originally the common law divided those crimes which were "wrong in themselves" (**mala in se**) from those which were "wrong because they were prohibited" (**mala prohibita**), that is, any act forbidden by statute but which otherwise did not seem to shock the conscience of the community. Such a classification finds little support from contemporary legal authorities or criminologists, who tend to regard the distinction as oversimplified and naive.

Other classifications of crime include "crimes against nature" which, in its broadest sense, includes carnal knowledge of an animal, or, when applied to human sexual experience, sodomy, fellatio, cunnilingus, or intercourse (even between legally married partners) in any but the vis-à-vis position. The reference to these acts as "crimes against nature" does not, of course, represent an indictment from "nature" itself but a value judgment on the part of some legislative body as to what is "natural." If we can repose any confidence in a lengthy series of investigations of sexual behavior, from Alfred Kinsey to Masters and Johnson, a type of sexual experience that is regarded as "unnatural" in one segment of our society may actually be the norm in another social group.

"Crimes against humanity" is a classification developed at the end of World War II and used by the victorious Allies in their trial of Nazi leaders at Nuremberg. These offenses, which included genocide, were seen as being of such magnitude and severity that the offenders should be compelled to answer to all mankind, rather than to a specific country or jurisdiction. Years later, European peace groups applied this same concept to President Lyndon B. Johnson and other members of his administration and tried them *in absentia* for alleged war crimes in Vietnam.

Offenses may also be classified as a *private wrong*, called a "civil injury" or *tort*, or a *public wrong*, which falls under the rubric of criminal law. A public wrong is a violation of public order for which the community may take action. The punishment imposed is for the protection of the community, not for the redress of injury to the individual. Private parties must seek redress through a civil court action. When an individual or organization sues another to obtain a remedy or recompense for an alleged injury, the case is a civil action. When the state prosecutes an individual or organization for the violation of a legislative statute, the case is usually a criminal action.

The same offense may give rise to both civil and criminal actions. Assault and battery may result in a civil action by the victim to secure damages for the injuries received and also in criminal charges filed by the state to punish the guilty party by a fine or imprisonment.

CRIMINOLOGY AS A DISCIPLINE

It is obvious that as long as crime has existed, there have been people willing to devote time and effort to its study. Those who studied crime in earlier times tended to be directly concerned on a daily basis with crime and criminals: attorneys, judges, police officers and administrators, and correctional personnel. The criminologist was not someone who earned a living from the full-time study of crime. Criminology as a field of professional endeavor was a twentieth-century development.

Criminology was regarded, until recently, as an area of specialization within sociology. Courses in criminology were offered through departments of sociology in most American colleges and universities; a separate department of criminology was a rarity on campuses in the United States. Criminologists recognized sociology as their primary professional affiliation and were identified as sociologists by members of other disciplines.

Although many contemporary criminologists have come from the ranks of sociologists, it is no longer accurate to identify criminology as a specialized field of inquiry in sociology. Today, departments of criminology may include within their roster of faculty members psychologists, psychiatrists, attorneys, political scientists, biologists, and representatives of other professions. Criminology is increasingly viewed as an interdisciplinary endeavor which seeks to incorporate the approaches and contributions of many fields—law, medicine, philosophy, and the social and behavioral sciences, to name only a few—as these relate to the study of crime, criminals, and the administration of justice. Criminologists have assumed the principal responsibility for providing a theoretical framework to explain and interpret the findings of researchers in a variety of disciplines.

Sociology helps us to understand the complex social and cultural processes accounting for differences in the types of crimes and their commission within various groups in our society. Psychology aims at identifying variables which affect the occurrence of behavior and the means by which the deviant behavior of specific persons can be modified. History supplies a perspective on the past events which have played a significant part in shaping our current crime problem. Chemistry, physics, biology, and other branches of natural science contribute to *criminalistics,* the generic term for the science and technology of criminal investigation and detection. Studies in criminal law help to explain the operation of the courts in meting out justice. Political science experts address themselves to the analysis of relationships between the criminal justice system and the democratic process. Religion and ethics may furnish insights into contemporary morality and other issues of conduct that lead to societal disapproval. Social casework can help equip people with methods and skills for dealing with offenders, both in the correctional institution and in community-based facilities and programs. Each of these disciplines makes a contribution to the body of organized knowledge known as criminology.

As an interdisciplinary endeavor, criminology is scientific in its major orientation and emphases. Many criminologists were originally trained as behavioral scientists or have come to accept scientific models as an appropriate framework for the integration of criminological data and theories. Nevertheless, it would be grossly inaccurate to equate "criminological" with "scientific" in contemporary criminology. Law, to take only one of several possible examples, represents an organized body of fact and theory that has developed its own type of systematic inquiry—a methodology both rigorous and exacting, despite the fact that the legal mode of inquiry is not scientific. The law is both a focus and a point of departure in criminology, but the specific nature of its concerns, subject matter, and adversary approach to investigation make it less suitable than behavioral science models as a potential frame of reference for the integration of diverse materials from a number of disciplines.

Criminal Justice and Criminology

A development with significant implications for American criminology was the raising of public consciousness that occurred during the 1960s with regard to the crime problem. The discovery by both presidential candidates in 1964 of "law and order" and "crime in the streets" as issues capable of generating even greater public concern than our deepening involvement in the internal politics of Southeast Asia made the respective campaigns sound at times like parodies of one another. At any rate, the newly reelected President Lyndon B. Johnson empaneled a commission of experts drawn from nearly every discipline, profession, or occupation that had anything to do with crime. This body was designated the President's Commission on Law Enforcement and Administration of Justice. It split itself into a series of task forces, each of which tackled a sector of the criminal justice system or an issue relating to the crime problem.

In 1967, the President's Commission (as was their abbreviated title) published the findings of the various task forces, together with an overall summary of the Commission's work entitled *The Challenge of Crime in a Free Society.* This report declared that financial resources at the local level were totally inadequate to deal with the necessity for innovation and change in approaches to crime and its control:

> Most local communities today are hardpressed just to improve their agencies of justice and other facilities at a rate that will meet increases in population and in crime. They cannot spare funds for experimental or innovative programs or plan beyond the emergencies of the day. Federal collaboration can give State and local agencies an opportunity to gain on crime rather than barely stay abreast of it by making funds, research, and technical assistance available and thereby encouraging changes that in time may make criminal administration more effective and more fair [p. 284].

The impact of this study was made apparent in the following year, when the Congress passed the Omnibus Crime Control and Safe Streets Act. Although a modest law enforcement grant program had been in existence since 1965, the Crime Control Act marked an historic first in our national experience: the massive infusion of federal monies into the improvement of the criminal justice system.

As subsequent events were to show, it is much easier to pass a bill than to create the means for seeing that its provisions are carried out. The Crime Control Act authorized the Department of Justice to create an agency called the Law Enforcement Assistance Administration (LEAA) to provide criminal justice planning and program grants to state and local governments, which were equally lacking in the personnel, knowledge, and experience to take full advantage of this sudden windfall. It also authorized the establishment of the National Institute of Law Enforcement and Criminal Justice in order to stimulate, promote, and encourage basic research in the areas of crime, criminal behavior, and the criminal justice system.

Education is a traditional American formula for dealing with problems of almost any kind. Thus, under the auspices of LEAA's Law Enforcement Education Program (LEEP), financial incentives in the form of subsidies and logistical support were provided to encourage criminal justice personnel to return to school in pursuit of further course work and degrees. What resulted in higher education circles was reminiscent, on a more modest scale, of the boom that occurred in the years immediately after World War II when veterans crowded college and university campuses in unanticipated and unprecedented numbers.

In a very short time, nearly every institution of higher learning managed to recruit a faculty and begin offering courses in criminal justice and criminology. Programs bore a variety of titles: "Criminal Justice," "Police Science," "Law Enforcement Administration," "Criminology and Corrections," "Administration of Justice," and so forth. Since there was no binding authority for what a criminal justice curriculum should include, course titles ranged from "Introduction to Criminal Justice" to offerings such as the one that appeared in the catalogue of a small college in East Texas: "Legal Aspects of the Law" (as contrasted, perhaps, with "Illegal Aspects of the Law"?).

The frenetic pace of program development has since slackened. Competent, thoroughly trained instructors are available in growing numbers to assume teaching responsibilities in the colleges and universities, and their contributions have already resulted in noteworthy improvements in the academic quality and rigor of criminal justice programs. Improvements have also resulted from the continuing efforts of organizations like the Academy of Criminal Justice Sciences and the International Association of Chiefs of Police to foster the growth of professional standards within the variegated fields of criminal justice.

Criminology has taken a prominent role in these developments. Criminologists, with their commitment to the goal of expanding the information base on crime and criminals, are significantly involved in the knowledge-generating processes of research and theory. The American Society of Criminology also strongly supports the increased participation of criminal justice practitioners in the professional activities of the ASC. Annual and regional conferences, seminars, and workshops afford many opportunities for criminal justice personnel and criminologists to meet and discuss topics of mutual interest and concern. Never before was the future outlook so optimistic with regard to the possibilities of fruitful collaboration between the researcher-theoretician and the practitioner.

SUMMARY

In order to understand the problem of crime, it is necessary to examine the broader issue of deviance from societal norms. Societies attempt to contain deviance through controls ranging from informal disapproval to the use of the police powers of the state. Antisocial attitudes, conduct norms, eccentricities, and odd behaviors may all be studied for their potential usefulness in helping to illuminate the factors involved in criminal conduct. All criminal acts are deviant, but not all deviants are criminals. Therefore, only those deviant acts which legislative bodies have defined by statute as criminal may legitimately be considered as crimes. The more serious crimes are classified as felonies, the less serious as misdemeanors. These categories also reflect a difference in the severity of the sanctions that society sees fit to impose in the punishment of such crimes.

Criminology emerged in the twentieth century as an interdisciplinary approach to the systematic study of crime, criminals, and criminal behavior. Although it is primarily scientific in its orientation and emphases, other nonscientific approaches occupy an important place in criminological inquiry. Since the passage of the Omnibus Crime Control and Safe Streets Act in 1968 which provided federal support for law enforcement, the courts, and corrections, the field of criminal justice has made considerable progress toward professionalization. Criminologists in their role of researchers and theoreticians contribute significantly to criminal justice by helping to provide the practitioner with new ideas, tools, and information.

DISCUSSION QUESTIONS

Find the answers to the following questions in the text.

1. Why do the authors maintain that the study of **deviant behavior** is more appropriate for the beginning student of criminology than is the more specific study of criminal and delinquent behavior?
2. How do we distinguish between **prescriptions** and **proscriptions** as forms of social sanctions?
3. Compare and contrast the value-consensus and value-conflict models of law.
4. Define and discuss **substantive criminal law** and **procedural criminal law.** What are the major sources of criminal law?
5. Identify four characteristics of the criminal law that distinguish it from other rules governing human conduct.
6. What are **felonies** and how do they differ from **misdemeanors**? Why is this such an important distinction in the administration of justice?
7. How do crimes differ from torts?
8. Why was the Omnibus Crime Control and Safe Streets Act such a landmark piece of legislation for criminal justice?

TERMS TO IDENTIFY AND REMEMBER

proscription
social sanction
mala in se
criminal procedure
substantive criminal law
value-consensus model
stare decisis
value-divergence model
law

felony
misdemeanor
mala prohibita
actus reus
procedural law
value-conflict model
penal sanction
uniformity
prescription

LEAA
socialization
strict liability offense
mens rea
lex talionis

common law
politicality
specificity
deviant behavior

REFERENCES

Chambliss, W. J. Elites and the creation of criminal law. In W. J. Chambliss (ed.), *Sociological Readings in the Conflict Perspective.* Reading, MA: Addison-Wesley, 1973.

Cunningham, W. C., and Taylor, T. H. *Research in Brief: The Growing Role of Private Security.* Washington, D.C.: National Institute of Justice, October 1984.

Durant, W. *Our Oriental Heritage.* New York: Simon & Schuster, 1954.

Eldefonso, E., and Coffey, A. R. *Criminal Law: History, Philosophy, Enforcement.* New York: Harper & Row, 1981

Hall, J. *General Principles of Criminal Law.* Indianapolis: Bobbs-Merrill, 1947.

LaFave, W. R., and Scott, A. W. *Criminal Law.* St. Paul, MN: West Publishing Company, 1972.

Law Enforcement Assistance Administration. *Manpower Survey of the Criminal Justice System: Executive Summary.* Washington, D.C.: U.S. Government Printing Office, 1978.

Makielski, S. J. *Pressure Politics in America.* Lanham, MD: University Press of America, 1980.

Perkins, R. M. *Criminal Law and Procedure.* Mineola, NY: The Foundation Press, 1966.

Quinney, R. *Critique of Legal Order: Crime Control in Capitalist Society.* Boston: Little, Brown, 1974.

Robin, G. D. *Introduction to the Criminal Justice System.* New York: Harper & Row, 1980.

Roby, Pamela A. Politics and criminal law. Revision of the New York State penal law on prostitution. *Social Problems,* 17 (1969): 83–109.

Sutherland, E. H., and Cressey, D. R. *Criminology.* Philadelphia: Lippincott, 1978.

Tappan, P. *Crime, Justice, and Correction.* New York: McGraw-Hill, 1966.

Williams, R. M. *American Society.* New York: Alfred A. Knopf, 1970.

chapter 2

CRIME STATISTICS IN THE UNITED STATES

Crime statistics serve a variety of purposes. They provide the public and government with a perspective on the nature and extent of the crime problem and its trends over time. Statistics also supply direct or implicit data on such characteristics as *age, race* or *ethnic background, sex, income level, family status,* and *occupation* of those who are arrested. This information is necessary in order to design crime prevention programs. Current statistics are important for planning, since they form the basis for projecting the nature and extent of crime in the future. They also provide baseline data for assessing the factors that contribute to the causes of crime and for the development of theories of criminality.

The budgets of criminal justice agencies are affected by crime statistics. Substantial increases in crime provide police departments with the justification for seeking additional patrol officers, equipment, and civilian employees. A steep rise in the number of arrests may support a request for more judges and court personnel.

Crime statistics also have an impact on laws and public policy. An increase in the rate of offenses involving the use of a gun may result in the passage of a law that establishes a mandatory minimum sentence for offenders who use firearms in the commission of a crime.

Increases in particular offenses may require criminal justice agencies to reallocate their resources. Police departments are constantly under public pressure to redeploy their officers in order to cope with increases in some types of street crimes. A rise in the incidence of robberies or a visible increase in street prostitutes and drug pushers typically results in public insistence that the police "do something about the problem." Police departments react by assigning more officers to make arrests and show the public that they are responsive to the needs of the community.

Action in one part of the criminal justice system has implications for the entire criminal justice system—an important point that is too often overlooked. More arrests result in a greater number of cases going to court, an increase in convictions, and more offenders being incarcerated. Thus, an additional strain is placed on the judicial and correctional components of the criminal justice system. Insensitivity to this problem is largely due to the fragmentation of the criminal justice system. Once the police have arrested and booked a suspect, the case becomes the responsibility of the prosecutor; once the judge has pronounced sentence, the defendant becomes the concern of correctional authorities. No one is responsible for keeping track of offenders as they proceed from phase to phase of the criminal process.

Increases or decreases in crime may also have consequences for specific agency programs. Large increases in juvenile delinquency and crime result in a call for more programs dealing with delinquency prevention and treatment. On one hand, support for crime prevention programs is usually based on increases in street crime, while, on the other hand, continued funding for these programs is justified by pointing to decreases in specific categories of offense.

Changes in the crime picture have important consequences for both politicians and agency administrators. "Crime in the streets" has been a major issue in a number of presidential campaigns as well as in campaigns on the local and state level. Mayors who fail to deal with a rising crime problem may be voted out of office at the end of their terms. Likewise, police chiefs may be terminated for failing to show progress toward combatting a rising crime rate.

Changes in the demographic characteristics of the offender population have significant ramifications for the whole system of criminal justice. Increases in female arrests have already resulted in changes in police procedures, as well as in increases in the number of programs specifically directed toward the female offender.

It is clear by now that crime statistics have a number of functions beyond simply providing an indication of the magnitude of the crime problem. Since criminal statistics affect the careers of political figures and have an impact on the funding of new programs and the continued operation of existing programs, they may on occasion be manipulated to suit specific purposes. This is one of the reasons the accuracy of official statistics has been questioned. We shall discuss this issue at greater length at a later point in this chapter.

SOURCES OF CRIME DATA

Information on the crime problem is obtained from a number of sources, the most important of which is official statistics. National police data are compiled by the Federal Bureau of Investigation (FBI) and published annually in the *Uniform Crime Reports (UCR),* which is the most widely used source of data on crime in the United States. This report includes statistics on "crimes known to the police" and information on the number, characteristics, distribution, and disposition of those who are arrested. The Federal Bureau of Prisons gathers data on persons incarcerated in federal and state prisons and publishes this information annually in *National Prisoner Statistics.* The Federal Bureau of Prisons also publishes other reports which provide information on such topics as the characteristics of state institutions, local jails, and persons under sentence of death.

The Youth Development and Deliquency Prevention Administration of the U.S. Department of Health Services is a major source of data on delinquency. Its annual publication, *Juvenile Court Statistics,* supplies information on the number of juvenile deliquency cases disposed of by the juvenile courts, broken down according to sex and age of offender, type of court, method of handling, jurisdiction of the court, and patterns over the years. The U.S. Department of Justice also furnishes data on several categories of state and local public juvenile facilities (shelters, detention centers, reception and diagnostic centers, training schools, forestry camps, ranches and farms, and group homes and halfway houses). Additional data are provided which cover private detention and correctional facilities.

In addition to official statistics, information concerning the crime problem is collected from other sources, which we shall describe and discuss later in this chapter. These include criminological studies directed toward both perpetrators and victims of crime who, for reasons explored later in this text, are not represented or are underrepresented in the *UCR* figures.

The *Uniform Crime Reports*

As early as 1920, August Vollmer, the well-known police executive, developed a plan for the establishment of a bureau of criminal records which included among its functions the collection of statistics on "crimes known to the police." In 1927, the

International Association of Chiefs of Police (IACP) established a committee whose purpose it was to develop a uniform crime reporting system. This committee published a manual which provided a model for the collection of crime statistics from local police departments. The proposed system was put into effect in June of that year with IACP serving as the national clearinghouse for the collection of criminal statistics from 400 cooperating agencies (Pittman and Handy, 1962). In 1930, by act of Congress, the FBI assumed responsibility for this system of crime reporting. These reports were first published monthly and then quarterly until 1941. From 1942 to 1957 they were issued semiannually and since 1958 these reports have been published on an annual basis.

The FBI has no power to require law enforcement agencies to provide it with crime data; instead, the Bureau is dependent upon the voluntary submission of data by police agencies. While in the past the FBI has obtained most of its data from individual law enforcement agencies, it now receives the majority of its information from state operated UCR programs. Currently, 41 states have programs of this kind in operation and others are in various stages of development.

The FBI uses several procedures to maintain the uniformity and accuracy of the data it receives. In order to insure that the data from all jurisdictions are comparable, the FBI provides all cooperating agencies with the *Uniform Crime Reporting Handbook* (1981), which outlines procedures for classifying and scoring offenses. Various procedures are employed to determine the reliability of the reports received from cooperating jurisdictions. Each report is examined not only for arithmetical accuracy, but also for any deviations or errors that might indicate an agency is not accurately reporting its crime statistics. In those cases where crime reporting procedures are found to be in part responsible for the variations in the level of crime, the questionable data are excluded from the current year's *UCR*. As of 1984, the UCR program received data from more than 16,000 law enforcement agencies, representing 96 percent of the total U.S. population. *Estimates are made for areas that fail to report and for those whose figures are incomplete.*

Law enforcement agencies are supposed to classify the offenses that come to their attention according to a schema that includes 29 categories, as shown in Table 2.1. These 29 offenses are grouped into Part I (Index) crimes and Part II crimes. The FBI makes use of the eight categories of crime included in Part I to measure the trends and distribution of criminality in the United States. In choosing offenses to be included in the Crime Index, the FBI is concerned with several factors: (1) not all offenses come to the attention of law enforcement; (2) not all crimes are significant enough to be of value in an index; and (3) not all crimes occur with sufficient regularity to be meaningful in the Crime Index (*UCR*, 1981). With these considerations in mind, the following offenses were selected to serve as an index: murder and nonnegligent manslaughter, forcible rape, robbery, aggravated assault, arson, burglary (breaking or entering), larceny-theft, and motor vehicle theft.

THE EXTENT OF KNOWN CRIME

The Crime Index of the *UCR*, as we pointed out earlier, covers eight major felonies which were chosen because they are the types of offenses most likely to be reported

Table 2.1 **CLASSIFICATION OF OFFENSES IN FBI** *UNIFORM CRIME REPORTS*

Part I (Index) Crimes

Criminal homicide: Burglary
  (a) Murder and nonnegligent   Larceny-theft
    manslaughter   Motor vehicle theft
  (b) Manslaughter by negligence   Arson
Forcible rape
Robbery
Aggravated assault

Part II Crimes

Other assaults   Gambling
Forgery and counterfeiting   Offenses against family and children
Fraud   Driving under the influence
Embezzlement   Liquor laws
Stolen property: buying, receiving,   Drunkenness
  possessing   Disorderly conduct
Vandalism   Vagrancy
Weapons: carrying, possessing   All other offenses (except traffic)
Prostitution and commercialized vice   Suspicion (not included in totals)
Sex offenses (except forcible rape,   Curfew and loitering law violations
  prostitution, and commercialized vice)   Runaways (limited to juveniles taken
Drug abuse violations   into protective custody)

Source: U.S. Department of Justice, *Uniform Crime Report—1984* (Washington, D.C.: U.S. Government Printing Office, 1985).

to the police. From information concerning the occurrence of these crimes that is forwarded to the Department of Justice from local law enforcement agencies, the *UCR* provides a figure representing the total number of Crime Index offenses estimated to have occurred in the United States in a given year. In 1984, this total was 11,881,755. This seems to be a shockingly large figure, but what does it mean?

Absolute numbers are notoriously misleading if they are unaccompanied by further information to help in interpreting their significance. For example, a score of 95 on a midterm examination sounds very impressive, until we learn that a perfect test received 200 points. Nearly twelve million crimes sounds impressive, too, in the absence of any additional data.

To help clarify the meaning of reported crime information, the FBI statisticians who compile the *UCR* construct crime *rates* by dividing the number of reported crimes by the number of people in the country and expressing the result as a crime rate per 100,000 people. For 1984, the population of the United States was estimated to be 236,158,000 people, and the total number of Index offenses was 11,881,755. Thus,

$$\frac{11,881,755}{236,158,000} \times 100,000 = 5,031.3 \text{ per } 100,000$$

The overall crime rate for Index offenses per 100,000 people in 1984 was about 5,000. We can then compare this figure with the crime rates for previous years to determine whether crime has increased, decreased, or remained the same.

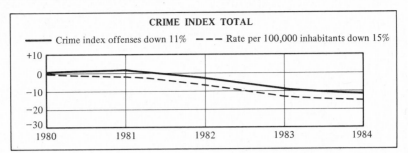

Figure 2.1   Decrease in reported rate of Index crimes during the period 1980 to 1984. (*Source:* U.S. Department of Justice, *Uniform Crime Reports—1984*. Washington, D.C.: U.S. Government Printing Office, 1985.

From 1976 to 1980, the Crime Index totals and rates increased about 18 percent. Between 1980 and 1984, however, there were decreases in the crime rate and in the total number of reported offenses, although the rate decrease was less than the reported drop in total offenses (see Figure 2.1). On the surface, this may suggest a for the first half of 1985 suggest an increase in crime rates, especially for violent crimes. Identifying crime trends is a ricky business. We shall return to this point in the Epilogue.

Clearance of Crimes by Arrest

Law enforcement agencies clear crimes by arrest or, in some circumstances, by exceptional means. An offense is cleared by arrest when at least one person is arrested, charged with the commission of the offense, and turned over to the court for prosecution. It should be noted that several crimes may be cleared by the arrest of one person, while the arrest of many persons may clear only one offense. Clearances by exceptional means are recorded in instances when some element beyond police control precludes the placing of formal charges against the offender: for example, the death of the offender by suicide or justifiably killed by the police; the victim's refusal to prosecute after the offender has been identified; or the denial of extradition because the offender committed another crime and is being prosecuted in a different jurisdiction. "In all exceptional clearance cases, law enforcement must identify the offender, have enough evidence to support arrest, and know the offender's location" (*UCR*, 1985, p. 152).

During 1984 law enforcement agencies nationwide reported that 21 percent of the total Crime Index offenses were cleared. Crimes against the person show consistently higher clearance rates than crimes against property, for several reasons: (1) the seriousness of crimes such as murder and rape results in more intensive investigative efforts; (2) the confrontation between the victims of crimes against the person are frequently acquainted with the offender; for example, 57 percent of the homicide cases in 1984 involved offenders who were relatives or individuals who were personally acquainted with the victim.

GEOGRAPHICAL AREA AND CRIME

Criminal activity is not distributed evenly throughout the United States. As shown by Table 2.2, the southern states led the nation in murder; the northeastern states had the highest rates of robbery and motor vehicle theft; and the western states topped the rest of the country in the commission of forcible rape, aggravated assault, burglary, and larceny-theft. No comparative data are given for the crime of arson. We will explore some of the factors that may help to explain these regional differences when we discuss specific crimes in later chapters of this book.

CHARACTERISTICS OF OFFENDERS

Analyses of crime data have usually assigned a prominent place to the variables of age, sex, and race. Crime in general has long been considered a predominantly youthful activity; this impression has been supported by *UCR* figures which have shown the highest rates for Crime Index offenses for people under the age of 25 years. Apart from such traditionally "female" crimes as prostitution, crime has also been a primarily male activity. Lastly, crime rates have been disproportionately high among black people, especially those who reside in the urban ghettos of America.

An examination of the 1984 *UCR* data shows that persons under the age of 25 years comprised 63 percent of those arrested for Crime Index offenses, 51 percent of those arrested for violent crimes, and 66 percent of those arrested for crimes against

Table 2.2   CRIME RATES, INDEX OFFENSES KNOWN TO THE POLICE BY REGION, 1984

Offense	Region				U.S. total
	Western states	Mid-Western states	Southern states	Northeastern states	
Crime Index total	6,210.4	4,674.8	4,898.5	4,561.9	5,031.3
Violent crime[1]	615.6	458.1	527.2	582.9	539.2
Property crime[2]	5,594.7	4,216.7	4,371.2	3,979.0	4,492.1
Murder	8.4	6.0	10.0	6.3	7.9
Forcible rape	43.9	32.9	37.7	27.9	35.7
Robbery	233.2	170.5	163.3	288.9	205.4
Aggravated assault	330.1	248.8	316.2	259.9	290.2
Burglary	1,628.8	1,103.9	1,277.7	1,055.6	1,263.7
Larceny-theft	3,447.1	2,683.0	2,729.3	2,375.9	2,791.3
Motor vehicle theft	488.9	429.0	344.2	547.5	437.1
Arson[3]					

Source: U.S. Department of Justice, *Uniform Crime Reports—1984* (Washington, D.C.: U.S. Government Printing Office, 1984. pp. 44–50).

[1] Violent crimes are offenses of murder, forcible rape, robbery, and aggravated assault.

[2] Property crimes are offenses of burglary, larceny-theft, and motor vehicle theft.

[3] No information is given on arson.

property. However, the period from 1980 to 1984 witnessed a drop of 11 percent in the arrests of persons under the age of 18 years. Criminal justice authorities had expressed a great deal of concern over the burgeoning rates of serious crimes among youths in this age bracket during the 1970s. It may be that we are seeing the beginnings of a downward trend in the crime rate that reflects the changing composition of the population. We appear to have passed the peak of the 11- to 25-year age category that was produced by the post–World War II "baby boom," with a proportional decrease in numbers of persons in that age group. The implications of this population shift for future crime trends are the subject of careful consideration in the concluding section of this book.

The impact of the sex variable on criminality raises all sorts of complex issues, many of which are dealt with in a later chapter on female offenders. Terms such as "startling" and "dramatic" have been applied to increases in crime rates for women during the decade from 1971 to 1980. As we try to emphasize in our analysis of trends in female crime, much if not most of the drama is lost when some attention is given to the actual numbers involved in the increases, rather than the rises in percentages. To take only one illustration, the female burglary rate rose nearly 300 percent between 1960 and 1975, as compared with a 100 percent increase for males during the same period. In absolute numbers, the increase was from 3,600 burglaries for women in 1960 to 14,000 in 1975, while the male burglary rate reflected an increase of 130,000 actual crimes!

Males continue to outnumber females in all categories of crime except prostitution and commercialized vice and running away from home. Even in the area of prostitution, we are seeing tendencies in some jurisdictions for laws against prostitution to be enforced against the male customers ("johns") of female prostitutes, a practice which has traditionally been winked at in most American cities. In addition, there are signs of increasingly vigorous enforcement of soliciting laws against youthful males who prostitute themselves to older homosexual customers.

According to the *UCR* (1985), blacks were arrested for 23.1 percent of all crimes committed in the United States and for 28.4 percent of the Crime Index offenses in 1984. Blacks accounted for 53 percent of violent crimes and 25.3 percent of property crimes. These crimes rates are far out of line with the actual proportion of black citizens in the total population of the United States. Trying to interpret the meaning of these rates, however, confronts us with some difficult and controversial issues.

There is one matter we can dismiss promptly; that is, the suggestion that high black crime rates are an indication of some genetic predisposition toward criminality. While there are bigots among us to whom such arguments are plausible, the criminologist maintains that race is related to crime only insofar as it affects the nature of social experiences and interactions.

A major problem in dealing with the variable of race is that it cuts across the variable of social class in contemporary American society to produce a high concentration of black people at the lowest end of the economic scale. Therefore, as soon as the factor of class in introduced into any analysis, the race issue is automatically dragged into the discussion because the two are next to impossible to separate in terms of their effects.

Within American cities, most whites reside in suburban rings, while the overwhelming majority of blacks are residents of the "central city"—a euphemism for "urban ghetto." In metropolitan areas of one million or more, black people comprise 30 percent or more of the central city population. This pattern is not an expression of choice but of necessity: blacks are subjected to discrimination in housing as a consequence of both financial hardship and racial prejudice. Black people are compelled to live under environmental conditions that are almost calculated to generate pressures toward deviance. Poor blacks are worse off today than they were a decade ago. Increased anger and alienation from a society that has failed to improve black living conditions have resulted in feelings that were expressed when James Forman of the Student Nonviolent Coordinating Committee told an angry SNCC audience: "If we can't sit at the table, let's knock the fucking legs off" (Silberman, 1979, p. 205). To these considerations must be added the undeniable and well-documented operation of persistent racism within the criminal justice system. These reasons are not an exhaustive explanation of why black crime rates have been disproportionately high, but they pose questions any theory of criminality must attempt to answer.

LIMITATIONS OF THE *UNIFORM CRIME REPORTS*

Statistics reported in the *UCR* should be interpreted with caution, for reasons we shall discuss in the two major sections that follow. In the first section, attention will be directed toward problems associated with the reporting and recording of crime events. The second section will examine some of the issues associated with the collection and analysis of these data.

The Production of Crime

Consider these three situations:

- A robber mugs a man on the street and takes his wallet containing $10, then flees without injuring him.
- A husband and wife get into a fight when the man comes home drunk. In the course of the argument, the man assaults his wife.
- A woman is raped in her home at night.

What factors determine whether the offenses described above will be incorporated into the *UCR*?

In order for an event to be included in the *UCR*, someone must observe it and report it, and it must be officially recorded by a law enforcement agency. The man who was mugged may decide not to report the robbery to the police because his loss was small and he lacks confidence in police effectiveness. The rape victim may not report her victimization because of embarrassment, fear, or even a desire to protect the offender if he happened to be known to her. In the case of the domestic disturbance, the police may attempt to arbitrate the dispute between husband and wife—

a procedure which usually results in no formal charges being filed. These examples suggest it is more realistic to view criminal statistics as emerging from the interactions of criminals, victims, and the police.

The reasons victims fail to report offenses to the police are many and varied:

1. *Some offenses may not be regarded as crimes by the victim or witnesses.* In the case of consensual crimes—prostitution, homosexual behavior, pornography—there is no victim in the traditional sense, since all parties to the transaction are willing participants. Inasmuch as these individuals are not likely to incriminate themselves, such offenses only tend to come to the attention of law enforcement authorities in those instances where the police are involved in the simultaneous detection of both the act and the offenders.

2. *Some offenses are supported or tolerated.* Center and Smith (1973) have made the point that the volume of crime reported by a community is directly affected by the community's *tolerance* for crime. All communities have a threshold beyond which they will not tolerate deviant behavior. Some communities, however, are willing to tolerate more criminal behavior than are others. Such communities may be said to have a *high threshold for crime* and would exhibit comparatively lower recorded crime rates than communities with low thresholds for crime. For example, certain types of violence within lower class neighborhoods may not be reported because of the support these acts receive from the community's standards.

3. *Businesses and industries may vary in their thresholds for crime.* Many employers are tolerant of workers who pilfer small amounts of material from the job and will only take action when the pilferage reaches sizeable proportions. This pattern is common both in the United States and abroad. Hood and Sparks (1970) cite an English study in which it was found that businesses made a distinction between "reasonable pilfering" and theft. Fully half of the firms contacted in the study indicated that they did not consider it theft when the value of the goods taken did not exceed $10.

4. *In some cases the circumstances may be embarrassing to the victim.* A married man who is robbed by a prostitute while on a business trip is not likely to report this offense for fear the illicit relationship would be disclosed to his wife. A business may fail to report employees who have embezzled funds from the firm because of concern that public knowledge of the crime would result in diminished confidence by customers in the ability of the firm to manage its own affairs. Embezzlement, as well as other offenses, is also not reported in those instances where the victims feel that little can be accomplished by making a formal complaint. For example, in cases of embezzlement involving substantial sums of money, it may be difficult if not impossible for offenders to make restitution. In these instances businesses may feel that it is in their best interests to simply fire the employee and write off the loss, rather than report the offense and become involved in a trial which would cost them money and not result in restitution.

5. *Victims may be reluctant to embarrass the perpetrator.* A recent victimization study found that 39.8 percent of the victims of violent offenses involving nonstrangers failed to report the crime because they felt it was a private or personal matter (U.S. Department of Justice, 1983).

6. *Some victims may be fearful of possible reprisals.* Victims may be intimidated; physically; through blackmail; or economically as a result of fear that their insurance may be canceled or the rates increased.

Many victims fail to report offenses to the police because they believe that nothing will be done due to lack of sufficient evidence to connect the offender to the offense. There is also evidence that a substantial number of victims fail to notify the police because they feel that the offense perpetrated against them was not important enough to justify its report.

On the other hand, in order to obtain a more complete picture of victim reporting practices, it is important to note some of the reasons people *do* report offenses to the authorities. First, Hawkins (1973) determined that people who are afraid of becoming victims of crime are the ones who are most likely to report an offense when they have been victimized. Second, the President's Crime Commission (1967) has suggested the sizeable increase in insurance coverage against theft is probably another factor that has increased the reporting of some crimes. Many citizens believe that they must report an offense to the police in order to collect insurance.

A third factor that has influenced reporting patterns is a change in attitude regarding the appropriateness of reporting offenses to the police. This is generally a function of a variety of factors, including changes in tolerance toward deviant behavior, changes in the degree to which people feel a need to call upon outside assistance in order to deal with deviant behavior, and changes in the extent to which people place confidence in the police. The President's Crime Commission (1967) indicated that changes in the expectations of the poor and minority group members regarding civil rights and social protection have increased their willingness to report crimes to the police.

Fourth, special programs directed toward specific offenses and groups and areas that are particularly vulnerable to crime may also have had an impact on the willingness of people to report crimes. Rape crisis programs, Crime Alert, and other crime prevention programs, as well as special programs directed toward dealing with crime against the elderly and crime in specific areas of the city, have all contributed to victim willingness to report offenses. These programs have also increased citizen awareness regarding crime prevention techniques which decrease victimization. For example, women are made aware of the conditions under which rape frequently occurs, and citizens are provided with information on "target hardening" their homes, cars, and businesses by means of closed circuit television monitors, electronic beepers, etc. As a result, the areas serviced by these programs may experience a real decrease in crime, which may be offset in the crime statistics by an increase in the reporting of offenses. This same condition may occur as a result of lack of public tolerance for certain offenses. This suggests the need for extreme caution in interpreting increases in reported crime.

THE ROLE OF THE POLICE

The police play an important part in determining the accuracy of crime statistics. When an offense is reported, it is their responsibility to determine whether a crime has actually been committed. Once this determination has been made, the police must record and classify the offense. It is apparent that the police make wide use of their discretion in officially recording an event as a crime and in classifying it.

Several factors have been identified which materially affect the accuracy of crime data. These include:

1. Police encounters with the public.
2. The effects of changes or variations in police practices and procedures.
3. The questionable use of certain crime statistics as measures of police performance.

Over the radio, the police will be given an address and a brief description such as "man lying in the gutter," "girl screaming," "juveniles fighting," "B and E (breaking and entering) in progress" and the like. In some cases the police may be given only a number which identifes a category of offenses. Upon arriving at the crime scene, the police have to ascertain whether, in fact, a crime has been committed, whether any of those present may have perpetrated the offense, and who is the victim. They are dependent upon the people who are present to provide details on the alleged offense. It is also important to note that the police have broad discretion with regard to the actions taken toward the offense. The exercise of this discretion has been found (e.g., by Black, 1970; Van Dine, Conrad, and Dinitz, 1979) to be affected by both the wishes of the complainants and by the demeanor of both complainants and suspects. That is, police are much more likely to file an official report when requested to do so by complainants. This request may be influenced by whether the complainants are antagonistic or disrespectful toward the police.

A second set of factors influencing crime statistics is changes and variations in police practices. Some of these changes have resulted from improvements in the quality of policing. The President's Crime Commission (1967) observed that over the past 25 years there has been notable progress in the professionalization of the police. Commission studies have shown that this has resulted in more formal action, more formal records, and less informal disposition of individual cases. It also seems likely that professionalization has affected the ability of the police to detect crime. Better methods for recording information, the use of more clerks and statistical personnel, and more intensive patrolling practices would tend to produce more accurate crime statistics. Additionally, major advances in police equipment have enhanced police efficiency and improved police response time, which has been found to positively affect the chances of noting and clearing crimes that come to the attention of the police (Maltz, 1975).

Other changes reflect political pressures and the influence of self-interest. Police departments are subject to the same political and community pressures that bear upon other government agencies. Substantial increases in street crime can create a fear among citizens for their personal safety and that of their property as well as affecting an area's tourist trade. In response to pressures to deal with specific offenses, police are likely to reallocate existing resources. This typically involves a proactive operation aimed at detecting and apprehending offenders. For instance, if muggings reach alarming proportions in an area police may respond by increasing the number of patrol officers in that neighborhood for purposes of deterring offenders and/or use decoys in an effort to apprehend offenders. A proactive effort on the part of police is likely to increase robbery rates but may also result in a decrease in arrest rates for other offenses which are receiving less attention. Thus, changes in offenses rates in particular jurisdictions may not reflect changes in the nature of the crime problem, but instead may simply result from a reallocation of police resources.

Crime statistics are also used as a measure of police performance. When a statistic is used in this way, the accuracy of the reported figures may be seriously affected. In 1949, the FBI rejected figures on crime supplied by the New York City Police Department (NYPD) because they were no longer credible. In the following year, the NYPD changed its procedures; reported robberies increased 400 percent and burglaries jumped 1300 percent. However, in the late 1950s, the department again adopted a "look good, don't rock the boat" policy and resumed the practice of underreporting crimes:

> "The unwritten law was," one high department official said, "that you were sup-posed to make things look good. You weren't supposed to report all the crimes that actually took place in the precinct—and, if you did, it could be your neck. I know captains who actually lost their commands because they turned in honest crime reports" [Cook, 1971, p. 27].

When John Lindsay became mayor, he directed the NYPD to provide an accurate picture of the crime problem. The result was that reported robberies rose from be-tween 7,000 and 8,000 a year to about 23,000 and burglaries leaped from 40,000 a year to 120,000.

By reducing the number of officially recorded offenses, a police department can portray its jurisdiction as more crime-free than it really is. It can also exaggerate its own efficiency when this is based on clearance rates, which are simply a ratio of crimes cleared (offenses in which the police have identified the perpetrator or perpe-trators) to recorded offenses. Table 2.3 provides an illustration of how comparisons between two police departments from similar jurisdictions may be extremely mis-leading because one department only records those offenses it considers to be actual crimes.

Internal pressure to appear efficient is not the only factor that affects the ma-nipulation of police statistics. Mayors, governors, and other political figures may pressure police to manipulate statistics in order to demonstrate the effectiveness of

Table 2.3 A COMPARISON OF REPORTED CRIME IN TWO CITIES, DEMONSTRATING HOW DIFFERENT RECORDING PROCEDURES CAN AFFECT CLEARANCE RATES

Offenses	City A	City B
Reported offenses	100,000	100,000
Less unfounded and suspicious circumstances, etc.	20,000	
Actual offenses	80,000	100,000
Clearances	20,000	20,000
Clearance rates	20,000 (25%)	20,000 (20%)
	80,000	100,000

> In one of the two California police departments he studied, Skolnick (1966) found that patrolmen and detectives were given a wide range of discretion in determining the legitimacy of a reported crime. Offenses were reported as "suspicious circumstances" when it appeared that a crime had been committed but one of its elements was missing; for example, a citizen reports that his home was burglarized and a camera was stolen, but no point of entry can be located. Offenses defined as suspicious circumstances are investigated by detectives who make the final determination as to whether a crime has actually occurred. Skolnick noted that 20 to 25 percent of the burglary complaints processed by patrol officers were defined as suspicious circumstances and given to detectives for a follow-up investigation. The detectives made the final determination as to whether these suspected offenses were recorded. Complaints remained "suspicious circumstances" not only when the detectives found that one or more of the elements of the alleged crime appeared to be missing but also when they believed that the complaint was unfounded, that is, the circumstances surrounding the offense were not believable. For instance, a delivery boy may claim to have been robbed while making a deposit for his employer at a local bank. Although the boy has a lump on his head and does not falter in his contention that he has been robbed, the detective still may not believe that he has been victimized. As a result, the detective will record this offense as a "suspicious circumstance" and it will never be recorded as an "offense known to the police."

their administrations. Police departments themselves may also inflate crime figures in order to justify the need for more equipment and/or personnel. It is difficult, if not impossible, to assess the extent to which crime rates are manipulated for these purposes.

SHORTCOMINGS OF *UCR* PROCEDURES

Many of the limitations of official statistics can be attributed to defects or difficulties in the collection, tabulation, analysis, and dissemination of crime data by the FBI. We shall try to identify some of these problems as we review a number of *UCR* procedures. Much of the criticism of the *UCR* concerns the extent to which it accurately portrays our crime problem. Critical comments have been directed toward the following considerations:

1. The use of the Index offenses as a measure of serious crime.
2. The practice of estimating crime for jurisdictions that fail to report to the FBI.
3. The construction of crime rates using the total adult population as a base.
4. Presentation of crime data by means which distort the information.
5. A system for use by the police in recording criminal events that fails to provide an accurate picture of the extent of the crime problem.

The Crime Index

It may be recalled that the rationale for the choice of the eight offenses which comprise the Crime Index included their frequency of occurrence, likelihood of coming to the attention of the police, and relatively serious nature. There is a real question, however, of whether the Crime Index is, in fact, a valid measure of serious crime, since the largest portion of the total Index crime rate comprises the less serious crimes of larceny and motor vehicle theft, while such serious offenses as kidnapping and assaults on police officers are omitted. The Index has also been attacked because it gives equal statistical weight to major and minor Index crimes. For *UCR* purposes, one reported petty larceny has the same effect on the crime rate as one reported murder or rape. Or, for example, the theft of a package of chewing gum has the same impact on the crime rate as the premeditated murder of a 5-year-old child. Furthermore, the Crime Index lumps together completed and attempted offenses for four of the eight Index crimes. This is a questionable practice in view of the major differences between crimes that are attempted and those that are successfully carried out.

The exclusion of white-collar/economic crimes is a serious shortcoming. Not only does the Crime Index ignore white-collar offenses, but the *UCR* in general fails to provide adequate information on these crimes. Many white-collar crimes are federal offenses and are handled by administrative agencies which have both investigative and adjudicatory powers. Thus, these crimes rarely come to the attention of the local police and are excluded from the *UCR*. It would be more accurate to call the annual volumes of the *Uniform Crime Reports* the "Uniform Conventional Crime Reports" or the "Uniform Street Crime Reports."

For all the reasons we have cited above, the Crime Index provides an imperfect picture of the crime problem. Savitz (1978) suggests that by making these eight offenses "major crimes," the *UCR* almost forces police to concentrate efforts and attention on their clearance, resulting in comparatively less attention being paid to non-Index offenses.

Estimating Crime Rates

The FBI engages in the highly questionable practice of estimating crime for jurisdictions that either fail to provide the Bureau with complete reports or with any information on crime. For those agencies that supply incomplete reports, estimates are made of the amount of crime occurring in these areas by examining the data from similar jurisdictions within the state. But it cannot be assumed that departments which fail to provide complete crime reports have sustained the same crime experiences as those which supply complete reports. However, crime statistics are not quite so badly distorted by this procedure as they are by the Bureau's practice of estimating data for those jurisdictions which fail to report any crime statistics whatsoever. In order to provide a comprehensive picture of crime, the Bureau inflates crime figures to account for these jurisdictions. This practice is of little consequence in cases where the state has reported data for 99 percent of its population. In the case of low reporting states, however, this procedure has serious consequences for the accuracy of reported crime data.

Use of the Total Population as Base

The *UCR* has been criticized for constructing crime rates (the number of crimes per unit of population) using the total adult population as a base (Reiss, 1967). By doing this, the *UCR* makes the dubious assumption that every person in the United States is equally likely to be a victim of a crime. Aside from the fact that it is inappropriate to view the total population as potential victims of most crimes, there are some crimes for which only some segments of the population are clearly eligible to be victims. Women, for instance, should be considered the population most at risk for the offenses of forcible rape and purse snatching.

Failure to make "environmental opportunities" the basis for determining the true risk groups for each crime, as suggested by Boggs (1965), means that the crime rates conveyed by the *UCR* do not provide an accurate indication of the risk of victimization associated with certain offenses. While the police, criminal justice specialists, and criminologists are concerned with the other data presented in the *UCR*, the public is primarily concerned with victimization rates. For this reason, some effort should be made to adjust this information so that it furnishes a more accurate picture of the risks connected with specific offenses.

Presentation of Crime Data

The manner in which some crime data are presented tends to distort it. While the *UCR* has been presenting crime rates based on population changes since 1958, crime data continue to be displayed in the form of "crime capsules," "crime calendars," "crime counts," and "crime clocks." Summaries of this kind are extremely misleading because they highlight changes in the absolute number of crimes while neglecting the crime rate, a far more important measure of the crime problem. Inasmuch as newspapers, television, local police departments, and civic groups typically use these charts to portray the crime picture, the public tends to receive a distorted impression of crime within a given city or community.

Variations in the population units used to construct different *UCR* tables make impossible table-to-table comparisons within the same report and year-to-year comparisons between different reports. In the 1985 *UCR*, for example, table 18 (Offense Analysis) was based on the reports of 13,156 agencies representing a population of 214,307,000; table 30 (Total Arrest Trends) was compiled from reports submitted by 18,658 agencies representing 162,547,000 people; and table 40 (Total Arrests, Distribution by Sex) was based on 9,879 agencies serving a population of 179,891,000.

Recording Procedures

The system developed by the *Uniform Crime Reports* for use by police to record criminal events involving index offenses distorts the volume and seriousness of our crime problem. This recording system uses a two-step process. First, police are required to "classify" a criminal event. The rule is that only the most serious offense occurring in a criminal event is to be recorded. Criminal homicide is ranked highest (most serious) among the Index offenses and motor vehicle theft is ranked lowest (least serious). The one exception to this hierarchical rule is arson, which is to be reported in all instances regardless of its commission in conjunction with other Index offenses (*UCR,* 1981, p. 36). This was done in recognition of the possibility that valuable information might be lost if the past procedure were followed.

The basic flaw in this system can easily be illustrated. Let us suppose that a robber holds up an all-night convenience store, kills the clerk, steals $50, and makes his getaway in a car belonging to one of the customers. On the same night a fight erupts at a local bar and one of the participants is killed. For *UCR* purposes, each of these events would be classified as a single nonnegligent homicide. It is clear that the holdup at the convenience store is more serious, since it involved not only a homicide but also a robbery and the theft of a motor vehicle. Thus, the system equates criminal events involving offenses of the same seriousness that may differ substantially with respect to the number of accompanying offenses. It is also clear that this system does not provide a true picture of the extent of the crime problem.

Second, the police are required to "score" the offense they identified as the most serious in the first phase. There are two rules: one applies to crimes against the person and the other to crimes against property. In the case of crimes against the person, the number of offenses to be recorded equals the number of persons raped, killed, maimed, wounded, or assaulted. For example, in the preceding illustrations, only one person was killed in each case, therefore one offense would be recorded for each of these events. If, however, the grocery store robber killed a clerk and an innocent bystander, then two offenses would be recorded for this event. Three aggravated assaults would be recorded if three people were seriously wounded as a result of being involved in the same fight. On the other hand, if four men forcibly raped one woman, then only one rape would be recorded because there was only one victim. In the case of offenses against property the rule is that one offense is recorded for each distinct operation (criminal event). If a nightclub were held up by armed bandits and all 25 patrons present at the time were deprived of their valuables, this would be construed as one distinct operation and would be recorded for *UCR* purposes as one robbery. This system of scoring recorded offenses even further distorts our picture of the crime problem. While it is certainly understandable that a simple system of this kind was necessary prior to the advent of the computer and sophisticated data management techniques, it is rather perplexing that the system is still employed today. Its use at the present time seems almost as incongruous as having the *UCR* printed on the Gutenberg press instead of using modern printing facilities.

Other Shortcomings of the *UCR*

Certain data gathered from cooperating agencies by the FBI are not published in the *UCR*. This includes information on the extent of injury and monetary loss, circumstances of the offense, victim-offender relationships, and the like (Hindelang, 1974). If this information were available, the data would improve our capability for carrying out a number of valuable kinds of criminological studies.

The *Uniform Crime Reports* provide little information beyond the police processing of offenders. Moreover, there is no single source or combination of sources that enables us to track offenders as they progress through the criminal justice system. The need for this type of system, appropriately labeled *Offender-Based Transac-*

tion Statistics, has been recognized for some time as a precondition for improving the operation of the criminal justice system.

A Perspective on Official Crime Statistics

Whatever the problems that have traditionally plagued those who sought to work with official crime data, there is little utility to endless laments about the inadequacies of the *UCR*. If this official source of data is, in effect, the only game in town, then this is the game in which one has to play or not play at all. Official crime statistics still represent the best approximation we have to the "dark figure" of crime, especially with regard to crimes against the person and property. We might even emphasize that there are no adequate substitutes for this kind of information. Some writers have suggested alternative views of official crime statistics which recognize their imperfections and limitations, yet provide a basis for making the fullest possible use of the information they convey.

Wheeler (1967) has suggested that *UCR* data can be viewed as rates of socially recognized deviant behavior. That is, official crime data are produced by official reactions to deviance; therefore, they constitute a barometer of community tolerance of deviant behavior. Wheeler sees crime data as resulting from the interaction of three elements: (1) the person who perpetrates the crime, (2) the victim or other citizens who may report the crime, and (3) the official agents of the state who are charged with the responsibility for controlling crime. Once again we see the importance of the process of social definition in the production of crime statistics. The recording of an event as a crime requires more than the mere occurrence of some particular action; it involves interaction among the above three elements. Thus, official crime data reflect the operation of social values in the very process by which an event becomes an officially recognized and recorded crime. We shall examine this process of labeling when we reach the section on criminological theories.

ALTERNATIVE SOURCES OF DATA ON CRIME

For a long time criminologists have recognized that the FBI *Uniform Crime Reports* provide a partial indication of the amount of crime which actually occurs because they are based only on "crimes known to the police." As we have tried to show, many crimes go undiscovered while others, when discovered, are not reported, or when reported are not recorded. It was also pointed out that there are problems with the types of analyses included in the *UCR*.

These considerations have prompted researchers to develop various methods to obtain more complete information on the crime problem. Some of these methods, such as **cohort analysis,** involve the analysis of reported crime; others, such as **self-report** and **victimization studies,** seek to provide an indication of the amount of unreported and unrecorded crime and delinquency.

Longitudinal Analysis (Cohort Analysis)

One of the major deficiencies of official statistical sources is that they fail to provide an adequate picture of **offender career patterns.** This makes it difficult to determine the proportion of the population involved in crime. The *UCR* only furnishes information on the number of arrests for each offense without giving any indication as to the number of people who are perpetrating these crimes. In 1977, nine million arrests were made for all *UCR* recorded offenses. At no point in the *UCR* is there any indication of the number of people who contributed to these arrest statistics. While it is fair to assume that at least some of these persons were arrested more than once, an accurate assessment is impossible. Data of this sort are indispensable for determining such factors as the length of a criminal career, extent of criminal specialization, and the characteristics of offenders with different kinds of commitments to crime. Absence of such data also limits the extent to which we can make sound decisions regarding appropriate programs and intervention points for various offender groups. For instance, analysis may show that intervention for some offender groups is pointless because their "criminal careers" are of very short duration and do not involve serious crimes. For others groups it may be best to intervene after they have perpetrated their first offense; in still other groups the appropriate intervention point may be after the second arrest. Obviously, information of this kind provides a much sounder basis for the allocation of criminal justice resources.

One method of obtaining information on offender careers is to follow a **cohort** for a specified period of time. A cohort is a group of individuals who have experienced the same event—for example, birth, prosecution, conviction for a crime, release on parole—within a specified time interval. This type of research is very rarely done because of the amount of time and resources it requires.

In one of the largest and most informative cohort studies ever conducted by criminologists, Marvin Wolfgang, Robert Figlio, and Thorsten Sellin (1972) traced the developmental histories of nearly ten thousand Philadelphia boys born in 1945, through the ages of 10 to 18 years. This project made it possible to study the careers of all the youths, including those who had one or more contact with the police.

Although approximately one-third of the boys experienced at least one contact with the police, nearly half of those involved single, one-time offenders, most of whom had committed **status offenses**—juvenile "crimes" such as truancy and running away from home for which there are no adult counterparts. A minority of 625 chronic offenders or recidivists (only 6.3 percent of the total birth cohort) committed 71 percent of the robberies, 62 percent of the property offenses (auto theft, burglary, and larceny), and 53 percent of the crimes against person (homicide, assault, and rape). Noting the disparity in delinquency rates between whites and nonwhites, the authors stressed the need for focusing attention and resources on nonwhite youths at the time of their first delinquency. In particular, such intervention might offer the possibility of reducing the number of assaultive and violent crimes committed by potentially chronic repeaters.

Self-report Studies with Juveniles

Early studies focused on agency records to determine the extent of "hidden delinquency," that is delinquent acts which may not appear in official statistics. In 1936, Robison found that over one-third of the cases of delinquency known to private agencies in New York were unknown to the juvenile court. During this period other studies confirmed these findings. A study of the case records of the boys participating in the Cambridge-Somerville Project (Murphy, Shirley, and Witmar, 1946) for over

Table 2.4   REPORTED DELINQUENT BEHAVIOR AMONG BOYS

Type of offense
Driven a car without a driver's license or permit
Skipped school
Had fist fight with one person
"Run away" from home
School probation or expulsion
Defied parents' authority
Driven too fast or recklessly
Taken little things (worth less than $2) that did not belong to you
Taken things of medium value ($2–$50)
Taken things of large value ($50)
Used force (strong-arm methods) to get money from another person
Taken part in "gang fights"
Taken a car for a ride without the owner's knowledge
Bought or drank beer, wine, or liquor (include drinking at home)
Bought or drank beer, wine, or liquor (outside your home)
Drank beer, wine, or liquor in your own home
Deliberate property damage
Used or sold narcotic drugs
Had sex relations with another person of the same sex (not masturbation)
Had sex relations with a person of the opposite sex
Gone hunting or fishing without a license (or violated other game laws)
Taken things you didn't want
"Beat up" on kids who hadn't done anything to you
Hurt someone to see them squirm

Source: J. F. Short, and F. I. Nye. Extent of unrecorded delinquency: Tentative conclusions. *Journal of Criminal Law, Criminology, and Police Science* 49 (1958): 297. Reproduced by permission of the authors and publisher.

five years revealed that nearly all of the youngsters in the project had committed numerous acts of delinquency of which only 1.5 percent ever resulted in official action.

In recent years, **self-report studies** have been the primary method used to assess hidden delinquency. These surveys have used two basic techniques to obtain information on delinquency. Most surveys request the subjects to complete a questionnaire which asks them to indicate their involvement in a variety of delinquent activities. (Table 2.4 provides a typical list of such activities.) In other cases, interviews are conducted with subjects to obtain information on on the extent of their delinquent behavior. Questionnaires are useful for gathering information on large samples in an anonymous fashion, while interviews permit the gathering of more detailed, and in some instances more accurate, information since the interviewer can probe the subject's answers and make a more accurate determination of which prior acts constitute delinquent behavior.

Self-report studies conducted in both the United States and abroad[1] have revealed that (1) the amount of undetected delinquency is enormous and (2) most delinquent behavior goes undetected. Almost every youngster in these studies had committed at least one delinquent act. Although the majority of these offenses were relatively minor, the small number of youths who admitted involvement in such

[1] Braithwaite (1981) identified 47 self-report and 53 official records studies in countries as diverse in culture as Yugoslavia and Argentina.

serious crimes as armed robbery was still much higher than was reported in official records (Empey, 1978). It is quite possible that this figure is even smaller than the true figure because young people are more likely to underreport or not report their involvement in serious offenses.

Although these studies have provided us with some useful information, their results have been questioned on a number of grounds. First, the data on delinquency that they have provided were not comparable to police and court data in terms of the number and seriousness of offenses examined. In this respect, their major flaw involved overemphasis of trivial offenses—for example, theft of less than $2 and truancy—and an underemphasis on serious offenses. Second, most of these studies did not use national samples; those that did failed to have a large enough sample to provide an adequate national picture of the limited range of juvenile behavior they examined.

Elliott, Huizinga, Knowles, and Canter (1983) designed a study that attempted to rectify some of the major deficiencies of prior research on self-reported delinquency, including the lack of comprehensive information on the frequency of juvenile involvement in crime. Using sophisticated sampling procedures, they drew a representative national sample of youths aged 11 to 17 years, of whom 1,725 agreed to participate in the study.[2] These youths were questioned each year for five years (1977–1981) by means of a survey instrument that included the full range of criminal activities covered by the FBI's *Uniform Crime Reports* (see Table 2.5).

First, we will report on the *prevalence* of delinquency in this population, that is, the number of youths that report committing one or more acts of delinquency. The vast majority of youths reported that they were involved in some type of delinquent activity during each of the five years they were questioned. Most of their offenses, however, were trivial or of a nonserious nature (i.e., status offenses and minor misdemeanors). Only a very small proportion of the youths reported any involvement in serious offenses and this declined as the population matured (see Figure 2.2). The *incidence* of delinquency—the average number of offenses per youth—in this population followed a similar pattern. There was a relatively high number of overall offenses per youth which rose from 36 in 1976 to 53 in 1980. But the incidence of serious (Crime Index) offenses was relatively low in 1976 (one per youth) and this declined over the term of the study. Although these figures may appear to suggest a low volume of serious delinquency when they are converted to estimates of actual volume of this behavior in the adolescent population, the figures are quite surprising. For example, if 12 percent of the youth population reported involvement on one or more Index offenses, this means that 3.5 million youths are committing serious offenses. An incidence rate of one Index offense per youth means that this population is accounting for 29 million serious offenses per year. As Elliott and his colleagues (1982) note, rates of this magnitude clearly suggest why the police and the juvenile justice system cannot deal adequately with all juvenile offenses.

Social Class, Race, and Delinquency   Elliott and Ageton (1980) have suggested that the failure by previous studies to find social class differences in self-reported delinquency could be related to the use of insufficient measures of this phenomenon. One

---

[2]By the end of the fifth year, the number of respondents participating had declined to 1,494. For the 5-year period, the cumulative loss was 13.4 percent.

Table 2.5 DELINQUENCY SCALES—NATIONAL YOUTH SURVEY

Offense-specific scales	Offense-category scales	Summary scales	

Felony Assault
(1) Aggravated assault
(2) Sexual assault
(3) Gang fights

Minor Assault
(1) Hit teacher
(2) Hit parent
(3) Hit students

Robbery
(1) Strongarmed
    students
(2) Strongarmed
    teachers
(3) Strongarmed others

Felony Theft
(1) Stole motor vehicle
(2) Stole something
    GT$50
(3) Broke into bldg/
    vehicle
(4) Bought stolen goods

Minor Theft
(1) Stole something
    LT$5
(2) Stole something
    $5–50
(3) Joyriding

Damaged Property[a]
(1) Damaged family
    property
(2) Damaged school
    property
(3) Damaged other
    property

Drug Use
(1) Hallucinogens
(2) Amphetamines
(3) Barbiturates
(4) Heroin
(5) Cocaine

Illegal Services
(1) Prostitution
(2) Sold marijuana
(3) Sold hard drugs

Public Disorder[a]
(1) Hitchhiked illegally
(2) Disorderly conduct
(3) Public drunkenness
(4) Panhandled
(5) Obscene calls

Status Offenses[a]
(1) Runaway
(2) Skipped classes
(3) Lied about age
(4) Sexual intercourse

Crimes Against Persons
(1) Aggravated assault
(2) Gang fights
(3) Hit teacher
(4) Hit parent
(5) Hit students
(6) Sexual assault
(7) Strongarmed
    students
(8) Strongarmed
    teachers
(9) Strongarmed others

General Theft
(1) Stole motor vehicle
(2) Stole something
    GT$50
(3) Bought stolen goods
(4) Stole something
    LT$5
(5) Stole something
    $5–50
(6) Broke into bldg/
    vehicle
(7) Joyriding

School Delinquency[a]
(1) Damaged school
    property
(2) Cheated on school
    tests
(3) Hit teacher
(4) Hit students
(5) Strongarmed
    students
(6) Strongarmed
    teachers
(7) Stole at school
(8) Skipped classes

Home Delinquency[a]
(1) Damaged family
    property
(2) Runaway
(3) Stole from family
(4) Hit parent

Index Offenses
(1) Aggravated assault
(2) Sexual assault
(3) Gang fights
(4) Stole motor vehicle
(5) Stole something
    GT$50
(6) Broke into bldg/
    vehicle
(7) Strongarmed
    students
(8) Strongarmed
    teachers
(9) Strongarmed others

General Delinquency A[a]
+(1) Damaged family
    property
+(2) Damaged school
    property
+(3) Damaged other
    property
(4) Stole motor vehicle
(5) Stole something
    GT$50
(6) Bought stolen goods
(7) Runaway
+(8) Lied about age
(9) Carried hidden
    weapon
(10) Stole something
    LT$5
(11) Aggravated assault
(12) Prostitution
(13) Sexual intercourse
(14) Gang fights
(15) Sold marijuana
+(16) Hitchhiked illegally
(17) Hit teacher
(18) Hit parent
(19) Hit students
(20) Disorderly conduct
(21) Sold hard drugs
(22) Joyriding
+(23) Bought liquor for
    minor
(24) Sexual assault
(25) Strongarmed
    students
(26) Strongarmed
    teachers
(27) Strongarmed others
+(28) Evaded payment
+(29) Public drunkenness
(30) Stole something
    $5–50
(31) Broke into bldg/
    vehicle
(32) Panhandled
+(33) Skipped classes
+(34) Didn't return
    change
+(35) Obscene calls

General Delinquency B
Same as General
    Delinquency A
except the + items omitted.

Source: D. S. Elliott and D. Huizinga. Social class and delinquency in a national youth panel. *Criminology* 21 (1983): 156–157. Reproduced by permission of the authors and publisher.
    [a]Not available for 1977.

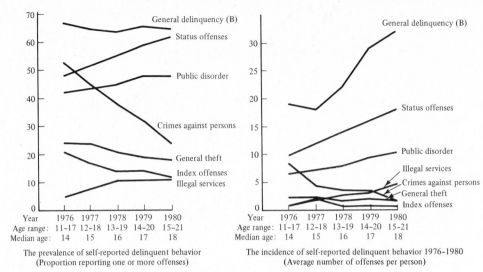

Figure 2.2 Prevalence and incidence of self-reported delinquent behavior. (*Source:* D. S. Elliott, D. Huizinga, B. A. Knowles, and R. J. Canter. *The Prevalence and Incidence of Delinquent Behavior: 1976–1980.* Boulder, CO: Behavioral Research Institute, 1983.) Reproduced by permission of the authors and publisher.)

of the major defects in prior self-reported delinquency (SRD) measures has been the limited representatives of items, that is, an underemphasis on serious offenses and overrepresentation of trivial offenses. Recognizing this problem, as we noted earlier, Elliott and his co-authors used a full range (46-item) self-report questionnaire in their national youth survey (see Table 2.5).

These new improved measures resulted in findings that showed some class differentials in delinquency. Elliott and Huizinga (1983) found that middle-class youths of both sexes reported less involvement in Crime Index offenses than working- or lower-class youths. Even those middle-class youths who were involved in Index crimes committed fewer offenses on the average than working- and lower-class youths. Despite class differences in both incidence and prevalence of serious offenses, the evidence for class differences in involvement in these offenses *was much stronger* when comparisons were made using incidence rates rather than prevalence measures. This means that the evidence is stronger for an involvement of lower- and working-class youths in more offenses per person as compared with their middle-class counterparts.

However, when overall involvement in delinquency was examined by class, there were few significant differences in the number of youths involved in one or more acts of delinquency. Some differences were found when general delinquency was examined by class and sex. Middle-class males reported substantially fewer acts per youth than did working- or lower-class males. This pattern was not found for females.

Studies examining official records have consistently reported a higher prevalence among blacks as compared with white delinquents (Hirschi, 1972; Wolfgang et al., 1972). On the other hand, most self-report studies have shown that the overall reported involvement of blacks and whites in one or more offenses is proportionately the same (Elliott and Voss, 1974; Hindelang, Hirschi, and Weis, 1981; Gold and Reimer, 1974; Institute for Juvenile Research, 1972; Williams and Gold, 1972), while a few studies have indicated slightly higher black rates of involvement in serious property crimes.

The more comprehensive nature of the Elliott et al. study (1983), with regard to both sampling procedures and improved SRD measures, provided an opportunity for further examination of this issue. These researchers examined the race variable both in terms of its effects on social class differences and as an independent dimension. With respect to social class, race was controlled to determine whether the class differences found were actually the result of differences between racial groups. A comparison of the incidence and prevalence rates of middle-class white subjects with their lower- and working-class counterparts still resulted in the types of class differences noted above. There were no major differences in the prevalence or incidence of general delinquency by race. Although blacks reported a significant involvement in violent offenses during the early years of this study, there was no evidence of constant racial variations in the incidence of these offenses; the initial differences in black prevalence had vanished by 1980. There was also no evidence of any racial differences in the prevalence or incidence of involvement in serious, nonviolent offenses. Both whites and blacks reported different incidence and prevalent rates on nonserious scales and offenses. For example, whites had higher levels of both incidence and prevalence rates for minor theft during the first few years of the study and for school-related offenses and drug use for the entire study, while blacks had higher rates of involvement in sex-related offenses.

Limitations of Self-report Studies on Delinquency   Like all of the other measures of crime that we have studied, delinquency self-report studies have their limitations. Until recently, there have been no efforts to conduct any nationwide studies of self-reported delinquency using measures that provide offense information comparable to that provided in official 1983 statistics. The 5-year study carried out by Elliott et al. (1983) represents a major effort to provide this type of data. Whether this type of research will be done on a regular basis remains to be seen. Until further studies of this magnitude are completed, we must view these findings with some degree of caution.

Two issues must be raised regarding the accuracy of SRD studies. First, if a given juvenile were administered the same questionnaire or interview at different times, would he or she give the same answers to the questions? Tests of the reliability of these measures have generally proven them to be reasonably adequate in this respect (Hindelang et al., 1981; Elliott et al., 1983). Second, it is necessary to determine the validity of the SRD measures, that is, the extent to which these measures obtain accurate information on the full range of delinquency and are free from systematic errors such as concealment or exaggeration of a youth's prior delinquency. Overall self-report studies appear to have a high level of validity (Elliott et al., 1983; Hindelang et al., 1981), but underreporting on the part of blacks appears to be a problem which threatens the validity of racial comparisons. Hindelang (1978), in an analysis of SRD data from several studies including his own research in Seattle (Hindelang, Hirschi, and Weis, 1982), found that a comparison of self-reported offenses by blacks with official data showed them to underreport at much higher levels than whites. Elliott and his colleagues (1983) questioned the validity of this technique for assessing racial differences in delinquency. Using an improved SRD measure and a more representative sampling, they found through a check of police records that while over one in five youths with records of arrests concealed part of their delinquent behavior, the amount of underreporting was much higher among blacks than whites and more frequently involved Crime Index offenses than nonserious offenses. These researchers believe that a small part of this underreporting can be attributed to errors in police records or in the matching of offenses in police records with self-reported offenses, rather than inaccurate recall or deliberate concealment on the part of subjects, but they still feel that it is a serious enough source of error to require that we exercise caution in interpreting racial differences. Finally, given the extensive underreporting of delinquency in official records, we agree with Elliott and his associates (1983) that although SRD measures may not provide the most valid indicator of delinquent behavior, they certainly provide a much more accurate picture of this problem than is conveyed by official statistics.

Self-report Studies with Adults

Our knowledge of undetected adult criminal behavior is extremely limited. It is much more difficult to secure representative samples of adults than of juveniles, which may help to account for the relative dearth of adult studies in this area. The earliest of these investigations was conducted by Wallerstein and Wyle (1947), who asked a sample of nearly 1,700 adults if they had committed any of 49 listed offenses, ranging from burglary and robbery to tax evasion and election fraud. Over 90 percent of the subjects admitted to the commission of one or more of these offenses after age 16 for which they would have received a jail or prison sentence. Men reported that they had committed an average of 18 offenses and women reported an average of 11 offenses. Nearly two-thirds of the men and one-third of the women admitted to the commission of at least one felony offense.

A more recent study by Tittle and Villemez (1977), using a sample of nearly two thousand adults in three states (New Jersey, Iowa, and Oregon), provides us with some additional information on the extent of undetected adult crime. The investigators not only asked their subjects to indicate their involvement in six offenses (theft $5, theft $50, illegal gambling, tax cheating, assault, and marijuana use) over the previous 4 years, but also elicited a statement from the respondents about the probability of their engaging in these offenses in the future.

Most adults reported that they had not engaged in either serious theft or assault and that they did not expect to commit such offenses in the future. On the other hand, a third of these respondents had gambled and slightly more expected to engage in this activity in the future. Also a proportionately small number of these adults reported past and expected marijuana use and involvement in petty theft. On tax cheating, the only white-collar crime for which information was requested, only 12 percent admitted past tax evasion and 23 percent indicated they might engage in it in the future. These figures are lower than one would expect, particularly in the case of marijuana use, petty theft, and tax cheating. Based on these figures, the authors have

Table 2.6 SELF-REPORTED CRIMINAL ACTS BY AGE

Act reported as occurring	Before 18 (%)	After 18 (%)	Before and after 18 (%)
1. Public intoxication	4	66	30
2. Driving while intoxicated	2	73	25
3. Auto theft	67	25	8
4. Breaking and entering	60	28	13
5. Armed robbery	11	66	23
6. Shoplifting	71	10	19
7. Stealing (face-to-face)	42	36	22
8. Illegal gambling	15	74	11
9. Bad checks	22	75	3
10. Forged prescriptions	3	92	5

Source: J. A. O'Donnell, H. L. Voss, R. R. Clayton, G. T. Slayton, and R. Room. *Young Men and Drugs—A Nationwide Survey.* NIDA Research Monograph 5 (Rockville, MD: National Institute on Drug Abuse, 1976). Reproduced by permission of the authors and the National Institute on Drug Abuse.

made estimates of the amount of unreported crime for the three states surveyed for at least the offenses of $50 theft and assault. It was estimated that for the 5-year period for which the respondents were asked to report their offenses, the FBI data considerably underreported crime. These authors also examined the relationship between reported criminal behavior and social status. There was no indication that the greatest propensities toward crime could be found among those in lower status groups.

Another study conducted in 1974 of a sample (N = 2,510) of American males 20 to 30 years old provides some additional data on undetected adult crime (O'Donnell et al., 1976). This study fills an important gap in our understanding of patterns of individual involvement in crime, because it looks at self-reported crime both during adolescence and young adulthood. The information provided in Table 2.6 indicates that, with the exception of armed robbery, most respondents reported that their involvement in conventional street crimes—auto theft, breaking and entering, shoplifting, face-to-face stealing—occurred before 18 years of age. On the other hand, involvement in alcohol- and drug-related offenses—public intoxication, driving while intoxicated, and forged prescriptions—were substantially more likely to occur after 18 years of age. This was also the case with running numbers and passing bad checks. The heaviest users of both alcohol and marijuana were more likely to report that they had committed each of these acts than did nonusers and light users.

VICTIMIZATION STUDIES

Victimization studies represent still another method of obtaining information on the nature and extent of the crime problem. While self-reporting studies ask people to provide information on the extent and nature of their involvement in criminal behavior, victim studies, on the other hand, ask people to indicate the frequency of occurrence and types of crimes which have been perpetrated against them. In addition to gathering information on selected crimes of violence and theft, victimization surveys also collect data on characteristics of victims and circumstances surrounding criminal acts, including victim-offender relationships, characteristics of offenders, victim self-protection, extent of victim injuries, time and place of occurrence, economic consequences to victims, use of weapons, whether the police were notified, and the reasons for not calling the police.

The first nationwide victimization studies were conducted by the National Opinion Research Center (NORC) for the President's Crime Commission on Law Enforcement and the Administration of Justice. In this broad-based and well-designed survey, interviews were conducted in 10,000 households throughout the continental United States. Researchers found that the estimated rate of victimization for index crimes was more than twice the rate reported by the *Uniform Crime Reports*.

A later series of victimization studies was carried out between 1972 and 1974 in 26 American cities (U.S. Department of Justice, 1974; 1975a, b). Decker (1977) combined the data from these studies and compared them with *UCR* data for the corresponding years. As Table 2.7 shows, he found that victims reported almost three times as many Crime Index offenses perpetrated against them as were recorded by the *Uniform Crime Reports*. Since victimization studies are not subject to the same reporting and recording problems that affect the *UCR*, they may be a more accurate barometer of crime increases than the *Uniform Crime Reports*.

Major Findings of Victimization Studies

In 1984, according to Bureau of Justice Statistics (BJS), estimated crimes in the United States dropped to the lowest point in 12 years. However, while crime in general decreased, violent crimes—murder, rape, robbery, and assault—remained

Table 2.7 DIFFERENCE OF MEANS TEST FOR OFFICIAL AND SURVEY ESTIMATES OF CRIME

	Mean rate (per 100,000)		*t* Value	Degrees of freedom	Significance
	VIC	UCR			
Rape	137	50	8.05	25	*a*
Robbery	1621	582	9.98	25	*a*
Aggravated assault	766	360	5.28	25	*a*
Larceny	9581	2737	8.92	25	*a*
Burglary	6187	2065	13.64	25	*a*
Motor vehicle theft	1073	1186	−1.68	25	0.10
Violent crime rate	2525	993	9.94	25	*a*
Property crime rate	16954	5875	10.94	25	*a*
Overall crime rate	19478	6868	11.11	25	*a*

Source: S. H. Decker, Official crime rates and victim surveys: An empirical comparison. *Journal of Criminal Justice* 5 (1977): 51. Reproduced by permission of the author and publisher.
[a]Significant beyond 0.0005.

about the same. BJS also reported that in 1984, 26 percent of the nation's households were touched by a crime of violence or theft, representing a 5 percent decline from 1983 and a 19 percent drop from 1975 (Bureau of Justice Statistics, June 1985).

Among their more specific findings, victimization surveys confirm that groups which are disproportionately involved in the perpetration of crimes—the young, the poor males, and blacks—are also the ones most likely to be victimized, both by crimes against the person and against property. In addition, residents of central city areas—our urban ghettos—are much more vulnerable to crime victimization than are those who live in nonmetroplitan areas or the suburbs. Among commercial victims, retail stores suffered the highest rates of burglary and robbery.

Personal crimes of violence predominantly involved members of the same race. In approximately two-thirds of these crimes, victims and perpetrators were strangers to one another. But some distinctions can be made within this category of personal crimes. Rape and robbery, for instance, more frequently involved strangers than did assault; and both white and black males were more likely than white and black females to have crimes of violence perpetrated against them by strangers. More than one-third of the white victims of sexual assault reported having been raped by someone they knew, as compared with only 13 percent of black rape victims.

Limitations of Victimization Studies

The value of information obtained from victimization studies rests on the accuracy and reliability of the survey techniques. A key issue is the adequacy of the sample on which the results are based. Other factors include the fallibility of memory of the crime victims and the truthfulness—or lack of it—which characterizes their responses to the members of the survey team.

Early victimization studies (those conducted for the President's Crime Commission in 1966) were criticized because approximately one-quarter of the people approached refused to be interviewed, thus introducing an immediate bias in the sample. The NORC study was also challenged because only one available adult in each household was questioned—a method which produced an overrepresentation of women and older persons (those more likely to be at home during the day). These problems were overcome in later victim surveys, which obtained nearly 100 percent participation of eligible persons and eliminated the excessive reliance on the responses of a single individual by interviewing everyone over the age of 12 in the households sampled.

Victims are not always able to remember the crimes that were perpetrated against them during a given period of time. In some instances, they may not even be aware that they *were* crime victims, for example, in such offenses as fraud, embezzlement, or buying stolen property. It is also possible that victimization figures are inflated by respondents who give false reports in order to justify illegal tax deductions or spurious insurance claims. To the best of our knowledge, there is no easy or simple way to gauge the extent to which victimization studies reflect an overreporting of crime for such reasons.

SUMMARY

Crime statistics have a variety of purposes, ranging from their use in helping to formulate laws and public policies to the design of programs aimed at reducing the incidence of offenses within particular groups. The most important source of official crime data is the FBI *Uniform Crime Reports (UCR)*. Based on information supplied by local law enforcement around the country, the *UCR* provides an annual tabulation of 29 categories of offenses grouped into Part I (Index) and Part II crimes.

For reasons which the chapter examines in some detail, the *UCR* is subject to a number of limitations which reflect shortcomings and problems involved in the collection, tabulation, and analysis of crime data. In addition, the use of questionable devices such as the "crime clock" for reporting on the number of offenses that occur in a given time period leads to distortions in the interpretation of crime statistics. In recognition of the limitations of official sources of crime data, criminologists have developed alternative sources of information on the crime problem, such as birth cohort analysis, self-reporting techniques, and victimization studies. Although these methods and approaches are subject to shortcomings and limitations of their own, they constitute a valuable additional source of information on the distribution and frequency of crime and delinquency in the United States.

DISCUSSION QUESTIONS

Find the answers to the following questions in the text.
1. What are some of the major purposes served by crime statistics?
2. How does the Federal Bureau of Investigation obtain the information which is published in the *Uniform Crime Reports*?
3. On what basis were the crimes selected for inclusion in the *UCR* Index on crimes? What are some of the **Part II offenses**?
4. Discuss some of the factors that help determine whether or not a particular criminal occurrence will be included in the *UCR*.
5. Identify some of the factors associated with the failure of a crime to come to the attention of the police.
6. How is the accuracy of crime statistics affected when they are used as a measure of police performance?
7. Cite a few of the reasons for questioning whether the Crime Index is, in fact, an index of "serious crimes."
8. Why do the authors suggest that the *Uniform Crime Reports* should be called the "Uniform Street Crimes Report"?
9. Indicate some of the ways that the *UCR* might be improved in order to afford a more accurate and reliable picture of the crime problem.
10. What can the method of **birth cohort analysis** contribute to an understanding of offender career patterns?
11. Discuss the two basic techniques (questionnaires and interviews) used to gather information in **self-report studies** and how they complement one another as data sources on delinquent activity.

12. Discuss the findings of self-report studies in relation to: frequency of delinquent activity; unofficial versus official delinquency; and the variables of social class, race, sex, and ethnic status.
13. What are some of the ways that investigators have sought to strengthen the reliability and validity of self-report studies of delinquency?
14. Summarize the major findings of **victimization studies.**
15. Discuss the major factors that limit the accuracy of information obtained through victimization studies.

TERMS TO IDENTIFY AND REMEMBER

Uniform Crime Reports (UCR)
birth cohort analysis
self-report studies
victimization studies
Part I (Index) offenses
Part II offenses
hidden delinquency

"dark figure of crime"
threshold for crime
crime rate
status offender
"crimes known to the police"
offender career patterns

REFERENCES

Akers, R. L. Socioeconomic status and delinquent behaviour: A retest. *Journal of Research in Crime and Delinquency* 1 (1964): 38–46.

Black, D. J. The production of crime rates. *American Sociological Review* 35 (1970): 733–48.

Boggs, S. L. Urban crime patterns. *American Sociological Review* 30 (1965): 899–908.

Braithwaite, J. The myth of social class and criminality reconsidered. *American Sociological Review* 46 (1981): 36–57.

Carter, R. M. *Middle-class Delinquency: An experiment in Community Control.* Berkeley: School of Criminology, University of California, 1968.

Center, L. J., and Smith, T. G. Criminal statistics—Can they be trusted? *The American Criminal Law Review* 11 (1973): 1045–86.

Cook, F. There's always a crime wave. In D. R. Cressey (ed.), *Crime and Criminal Justice.* Chicago: Quadrangle Books, 1971.

Decker, S. H. Official crime rates and victim surveys: An empirical comparison. *Journal of Criminal Justice* 5 (1977): 47–54.

Dentler, R. A., and Monroe, L. J. Social correlates of early adolescent theft. *American Sociological Review* 26 (1961): 733–43.

Elliott, D. S., and Huizinga, D. Social class and delinquency in a national youth panel. *Criminology* 21 (1983): 149–77.

Elliott, D. S., Huizinga, D., Knowles, B. A., and Canter, R. J. *The Prevalence and Incidence of Delinquent Behavior: 1976-1980.* Boulder, CO: Behavioral Research Institute, 1983.

Elliott, D. S., and Voss, H. L. *Delinquency and Dropout.* Lexington, MA: Lexington Books, 1974.

Empey, L. T. *American Delinquency: Its Meaning and Construction.* Homewood, IL: Dorsey Press, 1978.

Erickson, M. The changing relationship between official and self-reported measures of delinquency: An exploratory-predictive study. *Journal of Criminal Law, Criminology, and Police Science* 63, no. 3 (1972): 388–95.

Erickson, M. L. and Empey, L. T. Court records, undetected delinquency, and decision making. *Journal of Criminal Law, Criminology, and Police Science* 54 (1963): 456–69.

Farrington, D. P. Self-reports of deviant behavior: Predictive and stable? *Journal of Criminal Law and Criminology* 19 (1967): 99–110.

Gold, M., and Reimer, D. J. Changing patterns of delinquent behavior among Americans 13 through 16 years old: 1967–72. *Crime and Delinquency Literature* 7 (1975): 483–517.

Hawkins, R. O. Who called the cops? Decisions to report criminal victimization. *Law and Society* 7 (1973): 427–44.

Hindelang, M. J. Age, sex and versatility of delinquent involvement. *Social Problems* 20 (1971): 522–35.

———. The Uniform Crime Reports revisited. *Journal of Criminal Justice* 2 (1974): 1–17.

———. Race and involvement in common law personal crimes. *American Sociological Review* 43 (1978): 93–109.

Hindelang, M. J., Hirschi, T., and Weis, J. Correlates of delinquency: The illusion of discrepancy between self-report and official measures. *American Sociological Review* 44 (1979): 995–1014.

———. *Measuring Delinquency.* Beverly Hills, CA: Sage, 1981.

Hirschi, T. *Causes of Delinquency.* Berkeley: University of California Press, 1969.

Hood, R., and Sparks, R. *Key Issues in Criminology.* New York: World University Library, 1970.

Illinois Institute for Juvenile Research. *Juvenile Delinquency in Illinois.* Chicago: Illinois Department of Mental Health, 1972.

Maltz, M. D. Crime statistics: A mathematical perspective. *Journal of Criminal Justice,* 3, (1975): 177–94.

Murphy, F. J., Shirley, M. M., and Witmer, H. L. The incidence of hidden delinquency. *American Journal of Orthopsychiatry* 16 (1946): 686–96.

Nettler, G. N. *Explaining Crime.* New York: McGraw-Hill, 1978.

Nye, F. I., Short, J. F., and Olson, V. J. Socioeconomic status and delinquent behaviour. *American Journal of Sociology,* 63, (1958): 381–89.

O'Donnell, J. A., Voss, H. L., Clayton, R. R., Slayton, G. T., and Room, R. *Young Men and Drugs—A Nationwide Survey* (NIDA Research Monograph 5). Rockville, MD: National Institute on Drug Abuse, 1976.

Pittman, D. J., and Handy, W. F. Uniform crime reporting: suggested improvements. *Sociology and Social Research* 46 (1962): 135–43.

President's Commission on Law Enforcement and Administration of Justice. *The Challenge of Crime in a Free Society.* Washington, D.C.: U.S. Government Printing Office, 1967.

Reiss, A. J. Measurement of the amount and nature of crime. In President's Commission on Law Enforcement and Administration of Justice, Studies in Crime and Law Enforcement in Major Metropolitan Areas, *Field Surveys III,* no. 1. Washington, D.C.: U.S. Government Printing Office, 1967.

Robison, S. M. *Can Delinquency be Measured?* New York: Columbia University Press, 1936.

Savitz, L. Official police statistics and their limitations. In L. Savitz and N. Johnston (eds.), *Crime in Society.* New York: Wiley, 1978.

Short, J. F., and Nye, F. I. Extent of unrecorded delinquency: Tentative conclusions. *Journal of Criminal Law, Criminology, and Police Science* 49 (1958): 296–302.

Skolnick, J. H. *Justice Without Trial.* New York: Wiley, 1966.

Tittle, C. R., and Villemez, W. J. Social class and criminality. *Social Forces* 56 (1977): 474–502.

Tittle, C. R., Villemez, W. J., and Smith, D. A. The myth of social class and criminality: An empirical assessment of the empirical evidence. *American Sociological Review* 43 (1978): 643–56.

U.S. Department of Justice, Federal Bureau of Investigation. *Uniform Crime Reporting Handbook.* Washington, D.C.: U.S. Government Printing Office, 1981.

U.S. Department of Justice, Law Enforcement Assistance Administration, National Criminal Justice Information and Statistics Service. *Crimes and Victims: A Report of the Dayton-San Jose Pilot Surveys of Victimization.* Washington, D.C.: U.S. Government Printing Office, 1974.

———. *Criminal Victimization Surveys in the Nation's Five Largest Cities.* Washington, D.C.: U.S. Government Printing Office, 1975 *a.*

———. *Criminal Victimization Surveys in 13 American Cities.* Washington, D.C.: U.S. Government Printing Office, 1975 *b.*

———. *Criminal Victimization in the United States, 1975.* Washington, D.C.: U.S. Government Printing Office, 1977.

———. *Criminal Victimization in the U.S., 1978.* Washington, D.C.: U.S. Government Printing Office, 1980.

———. *Criminal Victimization of California Residents.* Washington, D.C.: U.S. Government Printing Office, 1981.

U.S. Department of Justice. *Criminal Victimization 1983. Bureau of Justice Standards Bulletin, June 1983.* Washington, D.C.: U.S. Government Printing Office, 1983.

———. *1973–1982 Trends, Criminal Victimization in the United States. Bureau of Justice Standards Bulletin, September 1983.* Washington, D.C.: U.S. Government Printing Office, 1983.

———. *Households Touched by Crime, 1984. Bureau of Justice Standards Bulletin,* June 1985. Washington, D.C.: U.S. Government Printing Office, 1985.

U.S. Department of Justice, Federal Bureau of Investigation. *Uniform Crime Reports—1984.* Washington, D.C.: U.S. Government Printing Office, 1985.

U.S. Department of Justice. *Advance Release.* Washington, D.C., April 7, 1985.

Van Dine, S. V., Conrad, J. P., and Dinitz, S. *Restraining the Wicked: The Incapacitation of the Dangerous Offender.* Lexington, MA: Lexington Books, 1979.

Vinter, R., Newcomb, T. M., and Kish, R. *Time out: A National Study of Juvenile Correctional Programs.* Ann Arbor: University of Michigan, Press , 1976.

Voss, H. L. Socioeconomic studies and reported delinquent behavior. *Social Problems* 13 (1966): 314–24.

Wallerstein, J. S., and Wyle, J. Our law-abiding law-breakers. *Probation* 25 (1947): 107–12.

Wheeler, S. Criminal statistics: A reformulation of the problem. *Journal of Criminal Law, Criminology, and Police Science* 58 (1967): 317–24.

Williams, J. R. and Gold, M. From delinquent behavior to official delinquency. *Social Problems* 20 (1972): 209–29.

Wolfgang, M. E., Figlio, R. M., and Sellin, T. *Delinquency in a Birth Cohort.* Chicago: University of Chicago Press, 1972.

chapter 3

RESEARCH AND THEORY IN CRIMINOLOGY

Research and theory are the two basic tools of social and behavioral science. They are the principal means by which criminologists seek answers to questions about crime, criminals, and the operations of the criminal justice system. Bartollas and Miller (1978) describe the close relationship between research and theory:

> Research finds methods to collect data, helps to identify variables to be studied, tests variables for their worth, analyzes related variables, and suggests new directions for theory. Theory points the way to new research, helps derive new variables, builds interconnections among variables, integrates new and old ideas, builds systems of thought, and leads the way to new social and theoretical conclusions. Research collects and theory analyzes; research discovers and theory explains; research disproves and theory reorders. The process is never ending. Without it, we would be doomed to wallow in ignorance, personal prejudice, and inaccurate information. We would also be doomed to repeat harmful and even dangerous practices [p. 384].

As the diagram in Figure 3.1 emphasizes, the relationship between research and theory is not only close—it is reciprocal. When criminologists speak of explaining crime and criminal behavior, it is this combination of facts gathered by research and the way they are interpreted by theory that provides the explanation.

Many of the elaborate methods and much of the technical vocabulary that characterize scientific inquiry originated in the scientist's efforts to deal with two simple but crucially important questions: "What do you mean?" and "How do you know?" The former question raises the issue of the meaning of terms and concepts and establishes the necessity for the lengths to which researchers often must go in order to clarify the object, event, or relationship they are trying to investigate. The latter question goes to the very heart of scientific inquiry. The use of scientific methods places a premium on objectivity, impersonality, quantification, and the ability to replicate results.

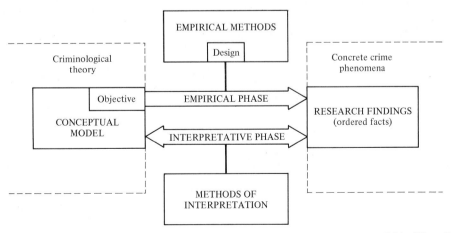

Figure 3.1 Diagram of the research process. (*Source:* Adapted from Matilda White Riley, *Sociological Research I: A Case Approach.* New York: Harcourt Brace and World, 1963, p. 4. Reproduced by permission of the author and publisher.)

In the first part of this chapter, we will discuss some of the fundamentals of scientific inquiry and how they relate to criminological research. Without an understanding of the research process, it is difficult to read critically the published research reports in the professional literature or to evaluate claims based on such reports. Much material that passes for research does not meet the minimum standards by which scientific investigations are judged.

The second part of the chapter is devoted to a brief consideration of how the fruits of research are utilized by criminologists in their attempts to formulate explanations of crime and criminal behavior. In a later section of the book, we shall look closely and critically at past and present theory-building efforts of criminologists. We hope that the present discussion will help to make clear the relationship between research and theory as two inseparable components of the knowledge-generating process in criminology.

SCIENTIFIC INQUIRY

Science is concerned with acquiring knowledge. Scientists are engaged in a constant search for explanations of what things are made of, how they are put together, and what makes them operate. To accomplish these purposes, scientists strive to keep the methods they employ self-correcting. In scientific inquiry, as the eminent physicist Percy Bridgman (1950) put it, "no special privileges are accorded to authority or tradition. . . . personal prejudices are carefully guarded against. . . . one makes a continual check to assure oneself that one is not making mistakes, and that any line of inquiry will be followed that appears promising" (p. 370). Instead of looking only for facts to support a particular viewpoint or opinion, scientists strive toward an objective understanding of the phenomena they study.

Precise observation and cautious interpretation have become trademarks of the scientist. According to an anecdote of dubious authenticity, a scientist and his friend were traveling by train and went through a pasture where sheep were grazing. "Oh look," said the friend, "those sheep have just been sheared." "Well, at least on *this* side," replied the scientist.

The scientist is properly skeptical of observations which have not been verified. Until or unless observations have been *empirically* verified—that is, by subjecting them to some sort of test in the real world—they do not qualify as **facts.** And it is facts that provide the building blocks, the structural materials, that scientists use in fashioning explanations of phenomena.

Scientists are also careful to distinguish between observations and **inferences.** What we can see, hear, feel, taste, and smell—what we can grasp with our senses—are observations. When we make a leap from something we can see to something we merely assume is there, we are going from the level of observation to the level of inference. We observe the wet pavement when we leave the house in the morning; we infer that it rained last night. But perhaps the street is wet because a sprinkler truck was working in the neighborhood, or because of a broken water main. Our leaps from observation to inference may not be as misguided as the one the research director made in his report on the flea (see the box on the facing page), but in daily life we tend to be considerably more careless about the distinction between observation and inference than the scientist can afford to be.

> The research director of a major agency was ordered to prepare a study about fleas. He put a flea on his desk and trained it to jump over his finger at his command. Then he pulled out two of the flea's six legs. "Jump," he ordered, and the flea still jumped. Two more legs came off. Again, "Jump," he commanded. Again the flea jumped. Finally, he pulled off the last two legs. "Jump," he commanded. The flea did not move. With that, the research director wrote his report: "When a flea loses all six legs, it becomes deaf."
>
> *Time,* November 25, 1957, Vol. 70, p. 112

In order to be of value in explaining phenomena, observations must be made under conditions that help to insure their accuracy. The earliest stage at which error is likely to occur is in the very meaning or definition of the phenomena the scientist wishes to investigate. Scientists are not nitpicking when they insist on precise definitions. If two scientists mean completely different things by the same term, the resulting confusion rules out the possibility of obtaining adequate observations.

Scientists employ the procedure of **operationalization** to reduce as far as possible the ambiguity of meaning. An operational definition consists of a statement of the methods and materials required to carry out the observations given in sufficient detail that someone else could duplicate this process. As a psychologist named Bachrach (1962) has noted, "the operational definition of a dish . . . is its recipe" (p. 74). If we ask the waiter, "What is this?" and he replies, "Fish chowder," we may be just as puzzled by the contents of the bowl as we were before we asked. But if the chef responds to the same question with a recital of the ingredients and instructions for their preparation, we have not only learned what it is but also how to make it ourselves.

A further step toward making observations specific and public enough to be duplicated by another scientist is the identification of **variables** that are relevant to the phenomenon in question. A variable can be defined as a factor or element that is inconstant and is subject to change from situation to situation. For example, people differ from one another in age, sex, height, and weight. These are physical variables which reflect underlying biological differences. They would have to be considered in nearly every kind of research involving human subjects. Other variables—for example, occupation, income, religious affiliation, or ethnic origin—reflect important social differences among people. Both kinds of variables—physical and social—are crucial to the conduct of criminological research.

Variables enter into criminological research in several ways. If criminologists are trying to gauge the effect of a particular variable, say academic success, on the frequency of delinquent behavior among 14-year-old male adolescents, it is not enough merely to pick two groups of youngsters—those with excellent school records and those with poor records—and compare them for the number of delinquent acts they have committed within the same period of time. There may be other factors in addition to academic success that could help account for any observed differences between the groups. For example, family size—are the families of delinquent youngsters larger or smaller than the families of nondelinquents? Income level—do delinquents come from families that are financially better or worse off than the families of nondelinquents? These variables and others may have an indirect or direct effect on what the researcher is attempting to investigate. Researchers are therefore obliged to **control** the operation of such **independent variables** so they can isolate the influence of a particular factor on the **dependent variable** they are investigating—in this case, the delinquent behavior of their subjects.

These two terms are easy to differentiate: Independent variables are those the investigator has reason to suspect may significantly influence the phenomenon being studied, which in criminological research is usually behavior of some kind. The terms independent and dependent variables provide researchers with a simple distinction without having to spell out the details in each specific instance.

Much more important is the matter of control, which is a key issue in research. Investigators must be able to conclude with confidence that the changes observed in the dependent variable they are studying are due to the influence of the particular variable they have isolated and not some other factor. Failure to control such factors leaves the way open for a **confounded variable.** As shown in Figure 3.2, a confounded variable in a research project has the capacity to ruin the results of careful observations and completely upset calculations. It is something like introducing a "wild card" into a game of poker.

The efforts researchers have made to deal with the problems of control have had important consequences for the ways studies are planned and carried out. Research designs can be relatively simple or extremely complex, depending on the

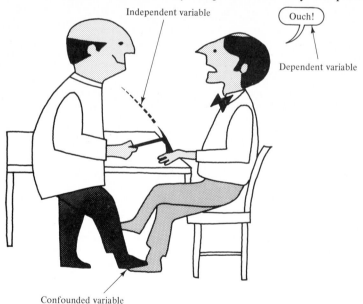

Figure 3.2 Relationship of independent, dependent, and confounded variables. The experimenter deliberately manipulates the independent variable and indirectly produces a change in the subject's behavior. If a confounded variable is inadvertently introduced, there is no way to tell whether the independent variable or the confounded variable produced the behavior change. (*Source:* Charles L. Sheridan, *Fundamentals of Experimental Psychology.* New York: Holt, Rinehart and Winston, 1971, p. 38. Reproduced by permission of the author and publisher.)

amenability to control of the variables which are related to the phenomenon under investigation. Criminologists are at a decided disadvantage in comparison with their colleagues in the natural sciences. The chemist, physicist, and biologist are able to create or reproduce in the controlled environment of the laboratory many conditions which permit them to carry out observations under fairly precise control. Criminologists, on the other hand, must make their observations of criminal behavior under circumstances of little or no control.

PURPOSES AND TYPES OF RESEARCH

Although a variety of techniques and procedures may be used in scientific inquiry, most research is intended to serve one or several of the following functions:

1. *To assess the status of given past or present phenomena.* A criminologist may look at how fluctuations in the country's economy appear to be related to past and present crime rates.
2. *To study the properties, characteristics, or components of given phenomena.* Criminological research may be directed toward examining such factors as birth order, school failure, or broken homes and their apparent effects upon juvenile delinquency.
3. *To examine the growth, development, historical background, or capacities for change of given phenomena.* Criminologists seek to investigate some of the major changes that have taken place over the past century in our approach to controlling criminal behavior.
4. *To investigate cause-and-effect relationships between or among given phenomena.* Criminologists may examine relationships between mental illness and violent crime.

Research can be categorized in a number of ways. One way is to classify research as **pure** or **applied.** Pure research is motivated by intellectual interest or curiosity; there is no expectation that the findings will ever have any kind of practical application. Applied research is directed toward solving a particular problem, despite the fact that a successful solution may not lead to any new knowledge.

If a team of researchers wished to discover whether officially adjudicated delinquent boys perform better or worse on intelligence tests than nondelinquent boys of comparable age, the study designed to investigate this question could be considered "pure" research. If, on the other hand, they were interested in testing the effectiveness of one type of parole supervision against another, their research would probably be classified as "applied." In the latter case, the problem has a specific and practical aspect: that is, the study is intended to provide an answer that is relevant and significant to the researcher within a pragmatic context.

We must caution that such distinctions as those made between pure and applied research are rather artificial. The history of science is filled with examples of pure research that turned out to have profoundly significant practical consequences; for example, the studies which led to the development of nuclear energy and space flight in our century. By the same token, applied research may open doors to possibilities and implications that extend far beyond the limits of the practical problem the investigator originally set out to solve. For instance, some extremely important developments in organization psychology can be traced back to a study in which researchers set out to measure the effect of changes in illumination on employee work habits in an industrial plant and discovered, instead, the power and influence of employee morale as a key factor in work productivity.

It is more helpful to classify research in criminology as **archival, descriptive, experimental,** and **quasi-experimental research.**

Archival Research[1]

The purpose of archival research is to collate, integrate, and interpret information concerning past events or persons. Students who have written term papers are likely to have performed archival research, although they may not have called it such. The writing of a term paper generally involves spending time in the library to gain access to available written and published materials. With or without the aid of services provided by a skilled reference librarian, the student may do an extremely creditable job of locating, gathering, and interpreting these materials in order to explore a hunch or substantiate an idea.

An archival researcher makes every effort to secure data from **primary** rather than **secondary** sources. A primary source can be the firsthand account of an actual witness to a particular event, an original document, or a surviving artifact. In doing a paper on Lombroso, for example, the student would read the works of Lombroso (probably in translation), rather than comments on Lombroso by some other writer. A secondary source may consist of a report by someone who received the testimony of an eyewitness or the replica of an original document. Sources of archival data in criminology include case reports, manuscripts, institutional files, and the like.

Evaluating the sources of the data calls for critical judgment on the part of the researcher. Validation involves two components: **extrinsic** and **intrinsic** validity. Extrinsic validity refers to the conditions by which the investigator seeks to establish the authenticity of a given document or piece of evidence. Determining the validity of documents, for example, may require exhaustive, detailed, and painstaking analyses of the materials which make up such documents.

Once they have managed to establish the authenticity of their data source, archival researchers must deal with the issue of intrinsic validity. Did the person identified as the author of a letter or report actually write it? Was the ransom note received by Colonel and Mrs. Charles Lindbergh written by Bruno Hauptmann or someone else? In the case of documents which purport to be original, inconsistencies in language, discrepancies in dates, and lack of agreement with previously authenticated documents must all be considered when challenging the genuineness of a given item.

---

[1]The term *historical research* is often used to refer to the kind of investigation we have designated here as *archival research.* We feel the latter term is more accurately descriptive of what is actually involved in this kind of research than the expression *historical research.* We should like to point out that legal research, which involves the search for statutory and case law precedents and the tracing of the judicial background of a point of law, also fits the designation *archival research.*

Descriptive Research

The several types of descriptive research employed in the social and behavioral sciences—surveys, case analyses, correlational studies, developmental research—possess the common characteristics of dealing with current situations. It is worth keeping in mind as we briefly review these various kinds of descriptive research that they are all, in a sense, status studies, that is, they attempt to obtain information about a particular question or issue.

Surveys Most people are familiar with the reported results, if not the actual methods, of polls that predict the outcome of presidential elections or surveys which seek to measure the unpopularity of proposals to finance civic improvements by selling municipal bonds. Often the results of such polls are reported in the daily newspapers in the form of graphs, tables, or charts. The principal tool used by the pollster is a **questionnaire.** Not too long ago, Americans had occasion to become familiar with the questionnaire, which they received through the mail from the U.S. Bureau of the Census.

Criminologists gather data each year from hundreds or even thousands of questionnaires. The items they include are likely to be more complex than the simple question about the number, age, relationships, and nature of employment of residents in the Census questionnaire, although their form in many instances may be similar. Constructing an effective questionnaire is a much more difficult task than it might appear, and it is one that calls for careful planning and thorough preparation. It is a well-known fact in behavioral science research that an investigator is lucky to get back as many as one-third of the questionnaires that were originally distributed in a study. One of the factors that undoubtedly contributes to this dismally low return rate is the high percentage of poorly constructed questionnaires that reach intended respondents. These instruments contain questions that are ambiguously worded, difficult to understand, and puzzling or confusing to the respondent.

Other instruments available to the researcher include attitude scales, tests of various types, inventories, and checklists. The interview is also a technique for gathering data. When it is used for this purpose, the interviewer usually tries to follow a schedule of questions that has been worked out in advance in order to insure a standardized procedure.

Field Research Most of the phenomena criminologists consider worth investigating present difficulties with regard to obtaining information through controlled experimentation. They are therefore obliged to study a good deal of criminal behavior in its natural setting—on the street, in jail, in court, or in prison. One way to do this is for the criminologist to act as a **participant-observer.** In a study considered a classic, the graduate assistant to a criminologist named David Maurer lived with the members of a group of pickpockets—a "whiz mob"—in Louisville, Kentucky, in order to amass information on the distinctive language and behavior patterns of the group. Similarly, William F. Whyte (1943) gathered data as a participant-observer of casual group interactions among pre–World War II gang youths in Boston.

Field study is subject to several pitfalls as a research technique. One is the tendency to become so involved with the group being studied that the investigator becomes immersed in their affairs and suffers a loss of objectivity and sense of original purpose. Field research seems to be best suited to the requirements of exploratory studies, which allow for the identification of major factors in a situation and some of their possible relationships; it is unsuited to the more rigorous requirements of controlled research.

Case Study   Criminologists in the 1920s and 1930s used the case study technique extensively to conduct in-depth analyses of single delinquent or criminal offenders (e.g., Shaw, 1930, 1931; Sutherland, 1938). More recently, Klockars (1974) has contributed a thorough case study of a professional "fence." This technique is widely practiced in medicine, psychiatry, and social work. Sigmund Freud, for example, developed his psychoanalytic theories of personality on the basis of day-to-day observations of the behavior of patients he was treating.

A researcher may employ an array of procedures and instruments to secure life-history information and psychological or physiological data concerning several case studies simultaneously. In the pursuit of relevant information, the researcher usually is obliged to seek the help of other professional workers—teachers, social workers, clergymen, physicians—who may have had the opportunity to become acquainted with the subject under a variety of circumstances.

One of the values of case study research is that it provides some basic information on factors that might help explain various kinds of behavior.

Correlational Studies   Much of the research in criminology is devoted to an examination of how one factor is related to another. We may try to do this by seeing how two factors *co-vary;* that is as one factor changes (increases or decreases), we examine how the second factor changes in the same way. Thus a criminologist may study co-variation between unemployment and property crime rates. There has been a noteworthy increase in this kind of research since the advent of electronic data processing, which permits the rapid analysis of large amounts of data. Before such methods became available, correlational studies required laborious and time-consuming computations in order to achieve results that can be obtained today in a matter of minutes with a computer.

Developmental Study   This type of research consists of studies in which the investigator examines changes that take place within an individual or group of subjects over a period of time. Observations or measurements are made of the physical or behavioral characteristics that are of concern to the researcher. It is not uncommon for a project of this kind, however, to turn up valuable information that is incidental to the main purpose of the investigation. Since this research design involves tracking a subject or subjects for a period of time that may be measured in years, it is often called a **longitudinal study.** This name distinguishes it from a **cross-sectional study,** which compares at the same point in time a number of different subjects who represent various stages in development, that is, a group of 13-year-olds, a group of 14-year-olds, and so on.

The Cambridge-Somerville Youth Study

One of the most famous developmental studies in criminology combined research with treatment. Based on a delinquency prevention project that was started in 1937 in two cities near Boston, a group of 325 high-risk boys were selected for the study by teachers and police officers to receive intensive personalized counseling. A control group of 325 boys living in the same area did not receive counseling. Although the project was curtailed by the entrance of the United States into World War II in 1941, the research continued with some changes until 1945. Over the years, a massive fund of observations and data was collected for each of the 650 boys originally in the project. Social workers, psychologists, and psychiatrists investigated the homes of the boys, conducted extensive interviews with their families and neighbors, checked on school progress, and administered tests of intelligence and personality to the subjects.

In addition to revealing an enormous amount of "hidden delinquency," as we noted in the previous chapter, the Cambridge-Somerville Study demonstrated that intensive personalized counseling over a five-year period failed to reduce recidivism among the boys in the treatment group, as compared with the boys in the control group who received no counseling (Powers and Witmer, 1951).

Descriptive research is sometimes, unfairly and without justification, trivialized as a mere matter of head-counts or tallies. However, descriptive research is subject to the same rigorous requirements in planning and implementation that govern research of other kinds. If a given piece of descriptive research suffers from inadequacies in design, execution, and interpretation, the fault is more apt to be found with the researcher than with the method.

Experimental Research

In a controlled experiment in the social and behavioral sciences, an investigator tries to determine what effect if any a given factor has on the behavior of a particular group of people. Criminological researchers may, for example, be interested in testing the effects of a new drug, whose inventors claim has the capability of dramatically improving memory in mental retardates, by administering the drug to a group of institutionalized mentally retarded delinquents. The investigators may begin by randomly dividing the mentally retarded delinquents into two groups of approximately equal size. Each group is tested for memory span by means of some standard instrument such as the Digit Span subtest on the Wechsler Adult Intelligence Scale, a widely used individual test of intelligence. One group, designated the experimental group, is then given the drug; the other group, called the control group, is administered a **placebo** (an inert substance) for purposes of dealing with the possible effects of suggestion. An even greater measure of control would be introduced into the experiment if both the drug and the placebo were given to the subjects according to a procedure called "double blind," which establishes that neither the subjects nor the persons responsible for administering the drug and placebo are aware of what they are receiving or dispensing. All other conditions—the physical setting, health and medical status of the subjects, length of time permitted for the test, nature of the instructions—are held as near to identical as possible for both groups. The test of memory span is then repeated. If the group that received the drug performs in a manner that is significantly better than those in the control group, the investigator can ascribe this difference to the effects of the drug.

In this experiment, the drug is the independent variable the investigator manipulates and the test of memory span is the dependent variable. Control is illustrated by the random assignment of subjects, common setting, identical instructions, and similar aspects of the procedure.

The source of power of the controlled experiment is in the control of all variables except the independent variable. But while the experimental technique is very powerful, it is not perfect; it has its problems and limitations. Being subjected to experimental procedure may actually modify or distort what is being measured. In the situation depicted in Figure 3.3, the attractive lady experimenter's physical assets introduce a confounding variable into the research!

Sometimes experimentation is impossible for either practical or ethical reasons. In other cases, experimental conditions may be so artificial or contrived that they bear little resemblance to conditions found in the real world. Nevertheless, despite its

Figure 3.3 The experimenter may inadvertently influence his or her results. (*Source:* Charles L. Sherida, *Fundamentals of Experimental Psychology.* New York: Holt, Rinehart and Winston, 1971, p. 10. Reproduced by permission of the author and publisher.)

limitations the controlled experiment is still the most direct means at our disposal for determining causal relationships between variables. As such, it has assumed increasing importance in criminological research.

Quasi-experimental Research

Many criminological studies are conducted in prisons, jails, training schools, and other types of institutional settings which do not lend themselves to the precise control of variables that is essential to conduct a true experiment. We shall refer to such studies as **quasi-experimental research.**

THE NATURE AND PURPOSES OF CRIMINOLOGICAL THEORY

Now that we have described some of the methods that criminologists use to gather reliable and valid information about crime, criminals, criminal behavior, and the criminal justice system, we may take a careful look at how this information can be organized in such a way as to help us understand these phenomena. The data yielded by research are like the pieces of a puzzle that need to be fitted together in order to provide a coherent, recognizable picture or pattern. This pattern is what we shall call a theory. We can say the same thing in more formal language, but it does not change the basic nature of the relationship between the theory (picture) and the data (pieces of the puzzle).

Putting facts together in some orderly fashion is only one of the advantages of theory. There is another advantage which we can illustrate by pursuing the puzzle analogy a bit further. As we assemble the puzzle, a picture begins to emerge of how the puzzle will appear when it is complete. When this has happened, the search for remaining pieces begins to take on a new and different aspect. Instead of groping for pieces that *appear* to fit, we now begin to look for pieces with specific colors, shapes, and sizes. The more the puzzle takes shape, the more are we aided in this search.

This process resembles what takes place in the development of a theory. The pattern that was imposed initially on the previous findings or observations helps to organize these findings in a coherent way. The pattern then yields some directions which further investigation can follow in order to fill in gaps left in the initial pattern or provide answers to previously unanswered questions.

Kerlinger (1964) identifies a theory as "a set of interrelated constructs (concepts), definitions, and propositions that presents a systematic view of phenomena by specifying relations among variables, with the purpose of explaining and predicting the phenomena" (pp. 10–11).

A **construct,** as a scientist uses the term, is understood to be more specific and precise than a mere idea. The construct of socioeconomic class, for instance, includes the dimensions of income and occupation as they help define a person's status in society. **Propositions** are statements that express a relationship between two or more variables; for example, "criminality is primarily a lower-class phenomenon in contemporary American society."

Finally, the above definition refers to **prediction.** Scientists regard the ability to accurately predict phenomena as the most demanding test of a theory that can be devised. Unfortunately, theories have not reached the level of sophistication in criminology that allows us to make the sort of predictions that are commonplace in the natural sciences. One of the reasons for this is the sheer complexity of the phenomena involved in crime and criminal behavior. Nevertheless, criminological research makes extensive use of predictive statements in the form of **testable hypotheses.**

Formulating Testable Hypotheses

A hypothesis can be regarded as a *stated prediction of a research outcome.* The following are a few examples of research hypotheses:

- There is a systematic relationship between urban residential area and the incidence of homicidal assault.
- There is a high positive correlation between severity and certainty of punishment for a particular criminal offense and the probability of occurrence of that offense.
- There is no significant difference in the incidence of violent crimes between high and low scorers on a test that purports to measure aggressive tendencies.

The last hypothesis is stated in the form of a **null hypothesis,** that is, as a prediction that there will be no true difference between groups on some particular measure. In the case of this null hypothesis, the implication is that any difference in the violent-crime rate between those who score high and low on the test of aggressive tendencies can be attributed to chance. Research hypotheses are often stated in this form.

Research hypotheses may originate in a formal theory. Many years ago, criminologist Walter C. Reckless formulated what was called **containment theory,** which sought to account for delinquent and criminal behavior in terms of both external, observable factors such as family, school, and community influences and internal constructs such as self-concept, goal direction, and frustration tolerance. One of the hypotheses formulated by Reckless was that communities in which strong external control was manifested by mutual support among neighbors and a readiness to discipline one another's children when they misbehaved, would exhibit little delinquency. A second hypothesis was that in these communities, internal factors were less important in controlling youthful behavior.

In this example, we can see that the hypotheses advanced by Reckless form a direct propositional link with his containment theory. These hypotheses about delinquency and control are statements about possible relationships between independent variables (e.g., neighborhood control) and the dependent variable (delinquency). The test of containment theory involves the task of investigating these potential relationships in an actual setting. As long as the relationships are merely expressed rather than verified through actual observation, we are in no position to say whether containment theory is a valid basis for explaining delinquency. When the relationships are systematically examined in a particular community and the findings provide corroboration for the research hypotheses, these results help to confirm the theory. If the findings fail to support the predictions, there are at least two possible explana-

---

Hypothesis Testing: A Parable from the Old West

A gunslinger of the Old West rides into a town and the terrified inhabitants form the hypothesis that "Joe is the fastest gun in the territory." The clear implication of this position is that in a contest against any other gunman, Joe's gun will be fired first. The expectation can be "proved" only one way—that is, by showing that alternative hypotheses (that other gunmen are faster) are incorrect. Each time Joe's skill is pitted against that of someone else and the predicted outcome is obtained, the theoretical allegation gains credibility. . . . However, if on just one occasion Joe's gun fires second (or not at all) in such a contest, a logical alternative suggests itself . . . namely, that "Joe was fast, but Harry is faster."

Today, a scientist rides into town and proposes the hypothesis that X causes Y. Others dispute this, claiming that A causes Y, or B causes Y, or C causes Y. Some of these alternatives will be clearly implausible, and the scientist will have little trouble discrediting them. If, however, his explanation holds up against a number of highly plausible alternative explanations, he will have strengthened his case considerably. Like the gunman, unfortunately, the scientist can never be completely sure that the competitive process has eliminated *all* rivals.

Source: W. D. Crano and M. B. Brewer, *Principles of Research in Social Psychology.* New York: McGraw-Hill, 1973, p. 10. Reproduced by permission of the authors and publisher.

---

tions for this failure. One is that the actual test or investigation was faulty for one reason or another; a second explanation is that the theory in its present form needs revision.

Research hypotheses can be derived from theories which yield contrasting or conflicting predictions. Although this happens much less frequently in criminology than the amusing boxed illustration might suggest, such empirical tests play an indispensable role in the advancement of knowledge. They provide one of the most cogent reasons theories are of such importance in criminology.

Criminological research is not confined to the testing of hypotheses that originate in formal theories. A good deal of exploratory research is directed toward a kind of free inquiry in which a general statement of objectives or purposes takes the place of specific hypotheses. Such research may result from a perception on the part of a criminologist of what appears to be a significant relationship between factors, from an apparent void or gap in observations of particular events, or merely from the conviction that current theories do not provide a satisfactory explanation for given phenomena.

It is difficult to be doctrinaire about these matters. Theory-based hypotheses are very important in formulating the research problem to be investigated, in constructing the design of the study, and in selecting appropriate research techniques. On the other hand, much valuable information has been gathered under the informal conditions of empirically based research. Given the kinds of problems which confront the criminologist, both types of investigation contribute significantly to our growing knowledge and understanding of crime and criminal behavior.

SUMMARY

Research and theory are the two principal ways in which knowledge is generated by scientists. Research supplies the facts which theory organizes and integrates in order to provide explanations for phenomena. Criminological research is conducted according to scientific methods which emphasize objectivity, freedom from bias, quantification, and the reproducibility of results.

Among the kinds of research performed by criminologists, we identified archival, descriptive, experimental, and quasi-experimental research. Archival research makes use of documents, case reports, manuscripts, and similar materials in an effort to interpret past events. Descriptive research, which employs such techniques as surveys, case analyses, and correlational and developmental studies, provides information on criminal behavior that is gathered in jails, prisons, and other "natural" settings. Experimental and quasi-experimental methods offer scientists the greatest measure of control over the variables they wish to investigate, but the use of such methods in criminological research is subject to several limitations. Nevertheless, criminologists are constantly seeking ways to utilize experimentation in their research.

The main task of criminological theory is to fashion a framework for organizing the data supplied by research into a coherent pattern, from which it is possible to derive testable hypotheses or stated predictions of research outcomes to guide further investigations of phenomena. Thus, theory and research operate in a mutually supportive fashion to increase our knowledge and understanding of crime, criminals, criminal behavior, and the functioning of the criminal justice system.

DISCUSSION QUESTIONS

Find the answers to the following questions in the text.
1. What are the respective roles played by research and theory in the explanation of crime and criminal behavior?
2. Discuss the characteristics of scientific method as a process for acquiring knowledge as compared with any other approaches. How are observations distinguished from inferences?
3. Why does operationalization constitute such an important part of scientific inquiry? Give an example of what might be required in trying to operationalize a concept such as "the college crime rate" in the United States.
4. What is a **"confounded variable"** in research?
5. Briefly summarize the major objectives of **archival research.** What is the concern of the archival researcher for **primary and secondary sources**?
6. Compare and contrast the purposes and methods of descriptive and experimental research. What are some of the problems encountered by the investigator in one type of research that are not encountered in the other area?

7. Define hypothesis and indicate how **testable hypotheses** might be derived from formal theory. What are the possible explanations for the failure of an hypothesis to be confirmed in a given study?

TERMS TO IDENTIFY AND REMEMBER

independent variable *pg. 64*

dependent variable

pure research

primary source

intrinsic validity

testable hypothesis

survey

field research

case study

prediction

archival research

"confounded variable"

applied research

secondary source

extrinsic validity

null hypothesis

questionnaire

participant-observer

correlational study

containment theory

experimental research

placebo

quasi-experimental research

construct

REFERENCES

Bachrach, A. J. *Psychological Research: An Introduction.* New York: Random House, 1962.

Bartollas, C., and Miller, S. J. *The Juvenile Offender: Control, Correction, and Treatment.* Boston: Allyn & Bacon, 1978.

Bridgman, P. W. *Reflections of a Physicist.* New York: Philosophical Library, 1950.

Campbell, D. T., and Stanley, J. C. *Experimental and Quasi-experimental Designs for Research.* Chicago: Rand McNally, 1963.

Kerlinger, F. N. *Foundations of Behavioral Research.* New York: Holt, Rinehart and Winston, 1973.

Klockars, C. B. *The Professional Fence.* New York: The Free Press, 1974.

Powers, E., and Witmer, H. *An Experiment in the Prevention of Delinquency: The Cambridge-Somerville Youth Study.* New York: Columbia University Press, 1951.

Shaw, C. *The Jack-Roller.* Chicago: University of Chicago Press, 1930.

———— . *The Natural History of a Delinquent Career.* Chicago: University of Chicago Press, 1931.

Sutherland, E. H. (ed.) *The Professional Thief.* Chicago: University of Chicago Press, 1937.

Whyte, W. F. *Street Corner Society.* Chicago: University of Chicago Press, 1943.

TWO

PATTERNS OF CRIMINAL BEHAVIOR

Classifications and typologies are used in an attempt to understand one another and the world around us. Finding similarities and differences among objects and events is the first step toward determining their composition, functions, and causes. The notion of type involves a reduction from the complex to the simple— or at least to the less complex. This term implies that phenomena possess some relatively enduring properties or characteristics which allow them to be grouped together as members of the same category. That is, membership in a group is based on sharing certain common features that distinguish an identifiable type or class.

Perhaps the simplest typology in criminal justice is one which involves the classification of individuals according to offense. As we saw earlier, classifying crimes into felonies and misdemeanors represents an evaluation of the seriousness of these crimes in terms of their impact on society. A further breakdown divides offenses into crimes against the person, crimes against property, public order crimes, political crimes, and *consensual* crimes (e.g., prostitution). We have noted that the *Uniform Crime Reports* list 29 types of criminal offenses.

Legal typologies have no pretense to universal validity, nor are they so regarded by the criminal justice system. As national or local classifications of crime, they are technical categories which possess some administrative usefulness; they are not presented as explanations of criminal behavior.

In addition to typologies which seek to classify offenses, we may identify typologies that seek to classify offenders. Statutes which impose criminal sanctions for specified acts of commission or omission reflect a system of classification based primarily on the nature and seriousness of the crimes. Left out are the personality of the offenders, their motives and individual characteristics, their relationships with victims, and their personal histories. These factors are not ignored by the law. On the contrary, they may weigh heavily in the determination of the guilt or innocence of the accused. But they are not built into the typological framework of the criminal law itself. Such factors, however, may impress the criminologist as being equal in importance to the nature of the offense; and criminologists may devote a great deal of attention to these considerations in their efforts to construct a meaningful and workable typology of criminal behavior. A glance at what comprises crimes against the person in the legal view indicates that the law tries to distinguish between offenses in which the confrontation between perpetrator and victim is face-to-face and often within the context of coercion or violence, and those offenses in which the relationship between offender and victim is remote and impersonal, as in the case of white-collar/economic crimes. In consensual or "victimless" crimes, the relations between criminal and victim usually involve cooperation in the exchange of services or substances; the real victim, if any, is the public rather than one of the participants.

Four of the FBI Index, or Part I, crimes—homicide, forcible rape, aggravated assault, and robbery—are crimes against the person that are also characterized as violent crimes. With regard to forcible rape, there has been an unfortunate tendency to emphasize the sexual component of this criminal offense at the expense of minimizing the violence to which the victim is subjected. However, legislative changes in the penal codes of a number of states have altered this situation: forcible rape has been redefined as "sexual battery" and carries with it a series of penal sanctions that are scaled in terms of the severity of the violence suffered by the victim.

Crimes against property make up the bulk of the more than twelve million crimes reported annually in official statistics in recent years. Property offenders have been categorized as occasional, ordinary, and professional criminals. Occasional property offenders do not view themselves as criminals because, as a rule, they do not develop the rationalizations, group affiliations, and sustained contact with the criminal justice system that promote the acquisition of a criminal self-image. These offenders are usually involved in such crimes as shoplifting, vandalism, auto joy-riding, and employee theft. Ordinary property offenders commit the majority of property crimes and make up the majority of the prison population in the United States. Crime represents a substantial portion of the life activities of these offenders. They augment their income or make their entire living by larceny, robbery, or burglary. Professional property offenders comprise a small group of highly proficient criminals who exhibit the most fully developed criminal careers and enjoy the top status within the criminal community. Their skills, as compared with those of other offenders, permit them to escape detection; hence, they are likely to spend little time in prison. In the past, professional criminals tended to limit their activities to pickpocketing, check forgery, shoplifting, and confidence or bunco games, but today there is a new class of "heavy offenders" who engage in such crimes as armed robbery.

Traditionally, criminology focused on the individual characteristics of such crimes as theft. Economic, syndicated, and political crimes are more meaningfully approached from an organizational perspective. Specific types of economic offenses, such as corporate or business crimes, involve price-fixing, commercial bribery, and other illegal practices. In these offenses, the organizational aspect is fundamental to the commission of the crime. But even in such "personal" economic crimes as bankruptcy fraud, the economic criminal is rarely an isolated actor.

Organization is the keynote of syndicated crime. In fact, *organized crime* is a much more familiar expression which covers the diversity of illegal activities carried on by syndicate criminals. Syndicated crime is a continuing and self-perpetuating conspiracy that relies heavily on fear and corruption in order to carry on its enterprises. The roots of syndicated crime reach far back into our national history. At one time or another, nearly every nationality or ethnic group has been represented in the ranks of syndicated crime. This fact has given rise to the hotly disputed concept of *ethnic succession,* according to which later immigrant arrivals replace the older and earlier groups as the latter find safer and more attractive opportunities in the legitimate business sector. While black and Hispanic groups have become heavily involved in the illicit drug traffic in the past two decades, the Italian-Sicilian syndicates still dominate the crime scene.

The illegal importation and distribution of cocaine, heroin, marijuana, and other "controlled substances" is a multibillion-dollar enterprise which has probably surpassed gambling as the principal revenue source for syndicated crime. But syndicated crime has also infiltrated many areas of legitimate business, where its activities have included bankruptcy fraud, the manipulation of stocks and bonds, and labor racketeering.

Traditionally, the term *political crime* referred to such offenses against the government as treason, sedition, rebellion, and assassination. In the post-Watergate and Abscam era, the expression is used increasingly to cover offenses committed by agents of the government against individuals, groups, organizations, the general public, and even foreign governments. Political crimes of terrorism, which include the seizure of American embassy personnel and civilians by Iranian revolutionaries, go beyond violations of the recognized canons of international law and approach the category of "crimes against humanity" for which Nazi leaders were prosecuted in the trials held at Nuremberg following the end of World War II. After three-quarters of a century of neglect by criminology, political crimes are currently a focus of intense interest and concern among criminologists.

While few people would question the necessity for legal sanctions against such crimes as rape and robbery, many have serious reservations about gambling, homosexual behavior between consenting adults, deviant drug use, and commercialized vice and pornography. In the view of people with divergent ideological convictions, to subject such types of conduct to societal regulation by means of criminal sanctions is an unwarranted intrusion of privacy and an indefensible extension of governmental authority into matters more properly dealt with by informal social sanctions. In the case of alcoholism and deviant drug use, the criminal justice system itself is seen as a significant causal factor in the social problems associated with these patterns of behavior.

Acts that are subsumed under the heading of consensual crimes may be regarded as shameful, immoral, or even injurious, but their status as crimes—as violations of the criminal law—is often equivocal. Abortion, for example, is not presently subject to criminal sanctions, although it was in the recent past and may be "recriminalized" at some point in the future if the forces of the antiabortion movement prevail. The term *consensual crime* is gaining wider acceptance as an alternative to the older and more controversial expression "victimless crime." It has been argued that victimless crime is a misnomer because such offenses as prostitution victimize a broad range of people, from the offenders themselves to society in general.

The female offender, until quite recently, had been neglected by all but a handful of criminologists; and cultural biases and sex-role stereotypes have often appeared in the guise of "explanations" of female criminality. Following a brief but critical review of criminological research and theories pertaining to female crime and criminals, we will discuss the problems involved in the accurate assessment of the frequency and distribution of female crime, together with the issues raised by the processing of female offenders within a criminal justice system that is primarily equipped to deal with adult male criminals. Noteworthy is the inclusion of the important but often neglected topic of delinquency in girls and its relationship to adult female crime. The chapter closes with a consideration of new trends and developments in female corrections.

chapter 4

CRIMES AGAINST THE PERSON

Crimes against the person may include both nonviolent and violent crimes. In addition to such violent offenses as murder, assault and battery, forcible rape, and robbery, we can distinguish the nonviolent crimes of statutory rape, indecent exposure, "peeping," and frottage (deriving sexual gratification from rubbing against a person of the opposite sex in a public place). Child molesting can be either violent or nonviolent, depending on circumstances.

The Staff Report of the President's Commission on Causes and Prevention of Violence (Mulvihill, Tumin, and Curtis, 1969) defined violent crimes as "the use or threatened use of force to secure one's own end against the will of another that results, or can result, in the destruction or harm of person or property or in the deprivation of individual freedom" (p. 4). This definition marks a departure from the tendency to restrict violent crimes to crimes against the person, a practice which American criminology inherited from European usage. It also identifies criminal violence with situations in which people are taken captive and held for ransom (kidnapping) or as hostages, regardless of whether or not the temporary deprivation of freedom is accompanied by, or results in, actual harm or destruction to the person or property of the victim(s).

The perspective suggested by this definition seems consistent with the FBI's decision to include arson, a crime against property, among the Part I or Crime Index offenses in the *Uniform Crime Reports,* beginning with the 1980 edition. It also directs attention to the problem of terrorism. While the actions of terrorists often compress a series of violent crimes—murder, kidnapping, assault—into a single episode, the political or ideological motivation for such crimes differs in important ways from that which characterizes more conventional crimes of violence. Therefore, we have chosen to discuss terrorism within the context of political crimes. Arson, on the other hand, is included among other crimes against property in the following chapter.

A PERSPECTIVE ON VIOLENT OFFENDERS

Typologies of violent offenders have been developed by a number of investigators (e.g., Guttmacher, 1960; MacDonald, 1961). The following typology was devised by John Conrad of Ohio State University and used by Spencer (1966) to classify offenders who had committed crimes of violence. By means of an aggressive history profile (AHP) constructed by Conrad, offenders can be categorized into groups that are hypothesized to differ in motivation, treatment needs, and parole prospects. Spencer employed the AHP to classify 704 offenders according to Conrad's typology for purposes of examining the criminal career, occupational history, and demographic characteristics of offenders in each category.

Culturally Violent Offenders

These individuals grow up in a subculture where violence is an accepted way of life. Among their distinguishing characteristics are: (1) the aggression was perpetrated for its own sake, as frequently seen in assault and battery, and not for other ends, as in robbery, and (2) the victim was a chance acquaintance or someone not well known to the offender.

Background Dimensions   With slightly more than half belonging to racial minorities, the culturally violent tended to concentrate in urban areas where they had been exposed to their subculture for a relatively long time. Compared to other types of offenders, juvenile delinquency had been high and tended more toward crimes of violence. Schooling was minimal and the group did not do well on pencil-and-paper tests of ability. The lack of skills to cope with society was reflected in their low occupational level, lack of employment, and job instability.

These juveniles turned to alcohol, drugs, and petty crimes and vented their frustrations in aggressive assault and barroom brawls. There was a record of misdemeanant convictions. A few came to institutions on charges of homicide, robbery, and felonious assault but most of the present commitment offenses were nonviolent. Their behavior may be characterized as chaotic, acting out of frustrations against society from which they were unable to gain normal satisfactions and rewards.

Criminally Violent Offenders

These offenders are those who commit violence if necessary to gain some end, as in robbery. Distinguishing characteristics are: (1) violence was used as a tool in carrying out some criminal act, usually robbery, and (2) the offender carried concealed weapons and was not classifiable under the other types.

Background Dimensions   The criminally violent channel their aggression into profitable avenues of robbery rather than into impulsive assaults. The criminally violent offender's lower percentage of arrests and higher percentage of prison terms suggest that his or her offenses are likely to be deliberate felonies. The high rate of escape attempts by this offender may be another indication of aptitude for planning a criminal act. Compared to the culturally violent, criminally violent offenders are better educated, have learned how to make better scores on group intelligence tests, and have worked more often at white-collar jobs. However, their talents generally serve illegal ends and their failure to assimilate into normal society is evident in their poor occupational record.

Pathologically Violent Offenders

These individuals committed offenses that were diagnostically related to a psychosis, brain damage (including convulsive disorder), or other major psychological disability. Distinguishing characteristics are: (1) the crime was a sex offense in which violence occurred and (2) the harm inflicted was bizarre or sadistic.

Background Dimensions   Characteristics of the pathologically violent form a distinct pattern: a relatively conservative offense frequency record and a favorable occupational record, along with indications of deviant instability such as a comparatively high homicide rate in present commitment offense, excessive use of alcohol, suicidal tendencies, marked underachievement in school, and the tentative indication of an atypical recurrence of offenses in the high age ranges.

Situationally Violent Offenders

This category of offender was distinguishable by the fact that the victim was related to the offender by blood or marriage or was a person with whom he or she had established close personal ties.

Background Dimensions   The situationally violent type of offender shows fewer offenses, a more socially conforming life pattern, and better parole prospects than fellow offenders. Compared to other types, including the nonviolent, he or she has less juvenile delinquency, fewer prison terms, less institutional violence, fewer escape attempts, higher occupational level, greater job stability, better military record, and a greater degree of schooling (Vetter and Silverman, 1978, pp. 64–67).

On the basis of the descriptive criteria supplied above, this typology would appear to be adequate to handle the categories of arsonist and terrorist we identified in our previous discussion.

✦ DOMESTIC VIOLENCE: THE BATTERING FAMILY

While violent crimes have been a perennial source of interest for both criminologists and the public, the issue of family violence has only recently attracted professional and public attention. Family life in the United States has traditionally been seen as the center of love and tranquility. As Gelles (1978) observes, "the semi-sacred nature of the American family as a social institution tended to create a smokescreen which obscured violence from the attention of the public and social scientists" (p. 170). Now that the smokescreen has been penetrated, we are discovering that violence is a fundamental and pervasive part of American family life. Husbands batter wives; parents batter children; sons and daughters batter their parents; the young batter the elderly. "People are more likely to be hit, beat up physically, injured, or even killed in their own homes by another family member than anywhere else, and by anyone else, in our society" (Gelles, 1979, p. 11).

The Battered Spouse

Throughout history, men have had the legal right and social sanction to control their wives (often regarded as their chattel or property) as they desired (NiCarthy, 1982; Saline, 1984). Men today in nearly every country continue a tradition of using whatever force they consider necessary to maintain dominance over their wives or intimate partners. According to Saline (1984):

> Many men continue to believe that as the major wage earners, they are entitled to have things at home done *their* way. While most of the laws supporting the husband's power to physically punish his spouse have been abolished, the social tradition lingers on. Up until fairly recently, after all, the woman's part in a tradi-

tional wedding ceremony contained the promise to honor and *obey* her husband [p. 82].

The idea that a marriage license is a "hitting license" is reinforced by society's tacit approval of such behavior.

The incidence of **spouse abuse** is very difficult to gauge with anything approaching accuracy. The Bureau of Justice Statistics report on family violence (1984) indicates that women were victims of abuse by husbands or former husbands at a rate of 2.7 per 1,000, while men were victims of abuse by wives or ex-wives at a rate of 0.2 per 1,000. These figures provide empirical support for the estimates of spouse abuse by Langley and Levy (1977), Martin (1976), and Moore (1979). Gelles and Straus (1979) reported that 16 percent of the families in their national survey had experienced spouse assaults, typically violence directed against a wife by a husband or ex-husband. It is worth mentioning that domestic disturbance calls account for more than two-thirds of all calls received by urban law enforcement agencies after 5:00 PM.

Among the factors that investigators have implicated as sources of spouse abuse are:

1. *Mental illness,* that is, that batterers are suffering from pathological personality disorders. Research strongly suggests that spouse abusers do not exhibit a higher profile of psychological illness than the normal population.
2. *The influence of alcohol.* The current view is that alcohol does not *cause* violence, but rather *permits* it by lowering restraints against its expression.
3. *Sexual inequality.* Family violence is more likely to occur when the man perceives himself as being unable to maintain himself in a position of dominance.
4. *Stress.* Frustration and other forces of personal stress in a man's life may lead him to abusive behavior if he cannot utilize more effective coping mechanisms.
5. *Compulsive masulinity.* Although not all abusive actions are motivated primarily by a need for external approval, at least some battering behavior appears to be an effort on the part of the abuser to bolster his self-esteem by showing that he is a "real man."

There is considerable agreement among researchers on the importance of learning in the intergenerational cycle of abuse. Families are the training ground for acquiring both stereotypical role behavior and the acceptability of violence. Thus, NiCarthy (1982) claims that nearly two-thirds of the men who batter their wives and/or children themselves grew up in homes where they were beaten or witnessed one parent battering another.

As a consequence of growing public awareness of the size and seriousness of the spouse abuse problem, refuges for the battered spouse have been opened in most cities. In many instances, they are operated by a female staff whose members are former victims of spouse abuse. In addition to offering a confidential and secure shelter, these centers usually provide a 24-hour hotline, telephone crisis counseling, food and transportation, child day care, and community resource referrals. Also, many states have adopted legislation intended to strengthen the legal protections afforded to women from battering husbands or boyfriends.

Abused and Neglected Children

"Child maltreatment, child abuse and neglect, is a serious and tragic problem" (Mayhall and Norgard, 1983, p. 70). Having made this statement, the authors go on to observe that it is almost the only statement that can be made about this topic which is not controversial. Some of the sources of controversy are semantic; others are conceptual; still others are methodological.

Physical assaults on children are part of the broader problem of **child abuse.** Parents who do not actually inflict injury on their children by beatings and other acts of violence may nevertheless deprive them of food, clothing, shelter, and medical treatment (physical neglect) or expose them to severe rejection in the form of excessive criticism, scapegoating, and terrorization (emotional neglect). A further dimension of child abuse is the sexual exploitation of children by parents or other adults through incest, rape, subjects of pornography, or other forms of molestation. We shall discuss these aspects of child abuse when we deal with sexual offenses later in this chapter.

As we have already seen in the case of spouse abuse, estimates of the incidence of child abuse in the several categories mentioned above vary widely. Gelles and Straus (1979) reported that between 1.4 and 1.9 million children in the United States are subjected to physical abuse from their parents in a given year. The authors of this national survey also pointed out that physical abuse is a continuing phenomenon: the average number of assaults per year was 10.5 and the median 4.5. The Bureau of Justice Statistics of the U.S. Department of Justice (1984) report puts the total figure of abused and neglected children at close to four million.

"Typical" abusive parents have been described as coming from backgrounds where they were unloved or abused and where homes were characterized by high levels of tension and frequent episodes of violent behavior. They are often engaged in destructive relationships with their own families. They have difficulty trusting others and are otherwise socially isolated. They are lacking in self-esteem and lack knowledge of a child's developmental stages or what is expected of themselves as parents. They have poor impulse control and are prone to project their hostilities onto the child. Abusive parents may also be under excessive personal stress as a consequence of poverty, unemployment, illness, alcoholism, or drug abuse.

Abuse of the Elderly

Some experts believe that abuse of the elderly is as prevalent as child abuse. However, no one knows for certain because victims are rarely seen by outsiders. It is estimated that between five hundred thousand and one million older people—4 percent of the nation's elderly—are victims of this form of family violence each year.

Gerontologists believe that, although the percentage of abused elderly is small, the problem is an extreme example of society's failure to care for its aged population. Demographic changes are contributing to the apparent increase in the abuse of the elderly and may be a harbinger of worse things to come. The population of those over 65 years of age grew twice as fast as the rest of the population during the past two decades, according to the Census Bureau.

Abuse of the elderly generally takes four forms: (1) physical abuse, including beatings, burnings, and sexual molestation; (2) psychological abuse, including threats of violence; (3) neglect, where the elderly person is left alone or locked up for long periods of time or denied food, medicine, and other assistance; and (4) financial exploitation, when a family member may steal money or property belonging to the older person. Research differs on whether physical abuse or psychological abuse is the more frequent form, but it is generally agreed that victims suffer from more than one kind of abuse.

The typical victim is a disabled middle-class woman over the age of 75 years. A major study (cited by Garland, 1984) found that a majority of abusers were women in their forties or fifties—very often daughters overwhelmed by the demands that caring for an older person entails. The decision to provide care is often made in the midst of a crisis; and despite good intentions, caretakers find themselves caught between the demands of children and husband and those of the older relative. People who looked forward to middle age as a time to enjoy freedom from parental responsibilities may resent the sudden unremitting burden of caring for a frail adult.

In some ways, abuse of the elderly is more difficult to deal with than child abuse, according to some experts. Because the aged are isolated, their mistreatment is less likely to be noticed by outsiders. Their status as adults makes it difficult for government authorities to intervene if the older person declines help. The elderly rarely report abuse. Growing old is a season of loss, when one's emotional world becomes constricted. The terrible fear of being left alone and more helpless and neglected is a powerful incentive against reporting abuse.

VIOLENT CRIME IN THE UNITED STATES

The volume of violent crime in the United States doubled between 1960 and 1975. In 1984, more than 1.25 million crimes of violence were reported to the police (*UCR*, 1985). These crimes were tallied as follows:

Murder and nonnegligent manslaughter	18,692
Forcible rape	84,233
Aggravated assault	685,349
Robbery	485,008

It should be emphasized that these are the official statistics and, as such, are subject to all of the constraints we have already identified and discussed in Chapter 2.

CRIMINAL HOMICIDE

Homicide is the killing of one human being by another. As a legal category, homicide can be criminal or noncriminal. Criminal homicide is generally considered first-degree murder when one person causes the death of another with premeditation and intent, or second-degree murder when death occurs with malice and intent, but without premeditation. Voluntary manslaughter usually involves intent to inflict bodily injury, but without deliberate intent to kill. Involuntary manslaughter is reckless or negligent killing without intent to harm. Noncriminal homicides include excusable homicides, usually in self-defense, or justifiable homicides, for example, the killing of an individual by a police officer in the line of duty (*UCR*, 1984).

Wolfgang and Zahn (1983) have cautioned that the classification of any homicide as either criminal or noncriminal—or a death as either a homicide, an accident, or a natural death—is not uniform across all time periods or across legal jurisdictions:

> What is considered a homicide death varies historically by the legal code of given jurisdictions, and by the interpretations and practices of agencies responsible for reporting death. When cars were first introduced into the United States, for example, deaths resulting from them were classified by some coroners as homicides, although now they are generally labelled accidental deaths unless caused by negligence. An abortion may be considered a criminal homicide or as the exercise of women's reproductive choice. Homicide statistics, like many other crimes, reflect definitions and legal interpretations that vary over time and space [p. 850].

"Normal" Murderers

Psychiatrist Manfred Guttmacher (1967) claims that most murders are committed by normal people—those who do not exhibit obvious signs of severe mental disturbance. Unlike many offenders, **"normal" murderers** generally do not have a history of criminal activities. They are rarely motivated by long-range plans or conscious desires; they kill on sudden impulse, often during a quarrel that began over some trivial incident, in circumstances where reasoning and judgment are overcome by strong emotions. Typically these situations involve relatives or friends and the killing is preceded by interpersonal stress and mounting tension. When murder occurs under such circumstances, there is little doubt about the identity of the perpetrator. In many instances, it is the murderer himself or herself who summons the police, then sits down and waits quietly for them to arrive.

Official statistics for calendar year 1984 identify 2.4 percent of homicides as the result of romantic triangles or lovers' quarrels (*UCR*, 1985). "Other arguments" were cited as the cause of 34 percent of the murders. This category includes killings by friends or acquaintances in barroom brawls, backyard arguments, stairwell confrontations, or violence in the murderer's or victim's own living room.

Felony Murderers

Felony murders are defined as those killings resulting from robbery, burglary, sex motives, gangland and institutional slaying and all other felonies. Felony murders

"Crimes of Passion"

In many so-called crimes of passion, the homicide victim is the third party in a romantic triangle. Lundsgaarde (1977) describes a case which exhibits features that are typical of this kind of slaying:

The killer, Mr. Jones, a 27-year-old white male, and his wife, age 32, had been very good friends of the victim, Mr. Russell, age 47, until the fatal episode that took place around midnight some time in October, 1969. When the police arrived at the scene of the killing they were met by Mr. Jones who calmly informed them that "I caught him with my wife and I shot him." The weapon, a .22 caliber rifle, was on top of the car in which Mr. Russell was shot. The relationships . . . among the three principals, together with the final events leading to the homicidal episode, are vividly summarized in an affidavit submitted to the police by the principal eyewitness, Mrs. Jones:

Last night, at about 11:30 PM, I called Russell at his home. I called to ask if I could borrow some money from him to pay the rent and the utilities. He said that he would lend me the money and that he would let me have about $55. He said he would be over as soon as he found a service station open as his tank was nearly empty. I guess it was about five minutes to midnight when he got to my house. I opened the front door and told him to come in. He said, "No, it's late and I have to get on back home." After he said this he walked up on the porch and we were just standing there talking about different things and the troubles me and Jones were having. About this time Russell made some remark about my husband being down at some joint watching gogo girls and that he could not stay as he had to work in the morning. About this time some cars passed the house and Russell said that I was going to be the talk of the neighborhood because I was standing out front talking to a bachelor. I said, "Let's go in the living room," but Russell said he wouldn't and that it wouldn't look too good so he said "Let's just sit in the car and talk for a few minutes." We got in the car and talked for a few minutes. After a while Russell teased me about how my hair looked and he kissed me a few times and then I kissed him back a few times. I kidded him about wrinkling his white shirt and he said that he wasn't worried about his shirt and that it was his tight black pants that were bothering him. This is when he said he would get comfortable and that's when he pulled his pants down around his knees. His shorts were down, too. When he said his pants were too tight, I told him to let me see and I felt and he had an erection. This is when he pulled his pants down and he took his left leg out of his britches. He then reached over and kissed me. At this time I was sitting under the steering wheel and Russell was over on the passenger's side. This is when Russell told me, "It's too late to send me home now." He reached over and kissed me. About this time I looked over Russell's shoulder and saw my husband. He had a gun. I think it was a .22 caliber rifle and my husband said something and then Russell said, "Now listen, Jones" or "Wait, Jones" and this is when my husband shot him. I jumed out of the car and

> ran around to the front and my husband had the gun pointed at me. I asked him not to shoot me and to think of our daughter. Then he said he wasn't going to kill me and that I wasn't fit to kill and that he was just going to beat the hell out of me . . . [pp. 107–8].

and suspected felony murders have doubled in the last two decades. In 1984, 9.3 percent of these killings occurred in connection with robberies; prostitution, commercialized vice, rape, and sex offenses accounted for 1.6 percent; narcotics law offenses comprised 2.7 percent. The killer in felony murders is usually male; he kills for money, sex, drugs, or to escape detection for a crime.

Multiple Murderers

There are two types of multiple murderers: the **mass murderer,** who kills a number of persons in one episode, and the **serial murderer,** who kills a series of victims—one, two, or more individuals per event over a period of time and often in different places. A recent intensive study of multiple murderers revealed that they are usually white, male, and older than the single-victim murderer (Berger, 1984).

Mass Murderer   On July 18, 1984, an out-of-work security guard named James Huberty entered a McDonald's Restaurant in San Ysidro, California, and engaged in a shooting spree which claimed the lives of 24 victims. This mass murder was the worst episode of its kind in American history. Although our knowledge of these murderers is not extensive, experts agree on several characteristics that appear to be common to this type of offender (Berger, 1984). Despite the sensational nature of their offenses, these killers are extraordinarily ordinary in appearance. They do not have the glassy-eyed appearance of lunatics nor would they stand out in a crowd. According to John Liebert, a psychologist at the University of Washington in Seattle, these individuals tend to be paranoid personalities who have been pushed over their threshold of self-control by some set of circumstances. For example, a threat of divorce may drive an unstable man to murder not only his wife but also their children and himself. In the case of James Huberty, the loss of his job as a security guard may well have been the event that caused him to drive to the McDonald's in order to "even the score with society" that in general had so often frustrated his efforts. Most mass murderers are believed to be psychotics. Ralph Tenay, forensic psychiatrist at Wayne State University, suggests that these individuals "have lost contact with or have a defective sense of reality" (as cited by Berger, 1984, p. 9). Their disorganized mental state leaves such individuals dissatisfied with expressing their aggression against one individual. Tenay contends that had Huberty been rational, he might have confined his need for revenge to the individual that fired him from his job. He further argues that one of the reasons the number of mass murderers has increased in recent years is a national policy of releasing large numbers of the mentally ill back into communities in many parts of the United States where weapons such as the Uzi automatic rifle that was used by Huberty are readily available.

Serial Murderers Serial murderers such as the Yorkshire Ripper, Ted Bundy, or Henry Lee Lucas may scatter their violent acts across a span of months or even years as they move about from place to place; others such as John Wayne Gacy may perpetrate most of their crimes in a rather restricted locale—a single town or city. These offenders are believed to represent a distinctive personality type. Experts believe that these individuals are sexual sadists whose psychological problems date back to their early childhoods. David Lunde, a forensic psychiatrist, characterized the serial murderer in an interview on ABC's "20/20" as an individual who is fulfilling violent sexual fantasies that they have had since childhood. He indicates that after each killing the offenders can satisfy their sexual urges and needs by thinking about what they had just done. However, after a period of time usually measured in weeks, the effect of the last killing begins to wear off and these offenders need to begin looking for a new victim. This behavior is consistent with 30 or more serial murderers who have recently come to public attention including Ted Bundy, who bludgeoned to death two young girls in a Florida sorority house and is suspected of having killed at least 33 young women in various parts of the country; the "Hillside Stranglers," two cousins—Angelo Buono and Ken Bianchi—who were responsible for the deaths of at least 10 women between 1977 and 1978; Son of Sam (David Berkowitz), who shot and killed six women over a 12-month period in New York; and Henry Lee Lucas who claims responsibility for 360 murders and is linked to approximately 150 victims by law enforcement officials.

Mass murderers are much easier to apprehend because they kill a number of people at once, often publicly, but the sporadic pattern of serial murderers as well as their movement from place to place makes it very difficult to identify them. A brief look at a typical six-week itinerary of serial murderer Henry Lee Lucas illustrates this pattern: Odessa, Texas, March 31, 1981—woman strangled to death; Monroe, Louisiana, April 4th—victim raped and shot; Jacksonville, Florida, April 14th—victim raped and stabbed; Big Spring, Texas, April 27th—woman bludgeoned to death ("ABC News," July 5, 1984). All of these homicides occurred in widely separated police jurisdictions. There was no reason for detectives in these areas to suspect that these murders were tied together. Furthermore, jealousy and distrust have been major impediments to cooperation between local law enforcement agencies as well as cooperation between these agencies and those on the federal level. There is, however, some reason for hope. Recently, the Federal Bureau of Investigation has begun a program called Violent Criminal Apprehension Program (VICAP) which seeks to coordinate efforts nationwide to more quickly identify serial murders. Under this program, the FBI is requesting that all jurisdictions report to them information on all unsolved murders in the United States. Under this system, information on any motiveless, senseless murder (of which about four thousand occur a year) would be fed into a central computer. It would then be possible to sort out all cases that show some similiarities and in turn to notify each jurisdiction that the case it reported was similar to that which occurred in several other places. Also, by pooling all the information from similar cases, they might be able to develop a profile which would increase the probability of apprehending these offenders. However, given the fact that many of these individuals are intelligent, have few visible signs of derangement even under expert examination, and follow a migratory lifestyle which makes them perpetual strangers in the communities they frequent, the task of identifying them will still be a monumental one. Up to this point, most of these offenders have been apprehended quite by accident, usually as a result of their own carelessness.

Juvenile Murderers

Heide (1984) has provided an interim report of research in progress on a sample of 60 youths convicted of murder or attempted murder. Her project was prompted by media depiction of an increase in violent behavior allegedly perpetrated by a "new breed" of ruthless, remorseless juveniles during the past decade. Her examination of arrest trend data from 1960 to 1982 revealed that arrests of juveniles for homicide has increased appreciably since 1960. Perusal of these data for more recent time frames, however, suggested that the number of homicides committed by juveniles, in contrast to those committed by adults, has stabilized over time. The proportionate involvement of juveniles in arrests for homicide appears to show a decreasing trend over the last decade, suggesting if a new breed of murderer exists, age may not be an adequate discriminator.

Based on a detailed examination of the first half of the sample ($n = 30$), Heide's data reveal that several distinct personality subtypes can be identified: "the player," who appears to embrace the role of street kid (i.e., enjoys hanging around with friends who are into the fast life, drinking, doing drugs, and participating in crime); "the lost child," who associates with delinquent peers but honestly appears to be at least partially unaware of events as they transpire, even when he is a participant in them; "the escapist," who tries to overcome his anxiety and bad feelings about himself by maintaining a strong front and embracing a delinquent role; and "the angry young man," who seems to "explode with anger and, even if the killing had not been planned, the amount of violence inflicted during the incident virtually ensures that the victim will not survive the attack" (p. 22). Heide notes that "the nihilistic killer," who kills people or animals casually and who derives satisfaction from hurting or destroying others does in fact exist, but in small numbers. At this time, Heide emphasizes the tentative character of her conclusions in view of the relatively small number of subjects analyzed thus far.

Rate of Criminal Homicide

Although the FBI did not begin compiling statistics until 1933, other sources indicate that the homicide rate in the United States moved steadily upward from 1900 until the 1930s (Bloch and Geis, 1970). Trend studies (Klebba, 1975; Farley, 1980) and comparative analyses in different time periods (Zahn, 1980) indicate that homicide rates dropped from the mid-1930s to the end of World War II, at which point there was a brief (3-year) upswing, followed by a drop to pre–World War II levels. Homicide in the United States was at a minimum during the 1950s (Farley, 1980), but began to rise and continued increasing at a steeper rate during the 1960s and 1970s. By 1980, homicide rates had reached a high of 10.2 per 100,000 population, declining

Profile of a Serial Murderer: "Pogo the Clown"

In late December of 1978, in Des Plaines, Illinois, Mrs. Elizabeth Piest drove to a nearby pharmacy where her 15-year-old son Robert was working. It was her 46th birthday, and her family had delayed cutting the birthday cake until Robert finished work. As Mrs. Piest and her son were leaving the store, Robert told her, "Mom, I've got to talk to a contractor about a summer job that will pay me $5 an hour." That was the last Mrs. Piest saw of her son.

The search for Robert Piest led police to the home of John Wayne Gacy, a 36-year-old contractor who lived in the Chicago suburb of Norwood Park. Armed with a warrant, they searched Gacy's tidy yellow brick home. There in the crawl space under the house and under the floor of the garage, investigators discovered the first skeletal remains of what eventually proved to be 27 bodies of boys and young men whom Gacy had sexually molested then strangled. Some of the bodies were found with ropes still around their necks. Gacy broke down and confessed to 32 murders—a toll which exceeded the 27 deaths claimed by Dean Corll's homosexual torture ring in Houston in 1974 and the 25 murders attributed to Juan Corona in California in the previous year.

Gacy, a short, husky man with a mustache, liked to dress up in costume as Pogo the Clown and entertain children. An active worker in the Democratic party, he was always available for doing chores and helping out at picnics. Everyone liked him. Similar attitudes toward Gacy had been held by people who knew him back in Waterloo, Iowa, ten years earlier. Consequently they were shocked when he was convicted of sodomy with a 16-year-old youth and sentenced to ten years in prison. His wife obtained a divorce while he was still serving time, but he was a model prisoner and was paroled after only 18 months. He moved to Chicago where he was arrested on another sodomy charge in 1971. The charge was dropped, however, when the youth failed to appear in court. A year later, Gacy remarried. Gacy's violent temper and outbursts of rage led his second wife to secure a divorce in 1976.

Gacy's mother-in-law, who had lived with them, recalled complaining of a foul smell in the house, "like dead rats," which Gacy explained came from stagnant water trapped in the crawl space. His former wife told the police, "I think now, if there were murders, some of them must have taken place while I was in that house." Two young men who escaped becoming victims of Gacy explained to police how he managed to trap his prey. First he would put handcuffs on himself and release them. Then he would encourage the boys to join in the game, but without showing them how to unlock the cuffs. The two survivors refused to play Gacy's lethal game.

Gacy once left a friend of his puzzled when he told him, "I do a lot of rotten, horrible things, but I do a lot of good things, too." The bodies of five of Gacy's victims, including that of Robert Piest, will probably never be recovered because they were thrown into the Des Plaines river.

Source: From information provided in *Time*, January 8, 1979, Vol. 113, No. 2, p. 23; *Newsweek*, January 8, 1979, Vol. 93, No. 2, pp. 24, 26.

to 8.3 in 1984. It is not clear, however, whether this decline is the beginning of a downward trend or merely a temporary fluctuation.

Research on Criminal Homicide

The germinal study of criminal homicide in the United States was conducted more than 25 years ago by Marvin E. Wolfgang (1958). His research covered 588 cases of criminal homicide which occurred during a 5-year period, from 1948 to 1952 in Philadelphia. His results indicated that: (1) black males, aged 20 to 24 years, had homicide rates that far exceeded their proportion in the general population, while the 25- to 34-year-old group of black males had the highest victimization rate; (2) stabbing was the most frequent method of inflicting death (39 percent) by black males, as compared with death by beating (22 percent) among white males; (3) murder is most likely to be committed in a public place (street or alley) on a weekend, between the hours of 8:00 PM on Friday and midnight on Sunday; (4) perpetrators and/or victims in nearly two-thirds of the cases had criminal histories and had been drinking prior to the murder; and (5) the crime usually resulted from an argument, fight, or robbery attempt. In the overwhelming majority of the cases, the victims and offenders were members of the same race and were close friends, relatives, or acquaintances.

Much of the subsequent research on criminal homicide consists of reexaminations of the variables and relationships that Wolfgang explored in his original study: type of weapon used; influences of race, sex, alcohol, and drugs; and the relationship between offenders and victims. Some of Wolfgang's findings have been confirmed by later research. For example, homicide rates were highest among young black males in the urban population Wolfgang studied and this pattern has remained consistent. Farley (1980) reports that the highest at-risk population is the group between 25 and 35 years of age and homicide is the leading cause of death among nonwhites between the ages of 20 and 30 years. Other findings, however, have changed. Stabbing and death by beating, which were the most frequent means of inflicting death among blacks and whites, respectively, in the 1958 study have been replaced by shooting as the major cause of death in later research on criminal homicide.

The involvement of alcohol or dugs in homicide remains a matter of controversy. Alcohol was present in either the victim or the offender in nearly two-thirds of the murders Wolfgang examined, but other studies (e.g., Greenberg, 1981) have found different percentages. In any event, Wolfgang originally cautioned against the assumption of a direct causal connection between the consumption of alcohol and the occurrence of criminal homicide; and this caveat was reiterated by the National Commission on the Causes and Prevention of Violence (1969).

The relationship between homicide and drugs other than alcohol is subject to many of the same difficulties of interpretation. Goldstein (1982) suggests that drugs may be involved in homicide in one of three ways: (1) offenders or victims under the influence of drugs may be more prone to engage in violent behavior; (2) drug abusers may engage accidentally in violent behavior during the commission of crimes aimed at securing the means to purchase drugs; and (3) homicide may occur as a result of territorial conflicts between drug dealers or as settlement for bad debts. Goldstein acknowledges that it is impossible to conclude which of these three factors contributes most to the relationship between homicide and drugs.

ASSAULT AND BATTERY

Most offenses against the person that do not result in death—apart from some sex offenses—include as an element some form of assault and battery. Technically speaking, **assault** is only the threat, with or without a verbal gesture, to do bodily harm to another person, while the actual injury is referred to as **battery.** Thus, if someone brandishes a two-by-four or a length of lead pipe against another, the former could be charged with assault, even though no injury occurred. Jurisdictions vary according to the inclusion of "battery" in the labeling of offenses falling within this category. Typically the more serious offenses, designated as felonies, are labeled **aggravated assault, assault with a deadly weapon,** or **assault with intent to commit murder,** while those classified as misdemeanors bear such labels as **simple assault** and **fighting.**

Aggravated assault is the leading crime of violence. In 1984, this offense accounted for 6 percent of the total Crime Index and 54 percent of the violent crimes. Research on assault is comparatively meager, perhaps because it is viewed as a run-of-the-mill offense. Most people do not appear to take threats seriously because most of them are uttered in anger with no real intention of carrying them out. Threats tend to be reported only when the potential victim has reason to believe that they will be carried out, for example, an estranged wife threatened by her husband. In the case of assaults involving injuries, these are not reported unless there is serious injury or property damage, which may be the case in bar fights. Most assaults involving injuries occur in communities that subscribe to what we have already identified as a subculture of violence. Within such communities, injuries are regarded as a private matter. There is, in addition, a distrust of the police and the feeling that "they would not do anything" if the offenses were reported.

Research on Aggravated Assault

Pittman and Handy (1964) studied a random 25 percent sample of 900 aggravated assault cases seen in 1961 by the St. Louis police. They analyzed their sample in terms of such variables as time and place of occurrence, relationship and kinship status of the offender and victim, the type of force employed, and disposition of the offender. The emergent pattern which characterized the typical case was that assailant and victim were male, black, and between the ages of 25 and 29 years. The peak day of occurrence was Saturday and the peak hours of occurrence were between 5:00 PM and 2:00 AM. The authors concluded that homicide and aggravated assault were similar enough in all major respects to be considered essentially the same type of crime: the dividing line between the two offenses was often determined by how rapidly the ambulance managed to get the victim to the hospital. Subsequent research (Curtis, 1974; Podlesny, 1973; Pokorny, 1970; Wallace, 1973; Waymire, 1979) has largely confirmed this conclusion.

ROBBERY

Robbery was identified by the President's Crime Commission (1967) and, more recently, by President Reagan's Task Force on Violent Crime (1981) as the type of offense that is most feared by the public. It is this "crime in the streets," along with burglary, that is a significant factor in public anxiety and alarm over crime. It is abundantly clear why people dread being victims of this offense. Robbery is almost invariably committed by a stranger in an unexpected and threatening way. In addition to the loss of money or property, victims are threatened with, or actually subjected to, bodily injury.

Characteristics of Offenders and Victims

Robbery is a crime in which blacks are involved as both perpetrators and victims in numbers that far exceed their proportion within the population, according to research by Normandeau (1968) and continuing data from the *Uniform Crime Reports* during the period from 1968 to the present. In the Normandeau study, which was based on robbery data in Philadelphia, three times as many blacks were apprehended as robbers and twice as many blacks were victims of robbery as were represented by population percentages, and these figures are paralleled by national data from the *UCR.* In addition, robbery is a youthful offense: more than half of the persons arrested for robbery in a given year are under the age of 25 years.

Conklin (1972) has formulated a typology of robbers which includes: (1) the professional, (2) the opportunist, (3) the addict, and (4) the alcoholic. According to the author, **professional robbers** have a long-term commitment to crime as a source of livelihood. They employ sophisticated planning, and although they usually work with accomplices, the structure of their gangs is generally temporary and fluid. Targets tend to be commercial establishments, and firearms are usually employed. Since these offenders are generally unemployed, they depend upon robbery for their livelihood. They spend money quickly on various luxuries and develop plans to commit other robberies only when they have exhausted their resources.

Opportunist robbers, on the other hand, are rarely committed to robbery. They tend to be younger, black, and from a lower socioeconomic background. The robberies they commit are not elaborately planned and frequently involve noncommercial targets. They are not dependent upon robbery as a primary source of income, and therefore the money they acquire from these offenses can be considered supplementary income. These offenders rarely carry a weapon of any kind, but because they tend to commit these offenses with accomplices, the group itself becomes the "weapon."

Addict robbers, although committed to theft, are not committed to robbery. In fact, given the opportunity to secure funds through other offenses—theft, drug selling—that involve less risk of being identified and arrested, these offenders will opt for these choices. However, in desperation for funds to support their habit, they are occasionally forced to engage in robbery. Their desperation may result in little planning and a careless selection of targets, which increases their chances of being apprehended. If an addict robber carries a weapon, which is unusual, it is likely to be an unloaded gun.

Although random circumstances and lack of planning may cause the offenses committed by **alcoholic robbers** to appear to be similar to those of the opportunists, the situational nature of the offenses distinguishes them from the latter category. Alcoholics do not seek out a victim and rarely employ a weapon. Frequently these offenses occur in an assaultive situation, where theft is an afterthought. For acloholic robbers, there is no commitment to crime, even though almost all of them have participated in a minimal amount of juvenile theft.

Female Robbers   Fortune, Vega, and Silverman (1980) interviewed 33 female robbers who were incarcerated in a correctional institution in the state of Florida. The majority of the women were black, single, under 30 years old, and of average intelligence. They were found to have operated with an accomplice and to have used a gun in the commission of their offenses.

The authors proposed a preliminary typology featuring the two categories— **situational robber** and **career robber.** In the case of the former, the circumstances which led to the robbery appeared to be external to the offender and involved a set of pressures or cues (distortion of judgment attributable to intoxicants, severe economic crises, peer pressures) which resulted in the commission of the offense. By way of contrast, the offenses committed by career robbers appeared to be part of an internalized and continuing pattern of criminal activity. All of the 18 offenders in this category had extensive prior arrest records and a history of robbery.

SEXUAL OFFENSES AND OFFENDERS

Sex offenders vary widely in terms of who they are and what they do. They range from violent sadists to "flashers" whose behavior is apt to leave people more amused than terrified. The offender may have assaulted only one victim, a new victim every day, or the same victim repeatedly over a period of years. Emotional impact on the victim can range from none to totally disabling. The victim may be a family member, a casual acquaintance, a close friend, or a total stranger. The crime may have been fantasized and rehearsed in growing detail over a period of months or it may have been committed impulsively, with sudden loss of control and no forethought. It may be the offender's first offense or his hundredth.

While many sex offenders may show an increase over time in the degree of violence they inflict on their victims, many others seem to stabilize in one pattern. The acts committed by sex offenders include not only forced vaginal intercourse between male and female, but also the exploitation of children through fondling (clothed or unclothed), window peeping, flashing, and physical contact in public places. Much of our information comes from studies of convicted sex offenders, especially those in treatment or research programs. We know relatively little about sex offenders who do not end up in the criminal justice system or who are not labeled as sex offenders, for example, most female sex offenders, many juvenile offenders, and the "less serious" offenders who have not yet progressed to the point where their offenses are prosecuted.

Sexual assault is probably the most damaging, short of murder, of all crimes against the person. It often affects for years the self-image of the victims, their sense of control over their lives, and their relationships with others. The fears and emotional difficulties created by sexual assault may be passed on to children and families of the victims. Sexual assault is also probably the least understood by the public of all crimes and this lack of understanding may often lead to further trauma for the victims. For example, police, families, friends, and jurors may believe that the child who has been sexually molested is making up stories.

Not all sex offenders are evil, strange monsters lurking in dark alleys. Many of them knew their victims before molesting them and many are relatives. Most sex offenders are not insane or sex maniacs and are not "crazy" in the traditional sense of the term. They do, however, have a serious psychological disturbance which usually began when they were young children. Eighty percent of sex offenders were victims of sexual assault when they were children (*Report on Treatment Programs for Sex Offenders,* 1984). Sex offenders come from all walks of life; many of them are married, gainfully employed, and supporting a family.

Many child molesters and incest offenders genuinely care for the children they molest; they use no force and intend no harm. Their thinking is generally distorted to the point that they believe that they are not injuring the children. Sexual offenders' psychological dynamics are such that they tend to victimize women and children out of a deep psychological need to dominate and control others, a need to be accepted by others, in spite of the fact which is clear to emotionally healthy people, that molestation does not lead to acceptance, and a deep need to release anger and hostility. In many cases the rapist is an angry, violent person who at some level desires to hurt, subjugate, control, and frighten his victims; or a person whose need to rape is fed by his distorted perceptions of others and their reactions toward him, who cannot express his growing rage in normal communication and thus resolve it. Eventually his anger manifests itself in sexual violence against the most available and vulnerable person. Often the rapist, when he is not committing sexual assault, is a charming individual. In many cases the child molester is an insecure, timid person who feels profoundly inadequate and alone, a person whose molestation of children is motivated by his need for intimacy and acceptance, his fear of rejection, and his distorted perceptions of children's reactions to him. Sex offenders almost never sexually molest their victims simply because of a need for sexual release.

Sexual Offenses and the *Uniform Crime Reports*

During 1984, there were 246,700 arrests for sex crimes in the United States, according to the *Uniform Crime Reports* (1985). These arrests can be tallied as follows:

Forcible rape	36,700
Prostitution and commercialized vice	112,200
All other sex offenses	97,800

The last category above includes **statutory rape,** which is defined as sexual intercourse with a female who is under the specified legal age, regardless of consent. The total number of *reported* cases (as distinguished from arrests) of forcible rape for this same period was 84,233. Since 1975, the rate of forcible rape has increased 35.7 percent.

The definition by the *UCR* of forcible rape as "the carnal knowledge of a female forcibly and against her will" (1985, p. 13) makes no allowance for those rare instances in which a male claims to have been victimized by a female rapist. More important, it excludes homosexual rape, a problem that has reached crisis proportions in our jails and prisons. In this respect, the *UCR* is not representative of the trend exhibited by state legislatures to replace the term and concept **forcible rape** with the broader and more realistic crime category of **sexual battery.**

Forcible Rape

Criminologists have repeatedly warned against uncritical acceptance of *UCR* statistics on racial factors in rape because they are based on reported rapes. However, women are showing a greater willingness to report rapes than was formerly the case. As the results of the NILECJ (1977) survey demonstrate, several factors appear to have contributed to this tendency: sexual permissiveness and women's liberation (suggesting a belief that women are less reluctant than before to place themselves in precarious situations); increased public awareness of rape as a result of extensive media coverage; and a change in attitudes toward reporting that reflects a perception of more sensitive treatment of the rape victim by the criminal justice system. This perception is undoubtedly linked with the publicity that has been given to improvements in the training of criminal justice personnel in rape crisis intervention methods. In addition, there has been a considerable growth in the establishment and development of rape crisis centers in metropolitan areas across the country.

Characteristics of Offenders and Victims   A series of studies (Amir, 1971; Chappell and Singer, 1973; Nelson, Silverman, and Vega, 1977; National Institute of Law Enforcement and Criminal Justice [NILECJ] 1977; Peters et al., as reported by Krasner, Meyer, and Carroll, 1977) have provided us with a wealth of detailed information on the nature of the rape offense. We will present an overview of the patterns that have emerged from this research with regard to factors such as race, age, criminal record, and the victim-offender relationship.

Race   All major studies have shown that rape is predominantly intraracial in character, that is, it is committed by white men against white women and by black men against black women. Furthermore, rape occurs with greater frequency among blacks than among whites. Almost half of the cases of rape reported each year involve black victims and offenders—a rate which is more than four times the black proportion in the U.S. population.

Age   Most rapists are young. Amir (1971) found that about two-thirds of the offenders in his study were between 15 and 24 years of age. Comparable findings were reported by Chappell and Singer (1973).

Rape victims range in age from several months to 85 years of age; and Krasner et al. (1977) mention that the Center for Rape Concern (CRC) at Philadelphia General Hospital has treated a 97-year-old victim. Despite variations from study to study, victims tend to concentrate in the 16- to 24-year age range. The National Crime Survey (NCS) for 1973–1982 found that young women in this age range were two to three times more likely to be victims of rape or attempted rape than women in general (Bureau of Justice Statistics, 1985). Thus, it would appear that rape victims and offenders tend to occupy roughly the same age bracket.

Victim-Offender Relationship   Rape by a stranger is the most frightening form of rape. This is also the most common form, accounting for 68 percent of the rapes reported to the National Crime Survey between 1973 and 1982. It has been suggested that victims are less likely to report rape by a known assailant to either the police or a survey interviewer because they feel embarrassed, wish to protect a friend or family member, fear reprisal from the attacker, or fear that their account of the rape will not be believed. This view is supported by NCS data showing that for nonstranger rapes or attempted rapes, victims only reported the incident to the police in 47.7 percent of the cases, as compared with a 56 percent reporting rate for stranger rapes (Bureau of Justice Statistics, 1984).

Criminal record   Approximately half the offenders in Amir's study had a record of previous crimes. Subsequent research has reported prior arrest rates that range between one-third and one-half the offenders sampled. The NILECJ study noted that the offender is likely to have a record that includes previous crimes of violence or sexual offenses, among them prior rapes. Black rapists were more likely than white rapists to have a criminal record.

A Typology of Rapists   A typology of rapists and rape incidents has been proposed by Groth and his associates (Groth, Burgess, and Holmstrom, 1977; Groth and Birnbaum, 1979), which incorporates a number of the sexual and aggressive elements in the motivation for sexual assault identified by earlier researchers (Cohen, Seghorn, and Calmas, 1969; Cohen, Garofalo, Boucher, and Seghorn, 1972) and has the additional value of more adequate sampling. Groth and his colleagues sought to establish the dominant motive of the rapist in each incident of sexual assault (i.e., power, anger, or sexuality). Their classification system consists of the following types:

1. *Power-assertive type.*   Rapes in which power motives predominate are characterized by the use of coercion based on threats or mild physical force to achieve control over the victim. Rapists of this kind, who constituted nearly half the sample, often have a history of "compulsive masculinity," which manifests itself in the attempt to establish domination over everyone with whom they come into contact.
2. *Power-reassurance type.*   This rapist, like his power-assertive counterpart, also attempts to establish control over his victim by means of intimidation. The major difference is that weakness, inadequacy, and underlying problems of gender identity are more pronounced among power-reassurance rapists. In fact, as Groth and his colleagues noted, sexual assaults in this group tended to occur as an aftermath to an incident in which the rapist had experienced humiliation, embarrassment, or some other affront to his feel-

---

Can a Husband Rape His Wife?

On October 10, 1978, Greta Rideout of Salem, Oregon, called the Women's Crisis Service and reported that she had been raped by her husband, John. She was advised to call the police, which she did. John, a 21-year-old unemployed cook, was arrested and charged with rape. He found himself facing a jury trial and the prospect of a 20-year prison sentence if convicted.

Greta Rideout claimed that her husband had chased her through a field near their apartment building, caught her and dragged her inside and raped her in the presence of their 2 1/2-year-old daughter. His defense counsel admitted that sexual intercourse had taken place but denied that John Rideout had used coercion. Greta was depicted to the jury as a woman with a history of sexual difficulties that included several extramarital affairs and a lesbian relationship. Husband John, on the other hand, was painted as an average man who sincerely believed that marriage constituted a guarantee of sexual access to one's spouse. The jury evidently agreed because it returned a verdict of not guilty.

Six years after Greta Rideout became a "sacrificial lamb," more and more states are making it illegal for men to force their wives into sex. Experts disagree, however, over the effectiveness of the laws and whether the nationally publicized Rideout trial helped or hurt efforts to pass marital-rape legislation. Husbands can now be prosecuted in 20 states and the District of Columbia. In another 26 states, including New York, Pennsylvania, Ohio, and Michigan, prosecution is possible only if the man and woman are living apart or have filed for separation or divorce. Four states—Alabama, South Dakota, Vermont, and West Virginia—do not recognize marital rape as a crime.

---

ings of self-esteem. Rapists of this type accounted for 21 percent of the sample.

3. *Anger-retaliation type.* Unlike power-oriented rapists, who rarely inflict physical injury on their victims, rapists who are driven by anger and hostility may inflict severe damage on their victims. These rapists may regard normal sexual experience with feelings of disgust and revulsion. Rape for such individuals is an act which expresses hatred toward all women: the dominant motive is revenge for real or imaginary slights suffered at the hands of women. Thirty percent of the rapists fit this pattern.

4. *Anger-excitation type.* Rapists of this kind, who accounted for only 5 percent of the cases, exhibited a pattern which might be characterized as pathological sadism. These men are "turned on" by inflicting suffering and humiliation on their victims. Typically, anger-excitation rapists use violence only as a means of arousal; thus, there is no need for further violence after intercourse has been completed.

Other kinds of severe psychopathology may be present in some rapists. The breakdown of moral and ethical restraints that frequently accompanies schizophrenia, manic reactions, and organic psychoses of certain types may lead to the expression of illicit sexual impulses. However, as Coleman notes, "during acute psychotic episodes the individual is likely to be so disorganized as to be capable only of indiscriminate physical assault rather than the coordinated behavior required for forcible rape" (1980, p. 582).

Homosexual Rape

William Laite, a businessman and former Georgia legislator, was convicted in Texas of perjury in connection with a contract he had negotiated with the Federal Administration Housing Authority. Laite was sentenced to a jail term in Fort Worth. The minute he entered the "tank" or dayroom, he was approached by five men. One of them said, "I wonder if he has any guts. We'll find out tonight, won't we? Reckon what her name is; she looks ready for about six or eight inches. You figure she'll make us fight for it, or is she going to give it to us nice and sweet, like a good little girl? Naw, we'll have to work her over first, but hell, that's half the fun, isn't it?"

Laite was terrified. "I couldn't move. This couldn't be happening to me," he recalled. But Laite was saved from forcible homosexual rape: a 17-year-old youth was admitted to the dayroom just as the five men were about to begin their assault. The men turned on the youngster viciously, knocking him unconscious. They were on him at once, "like jackals, ripping the coveralls off his limp body. Then as I watched in frozen fascination and horror, they sexually assaulted him, savagely and brutally like starving animals after a piece of raw meat. Then I knew what they meant about giving me six or eight inches."

But the attack did not end there. While the youth was still unconscious, the attackers jabbed his limp body with the burning tips of pencil erasers, making it twitch—and thereby increasing the sexual excitement of the rapists. In a final sadistic gesture, one of the attackers "shoved his fingers deep into the boy's rectum and ripped out a bloody mass of hemorrhoids" (Laite, 1972, pp. 42–44).

It is noteworthy that this homosexual rape occurred in a jail. Rape is much more pervasive in jails, detention centers, and training schools than in prisons, where control is tighter and inmates are subjected to greater physical restraint. Jails usually contain both inmates who are serving sentences of less than one year for misdemeanor offenses and those who are awaiting trial for serious felony offenses such as murder, robbery, and rape. Also housed in jails are "bound-overs," offenders who have been sentenced to prison terms and are awaiting transfer. Homosexual rapists in the jails are chiefly found among the latter two categories of prisoners.

Davis (1968) interviewed 3,304 inmates out of 60,000 who passed through the Philadelphia corrections system in a two-year period (1966–1968). He also interviewed custodial employees. His study revealed that sexual assaults were epidemic: approximately 2,000 of the inmates he interviewed admitted to having been victims of homosexual rape. Of this number, only 156 cases were documented; and of those cases, only 96 had been reported to the correctional authorities and a mere 26 cases had been reported to criminal justice agencies outside the corrections system. Reporting is discouraged by unwritten laws of prison culture and the fear of brutal reprisal.

Davis observes that sexual assaults, as contrasted with consensual homosexuality, are not caused by sexual deprivation: "They are expressions of anger and aggression prompted by the same basic frustrations that exist in the community, and which very probably were significant factors in producing the rapes, robberies, and other violent offenses for which the bulk of the aggressors were convicted" (1968, p. 16). Rather, as Scacco (1975) points out, racism is the central factor in sexual assaults within correctional institutions. Black aggressors and white victims are found in disproportionate numbers in every study of sexual assault in jails and prisons. Blacks rape whites to humiliate and degrade them—to give members of the white majority a taste of what blacks experience as members of a minority community. The same pattern is evident with regard to Hispanic minorities and whites. Rarely do blacks and Hispanics rape one another.

Status also plays a major role in homosexual rape in correctional institutions. Status in prison is a mark of survival. (It was not uncommon in Biblical times for an invading army to sodomize males in the conquered land to demonstrate their dominance.) The higher an inmate's status, the lower the incidence of attack against that inmate. Status in prison is usually related to a hierarchy based upon an inmate's resources, including physical strength, gang affiliation, access to contraband, crime of record, and institutional reputation (Cotton and Groth, 1982). Thus, the inmates who are most likely to be raped are white, middle class, young, inexperienced offenders of slight build, convicted of minor property crimes (Bowker, 1980).

Thus, it appears that homosexual rape is not committed for sexual relief. Rather, inmates rape one another for the same reason that men often rape women— to exert control and dominance and to degrade the victim. Race is a major factor in homosexual rape and certain types of inmates are much more likely to get raped than others.

VOYEURISM AND INDECENT EXPOSURE

Certain acts that offend individual or community tastes and values, as Lorensen (1983) observes, lie at "the outer fringes of criminal law regulation of sexual conduct" (p. 1493). Included within this category are **voyeurism ("peeping"),** indecent exposure, "flashing," and other acts of social or commercial nudity. In most jurisdictions, such acts are treated as misdemeanors, although a number of states deal more harshly with indecent exposure to children.

Voyeurism ("Peeping")

Voyeurism is a type of sexual deviation in which sexual gratification is obtained by observing a nude woman or some part of the nude female body without consent of the woman involved. More commonly the voyeur is called a "peeping Tom," a term derived from the legend of Lady Godiva, who rode naked through the public square of Coventry, England, in order to dramatize the plight of the overtaxed townspeople. All of the citizens remained indoors with their windows shuttered, but a tailor named Tom broke the pledge and peeped (Mathis, 1972).

Most peepers are interested in looking at attractive women, preferably engaged in some sort of erotic or provocative activity. But some peepers have more specific criteria: observing a partially clad woman engaged in lovemaking with another woman; watching a female perform fellatio; or looking at a woman and man engaged in mutual masturbation. Peepers are apt to be optimists and persevere in their activities in the expectation that something more erotically stimulating is just around the corner.

According to Gebhard et al. (1965), peepers are not prone to serious antisocial behavior but are much given to minor criminal acts; their criminal records usually feature arrests for habitual peeping and some exhibitionism. Unlike exhibitionists, the majority of peepers try to avoid detection. Those few voyeurs who attract attention to themselves generally wish to frighten or humiliate the victim or, in some instances, elicit some reciprocal interest—characteristics that are common to exhibitionists. Gebhard and his associates further suggest that "peepers who enter homes or other buildings in order to peep and peepers who deliberately attract the female's attention (tapping on windows, leaving notes) are more likely to become rapists than are the others" (p. 378).

Indecent Exposure

Exhibitionism (indecent exposure) is the "expressed impulse to expose the male genitals to an unsuspecting female as a final sexual gratification" (Mohr, Turner, and Jerry, 1964). This definition excludes exposure which precedes sexual contact, occurs in the context of public urination or intoxication, or results from severe mental disorders or retardation (Cox and Daitzmann, 1980). Following completion of his act, the exhibitionist often feels a sense of shame or guilt, combined with a fear of the possibility of apprehension and its accompanying publicity that may result in a loss of job and public disgrace. Given the compulsive nature of this offense and the offender's need for public exposure, it is not surprising that exhibitionists have the highest conviction rates among sex offenders (Cox and Daitzmann, 1980; Gebhard et al., 1965).

The Nature of the Act   The great majority of indecent exposures occur in public and semipublic places—in the street, in parks, within buildings, and in parked vehicles. The act itself is quite variable, ranging from the exposure of the flaccid penis without sexual satisfaction to exposure of the erect penis, often accompanied by masturbation and intense sexual satisfaction. The nature of the act can differ with the same individual according to circumstances and the intensity of the sexual urge. However, very little is really sexual about exhibitionism. That is, the exhibitionist does not expose himself as a prelude to sex or as an invitation to intercourse. Rather, the exhibitionist seems more intent on evoking fear or shock. In many cases, the offender is attempting to get his victim to acknowledge the fact of his masculinity by eliciting a reaction of shock, fear, or embarrassment. It is also generally agreed that the exhibitionist does not usually seek further contact with his victim and may, in fact, even fear it. With regard to choice of victim, the exhibitionist usually chooses a stranger and in some instances may choose multiple victims as is the case with exposures on playgrounds, crowded streets, and in public parks. It has also been noticed that some exhibitionists prefer particular types of victims. Thus, some choose mature females, still other choose adolescents, and some even choose young children. The proportion of children as victims of exposure varies between 20 and 50 percent of the total number. Mohr et al. (1964) noted, however, that the proportion of child victims may be higher among those charged as offenders because exposure to children is regarded more seriously and is more likely to be prosecuted.

CHILD MOLESTATION

Beyond our societal taboos against sexual acts involving children, the vulnerability of children and their inability to defend themselves arouses considerable personal anguish and public anger toward the child molester. However, many of the stereotypes of the child molester have little or no basis in fact. Groth, Burgess, Birnbaum, and Gary (1978) conducted a study of child molesters in Massachusetts and their findings contradicted the following specific myths of the child molester:

- Child molesters are generally "dirty old men";
- Offenders are strangers to their victims;
- Molesters are mentally retarded, alcoholic, or psychotic;
- Child molesters are sexually frustrated;
- Molesters progress over time to increasingly violent acts;
- Children are at greater risk from homosexual than from heterosexual adults.

The profile of the child molester that emerged from the Groth et al. study is a relatively young heterosexual male who is not insane, retarded, or sexually frustrated. He is more concerned about controlling than injuring the child and more often poses a psychological risk than a physical risk to the victim. His behavior is highly repetitive, often to the point of compulsion, rather than the result of a temporary lapse of judgment while under the influence of drugs or alcohol.

Mythology notwithstanding, in 1984 news stories of cases involving sexual abuse of children at day care centers throughout the United States capped a year which began with reports by the Federal Bureau of Investigation on sexual exploitation of children (Goldstein, 1984), incest (Barry, 1984), and the operation of child pornography and sex rings (Lanning and Burgess, 1984). In addition to the new light these and other reports shed on the magnitude of the problem of sexual abuse and exploitation of children, perhaps the feature that evoked the strongest public reaction was the age of many child victims—in some cases, infants less than 1-year-old.

Dr. Vincent DeFrancis of the Children's Division of the American Humane Association has cautioned that the emotional trauma experienced by children who have been sexually abused may be attributed at least in part to parental responses to their victimization. In some cases, children may be harmed more by parental overreaction, interrogation by criminal justice personnel, and medical examination following a sexual episode than by the act itself. DeFrancis (1969) suggests that parents can avoid unnecessarily traumatizing children who are sexual abuse victims by handling the incident calmly and with an absence of hysteria or excitement.

Child Rape

Many of the other elements commonly associated with rape do not apply to child rape. Almost two-thirds of the time, the rape is committed during daylight or dusk, the largest percentage (56 percent) between noon and 8 PM. On the other hand, about one-third of the rapes occurred between 8 PM and midnight, when the child was attacked by someone supposedly caring for him or her, such as a babysitter.

The incidents, as the children described them, were usually of short duration, occurred mostly indoors (35 percent at home, 21.7 percent in the offender's home—which is hardly surprising, considering the degree of acquaintance).

Tempting was used in almost 25 percent of the cases. . . . Coercion was used in 31 percent of the cases. Many victims said they were threatened with harm. Often the child was told that if he or she did not submit, the offender would harm younger brothers or sisters present.

Application of actual physical force was less frequent for children than for other groups (i.e., adolescents or mature women). No force at all was used in over 54 percent of the incidents. Roughness, such as pushing or shoving, was present in 30.5 percent; 16 percent of the victims were beaten by means such as slapping, but not brutally. Only 13.6 percent reported actual brutality; 8.5 percent slugging, kicking, beating, and the like; and 5.1 percent choking or gagging.

The definitions of rape are very pertinent in evaluating child molestation. Only 36.7 percent of the children were subjected to what most people, and the law, consider rape: forced penile-vaginal intercourse. (This compares with 86.4 percent of adolescent and over 95 percent of adult rapes.) According to the children, fondling or caressing occurred almost 30 percent of the time, penile-vaginal contact without penetration almost 20 percent, and oral intercourse or contact 6.6 percent. Incidence of rectal intercourse was 11.4 percent. (This was highest for any group, but could have been in error, since children have difficulty distinguishing between vaginal and rectal contact.) Other sexual acts, such as masturbation, occurred in almost 20 percent of the cases.

Source: W. Krasner, Linda C. Meyer, and Nancy E. Carroll, *Victims of Rape.* Washington, D.C.: U.S. Government Printing Office, 1977, pp. 7–8. Reproduced by permission of the U.S. Department of Health, Education and Welfare, and the authors.

SUMMARY

Crimes against the person include such violent offenses as homicide, assault and battery, robbery, and rape, and nonviolent crimes such as voyeurism ("peeping") and exhibitionism, which are often referred to as public order crimes. Child molestation may be either violent or nonviolent. In this chapter, we have examined official statistics and the results of systematic research in an effort to identify consistencies and patterns which may help explain such offenses and contribute toward the formulation of policies aimed at coping more effectively with these crimes.

Criminal homicide—the killing of one human being by another—is perpetrated by a variety of people, ranging from normal persons to individuals who are extremely disturbed. Recent attention has been directed toward serial murderers, whose crimes are distributed over time and whose victims tend to fit a particular pattern of physical and behavioral characteristics; and mass murderers, who kill a number of victims in a single explosive outburst of violence. Research on criminal homicide has confirmed certain earlier findings (e.g., homicide rates are highest among young, urban blacks) and failed to support other findings (e.g., handguns have replaced knives as the principal weapon in criminal homicide). The relationship between alcohol and drug abuse and criminal homicide is complex and controversial.

The discussion of assault and battery pointed out that this is an underreported offense. Threats are often not taken seriously and assaults involving injuries may only be reported when there is serious personal or property damage. A comparison of aggravated assault and robbery suggests that these offenses show a number of similar features.

This chapter also examined the patterns associated with robbery. Although robbery is classified as a crime against the person, its principal objective is financial gain; injuries to victims are minimal. Nevertheless, robbery is properly considered a crime against the person because it involves a direct threat of injury or even death to the victim. Four types of robbers were identified and discussed: professional, opportunist, addict, and alcoholic robbers.

A number of myths concerning sexual offenders were dispelled and a typology of rapists was supplied, based primarily on the motivational components of the act. The compulsive nature of voyeurism ("peeping") and indecent exposure was examined, along with the distinctive features of both of these offenses against public order. It was pointed out that these offenders rarely assault their victims, since the perpetrators derive sexual gratification principally from the exhibitionist or voyeuristic act itself. The sexual molestation of children was also discussed in the context of current concerns that child sexual abuse may be a much more widespread phenomenon than had previously been suspected.

DISCUSSION QUESTIONS

Find the answers to the following questions in the text.
1. What types of offenses are included in the category **crimes against the person**?
2. Indicate some of the factors that investigators have identified as possibly contributing to **spouse abuse** and **child abuse.**
3. What are the similarities and differences between **serial** and **mass murderers**?
4. Summarize the conclusions reached by Wolfgang in his 1958 study of **criminal homicide.** Has later research tended to confirm or refute his original findings?
5. Identify the characteristics of offenders in Conklin's fourfold typology of robbers.
6. Distinguish between **statutory rape** and **forcible rape.** Why is a term such as "involuntary sexual battery" seen as a more accurate characterization for the latter type of sex offense?
7. Discuss the principal research findings on rapists and their victims.
8. Where is **homosexual rape** most likely to occur within our criminal justice system and who are the most likely to be potential victims?
9. Does research on child molestation confirm or contradict prevailing stereotypes of child sexual abusers?

TERMS TO IDENTIFY AND REMEMBER

crimes against the person

child abuse

"normal" murderer

mass murderer – *alot at one (McDonald)*

assault and battery

robbery – *theft*

statutory rape

power-assertive rapist

anger-retaliation rapist

indecent exposure

child molestation

career robber

spouse abuse

criminal homicide

felony murderer

serial murderer

aggravated assault

forcible rape

homosexual rape

power-reassurance rapist

anger-excitation rapist

voyeurism ("peeping")

situational robber

REFERENCES

Abel, G. G., Blanchard, E. B., Becker, J. V., and Djenderedjian, A. Differentiating sexual aggressives with penile measures. *Criminal Justice and Behavior* 5 (1978): 315–32.

Amir, M. *Patterns of Forcible Rape.* Chicago: University of Chicago Press, 1971.

Barry, R. J. Incest: The last taboo. *FBI Law Enforcement Bulletin* 53 (1984): 2–9.

Berger, J. Traits shared by mass murderers remain unknown to experts. *New York Times,* August 27, 1984, pp. 1, 9.

Bloch, H. A., and Geis, G. *Man, Crime, and Society.* New York: Random House, 1970.

Block, R. *Violent Crime.* Lexington, MA: Lexington Books, 1977.

Bowker, L. H. *Prison Victimization.* New York: Elsevier North Holland, 1980.

Bureau of Justice Statistics: *Criminal Victimization in the United States, 1982.* Washington, D.C.: U.S. Department of Justice, 1982.

Bureau of Justice Statistics Special Report: *Family Violence.* Washington, D.C.: U.S. Department of Justice, April 1984.

Bureau of Justice Statistics Bulletin: *The Crime of Rape.* Washington, D.C.: U.S. Department of Justice, Washington 1985.

Chappell, D., and Singer, S. *Rape in New York City: A Study of Material in the Police Files and its Meaning.* Albany: State University of New York Press, 1973.

Cohen, M., Seghorn, T., and Calmas, M. Sociometric study of the sex offender. *Journal of Abnormal Psychology* 74 (1969): 249–255.

Cohen, M., Garofalo, M. A., Boucher, R., and Seghorn, T. The psychology of rapists. *Seminars in Psychiatry* 3 (1972): 307–27.

Coleman, J. C. *Abnormal Psychology and Modern Life.* Glenview, IL: Scott, Foresman, 1980.

Conklin, J. E. *Robbery and the Criminal Justice System.* Philadelphia: Lippincott, 1972.

Conrad, J. P., and Dinitz, S. *In Fear of Each Other.* Lexington, MA: Lexington Books, 1978.

Cotton, D. J., and Groth, A. N. Inmate rape: Prevention and intervention. *Journal of Prison and Jail Health* 2 (1982): 47–57.

Cox, D. J., and Daitzmann, R. J. *Exhibitionism: Description, Assessment, and Treatment.* New York: Garland STPM Press, 1980.

Curtis, A. *Violence, Race, and Culture.* Lexington, MA: D. C. Heath and Company, 1975.

Curtis, L. A. *Criminal Violence: National Patterns and Behavior.* Lexington, MA: Lexington Books, 1974.

Davis, A. J. Sexual assaults in the Philadelphia prison system and sheriffs' vans. *Trans-Action* 6 (1968): 9–17.

DeFrancis, V. Protecting the child victim of sex crimes committed by adults. Denver: American Humane Association, Children's Division, 1969.

Ellis, A., and Abarbanel, A. *The Encyclopedia of Sexual Behavior.* New York: Hawthorne Books, 1967.

Ellis, A., and Gullo, J. M. *Murder and Assassination.* New York: Lyle Stuart, 1971.

Erlanger, H. The empirical status of the subculture of violence thesis. *Social Problems* 22, no. 2 (1974): 280–92.

Farley, R. Homicide trends in the United States. *Demography* 17 (1980): 177–88.

Finkelhor, D. Common features of family abuse. In D. Finkelhor, R. J. Gelles, G. T. Hotaling, and M. A. Straus (eds.), *The Dark Side of Families.* Beverly Hills, CA: Sage, 1983.

Finkelhor, D., R. J. Gelles, G. T. Hotaling, and M. A. Straus (eds), *The Dark Side of Families.* Beverly Hills, CA: Sage, 1983.

Florida Mental Health Institute. Report on Treatment Program for Sex Offenders. Tampa, FL: FMHI, 1984.

Fortune, E. P., Vega, M., and Silverman, I. J. A study of female robbers in a Southern correctional institution. *Journal of Criminal Justice* 8 (1980): 317–25.

Gager, N., and Schurr, C. *Sexual Assault: Confronting Rape in America.* New York: Grosset and Dunlap, 1976.

Garland, S. B. Intervention helps in abuse of elderly. *Tampa Tribune,* August 4, 1984, p. 6-A.

Gastil, R. D. Homicide and a regional culture of violence. *American Sociological Review* 36 (1971): 412–37.

Gebhard, P. H., Gagnon, J. H., Pomeroy, W. B., and Christenson, C. V. *Sex Offenders.* New York: Harper & Row, 1965.

Gelles, R. J. *The Violent Home: A Study of Physical Aggression between Husbands and Wives.* vol. 13. Beverly Hills, CA: Sage, 1972.

Gelles, R. J., and Straus, M. A. Determinants of violence in the family: Toward a theoretical integration. In W. R. Burr, R. Hill, F. I. Nye, and I. L. Reiss (eds.), *Contemporary Theories about the Family.* New York: The Free Press, 1979.

Gigeroff, A., Mohr, J., and Turner, J. Sex offenders on probation: The exhibitionist. *Federal Probation,* 32 (1968): 18–21.

Goldstein, P. J. Drugs and violent behavior. Paper presented to the Academy of Criminal Justice Sciences, Louisville KY, March 1982.

Goldstein, S. L. Investigating child sexual exploitation: Law enforcement's role. *FBI Law Enforcement Bulletin* 53 (1984): 22–31.

Greenberg, S. W. Alcohol and crime: A methodological critique of the literature. In J. J. Collins (ed.), *Research on the Relationship Between Alcohol and Crime.* New York: Guilford Press, 1981.

Gorth, A. N. *Men Who Rape: The Psychology of the Offender.* With H. J. Birnbaum. New York: Plenum Press, 1979.

Groth, A. N., Burgess, A. W., Birnbaum, H. J., and Gary, T. S. A study of the child molester: Myths and realities. *LAE Journal of the American Criminal Justice Association* 41 (1978): 17–22.

Groth, A. N., Burgess, A. W., and Holmstrom, L. L. Rape: Power, anger, and sexuality. *American Journal of Psychiatry* 134 (1977): 1239–43.

Guttmacher, M. S. *Mind of the Murderer.* New York: Farrar, Straus and Cudahy, 1960.

Guttmacher, M. (ed.), *Studies in Murder.* New York: Harper & Row, 1967.

Heide, K. A preliminary identification of types of adolescent murderers. Paper presented at the Thirty-Sixth Annual Meeting of the American Society of Criminology, November 1984, Cincinnati.

Klebba, A. J. Homicide trends in the United States, 1900–1974. *Public Health Reports* 90, no. 3 (May–June 1975): 195–204.

Kopp, S. B. The character structure of sex offenders. *American Journal of Psychotherapy* 16 (1962): 64–70.

Krasner, W., Meyer, L. C., and Carroll, N. E. *Victims of Rape.* Washington, D.C.: U.S. Government Printing Office, 1977.

LaFave, W. R., and Scott, A. W. *Criminal Law.* St. Paul, MN: West, 1972.

Laite, W. *The United States vs. William Harte.* Washington, D.C.: Acropolis Books, 1972.

Langley, R., and Levy, R. C. *Wife Beating: The Silent Crisis.* New York: Pocket Books, 1977.

Lanning, K. V., and Burgess, A. W. Child pornography and sex rings. *FBI Law Enforcement Bulletin* 53 (1984): 10–16.

Lester, D. *Crime and Passion: Murder and the Murderer.* Chicago: Nelson Hall, 1975.

Loftin, C., and Hill, R. H. Regional subculture and homicide: An examination of the Gastil-Hackney thesis. *American Sociological Review,* 39, (1974),: 714–24.

Lorensen, W. D. Sex offenses: Voyeurism and indecent exposure. In S. Kadish (ed.), *Encyclopedia of Crime and Justice.* New York: The Free Press, 1983.

Luckenbill, D. F. Criminal homicide as a situated transaction. *Social Problems* 25 (1977): 176–86.

Lunde, D. T. Hot blood's record month: Our murder room. *Psychology Today* 9 (1975): 35–42.

———. *Murder and Madness.* San Francisco: Book Company, 1976.

Lundsgaarde, H. P. *Murder in Space City.* New York: Oxford University Press, 1977.

MacDonald, J. M. *The Murderer and His Victim.* Springfield, IL: Charles C. Thomas, 1961.

———. *Rape Offenders and Their Victims.* Springfield, Il: Charles C. Thomas, 1971.

Macnamara, D. E. J., and Sagarin, E. *Sex, Crime, and the Law.* New York: The Free Press, 1977.

Martin, D. *Battered Wives.* New York: Pocket Books, 1976.

Mathis, J. L. *Clear Thinking about Sexual Deviations.* Chicago: Nelson Hall, 1972.

Mayhall, P. D., and Norgard, K. E. *Child Abuse and Neglect: Sharing Responsibility.* New York: Wiley, 1983.

Medea, A., and Thompson, K. *Against Rape.* New York: Farrar, Straus & Giroux, 1974.

Mohr, J., Turner, E. R., and Ball, R. B. Exhibitionism and pedophilia. *Corrective Psychiatric Journal of Social Therapy,* 8, (1962),: 172–86.

Mohr, J., Turner, E. R., and Jerry, M. *Pedophilia and Exhibitionism.* Toronto: University of Toronto Press, 1964.

Moore, D. M. (ed.). *Battered Women.* Beverly Hills, CA: Sage, 1979.

Mulvihill, D. J., Tumin, M. M., and Curtis, L. A. *Crimes of Violence,* vol. 11, Staff Report to the President's Commission on Causes and Prevention of Violence. Washington, D.C.: U.S. Government Printing Office, 1969.

National Commission on the Causes and Prevention of Violence: Final Report. New York: Praeger, 1970.

National Institute on Law Enforcement and Criminal Justice. *Forcible Rape: A National Survey of the Response by Prosecutors.* Prosecutors' Volume I. Washington, D.C.: U.S. Government Printing Office, 1977.

NiCarthy, G. N. *Getting Free: A Handbook for Women in Abusive Relationships.* Seattle: Seal Press, 1982.

Normandeau, A. Patterns in robbery. *Criminologica* 1 (1968): 2–13.

Parker, R. N., and Smith, M. D. Deterrence, poverty, and type of homicide. *American Journal of Sociology* 85 (1979),: 614–24.

Peters, J. J. Children who are victims of sexual assault and the psychology of offenders. *American Journal of Psychotherapy* 30 (1976),: 398–421.

Peters, J. J., Meyer, L. C., and Carroll, N. E. The Philadelphia assault victim study. Research report submitted to the NIMH in partial fulfillment of Grant No. 21304. Unpublished manuscript, Center for Rape Concern, 1976.

Pittman, D. J., and Handy, W. J. Patterns in criminal aggravated assult. In B. Cohen (ed.), *Crime in America.* Itasca, Il: F. E. Peacock, 1970.

Podlesny, J. A. *Some Characteristics of Burglars, Larcenists, Assaulters, and Drug Offenders in Wyoming.* Washington, D.C.: U.S. Government Printing Office, 1973.

Pokorny, A. D. Human violence: A comparison of homicide, aggravated assault, suicide, and attempted homicide. In B. Cohen (ed.), *Crime in America.* Itasca, Il: F. E. Peacock, 1970.

President's Crime Commission on Law Enforcement and Administration of Justice. *The Challenge of Crime in a Free Society.* Washington, D.C.: U.S. Government Printing Office, 1967.

Reinhardt, J. M. *Sex Perversions and Sex Crimes.* Springfield, IL: Charles C. Thomas, 1957.

Saline, C. Bleeding in the suburbs. *Philadelphia Magazine* 75 (1984): 81–86.

Selkin, J. Rape. *Psychology Today* 8 (1975),: 70–72.

Spencer, C. *A Typology of Violent Offenders.* Administrative Abstract No. 23, California Department of Corrections, 1966.

Stoller, R. Sexual deviations. In F. Beach (ed.), *Human Sexuality in Four Perspectives.* Baltimore: Johns Hopkins University Press, 1977.

Sutherland, S., and Scherl, D. J. Patterns of response among victims of rape. *American Journal of Orthopsychiatry* 40 (1970): 503–11.

U.S. Department of Justice. *Crime in the United States: Uniform crime reports—1979.* Washington, D.C.: U.S. Government Printing Office, 1980.

Vetter, H. J., and Silverman, I. *The Nature of Crime.* Philadelphia: Saunders, 1978.

Wallace, S. E. Patterns of violence in San Juan. In W. C. Reckless, *The Crime Problem.* Englewood Cliffs, NJ: Prentice-Hall, 1973.

Warner, C. G. *Rape and Sexual Assault: Management and Intervention.* Germantown, MD: Aspen Systems Corporation, 1980.

Waymire, R. V. Aggravated assault: Prediction factors and intervention point. NOVA University, September 21, 1979. Practicum presented in partial fulfillment of the requirements for the M.S. in Criminal Justice.

Wolfgang, M. E. *Patterns in Criminal Homicide.* Philadelphia: University of Pennsylvania Press, 1958.

———. Criminal homicide and the subculture of violence. In M. E. Wolfgang (ed.), *Studies in Homicide.* New York: Harper & Row, 1967*a.*

———. Victim precipitated criminal homicide. In M. E. Wolfgang (ed.), *Studies in Homicide.* New York: Harper & Row, 1967*b.*

Wolfgang, M. E., and Ferracuti, F. *The Subculture of Violence.* London: Tavistock Publications, 1969.

Wolfgang, M. E., and Zahn, M. Homicide: Behavioral aspects. In S. Kadish (ed.), *Encyclopedia of Crime and Justice.* New York: The Free Press, 1984.

Zahn, M. A. Homicide in the twentieth century United States. In J. A. Inciardi and C. E. Faupel (eds.), *History and Crime.* Beverly Hills, CA: Sage, 1980.

Zahn, M. A., and Riedel, M. Homicide in eight American Cities. Unpublished manuscript, 1982.

Chapter 5

CRIMES AGAINST PROPERTY

Property offenses, which include burglary, larceny, motor vehicle theft, arson, and fraud, comprise the major portion of our conventional crime problem. In any given year, property offenses make up about 90 percent of the volume of Index crimes. The individuals who perpetrate these offenses vary in their attachment to the norms of conventional society, in the extent to which they depend upon crime for their livelihood, and in the planning, techniques, and skill they employ in their criminal activity. Three types of property offenders can be identified: **occasional property offenders, ordinary career criminals,** and **professional criminals.**

In the section which concludes this chapter, we shall discuss the work of Chaiken and Chaiken (1982) which deals with criminal careers. Their research addresses a number of significant issues, among them the concept of criminal specialization; the important part played by a combination of alcohol, barbiturates, and heroin in violent property crimes; and the controversial role of selective incapacitation as a possible societal response to those whom the authors characterize as "violent predators."

OCCASIONAL PROPERTY OFFENDERS

Occasional property offenders generally have a criminal record that consists of a single offense or a few infrequently committed property offenses such as illegal joyriding, naive check forgery, shoplifting, vandalism, or employee theft. Crime is a minor part of the life-style of offenders in this group. The incidental nature of their criminal activity precludes the possibility of its being a principal means of support. The crimes committed by occasional property offenders show little skill or sophistication. Criminal activity is usually fortuitous in nature and committed alone, with few if any prior criminal contacts (e.g., membership in a delinquent gang).

Occasional criminals do not perceive themselves as criminals; they are able to develop rationalizations for their conduct which enable them to view their crimes as noncriminal acts. For instance, a man who is away from home on a drinking spree with friends may forge a check when he runs out of money but feels pressure to continue the drinking bout (Lemert, 1967). Thus, he can attribute the criminal action to the fact that he was too drunk to appreciate the nature and consequences of his behavior.

While the occasional offender commits a variety of offenses, vandalism and joyriding have been identified as offenses which are almost exclusively perpetrated by this group (Clinard, 1974). Vandalism involves the willful or malicious destruction of property and is generally committed by juveniles, who tend to regard their actions as "pranks." This image of themselves as pranksters rather than delinquents is reinforced by the fact that, in the majority of instances, nothing is stolen.

Like vandalism, joyriding is also not a career type of crime. Joyriding is usually a sporadic form of teenage activity; the vehicles taken are those in which the owners have left the keys or those that can be started by "jumping" the ignition with a hotwire. Typically, cars are borrowed, driven around town, and abandoned when the gas tank is empty. These youngsters do not, unlike the career auto thief, select a particular type of car, contact a "fence" to arrange a sale of the vehicle or its parts, or strip the car for their own use.

115

Social reactions to these offenders is not severe because the offenses they commit are not too serious and they usually have no prior criminal record—or at most a minor one. As a result, charges against them are often dismissed; or when convicted, these offenders are placed on probation or given a suspended sentence (Clinard and Quinney, 1973).

ORDINARY CAREER CRIMINALS

Offenders in this group commit the majority of the property offenses reported each year and make up the bulk of the prison population. Typically these offenders either augment their income or derive their entire livelihood from criminal activity (including primarily the crimes of burglary, larceny, and robbery). Crime is a major part of the life activities of the career criminal. These offenders develop a conception of themselves as criminals. They tend to progress from petty crimes to more serious offenses; during this progression, there is a continual acquisition of skills and rationalizations to justify their criminal behavior. They tend to either specialize in a few types of property crimes or in a particular kind of offense. However, they never reach the level of sophistication and skill of the professional criminal.

Career Patterns

Conventional property offenders begin their careers as juvenile delinquents (Clinard and Quinney, 1973). The early life histories of these career criminals tend to exhibit a pattern of truancy, street fighting, vandalism, and delinquent gang membership. As a rule, ordinary career criminals begin their careers in a gang with juveniles of similar backgrounds. The delinquent activities of these groups are not isolated acts; they represent a part of the way of life of the slum communities in which these youths usually reside.

Gang youths show a history of delinquency that begins, in some cases, as early as age 6 or 7 years; and there is evidence that, following the onset of delinquency, these youths proceed from juvenile offenses to adult crimes. Robin (1967) found that a large proportion of the gang members he studied were persistent and dangerous offenders as juveniles and went on to become even more serious adult criminals. It appears, however, that the adult criminal careers of these offenders are relatively short-lived. Many offenders discontinue their criminal activity at around 18 or 19 years of age, while most of the remainder terminate their careers by the time they reach their mid-twenties or early thirties.

It is difficult to pin down the precise reasons career offenders decide to discontinue their criminal activities. For many juveniles, reaching the age of 18 years signifies that getting caught for committing crimes no longer means a spell in training school but rather incarceration in a state prison. In fact, the first prison sentence may clearly mark the discontinuation of further criminal activity. "Doing time" is seen as too high a price to pay for the returns on crime.

Delinquent and criminal activities become less attractive as a young male matures, gets married, obtains a regular job, acquires noncriminal friends, and puts in a period of time in military service. Offenders who continue their careers beyond age

30 spend less and less time on the street and more and more time in prison, because with each subsequent conviction they tend to draw longer sentences and parole authorities become less willing to grant early release.

PROFESSIONAL CRIMINALS

The term *professional criminal* is applied to a small group of offenders who have the most highly developed criminal careers and the highest status and skill level. As compared with other offenders, they are usually able to avoid apprehension and rarely spend time in prison. In the past, professional criminals were found among the ranks of pickpockets, counterfeiters, forgers, and confidence men—people who lived by their wits, who acquired money or property from their victims by means of dexterity, deception, duplicity, or distraction. Professionals limited their activities to nonviolent forms of criminal enterprise.

Several authors (Clinard and Quinney, 1973; Conklin, 1972; Gibbons, 1973; Inciardi, 1975; McCaghy, 1976) have expanded the category of professional criminal to include a subgroup identified as *professional heavy criminals* who employ coercion, force, and the threat of violence. These offenders engage in motor vehicle theft, burglary, and armed robbery.

Recruitment and Training

Recruitment and training are two of the major factors that distinguish professional from ordinary criminals. Professional criminals are drawn from the ranks of the legitimately employed as well as from the underworld. Inciardi (1975) states that professionals are recruited from among trade and service workers—waiters in bars, cab drivers, bellhops, hotel clerks, and waitresses—who interact on a regular basis with offenders. Professionals also tend to be drawn from legitimate occupations which parallel their subsequent criminal pursuits. Thus, "the etcher becomes the counterfeiter; the skilled worker or foreman of a lock company becomes a safe-cracker; the worker in a stock broker's office gets into 'hot' bonds" (Reckless, 1973, pp. 258–259). Professionals recruited in this manner usually have not been juvenile delinquents and do not have records which exhibit gradual progression from petty delinquencies to serious crimes. On the other hand, there is evidence that some skilled thieves graduate from minor offenses to professional crime. These offenders have generally been reared in slum or working-class conditions where there is considerable exposure to the underworld (Inciardi, 1975).

Contact with and selection of individuals for training as professional offenders may occur in many locations: jails, prisons, bars, poolrooms, hotels, and boarding houses. Once selected, an individual receives informal training which involves the learning of the necessary skills, techniques, attitudes, and values. New recruits learn by doing, that is, crime is learned on the job, along with the values and norms of the criminal group. In addition, the recruit learns techniques for stealing and disposing of goods during the period of apprenticeship.

The novice also becomes acquainted with and gradually accepted by other professionals. Not all professionals go through an apprenticeship in order to acquire criminal skills. In some instances, professionals are self-taught, as were two California bank robbers:

> So we decided to go into crime, and, in order to decide which branch we wanted to go into, since we were both inexperienced criminals at the time, we decided to do as much research as we could and find out which made the most money the fastest and that percentagewise was the safest. I think that you will find that every public library in a city has statistics on the number of crimes committed the previous year, how much money each crime was, and you could figure out from the amounts stolen, the number of crooks caught, and the number of convictions, what you wanted to know. We spent four days at the public library and we researched, and we came up with armed robbery as the most likely for us [Jackson, 1969, p. 20].

BURGLARY

Burglary is the unlawful entry into a structure to commit a felony or theft (*UCR*, 1984). It is the most common of the major property offenses and one which the public finds very threatening. The use of force is not a requirement for burglary. In the FBI *Uniform Crime Reports,* burglary is divided into three categories: forcible entry, unlawful entry without force, and attempted forcible entry. Burglary is generally considered a crime of stealth and opportunity.

Two important aspects of burglary are its frequency and economic impact. This offense accounts for nearly a third of all reported property crimes. About two-thirds of all burglaries are residential burglaries; the rest are attacks on commercial establishments. Although there are more residential burglaries than commercial burglaries, a business has the greater chance of being victimized, simply because there are fewer of them. Burglaries of both homes and businesses occur most often on weekdays; a weekend burglary is more likely to occur at a business than at a residence (Pope, 1977).

The total annual loss dues to burglaries is $3.5 billion, with an average loss of $924 per burglary (Federal Bureau of Investigation, 1984). In nearly two-thirds of all instances where property is stolen in a burglary, the stolen items are hard-salable merchandise such as television or stereo sets. Next in order are cash, jewelry, and furs; soft-salable items such as clothing, guns, credit cards, checks, stocks, bonds, and drugs; and items taken from safes. Burglary has a low clearance rate, somewhat less than one in seven. As a rule, burglaries with very low or very high losses have greater clearance rates than the more frequent burglaries with losses in the middle range.

Burglaries are not the product of modern society: the tomb of the Egyptian pharaoh Tutankhamen was broken into shortly after he was interred and churches and abbeys were constantly victimized during the Middle Ages. Burglary, however, does change with time. Types that flourished in the recent past have disappeared: today, for example, transom, coal-slide, and dumbwaiter burglaries are virtually extinct. Another rapidly vanishing species is the so-called step-over burglary. Apartment dwellers often place screening or other coverings on widows that open into fire escapes, but they fail to cover the windows next to the escapes. A step-over burglar crosses from the fire escape to the ledge and enters an unprotected window. This technique has declined since the advent of interior fire escapes.

Although burglars tend to come from the lower socioeconomic classes and are often not well educated, there have been some notable exceptions. Burglaries have been committed by professors, police officers, probation officers, and psychiatrists. A South Carolina psychiatrist who held a law degree and earned up to $100,000 a year was once arrested and the arresting officers recovered $500,000 in stolen property, linking the psychiatrist to 150 burglaries in a single county (Swanson, Chamelin, and Territo, 1984).

Burglars can be clasified according to a number of variables: age, race or ethnic identity, drug addiction, preference for premises to be attacked, and types of property they will take (Reppetto, 1974; Scarr, 1973). The most useful classification is skill: burglars range from the amateur to the professional, but most are unskilled at their crime.

The Professional Burglar

Professional burglars may commit only four or five offenses each year. Despite the infrequency of their crimes, they are important to the police because of the large value of cash or property taken and their intimate knowledge of sophisticated fencing systems. In addition to the "big score," the hallmark of the professional is thorough planning preceding each burglary. Professionals refuse to place themselves in jeopardy for anything other than sizable gain and they do so only after weeks or months of painstaking study of a potential target. Because they know exactly what they want in advance, professionals do not ransack the premises at a burglary site. Thus, a stolen article might not be missed for some time. Working nationally—or, at the highest professional level, internationally—the professional burglar often operates for many years without being arrested (Swanson, Chamelin, and Territo, 1984).

LARCENY-THEFT

Larceny is the unlawful taking, carrying, or leading away of property from the possession or constructive possession of another without the use of force or fear. It includes such crimes as shoplifting, theft of parts and accessories for motor vehicles, boat theft, and the theft of agricultural products, livestock, and farm machinery or equipment.

Larcenies make up more than half of the total volume of Index crimes. Studies indicate that many offenses in this category, particularly when the value of stolen goods is low, never come to the attention of the police because victims do not report the thefts. In other cases, merchants and business owners are not aware of the total value of the thefts that occur; this is a common problem in shoplifting.

Shoplifting

The National Retail Merchants Association indicates that twelve cents of every dollar spent by consumers is an incremental cost due to shoplifting. Shoplifting accounts for 11 percent of all larceny crimes (*UCR,* 1984) and it produces losses exceeding $3.5 billion annually (Swanson, Chamelin, and Territo, 1984).

Shoplifters can be classified into two groups on the basis of their use of the merchandise they steal: the commercial shoplifter, or **booster,** steals merchandise for resale; the **pilferer** takes merchandise for private use (Cameron, 1964).

Two patterns have emerged in recent years: both the dollar amount of the merchandise recovered and the total number of apprehensions have increased substantially. These patterns suggest that more and more people are shoplifting and that the majority of them are amateurs. It has been estimated that as many as 95 percent of all shoplifters apprehended are amateurs who do not sell stolen merchandise yet often have no personal need for it (Curtis, 1972).

As might be expected, professional shoplifters are not only apprehended much less frequently than amateurs, but they also steal more per theft. The professional is frequently a member of a highly skilled and well-organized group. It is not uncommon to find teams of young men and women, ranging in number from three to five, who set out on carefully planned tours throughout the United States. Their itinerary, carefully laid out to the last detail, includes the names of all stores that will be visited in various cities.

Participants in shoplifting teams are thoroughly trained in shoplifting techniques and wear special clothing to conceal and carry stolen merchandise. For example, a specially constructed unit called a **booster box** can be ingeniously designed to hold whatever kind of merchandise the shoplifter intends to steal. To an observer, the box appears to be nothing more than a package prepared for mailing; but a slot in the side or bottom allows the shoplifter to insert a stolen item swiftly and surreptitiously. Booster skirts or booster bloomers are also occasionally used by women. A booster skirt, which can be designed to match current fashion, features a hammock-like bag suspended between the shoplifter's legs. Booster bloomers (old-fashioned bloomers with double rows of tight elastic at the knees) can be worn under booster skirts; slits or pockets in the skirt or dress or an elastic waistband allow merchandise to be stuffed into the concealing recesses of the bloomers. Coat linings tailored to hold merchandise inserted through openings in the bottom of the pockets can also be adapted for men or women. A large handbag, briefcase, or shopping bag is often the trademark of the shoplifter (Cameron, 1964; Wright, 1972).

Marine Theft

The theft of boats and marine equipment has become an increasingly serious problem in recent years, with estimates of losses in the millions of dollars annually. In 1985, there were 25,000 boats listed as stolen in the United States. Various factors contribute to the high rate of boat thefts: (1) identification numbers are easily removed or altered; (2) boat builders do not maintain a central registry of identification numbers as automobile manufacturers do; (3) boat thefts are often reported to police departments that do not have a marine unit, instead of the U.S. Coast Guard; and (4) boat owners fail to show proper concern for security (*Tampa Tribune,* May 28, 1985). As Lyford (1982) has observed, marine theft is a high-profit/low-risk business that grows with each passing year.

Agri-crime

Property crime is so thoroughly identified with the urban setting that it comes as something of a shock to learn how rapidly rural property crime has increased in recent years. According to Swanson and Territo (1980), serious rural crime has risen 43 percent *over the urban rate* during the past decade. Included among agricultural crime are thefts of livestock, lumber, grain and feed, pesticides, fruit, vegetables, trees, and farm equipment. There are also heavy costs involved in property damage from fires of incendiary origin and from vandalism. For example, in 1976, losses in national forest areas from fires amounted to $11 million.

One of the most lucrative enterprises for agricultural criminals is the theft of farm tractors, trucks, earthmovers, and other heavy farm equipment. Some of these vehicles and pieces of equipment are shipped out of the country to destinations in Central and South America, but the greater percentage remains here in the United States after it has been subjected to techniques designed to make detection and discovery extremely difficult. In some locations, with the "right" connections, it is even possible to place an order for a particular kind of vehicle or piece of equipment and have the order filled faster than it could be supplied by a dealer.

Cattle rustling conjures up images of cowpokes, cayuses, sheriffs' posses, and frontier justice meted out at the end of a lariat. Today's rustlers use helicopters, fixed-wing aircraft, and 18-wheeler trucks to steal animals that are butchered and sold within hours after their disappearance, making it nearly impossible to trace or recover the loot.

Assessing the Costs of Agri-crime   Trying to gauge the economic impact of agri-crime is every bit as difficult as trying to estimate the costs of other types of criminal activity. What is needed is more surveys of the kind conducted by Dunway (1974), which reported that 80 percent of a sample group of 477 Iowa farmers had been theft victims during the preceding three-year period. As Swanson and Territo (1980) observe:

> If $65 million—a conservative estimate—in reported vandalism, fraud, arson, and theft is 3 percent of the problem, and if agri-crime is only 25 percent underreported, then a direct figure loss of approximately $3 billion is obtained. This figures excludes the indirect costs of agri-crime, such as the higher prices ultimately paid by the consumer [p. 10].

The direct and indirect economic costs of agri-crime may be paralleled by adverse social impacts, as well. For instance, crime may be the principal factor in the decline of two hundred thousand acres of land per year farmed by blacks.

Coping With Agri-crime   Swanson and Territo have issued an eloquent plea for actions on the part of the criminal justice system and criminologists in response to the problem of agri-crime. They recommend the immediate inclusion of course work covering the detection and prevention of agricultural crimes in the training curricula of police academies, the addition of seminars and workshops on agri-crime as part of the in-service training of both municipal and rural law enforcement officers, and the establishment of regional and state centers for the dissemination of agricultural crime information. They are fully cognizant of the imperative need for research on agri-crime and proffer a list of issues that need to be addressed:

- How much and what types of agri-crime are there?
- How much agri-crime is reported?
- Are rural investigators actually gathering physical evidence?
- Which existing crime prevention efforts are most applicable and how do we diffuse them to the rural environment?
- What types of totally new crime prevention programs need to be developed?
- Can typologies of agri-crime offenses and offenders be developed?
- How sensitive are prosecutors to the problem?
- What appreciation do urban investigative agencies have with respect to their place in the network?
- What new patterns of interagency cooperation are most likely to have impact on the problem [p. 12]?

THE FENCE: CRIMINAL RECEIVER OF STOLEN GOODS

We noted earlier that a reliable "fence"—a criminal receiver of stolen merchandise—is crucial if the professional burglar or shoplifter expects to operate on more than a modest scale. They require ready access to quick and relatively safe transactions in which stolen property is exchanged for money, hence the importance of the service performed by the fence. For the juvenile thief and occasional property criminal, the fence may not only provide a market, but may also finance and even direct criminal activities (Klockars, 1974).

The significance of the fence has been recognized and acknowledged for more than two centuries, ever since the notorious Jonathan Wild elevated criminal receivership to something between skilled labor and an art form before he was hanged at Tyburn in 1725. The President's Crime Commission in 1967 identified the fence as one of the "essential relationships" that the professional criminal must establish in order to survive and flourish. It is rather remarkable, therefore, that so little information is available concerning criminal receivership, especially in a society where losses from theft are calculated each year in the billions of dollars.

Conventional studies of criminal receivership have tended to concentrate on the fence as an individual who knowingly buys, sells, or otherwise traffics in stolen property. Viewed from this perspective, fences differ with regard to the scope, method and specialization of their operations, and it would appear that there is a hierarchy among criminal receivers. At one extreme are the fences who deal directly with the thief and openly sell to the buyer. Included within this group are local merchants who buy stolen merchandise to supplement their inventories or sell stolen property as an adjunct to their businesses and people who sell small quantities of stolen property out of their homes or apartments. At another level is the fence who specializes in particular types of merchandise: electrical construction materials, automotive products, jewelry, airline tickets, securities, forged or stolen documents—anything, in short, for which there is a demand. At the top of the hierarchy is the

THE STOLEN PROPERTY SYSTEM VIEW OF PROPERTY THEFT

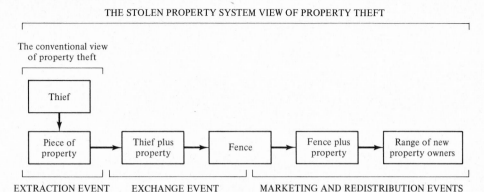

Figure 5.1 A schematic diagram of property theft events. (*Source:* Marilyn E. Walsh, *The Fence: A New Look at the World of Property Theft.* Westport, CT: Greenwood Press, 1977. Reproduced by permission of the author and publisher.)

master fence, who usually has no direct contact with the property he handles. Master fences typically operate as arrangers for the distribution of merchandise and conduct most of their transactions by telephone.

Our knowledge of the working relationship between property thieves and the criminal receiver is advanced by law enforcement initiatives such as "The Sting" operation described on page 124. Such operations, however, are limited for the most part to petty thieves, whose contacts are with small-time fences. These differ from professional thieves, who are seeking to dispose of stolen securities, expensive jewelry, or high-priced objects of art at a level requiring the investment of hundreds of thousands of dollars by the criminal receiver.

Of even greater importance, perhaps, is the fact that conventional studies which focus on the individual fence tend to sidetrack investigation from the much more significant issue of the organizational aspects of property crime. Theft, as Walsh (1977) points out, is "only the beginning of a very intricate system in which stolen property is acquired, converted, redistributed, and reintegrated into the legitimate property stream" (p. 174). The burglar who steals your television set is not interested in sitting down in front of it and watching his favorite programs; he steals it for its *negotiability,* its capacity to be exchanged for cash or drugs. The idiosyncrasies of the individual thief, or for that matter of the individual fence, are much less important than the **transfer function** performed by the criminal receiver and its place within the crime area that Walsh has entitled the Stolen Property System (SPS) (see Figure 5.1). This view of property theft moves beyond the extraction event (theft) to the exchange process and "continues to follow the crime to its intended resolution, to the transfer of stolen property to its new owner(s)" (p. 176).

The SPS conceptualization, Walsh notes, promotes at least two major shifts in our reactions to property theft:

> First, it counsels a heightened awareness of *property* itself as the critical element shaping the activities of theft principals. In other words, we realize that property, not an individual, creates markets, engenders distribution channels, determines

The Sting

Increasingly, the police are turning to undercover methods to control large-scale professional theft by posing as fences, or purchasers of stolen goods. One of the most successful and highly publicized such undertakings was The Sting, an undercover fencing operation in Washington, D.C., run by men from the Metropolitan Police Force, an FBI agent, and a Treasury man. For five months beginning in October 1975, the police used a warehouse as a site for the purchase of $2.4 million in stolen merchandise (for $67,000). To show their appreciation to their patrons, the stingpolice threw a party for the sellers of stolen goods, which ended in a mass arrest. Although many of the 180 arrested customers invoked the entrapment defense, it resulted in freeing just one defendant. The lone defendant was released because the circumstances of the case clearly showed that he was not predisposed to have committed the crime involved and that the police had gone too far in inducing him to do so. In the Return of the Sting operation four months later, the Washington police collared 150 more customers. The Sting model has since been successfully adopted in cities throughout the country.

Source: G. D. Robin, *Introduction to the Criminal Justice System.* New York: Harper & Row, 1980, p. 74. Reproduced by permission of the author and publisher.

pricing policies, and influences the content of theft statistics. Second, the stolen property system concept demands that greater attention be given to the key mechanism through which virtually all property-related decisions are made—the fence of stolen goods. In this way, the SPS view identifies the fence as the more strategic target for official intervention in the stolen property market-place [p. 177].

MOTOR VEHICLE THEFT

Motor vehicle theft is the theft or attempted theft of a motor vehicle for nontemporary use. This definition excludes the taking of a vehicle for temporary use by someone with lawful access. More than one million motor vehicles are stolen in a given year; motor vehicle thefts account for about 8 or 9 percent of the volume of Index crimes (*UCR,* 1984). Approximately three-quarters of the vehicles stolen are passenger cars; the remainder includes trucks, buses, and other types of vehicles. Approximately half of the vehicles stolen are 5 years old or less (model of vehicle) (*FBI Law Enforcement Bulletin,* 1975). These thefts are grouped into four categories: (1) joyriding, (2) thefts of vehicles for use in other crimes, (3) thefts for transportation, and (4) professional thefts.

Joyriding

Car thefts for joyriding constitute the majority of motor vehicle thefts. The perpetrators are usually teenagers, 15 to 19 years of age, who steal a car on a dare, as initiation into a gang, or for parts and accessories. Youths arrested for car thefts are often repeat offenders.

Theft for Use in Other Crimes

Criminals who plan to commit a nonauto crime often steal a car that can be abandoned immediately after the crime and therefore is very difficult to trace. The perpetrator usually steals the car as close to the time of the primary crime as possible, thus minimizing the possibility that the theft will be reported to the police. This minimizes the likelihood that a pickup order will be broadcast for the car while the thief is en route to or from the scene of the primary crime.

Thefts for Transportation

Thefts for transportation generally involve transients, hitchhikers, and runaways. Stolen cars are abandoned when the thief reaches his or her destination or runs out of gas (Horgan, 1974).

Professional Thefts

The professional auto thief steals with the specific intent of making a profit, either by altering the car for resale or dismantling the vehicle for parts. Professional motor vehicle theft rings, composed of specialists representing a variety of automotive skills, may use their own members to obtain cars or procure stolen vehicles from amateur thieves. Members of one East Coast ring, posing as prospective buyers, approached auto dealers with requests to "test drive" new cars. Their real purpose was to secure the serial number of the ignition key in order to have a duplicate made so that they could return later and steal the car at their leisure (*FBI Law Enforcement Bulletin,* 1971).

As a by-product of motor vehicle theft, garages now have a source of auto parts—the "chop shop"—which is faster and much cheaper than ordering parts from a car manufacturer or auto parts dealer. Chop shops obtain stolen cars from teenaged auto thieves or professional thieves in their own employ. The vehicles are hustled into a garage where, with pit-stop efficiency, they are dismantled in a matter of hours. Most operations are so smooth that a car can be vivisected into salable parts in a couple of days. Overhead is low, detection is difficult, supply is plentiful, and demand is great. The FBI considers the chop shop to be one of the most lucrative illegitimate businesses operating today (Sniffen, 1978).

One possible reason for such assembly-line efficiency may be the growing involvement of syndicated crime in chop shop operations. The enormous potential for profit in these activities—estimated at $4 billion annually (Rozzi and Mueller, 1980)—has proven an irresistible attraction for syndicated crime. For the auto thief who deals with the chop shop, there is the advantage that he is not subject to federal jurisdiction as long as the car is not shipped across state lines or the value of the stolen parts does not exceed $5,000.

ARSON

Arson is defined as any willful or malicious burning or attempt to burn—with or without intent to defraud—a dwelling, public building, motor vehicle, aircraft, or personal property of another (*UCR*, 1984). Only fires determined through investigation to have been willfully or maliciously set are classified as arson. Fires of suspicious or unknown origin are excluded. Official data show that arson is primarily an urban crime. In addition, despite an apparent heightened concern for arson and predictions of increases in its incidence and cost to the American public, four years of *UCR* arson figures suggest that arson is declining rather than increasing (Akiyama and Pfeiffer, 1984).

In 1984, 101,836 arson offenses were reported to the FBI, representing a 2 percent increase over 1983. Arson arrests for this period totaled 19,000, with males outnumbering females at a ratio of close to 9:1, whites outnumbering blacks at more than 8:1, and males over 25 years of age outnumbering those under 25 years of age at more than 6:4 (FBI, 1985).

Arrest and conviction rates for arson are low: about nine persons are arrested, two convicted, and less than one incarcerated for every one hundred fires classified as incendiary or suspicious. A number of factors contribute to this low rate of arrest and conviction, including the acute and continuing shortage of trained investigators, lack of witnesses, investigative difficulties, and the necessity for the prosecution to rely heavily upon circumstantial evidence when physical evidence is meager.

Arsonists

While almost anyone could conceivably commit arson under particular circumstances, those who actually become arsonists tend to fit one of three categories: (1) arsonists-for-profit, (2) arsonists-for-spite, and (3) arsonists-for-"kicks" (Kirk, 1969).

Arsonists-for-profit are the largest group of incendiaries or firesetters: people who burn their own property for purposes of collecting on insurance or arsonists who burn other people's property for hire. This type of arson is a calculated criminal act that is similar to burglary or robbery, although its perpetrators tend to feel less criminal and more justified by the "unfortunate" aspects of their financial situation—and by the rationalization that the insurance company, a large and affluent corporation, can sustain the loss.

Some "white-collar" arsonists may engage in firesetting for reasons other than defrauding the insurance company. Some of these reasons include getting rid of a business competitor, liquidation of real estate before it is turned over in inheritance, making salvage profits to offset heavy storage charges, or creating the potential for securing a rebuilding contract.

Often automobile fires are the result of arson. The owner may have incurred expensive auto repair bills that cannot be met or is facing repossession of the car. A common mistake which aids detection is the removal of valuables and accessories from the vehicle before burning it.

Perhaps the purest example of the arsonist-for-profit is the **torch,** or hired arsonist. The range of expertise exhibited by torches is broad, ranging from the highly skilled professional who can command a fee of thousands of dollars to the ghetto youths described by New York City Fire Marshal Barracato (in Barracato and Michelmore, 1976), who would burn down a tenement for as little as $100. The real pro has the pride of the true craftsman in his work: his fires are well planned; he generally works alone; he provides the property owner who hires him with a steelclad alibi; and he may even supply a guarantee for his services—money back if arson is detected, no questions asked.

The period of the Great Depression (1930–1935) was notorious for torch rings—syndicated groups of professional arsonists who let their services for bids. Hormachea (1974) refers to the "infamous Brooklyn Arson Ring," which included a broker who gained the reputation of being able to guarantee a fire with every policy he wrote. Shapiro (1976) tells of how a fire marshal named Tony Russo spent five months working undercover as "Tony the Torch." He was able to gain the confidence of an arson ring that numbered among its more than a dozen members two sisters aged 66 and 73. They were involved in an "arson and old lace" conspiracy to burn 500 buildings for insurance fraud profit.

Revenge is a powerful motive for setting fires. The arsonist-for-spite may harbor a grudge against someone—a neighbor, relative, employer, or business rival—for years before seeking to get even by setting fire to his home or place of business. The local store owner may try to dispose of his competitor by burning him out or the disgruntled worker who was fired from his job may retaliate by torching his former employer's property. In many instances, however, the victim may be completely unaware of the arsonist's enmity toward him.

The psychotic arsonist directs his firesetting against people whom he identifies in his persecutory delusions as enemies—the members of a "paranoid pseudocommunity." The term *pyromaniac* may be applied to a person of this kind, although it is more commonly used in reference to the individual who appears to derive sexual stimulation and/or gratification from arson. Lack of apparent motive is the trademark of the pyromaniac of either type; and when fires are found to be senseless but deliberately set, the investigator is apt to seek the explanation in the disturbed emotional state of the arsonist.

The arsonist for whom firesetting provides sexual excitement has been dubbed a **firebug** by arson investigators. Shapiro (1976) cites the case of a female arsonist who would run naked through the corridors of her apartment building; when a crowd had gathered, she would light bags of rubbish, then return to her apartment and experience an orgasm. Barracato and Michelmore (1976) mention the numerous cases on file of men and women who achieved orgasm "over the licking flames of fires they had created themselves" (p. 18). It should be noted, however, that these impressionistic accounts of the sexually motivated pyromaniac or "firebug" have not been substantiated by evidence from clinical research, This would appear to be an interesting area for systematic inquiry.

Fires may be set in order to conceal or destroy evidence that a crime had been committed. An embezzler might attempt to cover up illegal financial manipulations by burning the office—and the ledgers and account books along with it. A murderer might set a fire in the hope that the victim's remains would be consumed in the blaze. If the criminal has already committed a serious felony, it is doubtful whether he or she would stop at arson.

CONFIDENCE GAMES

Maurer (1974) claims that, "Of all the grifters (practitioners of professional crime), the confidence man is the aristocrat" (p. 3). If this claim is accurate, it is due in no small part to the fact that the "marks" (victims) hand over their money or property to the con artist because of their trust and confidence in him. The exploits of some of the most famous con men—Victor "The Count" Lustig, the man who sold the Eiffel Tower, not once but several times; German-born sharper Walter Hohenau, who fleeced Texans out of a fortune selling a contraption which he claimed could turn water into gasoline; Robert S. Trippet, slick operator of the $130-million Home-Stake Production Company fraud, whose victims included Barbra Streisand, Liza Minnelli, and Barbara Walters—are an impressive testimonial to the plausibility, ingenuity, and audacity of those whom Maurer places at the top of the criminal hierarchy.

The distinction between confidence games and swindles, such as those we shall describe in Chapter 6 on economic or white-collar crimes, is based on the nature of the victim's involvement. Confidence games depend on the greed and willingness to engage in dishonest behavior of the potential victim. The element common to all con games is showing the mark a way to make money or gain some other benefit by fraudulent means, then taking advantage of the mark's dishonesty. Thus, a true "scam" leaves no innocent victims. On the other hand, swindlers prey on the victim's innocence, ignorance, and gullibility. But this is a tenuous distinction, at best, particularly in the case of elderly victims. A New York detective who had been convinced that only the greedy were victimized by swindlers told a reporter of his changed viewpoint after spending several years on the bunco squad:

> For old people, especially the ones with nothing but a bank account and Social Security, that amount they have in the bank is like an index of how long they are going to live. A hope of another $3,000 means another year of life (Kaufman, 1973, p. 49).

The number of successfully operated con games and the monetary losses they represent are impossible to estimate because the victim's embarrassment and possible culpability mean that successful schemes go unreported. There are numerous confidence games, but among the ones that enjoy perennial popularity are the pigeon drop, the bank examiner scheme, and the Cuban (or Spanish) Charities scam.

The Pigeon Drop

The confidence game known as the **pigeon drop** is operated by two people. A lone victim, usually elderly, is approached on the street by one of the con operators, who strikes up a conversation. A wallet, envelope, or other item which could possibly contain cash is placed on the ground or a bench in such a way that it can be readily observed by the passerby. A second con operator walks past the potential victim and his cohort and picks up the wallet or envelope within full view of the pair standing nearby. After making certain that the victim has observed the pickup, the swindler approaches his partner and the victim and indicates that he has found a large sum of money which he is willing to divide with them. First, however, he requests that the two must produce a large sum of money to show "good faith." The victim is never permitted time to think about the proposition and is urged on by the first swindler to withdraw some "good faith" money from a savings account. When the money is withdrawn by the victim, he places it in an envelope provided by the first swindler. It is then shown to the second swindler who, by sleight of hand, switches envelopes, returning an identical envelope filled with worthless strips of scrap paper to the victim. Both swindlers then depart and the victim does not know that his money has been stolen until he goes to redeposit his savings.

The Bank Examiner Scheme

The **bank examiner scheme** is one of the more sophisticated con games and requires a little research about potential targets to determine where they bank. The con artist, usually a man in this scheme, calls the potential victim—let us say an elderly woman—and introduces himself as a federal bank examiner. He says that there has been a computer breakdown at the bank and that he wants to verify when she last deposited or withdrew money, plus her current balance. If the potential victim replies, for example, that there should be $8,000 in the account, the caller then indicates that the bank records show a lesser amount, say $2,000. The caller may then suggest that some dishonest teller may be tampering with the account and proceeds to ask for assistance in apprehending the dishonest employee.

Once the would-be victim agrees to cooperate, the caller advises that they will send a cab to the house to get her and take her to the bank. She is instructed that once she arrives at the bank, she should withdraw $7,000. One con man stays in the approximate vicinity of the victim's house and observes her enter the cab. Another con man waits at the bank to verify the withdrawal and to be certain that the bank officials or police are not alerted. After withdrawing the money, the woman gets back into the waiting cab and returns home. As she walks back into her home, one of the con men telephones her and begins to discuss the next phase of the bank's investigation. While still on the phone, the second con man knocks on the door. The woman is likely to indicate to the caller that someone is at the door, at which time the con man on the phone will instruct her not hang up—that the person at the door is probably one of the bank employees and, if so, he wants to speak to him. The con man at the front door does indeed identify himself as a bank employee, and the woman allows the con man in, who then talks to the other con man on the telephone. After a short conversation, the con man hands the phone back to the woman, whereupon the caller instructs her to give her money to the bank employee so that he can deposit it with the suspected teller. The money is then taken from the victim and she may even be given a receipt.

Cuban (Spanish) Charities

The **Cuban (or Spanish) charities** confidence game is similar to the pigeon drop, but instead of playing on the victim's greed, it appeals to his or her sympathy. The scheme has many variations, but in a recent case it worked something like this: A man stood crying outside the Miami Cuban Medical Clinic. A man in his sixties stopped and asked the crying man, "What's the matter? Can I help you? Are you sick?" The crying man told the sympathetic passerby that he had just arrived from a South American country, where his father was dying. He then explained that some years ago, while living in Miami, his father had stolen some money, but since that time he had moved to the country where he was living at present and had made a fortune. Now, he said, his father wanted to atone for his earlier dishonesty and had given him $10,000 in cash to donate to charities in Miami in his name. But because he was a stranger, alone in Miami, and grief-stricken over the impending loss of his beloved parent, he didn't know what to do with the money.

During this conversation another stranger (who was actually an accomplice) joined the conversation and after a few minutes the bereaved man said, "You both seem to be fine people. I'll give you the money to distribute, but how do I know I can trust you?" The second accomplice insisted that he was trustworthy and offered to withdraw money from his savings account as a gesture of good faith. The would-be victim agreed to the fairness of this gesture and volunteered to do likewise. They went to the bank, where the victim withdrew several thousand dollars. All three men put their money in an envelope, which was then turned over to the sympathetic stranger who was supposed to select the charities to receive the cash donation. They parted and the victim discovered that the envelope contained nothing but cut-up newspapers (Swanson, Chamelin, and Territo, 1984).

CRIMINAL CAREERS

An individual's commitment to a criminal career—a persistent pattern of law-violating behavior extended over a lengthy period of time—is one of the most important issues confronting the criminal justice system, especially with regard to sentencing and disposition. Studies by Wolfgang, Figlio, and Sellin (1972) and Petersilia, Greenwood, and Lavin (1977) have indicated that a relatively small number of offenders account for a disproportionately large share of delinquency and crime. Later research by Chiaken and Chaiken (1982) has made significant additions to our understanding of criminal careers and their implications for policies affecting the administration of justice.

The Chaikens' study, which was based on a sample of more than two thousand jail and prison inmates in three states (California, Texas, and Michigan), obtained information on criminal characteristics and career patterns among offenders from two sources: (1) questionnaires and (2) official records. The authors of this study assume that criminal behavior, like other forms of learned behavior, progresses from simple to more complex forms; for example, the theft of a pack of cigarettes from a convenience store requires much less skill than highjacking an interstate shipment of cigarettes transported by a trailer truck. In addition, people acquire the skills necessary to commit crimes without being apprehended, they acquire justifications and rationalizations for criminal conduct, and they become attuned to opportunities for perpetrating crimes. These ideas are either explicit or implicit in some of the theories which will be discussed in later chapters.

It is important to note at the outset that Chaiken and Chaiken did not attempt to cover all categories of crime, but instead asked inmates to indicate their involvement in ten specific types of criminal behavior: burglary, business robbery, person robbery, assault during robbery, other assaults, theft, auto theft, forgery, credit card swindles, and drug dealing. Approximately 13 percent of the sample stated that they had not committed any of these offenses. Official records indicated that these offenders were involved in such crimes as kidnapping, arson, forcible rape, and other sex crimes. After analyzing the various combinations of crimes reported by each subject, the Chaikens developed a typology of offender behavior in order of the seriousness of the behavior as perceived by the public. Not only does the table indicate the crimes in which the offenders participated; it also reflects their probable lack of involvement in other crimes (see Table 5.1).

These researchers also addressed the very important issue of criminal specialization. Much research has suggested that offenders do not specialize in a single type of crime; instead their criminal careers involve a variety of offenses (Figlio, 1981;

Table 5.1   DEFINITION OF HIERARCHICAL SUBGROUPS OF OFFENDERS

Group	Robbery	Assault[a]	Burglary	Theft,[b] fraud, forgery, credit card crimes	Drug deals	Percent of study sample[c]
Violent predators (robber-assaulter-dealers)	+	+	?	?	+	15
Robber-assaulters	+	+	?	?	0	8
Robber-dealers	+	0	?	?	+	9
Low-level robbers	+	0	?	?	0	12
Mere assaulters	0	+	0	0	0	5
Burglar-dealers	0	??	+	?	+	10
Low-level burglars	0	0	+	?	0	8
Property & drug offenders	0	??	0	+	+	6
Low-level property offenders	0	0	0	+	0	8
Drug dealers	0	0	0	0	+	6

Note: + = Group member commits this crime, by definition.

　　0 = Group member does not commit this crime, by definition.

　　? = Group member may or may not commit this crime. Analysis shows that nearly all members of the group do.

　　?? = Group member may or may not commit this crime. Most don't.

[a]Assault includes homicide arising out of assault or robbery.

[b]Theft includes auto theft.

[c]Percentages add to 87 percent. The remaining 13 percent did not report committing any of the crimes studied. Some serious crimes (e.g., rape, kidnap) were not included in the self-report survey. Respondents with missing data (150 out of 2,190) were excluded in calculation of percentages.

Source: J. Chaiken and M. R. Chaiken, *Varieties of Criminal Behavior* (Santa Monica, CA: Rand Corporation, 1982, p. 3). Reproduced by permission of authors and publisher.

Peterson and Braiker, 1981). Chaiken and Chaiken suggest that these conclusions result from a conception of specialization involving participation in only one offense (e.g., robbery) and/or the use of arrest or conviction records which only represent a small and often atypical sample of the totality of criminal acts committed by an individual. By using self-reports they were able to obtain much more information on a given individual; by defining specialization in terms of combinations of offenses they were able to find evidence of specialization.

In order to understand criminal specialization as defined by Chaiken and Chaiken, it must be viewed within the context of an offender's criminal career. As we pointed out earlier, some elementary forms of crime are common to the performance of more complex and serious types of criminal behavior. Theft is the most elementary form of criminal behavior; therefore, it is not surprising that most offenders in the study reported engaging in this type of behavior. Even if they have advanced to more complex forms of behavior such as burglary, offenders may from time to time, because of opportunity or need, commit an occasional theft. This should not rule out their classification as a burglary specialist if most of their criminal activity involves burglary. Occasional theft on the part of a burglar is much the same as the surgeon who occasionally performs the task of an intern or a nurse by taking a patient's blood pressure or temperature. Thus, with the exception of assault, there was a tendency for those involved in the higher-level types of offenses to commit one or more of the crimes that were below them in seriousness. It was found that 81 percent of the offenders who were involved in robbery, assault, and drug dealing also committed burglary, and 71 percent of them were involved in theft.

Another issue in criminal specialization is the extent to which offenders maintain their involvement in one or a series of related offenses over a period of time. This study suggests that, if offenders make changes, they usually move to a more serious complex of offenses or else they stop their involvement in crime altogether. Chaiken and Chaiken are quick to point out their data on upward transitions are very tentative, because the nature of the research was not well suited to study this phenomenon.

Also, with the exception of *mere assaulters,* as one moves up the list from the less to more serious offense categories, there is an increase not only in the seriousness but also in the amount of crime committed. Those at the top of the list not only commit more serious offenses but also commit more types of crimes than those in the lower varieties and are more likely to engage in both serious and less serious offenses at a higher annual rate. The data presented in Table 5.2 provide a picture of the offense patterns of the top 10 percent of the offenders in each category. Violent predators are much more likely to commit burglaries at a higher rate than those who restrict their activity to burglary. Finally, as a result of collecting background information from these offenders, the researchers were able to develop portraits of offenders in each category, as presented in Tables 5.3 and 5.4.

Violent Offenders

The offenders who make up the category of **violent predators** are predominantly white or Hispanic, single, have unstable work histories, and resemble the prisoners

Table 5.2 COMPARISON OF COMMISSION RATES OF HIGH-RATE OFFENDERS AMONG VARIETIES OF CRIMINAL BEHAVIOR

Variety of criminal behavior	Robbery			Assault	Burglary	Theft	Forgery & credit cards	Fraud	Drug dealing
	All[a]	Business	Person						
Violent predators	135	96	82	18	516	517	200	278	4088
Robber-assaulters	65	46	38	14	315	726	27	293	—
Robber-dealers	41	60	32	—	377	407	255	106	2931
Low-level robbers	10	15	9	—	206	189	78	811	—
Mere assaulters	—	—	—	3.5	—	—	—	—	—
Burglar-dealers	—	—	—	6	113	406	274	64	2890
Low-level burglars	—	—	—	—	105	97	62	36	—
Property & drug offenders	—	—	—	9	—	663	283	264	3302
Low-level property offenders	—	—	—	—	—	560	486	1160	—
Drug dealers	—	—	—	—	—	—	—	—	3035
Significant difference across varieties? (all crime rates considered)[b]	Yes	Yes	Yes	Yes	Yes	Yes	No	No	Yes

Note: Ninetieth percentile value of annualized crime rate.

Ten percent of the respondents in the crime variety who commit the crime commit it at or above the rate indicated in the table (a different 10 percent for each crime). Table 2.6 shows the percentage by age of who commit the crimes.

[a]"All" robbery is not the sum of business and person robbery. It also includes robberies that were reported as outgrowths of burglary and could not be classified as either business or person robbery.

[b]Significance test is by grouped χ^2 at the .01 level. The test does not refer to the 90th percentiles. Respondents who did not commit the crime are excluded in the test.

Source: J. Chaiken and M. R. Chaiken, *Varieties of Criminal Behavior* (Santa Monica, CA: Rand Corporation, 1982. p. 56). Reproduced by permission of authors and publisher.

Irwin (1980) called "state-raised youths," because they had a lengthy history of commitment to state juvenile facilities. Costly and intensive drug use leads violent offenders to perpetrate a variety of crimes at high rates; and it is the nature of the drugs they use—heroin and barbiturates, barbiturates and alcohol, heroin and amphetamines, or multiple combinations of these drugs—that is directly related to their involvement in certain kinds of crimes.

Most research on crimes of violence and violent offenders, as we saw in the preceding chapter, has tended to show that interpersonal violence is most likely to occur within the context of personal disputes involving friends, acquaintances, or relatives. Chaiken and Chaiken point out that the violence associated with the offenses perpetrated by the violent predator is an integral part of their deviant activity rather than a response provoked by particular individuals or circumstances. This seems to suggest that they are prone to use violence when provoked or when it seems to facilitate their accomplishment of the criminal objective. This makes them exceedingly dangerous since they are unpredictable in the employment of violence on their victims. The need for criminal justice professionals to identify these offenders is therefore obvious. However, it is difficult to identify these offenders from their offi-

Table 5.3 CHARACTERISTICS OF VIOLENT OFFENDERS

Types of offenders	Profile of distinguishing characteristics
Violent predators	Young (average age 23)
	Higher rate of total arrests for both violent and property offenders
	Extensive juvenile offense record in terms of both property and violent crimes at or before age 16
	History of heavy multiple drug use (combination of alcohol, barbiturates, heroin) including the addictive use of heroin beginning as juveniles
	Heroin habit exceeding $50 per day
	Irregular, unstable work history
	Predominantly Hispanic or white
	Single
	No extensive adult criminal record
	"State-raised youths" (i.e., lengthy history of commitment to foster homes, detention homes, state training schools, etc.)
	Unstable social background (poor job history; no family obligations)
	Violence is an integral part of their deviant activity
Robber assaulters	Young
	History of violent crime as juveniles and multiple commitments to state juvenile facilities
	Less likely to be addicted to heroin and to have $50 daily habits to support
	Do not have long records of arrests
Nonassaultive robber dealers	Multiple commitments to state facilities ("state raised")
	History of nonemployment (i.e., no work history)
	Began careers before 16 but restricted early activity to property offenses
	Heroin habit of over $50
	Multiple drug use beginning at adolescence but as adults did not mix high doses of drugs to the same extent as violent predators
Low-level robbers	Higher percentage of blacks
	Lower robbery rate
	Lower rate of general drug use
	Less likelihood of barbiturate use
Mere assaulters	Older (average age 28)
	Married
	Steady employment record
	Lower likelihood of multiple arrest pattern
	Drug use limited to small quantities of barbiturates or amphetamines; and barbiturates and alcohol

Source: Based on material by J. Chaiken and M. R. Chaiken, *Varieties of Criminal Behavior* (Santa Monica, CA.: Rand Corporation, 1982.) Reproduced by permission of authors and publisher.

Table 5.4   CHARACTERISTICS OF PROPERTY OFFENDERS

Types of offenders	Profile of distinguishing characteristics
Burglar dealers	White
	Heavily involved in property but not violent crime before age 16
	Multiple drug use including $50 a day heroin habit but less likely to use combinations of drugs frequently
	Compared to other inmates they have normal employment records, education, marital histories
Low-level burglars	Late starters—began criminal career after age 16
	Juvenile offenses limited to property offenses
	Lesss likely to have used drugs in the 4- to 5-year period prior to arrest
Drug and property offenders	Drug use in 4- to 5-year period preceding arrest; $50 a day heroin habit for up to 1 year before apprehension
	Higher educational levels and more stable relationships
Low-level property offenders	Older
	Less likely to use drugs in the 4- to 5-year period prior to current arrest
	More likely than other inmates to report serving several terms in adult prison

Source: Based on material presented by J. Chaiken and M. R. Chaiken, *Varities of Criminal Behavior* (Santa Monica, CA: Rand Corporation, 1982). Reproduced by permission of authors and publishers.

cial records. First, as a result of the fact that they are so young, they usually do not have extensive records of adult criminal activity. In addition, their official juvenile records do not offer much greater assistance. Although many of these offenders report extensive drug use and frequent violent criminal activity as juveniles, which should have made them highly visible to their neighbors, teachers, and other school mates, some appear to have no official records of involvement in delinquency. Even in those instances where juvenile records are available, they usually fail to indicate the seriousness or rate of their self-reported involvement in criminal activities. The Chaikens suggest that a variety of factors including imprecise definitions of drug use, the successful evasion of arrest and conviction, and plea bargaining, make it all but impossible to successfully identify these offenders from official records.

Other types of robbers differ from violent predators. Perhaps the most striking differences are those between violent predators and mere assaulters. The latter are older and more likely to be married, to have been employed steadily during the measurement period, and to have been able to hold on to one job, although they were less likely to have completed high school than other respondents. As juveniles, these offenders were much less likely to have used drugs; in fact, the only drug-use patterns they have in common with the violent predator involved a combination of barbiturate and amphetamine use and barbiturate and alcohol use in relatively small quantities. This group is also notable in that they are much less likely than other "violent offenders" to have records of multiple arrests or to have been placed on probation.

Property Offenders

Burglar dealers show a number of similarities to *robber dealers*: they are predominantly white, report involvement in property crime (but not violent crime) prior to age 16 years, and have been involved in heavy drug use in the period immediately preceding their arrest. Unlike robber dealers, they do not have a juvenile history of hard drug use and addiction to heroin, nor do they show the same record of multiple commitment to state facilities. Also, in contrast to other offenders in this study, they appear to have normal employment records, levels of education, and stable marital histories (see Table 5.2).

Low-level burglars can be categorized as the opposite end of the continuum from violent predators: they were relatively late starters, were significantly less likely than serious offenders to become involved in violent crime as juveniles, and had substantially less involvement in drug use. In contrast to low-rate burglars, *high-rate burglars* are usually older men who are either heroin addicts with costly habits or users of nonopiate drugs such as amphetamines or barbiturates, which tends to make them occupationally unstable. Furthermore, these offenders have criminal records which include long histories of arrest, conviction, and imprisonment. In short, the overall high rate of drug use by this group makes it difficult for them to hold a job, and in order to support their drug habit and/or to survive, they must engage in crime.

Conclusions and Policy Implications

The relationship between drug use and crime, as this study indicates, is often of long duration, originating in the juvenile years. Specific drug use patterns are related to certain types of crimes and the rates at which these offenses are committed. While heroin use in the past was considered to be a major factor in serious crime, today the multiple use of alcohol, barbiturates, and heroin appears to be significantly related to high rates of involvement in violent crimes. Official records fail to provide an accurate basis for distinguishing violent predators from other serious offenders, raising the possibility that resources may often be diverted to the wrong targets.

On the basis of these and other findings, Chaiken and Chaiken conclude their analysis with some suggestions for further research and recommendations concerning criminal justice policy that include the following:

1. The collection of data on juvenile criminal activity and drug use to assist criminal justice personnel in making sharper discriminations among offenders than are possible at present.
2. Routine drug testing of all arrestees in order to collect relevant information on the drug use history of offenders.
3. Prevention programs should be directed toward juveniles rather than adult offenders and should be aimed primarily at nonviolent property offenders, for many of whom crime is simply a substitute for conventional sources of income. Such offenders would probably benefit from vocational training programs which both provide them with marketable job skills and give them experience in working at a steady job.

These authors emphasize that drug use and crime must be viewed as parts of a complex lifestyle, and that the dynamics of the interrelationship can only be understood by examining both environmental factors and individual characteristics and the ways in which these interact in producing various kinds of criminal behavior. While the characteristics of those identified as violent predators suggest that long-term imprisonment is the only feasible policy at present that appears to have any potential for reducing their high rate of commission of violent offenses, Chaiken and Chaiken caution that this does not constitute a blanket endorsement of incapacitation. Current models for identifying violent predators are not precise enough to provide a reliable and valid basis for sentencing decisions which discriminate between nonviolent and violent offenders.

Given that this is the case and that most of the offenders who are incarcerated at present are not violent predators, it is necessary to wait until our methods of identifying violent predators have undergone considerable improvement. The fact that violent predators are not common among older prison populations suggests that, if left on the street, these offenders either die young or as they grow older decide to go straight. At any rate, until or unless this phenomenon is better understood, selective incapacitation of violent predators is impossible to justify on pragmatic as well as on legal grounds.

The best hope for dealing with violent predators, as Chaiken and Chaiken suggest, is through the development of an effective prevention program that attempts to identify these offenders at an early age and then focuses on controlling the factors that increase their likelihood of becoming violent predators. In other words they feel it is far more sensible to attempt to prevent individuals from becoming violent predators than to try to change adult offenders with well-established patterns of drug use and crime. They suggest that research directed toward prevention although difficult will prove more fruitful than similar efforts directed toward the development of rehabilitation programs for such offenders.

Finally, results from this study suggest the possible role of different environments and criminal justice practices in the development of certain patterns of criminal behavior. This study found that the Texas sample, when compared with the Michigan and particularly the California sample, had a smaller proportion both of offenders that committed crimes at high rates and of violent predators. In addition, the Texas sample reported much less serious drug use and much higher rates of employment. It is clear then that Texas, as compared with California and Michigan, sentences a greater proportion of less serious offenders to either jail or prison. In order to account for the differences between these states, these researchers controlled for a number of personal factors, including drug use, and still found that Texas inmates had significantly lower rates of robbery than the offenders in other states. These researchers believe that the reason for the lower robbery rates in Texas becomes clear when one looks at inmate responses to the following question: "Do you think you could do the same crime(s) again without getting caught?" While Texas inmates who, as a group, committed less serious offenses are most likely to answer no, those in California who committed more serious crimes are most likely to answer yes. Chaiken and Chaiken conclude that these findings

> suggest that some environments tolerate lifestyles comprising frequent criminal acts and hard drug use while others condemn them, that these disparate attitudes manifest themselves in different criminal justice policies and practices, and

that the difference in these policies and practices explain why some environments have a more similar criminal problem than other [p. 29].

Recognizing the highly tentative nature of their conclusions, Chaiken and Chaiken
suggest that their potential implications for criminal justice policy make a worthwhile topic for future research.

SUMMARY

This chapter has dealt with conventional property offenses and offenders. Three
types of property offenders were identified: occasional offenders, ordinary career
criminals, and professional offenders. Differences between these types with respect to
training, skill level, specialization, and commitment to criminality were noted and
discussed.

The Index crimes of burglary, larceny-theft, motor vehicle theft, and arson were
outlined and briefly described. Conventional and professional burglars were discussed; and attention was devoted to the specific offense patterns which characterize
the larceny-theft crimes of shoplifting, marine theft, and agri-crime. Emphasis was
put on the importance of the fence (criminal receiver of stolen goods) as a key figure
in the disposal of stolen property—a prerequisite for successful large-scale theft.

In the discussion of motor vehicle theft, the operations of "chop shops" and
their connections with professional auto theft rings were indicated. Arson, which was
included as an 8th Index crime by the FBI's *Uniform Crime Reports* in 1978, appears
to be an offense which is decreasing rather than increasing, despite impressions to the
contrary conveyed by the media. Coverage of property crimes also included a discussion of confidence games; several of the more typical examples (the pigeon drop, the
bank examiner scheme, and the Spanish charities scam) were described.

The chapter concluded with a discussion of criminal careers and the importance of research on the offender whose pattern of criminality shows persistence and
commitment over time. The conclusions reached by Chaiken and Chaiken (1982) in
their three-state study of incarcerated offenders and their implications for criminal
justice policy with regard to incapacitation were carefully explored.

DISCUSSION QUESTIONS

Find the answers to the following questions in the text.
1. Identify and briefly describe the **occasional property offender,** the **ordinary career criminal,**
   and the **professional criminal.**
2. What are the two major types of shoplifter identified by the terms **booster** and **pilferer?**
   What are the main differences between them?
3. Discuss the principal issues that need to be addressed in research on **agri-crime.**
4. Why is the **fence** (the criminal receiver of stolen goods) a key figure in successful theft?
5. Summarize the main types of motor vehicle theft. Why have "chop shops" become big
   business in property crime?
6. Discuss the motivational patterns in the crime of arson. What features of the crime contribute to the difficulties in the investigation and prosecution of arsonists?

7. Briefly outline the basic strategy employed by the confidence man in such con games as the **pigeon drop** and the **bank examiner scheme.**
8. Summarize the main findings of the research by Chaiken and Chaiken and discuss their policy implications for the criminal justice system.

TERMS TO IDENTIFY AND REMEMBER

occasional offender

professional criminal

pilferer

booster box

SPS

pigeon drop

firebug

Cuban (Spanish) charities

ordinary career criminal

booster

agri-crime

master fence

transfer function

"torch"

bank examiner scheme

violent predator

REFERENCES

Akiyama, Y., and Pfeiffer, P. C. Arson: A statistical profile. *FBI Law Enforcement Bulletin* 53 (1984): 8–13.

Alexander, A., and Moolman, V. *Stealing.* New York: Copperstone Library, 1969.

Barracato, J., and Michelmore, P. *Arson!* New York: Norton, 1976.

Bates, E. B. *Elements of Fire and Arson Investigation.* Santa Cruz, CA: Davis, 1975.

Blum, R. *Deceivers and Deceived.* Springfield, IL: Charles C. Thomas, 1972.

Cameron, M. O. *The Booster and the Snitch.* Glencoe, IL: The Free Press, 1964.

Chaiken, J., and Chaiken, M. R. *Varieties of Criminal Behavior.* Santa Monica, CA: Rand Corporation, 1982.

Clinard, M. B. *Sociology of Deviant Behavior.* New York: Holt, Rinehart and Winston, 1974.

Clinard, M. B., and Quinney, R. *Criminal Behavior Systems: A Typology.* New York: Holt, Rinehart and Winston, 1973.

Conklin, J. E. *Robbery and the Criminal Justice System.* Philadelphia: Lippincott, 1972.

Curtis, S. J. *Modern Retail Security.* Springfield, IL: Charles C. Thomas, 1972.

Dunway, B. Theft is a big problem on farms. *Wallace's Farmer,* Feb. 23, 1974, p. 80.

Federal Bureau of Investigation. Auto theft rings. *FBI Law Enforcement Bulletin* 40 (1971): 6–9.

————. Motor vehicle thefts—A Uniform Crime Reporting survey. *FBI Law Enforcement Bulletin* 44 (1975): 7–10.

Fitch, R. D., and Porter, E. A. *Accidental or Incendiary?* Springfield, IL: Charles C. Thomas, 1968.

Gibbons, D. C. *Society, Crime, and Criminal Careers.* Englewood Cliffs, NJ: Prentice-Hall, 1977.

Greenwood, P. W., and Inciardi, J. Criminal careers. In S. Kadish (ed.), *Encyclopedia of Crime and Justice.* New York: The Free Press, 1983.

Horgan, J. J. *Criminal Investigation.* New York: McGraw-Hill, 1974.

Hormachea, C. R. *Sourcebook in Criminalistics.* Reston, VA: Reston Publishing Company, 1975.

Inciardi, J. A. *Careers in Crime.* Chicago: Rand McNally, 1975.

Jackson, B. *In the Life: Versions of the Criminal Experience.* New York: Holt, Rinehart and Winston, 1972.

Kaufman, M. T. Elderly warned of con games as complaints rise. *New York Times,* March 28, 1973, p. 49.

Kirk, P. L. *Fire Investigation.* New York: Wiley, 1969.

Klockars, C. B. *The Professional Fence.* New York: The Free Press, 1974.

Lemert, E. M. *Human Deviance, Social Problems, and Social Control.* Englewood Cliffs, NJ: Prentice-Hall, 1967.

Lyford, G. J. Boat theft—A high profit/low risk business. *FBI Law Enforcement Bulletin* 51 (1982): 1–5.

Maurer, D. W. *The American Confidence Man.* Springfield, IL: Charles C. Thomas, 1974.

Mydans, S. Shoplifting: A fast growing crime. *Tampa Tribune,* Dec. 12, 1975, p. 3-A.

Nash, J. R. *Hustlers and Con Men.* New York: Evans, 1976.

Petersilia, J., Greenwood, P. W., and Lavin, M. *Criminal Careers of Habitual Felons.* Santa Monica, CA: Rand Corporation, 1977.

Pope, C. E. *Crime Specific Analysis: The Characteristics of Burglary Incidents.* Washington, D.C.: U.S. Government Printing Office, 1977.

Reckless, W. C. *The Crime Problem.* New York: Appleton-Century-Crofts, 1973.

Reppetto, T. A. *Residential Crime.* Cambridge, MA: Ballinger, 1974.

Rhode Island Marine Advisory Service. *Boat and Marine Equipment Theft.* Narragansett, RI: Rhode Island Marine Advisory Service, 1980.

Robin, G. D. Gang delinquency in Philadelphia. In M. W. Klein (ed.), *Juvenile Gangs in Context: Theory, Research and Action.* Englewood Cliffs, NJ: Prentice-Hall, 1967.

Robin, G. D. *Introduction to the Criminal Justice System.* New York: Harper & Row, 1980.

Roebuck, J. B., and Johnson, R. C. The "short con" man. In B. J. Cohen (ed.), *Crime in America: Perspectives on Criminal and Delinquent Behavior.* Itasca, IL: F. E. Peacock, 1970.

Rozzi, S. J., and Mueller, R. Automobile theft: An increasing crime problem. *FBI Law Enforcement Bulletin* 49 (1980): 9–13.

Scarr, H. A. *Patterns of Burglary.* Washington, D.C.: U.S. Government Printing Office, 1973.

Shapiro, F. C. *Raking the Ashes of the Epidemic of Flame.* New York: New York Times Reprint, 1976.

Shover, N. Structures and careers in burglary. *Journal of Criminal Law, Criminology and Police Science* 63 (1972): 540–48.

Sniffen, M. Today's auto thieves put their goods on the chopping block. *Tampa Tribune,* Nov. 7, 1978, p. 3-A.

Swanson, C. R., Chamelin, N. C., and Territo, L. *Criminal Investigation.* New York: Random House, 1984.

Swanson, C. R., and Territo, L. Agricultural crime: Its extent, prevention, and control. *FBI Law Enforcement Bulletin* 49 (1980), 8–12.

U.S. Department of Justice, Federal Bureau of Investigation. *Uniform Crime Reports—1984.* Washington, D.C.: U.S. Government Printing Office, 1985.

Walsh, M. *The Fence: A New Look at the World of Property Theft.* Westport, CT: Greenwood Press, 1977.

Wolfgang, M. E., Figlio, R. M., and Sellin, T. *Delinquency in a Birth Cohort.* Chicago: University of Chicago Press, 1972.

Wright, R. A. Nation's retail merchants mobilize security systems to control fast-growing shoplifting trend. *New York Times,* May 21, 1972.

Chapter 6

ECONOMIC, SYNDICATED, AND POLITICAL CRIME

Crimes against the person and conventional property offenses are perpetrated, for the most part, by individuals or by groups that have come together temporarily for a specific purpose, such as robbing a bank. In contrast, the economic, syndicated, and political crimes we shall discuss in this chapter are generally committed—with exceptions that will be noted—within an organizational context or setting. They represent "illegal actions taken in accordance with operative organizational goals which do harm, either economic or physical, to employees, to consumers, or the general public" (Schrager and Short, 1978, p. 407).

The characteristics of organizations create special difficulties for the systematic study of criminal behavior in organizational settings. Apart from the obvious hazards of attempting to conduct an unsponsored investigation of some syndicated crime "family," there are formidable problems of a methodological nature that confront the researcher. Dinitz (1977), for example, has referred to economic crime as a "more or less nonresearchable area in the conventional sense of research as an analytic and not merely descriptive enterprise" (p. 49), citing reasons that range from the laundering of money, shredding of records, and the "uncommonly high rate of amnesia for specific events" among economic criminals, to the lack of funding for economic crimes research. In addition, Schrager and Short (1978) have identified such problems as the difficulty of establishing criminal intent, of determining criminal responsibility of individual perpetrators, and of applying the civil/criminal distinction to organizational behavior.

Despite these and other difficulties, which we shall try to identify and discuss where appropriate throughout this chapter, criminologists cannot afford to ignore organizational crimes. As measured by economic factors alone, the impact of such offenses exceeds by far the costs of conventional property crimes. Of even greater importance, only recently has there been a growth in public awareness of the serious, even fatal, consequences that may result from criminal organizational acts.

With the recognition of the power of large organizations to exploit and injure ordinary citizens and to evade or disregard all but the most rigorous efforts at regulation, the distinctions between economic, or white-collar, and political crimes become more blurred. Where can the line be drawn between abuses of private corporate power and abuses of governmental and political power? The element common to both of these categories of offenses, as Moore (1980) points out, is that "they are committed with relative impunity by people in powerful institutional positions—sometimes for their own purposes and sometimes to further the interests of their institutions" (p. 22).

Sagarin (1973) emphasizes that "all crime is political because it is a political body (in America, the legislature) that defines an act as criminal" (p. vii) and other political bodies—the courts and correctional systems—which decide whether or not the individual has actually committed the act and apply the mandated penal sanctions. To these distinctions, Roebuck and Weeber (1978) have added the further qualification that political crimes occur in an *organizational* context, that is, "are committed by persons or groups of persons during the normal course of their activities as employees or members of formal organizations" (p. 7). Whether the crimes are committed against the government or by agents or representatives of the govern-

ment, whether individuals or groups advance
tional careers, the "one objective must be organ
must be engendered and supported by the inte
tion, and peer groups within the organization
based upon those norms" (p. 7). This charact(
written for syndicated crime, as the followir

ECONOMIC CRIMES

"White collar crime is a widespread patte
materially motivated and affects personal, business, a.... ₅
local, national, and international levels. It is observable in socialist countries ....
than in those that operate under the free enterprise system" (Edelhertz, 1978, p. 15).
White-collar, or economic, crime is a sociological rather than a legal category. Thus,
the types of acts that are considered white-collar/economic crimes may vary according to such factors as the perpetrator's occupation, educational attainments, and
personal experiences. Criminologist Edwin H. Sutherland introduced the concept of
white-collar crime nearly 50 years ago in order to direct attention to the crimes of the
"upper world," in contrast to conventional crimes committed mostly by the lower
classes. He defined white-collar crimes as offenses perpetrated by persons of respectability and high-school status in the course of their occupations.

Others have found Sutherland's definition too narrow because it fails to acknowledge that white-collar crimes are committed by persons outside their occupations (e.g., falsifying income tax returns) and it fails to take into account businesses
in which crime is an essential activity (e.g., fraudulent land sales companies). The
definition provided by Edelhertz (1970) rectifies this problem. He defines white-collar
crime as "an illegal act or a series of illegal acts committed by non-physical means
and by concealment or guile to obtain money or property, or to obtain business or
personal advantage" (p. 3).

The Edelhertz definition recognizes that white-collar/economic crime offenses
are not committed by people of a given occupational, educational, or social level. It
also suggests the method by which these offenses are committed. While conventional
offenders may use force or threats of violence to accomplish their criminal objectives,
white-collar/economic criminals achieve thier criminal objectives by disguising the
purpose of their actions. Deception may be written, verbal, or both. Illustrations
include deceptive advertising—companies making false claims about their products—and salespeople who make false claims about the products they are selling.
Finally, this definition suggests the reason people engage in this behavior: to achieve
some economic advantage.

Finn and Hoffman (1976) have suggested that we call this type of criminal
activity "economic crime" rather than white-collar crime, because the term *economic
crime* more accurately reflects the objective of this category of offense—economic
gain—and does not imply that such crimes are perpetrated exclusively by the wealthy
or those in executive positions. It seems probable that this label will eventu-

...place the term white-collar crime as a designation for this kind of criminal behavior.

Economic Crimes

In this section we shall utilize Edelhertz's four-part typology of white-collar crime schemes to illustrate the broad range of offenses that fall within this area of criminal activity.

Personal Crimes   The category of personal crimes involves crimes committed by persons operating on an individual or ad hoc basis. These offenses are perpetrated by persons pursuing some individual objective and usually do not involve face-to-face contact with the victims. Examples include individual income tax violations, Social Security fraud, welfare fraud, and bankruptcy frauds. The accomplishment of these offenses is relatively easy while their prevention and detection is hampered by the fact that government and corporate victims deal with a large anonymous population of consumers (Edelhertz, 1982). The feature common to all of these personal crimes is that they are practiced as a form of criminal entrepreneurship.

One of the newest areas of criminal initiative under this category is the use of credit cards to defraud. With millions of credit cards in circulation, the chairman of the House Banking Committee estimated losses from credit card fraud in 1982 at one billion dollars (Feldman, 1983).

In obtaining credit cards to defraud, the simplest way is usually the easiest and safest: 60 percent of cards used fraudulently were either lost or stolen. Twenty percent of fraud-related losses represent cards that were issued to, but never received by, legitimate applicants, and the remaining 20 percent are cards obtained by fraudulent application. Counterfeiting of credit cards is extremely rare, but there is growing concern that it will develop into a major problem as the more traditional methods of credit card fraud become less and less successful.

Most credit card frauds are variations on two basic forms of transaction: the use of the stolen or fraudulent credit card to "purchase" goods for resale, or the illegal use of the card to obtain a cash advance. The criminal may simply use a stolen or phony card as long as he thinks he can do so with relative safety in order to amass a pile of merchandise which can be sold or fenced. Or he may enter into collusion with the owner or an employee of a store to make a fraudulent purchase and then split the proceeds from the transaction. One witness before the Senate Banking Committee claimed that it was possible to charge up to $10,000 to a single card account simply by keeping the purchases at individual stores below the amount that requires employees to obtain authorization from the credit card company. This witness, who had become a police informant, stated that credit card fraud constituted his full-time employment (Feldman, 1983).

An employee may engage in the practice known as "double-slipping," that is, he or she imprints two charge slips, one for the correct amount and the other to be filled out later. The employee then fills in the amount, forges the customer's signature, pockets the cash paid by another customer, and puts the forged charge slip into the cash register. Other employee frauds are perpetrated by raising the amount on charge slips and pocketing the difference in cash.

As a convenience to their card holders, credit card companies guarantee payment on checks cashed in one of their outlets. A fraudulent credit card may be used by the criminal to cash books of checks underwritten by the credit company guarantee. If there is a limit as to amount, then the check may be written just under this limit (Farr, 1975).

Abuses of Trust The category of abuses of trust involves crimes committed by individuals in the course of their occupations operating inside business, government, or other establishments in violation of their duty, loyalty, or fidelity to an employer or client. Examples of these offenses include employee embezzlement, the acceptance of bribes or other favors by government or corporate agents in exchange for awarding contracts to particular companies, misuse of labor pension funds, employee theft, securities fraud, and payroll and expense account padding. In all of these cases, the employee or agent has the ability to cause harm by virtue of his or her position and, through the manipulation and control of paper or computer records, can temporarily or permanently bury any evidence that a crime has been committed (Edelhertz, 1982).

Employee Theft Inventory shrinkage—an accounting euphemism for losses due to employee pilferage—has been estimated as costing American business between $5 billion and $10 billion a year (*Tampa Tribune,* June 11, 1983). The pilferer may be an individual who steals from petty cash or may be part of an extensive and well-organized operation that systematically loots thousands of dollars worth of goods or merchandise from the firm. Whatever the *modus operandi,* the pilferer helps contribute to the bankruptcy of nearly one thousand businesses each year (Barmash, 1973).

Who are the pilferers? According to Lipman (1973):

> Some are punks and some are executives, but the average company thief is a married man, has two or three children, lives in a fairly good community, plays bridge with his neighbors, goes to church regularly, is well thought of by his boss. He is highly trusted and a good worker, one of the best in the plant. That's why he can steal so much over such long periods and why it's so hard to discover his identity [p. 160].

According to the author of a text on business and industrial security (Fisher, 1979), many security practitioners believe that from 70 to 80 percent of *all* employees steal on at least an occasional basis. Furthermore, it is also believed that from 20 to 30 percent of employees will not steal under any circumstances, "whereas 30 percent will steal regardless of any security barriers placed in their path, and the remainder will steal at least occasionally if given the opportunity" (p. 227).

Computer Abuse   Few areas of scientific and technological development can match the impact of the computer revolution. Already the computer has begun to reshape the world, and there is every reason to believe it will have comparable effects on crime. The advent of the computer made the crime of embezzlement easier to commit and harder to detect. The theft of computer time has created variants on the older common law crimes of larceny and trespass. While computers represent a valuable resource to business, industry, and government, they provide matchless opportunities for criminal exploitation. **Electronic data processing (EDP)** crimes are wide-ranging because computer data banks generally contain information encompassing the full scope of business operations. Consequently, computer abuse "can take the form of embezzlement, misappropriation of computer time, theft of programs, and illegal acquisition of such proprietary information as marketing plans and forecasts, product design, secret manufacturing processes, and confidential technical data (U.S. Chamber of Commerce, 1974, p. 20). Whatever the cost incurred by computer crime—and it has been estimated in the billions of dollars—it seems likely that it will go on increasing. More than 3 percent of the total work force in the country is employed in computer-related jobs, and the figure continues to grow.

EDP crimes offer scope for a much higher level of sophistication and technical skill than those required by the more commonplace forms of theft. The typical "electronic criminal" is male, highly motivated, bright, energetic, and generally young (18 to 30 years old) (Parker and Nycum, 1974). He is often the master of a body of technical expertise that borders on the esoteric. In fact, he may find it difficult to explain the details of his crime to someone lacking extensive knowledge of computer operations (Farr, 1975).

Some of the possibilities the computer offers for the development of new con games are suggested by the following case:

> At Citibank cash dispensers in New York City and surrounding suburbs, an imaginative con man's scheme depleted accounts of $92,000—with the unwitting assistance of the victims. The scheme worked like this: the con man, posing as a customer, stands between two cash terminals and pretends to be talking on the service phone. A legitimate customer comes in and inserts his card into one of the terminals, only to be told by the con man that the machine isn't working. The customer withdraws his card, leaving the first machine activated, and inserts his card into the second machine. The con man looks on surreptitiously as the customer enters his personal identification number and completes his transaction. Then, still holding the phone, the con man enters the same number and a withdrawal order on the first machine. To complete the theft, he must get the legitimate customer to insert the card once more into the first machine, and he does this by claiming that customer service thinks there is something wrong with his card. Three hundred seventy-four customers cooperated, and the courteous, well-spoken con man got away with their money [Coniff, 1982, p. 62].

The nature of evidence in computer offenses creates special difficulties from the standpoint of detection and investigation. For example, a single computer tape may contain more information than an entire shelf of books. Not only does this make the task of evaluation more difficult, but also evidence can later be destroyed with ease or the information "boobytrapped" so that an attempt by the investigator to retrieve the material results in automatic loss. For instance, when the perpetrators of the famous Equity Funding swindle—which fabricated 64,000 phony insurance policies worth $1 billion—were caught, they had a computer program available which could have erased all of the evidence.

The problems of computer crime have prompted a search for new and increasingly sophisticated approaches to computer security. One method is to code or encrypt information so that only those with keys can unscramble the data. Such systems are available for protecting stored information and even personal computer owners can buy encryption devices to keep their affairs private. But, as Peterson (1982) points out, there is no absolute security in electronic safeguards: in the end, the human element is the ultimate weakness. Quoting a well-known expert in the field, he claims that "the most effective way to break into a secure computer system is with a bribe or by introducing a pretty woman or a handsome man to the right computer operator" (p. 14).

Business Crimes The third category, business crimes—called by some "**crimes in the suites**"—may well be the most troublesome, as Edelhertz (1982) notes, because they involve individuals who rarely think of themselves as either criminals or abusers of society. The high social status of these individuals may make them feel that they can set standards and are not subject to the same rules and regulations that are required of others in society. The offenses committed by these individuals are a part, but not the central purpose, of the organization's business. Examples include antitrust violations, collusive bidding for public contracts, tax violations, food and drug violations, commercial espionage, and deceptive advertising. On a much smaller scale there are such violations as fraudulent Medicare or Medicaid claims, the "thumb on the grocer's scale," and the submission of a misleading financial statement in order to obtain credit for a business that otherwise would not be entitled to it. These crimes are particularly difficult to deal with because they are hidden within a mass of legitimate activities. Many of those in the business community fail to see these acts as crimes, but view them instead as simply part of what is required for conducting business.

The Impact of Corporate Crime When one considers what corporate crime costs consumers, the government, and the environment in terms of dollar amounts, the impact is staggering. Consumer advocates claim that corporate crime costs the economy $200 billion per year in inflated prices; poisoned air, land, and water; corruption of government officials; and evaded taxes. Price fixing alone is believed to cost consumers $60 billion a year (*U.S. News & World Report*, 1982).

The Judiciary Subcommittee on Antitrust and Monopoly estimated that faulty goods, monopolistic practices, and other violations annually cost consumers between $174 and $231 billion. The Department of Justice estimated the total annual loss to taxpayers from reported and unreported violations of federal regulations by corporations at $10 to $20 billion, and the Internal Revenue Service estimated that about $1.2 billion goes unreported each year in corporate tax returns (Shostak, 1974).

Kidnapping—By Computer

At age 24 and with 6 arrests on his record, Masatoshi Tashiro was one of Tokyo's petty thieves, no more, no less. It wasn't likely that he would commit the Crime of the Century. Not of *this* century, anyway. But Tashiro did make himself a harbinger of the way criminals will work, and (to his chagrin) of the way criminals will be foiled, in the electronic world of the year 2000. He did it by computerizing the ancient crime of kidnapping, a centuries-old felony.

It started with a cash-card account, which he opened under a false name and address at a major Tokyo bank. With this magnetically coded card, depositors could make withdrawals as large as $1,000 at a time from any of 348 automatic cash dispensers located throughout Japan. Tashiro made several test withdrawals. By phoning the bank afterward, he determined that it took the computer system at least 20 minutes to tell the bank which cash dispenser station he had used. That crucial lag would be his getaway time.

Tashiro chose as his victim the four-month-old daughter of a well-known Japanese movie actor. The abduction itself was conventional—a break-in and escape while the family slept—but the ransom demand was brilliantly original. The parents were to deposit $16,500 in Tashiro's cash-card account; he gave them the account number and the false name as calmly as if he were making a real-estate deal.

His reasoning quickly became apparent to the police. They might be able to cover 348 cash dispenser stations, but they would not know the one from which the kidnapper was operating until the computer told them so at least 20 minutes too late. Under the circumstances, the missing child's parents had little choice except to deposit the ransom money. First, though, the police made a countermove: they had the bank computer reprogrammed. Its new instructions were to trace any withdrawal from the ransom account instantly. When Tashiro made his first withdrawal, word flashed immediately to the central computer and from there, by radio, back to a stakeout team. The kidnapper was arrested as he strolled out of the dispenser station with the card and the cash in his hands. Shortly afterward, police recovered the missing baby from his home.

R. Coniff, 21st century crime-stoppers. *Science Digest* 90 (1982): 61. Reproduced by permission of the author and publisher.

Extent of Corporate Crime In the last 10 years 115 of America's 500 largest corporations have been convicted of at least one major crime or have paid civil penalties for serious misbehavior.

The extent of violations by corporations has been revealed by many government investigative agencies and committees on both a state and federal level. These agencies have found violations in banking institutions; stock exchange operations; and railroad, oil, food, and drug industries. In addition, investigations have uncovered widespread corporate domestic and foreign payoffs and illegal political contributions.

Reports filed with the Securities and Exchange Commission (SEC) by the nation's 25 largest corporations show that 7 firms have been convicted of, or have pled *nolo contendere* (no contest) to, at least one crime since 1976, and 7 more have been forced into settlements of major noncriminal charges—which totals 56 percent of the proportion of top firms linked to some form of serious misbehavior. Further, during the 10 years between 1971 and 1980, at least 2,690 corporations of all sizes were convicted of federal criminal offenses (*U.S. News & World Report,* 1982).

In a study conducted by *Fortune* magazine, Ross (1980) found that 117 of the 1,043 companies surveyed had been involved in at least one major offense between 1970 and 1980. Of the 188 citations by these companies, there were 98 antitrust violations; 28 cases of kickbacks, bribery, or illegal rebates; 21 instances of illegal political contributions; 11 cases of fraud; and 5 cases of tax evasion. An official with the SEC reported to the Senate Judiciary Committee that (as of 1977) more than 350 public corporations had made illegal or questionable payments in the conduct of their foreign or domestic business (Payne, 1978).

The most comprehensive, scientific study of large-scale corporate crime was conducted by Marshall Clinard and his colleagues at the University of Wisconsin at Madison (Clinard, 1979; Clinard and Yeager, 1980). The study focused on 477 of our nation's largest publicly owned manufacturing corporations, with sales in 1975 ranging from $300 million to more than $45 billion. The study examined violations that were identified in legal actions taken by 25 federal regulatory agencies between 1975 and 1976. These included unfair trade practices (e.g., price fixing), manufacturing violations relating to product safety, environmental violations (e.g., air and water pollution), labor violations (e.g., discriminatory hiring practices), and occupational safety and health hazards.

Clinard found that more than 60 percent of these corporations had at least one enforcement action initiated against them between 1975 and 1976. The fact that 40 percent of the corporations in his study had no legal action taken against them during this period suggests, according to Clinard, that illegal behavior is not necessarily required in order to compete successfully in the world of giant corporations. On the other hand, 42 percent of these companies were charged with multiple violations. Moreover, it is important to note that while a single conventional crime violation is not viewed as particularly significant in the instance of corporate crime, a single violation may involve millions of dollars and can affect the lives of thousands of citizens.

Antitrust Violations   Beginning with the passage of the Sherman Antitrust Act in 1890, the federal government has sought to bring under legal sanction a broad spectrum of inimical trade practices, ranging from monopoly formation to price fixing. These business crimes are known in the aggregate as **antitrust violations.** The three principal types of antitrust violations are boycott, price collusion, and agreement to refrain from competition. In addition to these violations are practices which, if not actually illegal, are at the very least unethical.

Boycott, or restraint of trade, has been defined as "a conspiracy or confederation to prevent the carrying on of business, or to injure the business of anyone by preventing potential customers from doing business with him or employing the representatives of said business, by threats, intimidation, coercion, etc." (*Black's Law Dictionary,* 1979, p. 234). For example, Store A advertises and sells a name-brand recliner for a certain price. Store B obtains the style number and advertises the same item at a considerably lower price. Store A, which has been doing a substantial business with the name-brand recliner firm for quite some time, informs the name-brand company that unless they discontinue shipments to Store B, all of the Store A accounts will be terminated. The name-brand company agrees, resulting in an antitrust violation.

Price collusion or price fixing can take many forms and may occur at almost any level of retail transactions. A fairly common method by which price fixing is accomplished occurs in the setting of prices for new merchandise. A retail store may set a price on an item that is as much as 150 percent higher than the wholesale price for which the item was purchased. Even when advertised at an alleged "lower sale price," the item may cost the customer nearly twice as much as the store paid for it.

The third major violation of antitrust statutes comes under the heading of "agreement to refrain from competition." On a large scale, this would include monopolies, mergers, and cartels. By vertical integration, a large corporation virtually swallows up competing dealers. Another merger method occurs through **diversification.** In this way an already complex corporate structure creates new business under its control in new areas. An example might be a franchise operation which primarily retails fast food preparations. After diversification it might also produce brand-name supplies, T-shirts, and decals which advertise the products.

Manufacturing Violations: Faulty Products   A major consumer concern is the safety of the products we purchase. The hazards resulting from unsafe products range from minor, temporary injuries to injuries involving permanent damage and death. Three government agencies are responsible for enforcing regulations involving the manufacture of safe products. The Consumer Product Safety Commission is responsible for removing unsafe products from the market and responding to reports of violations including those involving electric shock hazards, chemical, and environmental hazards, and fire and thermo burn hazards. The National Highway Traffic Safety Administration is responsible for, among other things, making sure that once defects in automobiles are discovered manufacturers correct them. The Food and Drug Administration is required to protect the public from unsafe, unsanitary, or falsely labeled food, drugs, cosmetics, or therapeutic devices (Clinard, 1979). The potential dangers associated with unsafe products and the apparent indifference of some corporate officials to these dangers are illustrated in the Ford Motor Company's handling of the Pinto.

Con Games   Con games, another category of economic crime, involve white-collar crime as a business or as the central activity of a business. These types of offenses are the easiest for the public to understand because they deal with the business of cheating. It is impossible to find any justification for a swindler who expects to reap a

The Case Against the Ford Pinto

In the early 1970s, in order to compete with the Volkswagen in the lucrative small-car market, Ford Motor Company rushed through the design and production of the Pinto. According to Dowie (1979), the company knowingly produced and marketed a vehicle which tests had shown possessed a dangerous flaw—a design defect in the placement of the gas tank that ruptured and burned when the Pinto was struck in the rear end. Ford calculated that the cost of an $11 safety improvement, which would have made the Pinto less likely to catch fire in a rear end collision, was more expensive than paying for the deaths ($200,000 per death) and injuries ($67,000 per burn injury) resulting from the failure to improve the safety of the vehicle.

By 1980, Ford had paid out millions of dollars in claims resulting from death and injury suits. Then in January of that year, Ford Motor Company was put on trial in Indiana on charges of three counts of reckless homicide which carries a maximum penalty of $30,000 under an Indiana law. The case against Ford stemmed from an incident in which three young women were killed when their Ford Pinto exploded into flames after being struck in the rear by a van. The prosecution charged that the company had manufactured a dangerous gas tank system, had known it to be defective, and had failed to correct it or to provide car owners with proper warning of its danger. This case is unique because it represents the first time in our history that a corporation had been criminally prosecuted for producing a faulty product. The prosecution was able to charge Ford with reckless homicide as a result of a 1977 revision of the Indiana Penal Code that permits a corporation to be viewed as a person for purposes of bringing criminal charges (Subcommittee on Crime, May 1980). In March 1980, after a two-month trial, the jury found Ford not guilty.

Despite Ford's acquittal, it was felt by many observers that the case had a positive impact because it made companies more aware of their responsibilities, not only in the automobile industry, but in other industries, as well. In effect, the Pinto case serves as a warning to corporations of the potential criminal liability that may arise in matters of product safety. As one expert noted, corporations will be more likely to examine closely the costs versus the benefits of safety and manufacturers may more quickly recall defective vehicles and voluntarily upgrade safety standards (Clinard, 1980).

large return while providing little or nothing to his victims. In some instances, these schemes may come very close to simply picking the victim's pocket, as is the case with the street pigeon drop that victimizes any gullible passerby. In other cases, such as pyramid schemes, the con games are more complex and involve well-orchestrated presentations which prey on individuals who are looking to be self-employed and/or to get rich quick. These schemes not only victimize individuals but business and government as well. Every year the government is defrauded by individuals who submit fabricated W-2 forms under assumed names and receive refunds to which they are not entitled. On the other hand, businesses lose many millions of dollars by selling merchandise on credit to bankruptcy fraud artists who buy or establish a business, obtain credit from manufacturers, then resell the merchandise they receive and disappear with the proceeds, leaving manufacturers with an empty, bankrupt shell.

Home Improvement Frauds   Home improvement or repair complaints are close to the top of the list of complaints received by consumer protection agencies in the United States (Nader, 1974). Frauds in this area are not only perpetrated with regard to the agreed-upon work but also involve deceptive financing arrangements. Among the most frequent complaints filed are phony bargain prices where no real bargain is offered, false claims on products and guarantees, and promises of prizes or refunds for referring friends to the building contractor. Other complaints involve misrepresentation of interest charges in "low monthly installments," obtaining signatures on blank completion certificates before the transaction is actually completed, adding unauthorized charges to contracts that have already been signed, and even executing second mortgages without the full knowledge of the home owner.

Many home improvements are once-in-a-lifetime projects and the homeowner may have had no previous experience with the specific type of contractor. Hence, when the homeowner seeks to have work done, anyone calling himself or herself a contractor competes on an equal basis. Also, few people have any capability of determining what is a reasonable price for home improvements. When the average person shops for a car or a television set, he or she is able to inspect the finished product before making a choice and can shop around and compare prices of the various retailers. In contrast, home improvement projects involve work that is yet to be done. It is difficult to make price comparisons since the quality of workmanship and materials used can vary greatly. The typical homeowner is therefore vulnerable to:

1. Overcharging, if the contractor does the work at all;
2. An unsatisfactory job, where the contractor has quoted a low price in order to secure the commission and then has used the cheapest materials and slapdash work methods;
3. Outright loss, for example, in instances where extremely low bids are submitted because the contractor has no intentions of performing the work.

Offender Justifications, Public Perceptions, and Costs of Economic Crimes

One of the major problems in dealing with white-collar/economic crimes is that neither the offenders themselves nor the public in many instances views these acts as prosecutable offenses (Dinitz, 1980). Economic crimes involve behavior that occurs in what appears to be thoroughly legitimate situations (Edelhertz, 1982). For example, while it is legitimate to sell stocks, it is illegal to deliberately misrepresent what

The "Terrible Williamsons"

The Williamson Gang, numbering about five thousand, has been labeled by authorities as one of the most elusive and well-organized group of rip-off artists in this country (Hawkins, 1983). This group typically operates in older neighborhoods where residents are more likely to be elderly and widowed. Often the first contact is made by a young boy who is polite, well spoken, and cleancut. His pitch is that his daddy has some extra asphalt or roofing material left over from a nearby job and, therefore, can resurface their driveway or repair their roof for a very reasonable price.

For roof repairs and driveway coatings, gang members frequently use crankcase oil, aluminum paint, or gasoline. To further persuade their victims, gang members offer verbal guarantees and claims that the goop they apply will seal all leaks and cracks. However, with the first rainfall, the material they use is washed away. Termite inspection frauds follow a similar pattern: a potential victim will be approached with the story that they have just completed protecting a neighbor's house against termites and wouldn't he or she be interested in similar protection. In order to frighten victims into purchasing their termite eradication program, gang members frequently smuggle pieces of termite infested wood into the victim's home. The eradication program consists of using the same material that is used on the roof or the house's foundation.

The victims of these fraudulent home repair schemes are frequently retired, middle-class homeowners who, in many cases, have poor hearing and eyesight and are thus not able to understand or see what they are being offered. Further, due to their advancing age and physical condition, they are frequently unable to inspect the work done by this group after it is completed. It is not until later that they realize that they have been swindled and often they are too embarrassed to report these incidents to the police.

A less well-publicized activity of this gang involves buying substandard travel trailers in Indiana and then transporting them to other parts of the country such as Florida, Texas, or California for resale. The trailers are parked in a local trailer park, gas station, or motel parking lot with a for sale sign on them. Interested customers are told that the trailer must be sold due to unemployment, an emergency operation, a dying son, and the like. Buyers are told that the trailer is worth up to $15,000, but under the circumstances it will be sacrificed for $8,000 when in reality the trailer was probably purchased by the gang for only $5,000.

is being offered for sale. When a robber holds up someone on the street, his intent is clearly to deprive the person illegally of his or her money and other valuables. However, in the sale of misrepresented stocks, it is not obvious in most cases that the seller is trying to defraud the customer.

As Edelhertz (1978) notes, economic criminals tend to see themselves as doing things which are part of the regular course of doing business. The rationalizations they use to justify their behavior may fit one of the following categories:

1. Their acts do not bear any resemblance to street crimes.
2. The government does not understand the kinds of pressures under which businesses operate; otherwise, they would not pass laws that make it impossible to compete successfully in the marketplace.
3. Illegal acts are the result of "genuine need"—the only way capital can be obtained to stay in business.
4. "Everyone else is doing it, so why shouldn't I?"

The conventional view that members of the public do not consider white-collar violations as serious, in contrast to ordinary crimes, was summarized in the President's Commission on Law Enforcement and the Administration of Justice (1967): "The public tends to be indifferent to business crime or even to sympathize with offenders when they have been caught" (p. 48). This may have been an accurate assessment in 1967, but subsequent studies (Cullen, Link, and Polanzi, 1980; Gibbons, 1969; Schrager and Short, 1980; Wolfgang, 1980) clearly show that, rather than being indifferent to economic crimes, people are increasingly prone to view such offenses as more serious than those committed by conventional offenders. A recent *New York Times*/CBS poll (Clymen, 1985) showed that 55 percent of the public views corporate executives as dishonest. The same poll indicated that 85 percent of the public feels that corporate white-collar offenders get away with their crimes.

Estimates of the losses from economic crimes in this country range from $3 to $60 billion per year and depend upon the crimes that are included in the estimates as well as how the analysts project actual losses from the relatively small number of incidents which are detected. Edelhertz (1978) contends that regardless of the basis upon which these estimates are made it can be confidently stated that the monetary losses from frauds on government programs, consumer frauds, and procurement frauds "dwarf to insignificance direct monetary loss stemming from common crimes" (p. 6). The Joint Economic Committee of the United States Congress (1977) estimated that the cost to our economy from white-collar crime was $44 billion a year, in comparison to the costs of crimes against property such as robbery and breaking and entering, which were estimated at $4 billion annually. The broader social consequences of economic crime are even more damaging than the monetary costs to individual victims, to communities, to businesses, and to governments.

Conclusions

After having been almost neglected by the criminal justice system in the years since Sutherland coined the term white-collar crime in the 1930s, economic crime is receiving long-deferred attention. It is interesting to reflect on some of the possible reasons economic crimes have become a national issue in recent times. Consumer advocacy has undoubtedly been a powerful stimulus to raising public consciousness regarding economic crime. Complaints about the rudeness, stridency, and partisan zeal of groups such as "Nader's Raiders" can probably be taken as a testimonial to the effectiveness of their activities—and an indication that many of their barbs manage to hit the mark. Civil rights activism also seems to have played an important role in arousing indignation over gross disparities in the sentences handed out to poor minority persons convicted of conventional property crimes and middle-class or affluent whites convicted of white-collar crimes. Indeed, the ideological polarization that led to the emergence of radical criminology would appear to be one of the direct consequences of long-standing judicial inequity.

Ecology and environmental protection advocates have made substantial contributions toward increasing public awareness of economic crime. Ever since the offshore oil spill that blackened the beaches of Santa Barbara, California, organizations like the Sierra Club and Common Cause have brought unrelenting pressure to bear on the government for the passage of legislation, or the effective enforcement of existing legislation, intended to prevent further despoliation of irreplaceable natural resources. The major focus of their efforts has been the concept of corporate accountability.

Recent accusations of criminal practices against well-known firms such as General Electric, General Dynamics, E. F. Hutton, and the Bank of Boston, plus the conviction of such notables as Paul Thayer, former Deputy Secretary of Defense and member of the Reagan administration, and Jake Butcher, a prominent Tennessee financier and political figure, have turned the spotlight of publicity on economic crimes and those who commit them. As recently as the 1970s, prison terms for economic offenders, especially persons of high status, were extremely rare; today, judges show a greater willingness to impose prison sentences upon socially and politically prominent offenders. Members of the judiciary cite the need to deter others from perpetrating such crimes and to dispel the common view that the wealthy and powerful are immune from the harsh penalties inflicted on conventional offenders (Taylor, 1985).

SYNDICATED (ORGANIZED) CRIME

There is a great deal of confusion regarding the nature of organized crime. Some people tend to view organized crime as an Italian-dominated, cohesive, national organization (variously called the **Mafia,** the "mob," or La Cosa Nostra); others, including some criminologists, see the Mafia as largely a myth and organized crime as a loose, informal confederation of diverse groups of criminal organizations. A primary source of confusion is the indiscriminate use of the term *organized crime* to refer to criminal groups or organizations which share a few similarities but also exhibit major differences. Blakely, Goldstock, and Rogovin (1978) have distinguished the following three types of criminal organizations.

On the lowest level is a **venture,** which involves a group of offenders who have come together for a short period of time in order to carry out a single crime (e.g., the hijacking of a truck or the robbery of several retail stores). A **criminal enterprise** provides illicit goods and services on a regular basis (e.g., a narcotics wholesaler who produces heroin and has a crew that dilutes the drug and packages it for retail sale). These two categories of criminal activity are not organized crime unless the individuals involved have ties to a criminal syndicate.

An **organized crime syndicate,** on the highest level, is a criminal organization that governs relationships between individual enterprises, regulates prices of illegal goods and services, allocates territory, settles disputes, and offers protection from rival groups and from prosecution. There are two types of syndicates: those that operate on national or international levels and limit their criminal activity to a particular field of endeavor and those that engage in a variety of illegal and legal enterprises.

The distinctive features that make syndicated crime not only a greater threat than conventional criminal activity to our society but also more difficult to control through conventional law enforcement practices are highlighted by the following statement, which was formulated by crime authorities and experts at a conference held at Oyster Bay, New York, 1965. It defines organized crime as "A self-perpetuating continuing criminal conspiracy for power and profit using fear and corruption and seeking immunity from the law" (Salerno and Tompkins, 1969, p. 303).

Several elements of this definition are worthy of note. One of the factors that distinguishes syndicates from other types of criminal groups is that syndicates are "self-perpetuating"; that is, if any of the leaders die or are sent to prison, the organization continues to operate—in much the same way that a corporation such as General Motors would continue to function if its president were to die or be incapacitated. That syndicated crime is a "continuing criminal conspiracy" refers to the fact that syndicate members have agreed to operate their enterprises according to certain procedures in order to maximize profits and to minimize detection by law enforcement.

Finally, attention must be given to the role played by fear and corruption in syndicate operations. Corruption is essential to the successful functioning of both legal and illegal syndicate enterprises because it enables organized crime to provide illicit goods and services relatively free from the risks incurred by conventional offenders who violate the law. Also, it is used in legal endeavors to gain contracts, to operate businesses in violation of licensing laws and other regulations, and to cover up the use of inferior material in construction projects or in products provided to both government and industry. Syndicates reach government at all levels, from patrol officers on the street to federal and state judges and legislators. The service provided by each functionary depends upon his or her position and influence while the compensation he or she receives is based on his or her position and the importance that the syndicate attaches to the services performed.

Fear and, in some cases, violence are two other methods employed by the syndicate to ensure the success of its operations. Threats of bodily harm and destruction of property are used to eliminate competition, to ensure the payment of overdue loans, to dissuade witnesses from giving damaging testimony, to assure cooperation, and to persuade businesspeople of the need for "protection." More specifically, threats as well as the actual commission of such offenses as arson, assault, coercion, mayhem, sabotage, and even murder may be used to gain control of a city's garbage collection business, to take over independent bookmakers, and to dominate the restaurant supply industry in a particular area. While the more established Italian syndicates are less likely to use violence because it draws more attention to their operation, this is not the case among some of the newer syndicates such as the biker groups and Colombians ("cocaine cowboys").

History and Development of Syndicated Crime in the United States

Early journalistic accounts of organized crime focused exclusively on Italian criminal groups and suggested that these syndicates represented U.S. branch offices of the Sicilian Mafia. While some members of the Sicilian Mafia did become associated with Italian criminal groups when they migrated to the United States in the late 1800s and early 1900s, conditions in the urban areas where U.S. syndicates flourished were as unsuited to the transplantation of groups from rural Sicily as New York City would have been to a tribe of American Indians from the western plains. This view also fails to recognize that syndicated crime in the United States has not been limited to those of Italian or Sicilian origin. A closer look at the history of syndicated crime indicates that its origins and development can be traced to social conditions that were inherent in American society.

The roots of syndicated crime extend far back in our history to the street gangs of hoodlums that appeared in New York City as early as the late 1700s. The Irish were the first immigrant group to become involved in organized crime on a large scale. After the Irish, the Jews dominated organized crime for a rather brief period, and the names of Arnold Rothstein, Louis "Lepke" Buchalter, and "Gurrah" Shapiro figured prominently in gambling and labor racketeering for about a decade. But most of the Jews moved quickly into the world of business and finance and were replaced by the Italians and Sicilians.

Operations on this scale required huge sums of money and necessitated the establishment of appropriate connections with government agents. More important, the struggle for control of the alcohol supply resulted in tight interstate and international alliances. The major figures in organized crime developed national objectives, the growth of which initiated the development of a coast-to-coast network to bring together the various ethnic groups. See Figure 6.1 for the location of major syndicate operations in the United States.

The current structure and organization of the Italian criminal syndicate (referred to in official Department of Justice communications as **La Cosa Nostra,** or abbreviated **LCN**) emerged from a bloody struggle in 1930 and 1931 known as the "Castellamarese War" which started between Italian and Sicilian gangs in New York and eventually spread throughout the country. After the fighting ended, a meeting was held among the leaders of all of the syndicates at which it was decided to form a national cartel. In a later meeting held at the Waldorf Astoria Hotel in New York City in 1934, the non-Italians—including such groups as the Bugs and Meyer Mob, the Cleveland syndicate headed by Moe Dalitz—became part of the cartel. In light of the involvement of these other groups, there may be some question regarding the applicability of the label *La Cosa Nostra* ("this thing of ours"), which is often used to refer to this collectivity. La Cosa Nostra only applies to the inner core of organized

Figure 6.1 Location of major syndicate operations in the United States. (*Source:* R. Salerno and J. S. Tompkins, *The Crime Federation.* New York: Doubleday and Company, 1969, p. 167. Reproduced by permission of the authors and publisher.)

158

crime which is composed of those of Italian parentage who are members of the Italian syndicate. Even the term *La Cosa Nostra,* which was popularized by the testimony of Joseph Valachi before the McClellan Committee, is not a correct label for the Italian criminal syndicate because it is only used in the New York metropolitan area. In New England the Italian syndicate is referred to as "the Office," in Chicago it is called "the Outfit," and in Buffalo it is known as "the Arm" (Messick, 1971).

Ethnic Succession   Bell (1963) and Ianni (1973) have suggested that the development of syndicated crime in the United States can be traced to the process of ethnic succession, whereby each new immigrant group used organized crime as the means of acquiring wealth and power before gaining a foothold in legitimate business. In other words, as Bell (1963) expressed the notion, each immigrant group handed to the next a "queer ladder of social mobility" for which organized crime was the first couple of rungs.

Lupsha (1981) offers a different and more plausible interpretation of this process. He suggests that involvement in syndicated crime does not result from limited choice or opportunities for social mobility on the part of particular ethnic group members, but rather represents a rational choice based on their attachment to a certain configuration of perverse values which are firmly rooted in American culture. For "straights," the path to success involves a combination of education and hard work. For "wise guys" (lower-ranking syndicate members), the way to success is through criminal pursuits. Their goal is an "easy buck"; hard work and education are for "suckers" and the stupid. For these individuals, the choice to pursue success initially through the illicit opportunity structure is a decision which is reinforced by their experience, peers, and capacity for violence. "Wise guys" are no more deprived than those who decide to be "straight" and pursue success by climbing the narrower and more crowded legitimate social mobility ladder.

The ethnic succession thesis also contends that when an ethnic or racial group acquires wealth and status through criminal pursuits, it relinquishes its control of illicit activities to a newer immigrant group lower on the status ladder. That is, the syndicate criminal "goes legit": he moves into a reputable sector of the economy, he adopts a life-style of respectability, and his children are reared in circumstances that provide a solid identification with conventional middle-class values. All of these consequences flow naturally from the assumption that the syndicate criminal's desire for respectability is so intense that he is willing to give up his lucrative illicit connections and interests in order to achieve it. This is, to say the least, a rather naive view. Bell and others who have advanced the ethnic succession thesis appear to have ignored the ancient Latin dictum: *Pecunia non olet* ("money does not stink"). Money can buy respectability. For one thing, the major syndicates are structured in such a way that the upper echelon members are insulated from direct contact with their illegal operations and enterprises. In addition, syndicate members long ago recognized the advantages of having legitimate business fronts in order to show a source of income and payment of taxes, thereby avoiding prosecution for income tax evasion.

Contemporary Syndicates

Italian-dominated Syndicates   The crime federation which encompasses the Italian-dominated syndicates (or LCN groups) is the leading criminal organization in the United States because of its wealth, status, power, influence, and national scope. The structure of this organization has not changed essentially since the 1930s; today it consists of 25 "families" which are based for the most part in the Northeast and Midwest but have members and operations in most states (see Figure 6.2). A "family" is organized as a hierarchy, which shields those at the top from direct involvement in criminal activities. This feature along with a code that requires loyalty and

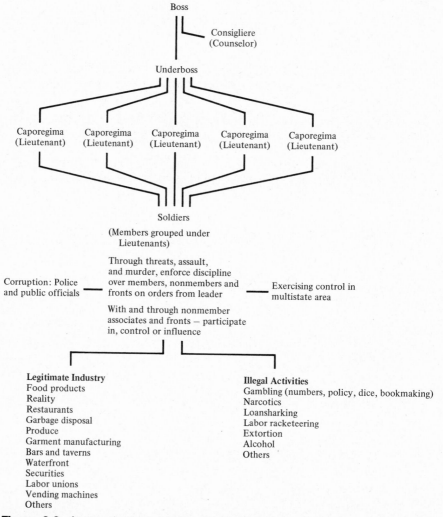

Figure 6.2   An organized crime family. (*Source:* President's Commission on Law Enforcement and Administration of Justice. *Task Force Report: Organized Crime.* Washington, D.C.: U.S. Government Printing Office, 1967, p. 9.)

silence (*omertá*) and is backed up by threats and violence, have made it difficult in the past to use traditional law enforcement methods to convict syndicate members, especially those in high positions.

Each family is headed by a boss (**capo**), whose authority is absolute and unquestioned within his group, area, or any extended territory under his influence which does not conflict with other syndicates. The boss is assisted by an underboss (**sottocapo**), or vice president, whose responsibilities include relaying instructions and collecting information. On the same level as the underboss is the **buffer,** who functions in much the same manner as an administrative assistant; therefore his title does not appear on the organizational chart. He is the boss's aide and may also on occasion serve as his driver, messenger, bodyguard, or counselor. The buffer provides insulation for the boss by serving as a go-between to whom money, commands, information, and complaints can flow back and forth from the lower ranks to the boss.

The boss is also advised by a counselor (**consigliere**), an elder statesman who is partially or fully retired. Below the underboss are the lieutenants and unit bosses who are usually responsible for a unit of approximately ten "soldiers," often referred to as "bottom men," "wise guys," or "made members." "Made men" may operate illicit enterprises for their bosses on a commission basis or they may "own their own business" and pay a percentage to the boss for the right to operate. Partnerships between two or more soldiers and men higher up in the command structure are quite common. "Made men" frequently have nonmember associates who work within given enterprises. While LCN members are all males of Italian origin, their associates may be of any race, creed, or national origin. It is estimated that there are two thousand initiated members. But the FBI indicates that the full extent of this multiservice syndicate cannot be appreciated unless we multiply this number by 10 to take into account the associates who are fully affiliated in their criminal enterprise (Webster, 1983).

The syndicates are governed by a commission which, over the years, has consisted of 9 to 12 bosses of the most powerful local syndicates. The main functions of the commission are to settle disputes between members and bosses and between families, to provide advice, to approve new bosses, and to establish overall policies. It should be emphasized that the commission does not attempt to run the day-to-day operations of the syndicates, but only tries to maintain harmony among the families.

Over the years, syndicate members have become more heavily involved in legitimate business. Today, syndicate members own or have interests in companies involved in garbage and waste disposal, dairy products, meat processing, bagels, kosher meat provision, construction, banking, and the lunch wagon industry. There are few profitable markets that syndicate members have failed to infiltrate. They have also centered attention on complex crime schemes and endeavors requiring involved political corruption arrangements (e.g., the theft of securities from brokerage houses and their disposal through a variety of legitimate outlets). Of course, these syndicates continue to be heavily involved in illicit activities, including gambling, loansharking, drugs, labor racketeering, and pornography.

In recent years, however, there have been changes in the extent to which the LCN has been able to dominate illegal activities in various racial or ethnic areas.

Ethnic awareness, especially in the black community, together with recognition of the huge profits to be made from illicit drugs, provided the impetus for the development of syndicates among blacks, Puerto Ricans, and Cubans. These syndicates have taken control of criminal enterprises in their respective areas. In some instances this has been a peaceful process, with the Italians leasing or franchising such operations as numbers (policy) to black or Puerto Rican groups. (The numbers game is a daily illegal lottery in which a player bets small sums on certain numbers or combinations of numbers derived from some readily accessible source in the newspaper, such as the U.S. Treasury balance or the payoffs at the race track.) In these arrangements the Italian family provides financing and protection, while the blacks and Puerto Ricans run the operation. In other cases the LCN families have been pushed out by blacks and Puerto Ricans who seek a monopoly in their own area.

Emerging Organized Crime Groups

At hearings on organized crime held by the Senate Committee on the Judiciary, FBI Director Webster (1983) gave testimony on the growth and development of new organized crime groups that vary according to ethnic and racial background, geographic area, and the types of illegal activities in which they are engaged. Like the LCN, these groups protect themselves with vows of secrecy and loyalty and enforce strict discipline by means of threats and violence. As relative newcomers, such groups have not achieved the wealth, power, status, or influence of the LCN groups—a situation which, as Rogovin (1983) has suggested, provides the authorities with "a unique opportunity to inhibit their growth" before they acquire the power and sophistication of the LCN.

Outlaw Bikers   Second only to LCN groups in terms of their increasing sophistication and importance within the constellation of organized crime groups are the *outlaw bikers* (Lazin, 1983; Rogovin, 1983). Outlaw motorcycle gangs originated in California after World War II among restless veterans who found it difficult to adjust to peacetime conditions and sought comrades with an interest in excitement and similar types of recreation (Katz, 1983). These clubs gained national notoriety when the Hell's Angels Motorcycle Club was organized in 1950. The activities of their members were glorified by such movies as *The Wild Ones,* which not only helped create a gang mystique but also encouraged young males who were dissatisfied with a traditional life-style to seek membership in these groups.

The 1950s and 1960s saw the continued development of the Hell's Angels and the emergence of the Pagans in 1954, the Outlaws in 1959, and the Bandidos in 1966 (McGuire, 1983). During this time, major gangs pushed aside or absorbed smaller ones and roaming chapter members, called "nomads," established new chapters across the country. Gang alliances were made, formal group structures were established, and leaders evolved within these groups. Although these gangs were capable of significant criminal activity during this period, their lawbreaking lacked a central goal or purpose; although they were dangerous, their outbreaks of violence around the country were isolated and sporadic.

Outlaw bikers became involved in the 1960s drug subculture and progressed from consumers of drugs to manufacturers and suppliers. By the 1970s, these gangs had changed from antisocial enclaves to multiservice syndicates and had taken their place as major organizations in the illicit drug trafficking business, particularly meth-amphetamines, from which they are making millions. Although drug trafficking is the principal activity of these groups, they are also involved in a variety of other criminal and legal enterprises.

The four major outlaw biker gangs in the United States—Hell's Angels, Out-laws, Pagans, and Bandidos—have an estimated total membership of more than 4,000, with 40,000 associates (Katz, 1983). Table 6.1 provides a summary of the major identifying information for each of these groups. In addition to these gangs, there are 800 to 1,000 smaller gangs operating in various parts of the country, 25 of which have chapters in 5 or more states.

Despite their uncouth manners and deceptively free-wheeling appearance, bi-ker gangs are highly structured organizations with national officers, policy-making boards, written constitutions, and strict procedures for admission and expulsion of members. They are most emphatically not composed of juvenile delinquents: more than half of these gang members are over 35 years old and their presidents range in age from 38 to 44 years. They possess production arsenals and sophisticated weap-onry that includes plastic explosives, remote control detonators, antitank rockets, and the latest in state-of-the-art automatic rifles and pistols; and there is evidence that they are marketing these weapons.

Gangs such as Hell's Angels have developed intelligence capabilities which compare with those of law enforcement. They have been able to place only women informants in courthouses, police department criminal records and communication sections, the state motor vehicle administration, and even the telephone company (Katz, 1983). This has provided them with advanced information on search warrants, wire taps, arrest warrants, and raids, as well as with blank drivers' licenses for phony identification (Jackson, 1983). These gangs have also developed the capability to detect the presence of electronic surveillance equipment and they use scanners to monitor police frequencies in the areas in which they operate (Katz, 1983). There is also some indication that these groups are beginning to store intelligence information on computer tapes (Higgins, 1983).

Table 6.1 MAJOR OUTLAW BIKER GROUPS

Biker group	Headquarters of "mother chapter"	Estimated membership	Principal operating area
Hell's Angels	Oakland, CA	500–2000	West Coast and abroad
Outlaws	Chicago, IL	1–2000	Southeast, South, and Canada
Pagans	*a	450–800	East Coast
Bandidos	Corpus Christi, TX	500–1000	Southwest, South

aUnlike the other groups, the Pagans do not designate a specific chapter as their headquarters. Instead, they have a president and vice-president and a group of approximately 20 of the most powerful and respected members who function as "area presidents" and comprise their "mother chapter."

Source: Based on material presented in testimony to the U.S. Congress, *U.S. Senate Permanent Subcommittee on Investigations,* 1983.

The most disturbing feature of the biker gangs is their propensity for violence. Initiation into the Hell's Angels is reputed to require that the new member kill someone—"roll their bones"—and failure to fulfill this requirement results in the death of the neophyte member. A former Hell's Angels member told the Senate Committee of incidents in which people wearing phony Hell's Angels tattoos on their arms had them removed by knife—along with the arm. An ex-Pagan testified that a gang member who had crossed other Pagans was welded inside an oil drum which was then shot full of holes and tossed into the bay. Unlike the LCN, outlaw bikers do not draw the line at carrying out murderous attacks on police officers (Ellis, 1983).

There are many indications of growing associations, as well as some conflicts, between LCN families and biker groups. The LCN has used biker gang members as "muscle" in the collection of loanshark debts and the intimidation of trade unions, as contract killers ("hit men"), and as bodyguards. One former Pagan (Jackson, 1983) testified that his group worked closely with an associate of a New York LCN family in operations involving counterfeiting, extortion, stolen automobiles, and in a variety of legitimate business enterprises. As a Washington law enforcement official put it these gangs have not successfully imitated Marlon Brando's change in roles from outlaw motorcycle rider in *The Wild Ones* to LCN Don in *The Godfather,* but they are certainly moving in that direction (McGuire, 1983, p. 385).

Other Organized Crime Groups   In addition to outlaw biker gangs, law enforcement officials have identified a number of other groups that have the potentiality or ability to develop as competitors in organized crime. These include: Russian emigres; the "Israeli Mafia"; Chinese triads (tongs); the Japanese Yakuza; Hispanic syndicates (Colombians, Puerto Ricans, Cubans, Mexicans); American black syndicates; and the Jamaican-based Rastafarians, a quasi-religious cult (U.S. Senate Committee on the Judiciary, 1983).

The Latin or Hispanic syndicates resemble the LCN with respect to their emphasis on kinship ties. Until the 1970s, Cubans were major importers of cocaine, marijuana, and counterfeit quaaludes, which they obtained from Colombian syndicates. By the mid-1970s, the Colombians had become dissatisfied with merely serving as suppliers for the Cubans, who not only made most of the money but also short-changed them. Moreover, as one undercover agent put it, "for $10 million a month, who needs the Cubans?" (Kalwary, 1979). The Colombians imported young enforcers to eliminate any Cuban opposition to their right to import and distribute in the United States.

There are 17 Colombian crime families who collectively control the cocaine trafficking in this country (Florida Governor's Council on Organized Crime). It is appropriate to call these groups families because its members are typically related by blood. They appear to be well-organized and sophisticated groups which is attested to by the fact that they have continued their criminal activity even though, in some instances, their leaders have been incarcerated.

Colombian drug dealers have been dubbed "cocaine cowboys" by the police because of their penchant for daring daylight shootouts involving the use of automatic weapons and heavily armored "war wagons" (Smith, 1979). Violence is not limited to attacks upon the Cubans: there is fighting among the various Colombian families involved in the drug trade. Thus, like the bikers, these groups display little concern for anyone who gets in their way. By 1981, Miami became known as Dodge City because of homicides resulting from Old West–type shootouts (Smith, 1983).

American blacks have been involved in organized crime activities since before the turn of the century. In some cities, blacks were able to control gambling and prostitution in their areas until some of the more powerful bootlegging and LCN syndicates recognized the potential of these enterprises and took over control of their operations (Haller, 1979; Ianni, 1974).

Blacks have always been involved with the LCN as lower echelon employees in gambling, as numbers runners, and as pushers in drug trafficking. According to Salerno and Thompkins (1969), some blacks had risen to the junior partner level in syndicate enterprises by the 1960s in cities like Buffalo, Chicago, and Detroit. During the Vietnam war, black syndicates developed their own southeast Asian pipelines for the importation of heroin. Thus, these syndicates have become major drug enterprises capable of importing, processing, cutting, and distributing drugs (Abadinsky, 1981). The growth of these groups into structured criminal organizations with substantial financial assets and political contacts necessitates that they be watched closely by law enforcement agents and, if possible, kept from developing into major crime syndicates by means of forceful prosecution.

Syndicate Enterprises

At the end of the nineteenth century, most of the money acquired by the American underworld was gained through extortion, blackmail, and dock racketeering. By the 1920s, the chief source of income had changed to bootlegging, which supplied organized crime with the funds and expertise to operate multimillion-dollar enterprises (Bequai, 1979). Today, it is estimated that organized crime has invested more than $20 billion in from 15,000 to 50,000 business establishments in the United States (Kaplan and Kessler, 1976). The scope of penetration into the legitimate business sector by organized crime has confronted the American public with a new fact of everyday life: "If we buy clothes, purchase imported goods, eat at restaurants with linen napkins, shop in stores that use private garbage services, gamble in casinos, invest in high-flying stocks, have an itch for dirty books, can't start the day without a fresh bagel or finish it without a piece of pizza, it is likely that organized criminals are involved to some extent in providing our goods and services—for which we have to pay higher prices than are necessary" (Thio, 1983, p. 392).

For a long time the principal revenue soruce for syndicated crime was gambling, with an annual take estimated in billions of dollars. Other lucrative activities included prostitution, pornography, loansharking, bankruptcy fraud, and labor racketeering. At present, drug trafficking is the primary activity and source of income for new emerging syndicates, and there are some indications that drug trade may be replacing gambling as the main source of income for some LCN syndicates, as well. Former Attorney General William French Smith (1983) claims that illicit drug sales in the United States in 1982 totaled $79 billion—a sum that is approximately equal to the combined profits reported that same year by the five hundred largest industrial corporations in the country. In the same way that Prohibition produced the funding base for the LCN, drug money serves to provide the financial base for emerging multiservice criminal syndicates. And in the same way that the demand for illegal beverage alcohol resulted in coalitions among groups involved in its manufacture, distribution, and sale, the demand for illicit drugs has spawned coalitions among groups in the United States and other countries to handle the volume of drug traffic.

✳ POLITICAL CRIMES

In a remarkable book entitled *Political Crime,* which was published in 1898, a French jurist named Louis Proal (1973) distinguished between crimes against the government such as treason, insurrection, and rebellion, and crimes "perpetrated by governments for alleged reasons of state, and by politicians for alleged reasons of expediency or for political advantage" (pp. xvii–xviii). The book provides detailed coverage of the latter type of crimes and deals with such topics as electoral corruption, the corruption of law and justice by politics, corruption of public morals, and "political spoliation."

After 75 years of neglect by criminology, which Edward Sagarin in his introduction to the reprint edition (1973) of Judge Proal's book calls "astonishing and, at the same time, inevitable," criminologists have rediscovered political crime as a legitimate and significant topic for systematic inquiry. Until recently, the term *political crime* connoted the kinds of traditional offenses against established government as those which Proal identified in his first category above. In the post-Watergate period, interest among criminologists in political criminality has been increasingly directed toward Proal's second category—crimes committed by agents of government against individuals, groups, organizations, and the general public. While Schafer's (1974) assertion that political criminality is "the most undernourished area of sociology and criminology" (p. 8) is still qualifiedly true, some important first steps have been taken to absorb political crimes and their study into mainstream criminological research and theory. We shall refer to these efforts in the discussion that follows.

Typologies of Political Crime

Roebuck and Weeber (1978) have delineated seven categories or specific types of political crimes: (1) domestic intervention by government (e.g., Watergate, the FBI campaign against Dr. Martin Luther King); (2) foreign intervention by government (e.g., the Vietnam war, CIA intervention in Chile); (3) intervention against the government (e.g., the Weathermen faction of the Students for a Democratic Society, the Symbionese Liberation Army); (4) domestic surveillance (e.g., FBI wiretaps and bugging, surveillance by the Internal Revenue Service); (5) domestic confrontation (e.g., Kent State, the suppression of the Attica insurrection); (6) evasion and collusion by the government (e.g., Kennedy's denial of the Bay of Pigs incursion, the Nixon administration's cover-up of the Watergate break-in); and (7) evasion and collusion against government (e.g., income tax evasion, military draft resistance, military desertion).

Each of these major types of political crime is examined within the framework of four dimensions of study: action patterns, goal of the offender(s), legal status of the offense, and the nature of the offense. Action patterns, which the authors consider the most important part of the typology, comprise illegal actions undertaken either to maintain and enhance the existing economic and political power structure or to change the existing structure of economic and political power.

Another approach to the construction of a typology of political criminal behavior is offered by Clinard and Quinney (1973), who distinguish between crimes against the government and crimes by agents of government. The former consists of attempts to "protest, express beliefs about, or alter in some way" the social structure—by which is meant the economic and political power structure that Roebuck and Weeber identify in their analysis. Crimes against government span a wide range of behavior that includes treason, sedition, sabotage, assassination, violation of military draft regulations, civil rights violations, student protests, violations resulting from the advocacy of "radical" ideas and actions, and refusal to conform to certain laws because of religious beliefs.

The second category, crimes committed by agents of government, is divided into (1) "violations of the civil liberties and rights of the citizens, as in the violation of constitutional guarantees and civil rights legislation by various government officials; (2) criminal acts committed in the course of enforcing the laws of the state, as in the example of assault and murder by police and prison guards; (3) violations of higher laws by governments, particularly the violation of the international laws of warfare" (p. 154).

The above categories of political crime are examined within a schema that includes legal aspects of selected offenses, group support of criminal behavior, correspondence between criminal and legitimate behavior, societal reaction and legal processing, and criminal career of the offender.

There are two points which need to be made with regard to political crimes. First, ordinary crimes can be invested with political meaning and used as symbolic means of expressing dissent toward the existing political structure. Political dissent which leads to crimes against the government can be viewed as *principled deviance,* according to Clinard and Quinney, because it often represents deliberate law violation for the purpose of demonstrating the unfairness of a given law. This can be an isolated individual act, of course, but it is more likely to be a group process. As we shall see when we examine the phenomenon of terrorism, both individual and group actions have been employed as expressions of dissent.

Second, the distinctions between political crimes and other, more conventional kinds of criminal activity are easily blurred when selected legal codes are applied punitively for politically motivated social control. As Roebuck and Weeber (1978) observe, "There may be nothing inherently illegal in an act; but the actor is criminalized when persons in power attach the illegal label to his behavior" (p. 20). Thus, political dissenters may be arrested for disorderly conduct, trespassing, parading without a permit, or violations of fire ordinances.

Terrorism

The kind of political crime that has received the most attention from the media, if not from criminologists, falls under the popular heading of terrorism. **Terrorism** and

terrorist are terms of limited usefulness, at best, and are prone to considerable confusion. Terrorism comprises both violent acts and threats of violence; it lumps together acts committed by criminals, psychotics, self-proclaimed patriots, and others with extreme ideological convictions; it makes no distinctions between acts carried out by individuals, groups, or even by governments. It may encompass the capture of an airliner and its passengers, the explosion of a bomb in a crowded shopping center, the murder of a prominent person or government official, and the seizure of a public building and its occupants as hostages. These and similar actions are done with the explicit objective of focusing attention on a cause or grievance; and to accomplish this aim, little heed is given to the victims of terrorist acts. They may be persons carefully selected according to plan or innocents unfortunate enough to be caught in the path of random violence.

According to one assessment (Anable, 1976), there were nearly 700 incidents of international terrorism between 1968 and 1975, accounting for 700 dead and 1,700 injured. This toll is dwarfed by the fighting in Lebanon or in Northern Ireland, and is almost trivial in comparison with the losses in an industrial society from accidents or crime. As we have already seen, the death toll from criminal homicide in the United States in 1978 topped 19,000. The total dollar loss, in terms of ransom payments and airplanes blown up or burned, is less than the annual loss in this country from shoplifting.

The consequences of these actions, however, are anything but trivial. Incidents that directly affect only a small number of people are given psychological impact by the perverse but skilled use of violence and terror, whose shock waves then reach millions. Terrorist actions prompt costly and sometimes disruptive security precautions. In some countries they lead to repressive retaliation and the erosion of civil liberties. They can even present a challenge to the accepted international order among sovereign nations.

The Terrorist Heritage   Although terrorism has been traced to the killing of tyrants (e.g., Brutus and Caesar, Charlotte Corday and Marat), the origins are lost in antiquity. Some notable historical examples of the calculated use of terrorism in the service of military conquest are Attila and the Huns, Genghis Khan and the Mongols, Tamerlane and the Seljuk Turks. As an ancient Chinese proverb puts it, "Kill one person, frighten ten thousand." These were the forerunners of the later German practice of *Schrecklichkeit* ("frightfulness") in attempting to cow and subdue captive populations in the two world wars.

Terrorism and the term *terrorist* are said to date from the French Revolution, during the period (1793–1794) when Maximilian Robespierre held dictatorial powers. Together with his satellites, St. Just and St. Couthon, Robespierre dominated the all-powerful Committee of Public Safety. By the mere threat of an accusation, they were able to control the political machinery of the French Republic.

The eighteenth-century contribution of colonial America to terrorism and terrorist tactics was the Sons of Liberty, part ruffian and part patriot, who helped fan the fires of resistance to the Crown and thus were instrumental in bringing about the coercive countermeasures by George III and the British Parliament which led to the Revolutionary War.

The modern era of terrorism began with the Anarchist movement in Europe during the nineteenth century. A "daydream of desperate romantics," as it was called by an historian of revolt, Anarchism sought the destruction of all existing governments and the abolition of private property. It called for a "propaganda of the deed," and its symbol was a bomb with a lighted fuse. In pursuit of this impossible dream, six heads of state lost their lives in the two decades which preceded World War I. Among them was President McKinley of the United States.

It was in Russia during this period that writers developed doctrines which proclaimed the virtue of terror. One of these was Serge Nachaeyev, whose "Revolutionary Catechism" contains the following statements regarding the duties of the revolutionary:

> The revolutionary is a dedicated man. He has no personal inclinations, no business affairs, no emotions, no attachments, no property, and no name. Everything in him is subordinated towards a single exclusive attachment, a single thought, and a single passion—the revolution.
>
> In the very depths of his being, not only in words but also in deeds, he has torn himself away from the bonds which tie him to the social order and to the cultivated world, with all its laws, moralities, and customs and with all its generally accepted conventions. He is their implacable enemy, and if he continues to live with them it is only in order to destroy them more quickly.
>
> The revolutionary despises all dogmas and refuses to accept the mundane sciences, leaving them for future generations. He knows only one science: the science of destruction. For this reason, and only for this reason, he will study mechanics, physics, chemistry, and perhaps medicine. But all day and night he studies the living science of peoples, their characteristics and circumstances, and all the phenomena of the present social order. The object is the same: the prompt destruction of this filthy order.

Fueled by such ideas, the *Narodniki*—members of the nihilist group called *Narodnaya Volya*—assassinated Czar Alexander II.

In 1884, Johannes Most, a German Social-Democrat-turned-anarchist, published in New York a manual entitled *Revolutionary (Urban) Warfare,* which bore the rather alarming subtitle: "A Handbook of Instruction Regarding the Use and Manufacture of Nitroglycerine, Dynamite, Guncotton, Fulminating Mercury, Bombs, Arson, Poisons, etc." Most pioneered the idea of the letter bomb and argued that the liquidation of "pigs" was not murder because murder was the willful killing of a human being—a category to which policemen did not belong.

It is readily apparent from this brief historical sketch that not only terrorist doctrines and ideals but also their techniques and methods have been around for more than a century.

Who Are the Terrorists? At first glance it seems possible to identify terrorists in terms of their political or ideological objectives: the Irish Republican Army, the Palestine Liberation Organization, the Basque separatist movement, the South Moluccans in Holland, the Croatians in the United States, the Tupamaro movement in

Uruguay, the Irgun Zvai Leumi in the days before the emergence of Israel as a modern state. In the case of revolutionaries who claim to represent the aspirations of oppressed and persecuted minorities, it is understandable that such persons could be regarded as heroes, even while their methods were deplored.

This description breaks down, however, when we consider groups like the Red Army Faction in Germany or Italy's Red Brigade. The alienated young persons who became members of these radical underground groups were not selfless revolutionaries seeking to strike a blow for freedom, nor were the groups they joined united by common commitment to some coherent political or ideological goal. What united the members was a deepseated, almost pathological hatred of present society. Although they claimed to speak for the working class, young urban terrorists came from upper-middle-class or upper-class families and were well educated and reared in comfort, even luxury. They spoke in the familiar jargon and clichés that form much of the rhetoric of the radical left, but they really endorsed no political theory or espoused no societal aims. Perhaps the simplest answer—that the act of violence for inadequate personalities is an end in itself, and that terror itself is a kind of ideology—is the correct answer. Or maybe the answer has to be sought in clinical psychology or psychiatry.

Experts have been careful to draw a line between the terrorist and the ordinary criminal. In a report by the Private Security Council of the Law Enforcement Assistance Administration (1976), terrorism was characterized by the commission of *criminal acts and/or threats by individuals or groups designed to achieve political or economic objectives by fear, intimidation, coercion, or violence.* Terrorism thus comprises acts which in themselves are crimes (murder, arson, robbery, kidnapping), but which differ from conventional criminal acts because they are carried out with the deliberate intention of producing fear. The distinguishing factor between terroristic acts and common forms of violent crime is that fear is not incidental to the terrorist's violence—it is its main objective.

Terrorism and crime are linked in various ways. It has become increasingly common to find criminal offenders who are ready to imitate the tactics of the revolutionary terrorist and swathe their criminal activities in revolutionary rhetoric. Eldridge Cleaver, George Jackson, Huey Newton, and Malcolm X developed their militant political consciousness while "doing time."

But relations between terrorist and criminal elements are not merely a matter of different interests that may happen to coincide. As Rapoport (1971) notes:

> Recall that Nachaeyev held the criminal to be the only true revolutionary and that Jerry Rubin hailed Bonnie and Clyde as his generation's heroes. In France and Italy during the first terrorist wave at the turn of the century and in Venezuela more recently, men with long and vile criminal records suddenly declared themselves revolutionaries [p. 61].

Criminal justice officials in England have told the authors that a sizable number of Irish Republican Army (IRA) members currently incarcerated in British prisons have criminal histories that antedate their recruitment into revolutionary membership.

As measured by television and newspaper coverage, criminals are not the only persons who are stimulated by the "success" of terrorism to emulate the tactics of terrorists. Maladjusted, emotionally disturbed individuals have been involved in many incidents of skyjacking, sniping, and barricade and hostage taking. A young man named Dolpin Lain seized and held a hostage atop one of the highest buildings in Los Angeles in January of 1977. His purpose was to generate publicity for his antismoking campaign (his father had died of lung cancer), and he succeeded in getting the *Los Angeles Times* to print an interview with him under the title "Stop Smoking: The Media Got His Message." As J. Bowyer Bell (1978) points out:

> Only when the behavior, motivations, and rationalizations of those involved are so obviously aberrant that no rationalization is possible has there been a refusal to take the "terrorists" at their own valuation. The strange Charles Manson cult in California, whose members explained their murders as an effort to begin a race war—Helter Skelter—attracted vast interest because their deeds were so violently pointless. They had killed without reason, without remorse, without effect. They had terrified without being terrorists [p. 43].

Coping with Terrorism   Democratic, open societies are especially vulnerable to terrorism. Totalitarian regimes such as the Soviet Union, on the other hand, have been immune. Entry to Russia and other countries with similar regimes is rigidly controlled, and movement within the country is severely restricted. Foreigners are subjected to close scrutiny; their associations with citizens are viewed with suspicion; and they are denied access to many places tourists can visit freely in a democratic country.

Planning terrorism is very easy in an open society. Libraries are a source of readily available information on everything from the construction plans of public buildings to the cockpit design of a Boeing 747 jetliner. It is almost ridiculously easy to purchase firearms in quantity—pistols, rifles, shotguns, even automatic weapons—in the United States; and it is not particularly difficult to secure a supply of explosive materials to manufacture crude but effective bombs.

If they are caught, terrorists are prepared to take advantage of democratic freedoms which are designed to protect the rights of defendants and cannot be curtailed selectively. In West Germany, accused terrorists exploited the permissive judicial system of the Federal Republic by disrupting court proceedings and even planned new terrorist actions from within their prison cells, aided by radical lawyers. More than half of the 267 international terrorists who have been apprehended since 1970 managed to escape punishment by getting safe conduct to another country, were released from confinement on the demand of their fellow terrorists, or were released after serving relatively short prison sentences. No terrorist of the 1970s or 1980s has thus far been executed.

Modern technology has added a sinister and increasingly ominous dimension to terrorism. Automatic weapons, plastic explosives, and even rocket launchers like the SA-7 (the Soviet portable heat-seeking rocket) belong to the terrorist's arsenal. The National Advisory Commission on Criminal Justice Standards and Goals

(1976), in its task force report on disorders and terrorism, warned that the threat of attack by terrorists armed with nuclear, biological, or chemical weapons is very real and ought to be realistically and urgently faced.

A democratic and open society such as that in the United States faces deep divisions of opinion regarding national policy toward terrorism and terrorists. At one end of the political spectrum, there is a vociferous minority whose recommended reaction to terrorists is, "Nuke 'em till they glow." At the other end of the spectrum is the kind of graceful resignation suggested by Bell (1978):

> Indignation is expensive; outrage is dear. Make the best of a troubled world. Do not open bulky packages mailed from an unfamiliar address in Belfast. Avoid riding with controversial diplomats, applying for executive positions in troubled zones, or flying planes that accept unfiltered passengers in the Rome or Athens terminals [pp. 278–79].

In times of crisis like the seizure of American hostages in Iran or the hijacking of TWA Flight 847, there is a strong temptation to bend every effort to secure the release of captives unharmed. But if terrorism is to be contained, civilized nations must utilize the breathing spells between outrages to seek more effective ways of defending themselves.

There are relatively few steps the United States can take on its own to shake off the label of "helpless giant" in the face of international terrorism, but a great deal can be done with the cooperation of other nations. Tightening airport security, boycotting countries with airports that are notoriously unsafe, and bringing diplomatic pressure to bear through concerted action are among the most obvious and immediate approaches that can be made within the context of international cooperation. Beyond these measures, pooling intelligence resources to keep track of the movements of known terrorists and working cooperatively to develop clandestine capabilities and antiterrorism counterintelligence networks offer the possibility of warning against planned terrorist attacks. In the last resort, democratic governments must plan for, organize, equip, and train what experts call the "force option"—elite military units like the West German commandos. And they must be prepared to use this option when all other alternatives have been exhausted.

As Whitaker (1985) reports, none of the countermeasures available to the United States and other civilized nations is guaranteed to succeed. Few of them are easy and some may involve moral and political decisions that are sure to be controversial. But terrorism is on the increase throughout the world and dealing with terrorists cannot be left to improvisation. Effective defense against terrorism demands a coherent, consistent, and carefully considered national policy.

SUMMARY

This chapter has dealt with three categories of criminal activity—economic, syndicated, and political crimes—which share the common feature of being perpetrated within an organizational context. The term *economic crime* has been proposed as a more accurate and comprehensive alternative to Sutherland's white-collar crime as a designation for acts committed by individuals or business organizations to obtain money or property. Among the types of economic crimes considered in this chapter are *personal crimes, abuses of trust, business crimes,* and *con games.* Each of these categories is defined and illustrated and an attempt is made to gauge the economic and social impact of such criminal activities.

The history and organizational structure of syndicated crime are briefly described in this chapter. Syndicated (organized) crime can be seen as a continuing and self-perpetuating criminal conspiracy that relies heavily on fear and corruption to carry on its activities. The roots of syndicated crime stretch far back into our history. At various times, nearly every nationality or ethnic group has been represented in the ranks of organized crime. While the Italian-Sicilian syndicates have dominated the scene, there are indications that other groups—outlaw bikers, Russian emigrés, Israeli criminals, Oriental gangs such as the Japanese Yakuza and the Chinese triads (tongs), Latin syndicates, American and West Indian blacks—are moving into syndicated crime in increasing numbers, as a consequence of involvement in illicit drug trafficking. These emerging crime groups are primarily financed by proceeds from this drug trade, but they are organized as multiservice criminal syndicates.

Treason and sedition were once the major types of illicit activity identified as political crimes. Watergate focused national attention on crimes perpetrated by agents of the government against individuals or organizations in the pursuit of economic or political goals. The rising incidence and severity of armed attacks on political and economic institutions by small, cohesive, highly trained groups in the furtherance of ideological objectives has directed domestic and international attention to terrorism. As this chapter points out, an open, democratic society such as that of the United States is especially vulnerable to terrorism. There seems little doubt that self-defense against terrorist incidents will exact a toll in terms of some curtailment of features such as freedom of movement and security from surveillance which are among the most cherished values of a free society.

DISCUSSION QUESTIONS

Find the answers to the following questions in the text.
1. What are some of the major obstacles encountered by the investigator who wishes to conduct research on economic, syndicated, and political crimes?
2. How did criminologist Edwin H. Sutherland define the term **white-collar crime** when he introduced the concept back in the 1930s? On what grounds do contemporary criminologists object to the term?
3. Name the four categories of economic crimes identified by Edelhertz and give at least one example of each.
4. Define and illustrate **antitrust violations.**
5. What is the significance of the Ford Pinto case in the investigation and prosecution of corporate crimes?
6. Who are the "Terrible Williamsons" and how did they acquire their unsavory reputation?
7. Discuss the impact of economic crimes on American society.

8. Distinguish among **ventures, criminal enterprises,** and **organized crime syndicates.**

9. Identify the concept of **ethnic succession** and cite the reasons why Lupsha (1981) and others disagree with this idea of a "queer ladder of social mobility" for various ethnic groups in syndicated crime.

10. What are the functional roles performed by the boss, underboss, buffer, and counselor in an organized crime family?

11. How have **outlaw biker** gangs managed to become so important in organized crime that they are second only to the older and more well-established Italian crime syndicates?

12. Outline and describe the seven types of political crimes in the Roebuck-Weeber typology and give current examples of each.

13. What is likely to be the major objective of a terrorist attack on persons or property?

14. Is **terrorism** a legitimate and worthwhile target for study by criminologists?

TERMS TO IDENTIFY AND REMEMBER

white-collar crime	electronic data processing (EDP)
"double slipping"	crimes
price collusion	"crimes in the suites"
criminal enterprise	venture
La Cosa Nostra (LCN)	antitrust violation
capo (boss)	ethnic succession
consigliere (counselor)	*sottocapo* (underboss)
outlaw bikers	buffer
terrorism	diversification
con game	Mafia
organized crime syndicate	*nolo contendre*

REFERENCES

Abadinsky, H. *The Mafia in America: An Oral History.* New York: Praeger, 1981.

Albini, J. L. *The American Mafia: Genesis of a Legend.* New York: Appleton-Century-Crofts, 1971.

Anable, D. World terrorism: Tackling the international problem. *Current Affairs* 179 (1976): 51–60.

Anderson, A. G. *The Business of Organized Crime.* Stanford, CA: Hoover Institution Press, Stanford University, 1979.

A night of terror. *Time,* July 25, 1977, pp. 12–22.

Bacon, J. Is the French connection really dead? *Drug Enforcement* 8 (1981): 19–21.

Barmash, I. Pilferage abounds in the nation's stores. *New York Times,* Oct. 28, 1973, p. 9.

Bell, D. The myth of the Cosa Nostra. *New Leader* 46 (1963): 12–15. Crime as an American way of life. *Antioch Review* 13 (Summer 1963),: 131–154.

Bequai, A. *Organized Crime: The Fifth Estate.* Lexington, MA: D. C. Heath and Company, 1979.

Black's Law Dictionary. St. Paul, MN: West Publishing Company, 1968.

Blakely, G. R., Goldstock, R., and Rogovin, C. H. *Rackets Bureau: Investigation and Prosecution of Organized Crime.* Washington, D.C.: U.S. Government Printing Office, 1978.

Chamber of Commerce of the United States. *White Collar Crime: Everyone's Loss.* Washington, D.C., 1974.

Child pornography law upheld. *Tampa Tribune,* July 3, 1982, pp. 1A, 6-A.

Clinard, M. B. *Illegal Corporate Behavior.* Washington, D.C.: U.S. Government Printing Office, 1979.

Clinard, M. B., and Quinney, R. *Criminal Behavior Systems: A Typology.* New York: Holt, Rinehart and Winston, 1973.

Clinard, M. B., and Yeaker, P. C. *Corporate Crime.* New York: Free Press, 1980.

Clymen, A. Low marks for executive honesty. *New York Times,* June 9, 1985, pp. 1F, 6F.

The Colombian connection: How a billion dollar network smuggles pot and coke into the U.S. *Time,* Jan. 29, 1979, pp. 22–29.

Cullen, F. T., Link, B. G., and Polanyi, C. W. The seriousness of crime revisited: Have attitudes toward white collar crime changed? Unpublished manuscript, Department of Sociology, Western Illinois University, Macomb, IL, 1980.

Dowie, M. Pinto madness. In J. H. Skolnick and E. Currie (eds.), *Crisis in American Institutions.* Boston: Little, Brown, 1970.

Edelhertz, H. *The Nature, Impact, and Prosecution of White Collar Crime.* Washington, D.C.: U.S. Government Printing Office, 1970.

———. Testimony before the House Subcommittee on Crime. U.S. House of Representatives, Committee on the Judiciary, White Collar Crime. Hearings before 95th Congress, 2nd Session, Covering June 21, July 12 and 19, and December 21. Washington, D.C.: U.S. Government Printing Office, 1979 (Serial No. 69).

———. White collar and professional crime: Challenge for the 1980s. Paper presented at the annual meeting of the American Association for the Advancement of Science, Jan. 7, 1982.

Edelhertz, H., Stotland, E., Walsh, M., and Weinberg, M. The investigation of white collar crime: A manual for enforcement Agency. Washington, D.C.: U.S. Government Printing Office, 1977.

Ellis, G. A. Pennsylvania State Police. Testimony given in the Hearings Before the Permanent Subcommittee on Investigations of the Committee on Governmental Affairs, U.S. Senate, 98th Congress, 1st Session, February 15, 23, and 24, 1983. Washington, D.C.: U.S. Government Printing Office, 1983.

Farr, R. *The Electronic Criminal.* New York: McGraw-Hill, 1975.

Feldman, C. Panel learns about credit card fraud. *Tampa Tribune,* Tuesday, May 24, 1983, p. 5-A.

Finn, P., and Hoffman, A. R. *Prosecution of Economic Crime.* Washington, D.C.: U.S. Government Printing Office, 1976.

Fisher, J. A. *Security for Business and Industry.* Englewood Cliffs, NJ: Prentice-Hall, 1979.

Gibbons, D. C. Crime and punishment: A study in social attitudes. *Social Forces* 47 (1969): 391–397.

Ianni, F. A. J. *Ethnic Succession in Organized Crime.* Washington, D.C.: U.S. Government Printing Office, 1973.

Jackson, E. (fictitious name). Former mother club member of the Pagan Motorcycle Club. Testimony given before the U.S. Senate Permanent Subcommittee on Investigations. Washington, D.C.: U.S. Government Printing Office, 1984.

Kalwary, K. Drug war: Violent way of Colombian life transferred to streets of Miami. *Tampa Tribune,* Nov. 3, 1979, p. 1-A, 48.

Katz, L. *Uncle Frank: The Biography of Frank Costello.* New York: Pocket Books, 1975.

Katz, T. L. Maryland State Police. Testimony given before the U.S. Senate Permanent Sub-committee on Investigations. Washington, D.C.: U.S. Government Printing Office, 1983.

Lazin, M. L. Chairman of the Pennsylvania Crime Commission. Testimony given before the U.S. Senate Permanent Subcommittee on Investigations. Washington, D.C.: U.S. Government Printing Office, 1983.

Lipman, M. *How America's Employees Are Stealing Their Companies Blind.* New York: Harper's Magazine Press, 1973.

Lupsha, P.A. Individual choice, material culture and organized crime. *Criminology* 19 (1981): 3–24.

McCaghy, C. H. *Deviant Behavior.* New York: Macmillan, 1976.

Messick, H. *Lansky.* New York: Berkeley Medallion Books, 1971.

Mitchell, J. M. Organized Crime: Stolen Securities. Hearing before the Permanent Subcommittee on Investigations of the Committee on Government Operations. 92nd Congress, 1st Session, 1971, Part I, 8–35.

Nader, R. Home repair frauds. *Ladies Home Journal,* 61, (1974): 86–147.

National Advisory Committee on Criminal Justice, *Organized Crime.* Washington, D.C.: U.S. Government Printing Office, 1976.

The National Narcotics Intelligence Consumers Committee. The supply of drugs in the U.S. Illicit market from foreign and domestic sources in 1979 (with projections for 1980–83). Washington, D.C.: Drug Enforcement Administration, undated.

Nichols, W. How to protect yourself from home improvement frauds. *Good Housekeeping* 178 (1974): 155–156.

Pace, D. F., and Styles, J. *Organized Crime: Concepts and Control.* Englewood Cliffs, NJ: Prentice-Hall, 1983.

Parker, D. B., and Nycum, S. The new criminal. *Datamation* 20 (1974): 56–58.

Proal, L. J. C. *Political Crime.* Montclair, NJ: Patterson Smith, 1973.

Roebuck, J., and Weeber, S. C. *Political Crime in the United States: Analyzing Crime By and Against Government.* New York: Praeger, 1978.

Rogovin, C. H. Prepared statement given before the U.S. Senate Permanent Subcommittee on Investigations, Feb. 24, 1983. Washington, D.C.: U.S. Government Printing Office, 1983.

Salerno, R., and Thompkins, J. S. *The Crime Confederation: Cosa Nostra and Allied Operations in Organized Crime.* Garden City, NY: Doubleday, 1969.

Schafer, S. *The Political Criminal.* New York: The Free Press, 1974.

Schrager, L. S., and Short, J. F. How serious is crime? Perceptions of organizational and common crimes. In G. Geis and E. Stotland (eds.), *White Collar Theory and Research.* Beverly Hills, CA: Sage, 1980.

Smith, S. C. Cocaine cowboys: Drug smugglers in Dade County are fighting bloody, brazen gang wars. *Tampa Tribune-Times,* Sept. 30, 1979, p. 4-B.

Study: Employee pilferage costing billions. *Tampa Tribune,* June 11, 1983, p. 70.

Subcommittee on Crime, Committee on the Judiciary. *Corporate Crime.* 96th Congress, Second Session. Washington, D.C.: U.S. Government Printing Office, 1980.

Taylor, J. S. Stiffer sentences: Judges tougher with white collar crime, especially in cases that are in public eye. *New York Times,* May 9, 1985, p. 30.

Thio, A. *Deviant Behavior.* Boston: Houghton Mifflin, 1983.

Tyler, G. *Organized Crime: A Book of Readings.* Ann Arbor: University of Michigan Press, 1962.

U.S. Senate Committee on the Judiciary. *Hearings on Organized Crime in America.* 98th Congress, First Session. May 20, 1983 and July 1, 1983, Part Two. Washington, D.C.: U.S. Government Printing Office, 1983.

Whitaker, M. United States need not be helpless in face of terrorism. *Tampa Tribune,* July 14, 1985, pp. 1-E, 4-E.

Wolfgang, M. E. Crime and punishment. *New York Times,* Nov. 18, 1980, p. 21-E.

chapter 7

CONSENSUAL CRIMES

Consensual crimes are often compared and contrasted with more conventional offenses against person and property to demonstrate the futility of attempting to "legislate morality." If by this we mean the enactment of statutes which provide legal sanctions for dealing with deviations from certain normative standards of conduct, then legislating morality is precisely what criminal law seeks to do. Distinctions between the legal order and moral order would appear to rest primarily on the means by which conformity to normative standards is sought, rather than upon the standards themselves. Both law and morality reflect attempts to influence behavior in a desired direction.

In offenses such as robbery and rape, there is little or no conflict between morality and law because these actions are proscribed by both moral codes and legal statutes. But the kinds of behavior subsumed under the heading of consensual crimes are sometimes proscribed by one set of rules but not by the other. A Catholic bishop visiting Boston is reputed to have told a Protestant minister, "Gambling in moderation is not a sin." "That may be true," the minister replied, "but in this state it is a crime."

While few people would seriously question the necessity for legal sanctions against offenses such as robbery and rape, many have serious reservations about gambling, prostitution, or homosexual behavior involving consenting adults. In the view of people with widely divergent ideological convictions, to subject such types of behavior to societal regulation by means of criminal sanctions is an unwarranted intrusion upon privacy and an indefensible extension of governmental authority into matters that are more properly dealt with by *informal* social sanctions. The American Law Institute, in its Model Penal Code (1968), recommended the abolition of most consensual crimes. The earlier Wolfenden Report (1957), which addressed the specific issues of consensual adult homosexuality and prostitution, stated that society should not seek to equate "the sphere of crime with that of sin" and that "there must remain a realm of private morality and immorality which is, in brief and crude terms, not the law's business" (p. 24).

There are intense and continuing controversies surrounding the conceptualization and legal status of "crimes against public order," societal reactions to such offenses, and the difficulties that these crimes create for law enforcement, the courts, and corrections. In this chapter we shall try to discuss some of the more significant problems and issues raised by a selected group of these offenses that includes problem drinking, deviant drug use, prostitution, and gambling. While this list of offenses is not exhaustive, we believe that it is representative, and, therefore, that the conclusions reached have generality beyond the specific patterns of behavior with which the present discussion attempts to deal. To avoid a wearisome and irritating reiteration of synonyms ("crimes against public order," "victimless crimes," "transactional offenses," etc.), we shall refer to the offenses covered in this chapter as **consensual crimes.**

DEFINING CONSENSUAL CRIME

"Consensual" denotes agreement—something which definitely is *not* present among criminologists in their recognition of just which offenses should be considered "victimless." In an effort to find consistency among a variety of sources on the identification of "victimless" crimes, Bedau (in Schur and Bedau, 1974) produced the summary given in Table 7.1.

Bedau cautions that the absence of a check mark under an author's name for a particular offense does not necessarily imply that the author would exclude that offense from the category of "victimless" crimes. It merely indicates that the writer in question did not explicitly discuss or describe that particular offense in his coverage of "victimless" crimes. What the table does indicate, according to Bedau, is that (1) "no two lists of crimes without victims are the same" and (2) "the concept of victimless crime does not denote a stable class of offenses at all" (1974, pp. 61–62). The reason for these difficulties, Bedau suggests, may be the complexity of the processes involved in *victimization*. He goes on to analyze the various ways in which participants can be victimized in so-called victimless crimes and he identifies four major features of these offenses that have led criminologists and legal experts to emphasize their lack of "direct victims":

1. *consensual participation*
2. *absence of complainant-participants*
3. *self-judged harmlessness of the behavior*
4. *transactional or exchange nature of the activity*

If these criteria are treated in such a way that each of them is viewed as a *necessary condition* for identifying victimless crimes, then, according to Bedau, combining them as the *sufficient condition* yields the following definition:

> An activity is a victimless crime if and only if it is prohibited by the criminal code and made subject to penalty or punishment, and involves the exchange or trans-

Table 7.1 CRIMES WITHOUT VICTIMS

	Schur (1965)	Skolnick (1968)	Packer (1968)	Morris (1973)	New York State Bar Assn. Crim. J. Sec. (1973)
Abortion	X	X			
Bribery			X		
Drug addiction	X			X	
Espionage			X		
Fornication			X		
Gambling		X	X	X	
Homosexuality	X	X			
Loitering				X	
Marijuana use		X			X
Narcotic use		X	X		
Private fighting		X			
Prostitution		X		X	X
Public drunkenness				X	X
Vagrancy				X	

Source: From E. M. Schur, and H. A. Bedau, *Victimless Crimes* (Englewood Cliffs, N.J.: Prentice-Hall, 1974, p. 61). Reproduced by permission of the authors and publisher.

action of goods and services among consenting adults who regard themselves as unharmed by the activity and, accordingly, do not willingly inform the authorities of their participation in it (p. 73).

Despite the care and precision with which this definition was framed, it is not comprehensive enough to include such activities as abortion and public drunkenness. In Bedau's judgment, "There is no convenient remedy for this. . . . It is better to conclude simply that perhaps some activities currently against the law are similar to, but not exactly like, some other activities which truly are victimless crimes" (p.74).

CONSENSUAL CRIMES AND CRIMINAL JUSTICE

The criminal justice system is often in the unenviable position of attempting to carry out conflicting policies and enforce laws which are vague, overlapping, or even contradictory. At the same time, criminal justice personnel are subjected to heated criticism for their inability to perform tasks which verge on the impossible. These situations apply to the area of consensual crime.

Opposition to consensual crime statutes is manifold and varied, but objections to such laws have tended to concentrate on the following issues:

1. Consensual crime laws are essentially unenforceable. ✓

2. Apart from their failure to achieve desired ends, such laws appear to increase or worsen social ills rather than reduce them.

3. Attempts at enforcement preempt a great deal of the time, energy, and money available for other law enforcement activity.

4. Police are forced to adopt legally and morally questionable techniques in the investigation of these offenses.

5. The efforts at banning such transactions may actually encourage the growth of an illicit traffic and raise the price of the goods and services in question.

6. Some of these laws may produce *secondary crime* (i.e., other than the proscribed behavior itself) and all of them create new "criminals," many of whom are otherwise law abiding individuals.

7. The administration of consensual crime laws is arbitrary and discriminatory; certain segments of society feel their impact a great deal more than others.

8. The largely discretionary nature of their enforcement, along with other key features of consensual crime situations, invites corruption and exploitation and may throw the entire system of criminal justice into disrepute [Schur and Bedau, 1974, p. 9].

There is, finally, the issue of the disposition of consensual criminals. It is difficult to fashion a compelling argument in support of punishing the drug addict, and detoxification seems a more promising approach to the public inebriate than a continuation of the "revolving door" of arrest-sentencing-incarceration-rearrest. The punitive response has had little success in dealing with gambling and prostitution, nor has the treatment approach yielded much in the way of gains except for a minority of self-professed compulsive gamblers or women for whom prostitution may be symptomatic of serious emotional maladjustment. Once an abortion has been performed, one cannot restore life to the fetus; and it is unlikely that sentencing the mother to a prison term will have any lasting benefits for her or society. Even if we were able, through the techniques presently available, to alter the behavior of individuals who voluntarily practice a homosexual life-style, there are no grounds in law or morality for proceeding with such behavior modification against the consent of the individual. For these and other reasons, the issue of disposition may provide the advocates of decriminalization of consensual crimes with their most cogent and convincing arguments.

Frequency and Distribution of Consensual Crimes

If it is difficult, as we have already noted, to arrive at an accurate assessment of criminal offenses that are reported by official data sources like the *Uniform Crime Reports,* it is utterly impossible to estimate the magnitude of consensual crime. Victimization studies, which provide some independent check on the number of crimes that are actually reported, have been little help in determining the frequency of occurrence of "victimless" crimes—for reasons that we discussed in the preceding section. Self-report studies, another source of verification for official crime figures, are also of extremely limited value.

We are told by Clinard and Quinney (1973) that "crimes against public order outnumber other crimes" (p. 78), but no authority is cited to support this assertion. Much of the "evidence" presented by groups or individuals concerning the frequency of consensual crimes is suspect on the grounds that it is used to buttress arguments for decriminalization. For example, in 1984 the National Organization for the Reform of Marijuana Laws claimed that there are 28 million people in the United States who have tried marijuana and 13 million who are regular consumers of marijuana. *Gamblers Anonymous,* an organization that is devoted to providing help for compulsive gamblers, estimates that the number of people in the country for whom gambling is a critical problem is between one million and four million. Figures of this sort are practically meaningless.

With regard to alcohol abuse, discussions of frequency and distribution suffer chronically from the introduction of information which is of doubtful relevance and even more questionable validity. It may be interesting to learn that the Rutgers Center of Alcohol Studies (1984) has estimated that there are more than 85 million consumers of beverage alcohol in the United States and that 9 million of these consumers are "alcoholics and problem drinkers." But these estimates are not particularly useful because they do not indicate how many persons among those 9 million alcoholics and problem drinkers are involved in the public drunkenness offenses which make up such a substantial portion of the misdemeanor arrests in any given year.

The issue of frequency and distribution of consensual crimes would be of interest only to the academic criminologist if it were not involved with the overwhelmingly important matter of public policy toward the enforcement of consensual crime laws. Thus, the decision on allocation of societal resources to cope with "the drug problem" ought to be maximally responsive to whether the number of heroin addicts, for instance, is closer to 200,000 (Markham, 1972) or 4,200,000 (Hunt and Zinberg, 1975). In practice, policies toward the enforcement of laws governing drug use seem to have been formulated without too much concern for accurate statistics.

PROBLEM DRINKING

Beverage alcohol is America's drug of choice. Its widespread use and abuse are related to criminal behavior in two ways: (1) *directly,* in the case of public drunkenness or driving while under the influence of alcohol; and (2) *indirectly,* when alcohol consumption is a contributing or precipitating factor in the commission of serious crimes. Approximately one-third of the more than 13 million arrests made in 1982 were for the following offenses which involved alcohol:

> Public drunkenness
>
> Driving while under the influence
>
> Liquor law violations
>
> Disorderly conduct
>
> Vagrancy

As we noted earlier (Chapter 4), the involvement of alcohol consumption in criminal homicide is a complex matter. Wolfgang and Strohm (1956) found a significant relationship between drinking in the victim and/or offender in more than 60 percent of the cases they examined. Greenberg (1981) reported a wide range of variation in the research she surveyed on alcoholism and crime involvement. Langan and Greenfeld (1983) report data on alcohol and crime from a random sample (11,399) of those over 40 years of age who were incarcerated in 1979 in state prisons. They found that most of these offenders have serious problems with alcohol. Approximately half of the sample group were drinking at the time of their current offense; about one-third were drunk at that time; and nearly two-thirds had been in an alcohol abuse program at some period during their lifetime. Langan and Greenfeld concluded that their data "certainly raise the suspicion that alcohol use by these middle-aged men is somehow implicated in their criminal careers" (p. 7).

The recent history of societal responses to alcoholism in this country is dominated by efforts to decriminalize alcohol-related offenses by casting the offender in the role of mental health patient, that is, one who is "sick" from the "illness" of alcoholism and, therefore, not responsible for his or her behavior. If addiction to alcohol is an illness, then convicting someone of the "crime" of alcoholic addiction could be construed as a violation of that person's constitutional right to be protected against cruel and unusual punishment.

This argument was invoked in the case of *Driver* v. *Hinnant* (1966). Driver, a 59-year-old man, had been convicted more than 200 times of public intoxication and had spent nearly two-thirds of his life incarcerated for these infractions. In the instant case, while admitting the truth of the charge under a North Carolina statute, he appealed his conviction on the grounds that his alcoholism was a disease which had destroyed the power of his will to resist the constant, excessive consumption of alcohol; that his appearance in public in an inebriated condition was not of his own volition but was rather a compulsion symptomatic of that disease; and to stigmatize him as criminal for this situation constitute cruel and unusual punishment.

In *Powell* v. *Texas* (1968), the U.S. Supreme Court upheld the lower court conviction of Leroy Powell, who had been charged with being drunk in a public place. The defendant had presented evidence that he was a chronic alcoholic with an irresistible compulsion to drink and, once intoxicated, he had no control over his behavior. The lower court ruled that chronic alcoholism is not a defense to public drunkenness. Wright and Kitchens (1976) interpreted the Court's decision in *Powell* as a possible indication of concern that the defense of chronic alcoholism might be extended to cover more serious crimes committed by alcoholics. "Thus the Court has forbidden punishment for being an alcoholic, but permits punishment for being a drunk in public. This is analogous to forbidding punishment for having epilepsy, but permitting punishment for having a convulsion" (p. 111).

The "Revolving Door Syndrome"

Public drunkenness is a misdemeanor. Offenders are apprehended and prosecuted under a variety of statutes covering vagrancy, loitering, disorderly conduct and so forth, in addition to those statutes that specifically prohibit public inebriation. Although anyone who has had too much to drink and appears in a public place in an intoxicated state can be arrested as a public drunk, most arrests for public drunkenness involve skid-row derelicts with a lengthy history of chronic alcoholism. These people, mostly men, are arrested and rearrested in a dreary cycle that has been called the **revolving door syndrome** (Pittman and Gordon, 1958). Offenders are typically nonviolent and are often in a precarious condition of physical debilitation.

The most outstanding characteristic of the skid-row alcoholic is the *chronicity* of his offense—a feature that helps to account for the fact that public drunkenness arrests account for about 50 percent of all misdemeanor arrests made in this country in any given year. One study revealed that 6 offenders had spent a total of 125 years in various penal institutions, doing a "life sentence on the installment plan" (President's Commission on Law Enforcement and Administration of Justice, 1967). On any given night, drunks constitute from one-half to two-thirds of the jail population (about one million per year are arrested), and it is not unusual for a "drunk court" to parcel out "justice" at an average of one case every two minutes.

Alcoholism and Alcohol Addiction

An alcoholic, according to criteria established by the American Medical Association in 1972 for the diagnosis of alcoholism, is an individual who drinks to the extent that it interferes with any major area of his or her life, including social (interpersonal) relationships with family members, employment, the law and the criminal justice system, and health. Alcoholism is viewed as continuous and repetitive, although it is not necessary for an alcoholic to drink every day of his or her life; he or she may drink as little as once a year. The central issue is not how much or how often individual alcoholics drink, but rather what happens to them when they drink. The key to the misuse of alcohol, which is the same as the misuse or abuse of other drugs, is that the consumption of beverage alcohol is used to seek escape from emotional tensions or from solving personal problems, or to achieve objectives which nonabusers have learned to attain through other, more socially and personally acceptable ways.

The National Institute of Alcohol Abuse and Alcoholism (among others) uses the term **problem drinker** in preference to *alcoholic.* Jellinek (1960) introduced the expression **addictive drinker** to distinguish the "true alcoholic" from the habitual symptomatic excessive drinker. Some of the basic differences between these two categories of drinker have to do with the kinds of behavior changes that occur in their history of alcohol use, as well as some of the typical symptoms of alcoholism or addictive drinking.

Addictive drinkers tend to lose control: they drink themselves into oblivion almost every time they drink. Heavy drinkers typically do not drink to the point of passing out, but they do consume sufficient quantities of alcohol to leave the casual observer under no doubt that they are heavily under the influence. Also, addictive drinkers eventually move outside the cultural patterns of drinking whereas excessive drinkers or heavy drinkers typically do not. Addictive drinkers at some point begin to drink by themselves, hide their drinking, and associate only with other people who drink a great deal. The heavy or excessive drinker continues to drink in the party or other social situation, even though he or she may get just as intoxicated. Blackouts are common to most alcohol addicts, as is the tendency toward isolation, to make alcohol the purpose of their lives, and the ability to appear unintoxicated while they are drinking. Each of these behavior patterns is uncharacteristic of the habitual excessive drinker.

Alcoholism and Problem Drinking as "Disease"

The notion that alcoholism and problem drinking represent a disease appears to be thoroughly accepted by the American public, but the validity of the concept is questioned by many criminal justice personnel, especially among those directly involved in some working capacity with drinkers. The disease concept of alcoholism replaced the earlier image of the alcoholic or problem drinker as a shiftless, irresponsible degenerate or weakling who lacked the willpower or "backbone" to control his or her urge to drink. How did this take place? Who and what were involved in the discovery of the disease of alcoholism?

The answer is that alcoholism as disease was not discovered—it was *invented.* To be more precise, the American Medical Association (AMA) decided in 1956 *by formal vote* to classify alcoholism as a disease. Despite appearances, there is nothing unusual about this decision. (As we will see a bit later in this chapter, the American Psychiatric Association voted in 1974 to delete homosexuality from its list of mental disorders, a position it had held for nearly a century.) Jellinek (1960), a physiologist who had extensively researched alcoholism and problem drinking and whose views were extremely influential in the AMA's acceptance of the disease concept of alcoholism, stated that "a disease is what the medical profession recognizes as such" (p.

12). The U.S. Supreme Court noted in the *Powell* decision that "alcoholism has too many definitions and disease has practically none" (1968, p. 1262).

The most significant implication of the AMA decision was to identify the alcoholic and problem drinker as individuals to be handled by the mental health system rather than the criminal justice system. McCaghy (1976) quotes from a pamphlet entitled *Alcoholism Is a Disease,* written by Dr. Marvin A. Block, chairman of the AMA Committee on Alcoholism:

> Today the physician is equipped to help care for these sick people [alcoholics]. . . . Doctors can prescribe drugs to alleviate physical symptoms. In physical complications from excessive drinking, proper diet, vitamins and drugs can be used to restore the patient physically and usually he can return to his former physical fitness. When underlying psychological reasons can be discovered to account for the patient's escape into alcoholic oblivion, corrective therapy can be applied. Anxieties due to insecurity in financial, domestic or physical matters may be alleviated by psychotherapy. In his relationship with the physician, the alcoholic may be relieved of fears that have no foundation in fact, thus obviating the need for escape through alcohol. . . .
>
> It must be remembered that alcoholism is a disease, that habitual excessive drinking is an illness which the physician is ready to treat. His advice should be sought early. As with other diseases, the earlier it is detected and treatment begun, the greater the chance for recovery and happy living [pp. 277–278].

Altering the status of the problem drinker from criminal to patient—from someone deserving punishment to someone needing treatment—is difficult to criticize on humanitarian grounds. Unfortunately, recasting alcoholism as a medical or psychiatric entity has neither moved us appreciably closer to an understanding of the etiology of alcoholism nor provided the kinds of effective treatment that are suggested in Dr. Block's rather optimistic statements above.

NONMEDICAL DRUG USE

"Drug use" and "drug abuse" are expressions that communicate very little reliable and accurate information. The word *drug* itself is an omnibus term that refers to "any substance other than food that by its chemical nature affects the structure or function of the living organism" (National Commission on Marijuana and Drug Abuse, 1973, p. 9). This definition is roomy enough to include anything from aspirin for a headache or a Coke for "the pause that refreshes" to librium for nervous tension or cocaine as a ticket to Euphoria. It helps a bit to identify the nature of a drug and its intended effects on the user, for example, that the drug is an amphetamine—a stimulant—and is intended to help an individual lose weight through dieting. But amphetamines can be consumed for reasons that have nothing to do with diets—and it is this sort of usage that is apt to be identified as deviant.

The vocabulary of drug use is heavily loaded with value judgments and arbitrary meanings. During the "tune-in, turn-on, drop-out" heyday of the "acid" subculture, LSD was variously described as "mind expanding" by its proponents and "psychotomimetic"—imitating psychotic states in its hallucinatory effects—by its critics. For these terms, "good" and "bad" could just as easily have been substituted. "Narcotic," which refers to "any drug that induces profound sleep, lethargy, and relief of pain" (Webster, p. 975), tends to be restricted in medical use to opium derivatives (morphine, heroin, paregoric) and synthetics such as Demerol with similar effects. In federal and state laws, however, and in the official circles the term *narcotic* has become practically synonymous with "dangerous" and "illegal."

"Addiction," "dependence," "abuse," and "habituation" are also difficult to define with precision and are likely to be used in contexts that are emotionally loaded. The National Commission on Marijuana and Drug Abuse (1973), after a fruitless attempt to pin down the meaning of habituation and addiction, settled for a typology of drug dependence based upon a continuum ranging from experimentation with drugs out of curiosity to compulsive use of drugs in an effort to find emotional security (see Table 7.2). With regard to the value-laden term *drug abuse,* the Commission recommended that it be discarded:

> The term has no functional utility and has become no more than an arbitrary code word for drug use which is presently considered wrong . . . Drug abuse, or any similar term, creates an impression that all drug-using behavior falls in one of two clear-cut spheres: drug use which is good, safe, beneficial and without social consequences; and drug "abuse" which is bad, harmful, without benefit and carrying high social cost [pp. 13–14].

Drug Laws and the "Dope Addict" Stereotype

Most adults in the United States have had first-hand experience at one time or another with someone in an advanced state of inebriation. Drunken behavior can be extremely amusing when it is portrayed on television by a comic artist like Foster Brooke; in real life it is much more apt to be unpleasant, even disgusting. There is little to laugh about glazed eyes, a reeking breath, incoherent speech, a stream of profanity and obscenity, and the blind staggers, not to mention vomiting, involuntary urination, and passing out. To the extent that the average person finds public drunkenness objectionable, his or her attitudes at least tend to be grounded in personal knowledge, however sketchy that knowledge may be.

It is a different story, however, with regard to the behavior of someone who "abuses drugs." Few people who have not experimented with drugs themselves would be able to recognize the behavioral signs of a cocaine "kick," a heroin "high," or the combination of dreaminess, mild euphoria, and intensification of feelings that is sought by smoking marijuana.

Public attitudes toward deviant drug use are dominated by media portrayals of "dope addict" behavior and personalities: the blank-eyed, vacant-minded stare of the teenaged "zombie," "zapped out" on "angel dust"; the squalid, menacing figure of the user-pusher, seducing schoolchildren into the enslavement of drug dependency; the orgiastic, often violence-prone conduct of "turned on" audiences at rock concerts; and lingering echoes of yesterday's "flower children" generation. Racial bias also plays a role. Prior to the 1960s, when "the drug problem" was mostly restricted

Table 7.2   A TYPOLOGY OF DRUG DEPENDENCE

Type of use	Frequency of use	Dosage	Motivation	Consequences
Experimental	10 or fewer times (total)	Low	Curiosity	Generally none; occasional psychological or physiological damage
Social-recreational	Highly variable, but greater than experimental	Low-moderate	Sharing a pleasurable experience with friends	Generally none; possible escalation to greater frequency and dosage
Circumstantial-situational	Highly variable	Low-moderate	Adjusting to a situation—lowering stress, preparing for examinations, getting "up" for athletic contests, and so on	Possible reliance on drug for other situations leading to escalation of use
Intensified	At least daily	High	Achieving relief from persistent situation; to be "normal"	Possible decrease in efficiency for other functions
Compulsive	Continuous	Very high	Seeking continuous security or comfort either from situations leading to initial drug use or from later consequences of drug use—loss of job, breakup of family, withdrawal symptoms, and so on	Abandonment of other functions

Source: Derived from National Commission on Marihuana and Drug Abuse, *Drug Use in America: Problem in Perspective* (Washington, D.C.: U.S. Government Printing Office, 1973), pp. 94–98, 137.

to the urban ghetto, the American white middle class was remarkably complacent. But during the 1960s and early 1970s, when the college student sons and daughters of the white middle class became the "spaced out" generation, there was swift recognition of "the drug problem" among suburban parents.

It is hardly surprising to find that public views on deviant drug use are the product of ignorance and misinformation when one considers the extent to which ignorance and misinformation have helped shape the *official* response to deviant drug consumption. If Prohibition can be blamed for helping to create the alcohol problem—and, incidentally, giving a major boost to the growth and development of organized crime—it would be fair to say that federal and state laws on drug use bear a heavy responsibility for today's "drug problem" in the United States.

Prior to passage of the **Harrison Act** in 1914, many of the drugs which are now legally proscribed or available only by physician's prescription were readily obtainable across the counter. Patent medicines, especially those consumed in the symptomatic treatment of "female disorders," often contained opium derivatives such as morphine. The intent of the Harrison Act was not to punish people who had become addicted to opiates but rather to suppress the illicit manufacture and distribution of addictive drugs. In its *parens patriae* capacity, the federal government opened drug addiction treatment centers in Lexington, Kentucky, Buffalo, New York, and Fort Worth, Texas, where self-referrals were accepted on a voluntary basis.

If narcotic addiction was not quite a crime, neither was it exactly an illness. Physicians were beginning to discover that attitudes and values were more significant than physiology in trying to understand addiction; that the end of withdrawal distress did not terminate addiction; and that addicts, as a group, were among the world's least promising patients—intransigent, manipulative, exploitative, and prone to a low recovery and high relapse rate. As the medical profession fled the field, popular views of the addict as an unfortunate victim of circumstances were replaced by the conviction that the addict was either a weakling or a normal degenerate who *enjoyed being deviant.* After all, achieving abstinence was chiefly a matter of exerting willpower; hence, backsliding after treatment could only be interpreted as having chosen evil in place of good (O'Donnell, 1967).

Repeal of Prohibition in 1933, with its consequent loss of revenue from illegal beer and booze, led syndicated crime to move into the importation and distribution of morphine and heroin. Vigorous law enforcement, plus the abandonment of treatment efforts by the medical profession, helped to drive deviant drug use into the ghetto. By the middle of the 1930s, addiction rates had risen dramatically among young, male minority group members.

In 1937, marijuana was added to the list of legally controlled drugs. Despite the lack of any valid and reliable evidence linking marijuana consumption to opiate addiction, the Federal Bureau of Narcotics managed to mobilize enough support in the Congress to assure the passage of the Marijuana Tax Act. Accoring to Howard Becker (1963), the enactment of this legislation was almost entirely the result of intensive lobbying by Federal Bureau of Narcotics executives:

> While it is, of course, difficult to know what the motives of Bureau officials were, we need assume no more than that they perceived an area of wrongdoing that properly belonged in their jurisdiction and moved to put it there. The personal interest they satisfied in pressing for marijuana legislation was one common to many officials: the interest in successfully accomplishing the task one has been assigned and in acquiring the best tools with which to accomplish it. The Bureau's efforts took two forms: cooperating in the development of state legislation affecting the use of marijuana, and providing facts and figures for journalistic accounts of the problem. These are two important modes of action available to all entrepreneurs seeking the adoption of rules: they can enlist the support of other interested organizations and develop, through the use of the press and other communication media, a favorable public attitude toward the proposed rule. If the

efforts are successful, the public becomes aware of a definite problem and the appropriate organizations act in concert to produce the desired rule [pp. 138–39].

This interpretation of the bureau's actions may be perfectly satisfactory, yet one is left with the feeling that it does not adequately account for the zeal with which this matter was pursued. It seems extremely important to set this issue within the context of the times. Federal officers were encountering familiar faces in their enforcement efforts—faces that belonged to syndicated crime figures whose activities had already been the target of criminal investigation in connection with the illicit trade in beverage alcohol during Prohibition. A mystique had developed among federal agents: they saw themselves as forces of morality pitted against the satanic conspiracy of organized crime. Discussions with men who were federal law enforcement agents during this period leave one with the clear impression that their attitude toward drug traffic and drug addicts was shaped by the conviction that anything in which organized crime had a stake was categorically evil, and therefore had to be outlawed as a matter of course.

The Federal Narcotics Act of 1956 had the effect of erasing a distinction between the user and seller of drugs. On a first offense for illegal possession of drugs, a sentence of 2 to 10 years could be imposed; for a second offense, the penalty was 5 to 20 years; and for the third and later offenses, the possible sentence was 10 to 40 years. States followed the federal lead and punished the possessor of drugs severely for the first offense. As Lindesmith (1968) observes:

> Another interesting feature of our anti-narcotics legislation is that, whereas it purports to be aimed at the peddlar of the drug rather than at the user and does not specifically define the use of drugs as a crime, it does in fact make every addict in the United States a criminal unless he happens to be so old and infirm that withdrawal of the drug would cause death or unless he has an incurable disease. It is possible for a man to be a chronic alcoholic and to drink himself to death without violating the law or causing someone else to violate the law. As a consequence of the drug user's vulnerability to arrest, much of the punishment for the violation of the drug laws is handed out to the user of the drug rather than to the peddlar. The federal institutions and prisons are filled mainly with the victims of the drug traffic, not with those who profit from the traffic [p. 222].

Types of Drugs and Drug Use

The Narcotic Addiction Control Commission of the state of New York has identified five major categories of drugs: deliriants, hallucinating agents, amphetamines and other stimulants, barbiturates and other depressants, and opiates (see Table 7.3). While there are substantial differences among these types of drugs with regard to the effects they produce, Kaplan (1970) has identified some general patterns associated with drug use. He divides users into three types: *situational users, spree users,* and *hardcore users.*

Situational users tend to consume particular drugs for specific purposes, for example, to stay awake while cramming for a midterm exam or to suppress the

Table 7.3 CONTROLLED SUBSTANCES: USES AND EFFECTS

Drugs	Schedule	Often prescribed brand names	Medical uses	Dependence potential: Physical	Dependence potential: Psychological	Tolerance	Duration of effects (in hours)	Usual methods of administration	Possible effects	Effects of overdose	Withdrawal syndrome
Narcotics											
Opium	II	Dover's Powder, Paregoric	Analgesic, antidiarrheal	High	High	Yes	3 to 6	Oral, smoked	Euphoria, drowsiness, respiratory depression, constricted pupils, nausea	Slow and shallow breathing, clammy skin, convulsions, coma, possible death	Watery eyes, runny nose, yawning, loss of appetite, irritability, tremors, panic, chills and sweating, cramps, nausea
Morphine	II	Morphine	Analgesic	High	High	Yes	3 to 6	Injected, smoked			
Codeine	II III IV	Codeine	Analgesic, antitussive	Moderate	Moderate	Yes	3 to 6	Oral, injected			
Heroin	I	None	None	High	High	Yes	3 to 6	Injected, sniffed			
Meperidine (Pethidine)	II	Demerol, Pethadol	Analgesic	High	High	Yes	3 to 6	Oral, injected			
Methadone	II	Dolophine, Methadone, Methadose	Analgesic, heroin substitute	High	High	Yes	12 to 24	Oral, injected			
Other Narcotics	I II III V	Dilaudid, Leritine, Numorphan, Percodan	Analgesic, antidiarrheal, antitussive	High	High	Yes	3 to 6	Oral, injected			
Depressants											
Chloral Hydrate	IV	Noctec, Somnos	Hypnotic	Moderate	Moderate	Probable	5 to 8	Oral	Slurred speech, disorientation, drunken behavior without odor of alcohol	Shallow respiration, cold and clammy skin, dilated pupils, weak and rapid pulse, coma, possible death	Anxiety, insomnia, tremors, delirium, convulsions, possible death
Barbiturates	II III IV	Amytal, Butisol, Nembutal, Phenobarbital, Seconal, Tuinal	Anesthetic, anticonvulsant, sedation, sleep	High	High	Yes	1 to 16	Oral, injected			
Glutethimide	III	Doriden	Sedation, sleep	High	High	Yes	4 to 8	Oral			
Methaqualone	II	Optimil, Parest, Quaalude, Somnafac, Sopor	Sedation, sleep	High	High	Yes	4 to 8	Oral			
Tranquilizers	IV	Equanil, Librium, Miltown, Serax, Tranxene, Valium	Anti-anxiety, muscle relaxant, sedation	Moderate	Moderate	Yes	4 to 8	Oral			
Other Depressants	III IV	Clonopin, Dalmane, Dormate, Noludar, Placydil, Valmid	Anti-anxiety, sedation, sleep	Possible	Possible	Yes	4 to 8	Oral			
Stimulants											
Cocaine	II	Cocaine	Local anesthetic	Possible	High	Yes	2	Injected, sniffed	Increased alertness, excitation, euphoria, dilated pupils, increased pulse rate and blood pressure, insomnia, loss of appetite	Agitation, increase in body temperature, hallucinations, convulsions, possible death	Apathy, long periods of sleep, irritability, depression, disorientation
Amphetamines	II III	Benzedrine, Biphetamine, Desoxyn, Dexedrine	Hyperkinesis, narcolepsy, weight control	Possible	High	Yes	2 to 4	Oral, injected			
Phenmetrazine	II	Preludin	Weight control	Possible	High	Yes	2 to 4	Oral			
Methylphenidate	II	Ritalin	Hyperkinesis	Possible	High	Yes	2 to 4	Oral			
Other Stimulants	III IV	Bacarate, Cylert, Didrex, Ionamin, Plegine, Pondimin, Pre-sate, Sanorex, Voranil	Weight control	Possible	Possible	Yes	2 to 4	Oral			
Hallucinogens											
LSD	I	None	None	None	Degree unknown	Yes	Variable	Oral	Illusions and hallucinations (with exception of MDA), poor perception of time and distance	Longer, more intense "trip" episodes, psychosis, possible death	Withdrawal syndrome not reported
Mescaline	I	None	None	None	Degree unknown	Yes	Variable	Oral, injected			
Psilocybin-Psilocyn	I	None	None	None	Degree unknown	Yes	Variable	Oral			
MDA	I	None	None	None	Degree unknown	Yes	Variable	Oral, injected, sniffed			
PCP	III	Sernylan	Veterinary anesthetic	None	Degree unknown	Yes	Variable	Oral, injected, smoked			
Other Hallucinogens	I	None	None	None	Degree unknown	Yes	Variable	Oral, injected, sniffed			
Cannabis											
Marihuana, Hashish, Hashish Oil	I	None	None	Degree unknown	Moderate	Yes	2 to 4	Oral, smoked	Euphoria, related inhibitions, increased appetite, disoriented behavior	Fatigue, paranoia, possible psychosis	Insomnia, hyperactivity, and decreased appetite reported in a limited number of individuals

Source: Drug Enforcement Administration. *Drugs of Abuse* (Washington, D.C.: U.S. Government Printing Office, 1975).

appetite and remain energetic while dieting. Spree users consume certain drugs for kicks, usually in a social situation, and their motivation is aimed at producing an altered mental or emotional state. The hardcore user is an individual whose life is centered on drugs in much the same way as the problem drinker's life is wrapped up with alcohol; life becomes reduced to an endlessly repetitive cycle of drug seeking and drug taking, with everything else subordinated to these activities.

The addictive pattern of increasing tolerance for the drug may occur in the use of any or all of these substances in a manner comparable to its development in alcoholism. People first discover that they receive pleasant feelings from the drug. This discovery is soon followed by the use of the drug to solve problems, either to reduce anxiety or to cope with a difficult situation. Other forms of coping are eliminated; the drug is used with growing frequency and increasingly heavy dosage. Once a person gets into the phase of heavy and continued use, he or she develops a system of rationalizations for the drug consumption, becomes preoccupied with securing the drug, worries about protecting the sources of supply, and otherwise behaves in ways that are typical of the alcohol addict.

Deviant Drug Use and Crime

Drug use and crime are indissolubly linked in the public view, and to a considerable extent among criminal justice system personnel. Claims have been advanced that as much as half of the criminal activity in U.S. cities during a given year is directly related to drug abuse. The findings of recent research, however, raise some serious questions about this assumed relationship and whether, in fact, it actually exists.

Common sense underlies the argument that there are few people, certainly few addicts, who are sufficiently well off to afford a drug habit costing from $100 to $500 a day. It is especially difficult to support such a habit when the drug user is unemployed and intoxicated by drugs most of the time. It follows, then, that the drug user must turn to illegal activities—theft, burglary, robbery, or commercialized vice—in order to procure the means to maintain the habit.

Supported by funds from the National Institute of Drug Abuse (NIDA), Inciardi (1979) analyzed approximately 2500 interviews with known heroin users, users of other drugs, and criminal nonusers. The main issue which the research addressed was the *sequence and relationship* of drug use and street crime. What Inciardi found was criminal histories among addicts and histories of addiction among criminals. In a sample of 117 female and 239 male active heroin drug users in the South, he found all had criminal histories, although 50 percent of the males were legally employed. Most of the crime uncovered was drug support oriented, and there were relatively few arrests proportionate to the number of crimes the addicts and the criminals indicated they had committed. Approximately one out of every 400 crimes actually resulted in an arrest.

The notion that drug addiction produces crime is an oversimplification of an extremely complicated relationship. In Inciardi's subjects, alcohol use typically was present at first, followed by criminal activity, then drug use, then further criminal activity. Among the females in the sample, criminal histories long preceded drug-use histories. Inciardi's data indicate that perhaps several events are occurring concurrently: criminal histories are overlapping with addiction or drug-use histories. If that is the case, the combination of the two makes the deciphering of the relationship very difficult. Aside from crime which is oriented directly toward the support of the drug habit, there appears little documentable relationship at all between drug abuse history and criminal history.

In a study of juveniles, Tuchfeld (1979) made essentially the same discovery. That is, considering the question of whether drugs preceded or followed criminal behavior, the individuals in his sample showed histories of alcohol use, opiate abuse, and then crime. While the assumption was made that there was some link between them, the relationship was anything but simple and was difficult to unravel.

Polydrug Use

These studies and others bring into sharp focus the **polydrug user.** Information on polydrug use is quite scanty in the professional literature, but it would appear that drug-use histories are more frequently polydrug than single drug; hence, the study of alcohol alone, heroin alone, or marijuana alone is not going to provide the answers we are seeking. Motivation is crucially important in such efforts, and we have little data on criminal activity where drugs are used strictly to provide the courage to commit the offense, rather than the commission of the offense being required in order to support the drug habit.

Chaiken and Chaiken (1982), in the study of career criminals to which we referred in Chapter 5, found that offenders who deal in drugs are frequently users. In addition, they discovered that costly and intense drug use leads violent predators to commit a greater variety of crimes at much higher rates. What is particularly interesting is that the nature of the drugs used by these offenders seems to be directly related to the types of offenses they committed.

Offenders who were only addicted to heroin tended to commit property crimes rather than violent crimes and there was some indication that the cost of the drug rather than any of its physiological effects is what triggered offenses by these addicts. In fact, in the case of heavy users who had a cheap source of supply or could trade other services for their drugs, their heroin habits appeared to have no effect on their rate of criminal activity. However, it is important to note that the distinctive characteristic of violent predators was not merely their heavy involvement in drugs but their multiple drug use which included the following combinations: heroin and barbiturates, barbiturates and alcohol, heroin and amphetamine, barbiturates with amphetamine, amphetamine or alcohol or multiple combinations of these. This multiple drug use was directly related to their involvement in certain kinds of offenses. Thus, use of more than one drug (particularly barbiturates) and intermittent recreational use of heroin was related to involvement in assault; heavy use of nonopiate psychotropic drugs was found to be strongly associated with high rates of involvement in all crimes, excluding the nonviolent offenses of auto theft and burglary. Therefore, it was not surprising that white respondents committed assaults at a much higher rate than black respondents, given their more frequent use of barbiturates. Not only were these offenders likely to use drugs in high quantities, they also used them on a daily basis and were more likely than other offenders to have heroin habits exceeding $50 a day.

Fully 50 to 60 percent of the offenses for which drug abusers are arrested and prosecuted are for possession and sale of drugs. Should decriminalization become a reality, the crime rate "associated" with drugs would be radically reduced, and again we would be forced into the posture that if a relationship exists between criminal activity and drug abuse, it is quite complex and perhaps spurious.

Research suggests the progression to polydrug use involves availability and peer popularity. For example, alcohol use typically appears early in the history (at approximately 13 years of age), followed by some experimentation with marijuana, back to alcohol again, and then perhaps to other drugs. On the street, in the 1980s, the other hallucinogenic drugs have practically disappeared.

The most serious problem we have with drugs and drug-abuse histories is that our knowledge and our data are quite limited. This is occasioned by the fact that most of the substances are illegal and, therefore, it is difficult to obtain the kind of information required to make valid conclusions, develop intervention strategies, and devise effective treatment programs. Arguments for and against the decriminalization and/or legalization of various currently controlled substances are made on the basis of little knowledge, sparse data, extremely limited experience (most of which is personal, anecdotal, and self-reported), and a great deal of emotion. In this context, what we do and how we do it seems destined to be fraught with errors, miscalculations, and blunders. It is difficult to escape the conclusion that only after some efforts at decriminalization will there be enough individuals to gauge accurately the short-term and long-term effects of many used or abused drugs in order to determine what society's reaction and that of the treatment community toward deviant drug use ought to be.

PROSTITUTION

Prostitution can be defined as the repeated exchange of sexual stimulation for profit (primarily money) with many persons. This definition deliberately omits the requirement of sexual intercourse, because a great deal of what arouses individuals sexually, even to the point of orgasm, does not involve intercourse, and may not even require physical contact between the two or more parties. In addition, the definition emphasizes the repetitive nature of the act and specifies the involvement of many individuals. These two qualifications, while they eliminate the individual who occasionally accepts money for sexual favors, more clearly identify persons whose entire livelihood, or some part of their regular livelihood, comes from the exchange of sexual stimulation for financial rewards. The definition also recognizes that money is not necessarily the commodity in question. While the exchange of cash is the most common commodity, there can be other compensations. We have eliminated by this definition the housewife and those who are merely promiscuous. Those individuals clearly fall outside of the usual understanding of prostitution.

It would be inaccurate to entirely equate prostitution with mere sexual transactions for pay. Prostitution encompasses certain features of social identity or role, but criminal sanctions are most often invoked against the more specific acts involved in *soliciting in public.* It is the streetwalker or "common prostitute" rather than the high-priced call girl who is most likely to become the target of efforts by law enforcement agencies to "clean up our city" in response to pressures generated by community indignation. The more discreet and much less visible activities of the call girl, arranged by telephone and transacted in privacy, do not confront the community with an overt affront to civic sensibilities.

The Red-light District

During the period of westward expansion that followed the Civil War, the kind of establishment known variously as "house of ill repute," bordello, whorehouse, cathouse, and brothel was extremely popular. As many as a dozen or two of these establishments might be located in a section of the city or town identified as the **red-light district,** reputedly as a testimonial to the practice of advertising by means of a red lantern or light. Many of these houses and the women who worked in them were popularized in the late 1800s by Western paperback novels (James, Withers, Haft, and Theiss, 1975). The "whore with a heart of gold" became a Western legend and a standard character—disguised as a "dance hall girl"—in television shows such as "Bonanza" and "Gunsmoke."

While the Western whorehouse was being romanticized and was viewed, particularly in mining camps and other boom towns, as a necessity to be tolerated and supported, the East Coast was beginning to have second thoughts. The Mann Act (passed in 1910 as the Federal White Slave Act) heralded the beginning of the end of the red-light districts. The intent of the Mann Act was to curtail the recruitment of American young women into prostitution by prohibiting their transportation across state lines. In this way the East was reacting to what was believed to be the only source of supply for the Western part of the nation.

Primarily because of their visibility, the red-light districts became targets of groups whose religious persuasions or community spirit moved them to action. By 1939, the majority of the red-light districts had disappeared, although Galveston, Texas, was able to maintain an area populous enough to qualify as such well into the late 1960s.

Despite the passing of the red-light district, individual houses of prostitution continued to flourish. The typical establishment, which featured a complement of 16 to 20 young women and hosted the male clientele on the premises, decreased in size, and "outdates," where prostitutes traveled to some other location to meet their clients, became more common. Pauline's, in Bowling Green, Kentucky, is an example of the former, while Xaviera Hollander's in New York City is an example of the latter. Both of these establishments are now closed and both madames—operators of whorehouses—have retired.

Varieties of Prostitutes

Among the many current styles or modes of prostitution that can be identified in the United States today (James, 1983), three are especially important. The first of these is the **streetwalker,** or hustler. As we noted earlier, this person is the most visible type of prostitute because she plies her trade openly in bars, in doorways, or on the streets. She is also the most active, servicing perhaps as many as 10 to 20 "johns" (customers) in a given evening. Generally, streetwalkers are organized into groups, or "stables," each of which is handled by a pimp, or "main man." (In some localities the pimp is referred to as a "player.") In some cases the prostitues give all of their earnings to the pimp and receive, in return, money for expenses, while the rest goes into escrow and is split between the prostitute and the pimp whenever they decide to go their separate ways. In other instances, prostitutes are exploited by pimps and change stables at the risk of being beaten or even murdered. Streetwalkers have the lowest status among prostitutes. They are the most likely to become involved in drugs and other kinds of criminal activity, and they produce most of the horror stories popularized in the press detailing male exploitation of females.

The second level is composed of **part-time prostitutes,** who work out of small houses or perhaps share an apartment. This would also include the more creative prostitutes who ply their trade in mobile homes. A pimp or a madame may or may not be present, since many of these women freelance, getting their customers by word of mouth or by referral from one prostitute to another. Sexual activity is not as frequent at this level, although the individual "tricks" are more expensive on the average than they are for the streetwalker. Many of the prostitutes at this level have learned specialties and thus can charge higher prices. At this level, young women do not tend to be forced into the profession, but rather drift into it either because other alternatives do not seem to present themselves, because they were initially promiscuous, or simply because there is no other way to make the kind of money that can be made in prostitution. In more recent history this level has come to be populated in part by students and housewives, who are strictly using the profession for money to supplement incomes or more commonly for a more specific end (such as college or graduate school). Also included at this level are the full-timers who operate from massage parlors, model studios, and escort services. Through these forms, the idea of a "house" can still be maintained, while at the same time providing some screening as far as the customers are concerned.

The **call girl** is at the top of her profession. At this level there are almost no pimps or madames and the prostitutes tend to rely on referrals from each other as well as referrals from their customers. These prostitutes primarily service fairly wealthy clientele, adjusting their prices to the client's ability to pay. Sexual activity is the least frequent at this level, and the prices are the highest. Quite often, call girls will operate out of their own apartments or the apartment of a friend, and it is unusual for more than three to be residing in the same place at the same time. Many of these women (there are also male prostitutes at this level) have girlfriends or boyfriends whom they support or with whom they carry on a durable relationship. At least one study (Praeger and Clafflin, 1979) suggests that such outside relationships are necessary for emotional stability.

Entering "The Life"

While there are many accounts of teenagers being repeatedly raped and drugged in order to fill stables at the streetwalker level, it is difficult to document the frequency with which this practice occurs. Whatever the estimate, it is more common at the streetwalker level than at other levels. Frequently, girls learn the trade from working prostitutes. Many were initially promiscuous, and thus established a basis of experience which was not alien to that of the working prostitute. Second, they acquired motives and a rationale for the behavior. Since most prostitutes are made rather than born, they receive instruction from other prostitutes in the finer points of the profession. This involves not only the physical activities themselves, but also such details as how to set up an apartment, how to talk to a customer on the telephone, and how to collect the fee. During the course of the training, as well as through interaction with other prostitutes while working, prostitutes develop a number of justifications for their behavior. Primary among these is the financial return, although security, serving a societal need, and supporting children also become important rationalizations. Finally, there is a recognition of restrictive alternatives: there is simply no other way a person, particularly a woman, can make as much money in a short period of time, with the exception of drug dealing. A streetwalker can make $20 for less than 20 minutes' work (usually oral sex); on a bad night, she can make as much as $200. And the risks involved in drug trafficking are much greater than those in prostitution.

A Note About the Customers

Without customers prostitution would disappear. It is therefore appropriate to include a short discussion of what we know about that person. For the female prostitute, the customer is white, middle class, and 30 to 60 years old. Prostitution serves a function in business, government, and academia which is not met in other ways. If a wealthy client desires sexual favors as a condition of placing an order with the company, that company will see to it that the customer's wishes are granted. The practice is quite common throughout the industrialized world, not just the United States. One may find an individual in the corporate structure whose primary purpose is to see to it that these desires (whatever they are) are fulfilled, although more commonly it is up to the individual salesperson to keep his customers happy. In some cases, it is merely considered courteous to let the customer know that the service is available, should the customer desire it.

In government as well (as several famous scandals attest), being involved with a prostitute is not uncommon. While it is doubtful that American embassies across the country maintain stables for visiting dignitaries, the practice was quite common at the municipal, county, and state level throughout the history of our nation.

Prostitution can provide a number of things which may not be available elsewhere. One of the most obvious is variety both in sexual expression as well as in partners. Within the bonds of marriage, one is restricted to one partner, as well as a fairly limited repertoire of sexual experiences. Both of these limitations can be overcome through the services of a prostitute. One of prostitution's major advantages is the actor-and-actress nature of the job, that is, the prostitute and customer are able to act out any number of roles for the pleasure of the customer. In addition, the risk associated with soliciting a prostitute and then carrying through with the act has been reported by many customers as one of the reasons they were attracted to prostitutes. In addition, the prostitute is totally devoted to the client, at least during the time the client has purchased.

Paying for the service allows the customer his choice of gratification. In addition, there is no pretext involved, the transaction being almost as uncomplicated as purchasing a pair of shoes. There is no commitment beyond the time they are together and the individual is not risking an affair with an associate, or an associate's wife which may prove to be embarrassing, indelicate, or totally destructive to the individual's status and/or career. Furthermore, in many instances men find it cheaper to pay a prostitute for sexual gratification than to spend $50 to $100 bar-hopping and still end up with no "lay."

In addition, wives have traditionally responded in a much more neutral or less negative fashion to a husband's consorting with a prostitute than the husband's involvement in an extramarital affair. Basic to this reaction is the fact that emotional commitment, which is a common feature of extramarital affairs, is typically absent in the more casual relations with prostitutes. A mistress or lover presents a direct threat to the continued integrity of the marriage and family. It is precisely this fact, one may note, which allows prostitutes to suggest that they are actually a kind of insurance policy for the family unit.

Toward the Decriminalization of Prostitution

On Mother's Day in 1973, a group calling itself **COYOTE**—an acronym for "Cast Off Your Old Tired Ethics"—established a coalition of prostitutes and feminists to fight for legal change. Their first priority was the decriminalization of prostitution rather than its legalization. COYOTE believed that decriminalization would allow prostitution to be treated as a business and provide prostitutes the greatest freedom to ply their trade. Legalization, on the other hand, would require government intervention and control. Originally founded in California, chapters of COYOTE sprang up across the United States and included Association of Seattle Prostitutes (ASP), Prostitutes of New York (PONY), Dump Obscene Laws; Prove Hypocrisy Isn't Necessary (DOLPHIN), California Association of Trollops (CATS), and Prostitutes Union of Massachusetts Association (PUMA).

COYOTE no longer exists in its earlier organizational guise. In 1977 it became the National Task Force on Prostitution; among its 30,000 subscribers are prostitutes, ex-prostitutes, lawyers, women's groups, social service agencies, and the general public. Its major goal is still the decriminalization of prostitution, but the task force also seeks to protect working prostitutes from arrests for loitering and from entrapment by vice squad operatives. Its activities include lobbying in state legislatures, research and statistics, maintenance of a library on sex, women, and prostitution, and a speakers bureau. Possibly for reasons of sentiment, its newsletter is called *Coyote Howls.*

GAMBLING

Gambling is an activity which offers the chance or opportunity to obtain money or commodities in exchange for skill or luck in predicting outcomes. The American success formula calls for hard work, with a dash of luck thrown in. But luck alone, as Geis (1972) observes, is a magic shortcut:

> Gambling toys with and teases certain imperatives of our culture, particularly those concerned with what has been called the Puritan ethic, a set of postulates about human existence which maintain that man should prosper and enjoy the good . . .only by means of his own efforts, and not through the sheer intervention of chance or providence [p. 222].

According to this formula, it is a toss-up whether the "evils of gambling"—which are alluded to almost as often as are the "evils of drink"—are better represented by the winner than by the loser.

American attitudes toward gambling are markedly ambivalent. Folk and literary heroes (such as Damon Runyon's Sky Masterson) have come from the ranks of professional gamblers. Gambling is regarded at one and the same time as an art, a skill, an all-pervasive destructive force, a science, a sickness, a recreation, and a sure road to personal ruin. Most recently it has been viewed as an addiction. Unlike alcoholism and nonmedical drug use, individuals with this deviant pattern are not readily identifiable by alterations in their external composure or physical well-being.

Gambling is a perplexing problem for the criminal justice system. In almost every state, some forms of gambling are illegal while others are not only legal but are actively encouraged. Parimutuel betting is permitted in Florida at horse and dog tracks and at *jai alai* frontons; and bingo and some types of lotteries are also available in the state. Las Vegas and Reno in Nevada and Atlantic City, New Jersey, offer casino gambling with virtually no restrictions. More recently, Indian reservations have offered gambling, particularly bingo, to the public. At the same time, crap shooting and the numbers are almost universally illegal.

Mangione and Fowler (1979), in their study of the enforcement of antigambling laws in 16 American cities with populations of more than 25 million identified four main targets of gambling laws and enforcement practices: (1) noncommercial social gambling in private places; (2) social gambling in public places; (3) direct participation in operating an illegal gambling establishment for profit (e.g., taking bets on horses or operating an illegal casino); and (4) indirect participation in a commercial gambling operation. In all 16 of the jurisdictions covered by their study, Mangione and Fowler found that police officers assigned a low priority to gambling violations: "Consistently, the resources devoted to gambling law enforcement were modest, averaging less than 1% of the police force" (p. 119). But they also discovered that a number of departments pursued an aggressive arrest policy for street-level gambling violations—those which are highly visible—in the pursuit of public support and approval.

Lotteries

One of the most popular forms of organized gambling in the United States has been the **lottery.** Early in our history, many states and cities used lotteries—drawings from many tickets purchased at low cost to select a few winners—as a means of raising funds for public, educational, and charitable purposes (Blakey, 1979). Everything from founding a university to the construction of a church has been funded in this fashion; thus, the notion of lotteries on a larger scale was not difficult for Americans to accept. One of the largest lotteries that was ever organized in the United States, which drained as much as $500 million annually from its clientele, was the Louisiana State Lottery Company or the "Golden Octopus" (Robbins, 1980).

Critics of lotteries have claimed that revenues raised from lotteries are often spent for purposes other than those promised: money designated for education, road and bridge repairs, and salary raises for state employees ends up in the general fund. Opponents of lotteries also charge that they are much more expensive than taxes as a means of raising revenues. Most taxes cost the taxpayer about 5 cents for each dollar collected, while a lottery can cost between 15 and 40 cents for each dollar (Skolnick, 1983).

The U.S. National Gambling Commission (1976) reported that promotion costs and payoffs to players reduced the revenues raised by the twelve state lotteries operating in 1975 to less than 1 percent of the $90 billion required to run local and state governments in those states. However, the situation had changed dramatically by 1980. As a result of new technology and an expansion of lotteries, revenues rose to nearly $2.4 billion in 1980 and returned $1.4 billion to the state government that sponsored the lotteries. According to Skolnick (1983), electronic games which combine gambling with video technology will offer an increasingly large choice of gambling opportunities. Thus, we are left with the fundamental question of the propriety of the government's role in promoting this "voluntary" activity. Says Skolnick:

> Given the entrepreneurial imperatives that have come to be associated with the lottery, the public policy issue may not rest on whether gambling as such is moral, but on whether the government ought to promote an activity that is, if not immoral, at least not exemplary. If government is, in Justice Louis D. Brandeis's dictum, "an omnipresent teacher," is promotion of the lottery an appropriate state activity, comparable to the promotion of education, public health, and other conventionally salutary activities [p. 805]?

The question becomes even more pertinent with respect to state support for casino gambling—a much more controversial issue.

Legalization of Gambling

Based on information from places where gambling has been legalized, there is an immediate increase in the revenues collected by the government, limited only by the forms of gambling available, the economic circumstances of the gamblers, and the percentage taken by the government from bets and licensing fees paid by both gaming establishments and individual bookies. Inevitably, illegal interests are drawn by the lure of high profits, with the result that theft, fraud, graft, and other forms of corruption become visible in the public sector. Success or disaster with legalized gambling appears to be a function of the skill with which a government can plan for, monitor, and enforce its regulations, while preventing the encroachment of illegal interests (Skolnick, 1979; Weinstein and Deitch, 1974).

ABORTION

Prior to 1973, abortion—the termination of a pregnancy before the unborn child or fetus attains the capacity to live outside the womb—was subject to restrictive laws in nearly every jurisdiction in the country. One of the few exceptions allowed by such laws was therapeutic abortion, the intentional termination of pregnancy for reasons of medical necessity. As a consequence, there emerged professional criminal abortionists and an illicit traffic in abortions that was estimated to be the third largest illegal endeavor in the United States, surpassed only by drugs and gambling (Martin, 1961). Women who were in no position to haggle over fees were paying prices that averaged $400 or $500 in cities such as Chicago and could reach as high as $2,000.

As Schur (1965) noted, there was a good deal of confusion over the direction and purpose of these restrictive laws on abortion. Although they appeared to be primarily concerned with the prohibition of illegitimacy and promiscuity, they affected a much larger proportion of married women than unmarried women. An expert referred to by Schur estimated that 90 percent of the women who obtained criminal abortions were married women with children.

In 1973, the U.S. Supreme Court struck down all restrictive laws on abortion. In two related decisions (*Roe* v. *Wade* and *Doe* v. *Bolton*), the Court declared that abortion during the first three months (or trimester) of pregnancy is a matter for medical judgment of the woman and her physician and that, for the stage subsequent to approximately the end of the first trimester, the state may if it chooses regulate and even prohibit abortion. However, even during this period, the state must allow abortion where necessary in appropriate medical judgment to preserve the health or life of the mother.

During 1980 and 1984 Ronald Reagan campaigned on a strong profamily policy which favored public prayer in schools and opposed the Equal Rights Amendment and abortion. Profamily legislators in the U.S. Congress have been successful in limiting both Medicaid funds for abortion and the provision of family planning services to teenagers without parental approval. They are also supporting a constitutional amendment which states that life begins at conception. Passage of the Human Rights Federalism Amendment—commonly known as the **Hatch Act**—would make abortion murder, thus ending legally sanctioned, medically approved abortions.

Abortion is an issue that deeply troubles millions of Americans. A poll conducted by *Newsweek* in January 1985 indicated that 40 percent of all Americans wonder whether their own position on abortion is right, regardless of whether they support or oppose it. More than one-third of the public thinks that more restrictions on abortion are required because of modern medicine's ability to keep a fetus alive, although a somewhat larger plurality disagrees. As in past surveys, less than one-quarter of the respondents polled supports an absolute right to abortion.

The newest factor in the lengthy and continuing controversy over abortion is the introduction of violence. Since 1982 there have been 30 incidents of arson and bombings of abortion clinics, 24 of them in 1984. So far no one has been killed or injured. President Reagan has spoken out against the bombings and the National Right-to-Life Committee has condemned the use of violence as evil and counterproductive. More to the point, perhaps, a Florida court convicted two young couples who had participated in the bombings of abortion clinics in Pensacola; and the two young men involved received prison sentences.

According to *Newsweek's* account, much of the support for abortion appears to have strong roots in social class and in attitudes toward work. Referring to a study by a University of San Diego sociologist named Kristin Luker of 200 California women involved in pro- and antiabortion activities, the special feature describes the debate over abortion as a debate over motherhood and its place in society. Luker found that the average prochoice abortionist was 44 years of age, married to a professional, worked outside the home herself, had a college degree, two children, and an annual family income of $50,000. The average prolife activist was also 44 years old and married, had a high school education, three or more children, a family income of $30,000, and did not work outside the home. The abortion opponent believed in traditional sex roles and saw motherhood as her highest mission in life, while the abortion supporters saw herself more as her husband's equal and viewed the unavailability of birth control and abortion as limiting her competitive chances in the world.

With powerful emotional forces lined up on both sides of the abortion issue, an easing of hostilities seems remote. Abortion politics appear to be at a stalemate, at least for the time being. None of the proposed constitutional amendments to ban or restrict abortion has won approval in Congress, let alone has begun the arduous ratification process through 38 state legislatures. The movement to convene a constitutional amendment convention has been stalled since 1980, still 17 short of the necessary state legislatures. Nevertheless, as abortion proponents warned during the last presidential campaign, a shift of only two seats in the U.S. Supreme Court could reverse the decision of the Court in *Roe* v. *Wade,* with consequences that could include a revival of the practices of criminal abortion that led to the original decision.

DECRIMINALIZATION OF CONSENSUAL CRIMES

To a criminologist, one of the most intriguing aspects of consensual crime and its study is the remarkable persistence of attempts to employ criminal sanctions in the suppression or control of behavior regarded as sinful, immoral, or merely objectionable by some minority sufficiently powerful to influence the passage of appropriate laws. Winston Churchill, in one of the volumes in his *History of the English-speaking Peoples,* noted that the English Puritans during the Protectorate of Oliver Cromwell, like their American counterparts in Massachusetts, devoted themselves to the suppression of vice.

> All betting and gambling were forbidden. In 1650 a law was passed making adultery punishable by death, a ferocity mitigated by the fact that nothing would convince the juries of the guilt of the accused. Drunkenness was attacked vigorously and great numbers of alehouses were closed. Swearing was an offence punishable by a graduated scale of fines. . . .Christmas excited the most fervent hostility of these fanatics. Parliament was deeply concerned at the liberty which it gave to carnal and sensual delights. Soldiers were sent round London on Christmas Day before dinnertime to enter private houses without warrants and seize meat cooking in all kitchens and ovens. Everywhere was prying and spying.

All over the country the Maypoles were hewn down, lest old village dances around them should lead to immorality or at least to levity. Walking abroad on the Sabbath, except to go to church, was punished, and a man was fined for going to a neighbouring parish to hear a sermon. It was even proposed to forbid people sitting at their doors or leaning against them on them on the Sabbath. Bearbaiting and cockfighting were effectually ended by shooting the bears and wringing the necks of the cocks. All forms of athletic sports, horse racing, and wrestling were banned, and sumptuary laws sought to remove all ornaments from male and female attire [pp. 240–41].

The stifling effects of these innumerable petty tyrannies extended into every corner of life and made Cromwell's Protectorate despised and hated as no government has ever been hated, before or since, in England.

Despite its addiction to Old Testament rhetoric, Cromwell's government was a military dictatorship, with most of the characteristics we have come to identify with similar regimes in the twentieth century. In a dictatorship, deviance from official norms is harshly, even ruthlessly, suppressed. Dissenters may be sent to a labor camp, to a mental hospital, or even put to death. Conflicts between law and morality exhibit few of the properties we associate with consensual crime in our own society. It is virtually impossible to imagine a gay liberation movement or COYOTE in the Soviet Union.

In a relatively open, pluralistic society such as ours, composed of groups with divergent traditions, customs, belief systems, and values, conflicts between the law and the moral views of some group or other are inevitable. While agreement is possible among groups with diverse moral and ethical convictions across a broad spectrum of issues, certain key issues allow little or no grounds for compromise. It is on issues of this kind that groups are likely to seek the support of legal sanctions as a backstop for morality.

Legal scholar Herbert L. Packer (1968) has identified six conditions which ought to be present if criminal sanctions are to be imposed against behavior that endangers societal disapproval:

1. The conduct must be regarded by most people as socially threatening and must not be condoned by any significant segment of society.
2. Subjecting the conduct to criminal penalties must not be inconsistent with the goals of punishment.
3. Suppressing it will not inhibit socially desirable conduct.
4. It can be dealt with through evenhanded and nondiscriminatory law enforcement.
5. Controlling it through the criminal process will not expose that process to severe qualitative or quantitative strains.
6. No reasonable alternatives to the criminal sanction exist for dealing with it [p. 296].

We might ask whether any or all of these conditions are met by the kinds of behavior which we have described in the preceding sections of this chapter.

The most reasonable conclusion would seem to be that laws which cannot be enforced should not be enacted; and the corollary to this proposition is that behavior which is subject to such laws ought not to be legally proscribed. This does not necessarily imply that certain kinds of behavior that fit the above specifications should or can be exempt from adverse public opinion or other types of social disapproval. As Geis (1972) reminds us, "To the extent that a society thrusts from its core nonconformists and then takes harsh measures to repress them, it will create a resistant force in its midst." As an alternative, he suggests that "the most efficacious method of dealing with deviancy is to ignore, to the furthest point of our tolerance, those items which we find offensive" (pp. 260–61). This recommendation is made in the belief that an unwillingness to drive into isolation the individual who deviates allows an opportunity for those societal values to operate that may help renew the deviant individual's "stake in conformity."

SUMMARY

In this chapter, we have examined a number of offenses often characterized as "victimless" crimes. We have chosen, instead, to refer to them as *consensual* crimes to emphasize the common characteristics of these offenses: consensual participation, absence of complainant-participants, self-judged harmlessness of the behavior, and the transactional or exchange nature of the activity. The lack of community consensus regarding the need to prohibit these offenses, along with the consensual involvement of those who violate these statutes, make enforcement of these laws extremely difficult.

Attention has been focused on problem drinking, nonmedical drug use, prostitution, gambling, and abortion. Our discussion of problem drinking considers the direct and indirect relationship between alcohol consumption and crime. Attention was also given to court decisions that have affected our methods of handling the public inebriate. Types of alcoholics were identified and the concept of alcoholism as a disease and its implications for handling individuals with this problem were also discussed.

To help clarify the meaning of "drug abuse," the section on nonmedical drug use began with a typology of drug offenders which views drug use on a continuum from experimentation to compulsive use. It was noted that public opinion on nonmedical drug use is strongly influenced by ignorance and misinformation. To a large extent, this situation affected the passage of laws dealing with the problems of addiction. Turning to the topic of types of drugs and drug use, it was noted that, despite many differences among the main categories of drugs, it is possible to identify three patterns associated with their use. In our discussion of the relationship between drug addiction and crime, we suggest that the notion that drug addiction *produces* crime is an oversimplification of an extremely complicated relationship. It is far more accurate to view these patterns of behavior as overlapping rather than as one causing the other. Finally, in examining the issue of descriminalization of drugs, we note that our knowledge at this point is far from sufficient to draw any valid conclusions regarding the effects of this type of policy decision. Only after experimenting with the decriminalization of some of these drugs will we have sufficient data to determine both community reaction and its impact on users.

Our discussion of prostitution begins with a definition which describes this phenomenon as the repeated exchange of sexual stimulation for profit with many persons. Despite the passing of the red-light district, individual houses of prostitution continue to flourish. Three levels of prostitutes were identified: the streetwalker; part-time and full-time prostitutes who ply their trades at various locations including apartments, as well as through massage parlors, model studios, and escort services; and call girls. Entering prostitution is a matter of choice based on economics and the restrictive employment alternatives open to women. Those entering "the life" typically receive training from their more experienced "sisters." Businesses use prostitutes to please existing and potential clients while individuals use their services because they involve no commitment and provide a wide range of sexual activities that are often not available in conventional relationships.

Gambling is attractive to many segments of our society because of the opportunities it provides for excitement and financial return. Adversaries of gambling consider it to have many of the same ill effects as alcoholism. However, as in the case of alcoholism, it is important to make a distinction between the occasional or recreational gambler and the compulsive gambler. The controversy over legalizing various forms of gambling revolves around issues of morality, economics, and the state's ability to keep criminal elements out of legal operations.

The 1973 Supreme Court decisions in *Roe* v. *Wade* and *Doe* v. *Bolton* struck down restrictive laws against abortion which had helped to create a large and lucrative traffic in illegal abortions. Opponents of abortion, however, have continued their campaign to reverse the court's decision by seeking an amendment to the U.S. Constitution which would define life as beginning at conception rather than viability (the capacity of the unborn child or fetus to survive outside the womb). The abortion issue has recently produced acts of violence directed against abortion clinics by individuals whose actions have been repudiated by nearly every abolitionist organization. A growing body of medical evidence which sheds new light on fetal development may help support a political compromise that is acceptable to both pro- and antiabortion advocates.

The chapter concludes with a discussion of the decriminalization of consensual crimes. It is suggested that, in a pluralistic society such as ours, conflicts are inevitable when these types of behavior are made subject to criminal sanction. The passage of such legislation puts our society in the untenable position of having laws which are all but unenforceable. Furthermore, these laws tend to isolate from the mainstream of society groups which engage in such behavior.

DISCUSSION QUESTIONS

Find the answers to the following questions in the text.

1. Discuss some of the major issues surrounding the definition of **consensual crime.**
2. Describe the problems faced by criminal justice personnel in enforcing the laws that prohibit consensual crimes.
3. Identify and describe the recent court decisions that have affected our treatment of alcoholics. What is the current American Medical Association (AMA) definition of someone who suffers from alcoholism?
4. What are the characteristics of an **addictive drinker**?
5. What is the most significant of the decisions by the AMA to classify alcoholism as a disease?

6. Describe the characteristics of the typology of drug dependents developed by the National Commission on Marijuana and Drug Abuse.

7. How accurate are public perceptions of **nonmedical drug use**?

8. Briefly sketch the history of this country's response to the control and treatment of nonmedical drug use.

9. Identify the three general patterns associated with nonmedical drug use.

10. Discuss the relationship between nonmedical drug use and crime.

11. Define **prostitution** and identify some of its basic patterns.

12. Discuss the reasons women enter prostitution and the type of training they receive.

13. What are the principal arguments for and against state **lotteries**?

14. What are some of the factors that have moved abortion to the center of public attention during the past several years?

15. Discuss the issues surrounding the decriminalization of consensual crimes.

TERMS TO IDENTIFY AND REMEMBER

consensual crimes   nonmedical drug use
the revolving door syndrome   problem drinker
addictive drinker   the Harrison Act
polydrug user   prostitution
red-light district   streetwalkers
part-time prostitutes   call girls
COYOTE   gambling
therapeutic abortion   lotteries
Hatch Act

REFERENCES

American Law Institute. *Model Penal Code.* Philadelphia: American Law Institute, 1968.

America's abortion dilemma. *Newsweek,* January 14, 1985, pp. 20–29.

Beck, J. Science may find political solution to abortion crisis. *Tampa Tribune,* January 15, 1985, p. 11-A.

Becker, H. S. *Outsiders: Studies in the Sociology of Deviance.* New York: The Free Press, 1963.

Blakey, R. G. State conducted lotteries: History, problems, and promise, *Journal of Social Issues* 35 (1979): 62–86.

Chaiken, J., and Chaiken, M. R. *Varieties of Criminal Behavior.* Santa Monica, CA: Rand Corporation, 1982.

Churchill, W. S. *A History of the English-Speaking Peoples. Vol. II. The New World.* New York: Bantam Books, 1963.

Clinard, M. B., and Quinney, R. *Criminal Behaviour Systems: A Typology.* New York: Holt, Rinehart and Winston, 1973.

Doe v. *Bolton,* 410 U.S. 179 (1973).

Driver v. *Hinnant,* 356 F. 2d 761 (4th Cir. 1966).

Easter v. *District of Columbia,* 361 F. 2d 50 (D.C. Cir. 1966).

Geis, G. *Not the Law's Business.* Washington, D.C.: U.S. Government Printing Office, 1972.

Greenberg, S. W. Alcohol and crime: A methodological critique of the literature. In J. J. Collins (ed.), *Research on the Relationship Between Alcohol and Crime.* New York: Guilford Press, 1981.

Haskell, M., and Yablonsky, L. *Crime and Delinquency.* Chicago: Rand McNally, 1974.

Hunt, L. G., and Zinberg, N. E. *Prevalence of Active Heroin Use in the U.S.* Washington, D.C.: U.S. Government Printing Office, 1976.

Inciardi, J. A. Heroin use and street crime. Paper presented at the annual meeting of the Academy of Criminal Justice Sciences, Cincinnati, March 3–5, 1979.

James, J. Prostitution and commercialized vice. I. Social and organizational aspects. In S. Kadish (ed.), *Encyclopedia of Crime and Justice.* New York: The Free Press, 1983.

James, J., Withers, J., Haft, M., and Theiss, S. *The Politics of Prostitution.* Seattle: Social Research Associates, 1975.

Jellinek, E. M. *The Disease Concept of Alcoholism.* New Haven, CT: Yale University Press, 1960.

Kaplan, R. *Drug Abuse: Perspectives on Drugs.* Dubuque, IA: William C. Brown, 1970.

Langan, P. A., and Greenfield, L. A. *Career Patterns in Crime.* Bureau of Justice Statistics Special Report. Washington, D.C.: U.S. Department of Justice, June 1983.

Lindesmith, A. R. *Addiction and Opiates.* Chicago: Aldine, 1968.

McCaghy, C. H. *Deviant Behavior.* New York: Macmillan, 1976.

Markham, J. M. Heroin addicts numbers game. *New York Times,* June 6, 1972, p.8.

Martin, J. B. Abortion. *Saturday Evening Post,* May 20, 1961.

Mangione, T. W., and Fowler, F. J. Enforcing the gambling laws. *Journal of Social Issues* 35 (1979): 115–28.

National Commission on Marijuana and Drug Use. *Drug Use in America: Problem in Perspective.* Washington, D.C.: U.S. Government Printing Office, 1973.

O'Donnell, J. A. Narcotic addiction and crime. *Social Problems* 13 (1966): 374–85.

Packer, H. L. *The Limits of the Criminal Sanction.* Palo Alto, CA: Stanford University Press, 1968.

Pittman, D. J., and Gordon, W. C. *Revolving Door: A Study of the Chronic Police Case Inebriate.* New Brunswick, NJ: Rutgers Center of Alcoholism Studies, 1958.

Powell v. *Texas,* 392 U. S. 514 (1968).

President's Commission on Law Enforcement and Administration of Justice. *The Challenge of Crime in a Free Society.* Washington, D.C.: U.S. Government Printing Office, 1967.

Robbins, P. Louisiana lottery was so big it didn't have to be rigged. *Smithsonian* 10 (1980): 113–16, 118–25.

Roe v. *Wade,* 410 U.S. 113 (1973).

Schur, E. M. *Crimes Without Victims.* Englewood Cliffs, NJ: Prentice-Hall, 1965.

Schur, E. M., and Bedau, H. A. *Victimless Crime: Two Sides of a Controversy.* Englewood Cliffs, NJ: Prentice-Hall, 1974.

Skolnick, J. H. Gambling. In S. Kadish (ed.), *Encyclopedia of Crime and Justice.* New York: The Free Press, 1983.

———. The social risks of casino gambling. *Psychology Today* (July 1979): 52–58, 63–64.

Tuchfeld, B. S. Alcohol, opiates and the propensity for deviant and criminal behavior in adolescents. Paper presented at the annual meeting of the Academy of Criminal Justice Sciences, Cincinnati, March 3–5, 1979.

U.S. National Commission on the Review of the National Policy Toward Gambling. *Gambling in America; Final Report.* Washington, D.C.: U.S. Government Printing Office, 1976.

Webster's New World Dictionary of the American Language. New York: The World Publishing Company, 1964.

Weinstein, D., and Deitch, L. *The Impact of Legalized Gambling: The Socio-Economic Consequences of Lotteries and Off-Track Betting.* New York: Praeger, 1974.

The Wolfenden Report. Committee on Homosexual Offenses. New York: Lancer Books, 1964.

Wolfgang, M. E., and Strom, R. B. The relationship between alcohol and criminal homicide. *Quarterly Journal of Studies on Alcohol* 17 (1956): 411–25.

Wright, J., and Kitchens, J. A. *Social Problems in America.* Columbus, OH: Charles E. Merrill, 1976.

chapter **8**

FEMALE OFFENDERS

During the decade from 1960 to 1970, female arrests for Crime Index offenses increased 202 percent, as compared with a 73 percent increase for male arrests. Throughout the rest of the 1970s, arrests rose at a much faster rate for women than for men (*UCR*, 1980). Accounts in the popular media, as well as an examination of increased female involvement in the major offenses, would seem to suggest that we are experiencing a female crime wave. As we shall try to show in this chapter, this impression is misleading and has resulted from a superficial analysis of statistics on female crime. It is true that there have been large *percentage* increases in the number of women involved in crime as compared with two decades ago, but these increases represent relatively modest increases in actual numbers.

For reasons that feminists have ascribed to chauvinism on the part of members of a male-dominated profession, criminologists have been selectively inattentive to the problems of female criminality. Freda Adler (1975) maintains that for centuries men have approached the "mysteries" of feminine behavior as though women belonged to a wholly different species, as though women did not share male needs for security and status, as though the motivations of women were somehow alien. Female criminals were looked upon as freaks.

EXPLANATIONS OF FEMALE CRIMINALITY

Female crime has been attributed to a variety of conditions and causes. In this section we will examine the major explanations of female crime, which can be grouped into three categories: (1) individual factors; (2) sociological factors; and (3) female emancipation.

Individual Factors

Early nonscientific explanations of female crime tended to see the offender as having been led astray or corrupted by others (i.e., men); in only a few instances were women regarded as "evil" (Rasche, 1974). More scientific attempts at the explanation of female criminality emerged in the latter part of the nineteenth century and emphasized inherited physiological and psychological characteristics. For example, in 1875 Van der Warker suggested that men commit crimes when they are poor or hungry, while women commit crimes because of certain mental traits that drive them to do so (Pollock, 1978).

✓ Lombroso, the best known early advocate of the role of constitutional factors in crime, sought to generalize to women the thesis he had developed concerning the inherited criminality of men (Lombroso and Ferrero, 1897). But female criminals failed to manifest the *atavistic* ("criminal throwback") characteristics that he had postulated were symptoms of inherited criminal tendencies. He explained this "disappointing" finding by asserting that women have many traits in common with children: they are vindictive, jealous, inclined toward cruelty in their vengeance, and deficient in moral sensibilities. These properties are neutralized in most instances by maternity, piety, want of passion, sexual coldness, weakness, and underdeveloped intelligence. However, when piety and maternity are wanting, and in their place are strong passions, intensely erotic tendencies, and muscular strength—all of which are irritated by morbid psychical activity—the result, Lombroso maintained, is a female criminal who is a monster. Not only did she have to counter all of the normal influences that keep women on the straight and narrow, but also she is a double exception among civilized people; that is, criminals are an exception in civilized circles and women are a rarity among criminals, given that their natural form of deviance is prostitution, not crime. Occasional offenders, according to Lombroso, who account for the vast majority of female crime, become involved in criminal acitivity as a result of the absence of some, but not all, of the moral constraints that keep normal women on the path of virtue and prevent them from succumbing to temptation and the suggestions of others.

Other early research by Matthews, Burt, and Seagrave during the 1920s was directed toward factors such as physical size, sexual development, illness, and disease, but failed to uncover any noteworthy causal relationships.

Despite these negative findings, constitutional—particularly, sex-related—explanations have continually been advanced to explain crime. Pollak (1950) found that female crime has been attributed to physiological overdevelopment, pregnancy, menopause, and menstruation, although with the exception of menstrual stress, little evidence has been produced to support the alleged influence of these factors. Also, the research that shows a relationship between menstruation and crime has been questioned on such methodological grounds as sample size and reliability, as well as for its failure to determine whether these periodic mood changes may be characteristic of both sexes (Bowker, 1978). As evidence for this, a study by Hershey found that males experience regular periodic emotional changes which parallel those experienced by women during the menstrual cycle (as cited by Bowker, 1978).

Emphasis on the causal significance of constitutional factors has continued into modern times. Biological factors may eventually prove to have some relevance for explanations of crime, but there still appears to be a tendency to confuse biological differences with gender differences that result from social, psychological, and cultural influences. Bole and Tatro (1979) have noted that there are four sexual functions—impregnation, lactation, menstruation, and gestation—which biologically distinguish the sexes. As long as allowance is made for these basic reproductive functions, no particular sex role is unchangeable.

√Mental deficiency among offenders has also been considered a manifestation of constitutional inferiority. Some of the early research shows women offenders to be below average when compared to women generally and even to male offenders, but their scores in later research are more normally distributed and only slightly skewed toward the lower end. It is plausible that these lower scores result from the fact that sampling is limited to apprehended offenders who may disproportionately be mentally less gifted than their unapprehended counterparts.

Psychoanalytic explanations of female crime are, to a large extent, constitutionally based. That is, Freud and many of his followers assumed that female behavior and personality development resulted unvaryingly from biological and physical characteristics that made them inferior to males. The principal source of this inferiority was viewed as the female's lack of the male sex organ; and this "genital deficiency," in turn led to such problems as "penis envy," masochism, narcissism, and exhibitionism, as well as to the driving force behind a woman's desire to become a man.

Psychodynamic explanations of crime and delinquency generally stress the notion of arrested psychosexual development. Delinquency among girls is presumed to reflect fixation at a level of sexual immaturity; and the female delinquent is portrayed as a lonely girl with a warped conception of femininity, which usually results from a poor and inadequate relationship with her mother. While the psychological processes that produce these disturbances differ, they typically create conflicts which are acted out in promiscuous sexual relations that fail to provide resolution for the conflicts.

Changing definitions of appropriate sexual behavior among teenagers have forced psychoanalysts to consider premarital sexual experimentation pathological only when it is accompanied by depression, moodiness, or other indications of emotional disturbance (Blos, 1979). Note should also be made of Konopka's (1966) research on institutionalized girls aged 14 to 19 years. She concluded that four factors contributed to female delinquency: (1) biological onset of puberty; (2) complex identity problems; (3) changing cultural position of women which created role ambivalence; and (4) lack of meaningful adult relationships resulting in isolation and loneliness.

Another early approach to female crime focused on identifying biological and social factors associated with this offender population. One of the best-known studies in this tradition was conducted by Sheldon and Eleanor Glueck (1934). The research covered almost every conceivable aspect of the lives of 500 inmates incarcerated at the Women's Reformatory in Massachusetts, including personal, family, reformatory, parole, and postparole history. The Gluecks concluded that female involvement in crime was the result of a complex of biological and social factors that included mental abnormality, retardation in school, and economic insufficiency. They summarized the characteristics of their sample in the following passage:

> This swarm of defective, diseased, anti-social misfits, then, comprises the human material which the reformatory and parole system are required by society to transform into wholesome, decent, law-abiding citizens! Is it not a miracle that a proportion of them were actually rehabilitated? [Glueck and Glueck, 1934, p. 288].

Citing such undesirable social consequences as the unrestrained birth of illegitimate and underprivileged children, the spread of venereal infection, and the ill effects of unrestrained sexual indulgence, the Gluecks argued that community protection required extended, if not lifelong imprisonment, for many of these offenders. Further incarceration for the period of fertility or for sterilization of these offenders was advocated as a means of preventing their pregnancy since it was felt that they would transmit criminal tendencies to successive generations. They advocated that the jurisdiction over women be transferred to the juvenile court on the grounds that the irresponsibility of these women requires that they receive just as much protection and salvation as children—indeed, that many of them *were* children, psychologically speaking, in terms of their inability to assume social responsibilities.

Later, research focused primarily on identifying social background variables. Schulman (1961) indicated that court reported data showed delinquent girls to have more pathological family lives than boys as manifested by: greater dependency, inadaquate home furnishings, excessive family mobility, greater proportion of working mothers, proportionately more broken homes, and criminal patterns. Gibbons (1981) concludes his review of the research and literature on female delinquency by asserting that family tensions are a major factor in female delinquency, which, in conjunction with social class factors and social liabilities, apparently propel a girl toward delinquency involvement. However, a study conducted by Datesman and Scarpitti (1975) provides some evidence that a disruptive family environment (a broken home) is not unequally related to female delinquency except in cases of girls apprehended for ungovernability and running away from home. Since arrests for these offenses are based on a double standard, as we take a more egalitarian view of the sexes, they suggest there will be a decline in arrests for these offenses which should result in less marked differences in this respect between the sexes.

Social Factors in Female Criminality

The work of W. I. Thomas (1923) represents one of the earliest explanations of female crime in social, rather than biological, terms. Thomas maintained that human behavior is directed toward the satisfaction of four fundamental wishes: the desire for new experience, security, responsibility, and recognition. The determination of how these are satisfied is based on the individual's ties to the family and the community. Girls with strong ties choose conventional means, while those with weak ties are more likely to opt for means that are amoral and hedonistic. Thomas states that girls become involved in delinquency as a means of satisfying their desire for excitement, pretty clothes, or other amusements. In fact, he offers a utilitarian interpretation of their illicit sexual involvements, arguing that such involvements are typically seen by these girls in much the same way that they view occasional work or borrowing money; that is, sexual involvement in prostitution or other illicit affairs is a means to an end, a position consistent with contemporary views held by prostitutes.

For more than 50 years, the work of Shaw and McKay and their colleagues, which is described in Chapter 11 (Sociological Theories of Criminality), has provided a picture of male and female delinquency and associated conditions in Chicago and other cities. They found that girls are mostly brought to court for sex offenses and boys for larceny. High rates of female delinquency occur in the same lower-class depressed areas as those areas which exhibit high rates of male delinquency.

One of the earliest in-depth studies of female criminality was conducted by Otta Pollak (1950). His work challenged a number of widespread myths about the nature and extent of female involvement in crime. Pollak believed that women had received a great deal of undeserved praise for their significantly lower crime rate, when in fact their participation in crime compares with that of men. In his study, he sought the answers to three questions:

1. Are those crimes in which women seem to participate exclusively, or to a considerable extent, offenses which are known to be greatly underreported?

2. Are women offenders generally less often detected than are men offenders?

3. Do women, if apprehended, meet with more leniency than do men [p. 1]?

Pollak's analysis of the available statistics on female criminality led him to answer all three of these questions in the affirmative.

Shoplifting of a nonprofessional character, thefts by prostitutes, domestic thefts, and episodes involving disturbance of the peace are consistently underreported in official crime tallies. Shoplifting is an offense that seems especially accessible to women as it is not at all unusual for a woman to spend a good deal of the day shopping. Sometimes clothing styles make it relatively easy for a female shoplifter to conceal "boosted" merchandise on her person. Also, some offenses which typically lead to prosecution if the offender is male go unprosecuted if the offender is female (e.g., homosexual contacts between women, exhibitionism, and being an accessory to statutory rape).

Pollak contended that the criminal behavior of women is easily hidden or "masked" by the traditional roles assigned to women by our culture and society. In addition, he believed that women use more deceit than men in the commission of their crimes. Women are taught deceit for physiological reasons: faking orgasm and concealing menstruation, according to Pollak, give women practice in the art of deceit.

With regard to the third question, Pollak found plenty of evidence that women are given favorable, even preferential, treatment at every stage of the criminal justice system and process, from arrest to corrections. Reckless and Kay (1967) concluded their review of various explanations for low crime rates among women with observations that provide support for Pollak's contentions in this respect:

> Perhaps the most important factor in determining reported and acted-upon violational behavior of women is the chivalry factor. Victims or observers of female violators are unwilling to take action against the offender because she is a woman. Police are much less willing to make on-the-spot arrests of, or "book" and hold women for court action than men. Courts are also easy on women, because they are women. . . . Overlooking, letting-go, excusing, unwillingness to report and to hold, being easy on women are part of the differential handling of the adult females in the law enforcement process from original complaint to admission to prison. The differential law enforcement handling seems to be built into our basic attitudes toward women [p. 16].

Since the 1950s theory and associated research on crime have focused primarily on male delinquents with some criminologists giving attention to female delinquents as well. Cohen and Short (1958) explained the sexual delinquency of teenage girls as an attempt by girls with limited assets and abilities to hold the attention of males. Like males, they reject conventional yet unreachable status goals for satisfactions immediately attainable with present resources. In addition to sexually oriented subcultures, they found girls were also involved in violent and aggressive gangs and drug oriented subcultures which involve a vicious cycle of prostitution and addiction.

Short and Strodtbeck (1965) describe lower-class female delinquents in Chicago and explain that, like their male counterparts, these girls are inarticulate and unattractive in both appearance and behavior. They contend that delinquency among these youth results from their entrapment "in a cycle of limited social abilities and other skills, and experiences which further limits opportunities to acquire these skills or to exercise them if acquired" (p. 243). These social disabilities tend to contribute to the status dilemmas of these youths and in this manner contribute to their delinquency.

Research has also been directed toward determining the applicability of theories of male crime and delinquency to females. Datesman, Scarpitti, and Stephenson (1975) examined the applicability of self and opportunity theories to delinquent females. They found that delinquency and self-concept were related among black females but not among whites. Delinquency was also found to be more related to limited opportunity for females than for males. Both black and white females also perceived fewer opportunities than did their nondelinquent female counterparts. Public policy offenders (a category which, for girls, generally involves sex-related crimes) showed the lowest perceptions of opportunity. Datesman, Scarpitti, and Stephenson argue that the sexual behavior of these girls may represent a pursuit, through less than conventional means, of the marriage goal, or a rejection of it. A follow-up study by Cernkovich and Giordano (1979) reported that although lack of opportunities and perceived restrictions on opportunity based on being female were unrelated to female or male delinquency involvement, blocked general opportunity affected delinquency involvement for both sexes and had a greater impact on whites than blacks, regardless of sex.

Another study by Simon, Miller, and Aigner (1980) attempted to determine the applicability of the key variables associated with anomie, labeling, control, and differential association theories to female delinquency. They found that with the exception of anomie/opportunity theory, approximately as strong a relationship existed between these theories and self-reported delinquency for girls as for boys. While neither educational nor occupational opportunity was a strong predictor of delinquency for either sex, it was less so for females. This may occur because these factors are less important for teenage girls than boys, or females who are frustrated by blocked legitimate opportunities may also not have access to illegitimate opportunities. They also found that sex-related differences in delinquency rates appear to result from a reduced exposure to deviancy-related factors. In fact, when they controlled for these dissimilarities, the relationship between sex and delinquency was largely eliminated. This provides support for the **convergency hypothesis,** which argues that crime rate differences between the sexes will decrease as gender roles approach equality. These authors conclude that conventional theories of delinquency are adequate for explaining female criminality; however, these theories fail to adequately deal with the differential exposure of males and females to criminogenic factors which is anticipated by their middle-range scope. They assert that this requires explanation on a macro or sociological level which would specify how sex roles in contemporary society determine the manner in which the sexes are distributed in relation to the independent variables associated with each theory.

Female Emancipation

Changes in the volume and nature of female crime have also been tied to **female emancipation.** This raises several questions regarding changes in female involvement in the labor market. First, have there been substantial changes in the rate and pattern of female crime? The data presented later in this discussion show quite clearly that much of the apparent change in female crime and delinquency results from a look at gross percentage changes without reference to their numerical significance. These data also show that patterns of female crime and delinquency have not changed dramatically over the past two decades. Adult female crime continues to be primarily a matter of involvement in the offenses of larceny, embezzlement, fraud, and forgery. Official juvenile involvement has also remained relatively constant, with offenses of larceny and running away from home accounting for the vast majority of these offenders being taken into custody. While the juvenile self-reporting data do show a greater trend toward convergence than is evident in official statistics, this must be interpreted in light of other data that show that more serious and persistent delinquents are more likely to be arrested.

A second issue is whether there have been sufficient changes in the female role (i.e., expanded employment opportunities, more liberated or feminist attitudes toward self, and masculinization of female behavior) to affect female crime patterns. The attribution of crime to the masculinization of female behavior can be traced back to Lombroso; more recently, it has been linked to role convergence between the sexes. Although current research does show that female roles have become more egalitarian, other research indicates that traditional female role patterns emphasizing the wife and mother role are still dominant among both American males and females. Despite the fact that more women are entering male-dominated fields, attitudes still persist which make their active pursuit and acceptance in these areas a long way off. With respect to crime, while more women have not only become involved in but also become active participants rather than accessories in **male-dominated offenses,**[1] their numerical involvement is still relatively minor.

Another indication of the influence of female emancipation on crime is the extent to which female offenders subscribe to more liberal as opposed to traditional role definitions. Existing research on delinquency largely failed to find any positive relationship between these attitudes and crime with some research actually showing a negative relationship (Eve and Edmonds, 1978). A study by James and Thornton (1980) examined the relationship of attitudes toward feminism and delinquency as well as controlling for the influence of the women's movement on other delinquency related variables. They concluded that while increasing delinquency opportunity and reduced social controls "might contribute to the growth in the rate of delinquency and crime among females, our evidence suggests that the extent of crime among feminist women is similar to, or even less frequent than, that among their more traditional counterparts" (p. 243). Studies of adult females provide remarkably similar results. Leventhal (1977) found that female inmates were more likely to hold traditional attitudes toward the nature of women and their role expectations than were college students. However, their scores on the masculinity-femininity (MF) scale of the Minnesota Multiphasic Personality Inventory (MMPI) suggested that these inmates perceive themselves as being more masculine than the college sample. The Glick and Neto (1977) study found that the majority of incarcerated women still maintain traditional views regarding the role of women in society.

---

[1] See Table 8.1 later in this chapter for definition of male-dominated offenses.

An assessment of the role convergence argument also requires an examination of the extent to which the expanded participation of females in the labor market and particularly in male-dominated offenses can be related to changes in female crime. First, the evidence shows that expanded female employment is in traditional female rather than male-dominated occupations (Datesman and Scarpitti, 1980). Second, a study by Bartol (1979) using an economic game model, failed to find any significant relationship between increased female employment and crime. Her data showed that although increased employment among single women did positively affect property crime, this relationship did not hold for married women who represented the major portion of this group entering the labor force. Moreover, she found that married women were more likely to commit larceny, which she relates to their diminished legitimate opportunities and to the complementary nature of these crimes to certain household activities. Most importantly, she attributes the recent rise in female crime to a sharp reduction in "women's value of time at home" which in this case is measured by the number of preschool children in the home. In fact, her data show that the 58 percent increase in the female crime rate between 1960 and 1970 can be accounted for by a drop in the average number of preschool children per husband-wife family during this period.

A final related issue is whether expanded employment opportunities for women have put them in a position to be able to commit white-collar offenses. For example, one cannot commit computer fraud unless one has a job that makes access to computers possible. The data, however, show that women have only made slight gains in the managerial and professional categories. Even these slight gains are overshadowed by the fact that when women move into these higher status categories, they typically are employed in less prestigious and lower-status positions. Therefore, it would appear that women are in little better position now than in the past to perpetrate crimes requiring them to be in relatively high-trust positions. Thus, while female involvement in embezzlement has increased, it is likely, as we noted, that these offenses are committed by women in relatively low-status clerical or sales positions.

CURRENT ANALYSES OF FEMALE CRIME

Although official statistics have been used to convey a distorted picture of the nature and extent of female criminality, their proper utilization can afford some valuable insights into what is happening in this sector of the crime problem. We shall try to use this information, along with data from self-report studies, to examine trends in both adult female crime and juvenile female delinquency and criminality.

Adult Crime Data

It is possible to analyze changes in female crime by using either raw *UCR* arrest figures or by converting these data to arrest rates. The latter method is preferable, since it takes into consideration population size and composition and is not affected by differences in the base levels by arrest. Steffensmeier (1978, 1980) has made this conversion in *UCR* figures for the two time periods of 1960–1975 and 1965–1977. We shall make use of this newly computed arrest rate information to answer several questions about the nature and frequency of female criminality over the past two decades.

Table 8.1   AGGREGATE ARREST RATE PERCENTAGE CHANGES FOR ADULT MALES AND FEMALES, 1965 AND 1977

Type[a]	% FC[b]		% of female total		% of male total	
	1965	1977	1965	1977	1965	1977
Violent	9.9	10.8	7.8	8.2	8.1	10.9
Masculine	8.2	9.5	9.7	11.0	12.4	16.8
Male-dominated	7.7	8.7	50.6	38.5	69.3	65.0
Serious	14.7	21.1	15.0	25.5	9.9	15.4
Serious without larceny	7.4	8.5	4.4	5.1	6.3	8.9
Petty property	23.2	33.8	14.4	29.2	5.4	9.2

[a]Definitions are as follows:

Violent crimes are murder, aggravated assault, other assaults, weapons, and robbery.

Masculine crimes are murder, aggravated assault, other assaults, weapons, robbery, burglary, auto theft, vandalism, and arson.

Male-dominated crimes include the masculine crimes, plus stolen property, gambling, driving under influence, liquor law violations, drunkenness, narcotic drug law, sex offenses (except forcible rape and prostitution), and offenses against the family.

Serious crimes are murder, robbery, aggravated assault, burglary, larceny theft, and auto theft.

Petty property crimes are larceny-theft, fraud, forgery, and embezzlement.

[b]Percent that female rate contributes to the proportion of total arrests (male rate and female rate).

Source: Adapted from an article by D. Steffensmeier, Sex differences in patterns of adult crime, 1965–1977, a review and assessment, *Social Forces* 58 (June 1980): 1092. Reproduced by permission of the author and publisher.

1. How did female and male arrest patterns change for the periods of 1960–1975 and 1965–1977?
2. Have there been any major changes in the types of offenses committed by women during these periods, especially in terms of offenses considered violent, "male-dominated," "masculine," or serious offenses?
3. Is there any data support for the hypothesized relationship between expanded occupational opportunities and increased female crime, as reflected in economic/white-collar crimes?

Male and Female Arrest Patterns for 1960–1975 and 1965–1977   There were substantial increases during the first time-period in the rates of female involvement in violent crimes, but these increases were generally matched by those of males. Of greater significance was the fact that the percentage which females contributed (% FC) to total arrest during this period remained approximately the same. As a group and individually, property offenses (burglary, auto theft, fraud, embezzlement, larceny-theft) rose substantially. However, with the exception of larceny-theft and, to a lesser extent, fraud/embezzlement, these increases were the result of the relatively small size of the initial base (Steffensmeier, 1978).

In his examination of the second time period, 1965 to 1977, Steffensmeier (1980) dealt with 27 offenses.[2] During this period the gap between male and female offenses as measured by the percentage that women contributed to the total arrest figures changed less than 2 percent for most offenses. In answer to the question, therefore, of whether there were any significant changes in the types of offenses

[2]The offenses he examined included drunkenness, disorderly conduct, larceny-theft, prostitution, driving under the influence, liquor law violations, aggravated assault, vagrancy, fraud, gambling, narcotic drug violations, suspicion, sex offenses, offenses against family, forgery, burglary, weapons law violations, robbery, vandalism, auto theft, embezzlement, murder, receiving stolen property, arson, and negligent manslaughter.

committed by women during the period from 1965 to 1977, the data show no major shifts in categories of female crimes.

Feminine Participation in Violent, "Male-dominated," "Masculine," and Serious Offenses[3]   In offenses which have traditionally been considered violent, masculine, or male-dominated because they are viewed as requiring male skills, strength, or techniques, the percentage of female contribution to total arrest (% FC) figures from 1965 to 1977 changed very little. In the case of serious offenses, there was an apparent increase in the female contribution to total arrest figures. However, when larceny-theft (which in the case of female crime is largely a matter of shoplifting) is excluded from the category of serious crime—a procedure which is more than justified by the fact that shoplifting is primarily petty theft—the picture of comparative criminality is considerably changed. It is clear from the data that claims of increased female involvement in "serious offenses" are false and result from the inappropriate inclusion of petty theft in this category.

Female Involvement in White-Collar/Economic Crimes as a Function of Expanded Occupational Opportunities   Research on such white-collar/economic crimes as fraud, forgery, and embezzlement has suggested that these offenses are rarely committed by women in the course of their occupations (Hoffman-Bustamente, 1973; Klein and Kress, 1976; Greenwell, Silverman, and Vega, 1978; Klein and Montague, 1979; Denys, 1969). With regard to embezzlement, female perpetrators tend to be found in comparatively low-level positions as cashiers, bank tellers, sales clerks, and the like (Franklin, 1979). Thus, it is difficult to make a case that any increases in this offense are a reflection of increased employment opportunities for women. For these reasons, Steffensmeier has labeled those offenses petty property crimes. It should be noted (see Table 8.1) that *it is among these offenses, which primarily involve shoplifting, that the major changes in female crime patterns have actually occurred.*

Juvenile Female Crime and Delinquency

It has also been argued that the movement toward sexual egalitarianism has produced changes in the patterns of female delinquency to the extent that they now more closely approximate those of male juveniles (e.g., Adler, 1975; Weis, 1976). Changes in sex roles may not be reflected in patterns of adult criminality because of the traditional socialization patterns experienced by female offenders. If role convergence has, in fact, occurred, it is more likely to be mirrored in the socialization of juveniles and should result, therefore, in patterns of female delinquency that more closely parallel those of males.

Official Statistics   Steffensmeier and Steffensmeier (1980) computed arrest rates for juveniles on 29 offenses for the period 1965 to 1977, adding the categories of drugs/drinking, status, and sex-related offenses to the classifications used in the previous studies. Definitions of these categories are supplied in Table 8.2.

During this time period, arrest rates for male and female juvenile offenders

[3]Definitions for these categories can be found in Table 8.1.

Table 8.2 AGGREGATE ARREST RATE PERCENTAGE CHANGES FOR MALE AND FEMALE ADOLESCENTS, 1965 AND 1977

Type[a]	% FC[b]		Female % total		Male % total	
	1965	1977	1965	1977	1965	1977
Violent	10.5	15.0	3.4	5.5	6.3	8.9
Masculine	5.9	9.4	10.1	12.6	33.8	34.5
Serious	12.8	19.1	27.9	32.6	40.2	39.2
Serious without larceny	4.6	7.8	4.8	6.2	20.9	20.9
Petty property	20.2	28.7	23.6	28.0	20.0	19.8
Petty property without larceny		19.7 23.5	0.5	1.6	0.5	1.5
Status offenses	30.6	39.6	34.6	32.4	16.8	14.1
Sex-related offenses	14.4	19.2	9.3	5.3	11.8	6.4
Drugs/drinking	12.4	17.9	5.3	12.1	8.0	15.7

[a]Definitions are as follows:

Violent crimes are murder, aggravated assault, other assault, weapons, and robbery.

Masculine crimes include the violent offenses, plus burglary, auto theft, stolen property, vandalism, arson, and gambling.

Serious crimes are murder, robbery, aggravated assault, burglary, larceny-theft, and auto theft.

Petty property crimes are larceny-theft, fraud, forgery, and embezzlement.

Status offenses are runaways, curfew, and liquor law violations.

Sex-related offenses are disorderly conduct, suspicion, and vagrancy.

Drugs/drinking offenses are use of narcotic drugs, driving under the influence, drunkenness, and liquor law violations.

[b]This definition is found in Table 8.1.

Source: Adapted from an article by D. Steffensmeier, Trends in female delinquency, *Criminology* 20 (May 1980): 62. Reproduced by permission of the author and publisher.

showed minor and insignificant changes in most offenses. Larceny-theft and running away accounted for the largest numbers of juvenile females arrested, with each representing approximately 25 percent of the total arrests for this category. The categories of masculine and violent crime appeared to show increased female involvement, but this apparent increase is of little significance because it is largely the result of increases in "other assaults," which are relatively minor offenses. There were no major changes with regard to violent and "masculine" offenses. Once again, the inclusion of larceny-theft in the category of "serious crime" was just as questionable as it was in the case of adults and presents the same distorted picture of juvenile female involvement in this category. The apparent discrepancy between males and females disappears when larceny-theft is excluded from this category of crime.

The slight change in status offenses and sex-related crimes between 1965 and 1977 shows that our protective attitudes toward young girls did not change significantly during this period. Although arrest rates for drug-related offenses rose sharply for both males and females from 1965 to 1977, males still predominated in arrests for these offenses. However, there was a 5 percent increase in the extent to which females contributed to total arrests for this category. Changes in the relative involvement of females are due primarily to increases in liquor law violations and arrests for narcotic drug violations. It would appear from the self-report studies, which will be reviewed in the following section, as well as from other sources, that this increased involvement reflects a rise in the use of marijuana by this population (Steffensmeier and Steffensmeier, 1980).

Self-report Studies

Discussion up to this point has been limited to an examination of the information available from the *Uniform Crime Reports* and, as a result, suffers from all the short-comings and limitations on official statistics. There are enough self-report studies of crime and delinquency, however, to provide some insights on the extent to which male and female involvement in delinquency show increasing similarities. We can also discern from this material any significant changes in the nature of female delinquency.

Based on an examination of self-reporting data, it seems possible to conclude that differences in the delinquency of boys and girls are less pronounced than the official statistics indicate. Part of the reason for this disparity is that official statistics tend to overemphasize relatively minor **status offenses.** A recent study by Zimmerman and Broder (1980) shows that half again as many males as females (i.e., a ratio of 15 to 1) reported involvement in delinquency. However, the difference between boys and girls increases 2.4 to 1 for criminal offenses and rises even more sharply (4.7 to 1) for violent offenses.

Data from a variety of localized studies which span the period from the mid-1950s to the late 1970s indicate that the types of offenses committed by girls are similar to those committed by boys; the only difference is that girls show less involvement in serious personal and property offenses. Comparable studies conducted during this same period show that (1) involvement of boys and girls in status offenses remained essentially the same; (2) the difference in involvement in property crime dropped progressively; and (3) the difference in involvement in violent crime dropped substantially (Silverman, 1981).

Information from the first study that used a national sample (Gold and Reimer, 1975) shows that when drinking and drug use are excluded, there is no apparent change in the frequency of involvement of girls in the overall figures for delinquency. Moreover, a seriousness-of-crime index showed that while boys were involved in more serious delinquency than girls, male scores declined between 1965 and 1972; female scores, on the other hand, stayed about the same.

The Second National Youth Survey conducted by Elliott, Ageton, Huizinga, Knowles, and Canter (1983) for the period 1976-1980, as we noted in Chapter 2, used a comprehensive scale that included a full range of criminal activities. This study showed that females were less often involved in delinquent behavior (prevalence) and committed fewer offenses (incidence) than their male counterparts. With the exception of the incidence of runaway offenses for 1980, there were no offenses in any year where females reported incidence or prevalence rates that were significantly higher that those reported by males. Male/female differences in both incidence and prevalence were particularly great in the serious and violent offense scales.

Discussion

An examination of both official and unofficial crime data leads to the inescapable conclusion that the much discussed increase in female criminality is more apparent than real. In fact, the large percentage gains in the Crime Index offenses of the *UCR* have resulted from the relatively small size of the initial female base figures. For example, a 288 percent increase in the female burglary rate from 1960 to 1975 reflected an increase in actual numbers from 3,600 burglaries in 1960 to 14,000 in 1975 (U.S. Department of Justice, 1976). During this same period, the rise of 100 percent in the male burglary rate was based on an increase of 130,000 actual crimes, which tends to reduce to comparative insignificance the increase of slightly more than 10,000 female offenses for the same span of time.

There have been slight gains in female contributions to total violent, male-dominated, masculine, and serious (excluding larceny) offenses, but the only increases of more than 5 percent have been for the crimes of larceny-theft, embezzlement, fraud, forgery, and vagrancy. While the latter four offenses as a group might suggest that there have been increases in white-collar/economic crimes, a closer look at the circumstances surrounding them indicates that they are not occupationally related or are perpetrated by low-level employees and involve relatively small amounts of money. Increased participation of females in these offenses shows that women are still involved in the same offenses that they have traditionally committed; larceny-theft is the only offense in which females have made substantial gains of numerical significance. As noted, the gains resulted almost exclusively from arrests for shoplifting, which has always accounted for the predominant number of female arrests. Increased female involvement in this offense certainly cannot be attributed to changes in the female role but instead is more likely to have resulted from a combination of factors including changes in merchandising practices, changes in store policies regarding the arrest of shoplifters, women having more free time as a result of reduced family size, economic necessity resulting from spiraling inflation, and increases in the number of female-headed households.

Female adolescent involvement in crime has also not shown any truly remarkable changes. In only five cases did official statistics show a change in the relative gap of more than 5 percent with this increase amounting to no more than 9 percent in any instance. Larceny-theft and running away continue to account for almost 50 percent of the total female arrests. Further, when other assaults are excluded from "masculine" crime and larceny is excluded from serious crime, changes in these categories as well as violent offenses are minor and insignificant. It was also noted that increased female involvement in petty property crime is mostly a result of increased participation in larceny. The slight drop in the contribution of status and sex-related offenses to total female arrest appears to reflect increased female involvement in other offenses, and may also indicate a slow change in the paternalistic attitude toward female juveniles. The increased female participation in drug-related offenses was an anticipated consequence of the greater acceptability and accessibility of drugs within the teenage subculture.

The self-reporting data show a closer covergence between male/female participation in delinquency than do *UCR* data, but basic differences in these two data sets render any comparisons extremely questionable. Most of the self-reporting studies tend to overemphasize minor offenses and also the offense designations are not always comparable. The data presented substantiate this point because they show there is progressively greater disparity in self-reported rates between the sexes from status to property to violent offenses. In evaluating these findings, consideration must be given to data showing that youth involved in more persistent and serious delinquency are more likely to be apprehended. Considering these limitations, it is probably fair to conclude that the divergence in male/female involvement in crime is not quite as great as reflected in official statistics, yet not as close as self-reporting studies suggest. These studies also indicate that the types of offenses committed by both sexes are more similar than is reflected in official statistics, although girls report less participation in serious personal and property offenses. This provides support for the view that the "sexual nature of female delinquency" is to a large extent a function of society's protective attitudes toward adolescent girls.

FEMALE OFFENDERS AND THE CRIMINAL JUSTICE SYSTEM

We have already noted the claim by some criminologists (e.g., Pollak, 1950; Reckless and Kay, 1967) that women are accorded preferential treatment over male offenders, that is, they are less likely than men to be arrested or convicted of the same offense, and if convicted, are less likely than men to receive a prison sentence. One of the reasons cited for this difference in treatment is the "chivalry factor" (Reckless and Kay, 1967), which implies that male police officers are reluctant to place members of the so-called weaker sex "up against the wall" or to respond to force with equal force and that male judges are loath to expose women to the dehumanizing aspects of the criminal justice process by sentencing them to incarceration. If, in fact, women have enjoyed preferential handling by the criminal justice system, as they are arrested in greater numbers for crimes committed mainly by men, they can expect a rapid change in the paternalistic attitudes of judges.

An opposing view is that women may be treated more harshly than men because many male judges view the behavior of female defendants as much more discrepant from their conventional social role than that of male defendants. As Rita Simon (1976) observes:

> . . . women defendants pay for the judges' belief that it is more in man's nature to commit crimes than it is in women's. Thus, when a judge is convinced that the woman before him has committed a crime, he is more likely to overreact and punish her, not only for the specific offense but also for transgressing against his expectations of womanly behavior.
>
> The existence of such statutes as the indeterminate sentence for women, or the sanctioning of a procedure whereby only convicted male defendants have their minimum sentences determined by a judge at an open hearing and in the presence of counsel, while the woman's minimum sentence is decided by a parole board in a closed session in which she is not represented by counsel, are cited as evidence of the unfair, punitive treatment that is accorded to women in the court. [p. 50].

While statistics show that about 1 out of 5 persons arrested in the United States is a woman offender, only 1 woman out of every 30 arrested is sent to prison. For example, New York State has a population of about 18 million and nearly one million index crimes (*UCR,* 1984), but the State incarcerated a little over 1,000 women in 1984 (Bureau of Justice Statistics, 1985). Crime patterns are changing, albeit slowly, and a precipitous rise in the number of females placed in state correctional facilities should not be part of that change. The differential treatment accorded women in many cases does not automatically mean better treatment or consideration. As an alternative to differential treatment, the model of the male prison is sometimes copied, even to the point of ignoring the obvious physical differences of the female inmates. At the other extreme, the best programs of differential treatment, filled with compassionate understanding for the women residents, could serve as models for institutions housing either sex, or both in the same institution.

Arrest is the first point at which the female offender comes into contact with the criminal justice system. While arrest may be a disturbing experience for the male offender, it creates special problems for the female offender. It has been estimated that 80 percent of the female offenders in the United States have dependent children at home, and that a great percentage of these children have no one else to care for them. A recognition of the need to provide more pretrial services for female offenders has prompted many communities to develop volunteer programs to assist with the women's problems at home. It is important to remember that the *children* of female offenders often become residents of juvenile institutions as a result of the actions of their mothers. To the juveniles who are removed from the community and placed in what they perceive as a facility for other juveniles who have committed offenses, it becomes hard to accept that *protection*, not punishment, is the state's motivation.

Women in Confinement

The plight of the woman behind bars is often a difficult one. With respect to institutional arrangements and facilities, the male offender oriented criminal justice system may ignore the special requirements of the female offender. The nature of the punishment for female offenders has come a long way since the time when they were thrown into the holds of hulks[4] as diversion for incarcerated male felons, but much more progress is necessary before treatment of the female offender can be said to be an integrated part of the correctional system and process.

Problems with female prisoners start with the requirement for a search in a police station. Many large urban police departments are able to maintain a matron on duty and provide separate facilities for female detainees. However, in many jurisdictions, especially smaller ones, there are no matrons and no separate facilities; even the schedules of visiting hours for men and women may show gross inequities.

Confinement for women at the local level ranges from a few well-designed jail facilities for female use to whatever can be improvised, such as a separate cell next to those for male offenders. The screening process at the point of arrest creates great problems for jail personnel. Because only the most serious female offenders are selected for arrest and detention, there is a more immediate need for effective security measures. The problem is made more acute because of the lack of qualified personnel and adequate facilities to provide the extensive security required. To a large extent,

---

[4]Hulks were old ships retired from service and used as floating prisons (eighteenth and early nineteenth centuries).

this is a result of the relatively small number of women held in jails. For example, in 1983, only 15,330 women were confined in jails and lockups, as compared with 210,451 males (Bureau of Justice Statistics, 1984).

In addition, certain tangential problems relate to the detention of a woman. The first is what to do with her children, if she has any. If there is a husband at home, he is likely to be working during the day. Provision of adequate services for the dependent children requires close coordination with the local child welfare agencies. These services are often unavailable in the smaller jurisdictions, and although it requires an imaginative law enforcement effort to deal with such children, often the task is left to people who are untrained to handle them. Confinement itself is a problem in most jails, and it is often solved by making temporary use of a portion of the facility designed for male use. In some cases, law enforcement officials might make arrangements to house the female prisoner at a local hospital or mental institution for a short period of time. Others make arrangements with the larger urban departments to transfer the female prisoner to their facility until trial.

All of these temporary measures create problems for both the corrections administration and the offender. Security and logistics become a drain on resources not planned for such use. The defendant has problems with visiting, contact with counsel, and concern for the welfare of her family. All of these problems may be shared by the male defendant, but he is much less likely to have the woman's acute worry for her children. That is, if the male prisoner has children, there is probably a wife to take care of them, while the woman often has no husband or one that is away from home at work. In addition, some of the women are pregnant or require medical attention for other problems unique to their sex. The average small-town police station is scarcely prepared to handle this kind of situation. As a consequence of the almost total lack of standards for female confinement, the situation at the local jail or facility is only a token of the problems that characterize state prisons for women.

The "Forgotten Offender"

The woman in a correctional institution has been described by some authors (e.g., Simon, 1975) as a " **forgotten offender.**" There are at least three primary reasons for such a designation. First, very few women are incarcerated. By June 30, 1985, there were 22,646 women in state and federal institutions, as compared with 490,041 males (Bureau of Justice Statistics, 1985). While the number of women incarcerated has risen more than 300 percent (*New York Times,* September 16, 1985) since 1970, women still only constitute 4.5 percent of the prison population. Second, the plight of the female inmate has drawn little public or official attention because institutions for women have not experienced any major disturbances or riots. Thus, female prisoners have not employed the means used by male prisoners—the prison riot—to make their demands public; they suffer from neglect, therefore, when changes are considered by public officials. Finally, the offenses that women typically commit usually fail to receive much public attention because they are not serious, do not involve large numbers of people, and rarely cause members of society the kinds of problems created by the offenses committed by males.

A study conducted by the General Accounting Office (GAO) in 1980 described the typical female offender as young, poor, a member of an ethnic or racial minority, unskilled, unmarried, a parent, and the perpetrator of some form of consensual or economic crime. In testimony before the House Subcommittee on Courts, Civil Liberties, and the Administration of Justice, the director of the Federal Bureau of Prisons confirmed this description when he characterized the average female offender as 31 years old, black, single, the head of a household, and responsible for two children. He further indicated that the female offender usually does not have a high school diploma and probably has been committed for a drug-related or economic offense (GAO, 1980).

To fully understand the plight of the incarcerated female offender it is necessary to examine briefly the nature and extent of facilities for these women and to make some comparisons with their male counterparts. As we noted earlier, institutions for men far outnumber those for women. In fact, most jurisdictions have only one or at most two female institutions. This results in women not receiving equitable opportunities in terms of housing, services, and participation in programs and industries. In contrast to males, women may be placed in institutions that house inmates with a range of security levels. Women who are low security risks may have their freedom curtailed simply because no other facilities are available. This situation also means that women are much more likely to be incarcerated in an institution that is a long distance from their home and community.

The size and location of most institutions for women generally limit the number of programs and training opportunities for this population. For example, in one state the GAO (1980) study found that male inmates were given the chance to participate in a formal prerelease program just before the termination of their sentence. In this jurisdiction, inmates could request placement in this program or their participation could be required by the parole board as a condition of their release. Approximately half of the men released each year in this state participated in the program, with 85 percent of those involved having verified employment upon release. Women, on the other hand, lacked the opportunity to participate in a similar program and had to find their own jobs.

Female institutions do not provide women with the same opportunity for learning skills that will assist them in finding a job upon release. In one of the states covered in the GAO study, investigators found a wide disparity between the program offerings at the one female institution and those available at the two male institutions. Women had the option to receive training in food services and keypunching while one of the male institutions provided men access to 13 different on-the-job and vocational training programs, which included auto body repair, welding, drafting, computer programming, X-ray technology, and medical lab assistance. The other male institution provided inmates with 11 such programs.

Women are severely limited in the number of prison industries in which they can participate. Involvement in these programs gives inmates the opportunity to experience a work environment, receive training, and may provide inmates an hourly wage. Women incarcerated in the federal prison system have access to only 13 of the 84 industrial operations compared to males who have access to 82 of these operations. Industrial programs for women are equally limited on the state level. For example, the GAO (1980) study found in one state that women have the option of participating in only one industry—sewing. Men in the same system can work at a furniture factory, a dairy farm, a glove factory, a sewing machine repair shop, and an industrial laundry. Furthermore, while men can transfer from one facility to another to better utilize their skills, this option is not open to women.

Differences were found by the GAO study in the range of medical services available to males as compared to females. The study noted that in one state, there were no separate living units for emotionally disturbed women at their institution. This facility also lacked an infirmary and only provided inmates with the intermittent services of a dentist, physician, psychologist, and psychiatrist. In contrast the two male institutions had staffed infirmaries providing routine medical services and one even had both an inpatient mental health unit and an inpatient dependency program. In two other states the same study found that male inmates have a comprehensive treatment facility which is staffed by psychiatrists, while women inmates have to be transferred to state or local hospitals in instances in which their problems require extensive treatment.

On the level of the county jail, the problem faced by female inmates is not one of availability but rather of access, since usually males and females are housed in the same institution. At these facilities women requiring different security levels are usually housed in the same cell or cell block and not only have no access to recreational facilities but are frequently fed in their cells. Moreover, as a result of the fact that it is difficult to separate female inmates due to their small numbers, acutely psychotic women are sometimes kept with other inmates while waiting to be placed in a state mental health facility. The plight of the female held in our county jails is illustrated by the following circumstances experienced by women in one state.

> Within county institutions, female inmates were not segregated by security classification although male inmates were.
>
> Small or local jails often place women in the segregation or maximum security section as a means of meeting state requirements for the segregation of sexes.
>
> In one facility women on work release were strip searched each day upon return, because they were housed with the general female inmate population. At the same institution, men on work release were housed separately and were not subject to the daily strip search.
>
> At another facility an industry shop was provided for men but not for women inmates.
>
> At one institution men had access to a gym but women did not [GAO, 1980, pp. 16–17].

It is clear by now that there are large disparities between the types of facilities, programs, and services available to males as compared to females. While correctional officials have been able to ignore the female offender until now, recent court actions have changed this situation. Like their counterparts on the outside, female inmates are beginning to demand that they receive parity with their male counterparts (GAO, 1980). Suits filed by female inmates demand that correctional officials provide them with the same kinds of facilities, vocational training, educational programs and work/study programs that are currently available to men. Courts deciding in favor of female inmates are no longer accepting the traditional reasons given by correctional officials (e.g., the small number of female inmates, the expense of providing equal situations, administrative convenience) for maintaining these unequal conditions.

Decisions in favor of female inmates are based on various legal grounds. In some cases treating female inmates differently than males has been viewed as a violation of the Fourteenth Amendment. In other cases, this type of treatment was considered cruel and unusual punishment which is prohibited by the Eighth Amendment. In still other instances, inmates have protested that their circumstances of incarceration represent an extreme invasion or violation of privacy which is protected under the Fourth Amendment.

Given that the jurisdictions are now being required to provide improved facilities for women it is important to examine briefly the kinds of available alternatives that will provide women with more equitable treatment. The GAO (1980) study recommends four alternatives which are currently in use and provide equitable treatment for females without duplicating existing programs and services. **Shared facilities,** typically called co-correctional facilities, represent one of these alternatives. Under this concept male and female inmates are housed in the same institution with separation limited to their living quarters. It is interesting to note that this is not a particularly new idea since for centuries men and women were housed together in the same facilities. In fact, it was only during the 1870s that we moved toward the development of single-sex institutions—a situation that continued until the Bureau of Prisons opened its first co-correctional institution in 1971. Staff at one of the federal co-correctional institutions feel that the advantages of this type of program outweigh its disadvantages. They list the advantages as follows:

> A more normalized environment improves inmate language, dress, and grooming habits.
>
> Fewer fights and assaults result in a safer environment for staff and inmates.
>
> A more extensive range of programs increases the inmate's chances to improve.
>
> The presence of both sexes results in improved community transition upon release.
>
> Nontraditional training programs are available to females.
>
> Females can be located closer to their homes by increasing the number of locations where they can be housed [GAO, 1980, pp. 27–28].

They cite the following as disadvantages:

> The need for more staff for surveillance and control.
>
> A greater need for public relations within the community because of the greater risk of failure [GAO, 1980, p. 28].

The establishment or the expansion of community correctional programs for women represents a second alternative that can provide new and/or expanded opportunities for these offenders. The possible alternatives that are available to communities through either residential or nonresidential programs span the full spectrum of services available to most citizens and include educational and vocational training as well as medical treatment. By using existing vocational training programs in the community, the wide and varying needs, capabilities, and interests of most offenders can be met. These programs can also provide inmates with the opportunity for employment in a much greater variety of jobs than institutions can possibly offer. The same holds true in terms of the availability of medical services as well as educational programs. Also as a result of the fact that inmates can be employed in the community and receive marketplace wages, these programs can require inmates to provide either the community or their victims with some restitution for their offenses.

A third recommendation that would benefit female offenders is joint ventures which can include participation by federal, state, and local jurisdictions. As we have already noted, the small number of females in separate jurisdictions makes it exceedingly expensive to provide a wide range of programs and facilities for these offenders. However, by pooling federal, state, and local resources we can better utilize existing incarceration facilities and thereby provide more equitable environments for the female offender. The idea is for adjacent states and federal government to develop cooperative agreements whereby state, local, and federal facilities in a given region would be utilized in such a manner as to provide different levels of security as well as a greater variety of programs for female inmates in that region. Using this approach, jurisdictions would be better able to provide females with equivalent facilities and services without the need to duplicate existing resources in neighboring jurisdictions.

Finally, the GAO study recommends that institutions can at once increase the opportunities for work that they provide inmates, and their earnings as well through the involvement of private companies in prison industry programs. Under this arrangement private companies would come into the institutions with modern equipment designed to supply products and services that are currently in demand on the open market. This would not only provide more jobs for inmates but also offer them a much better potential for employment upon release. In addition, this would offer inmates the opportunity to earn money during incarceration which could be utilized for the support of dependents, restitution to victims, and/or to defray part of the cost of food and housing. By using a variety of these alternatives, jurisdictions can overcome the inequality that currently exists in correctional programs for women while at the same time avoiding court-imposed changes.

The Inmate Mother

The *National Study of Women's Correctional Programs* (Glick and Neto, 1977) reported that more than half of approximately 6300 women in prison in 14 states were mothers and nearly all of these had children, under the age of 18. Imprisonment for the **inmate mother** has a twofold adverse effect. In addition to the emotional loss and pangs of separation suffered by the mother, she faces the prospect of endless worry over the care and custody of her children while she is doing time. Her concern is usually justified. If there is no father/or close relative to assume responsibility for looking after the children, the most likely result is that the children's care will be taken over by a social welfare agency and the children may be placed in a foster home or put up for adoption.

Phyllis J. Baunach (1977) underscores the limitations on the inmate mother's participation in the decision-making process concerning the custody of her children:

> The careful arrangements made by women prior to incarceration for the care of their children may be reversed by authorities who "know what is best" for the child's welfare. For instance, a black inmate in Washington state had procured placement for her 8 children with white members of her congregation. Despite the inmate's efforts, and the help of her white friends, a young social worker decided that the children should be placed with black families. The inmate objected that her children would be happier with white friends than with black strangers, and responded, "They're not like kittens where you give half the litter away" [p. 8].

Arbitrary and capricious policies toward visitation can make it almost impossible for the inmate mother to maintain contact with her children. Some prisons for women provide facilities for female offenders to meet and spend time with their children in pleasant surroundings on or off the grounds; and others follow a liberal policy of furloughs for incarcerated offenders with children. But too many institutions are still operating with the kind of policy that Murton and Baunach (1973) encountered at the Washington, D.C. Detention Center, which permitted only two one-hour visits per week.

COMMUNITY CORRECTIONAL PROGRAMS FOR FEMALE OFFENDERS

Glick and Neto's National Study looked at 36 community-based programs that included 6 categories of residential facility:

1. halfway houses, including alternatives to incarceration
2. academic prerelease programs
3. work-release/prerelease centers
4. therapeutic communities for drug abusers
5. residential centers for alcoholics
6. mixed modality drug programs

The authors found that these programs exhibited several positive features: they tended to differ from institutional programs in terms of a closer resemblance between inmate and staff racial and cultural characteristics; a concentration on the use of ex-offenders as staff members; and the utilization of extensive family and community involvement. On the other hand, they reported that there were several dimensions in which many programs seemed little more than an extension of the criminal justice system:

> . . . the majority of all programs were control-oriented, which was typically manifested through use of room searches, urine tests, and, occasionally, body searches to maintain program control over residents, and a heavily structured treatment modality [p. 181].

Also, several of the programs were in the price range of $10,000 to $15,000 per year, which made them prohibitively costly for more than a very small number of carefully selected inmates.

The conclusion seems to be that community-based correctional programs for women are few in number, selective in their operations, and not particularly cost-effective. What is especially noteworthy is the apparent lack of any effort directed toward the employment problems of the female ex-offender. In most communities, former offenders have no central place to turn to for help in locating a job. Few employment agencies are sensitive to the problems of women ex-offenders. The development of a skills bank or employment clearinghouse service, together with some imaginative combination of vocational counseling and training, might be the best contribution our society could make to the reintegration of the female offender into the community.

SUMMARY

Until recently the relatively insignificant involvement of females in crime has resulted in few systematic explanations. Early biological, sociological, and psychological explanations of female crime were based on faulty concepts with respect to biological and social differences between the sexes. Putting these myths aside, recent research and theory has been directed toward applying existing theories to females as well as developing new theories that encompass the sex variable. Our analysis of the female emancipation concept as a causative factor in female crime revealed that it has had little or no influence on female crime patterns.

After examining both official and unofficial crime data, we come to the inescapable conclusion that the much discussed increase in female criminality is more apparent than real. While the *Uniform Crime Reports* have reflected large percentage gains in female involvement in crime index offenses over the last few decades, these increases have resulted primarily from the relatively small size of the initial female-based figures. Our analysis shows that for the most part the only increases of any significance have been in the area of property offenses including larceny-theft, embezzlement, fraud, and forgery. These are the types of offenses in which women have traditionally been involved and there is no indication their involvement will change in the near future. Our analysis of female adolescence also did not reveal any truly remarkable changes. This group is still primarily taken into custody for larceny-theft and running away from home. We also noted a slight drop in the contribution of status and sex-related offenses to total juvenile female arrests in line with the gradual change in our paternalistic attitude toward female juveniles while the increased participation in drug-related offenses by this group resulted from the greater acceptability and accessibility of drugs within the teenage subculture. The self-reporting data on juveniles suggest that there is a greater convergence between the sexes with respect to involvement in nonserious personal and property offenses than is reflected in official statistics.

The lower female crime rate, as well as the less serious nature of female involvement in crime, results in proportionately fewer women than men coming into contact with the criminal justice system, although this has changed as a result of changing attitudes toward women within our society. Fewer women in the criminal justice system means less adequate facilities and services for female offenders.

The discussion of the "forgotten" female offender focused on the plight of incarcerated women. The size of female inmate populations rarely justifies more than one or two institutions for women in each state. Consequently, women are not afforded the same opportunities for housing in institutions that are appropriate to their required level of security. The size and location of these institutions frequently restrict the number of training and industry programs in which they can participate. Also, these institutions fail to provide women with the same range of medical services that are available to men.

In county jails, where men and women are frequently housed in the same facilities, women are often denied access to the same services and programs that are supplied for men. If jurisdictions are to avoid litigation arising from failure to comply with court mandated changes, they are going to be compelled to provide more equitable treatment for women. This can be accomplished through the use of cocorrectional facilities, expansion of community correctional programs, joint jurisdictional ventures involving local, state, and federal cooperative efforts, and involvement of private industry in prison work programs.

Not only have we forgotten the female offender, we have also neglected to provide adequate opportunities for these women to maintain ties with their children.

It seems fair to conclude that the nature of female crime is not likely to change in the immediate future. The recent interest in this field—it is hoped—will result in improved, nonsexist explanations and interpretations of this phenomenon. Additionally, there is a recognition that we need to improve existing facilities for this offender population.

DISCUSSION QUESTIONS

Find the answers to the following questions in the text.
1. Have there been any major changes in the types of offenses committed by women during the last two decades? Identify the major patterns of female crime.
2. Have there been any changes in the nature of juvenile female crime over the past two decades? What are the major types of juvenile female crime?
3. Describe the early explanations of female crime and the criticisms of these approaches.
4. What are some of the more contemporary approaches to explaining female crime?
5. What has been the effect of **female emancipation** on female crime?
6. What is the nature of correctional programs for women?
7. What are some of the obstacles faced by women seeking rehabilitation?
8. Describe the plight of the **inmate mother.**

TERMS TO IDENTIFY AND REMEMBER

status offenses
inmate mother
female emancipation

"forgotten offender"
convergence hypothesis
shared facilities

REFERENCES

Adler, F. *Sisters in Crime.* New York: McGraw-Hill, 1975.

Bartol, A. Women and crime. *Economic Inquiry* 17 (January 1979): 29–51.

Baunach, P. J. Women offenders: A commentary current conceptions of women in crime. *Quarterly Journal of Corrections* (Fall 1977): 14–16.

Block, R. *Homicide in Chicago: A Ten-Year Study.* Paper presented at the meeting of the American Society of Criminology, Chicago, 1974.

Blos, P. *The Adolescent Passage: Developmental Issues.* New York: International Universities Press, 1979.

Bole, J., and Tatro, C. The female offender: The 1980s and beyond. In J. T. O'Brien and M. Marcus (eds.), *Crime and Justice in America: Critical Issues for the Future.* New York: Pergamon Press, 1979, pp. 255–82.

Bowker, L. H. *Menstruation and Female Criminality: A New Look at the Data.* Paper presented at the annual meeting of the American Society of Criminology, Dallas, November 1978.

Bureau of Justice Statistics Bulletin: Prisoners 1925–81. Washington, D.C.: U.S. Department of Justice, December 1982.

———. Bulletin: *The 1983 Jail Census.* Washington, D.C.: U.S. Department of Justice, November 1984.

Bureau of Justice Statistics Bulletin: *Prisoners in 1984.* Washington, D.C.: U.S. Department of Justice, April 1985.

Cernkovich, S. A., and Giordano, P. Delinquency, opportunity and gender. *The Journal of Criminal Law and Criminology* 70, no. 2 (1979): 143–51.

Cohen, A. K., and Short, J. F. Research in delinquent subcultures. *Journal of Social Issues,* 14, no. 3 (1958): 20–37.

Cottle, T. J. Children in jail. *Crime and Delinquency* 25 (1979): 318–34.

Cowie, J., Cowie, V., and Slater, E. *Delinquency in Girls.* London: Heineman, 1968.

Datesman, S. K., and Scarpitti, F. Women's crime and women's emancipation. In *Women, Crime and Justice.* New York: Oxford University Press, 1980.

———. Female delinquency and broken homes: A reassessment. *Criminology* 13, no. 1 (1975): 35–55.

Datesman, S. K., Scarpitti, F. K., and Stephenson, R. M. Female delinquency: An application of self and opportunity theories. *Journal of Research in Crime and Delinquency* 12, no. 2 (1975): 107–23.

Denys, R. G. Lady paperhangers. *Canadian Journal of Corrections* 52 (1969): 169–92.

Elliott, D. S., Ageton, S. S., Huizinga, D., Knowles, B. A., and Canter, R. J. *The Prevalence and Incidence of Delinquent Behavior: 1976–1980.* Boulder, CO: Behavioral Science Research Institute, 1983.

Eve, R., and Edmonds, K. R. *Women's Liberation and Female Criminality: Or Sister, Will You Give Me Back My Dime?* Paper presented at the meeting of the National Society of Social Problems, San Francisco, September 1978.

Franklin, A. Criminality in the work place: A comparison of male and female offenders. In F. Adler and R. J. Simon (eds.), *The Criminology of Women.* Boston: Houghton Mifflin, 1979, pp. 167–76.

General Accounting Office Report of the Comptroller General to the Congress of the United States. *Women in Prison: Inequitable Treatment Requires Action.* Washington, D.C.: U.S. Government Printing Office, 1980.

Giallombardo, R. *Society of Women: A Study of a Woman's Prison.* New York: Wiley, 1966.

Gibbons, D. C. *Delinquent Behavior.* Englewood Cliffs, NJ: Prentice-Hall, 1981.

Glick, R., and Neto, V. V. *National Study of Women's Correctional Programs.* U.S. Department of Justice. Washington, D.C.: U.S. Government Printing Office, 1977.

Glueck, S., and Glueck, E. *Five Hundred Delinquent Women.* New York: Alfred A. Knopf, 1934.

Gold, M., and Reimer, D. J. Changing patterns of delinquent behavior among Americans 13 through 16 years old: 1967–72. *Crime and Delinquency Literature* 7 (1975): 483–517.

Greenwell, R., Vega, M., and Silverman, I. J. *The Female Forger.* Paper presented at the meeting of the American Society of Criminology, Dallas, November 1978.

Hoffman-Bustamante, D. The nature of female criminality. *Issues in Criminology* 18 (1973): 117–36.

James, J., and Thornton, W. Women's liberation and the female delinquent. *Journal of Research in Crime and Delinquency* (July 1980): 230–44.

Kassebaum, G. Sex in prison. *Sexual Behavior* 2 (1972): 39–45.

Kempt, T. *Physical and Psychological Causes of Prostitution.* Geneva: League of Nations Advisory Committee on Social Questions, 1943.

Klein, D. The etiology of female crime: A review of the literature. *Issues in Criminology* 8 (1973): 3–30.

Klein, J. F., and Montague, A. *Check Forgers.* Lexington, MA.: D. C. Heath and Company, 1979.

Konopka, G. *The Adolescent Girl in Conflict.* Englewood Cliffs, NJ: Prentice-Hall, 1966.

Leventhal, G. Female criminality: Is "Women's Lib" to blame? *Psychological Reports* 41 (1977): 1179–82.

Lindsay, P. *The Mainspring of Murder.* London: John Lang, 1958.

Lombroso, C., and Ferrero, W. *The Female Offender.* New York: D. Appleton and Company, 1897.

McGowan, B., and Blumenthal, K. *Why Punish the Children? A Study of Children of Women Prisoners.* Hackensack, NJ: National Council on Crime and Delinquency, 1978.

Murton, T. O., and Baunach, P. J. Women in prison. *Free World Times* 2 (June–July 1973): 1–2.

Nation's prison population growing more quickly. *New York Times,* September 16, 1985, p.12.

Nau, E. Homicides by females. *International Criminal Justice Document of Translation.* U.S. Department of Justice, National Criminal Justice Reference Service, 1972.

Pollak, O. *The Criminality of Women.* Philadelphia: University of Pennsylvania Press, 1950, pp. 121–35.

Pollock, J. Early theories of female criminality. In L. H. Bowker (ed), *Women, Crime and the Criminal Justice System.* Lexington, MA: Lexington Books, 1978.

Rasche, C. E. The female offender as an object of criminological research. *Criminal Justice and Behavior* 1, no. 4 (1974): 301–20.

Reckless, W. C., and Kay, B. A. *The Female Offender.* Consultant report presented to the President's Commission on Law Enforcement and Administration of Justice, 1969.

Schulman, H. M. S. *Juvenile Delinquency in American Society.* New York: Harper & Row, 1961.

Short, J. F., and Strodtbeck, F. L. *Group Process and Gang Delinquency.* Chicago: University of Chicago Press, 1965.

Silverman, I. J. Female criminality: An assessment. In I. J. Barak and R. C. Huff (eds.), *The Mad, the Bad, and the Different: Essays in Honor of Simon Dinitz.* Lexington, MA: Lexington Books, 1981.

Simon, R. L. *The Contemporary Woman and Crime.* Rockville, MD: National Institute of Mental Health, 1975.

Simon, R. L., Martin, G., Miller, M. G., and Aigner, S. M. Contemporary theories of deviance and female delinquency: A comparison test. *Journal of Research in Crime and Delinquency* 17 (1980): 42–53.

Steffensmeier, D. J. Crime and the contemporary woman: An analysis of changing levels of female property crime, 1960–1975. *Social Forces* 57, no. 2 (1978): 566–83.

———. Sex differences in patterns of adult crime, 1965–1977: A review and assessment. *Social Forces* 58, no. 4 (1980): 1080–1108.

Steffensmeier D. and Steffensmeier, R. H. "Trends in female delinquency: An examination of arrest, juvenile court, self report and Field Data" *Criminology* 18 (May 1980): 62–85.

Thomas, W. I. *The Unadjusted Girl.* Boston: Little, Brown, 1923.

Trojanowicz, R. C. *Juvenile Delinquency Concepts and Control.* Englewood Cliffs, NJ: Prentice-Hall, 1978.

U.S. Department of Justice, Federal Bureau of Investigation, *Uniform Crime Reports, 1970.* Washington, D.C.: U.S. Government Printing Office, 1971.

———. *Uniform Crime Reports, 1975.* Washington D.C.: U.S. Government Printing Office, 1976.

———. *Uniform Crime Reports, 1979.* Washington, D.C.: U.S. Government Printing Office, 1980.

Ward, D. A., and Kassenbaum, G. G. *Women's Prison: Sex and Social Structure.* Chicago: Aldine, 1965.

Ward, D. A., Jackson, M., and Ward, R. E. Crime of violence by women. In D. J. Mulvihill and M. M. Tumin (eds.), *Crimes of Violence* (vol. 13). Washington, D.C.: U.S. Government Printing Office, 1969.

Weis, J. Liberation and crime: The invention of the new female criminal. *Crime and Social Justice* 6 (1976): 17–27.

Williams, V. L., and Fish, M. *Convicts, Codes, and Contraband: The Prison Life of Men and Women.* Cambridge, MA: Ballinger, 1974.

Wolfgang, M. *Patterns in Criminal Homicide.* Philadelphia: University of Pennsylvania Press, 1952.

Zahn, M., and Neilson, K. *Changing Patterns of Criminal Homicide: A Twenty-Year Follow-up.* Paper presented at the meeting of the American Society of Criminology, Tucson, 1976.

Zemmerman, J., and Broder, P. K. A comparison of differential delinquency measures devised from self-report data. *Journal of Criminal Justice,* no. 3 (1980): 147–62.

THREE

THEORETICAL PERSPECTIVES ON CRIME AND CRIMINALITY

Theories of criminality have a twofold purpose: they help organize existing information about criminal behavior into a coherent, systematic framework, and they serve to point out directions for further research by indicating potentially fruitful leads to be explored. In addition, theories of criminality may help establish some rational basis for programs aimed at controlling, reducing, eliminating, or preventing crime and delinquency.

The search for the causes of criminal behavior is ages old. But it was not until the latter part of the nineteenth century, when the methods of science became available to investigators, that the foundations were laid for the systematic acquisition of valid and reliable information about crime and criminals. Prior to that time, there were relatively few facts or theories. Knowledge of crime and criminals consisted mostly of anecdotes and speculative views concerning the causes of crime which were rooted in commonsense observations of criminal behavior.

Common sense suggests that people who act differently must *be* different, in some way or other. The notion of "differentness" extended in earliest times to include demoniacal possession—that the behavior of the criminal was controlled by some evil spirit which had taken over the individual's body and soul. Later speculations led to conclusions which stressed faulty biology or psychological disorder as the principal causes of crime.

The Classical School of criminology was less concerned with finding the determinants of criminality than in seeking reforms in criminal law and the administration of justice. Classical criminologists replaced the view of the human being as a marionette whose strings were pulled by supernatural powers with the conception of humans as rational beings who acted on the basis of judgment and reasoning and were therefore responsible for their behavior. While recognizing that a person's exercise of free will could be adversely affected by a variety of conditions, the Classical criminologist sought comparable rationality in the criminal laws and their administration. Beccaria, the most noted member of the Classical School, advocated the principle of equal punishment for a crime. In addition, he believed that crime prevention was more important than punishment.

Following the Classical School—and, to a considerable extent, as a reaction to it—the Positivist School of criminology rejected attempts to explain crime as the willful act of a rational being exercising free will. Positivist criminologists viewed criminal behavior as determined by forces largely beyond human control. These, they believed, could be discovered by scientific methods of inquiry of the kind that were already leading to swift advances in physics, chemistry, and biology. In opposition to the Classical School, Positivist criminologists directed their attention toward the *offender,* rather than toward the offense.

The causes of crime have been looked for both within and outside the offender. Physiology and heredity, mental disorders, personality characteristics, poverty, frustration, racism, and even the criminal justice system itself are all factors that have been examined as possible causes of criminal behavior.

The relationship between economic factors and criminality is extremely complex. Poverty can bring about crime, but its social conditions may be more important than the economic circumstances in producing crime. To the radical or critical criminologist, criminality is one of the consequences of the class struggle in a capitalist society. Criminal law and the criminal justice system are viewed as tools used by the power elites to maintain the status quo and exclude the poor and disenfranchised from sharing power and wealth.

The nature-nurture issue has never been dropped entirely from criminology theories since the time of Lombroso. But genetic studies of criminality have progressed considerably since the turn of the century, when investigators traced the genealogies of families distinguished by unusually high percentages of criminals, lunatics, and mental defectives. In addition to genetic studies, researchers have conducted wide-ranging investigations of abnormal physiological structures and their possible influence on criminal behavior. Nearly four decades of research has found certain consistent patterns of abnormal functioning in the brain waves, skin conductance, and cardiovascular responses of individuals identified as having antisocial personalities.

Psychiatrists have interpreted crime as a syndrome or category of mental illness. Psychologists, on the other hand, have tended to view criminality as behavior that is acquired in the same way as other patterns of learned behavior, that is, through reinforcement. The psychiatric approach has fostered two lines of inquiry: (1) the search for a "criminal personality," and (2) the assessment of psychiatric disorders among criminals. Both of these areas of research have failed to provide results which confirm the theories on which they are based. Neither clinical observations nor psychological tests have identified any cluster of psychological traits distinctive to the criminal. With the exception of alcoholism, drug addiction, and sociopathy or psychopathy—terms often defined with reference to the criminal behavior they are supposed to explain—psychiatric disorders appear to occur with about the same frequency in both criminal and noncriminal populations.

Approaches to criminality using learning theories, developed chiefly from laboratory studies of animal and human subjects, have provided some of the clearest theoretical accounts of how criminal behavior may be acquired, maintained, and changed. Attempts to modify criminal behavior by means of "psychotechnology," however, have generated intense opposition. Outrage over certain projects which seemed to reduce human beings to the level of animal subjects led in 1974 to the withdrawal of federal support from all projects involving "behavior modification." Current programs have dropped the language of psychotechnology and show a great deal of restraint in their claims and methods.

Sociological theories of criminality are directed toward finding answers to questions about collective rather than individual criminal behavior. There are two approaches to the exploration and interpretation of social factors in crime causation. The structural approach looks at the influence of social patterns of power or institutions on criminality. The subcultural approach emphasizes the role of conflict between the norms of the larger society and those which characterize lower class or ethnic subcultures. The latter approach maintains that when the norms of the subculture impose standards of conduct different from those prescribed by the larger culture, the resulting normative conflict can become the major source of criminal behavior.

Sociopsychological theories of criminality examine the processes by which people become delinquents or criminals, and the differential response factors that help explain why some people who are exposed to adverse environmental conditions engage in crime and delinquency while others do not. Sutherland's differential association theory suggests that crime is learned principally in primary groups. Reckless's containment theory attempts to consider both social and cultural factors (outer containment) and individual factors (inner containment) and the way these factors interact to produce crime and delinquency. Finally, the labeling perspective focuses on societal reactions to deviant behavior. The imposition of a deviant label may result in increasing, rather than decreasing, tendencies to engage in criminal behavior. According to this approach, formal treatment of deviant behavior may do more harm than good.

Despite some modest accomplishments, we are still groping for answers about the causes or determinants of crime. But it seems abundantly clear that *crime in general* cannot be explained by any particular factor. Sunday-supplement journalists are fond of "explaining" crime and delinquency as the result of poverty, broken homes, failure of the schools, or other single causes. But crime is a term that embraces vastly different acts—from the slayings by the serial murderer to the greedy maneuvers of corrupt politicians. It is extremely doubtful that the many varied behaviors that count as crimes could all be explained by any single or simple theory.

Increasingly, efforts to explain crime will be directed toward discovering what causes specific crimes. Solutions to the problems posed by crime and delinquency, however, will not come automatically with the discovery of the causes of criminality. Policies dealing with crime are affected indirectly, at best, by what criminologists have to say about the causes of crime. To cope effectively with the factors that research has already shown to be significantly implicated in many kinds of criminal activity requires social changes of a far more fundamental and pervasive nature than are within the present capabilities of the criminal justice system and other institutions and agencies of social control in contemporary U.S. society.

In Chapter 9, which begins this section, we take note of the revival of doctrines associated with the Classical School of criminology. Declaring that the rehabilitative approach is bankrupt, modern classical criminologists argue for an approach to crime and criminals which emphasizes the deterrent and preventive uses of punishment, including the death penalty, and reasserts the primacy of rational choice, free will, and responsibility for individual actions, in contrast with the determinism of scientific criminology. The pros and cons of these respective positions are carefully considered.

chapter **9**

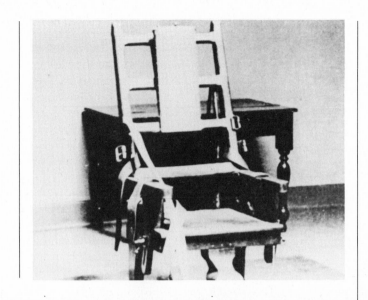

CLASSICAL, POSITIVIST, AND NEOCLASSICAL PERSPECTIVES

Over the course of time, criminal behavior has been attributed to almost every conceivable factor: race, climate, meteorological conditions, phases of the moon, alcohol, drugs, culture, movies, dancehalls, the breakdown of religious beliefs—even the confluence of the stars and planets. Medieval thought ascribed a wide range and variety of deviant behavior to demoniacal possession—an "explanation" which could be extended to include at least some forms of criminal deviance. The basic premise of this approach is that criminal conduct is caused by some "otherworld" power or spirit which transcends physical restrictions or limitations and is not subject to human understanding and control. Since such a spirit is beyond the comprehension of mortal humans, it provides a convenient explanation for any or all conditions that are baffling or hard to understand.

Throughout history, people have tended to rely on otherworldly spirits as a source of explanation for many natural as well as human actions and events. Primitive peoples believed that spirits possessed and controlled the actions of all objects and beings. Hebrew and Christian traditions supported the notion of an omniscient, omnipresent, all-powerful deity to whom anything was possible—from creating a rainbow to stopping the sun in its path. During the Middle Ages, otherworldly interpretations were used to account for political and social, as well as physical, events. Thus, the will of God explained not only birth and death, but why men became kings, priests, or paupers. Cultures which generally relied heavily on supernatural explanations tended to interpret criminal behavior as a result of being possessed or instigated by, or succumbing to the temptations of an evil spirit. Under the influence of the Judeo-Christian tradition, medieval interpretations attributed criminal behavior to the Devil.

This philosophical orientation continued well into the nineteenth century. Defendants indicted under English law were charged not only with violating the law but also with being "prompted and instigated by the Devil and not having the fear of God before his eyes." The Supreme Court of North Carolina, as recently as 1862, endorsed the notion of demoniacal possession in its declaration: "to know the right and still pursue the wrong proceeds from a perverse will brought about by the seductions of the Evil One" (Sutherland and Cressey, 1978, p. 54). Individuals who were viewed as demoniacally possessed were subjected to cruel tortures which were directed toward expelling or exorcizing the evil spirits or the Devil. In most of these cases, the individual was rescued from the clutches of the Devil, but usually died in the process. In other cases, people might be banished in order to protect the community from further outrages at the hands of the offending individual or to placate some vengeful supernatural power.

One of the contributions of the medieval church to criminological thought was the concept that crime and sin were synonymous. Thus, a crime was not merely an offense against the community or state—it was an offense against God. A second contribution of the church in the Middle Ages was the concept of free will—the idea that people choose their actions, good or bad, and hence can be held responsible for them. The religious doctrine of eternal punishment, atonement, and spiritual conversion rests on the assumption that people who have committed sins can act differently if they choose to do so.

These ecclesiastical views were reflected in secular interpretations of crime. Criminal law during the waning of the Middle Ages was largely concerned with *deterrence:* capital and corporal punishment were lavishly meted out for even the most commonplace and trivial offenses in the belief that public punishment would help to deter potential wrongdoers. As Schafer (1969) observed, "Every part of the human body was subjected to punishment. Whatever was left after mutilation of the body was destroyed by branding, stocks, pillory, or other sundry humbling or corporal measures" (p. 103). But no matter how vigorously society tried to "beat the Devil" out of offenders, the criminal who was most likely to be deterred by these barbarous punishments was the one who died from such torture. Later, philosophers and social critics began to seek more rational grounds for deterrence by means of investigation of its possible causes.

Viewpoints toward crime and criminals changed relatively little during the sixteenth and seventeenth centuries in England and in Europe. Sir Thomas More, Lord Chancellor to Henry VIII, and author of the influential and widely read *Utopia,* was skeptical of the well-entrenched doctrines of retributive justice. As one of the first major intellectual figures to question the notion that punishment is a deterrent to crime, he suggested that prevention might demand a closer examination of the conditions which helped to produce criminal behavior. His ideas on criminality, in addition to his views on a variety of other significant issues, were entirely too advanced for the times. It remained for later thinkers to pursue some of his lines of thought regarding the relationship between crime and punishment.

THE CLASSICAL SCHOOL OF CRIMINOLOGY

Criminal law in eighteenth-century Europe continued to be uncertain, repressive, and barbaric (Monachesi, 1970). Public officials had the power to deprive people of their freedom, property, or lives without recourse to any of the due process rights which are taken for granted today. Individuals could be imprisoned on the basis of secret accusations supported by the flimsiest evidence; and ingenious methods of torture were used to extract confessions from those who refused to cooperate.

Judges during this period had nearly unlimited discretion in punishing criminal offenders and frequently the sentences imposed depended upon the status and power of the accused. Poor and powerless offenders were subjected to cruel punishment, while the wealthy and powerful were treated leniently. The majority of criminal offenses at this time were punishable by death. In many cases, the individual was first subjected to excruciating torture before being executed. It was in reaction to these abuses, cruelties, and irrationalities that the classical criminologists proposed their reforms—and it is in appreciation of such conditions that the proposed reforms appear so revolutionary.

Cesare Beccaria

One of the principal figures of the Classical School was an Italian nobleman named **Cesare Bonesana, Marchese de Beccaria** (1738–1794). In his famous *Essay on Capital Crimes and Punishments,* which was published anonymously in 1764, Beccaria provided a manifesto for the Classical School. His book was a plea for the reform of judicial and penal systems of the time. In it he proposed a series of far-reaching reforms in criminal law that were intended to move it toward humanitarian goals. He opposed the use of torture and the death penalty; he criticized laws that were written so opaquely that they required extensive interpretation; he argued for the minimal punishments necessary to protect society; he was a spokesman for the defense of the accused against the capricious and arbitrary administration of justice.

To Beccaria the primary function of punishment was to insure the continued existence of society (Monachesi, 1970). The nature and amount of punishment inflicted against offenders should vary in proportion to the extent the individual's acts endanger the existence of society. The more threatening the crime to societal welfare and existence, the more severe should be the punishment inflicted upon the offender. Beccaria was against the use of punishment as a means of tormenting offenders or in order to undo a crime that was already committed. Instead he felt that punishment should function as a means of preventing offenders from doing further harm to society as well as preventing others from committing crimes. Thus from Beccaria's standpoint punishment was to serve as a deterrent rather than as a means of retribution. He looked on punishment as an educative process: the type of punishment selected and the means by which it is imposed should have the greatest impact and make the most enduring impression upon the offender while at the same time it should inflict the least amount of physical suffering. Beccaria felt that it was not the severity but rather the certainty of punishment that represented the most effective deterrent. In fact, he believed punishments which were severe, cruel, and inhumane not only failed to prevent crime but by brutalizing them, actually encouraged people to commit further offenses. In this respect he was against the use of capital punishment. A summary of Beccaria's views is given on the following page.

Beccaria's influence was considerable; his work was translated into many languages, his views received the respectful attention of leading social philosophers and critics like Voltaire in France, and his ideas led to legal reforms in a number of countries. In England, Jeremy Bentham, Samuel Romilly, and William Blackstone built upon the beginnings supplied by Beccaria. As Allen and Simonsen (1978) have noted, four of Beccaria's unprecedented ideas found their way into French criminal law as formulated in the Napoleonic Code:

1. An individual should be regarded as innocent until he is proven guilty.

2. An individual should not be forced to testify against himself.

3. An individual should have the right to employ counsel and to cross-examine the state's witnesses.

4. An individual should have the right to prompt and public trial and, in most cases, a trial by jury [p. 20].

These ideas have found an equally respected and durable place in the United States. The reader will recognize that they are incorporated in almost identical language within our own Constitution, as part of the Bill of Rights.

Beccaria on Capital Crime and Punishment

1. The basis for all social action must be the utilitarian conception of the greatest happiness for the greatest number.

2. Crime must be considered an injury to society, and the rational measure of crime is the extent of that injury.

3. Prevention of crime is more important than punishments for crimes; indeed, punishment is justifiable only on the supposition that it helps prevent criminal conduct. In preventing crime it is necessary to improve and publish the laws, so that the nation can understand and support them, to reward virtue, and to improve the public's education both in regard to legislation and to life.

4. In criminal procedure secret accusations and torture should be abolished. There should be speedy trials. The accused should be treated humanely before trial and must have every right and facility to bring forward evidence in his behalf. Turning state's evidence should be done away with, as it amounts to no more than the public authorization of treachery.

5. The purpose of punishment is to deter persons from the commission of crimes and not to provide social revenge. Not severity, but certainty and swiftness in punishment best secure this result. Punishment must be sure and swift and penalties determined strictly in accordance with the social damage wrought by the crime. Crimes against property should be punished solely by fines, or by imprisonment when the person is unable to pay the fine. Banishment is an excellent punishment for crimes against the state. There should be no capital punishment. Life imprisonment is a better deterrent. Capital punishment is irreparable and hence makes no provision for possible mistakes, and the desirability of later rectification.

6. Imprisonment should be more widely employed but its mode of application should be greatly improved through providing better physical quarters and by separating and classifying the prisoners as to age, sex, and degree of criminality.

Source: H. E. Barnes and N. K. Teeters, *New Horizons in Criminology.* Englewood Cliffs, NJ: Prentice-Hall, 1959, p. 322.

Jeremy Bentham and Utilitarianism

One of the most persistent notions in intellectual history is that human conduct depends to a large extent on a trade-off or balance between pleasure and pain. Common sense allows for the definition of happiness as maximizing pleasure and minimizing pain; this appeals to thoughtful and reflective persons of every age. This theme was already familiar and even commonplace at the time it became a central idea in the philosophy of **Jeremy Bentham** (1745–1832).

Bentham maintained that many, perhaps most, human actions can be understood with regard to what he called " **hedonistic** (or felicific) **calculus**," a term he devised to express the idea that "to achieve the most pleasure and the least pain is the main objective of an intelligent man." If this notion is applied to criminal conduct, it supports the contention that the main purpose of punishment ought to be to limit the pleasure or gain that the offender receives from his criminal acts and to inflict pain for his misconduct. Bentham believed that if more pain than pleasure resulted from crime, people would thus be deterred from committing criminal acts. Like Beccaria, Bentham felt that the primary purpose of punishment was deterrence and prevention. Similarly, he opposed excessive punishment of the offender and held that the punishment should "fit the crime." Bentham's objective was to reform the brutal, archaic English criminal code with its more than two hundred capital offenses into a system which employed graduated penal sanctions. Bentham's ideas were supplemented and implemented by four of his contemporaries, Romilly, Mackintosh, Peel, and Buxton (Barnes and Teeters, 1959).

Bentham is also known for his development of a utopian plan for the design of prisons. Described by Geis (1970) as an illustration of eccentricity in action, he points out that, to Bentham's credit, imprisonment at this time was a rather novel approach; the usual form of punishment included transportation, capital punishment, fines, and the like. Bentham called this institution a panopticon or "inspection house" (Barnes and Teeters, 1950). The plans for the institution called for the construction of a huge tank or domelike structure covered by a glass roof with cells on each tier of the outer circumference facing toward the center. A guard tower was built in the center with the idea that this would make it possible for all cells to be under constant scrutiny. Ironically no panopticon prisons were built in England or on the Continent, but several were built in the United States (Geis, 1970). The Western State Penitentiary in Pittsburgh was to some extent based on Bentham's plan. However only a few years after it was built, it was decided that this institution was wholly unsuited for anything but a fortress and was ordered rebuilt. The other institution that followed the panopticon plan was built at Stateville, Illinois, and is still standing. It is interesting to note that prison administrators discovered the impracticality of this design after four of the cell houses were built and occupied with the result that the remaining cell blocks were built following a more conventional plan. What Bentham failed to recognize was that while the center guard tower provided an opportunity for guards to watch inmates it likewise gave inmates an opportunity to know where guards were at all times.

The Legacy of the Enlightenment

The Classical School of criminology was heavily influenced by a philosophic viewpoint which helped identify the period as the Age of Enlightenment. It was contended that man was conceived as a rational and intelligent being capable of self-direction. He is not possessed by evil spirits or the Devil but is an individual with the capacity to understand his own actions and to behave in ways consistent with his best interests. Man, in short, is master of his fate and captain of his soul.

From the perspective of the Classical School, man was viewed as a self-determined being capable of learning from experience and using those lessons to change his own behavior or that of the groups to which he belongs. Criminal behavior, therefore, was judged in terms of the motives of the perpetrator, the degree of deliberate calculation or intent revealed by the act, and whether or not the offender could distinguish between right and wrong. Fundamental to this position was the belief that crime could be controlled by law, since people who can distinguish between right and wrong will reason that it is undesirable and unwise to do wrong.

The descriptive titles historians assign to periods or epochs are apt to be misleading in their oversimplification. The Age of Enlightenment, for example, had many stretches of darkness, despite the broad humanitarian reforms it introduced. The French Revolution toppled the *ancien régime* and liberated the energies of the common people of France, but it also gave the world Napoleon Bonaparte and twenty years of devastating warfare. It paved the way for the Industrial Revolution, but it generated violent currents of political reaction in a number of countries, especially Russia and Germany. Criminals, along with the mentally ill, were among the beneficiaries of social reforms that included the administration of justice, at least to the extent that some of the more savage forms of earlier punishment—breaking on the rack, mutilation, branding—were gradually abolished. But the nineteenth century was fairly well advanced before significant gains were made in alleviating the plight of the mentally ill patient and the incarcerated prisoner. This is a theme to which we shall return later.

The principal contributions to criminological thought of the Classical School were twofold: (1) belief in the rational nature of man, which supported the notion that the individual possesses innate powers to order his or her conduct in accordance with free choice between right and wrong, good and evil; and (2) the concept of *hedonism,* that is, that behavior is guided and dominated by tendencies to seek pleasure and avoid pain.

Contemporary concepts of criminal jurisprudence retain the basic assumption that man is a rational creature, is responsible for his actions, and is able to choose between right and wrong (free will). This is apparent in laws governing behavior that make allowance for partial or diminished responsibility: the insane person who was incapable of making a meaningful and behaviorally relevant distinction between right and wrong at the time the crime was committed is exempted from criminal sanctions. Hedonism perseveres in the more contemporary guise of the *pleasure principle* in psychoanalysis, which asserts almost the same ideas as those which Bentham expressed in the hedonistic calculus, and in modern reinforcement theory, where pleasure and pain are dealt with in terms of positive and negative reinforcing stimuli and responses.

If one of the major objectives of criminological theory is to direct the search for causes or determinants of criminal behavior, it must be said that the Classical School contributed relatively little to advancement toward this goal. As Vold (1979) observes:

> It seems fair . . . to characterize the classical school as administrative and legal criminology. Its great advantage was that it set up a procedure that was easy to

administer. It made the judge only an instrument to apply the law, and the law undertook to prescribe an exact penalty for every crime and every degree thereof. Puzzling questions about the reasons for or causes of behavior, the uncertainties of motive and intent, the unequal consequences of an arbitrary rule, these were all deliberately ignored for the sake of administrative uniformity. This was the classical conception of justice—an exact scale of punishments for equal acts without reference to the individual involved or the special circumstances in which the crime was committed [p. 26].

THE POSITIVIST SCHOOL OF CRIMINOLOGY

Attempts to identify the causes of crime in forces beyond human control—external as well as internal—which undermine a person's capacity to choose between right and wrong characterize the positivist approach in criminology. **Positivism** subscribes to the viewpoint that human conduct is dominated by environmental and psychological factors and that an understanding of these factors will provide the means to comprehend all human behavior, noncriminal as well as criminal. The ideas and approaches of the Positivist School constitute the bridge or transition from historical to contemporary theories of criminality. As the various disciplines of sociology, anthropology, psychology, and psychiatry began to develop, explanations of criminal behavior were sought in the psychological makeup of the individual and in the social and physical environment. Rationally ordered choice was increasingly rejected as a cause for either normal or deviant behavior. The emergence of the Positivist School of criminology, as Schafer (1969) observed, "symbolized clearly that the era of faith was over and the scientific age had begun" (p. 123).

Comte and Positivism

Auguste Comte (1798–1857) contributed the term *positivism* and articulated many of the basic tenets of positivist philosophy. He maintained that positive knowledge is acquired by reasoning and observation, duly combined, and that an explanation of facts is simply the establishment of a connection between single phenomena and some general facts, the number of which continually diminishes with the progress of science. In Comte's view, there can be no real knowledge but that which is based on observed facts.

In contrast to the speculative approach and introspective methods of the Classical School, positivism prescribed an approach to the *systematic acquisition of knowledge.* By extending to human behavior and social phenomena the scientific methods of observation and study that had already accounted for significant advances in the understanding of physical events and processes, Comte rejected the free will position of the Classical School in favor of *determinism,* that is, the position that all phenomena are susceptible to scientific explanation. This determinist position is shared by those whose contributions make up the Positivist School of criminology. The contrasts between the Classical and Positivist schools have been summarized by Jeffery (1960) in the following terms:

> The Classical School defined crime in legal terms; the Positive School rejected the legal definition of crime. The Classical School focused attention on crime as a legal entity; the Positive School focused attention on the act as a psychological entity. The Classical School emphasized free will; the Positive School emphasized determinism. The Classical School theorized that punishment had a deterrent effect; the Positive School said that punishment should be replaced by a scientific treatment of criminals calculated to protect society [p. 366].

Auguste Comte developed the concept of positivism, but the application of the positivist approach to the study of crime must be attributed to Cesare Lombroso, who is often called "the father of modern criminology," and his two associates, Enrico Ferri and Raffaele Garofalo (Schafer, 1969). In fact, their different emphases on the most important factors in crime causation—biological, (Lombroso), social, (Ferri) and psychological (Garofalo)—laid the groundwork for later theory and research into the major determinants of criminal behavior.

The Anthropological / Morphological Approach

✓ **Cesare Lombroso,** an Italian army physician, sought to establish a relationship between certain physical characteristics and criminal behavior. Like many intellectuals during the latter half of the nineteenth century, he was heavily influenced by Darwin's writings on organic evolution. Lombroso believed in the existence of a distinct anthropological type, the *born criminal,* who is likely or even bound to engage in crime. These congenital criminals represent **atavistic types**—a throwback to some earlier or more primitive type of contemporary man. According to Lombroso, these offenders are characterized by certain identifiable malformations of the skeleton and skull. These "stigmata of degeneracy" include an under- or over-sized brain, a receding forehead, large ears, and a projecting or receding jaw.

Lombroso's views underwent development and change. By the time the latest edition of his book *Criminal Man* was published in 1897, Lombroso had broadened his views on crime causation and restricted the number of those he identified as born criminals to about 35 percent of the criminal population. He recognized several additional categories of offenders. These are described below with additional comments quoted from the final version of *Criminal Man* prepared with the assistance of his daughter, Gina Lombroso-Ferrero, which was originally published in 1911 and later reprinted in 1972.

1. *Insane Criminals.* Included in this category of offenders are idiots, imbeciles, alcoholics, paranoiacs, and those suffering from general paresis, epilepsy, and hysteria. Individuals in this group may exhibit some stigmata and also show tendencies toward impulsivity and cruelty.
2. *Occasional Criminals.* This category includes the following subtypes:
   a. *Criminaloids:* These persons occupy a position in Lombroso's schema between the born criminal and the honest man. They were seen as predisposed to engage in criminal activity when opportunities were presented.

Lombroso indicated that they were a variety of born criminal, but exhibited less intensive organic tendencies and only a touch of degeneracy.

b. *Habitual Criminals:* Criminals in this category were viewed by Lombroso as lacking in innate abnormalities which produced criminal tendencies. Instead, they displayed the effects of inadequate socialization, for example, poor education, lack of parental guidance, and so forth. Lombroso further suggested that groups like the Mafia and Camorra contain members who were drawn into a life of crime as a result of association.

c. *Juridical Criminals:* This category comprises "individuals who break the law, not because of any natural depravity, nor owing to distressing circumstances, but by mere accident" (Lombroso-Ferrero, 1972, p. 115). Included are "authors of accidental misdeeds" such as involuntary homicide, and those who commit the kinds of crime that today would be regarded as public order or political offenses.

d. *Criminals of Passion:* These offenders represent "the ultra-violet ray of the criminal spectrum" (p. 118), as contrasted with the ultra-red of the vulgar criminal. According to Lombroso, "their abnormality consists in the excessive development of noble qualities, sensibility, altruism, integrity, affection, which if carried to an extreme, may result in actions forbidden by law, or worse still, dangerous to society" (p. 118).

Lombroso's hypotheses were based largely on intuition and speculation, and they failed to meet the test of empirical verification. Charles Goring, an English physician, obtained comparative anthropometric measurements on a large sample of British criminals and noncriminals. Goring (1913) concluded:

> We have exhaustively compared . . . different kinds of criminals with each other, and criminals as a class with the law-abiding public. From these comparisons no evidence has emerged confirming the existence of a physical criminal type such as Lombroso and his disciples have described. . . . Our results nowhere confirm evidence nor justify the allegations of criminal anthropologists. They challenge their evidence at almost every point. In fact, both with regard to measurement and physical anomalies in criminals, our statistics present a startling conformity with similar statistics of the law-abiding classes. The final conclusion we are bound to accept . . . must be that there is no such thing as a physical criminal type [quoted by Hardman, 1964, p. 202].

But Lombroso's theory was revived by an American anthropologist named Ernest Hooton, who conducted a massive study of male prisoners in ten states. Hooton attempted to account for the failure to demonstrate a relationship between physical features and criminality on the grounds that Lombroso had neglected to categorize criminals according to the type of offense they had committed. Said Hooton (1939):

> It is a remarkable fact that tall, thin men tend to murder and to rob, tall heavy men to kill and to commit forgery and fraud, undersized thin men to steal and to burglarize, short heavy men to assault, to rape, and to commit other sex crimes, whereas men of mediocre body build tend to break the law without obvious discrimination or preference [p. 376].

If Lombroso had incorporated these considerations, Hooton believed, his theory might have found confirmation. On the basis of his own findings, Hooton claimed that criminal behavior is a direct result of the impact of environment upon low-grade human organisms and that characteristic patterns of offense are committed by people of various races and nationalities. These results led him to the conclusion that "the elimination of crime can be effected only by the extirpation of the physically, mentally, and morally unfit or by their complete segregation in a socially acceptive environment" (p. 13).

Hooton's book, it should be emphasized, was published in 1939, the year Nazi Germany invaded Poland and ignited the conflagration known as World War II. It was not until six years later, in the rubble and wreckage of Hitler's Thousand Year Reich, that the world discovered the grisly evidence which remained from the Nazi attempt to carry out the sort of program Hooton seems to have advocated. Unfortunately—for Hooton, but not the rest of the world—the critics failed to agree with his conclusions. They found nearly as much to object to in Hooton's own work as they had found in Lombroso's writings, and they took Hooton to task for a variety of methodological flaws, ranging from ambiguous definitions of key concepts to systematic bias in his sampling procedures. For instance, his control group was composed of a fantastic conglomeration of noncriminals that included firemen from Nashville, Tennessee, members of a militia company, patrons of a bathing beach, college students, patients from a large urban hospital, and various others. Critics questioned whether these groups constituted a representative cross-section of the population.

A more complex approach to constitutional typology was made by William Sheldon (1949) in his characterization of three types of "biological delinquents." Sheldon's **somatotyping** described an individual's body build according to the predominance of a cerebral, visceral, or muscular component in the overall somatic index. Numerical values ranging from one to seven were given for each of these components, yielding a composite score which identified the individual as an *ectomorph* (thin, with a preponderance of skin and nervous tissue), *endomorph* (rotund, with a predominance of visceral and fatty tissue), *mesomorph* (robust, with a preponderance of muscle and bone tissue), or *average*.

Sheldon further postulated that temperament or prevailing mood could be measured along the three dimensions of *cerebrotonia*—a tendency toward solitary pleasures, sensitivity, preference for intellectual pursuits; *viscerotonia*—a predilection toward comfort, relaxation, sociability, and the pleasures of the table; and *somatotonia*—a penchant for activity, competition, and aggressiveness.

When Sheldon's approach was tested empirically in a study (1949) which compared nondelinquent and delinquent boys, he reported a preponderance of mesomorphy (stocky physique and muscular strength) among delinquents. This finding was confirmed in another study by Sheldon and Eleanor Glueck (1950).

Like his morphological predecessors, Sheldon was sharply criticized for numerous methodological shortcomings in his work: that the statistical treatment of his data was riddled with errors; that the system of somatotyping was contaminated (i.e., the same person who performed the classification of body types also carried out the personality typing); and that when objective tests are substituted for interviews, the correlations between personality and somatotype tend to disappear. In criticizing the

Gluecks for their use of Sheldon's approach, a noted physical anthropologist (Washburn, 1951) referred to somatotyping as "a new Phrenology in which the bumps of the buttocks take the place of the bumps on the skull" (p. 561).

A commonsense reaction to the reported finding that stocky, muscular, physically active boys outnumber thin intellectuals or fat comfort-lovers among the ranks of delinquents is likely to be, "So, what else is new?" After all, delinquent activity places a premium on the possession of physical strength and agility; and in the kind of "natural selection" process by which gang delinquents become leaders, the mesomorph has a decided advantage over endomorphs and ectomorphs. Lastly, as Hardman (1964) has pointed out, people tend to live up to cultural stereotypes of how thin, fat, or muscular types of individuals are supposed to behave. In short, it is not necessary to assume a direct causal relationship between body build and behavior in order to account for most of the correlations reported by Sheldon and the Gluecks.

SOCIAL FACTORS AND CRIMINALITY

In addition to concern with mentally ill and criminally disposed persons as individuals, investigators in growing numbers focused attention on *crime as a social phenomenon.* They sought to account for the demonstrable fact that crime is distributed unequally throughout the various populations and groupings which make up society; and their goal was to relate social factors to criminality as causes or determinants.

The Cartographic School

An approach to the study of crime and delinquency called the **Cartographic School** flourished in England and France from 1830 to 1880. The early proponents of this approach were concerned with the spatial distribution of crime and delinquency. They believed that before attempting to search for causes of crime or deal constructively with offenders, they must acquire detailed information about the frequency of occurrence of crimes, characteristics of offenders and the areas in which they live, and changes in crime patterns over time. Cartographic research was initially focused on identifying areas in which crime was concentrated, then making comparisons between these areas and others with respect to factors such as income, literacy, education, and population density.

Among the earliest cartographers were a French lawyer, Andre-Michel Guerry, and a Belgian mathematician and astronomer, Lambert A. J. Quetelet. Guerry, as McCaghy (1976) points out, published the first known work on criminology that can be considered scientific. Quetelet was the first to discover the application of the mathematical theory of probability to human measurements. From his statistical studies, Quetelet drew the conclusion that moral and intellectual qualities are measurable, and therefore a kind of "social physics" is possible.

Guerry and Quetelet paid careful attention to official statistics on phenomena such as the number of crimes committed in a given geographic area over a specific period of time and were able to confirm that crimes rates both vary from region to region and—more importantly—show interesting consistencies in particular areas from year to year. Quetelet (1842) was led to speculate:

> This remarkable constancy with which the same crimes appear annually in the same order, drawing down on their perpetrators the same punishments, in the same proportions, is a singular fact. . . . I have never failed annually to repeat that there is a *budget* which we pay with frightening regularity—it is that of prisons, dungeons, and scaffolds . . .we might even predict annually how many individuals will stain their hands with the blood of their fellow men, how many will be forgers, how many will deal in poison pretty nearly in the same way as we may foretell the annual births and deaths [p. 6].

Quetelet made it clear that his "annual budget of crime" made no provision for predicting the criminal behavior of any specific individual. By definition, a crime rate refers to a property or characteristic of a group; and the most that Quetelet would allow is that certain factors such as sex, occupation, age, and use of alcohol may be understood as "propensities" toward the commission of crimes. Nevertheless, Quetelet observed:

> Society includes within itself the germs of all the crimes committed, and at the same time the necessary facilities for their development. It is the social state, in some measure, which prepares these crimes, and the criminal is merely the instrument to execute them. Every social state supposes, then, a certain number and a certain order of crimes, these being merely the necessary consequences of its organization [p. 108].

The achievements of the Cartographic School were neglected until the emergence of the ecological approach in the twentieth century, which we will examine in Chapter 11 when we consider the contributions of the Chicago School of criminology. Some of the more important "discoveries" of the ecological approach, such as the observation that crime and delinquency tend to be concentrated in particular areas, were actually rediscoveries of phenomena that had already been studied by members of the Cartographic School.

Sociological Criminology

The school of sociological criminology numbers among its founding fathers the Italian social critic and reformer, **Enrico Ferri.** Ferri conceived of sociological criminology as being concerned not only with social conditions which produce, or help to produce, crime, but also with social policies toward crime control and prevention.

From Ferri's standpoint, crime was seen as resulting from multiple causes, which could be classified into three categories: (1) physical factors, such as climate, fertility and distribution of soil, the seasons, temperature, and so on; (2) anthropological or individual factors such as age, sex, education, social class, organic and mental characteristics, etc.; and (3) social factors, such as population changes, customs, religion, political, economic and industrial conditions, nature of the family, etc. While recognizing the role of anthropological and physical factors in crime causation, his research in France showing that crime had risen significantly led him to conclude that social factors were the most important cause of this increase, since physical and anthropological factors do not change substantially over a relatively brief period of time.

In line with his socialist political philosophy, Ferri advocated a number of "penal substitutes" for punishment on the grounds that incarceration had little if any effect on reducing or preventing crime. These penal substitutes included the abolition of monopolies, inexpensive housing for working-class people, the establishment of foundling homes, and state control over the manufacture of weapons.

Sociopsychological Factors and Crime

A French contemporary of Ferri, **Gabriel Tarde,** developed a theoretical approach which emphasized the interaction between social and psychological factors. Tarde acknowledged the importance of biological and physical factors in crime causation, but his research left him convinced that social environment was the most significant influence in producing criminal behavior. He also recognized the role played by chance in human affairs.

Tarde's approach anticipates the work of Edwin H. Sutherland, whose contributions will be examined later, in two important ways. First, Tarde viewed the professional criminal (murderer, pickpocket, swindler) as an individual who goes through a long period of apprenticeship in much the same way as a lawyer, physician, or nurse. His conception of professional criminals as members of a group who possessed a distinctive language and code of conduct bears a strong resemblance to Sutherland's description of the professional thief in his monograph by that title published in 1937.

Second, Tarde's "laws of imitation" anticipate Sutherland's *differential association theory.* Tarde believed that these laws applied not only to crime but to all aspects of social life. Tarde's analysis of criminal behavior identified three recurring patterns which, in turn, led to the formulation of three laws of imitation which sought to account for crime and delinquency as learned or adopted in a manner similar to the way that fashions are adopted within society. Parallels can be drawn between the adoption and spread of fads such as jogging, the mini-skirt, or "streaking" and crimes such as hijacking or the theft of CB radios. Tarde's (1912) basic premises were (1) man imitates others in proportion to the closeness and frequency of his contacts with them, which makes imitation more likely to occur in cities or other places where crowds assemble; (2) crime and deviance tend to spread from superiors to inferiors, that is, from the hoi polloi to the common folk, from great cities to the countryside; and (3) when two mutually exclusive patterns come together, one may be replaced by the other. For example, shooting has replaced stabbing and beating as a means of committing murder because this method is more likely to achieve the intended effect with less effort. Based on the operation of these principles, modern society with an increased standard of living generated by growing industrialization promotes rather than reduces propensities toward crime.

Psychological Factors and Crime

Raffaele Garofalo is the third member of criminology's "Holy Three" (Barnes and Teeters, 1959). Garofalo begins his analysis by developing a definition of crime. Dissatisfied with a strictly legal definition, he formulated a sociological concept of "natural crime," which consisted of unconventional conduct that offends the basic moral sentiments of *pity*—the normal reaction of revulsion that most people have toward the suffering of others—and *probity,* which involves respect for the property rights of others. Garofalo viewed the criminal as a person deficient in the development of these altruistic sensibilities; hence, he is given the psychic or moral freedom to commit crimes. This deficiency, in Garofalo's view, is not simply the result of adverse environmental circumstances, but is based upon some congential organic defect, the nature of which Garofalo never managed to specify.

Garofalo had served as a magistrate in the Italian courts and found himself in disagreement with the classification of criminals used by Ferri and Lombroso, a typology which he considered lacking in homogeneity, precision, and practical value. Garofalo offered a typology which classified criminals as: (1) typical criminals or murderers, (2) violent criminals, (3) criminals deficient in probity, and (4) lascivious criminals. Excluded from this typology were those whose violations of law do not harm the sentiments of society.

In a chapter entitled "The Law of Adaptation" in his book *Criminology* (1914), Garofalo proposed a theory of punishment which reflects the influence of Darwinian ideas on his thinking. Just as nature eliminates organisms that cannot adapt to the demands of their physical environment, society must eliminate those who demonstrate by their criminal behavior an inability to adapt to the demands of civilized life. Garofalo suggests three means of elimination: (1) *death* for those whose criminal acts stem from a moral anomaly which renders them permanently incapable of social living (e.g., egoistic murderers); (2) *partial elimination,* which includes long-term or life imprisonment or expulsion to a penal colony, for those who are only fit for living the life of nomadic hordes or primitive tribes (e.g., thieves and habitual criminals); and (3) *enforced reparation* for crimes committed by those who are lacking in altruistic sentiments, but under circumstances that are highly unlikely to recur (e.g., those who cause property damage or damage to reputations).

ECONOMIC CONDITIONS AND CRIMINALITY

Theories of criminality that view economic factors and influences as major causes of criminal behavior are probably among the oldest types of explanation that have a social, as opposed to individual, orientation. Schafer (1969) reminds us that economic explanations of crime were offered by the early Greek philosophers as well as by the later Roman writers Virgil and Horace. Many of the early criminologists we have already discussed in this chapter, while often attributing primary causality to other factors, still recognized the role of economic conditions in crime causation. Beccaria maintained that theft arises out of desperation and economic misery. Ferri included economic conditions among the social factors that contribute to criminality. Even Lombroso held that poverty was an important agent in crime causation.

The early statisticians, as a matter of course, examined the relationship between economic conditions and crime, using a variety of official and unofficial sources. For example, the Bavarian Georg Von Mayr, who worked with police statistics, noted a correlation between fluctuations in commodity prices and the incidence of crimes against person and property. Starke, in Prussia, found comparable relationships between food prices and crime rates. Perhaps the most thorough of these early studies was conducted by the Italian, di Verce, who analyzed the effect of economic influences on a wide variety of crimes, ranging from arson to horse stealing. Says Schafer (1969):

> Agricultural vicissitudes, fluctuations in the price of food, industrial crises and strikes, and conditions of the working class are only examples of the several variables di Verce used in his numerous correlations. He expressed the degree of influence of economic conditions in general terms, such as "much," "moderate," "little," "only slightly," and "not at all." One of his many findings was that crime was higher in those regions where wealth was above average; his explanation was that where there is wealth there is also poverty, and poverty induces use of criminal opportunities [p. 262].

Other social statisticians like Guerry and Quetelet did not conclude from their studies that economic depression and poverty were decisive factors in crime.

While there are other writers in addition to those mentioned who gave consideration to economic factors and used them to explain crime and other social problems, Marx and Engels stand out as the first to provide a thorough and comprehensive theory of economic determinism. According to this position, all social phenomena—religious, political, psychic, and material—are products of the existing economic system. The capitalist economic structure of Western Europe and the United States is implicated as the major cause of crime. The views of Marx and Engels were incorporated by the Dutch writer, Willem Adrian Bonger, into a formal theory of deviance. In Chapter 10, Bonger's contributions are examined in detail.

Conclusion

Earlier we referred to the Positivist School of criminology as a bridge between the past and present. The most distinctive feature of the positivist approach, as contrasted with the Classical School, was its adoption of the scientific method as the basis for attempting to identify the causes of criminal behavior. Without denying the brilliance and originality of theorists such as Beccaria, the significance of positivism as an advance lies with its methodology. That is, science constitutes an approach to the generation of knowledge which is both self-corrective and cumulative. Thus, the methods of scientific investigation are far more important than are the insights and achievements of individual scientists.

It must be emphasized, however, that the application of scientific methods furnishes no guarantees of infallibility. The knowledge-generating processes of scientific research can be painfully slow and subject to a variety of errors. But implicit in the nature and operations of science is the capability, over time, of freeing the conclusions of scientific research from the distortions introduced by either random or cumulative error. Modern criminological theory bears the stamp of this positivistic or scientific tradition.

MODERN CLASSICAL CRIMINOLOGY

In the 1970s and early 1980s, frustration produced by the failure of scientific criminology to formulate a comprehensive explanation of the causes of crime on which effective rehabilitation programs could be based led to a revival of concepts of punishment as a means of social control identified with the Classical School of criminology. This renewal of interest was spurred by rising crime rates, lethal outbursts of violence in the prisons, and a number of widely publicized reports on the failure of rehabilitation as a realistic and feasible goal of corrections. Instead of futile attempts to treat unregenerate criminals, modern classical or conservative criminologists (Bayer, 1981) support the abandonment of both the rhetoric and substance of the rehabilitative philosophy and advocate its replacement with punishment or retributive justice. Wrapped up in this agenda are several issues—among them, capital punishment—which we shall consider in the following pages.

In our coverage of the historical background of criminological theory, we pointed out that the Classical School was founded on the doctrines of free will and rational deviance. Human beings were seen as capable of making deliberate decisions to behave, based on calculations of pleasure and pain. Presumably it is from these characteristics that society emerges. In order to avoid continual chaos resulting from unchecked individual freedom, people enter into a social contract whereby they surrender part of their liberty in exchange for security under the laws of a state. The role of the state is to reduce crime. Beccaria believed that it is better to prevent crimes than punish them. In contrast to the positivist criminologists who were to dominate the scene for the next two centuries, Beccaria perceived human beings as equal, self-determining individuals whose freedom and responsibility are unaffected by personal characteristics, extenuating circumstances, and past experiences. Because of their rationality, people were regarded as equal before the law. Beccaria accepted literally the notion that the punishment should fit the crime.

Positivist criminology opposed the Classical School's belief in free will, offering in its place the principle of determinism—that all events, including human behavior, have causes. Criminal behavior, so the argument ran, is caused by factors beyond the control—or even the awareness—of the individual; treatment, not punishment, was seen as the proper approach to crime prevention. Crime became a problem in pathology; criminals were viewed as ill or maladjusted rather than pleasure-seeking and predatory. Positivism's "let the treatment fit the offender" replaced the Classical School's "let the punishment fit the crime." The differences between the two approaches are summarized in Table 9.1.

Punishment is familiar to us in all aspects of life. We are acquainted with its use in the family and in the school; we employ punishment of various kinds with our pets, our children, and with one another; we believe we understand its operations and generally can foresee its effects when it is employed. Through the use of positive sanctions (rewards, reinforcements), groups and societies seek to encourage conformity to various norms; by means of negative sanctions (punishments) attempts are made to discourage deviant behavior.

Reward and punishment as two of the principal techniques or processes for affecting behavior have been familiar to the philosopher—or indeed to any person with an inquisitive mind—since time immemorial. The notion that people seek to maximize pleasure and avoid pain or discomfort was already an ancient notion when it found its way into Jeremy Bentham's *hedonistic calculus.* Similar ideas had been expressed by the ancient Greek philosophers; and both Freud's *pleasure principle* and

Table 9.1 COMPARISON OF THE CLASSICAL AND POSITIVE SCHOOLS OF CRIMINOLOGY

	Classical	Positive
Date developed	Eighteenth century	Nineteenth century
Purpose	Reform of the judicial and penal systems	The application of scientific methods to the study of the criminal as an individual
Definition of behavior	Crime as defined by the legal code, *nullum crimen sine lege* (no crime without law)	Rejection of legal definitions by substituting "natural crime," "antisocial behavior," "offends sentiments of the community"
Explanation of behavior	Free will, rationality; deviants and nondeviants essentially similar	Determinism: biological, psychological, economic, genetic, etc. Deviants and nondeviants different
Method of behavior change	Fear of punishment as a deterrent	Scientific treatment

Source: Adapted in part from C. R. Jeffery, The historical development of criminology. In Hermann Mannheim (ed.), *Pioneers in Criminology* (Chicago: Quadrangle Books, 1960, pp. 366–67). Reproduced by permission of the author and publisher.

reality principle, and B. F. Skinner's views on reinforcement did little more than restate the idea in a somewhat more sophisticated form (Smith and Vetter, 1982).

As techniques for modifying behavior, neither reward nor punishment are exact and unvarying in their effects. Punishment often proves no more successful in discouraging some kinds of deviation than does reward in encouraging conformity to various norms. Their persistence in human affairs, however, argues that they serve important functions other than those of merely altering or otherwise affecting the behavior of others.

The use of punishment in dealing with norm violators has been supported traditionally by several types of justification or rationale:

1. *Retribution:* "You're going to get what's coming to you."
2. *Deterrence:* "We're going to punish you so that you won't do it again." This formula has a variation: "We're going to punish you so that *others* won't do it."
3. *Incapacitation:* "As long as we're punishing *you,* you won't be out doing something to *us.*"

As one can see, these rationalizations leave room for considerable overlap. For instance, locking a child who has been naughty in his or her room without supper may serve all three functions simultaneously. That is, it may communicate to the child that acting naughty will bring down the wrath of the parents and family; second, that it is no fun being locked up without supper, which gives one something to think about the next time an opportunity presents itself to act naughty; and third, that as long as one is locked up, there are few chances for further naughtiness. If a thoughtful brother or sister draws an appropriate conclusion from watching a sibling punished in the above manner, the punishment may manage to have deterrent effects of a general, as well as a specific, nature. These points should be borne in mind when considering the use of punishment for official purposes. The seriousness and magnitude of the punishment may differ, but the principle may remain the same.

Retribution

The punitive response is rooted in tradition and buttressed by common sense. **Retribution**—the word means "something for recompense"—is a rather primitive (one hesitates to call it "natural") human reaction: people who get hurt want to hurt back. It is not difficult, therefore, to understand why this justification for the use of punishment ("the law of just deserts") has received a good deal of popular support throughout the ages. During the Iranian crisis, practically every newspaper in the country received letters suggesting that the United States round up an equal number of hostages from among the Iranians who are here on student visas and place them under exactly the same conditions of captivity as those which our embassy personnel were forced to endure in Teheran. Similar messages, including those which verged on the obscene, festooned the bumpers of automobiles from Maine to California.

Deterrence

Deterrence, we noted, has a *specific* and a *general* aspect. When we punish malefactor A by imprisonment, we wish to deter A from committing further offenses, not only during A's period of incapacitation, but also following release from confinement. Our desire is reinforced by the belief that punishment brings about beneficial changes in the behavior of the person who is punished.

We also tend to believe that punishing A will have the additional desirable effect of deterring B and C from the commission of criminal offenses of a similar nature to those committed by A. Optimistically we hope that the example provided by A's punishment will have even broader effects in terms of deterring the commission of offenses *other than* those for which A received punishment.

Psychologists, sociologists, political scientists, economists, and other specialists have experimented extensively with the deterrent effects of punishment. Psychological studies have been conducted with both animal and human subjects and have generated a large volume of conflicting and often contradictory results. This is quite understandable, given the sheer complexity that involves even the simplest experiment on punishment, but it is of little help for the judge or correctional administrator. In particular, it is difficult to understand how criminal justice authorities could be expected to place much confidence in experimental findings from research involving animal subjects when a crucially important element in deterrence is the human capacity for reasoning about the probable outcome of one's actions (Newman, 1978).

Sociological studies of the deterrence effectiveness of punishment have dealt with variations in recidivism rates in relation to type and severity of sentencing. Sociologists have also focused on the issue of capital punishment as it appears to affect incidence rates in homicide. Economists, too, have devoted considerable attention to capital punishment and deterrence of violent crimes such as murder, but they have tended to employ extremely sophisticated mathematical models that are beyond the comprehension of almost anyone, save other economists or mathematicians. Despite the sophistication and complexity of the methodology, the results have not been appreciably different from those reached by the psychologists: namely, that some research supports the notion of deterrence and other research does not.

Experts on punishment have stressed the point that several factors seem to significantly affect the results or outcome of punishment—that is, are related to the success, partial success, or failure of punishment as an approach to deterrence. These factors are the (1) speed, (2) severity, and (3) certainty of punishment. Evidence from both informal anecdotes and laboratory experiment tends to indicate that certainty is a more influential variable than severity or speed, but it is difficult to arrive at an unqualified conclusion. All three factors are rarely present in any real-life situation; and even in the controlled environment of the laboratory, it is nearly impossible to conduct a rigorous and exacting comparison of the relative efficacy of one variable with the others.

According to Grünhut (1948), three components must be present if punishment is to operate as a reasonable means for curbing crime. First, "speedy and inescapable detection and prosecution" must convince the offender that crime does not pay. Second, after punishment has been meted out, the criminal must have a fair chance for a fresh start. Third, "the state which claims the right of punishment must uphold superior values which the offender can reasonably be expected to acknowledge" (p. 3).

Incapacitation (Restraint)

Punishment which involves imprisonment is justified on the grounds that as long as the offender is being held in confinement, he is not free to commit further crimes. Extreme forms of punishment, such as execution or life imprisonment, constitute total incapacitation. This rationale seems to be regarded by both supporters and critics of the punitive approach as the most plausible of the utilitarian arguments on the side of punishment.

Implicit in **incapacitation** is the belief that the best basis for predicting future behavior is past behavior. In the case of criminal behavior, the presumption is that the person who committed a particular type of crime is likely to commit more of those crimes or crimes of some other type. Packer (1968) points out that:

> This latter justification does not seem to figure largely in the justification for incapacitation as a mode of prevention. To the extent that we lock up burglars because we fear that they will commit further offenses, our prediction is not that they will if left unchecked violate the antitrust laws, or cheat on their income taxes, commit further burglaries, or other crimes associated with burglary, such as homicide or bodily injury. The premise is that the person may have a tendency to commit further crimes like the one for which he is now being punished and that punishing him will restrain him from doing so [p. 50].

In every case, Packer reminds us, it is an empirical question whether or not the prediction is valid.

Increased attention has been given to incapacitation as a potentially effective strategy to control crime because: (1) public confidence has waned in the ability of correctional programs to rehabilitate offenders; (2) public attitudes toward crime and criminals in recent years have become more punitive; and (3) prisons in the United States have reached an all-time peak population of 490,041 inmates and are operating at 10 percent overcapacity (Cohen, 1983; *New York Times,* Sept. 16, 1985).

These conditions, particularly overcrowding, have raised the issue of whether limited and expensive prison space can be used more effectively. This, in turn, raises the question of whether there are reliable and valid ways of determining who should be incarcerated and for how long. In theory, the incapacitation perspective provides an answer to this question. From this standpoint, long-term imprisonment would be reserved for those who are most likely to continue to commit serious crimes at relatively high rates. This idea has attracted supporters with a variety of views regarding the goals of corrections because it would reduce the number of people who require incarceration, lessen the period of time for the imprisonment of certain types of offenders, and lower the costs of operating the correctional system.

Two kinds of incapacitation strategies have been proposed: *collective incapacitation* and *selective incapacitation.* Under the collective incapacitation strategy, all individuals convicted of a certain offense (e.g., robbery) would receive the same sentence (e.g., 5 years). After reviewing research in this area, Cohen (1983) concluded that collective incapacitation would have only a modest impact (10 to 20 percent) on crime reduction and might double, triple, or increase even more dramatically the size of the prison population, depending on which categories of offenders were chosen for incapacitation. Van Dine, Conrad, and Dinitz (1979) found that using a policy of incarcerating, any offender convicted of a felony for 5 years would produce a 523 percent increase in the prison population from a single county in Ohio.

Selective incapacitation involves individual sentences which are based on predictions that certain offenders will commit serious offenses at higher rates than others convicted of the same types of crimes. Under this strategy, sentences would vary according to differences in predictions regarding an individual's probability of committing future crimes. This strategy permits quite different sentences for those committing the same offense because it is assumed that those who commit the same offense have different probabilities for future involvement in crime. The effectiveness of this strategy rests on our capability of identifying high-rate offenders at an early point in their careers and incarcerating them before they start committing most of their offenses. This strategy has a number of ethical problems, including the fact that we would be punishing people for crimes they have not as yet committed, and might not commit if they were released. However, even putting this aside, the problems of accurately identifying high-rate offenders are monumental. At this point studies focused on identifying high-rate violent offenders using a combination of offenses plus other characteristics have been able to predict future offenses correctly on the part of no more than 45 percent of the group studied (Cohen, 1983). In other words, at this point, using existing scales to identify high-rate offenders for purposes of incapacitation, we would be holding in prison 55 people out of 100 incarcerated who would not commit a violent offense. Obviously this level of accuracy is unacceptable. Cohen (1983) has offered a different approach to incapacitation which avoids many of the problems associated with selective incapacitation. This is called **criminal career inca-pacitation,** and has as its objective the identification of classes of offenders who on the average have active high rates of crime. Cohen's research in Washington, D.C., led her to conclude that individuals convicted of robbery and burglary are prime candidates for incapacitation, based on the fact that on the average they commit these offenses at relatively high rates and have relatively short careers. Short prison sentences for these offenders can potentially reduce large portions of their expected careers and thus reduce robbery and burglary rates. For example, her research showed that a 2-year prison sentence imposed on those convicted of robbery would reduce robberies by 8 percent and only increase the total prison population by 7 percent.

Without denying the importance of the considerations discussed above, the principal obstacle that has confronted proponents of incapacitation is the simple fact that those who are incapacitated by being placed in confinement do not stay there: they are released form prison or training school after varying periods of time, and then their subsequent behavior inevitably reflects the consequences of their experiences during confinement. Vachss and Bakal (1979), for example, contend that confinement of criminality-prone delinquents has the effect of *increasing,* rather than diminishing, their proclivities toward further commitment to a criminal career. Their argument is not directed toward the ineffectiveness of incapacitation as such, but rather the adverse results of confinement in existing types of juvenile correctional institutions.

There is nothing startling or novel in the discovery that imprisonment has both broad and deep effects upon those so confined. But it is necessary to point out that a substantial body of opinion within corrections supported *the belief that those effects were beneficial* for the inmate and society; that those effects were, in fact, the primary purpose for incarcerating the individual in the first place.

The Death Penalty

Discussions about capital punishment are usually dominated by emotional, rather than intellectual, considerations. The issues raised by the death penalty tap deep levels of primitive belief. Our answers to questions about the taking of human life in socially sanctioned circumstances are thus likely to express our primitive beliefs; and the intellectual arguments we use to justify our attitudes amount to rationalizations. It seems to us that this observation is equally valid for liberal and conservative ideological positions.

One of the principal forms of rationalization involves the deterrence argument. As we noted earlier in this chapter, the rationale for deterrence is that people will refrain from committing criminal acts because they fear the consequences of punishment. Supporters of the death penalty might argue, therefore, that because a fear of death is one of the most powerful motivations in human behavior, capital punishment provides a potent defense against any crime that incurs the death penalty. But opponents of the death penalty maintain that this position is based on a simplistic idea of human conduct—one that views human beings as rational creatures who can weigh the potential consequences of their actions and make informed choices among alternatives. Conservative or modern classical criminologists retort that this "simplistic" position incorporates the doctrine of free will on which criminal law is based.

At the beginning of 1985, the death row population in the United States had passed 1,500—the largest figure since recordkeeping began in 1953. Southern states held three-quarters of the condemned; and Florida, Georgia, and Texas accounted for more than half of the total.

In 1972, when the death row population stood at 631, the U.S. Supreme Court ruled in *Furman* v. *Georgia* (408 U.S. 238) that "the imposition and carrying out of the death penalty in the instant cases constitutes cruel and unusual punishment in violation of the Eighth and Fourteenth Amendments." As a result of the *Furman* decision, the death sentences of the 631 inmates on death row were set aside.

Had the Supreme Court struck a mortal blow to the advocates of capital punishment? No. There was no consensus by the Court in *Furman*. The decision was 5 to 4, and each of the nine justices wrote an opinion expressing his view on the constitutionality of the death penalty. Four of the justices stated that the imposition of the death penalty did not run afoul of the Constitution. Only two justices (Brennan and Marshall) stated that capital punishment was unconstitutional under all circumstances. And three justices agreed that the death penalty historically had been arbitrarily and capriciously imposed—especially against blacks, the poor, and men. However, they did not decide in *Furman* whether the death penalty could ever be imposed, given new legislative guidelines.

The legislative response to *Furman* was swift. Thirty-six jurisdictions (including the U.S. Congress) passed new legislation to remove the discrimination that had permeated the death penalty for many years. But the legislative packages were anything but uniform. Some states made the death penalty mandatory for a conviction of first-degree murder. Others left sentencing exclusively to the jury. And others permitted a sentencing recommendation from the jury, but left the final decision with the trial judge. However, most states did provide legislative guidelines to the juries and judges as to their sentencing authority in capital cases.

All of the occupants now on death row in the United States were convicted under post-*Furman* statutes. However, opponents of the death penalty, including the American Civil Liberties Union and Amnesty International, contend that sentencing under the new laws is as arbitrary and racially discriminatory as that which occurred before the *Furman* decision. One study—based on statistics from Texas, Ohio, Florida, and Georgia from 1972 through 1977—concluded that blacks convicted of murdering whites were sentenced to death, while only 3 of 341 whites convicted of murdering blacks received the death penalty.

Some occupants of death row have committed crimes so far outside the bounds of normal human experience that the perpetrators seem to belong to another species. Consider Lawrence Bittaker, who was sentenced to death for kidnapping and murdering five teenage girls. According to an account in *Time*,

> . . . he and a partner raped and sodomized four of them first, for hours and days at a time, sometimes in front of a camera. But that is not all. He tortured some of

the girls—pliers on nipples, ice picks in ears—and tape-recorded the screams. But that is not all. The last victim was strangled with a coat hanger, her genitals mutilated and her body tossed on a lawn so that he could watch the horror of its discovery [Andersen, 1982, p. 39].

Bittaker's prosecutor coined the term "mutants from hell" for Bittaker and his partner.

In December 1982, Charlie Brooks, Jr., was put to death in Texas, the first American ever to be executed by a lethal drug injection. The execution released a flood of speculation that we might be on the brink of a large-scale resumption of executions that could boost the execution rate to the level of the 1930s. These speculations are buttressed by public opinion polls that indicate a major shift from the 1960s, when only a minority of the public favored the death penalty. Today, a majority supports capital punishment. A 1985 media poll showed that 84 percent of Americans favor the death penalty. Twenty-nine percent of the respondents recommended its use in all murder cases, and 57 percent favored the death penalty only under certain circumstances (e.g., the sexual abuse and murder of a child). Half of those who support capital punishment, however, expressed the belief that the death penalty is not imposed fairly from case to case (Kilman, 1985). It should be pointed out that the editorial comments that often accompany poll reports convey the impression that most people are fed up with judicial delays and are impatient to push on with the distasteful but necessary task of executing condemned murderers.

In the end, the issue of capital punishment is fought on the question of whether the evidence supports or refutes the contention that the death penalty deters people from committing certain crimes. Supporters of capital punishment take refuge from accusations that they are barbaric and bloodthirsty by claiming that the death penalty works to reduce the incidence of heinous murders. And abolitionists, with Jove-like objectivity, ask for satisfactory scientific evidence that the death penalty is an effective deterrent against crime. Scores of studies by criminologists, psychologists, and economists have thus far failed to produce convincing scientific evidence, however, and some claim that such evidence is beyond the reach of scientific verification—now or ever.

PUNISHMENT OR REHABILITATION?

The idea of rehabilitation in corrections began as a matter of moral redemption of the offender. It was gradually co-opted by psychiatry, however, and transformed into a problem for psychotherapy. The goal of correctional treatment became the changing of the personality of the individual offender to achieve improvements in social behavior and personal adjustment. This was a praiseworthy objective; unfortunately, it was—and still is—expected to be pursued within a system whose representatives and practitioners are charged with a responsibility for protecting society that takes precedence over the rehabilitation of offenders.

Consider the issue of incarceration. Prisons continue to be the most visible manifestation of the correctional component of our criminal justice system. One of the major difficulties we face in trying to rehabilitate offenders in prison is that these institutions house a disproportionately high concentration of people who are socially deviant, emotionally unstable, psychologically disturbed, mentally retarded, and prone to aggression and violence. No longer are prison populations composed primarily of nonviolent offenders. Our constant search for alternatives to imprisonment has diverted into probation and other community-based correctional programs for many first offenders, minor property criminals, drug-bust cases, and similar types of persons, leaving mostly those who are perceived as a threat to public safety as candidates for incarceration. Thus, we have loaded our prisons with the highest concentration of dangerous and intractable offenders in our entire history of penology.

Aside from these considerations, the rehabilitative ideal was based on the assumption that we had the capability of identifying the causes of crime and developing programs to deal with these causes. Unfortunately, we still lack the theories and programs to fulfill the requirements of rehabilitation.

In addition, the shift in racial composition of the prison population during the 1960s and 1970s to the point where whites were a minority, along with changing attitudes on the part of ethnic minorities regarding their rights and newly found ability to intimidate whites (Silberman, 1983), significantly elevated tension levels in prisons. Thus, today inmates practice an informal, self-imposed segregation: whites and blacks stand in separate lines for meals, and whites, blacks, and Hispanics rarely sit together in the mess hall. White convicts with hostile attitudes toward blacks and Hispanics band together in a group, and blacks and Hispanics with antiwhite biases do likewise. The result is that all of them are constantly engaged in a struggle over the spoils of prison enterprises and violations of the prisoner's code which constitute slights against each group's honor. Such internecine strife creates potentially explosive conditions within the institution that can be fused by a single incident. This situation, combined with the fact that prisons are operating with populations that are over capacity, has forced correctional officials to concentrate on maintaining custodial control; under the circumstances, rehabilitative programs have become a matter of secondary concern.

Several other factors have contributed to the demise of the rehabilitative ideal in corrections. Public attitudes toward crime and criminals have become more punitive. Also, research that has received wide publicity has suggested that treatment programs are largely ineffectual. Perhaps the most notable of these studies was reported by Lipton, Martinson, and Wilks (1975), who conducted a massive review of over two hundred correctional treatment projects that spanned nearly 20 years. These projects were classified according to the intervention techniques or methods employed, including milieu therapy, group therapy, individual counseling, parole supervision, and medical treatment. Treatment outcomes were assessed by various measures: recidivism, personality and attitude change, and community adjustment. According to Martinson (1974), the principal conclusion that could be reached from this comprehensive survey was that *"with few and isolated exceptions, the rehabilitative efforts that have been reported thus far have had no appreciable effects on recidivism"* (p. 25). Research of this kind has resulted in the developments of views such as that expressed by James Q. Wilson, author of the widely read and much discussed book *Thinking About Crime* (1977), who made the following assessment of correctional treatment approaches and their results:

It does not seem to matter what form of treatment in the correctional system is attempted—whether vocational training or academic education; whether counseling inmates individually, in groups, or not at all; whether therapy is administered by social workers or psychiatrists; whether the institutional context of the treatment is custodial or benign; whether the person is placed on probation or released on parole; or whether the treatment takes place in the community or in institutions. Indeed, some forms of treatment—notably a few experiments with psychotherapy—actually produced an *increase* in the rate of recidivism [p. 159].

Dissent with these negative evaluations has been registered by Glaser (1975), who concluded from a survey of correctional treatment studies that certain programs appear to have successful outcomes for certain categories of offenders. Adams (1970) reported that an intensive counseling program carried out with inmates of a California penal institution—the so-called Pilot Intensive Counseling Organization (PICO) program—appeared to produce positive results with selected types of offenders. Shireman and his associates (1972) reviewed a dozen treatment studies that had been conducted in various institutions. They concluded that certain types of institutional therapy (e.g., short-term milieu therapy), together with a high staff morale situation, could yield results that were sufficiently strong to carry over into the postrelease period. They also found some evidence that positive results are associated with treatment programs aimed at youthful offenders, including intensive milieu therapy, group counseling techniques, and provision of plastic surgery for individuals with psychological problems related to facial deformation or disfigurement.

Gibbons and his colleagues (1977) maintain that correctional treatment has not yet been given a fair trial. At the same time, they contend, "it is likely that intervention efforts will need to move away from many of those earlier stratagems that were based on psychiatric images of offenders and on efforts to tinker with their mental health through some kind of individual counseling or therapy" (p. 106). This would seem to be an excellent first step toward divesting corrections of its overload of psychiatric jargon and illness models. Terms such as *treatment* ought to be reserved for medical procedures and psychiatrically neutral terms such as *intervention technique* used in their place. A meaningful and financially rewarding job or the chance to acquire further education are probably more valuable as an intervention activity than short-term or long-term psychotherapy in encouraging prosocial behavior in the criminal because they increase his "stake in conformity."

At the present time, we have practically no tried and proven way of "treating" antisocial behavior. Most of the research that has concerned itself with the durable effects of behavior change has involved relatively stable, reasonably motivated, middle-class patients or clients who have voluntarily sought opportunities for therapy. Even under these favorable circumstances, it has proven exceedingly difficult to achieve successful therapeutic outcomes, at least in terms of measures for which there is anything approaching professional consensus. To extrapolate from these findings to some of the clientele of the criminal justice system seems out of the question. As Silber (1974) reminds us, most of the prisoners in correctional institutions:

. . . are hostile, suspicious, and immature and tend to identify with subcultural values that are legally proscribed. They usually perceive their personality functioning to be acceptable. They are not, in general, likely to clamor for individual psychotherapy and usually are seen on referral. Thus, there is no strong sustained interest on the part of the prisoners themselves for treatment [p. 242].

Whether the individual pathology model of treatment has relevance for less serious offenders whose crimes have yet resulted in imprisonment remains to be established. As we saw from critical reviews of correctional treatment studies, the evidence is both pro and con. We believe that the middle-of-the-road position of Simon Dinitz and John Conrad represents a reasonable alternative. These criminologists suggest that rather than trying to rehabilitate every offender who enters prison, we provide sound programs and appropriate incentives for participation in such programs for offenders who wish to take advantage of opportunities for self-improvement. In this way, the prison can become hopeful without bearing the burden of attempting to change offenders who have no desire to be rehabilitated.

CONCLUDING OBSERVATIONS

If this were the best of all possible worlds, the problems of crime would resolve themselves into a simple process. Having been apprehended and convicted of criminal acts, offenders would express remorse for the wrongs they had inflicted and would seek to atone for their actions by undergoing appropriate punishment in a spirit of seeking self-redemption as a willing participant in a process of expiation. Once they had been put through this symbolic laundering, ex-offenders would emerge with clean hands, shining faces, their "debt to society" paid in full, and all guilt expunged from the record. They would then be ready to resume their place in society among the anonymous ranks of the "rest of us."

Not the least of the problems posed by this pleasant little formula is the fact that a distressingly large percentage of the people who are arrested and charged with criminal offenses are essentially unregenerate. They refuse to acknowledge their guilt or accept responsibility for their deeds. Furthermore, they see no need to change the way in which they make their living. Moreover, many of our fellow citizens—and, perhaps, on occasion, we ourselves—would like to see criminals do a little suffering before they embark on their quest for reformation. It is reminiscent of the poet Heinrich Heine's oft-quoted observation to the effect that all he really wanted out of life was a small cottage surrounded by trees—from which several of his enemies were hanging. To turn the other cheek may be a laudable objective for moral philosophers, but other alternatives have been a great deal more popular throughout the history of humankind's attempts to cope with crime and criminals.

The author of a well-known textbook in criminology stated that "one of the sources of the inconsistencies and administrative problems that plague police departments, courts, and correctional agencies has been identified as the preservation in the system of criminal justice of irreconcilable perspectives derived from the classical and positive schools" (Johnson, 1974). One is strongly tempted to point out that the "inconsistencies" in the criminal justice system are only a reflection of those which are basic to the human condition; and that the "irreconcilable perspectives" of the

Classical and Positive schools are derived, in turn, from views of criminality that both possess limited validity.

SUMMARY

In this chapter, we have discussed some of the reasons for the large number of theories in criminology. We questioned whether criminologists have been saying different things about the same phenomena or have been addressing different phenomena under the same terms, that is, that crime subsumes both criminal and delinquent behavior. A review of the theories covered in this section—individualistic theories (biology and psychology), social disorganization and anomie, subcultural explanations, control theories, societal reaction (labeling), conflict and radical theory—suggests that both tendencies are common to contemporary criminological theory. A brief assessment was made of each theoretical approach. The results of this appraisal provided confirmation and support for the contention that no single theory in criminology is adequate to account for the multiplicity and diversity of criminal behavior, and that criminological theory seems increasingly likely to move toward convergence, synthesis, and interdiciplinary integration.

The concluding section of the chapter is devoted to an examination of the perspective identified as modern classical or conservative criminology—a viewpoint associated with the ideological orientation of the New Right. The main tenets of this perspective are a repudiation of the deterministic doctrine of positivistic or scientific criminology and repudiation of the rehabilitative approach in favor of a return to the punitive approach identified with the Classical School of criminology. The empirical evidence available on the deterrent and incapacitating effects of punishment do not allow any clear conclusions about the effectiveness of punishment as an alternative to rehabilitation in the disposition of criminal offenders. Critics of the punitive approach argue that rehabilitation has never been given a fair trial in our correctional system and institutions, but public opinion seems to line up on the side of the position taken by the modern classical or conservative criminologists—at least for the foreseeable future.

DISCUSSION QUESTIONS

Find the answers to the following questions in the text.

1. What did the medieval Church contribute to criminological throught?
2. Identify the major views held by the Classical School of criminology. Who was **Beccaria** and why was his *Essay on Capital Crimes and Punishments* such an important work?
3. Compare and contrast the major tenets of the Positivist and Classical schools of criminology with regard to the issue of free will.
4. In addition to the concept of the "born criminal," what other categories of criminal offender did **Lombroso** recognize?
5. What was the **Cartographic School** and why was it so influential in the development of sociological and sociopsychological theories of criminality?
6. What is the basis for the claim that the Positivist School of criminology was a bridge between the past and present?

7. What are some of the factors that have led to a resurgence of interest in Classical criminology?

8. How do we distinguish between **general** and **special deterrence**? Does research support or refute arguments for the disposition of criminals based on **incapacitation**?

9. What is the probability that the controversy over punishment versus rehabilitation can be settled by means of evidence gathered through scientific research?

10. Why were the sentences of more than 600 death row inmates set aside by the U.S. Supreme Court decision in *Furman* v. *Georgia*?

11. Discuss the counterarguments to Martinson's claim that "almost nothing works" in corrections.

TERMS TO IDENTIFY AND REMEMBER

Comte	positivism
Bentham	Lombroso
Ferri	Beccaria
somatotype	hedonistic calculus
Cartographic School	Garofalo
atavistic types	Tarde
general deterrence	retribution
incapacitation (restraint)	special deterrence
criminal career incapacitation	*Furman* v. *Georgia*

REFERENCES

Adams, R. Differential association and learning principles revisited. *Social Problems* 20 (1973): 458–70.

———. The adequacy of differential association theory. *Journal of Research in Crime and Delinquency* 11 (1974): 1–8.

Adams, S. The PICO project. In N. Johnston, L. Savitz, and M. E. Wolfgang (eds.), *The Sociology of Punishment and Corrections.* New York: Wiley, 1970.

Allen, H. E., and Simonsen, C. E. *Corrections in America.* New York: Macmillan, 1982.

Andersen, K. An eye for an eye. *Time,* June 24, 1983, pp. 28–39.

Barnes, H. E., and Teeters, N. K. *New horizons in Criminology.* Englewood Cliffs, NJ: Prentice-Hall, 1959.

Bartol, C. R. *Criminal Behavior: A Psychological Approach.* Englewood Cliffs, NJ: Prentice-Hall, 1980.

Bayer, R. Crime, punishment, and the decline of liberal optimism. *Crime and Delinquency* 27 (1981): 190.

Burgess, R. L., and Akers, R. A. A differential association-reinforcement theory of criminal behavior. *Social Problems* 14 (1966): 128–47.

Cohen, J. *Incapacitating Criminals: Recent Research Findings.* Washington, D.C.: U.S. Department of justice, National Institute of Justice, 1983.

Cortes, J. B. and Gatti, F. M. *Delinquency and Crime.* New York: Seminar Press, 1972.

Durant, W. J. *The Mansions of Philosophy: A Survey of Human Life and Destiny.* New York: Garden City Publishing Company, 1929.

Eldefonso, E. *Law Enforcement and the Youthful Offender.* New York: Wiley, 1967.

Empey, L. T. The application of sociological theory to social action. *Social Problems* 12 (1964).

Fodor, E. M. Moral development and parent behavior antecedents in adolescent psychopaths. *Journal of Genetic Psychology* (1973) 37–43.

Fox, V. B. *Introduction to Criminology.* Englewood Cliffs, NJ: Prentice-Hall, 1977.

Galton, F. *Inquiries into Human Faculty and Its Development.* London: Macmillan, 1883.

Garofalo, R. *Criminology.* Boston: Little, Brown, 1914.

Geis, G. Jeremy Bentham. In H. Manneheim (ed.), *Pioneers in Criminology.* Montclair, NJ: Patterson Smith, 1970.

Gibbons, D. C., Thurman, J. L., Yospe, F., and Blake, G. F. *Criminal Justice Planning: An Introduction.* Englewood Cliffs, NJ: Prentice-Hall, 1977.

Glaser, D. Criminality theories and behavioral images. In D. R. Cressey and D. A. Ward (eds.), *Delinquency, Crime, and Social Process.* New York: Harper & Row, 1969.

Glaser, D. Maximizing the impact of evaluative research in corrections. In E. Viano (ed.), *Criminal Justice Research.* Lexington, MA: Lexington Books, 1975.

Glueck, E., and Glueck, S. *Unraveling Juvenile Delinquency.* New York: Commonwealth Fund, 1950.

Goffman, E. *Stigma.* Englewood Cliffs, NJ: Prentice-Hall, 1963.

Goring, C. *The English Convict.* London: H. M. Stationery Office, 1913.

Grünhut, M. *Penal Reform.* London: Oxford University Press, 1948.

Hardman, D. G. The case for eclecticism. *Crime and Delinquency* 10 (1964): 201–16.

Hooton, E. A. *Crime and the Man.* Cambridge, MA: Harvard University Press, 1939.

Jeffery, C. R. The historical development of criminology. In H. Mannheim (ed.), *Pioneers of Criminology.* London: Stevens, 1960.

Johnson, E. M. *Criminology and Corrections.* St. Louis: Mosby, 1974.

Kilman, L. Poll: U.S. backs the use of execution. *Tampa Tribune,* Jan. 29, 1985. p. 1.

Kohlberg, L. Moral stages and moralization: The cognitive developmental approach. In T. Lickona (ed.), *Moral Development and Behavior.* New York: Holt, Rinehart and Winston, 1976.

Korn, R. R., and McCorkle, L. W. *Criminology and Penology.* New York: Holt, Rinehart and Winston, 1961.

Lemert, E. M. *Human Deviance: Social Problems and Social Control.* Englewood Cliffs, NJ: Prentice-Hall, 1967.

Lickona, T. (ed.), *Moral Development and Behavior.* New York: Holt, Rinehart and Winston, 1976.

Lipton, D., Martinson, R., and Wilks, J. *The Effectiveness of Correctional Treatment—A Survey of Treatment Evaluation Studies.* Springfield, MA: Praeger, 1975.

Lombroso, C. *L'uomo delinquente (The Criminal Man).* Milano: Hoepli, 1876.

———. *L'uomo delinquente.* Torino: Fratelli Bocca, 1897.

Lombroso-Ferrero, G. *Criminal Man According to the Classification of Cesare Lombroso.* Montclair, NJ: Patterson Smith, 1972.

McCaghy, C. H. *Deviant Behavior: Crime, Conflict and Interest Groups.* New York: Macmillan, 1976.

Martinson, R. What works? Questions and answers about prison reform. *The Public Interest* 35 (Spring) 1974: 22–54.

Monachesi, E. Cesare Beccaria. In H. Mannheim (ed.), *Pioneers in Criminology.* Montclair, NJ: Patterson Smith, 1970.

Nassi, A. J. Therapy of the absurd: A study of punishment and treatment in California prisons and the roles of psychiatrists and psychologists. In H. J. Vetter and R. W. Rieber (eds.), *Contemporary Perspectives on Forensic Psychiatry and Psychology.* New York: John Jay Press, 1980.

Nation's prison population growing more quickly. *New York Times,* September 16, 1985, p. 16.

Nettler, G. *Explaining Crime.* New York: McGraw-Hill, 1978.

Newman, G. *The Punishment Response.* Philadelphia: Lippincott, 1978.

Packer, H. *The Limits of the Criminal Sanction.* Palo Alto, CA: Stanford University Press, 1968.

Paterson, D. G. *Physique and Intellect.* New York: Century, 1930.

Petersilia, J., Greenwood, P. W., and Lavin, M. *Criminal Careers of Habitual Felons.* Santa Monica, CA: Rand Corporation, 1977.

Quetelet, L. A. J. *A Treatise on Man and the Development of His Faculties.* A facsimile reproduction of the English translation of 1842. Gainesville, FL: Scholars' Facsimiles and Reprints, 1969.

Savitz, L., Turner, S. H., and Dickman, T. The origin of scientific criminology: Franz Joseph Gall as the first criminologist. In R. F. Meier (ed.), *Theory in Criminology: Contemporary Views.* Beverly Hills, CA: Sage, 1977.

Schafer, S. *Theories in Criminology.* New York: Random House, 1969.

Sheldon, W. H. *Varieties of Delinquent Youth: An Introduction to Constitutional Psychiatry.* New York: Harper and Brothers, 1949.

Shireman, C. H., Mann, K. B., Larsen, C., and Young, T. Findings from experiments in treatment in the correctional institution. *Social Service Review* 46 (1972): 38–59.

Silber, D. E. Controversy concerning the criminal justice system and the role of mental health workers. *American Psychologist* 29 (1974): 239–44.

Smith, B. D., and Vetter, H. J. *Theoretical Approaches to Personality.* Englewood Cliffs, NJ: Prentice-Hall, 1982.

Solomon, H. M. The dynamics of delinquency. In P. F. Cromwell, G. C. Killinger, R. C. Sarri, and H. M. Solomon (eds.), *Introduction to Juvenile Delinquency.* St. Paul, MN: West, 1978.

Tarde, G. *Social Laws: An Outline of Sociology.* New York: Macmillan, 1907.

Vachss, A. H., and Bakal, Y. *The Life-Style of the Violent Juvenile: The Secure Treatment Approach.* Lexington, MA: Lexington Books, 1979.

Van Dine, S., Conrad, J., and Dinitz, S. *Restraining the Wicked: The Dangerous Offender Project.* Lexington, MA: Lexington Books, 1979.

Vold, G. B. *Theoretical Criminology.* New York: Oxford University Press, 1958.

Vold, G. B., with the assistance of T. Bernard. *Theoretical Criminology* (rev. ed.). New York: Oxford University Press, 1979.

Washburn, S. L. Review of W. H. Sheldon's *Varieties of Delinquent Youth. American Anthropologist* 53 (1951): 561–63.

Wilson, J. Q. *Thinking About Crime.* New York: Vintage Books, 1977.

Wolfgang, M. E., Figlio, R. M., and Sellin, T. E. *Delinquency in a Birth Cohort.* Chicago: University of Chicago Press, 1972.

chapter 10

ECONOMIC CONDITIONS AND CRIMINALITY

necessities of life feel obliged to steal in order not to succumb to poverty. He felt that his position was supported by the fact that thefts increased during economic depression, were more common in the winter months, and were more prevalent among widows and divorcees than other women.

Crimes of cupidity—the desire for inordinate wealth—are identified with the occasional criminal. Although these offenders earn enough to satisfy their basic needs, their desires for luxury motivate them to steal when the opportunity presents itself. This desire is greatly increased when there is a division between the rich and poor because it heightens the latter group's awareness of the existence of a variety of goods that are not normally available to them. Capitalism widens the gap further between the classes. It also forces the use of advertising and the display of a large variety of goods in stores, which further enhances a person's desire for luxuries. Shoplifting and embezzlement are the kinds of crime included within this category.

Robbery and related offenses were seen as declining in modern industrial societies and being replaced by less serious crimes such as theft and fraud. Violent offenders were viewed as products of an environment in which children were introduced as both victims and observers of violence perpetrated by members of their immediate families. Bonger seems to have attributed the involvement of nonprofessional offenders in violent crimes to the influences of what the later criminologists Wolfgang and Ferracuti (1967, 1969) identified as a "subculture of violence," although Bonger did not refer to it in these terms. Professional offenders, on the other hand, become involved in violent crimes as a consequence of their criminal activities. Bonger noted that men who carry knives are likely to use them when threatened. At some point in their careers, these criminals are likely to be placed in a position where they have to use violence in order to obtain a criminal objective: "The man who has formed the habit of breaking into houses and bursting open safes is forcibly drawn, sooner or later, to rid himself of witnesses who surprise him at this work or of a victim who might recognize him" (Bonger, 1916, p. 598).

White-collar/Economic Crimes Bonger also dealt with a category of offenses that modern criminologists have designated *white-collar* or *economic crimes.* These include such offenses as fraudulent bankruptcy, exaggerated merchandise claims, unnecessary examinations by physicians, and similar types of crimes. These offenses are committed by middle-class persons for motives not essentially different from those in other forms of theft, that is, cupidity, professionalism, and poverty.

Business failure in the case of the middle class has the same effect as poverty for the lower classes. A man facing business failure will resort to crime not as a means of preventing absolute poverty but in order to maintain his current position and standard of living. Bonger contends that capitalism provides the impetus for this activity by emphasizing the principle of "every man for himself" as a means of achieving success. Thus, if a man is compelled to always pursue his own interests he can give very little thought to the interest of others. This enables a merchant to engage in fraudulent business practices in order to prevent the demise of his business with little concern for the impact of these practices on the consumers.

Bonger also notes that the penalties associated with these offenses, particularly relative to the greater harm from them, are relatively light as compared with those for ordinary offenses like theft. Further, he recognizes that only a limited number of these practices are punishable by law and argues for the formal sanctioning of more of these practices.

Sexual Crimes, Crimes of Vengeance, Political Crimes, and Degeneracy   *Sexual, political, and violent crimes,* according to Bonger (1916), are also related to economic conditions. Adultery is attributed to the organization of society in Bonger's time which made divorce difficult if not impossible. Rape and related acts involving both adult and child victims are viewed as a consequence of living conditions in the lower strata of society which teach children to view sex from primarily an animal point of view. Other contributing factors included the economic condition which prevents some individuals from marrying at a "natural" age, alcoholism, and the inferior social position of women.

Crimes of vengeance result from circumstances surrounding our economic and sexual lives. First, the desire for vengeance is generated by an economic system which is characterized by strife and competition, that is, doing injury to others. Examples of this include retailers being put out of business by large department stores, striking workers being replaced by strike breakers, and disputes over inheritance. Crimes of sexual vengeance are aroused by an economic climate in which women are viewed as property and men have great power over them. Alcoholism and poor early socialization are also mentioned as contributory factors. *Political crime* is directed toward injuring a ruling class in order to aid an oppressed class or to liberate a subjugated people from their oppressors.

Finally, Bonger even viewed economic and social conditions as important factors in the development of *degeneracy* which he in turn saw as a cause of criminality. Degernerates are individuals who suffer from mental diseases or diseases of the nervous system. Even in instances in which these conditions were regarded as due to heredity, he still contended that their basic cause could be traced to unfavorable environmental circumstances that have exerted their influence from generation to generation and have thus resulted in an individual who is abnormal at birth. Degeneracy and mental illness among the middle class is caused by the pressures created by the desire to maintain and/or improve one's economic position.

Summary   Bonger's work represents the first clear and comprehensive application of Marxist principles to the study of crime. Second, and of equal importance, it is one of the earliest attempts to identify specific types of crimes and the determinants of each category of offense. Bonger's discussion of the causes and career patterns of professional criminals shows a recognition of what later theorist Edwin H. Sutherland called "differential association"—the learning process involved in the acquisition of criminal patterns. Bonger emphasized the negative role of the prison in educating young offenders in the skills and attitudes associated with a developing criminal career.

Bonger also showed an understanding of the importance of socialization and of behavioral expectations in producing a disproportionate number of violent offenses in the lower classes. As we suggested, this represents an early identification of the role of the subculture of violence in producing violent behavior. Bonger identified, described, and offered explanations for crimes and deceptive practices that fall within the category labeled by modern criminologists as white-collar/economic crimes. Some of the explanations he offered for these offenses are as applicable today as they were when he identified them in the early part of this century. It is hard to deny that certain types of offenses in this category are attributable to fierce competition, conspicuous consumption, the low risk of apprehension, and the relatively light penalties associated with these violations. Thus, we see that the roots of many concepts and theories of modern criminology can be traced back to the work of this early pioneer.

RADICAL CRIMINOLOGY

This section is concerned with the views of a number of contemporary criminologists whose ideas derive from, or have been heavily influenced by, Marxist thought, and with certain other criminologists whose viewpoint is indebted to a conflict perspective. It has been the practice to lump all of these criminologists together as "radical criminologists." Bohm (1982) cautions that while people who are referred to as radical criminologists share certain ideas and assumptions, "there are important philosophical, theoretical, practical . . . and nominal differences . . . among them" that are "ignored by critics and enthusiasts alike" (p. 566). In our judgment, to continue to use the blanket term *radical criminology* is to perpetuate a source of major confusion for readers who are unlikely to be familiar with these various views. Therefore, it seems appropriate to begin this discussion where the previous discussion of Bonger left off: namely, with contemporary criminological positions which reflect the influence of Karl Marx, Friedrich Engels, and neo-Marxist figures such as Ralf Dahrendorf and others.

An Overview of Radical Criminology

Radical criminology requires a critical reappraisal and redefinition of the subject matter and concerns of crime (Meier, 1976; Platt, 1975). Radical criminologists examine more than crime as it is legally defined. Engels's proposition that crime is the result of demoralization produced by capitalism is further developed in radical criminology in the thesis that "self-determination, dignity, food and shelter, and freedom from exploitation" are human rights, the violation of which constitutes a crime (Klein and Kress, 1976, p. 36). Extension of this principle then logically includes such acts as racism, sexism, and imperialism as crimes. It is Quinney's (1974) contention that "capitalist societies violate human sensibilities and [thereby] induce rebellion by the populace" (p. 132). Deviance viewed in this perspective is understandably considered to be innately healthy.

Radical criminologists see criminality as primarily an expression of **class conflict.** According to their interpretation, behavior designated as "criminal" by the ruling classes is the inevitable product of a fundamentally corrupt and unjust society; law enforcement agencies are the domestic military apparatus used by the ruling classes to maintain themselves in power; the causes of crime lie within society and its legal system; therefore, crime will persist until or unless both are made to change.

The basic tenets of this position are outlined by Quinney (1974) in the following propositions.

1. *American society is based on an advanced capitalistic economic system.* All life in our society is influenced or determined by the capitalist mode of production. Even government is inseparable from and, in fact, is run by and for the large corporations.

2. *The state is organized to serve the interests of the dominant economic class, the capitalist ruling class.* As in other capitalist societies, there is a division in our society between the class that rules and those who are ruled. According to Quinney, the ruling class in a capitalist society is "that class which owns and controls the means of production and which is able, by virtue of the economic power thus conferred upon it, to use the state as an instrument for the domination of society" (1974, pp. 19–20). In the United States, this class is mainly composed of those who own and control the corporations and financial institutions; they comprise about 1 percent of the population, and own 40 percent of the nation's wealth. Although Quinney recognizes there are other classes (e.g., small businesspeople, office workers) and some which may cut across these two major classes, he maintains that it is this division between the leading class (ruling class) and the subordinate class (working class) which is the basis for the political, social, and economic ways of life in a capitalist society.

3. *Criminal law is an instrument of the state and ruling class to maintain and perpetuate the existing social and economic order.* Law is viewed as a vehicle that is created by the ruling class in order to secure their own interests. In other words laws are used to maintain and protect the property and interests of the ruling class. Moreover, as capitalist society becomes further threatened, criminal law comes to be increasingly employed to maintain domestic order. That is, it comes to be used as a means of suppressing dissent among the working classes. In short, the law is used by the ruling classes to control the rest of the population.

4. *Crime control in capitalist society is accomplished through a variety of institutions and agencies established and administered by a governmental elite, representing ruling-class interests for the purpose of establishing domestic order.* From this standpoint, our social control system is viewed as a means of protecting the status quo and preventing the underclass from becoming powerful.

5. *The contradictions of advanced capitalism—the disjunction between essence and existence—require that the subordinate classes remain oppressed by whatever means necessary, especially through coercion and violence of the legal system.* In order for the capitalist elite to maintain its superiority within our society, the underclass has to be held down or suppressed by any means available to the dominant class, including economic exploitation and political manipulation. As long as this precarious situation prevails (i.e., until or unless there is a revolution), the law and the criminal justice system operate as tools or instruments to perpetuate the dominant class. Coercion and violence are committed by the agents of social order against the hapless victims of the downtrodden underclass.

6. *Only with the collapse of capitalist society and the creation of a new society, based on socialist principles, will there be a solution to the crime problem.* Quinney contends that the crime problem is rooted in the disparities that are inherent in a capitalist system. From his standpoint, the problem will not be resolved until the present society collapses and is replaced by a new social order in which human

beings will no longer be compelled to suffer the alienation that is a fundamental part of living in a capitalist society. Says Quinney (1974): "when there is no longer the need for one class to dominate another, when there is no longer the need for a legal system to secure the interests of a capitalist ruling class, there will no longer be the need for crime" (p. 25).

Crime and Criminal Justice   Fundamental inequities of the American criminal justice system are divided into two principal categories: discriminatory treatment on the basis of class, and discriminatory treatment on the basis of race. While discrimination by race is fading to some degree in certain sectors of the system, it is still a clear and significant factor in the administration of justice. Discrimination by class is becoming more widespread than ever today, as the gap between classes widens with economic deterioration. Class and race are not, of course, mutually exclusive, as demonstrated in the position of poor blacks in relation to the process of justice.

Radical theoreticians reject the concept of individual guilt and responsibility for illegal acts committed by working-class people against the persons and property of the bourgeoisie. They see these crimes as wholly justified acts of rebellion by slaves against masters. In their view, this makes the bulk of property crimes "political" crimes, morally acceptable, indeed almost mandatory in view of the criminal nature of society itself.

Assaults and property crimes by proletarian people against other proletarian people are not justified by radical theory, but are understood as inevitable social distortions produced by capitalist society which breeds racial distrust among the poor, protects the person and property of the bourgeoisie much more effectively than those of workers, and produces poverty and alienation.

CRITICAL CRIMINOLOGY

A substantial number of criminologists included by others in the category of radical criminologists prefer to identify themselves more accurately as *critical criminologists.* One of the leading spokesmen for this position is Gresham Sykes, whose earlier work (with David Matza) on delinquency will be examined in Chapter 12. Sykes (1978) suggests that critical criminology has some of its roots in the social turbulence of the 1960s. American involvement in the Vietnam war; the development of a counterculture, one of whose themes was the use of drugs (especially marijuana); the emergence of, and reaction to, political protest; and a growing consumer advocacy movement led people to question many long-cherished assumptions about the impartiality of government and the criminal justice system.

The Themes of Critical Criminology

According to Sykes (1978), critical criminology endorsed three major themes. First, critical criminologists took issue with theories that viewed crime as a result of biological and psychological maladjustments and with sociological theories that relied on such factors as inadequate socialization, peer-group pressure, and the like. Instead, they argued that criminologists should focus on why some persons and not others are stigmatized with the label of criminal rather than the characteristics that distinguish criminals from noncriminals.

Second, this approach was marked by a dramatic shift in the assessment of the motives behind the actions of public officials who deal with the crime problem. There is little dispute that for a long time criminologists had pointed out that the "criminal justice processing system" is unfair and discriminatory, particularly to the poorer members of minority groups. However, few criminologists had been willing to go so far as to claim that the system was inherently unjust. Instead, the faults of major system agencies—police, courts, correctional institutions—were viewed as the result of such factors as lack of funds, individual stupidity, unenlightened policies, prejudice, and corruption. Critical criminologists, on the other hand, see the operation of the criminal justice system as either involving the deliberate use of laws for the purpose of maintaining the status quo for powerful members of society or as a means of serving the self-interests of those who operate these agencies (e.g., continuing to provide jobs and benefits for criminal justice system personnel). The unjust nature of the system is not seen as resulting from minor flaws or individual faults, but is attributed instead to the fact that these agencies function as instruments for the control of one class by another.

The third theme endorsed by critical criminology involves the "rightfulness" of the criminal law. Sykes (1978) suggests that, until the emergence of critical criminology, this dimension of law had not been considered a suitable question to be examined by the social scientist. Whereas a few aspects of the law such as the insanity plea, capital punishment, definitions of juvenile delinquency, and the prohibition of gambling were examined quite critically, most criminal law was viewed as embodying shared social values.

Critical criminology takes a different view of the law. These criminologists do not feel that criminal law should be viewed as the collective moral judgments of society which are put forth by a government that is defined as legitimate by almost all citizens. Instead, they feel that our society is best viewed as a "territorial group" under a regime imposed by the ruling few in the manner of a conquered province (Sykes, 1978, p. 17). This is not to suggest these criminologist consider offenses such as murder, rape, and robbery acceptable, but what they do question is the popular belief that there is uniform agreement regarding all the values that underlie our legal system, for example, the sanctity of property, the sanctity of the person, and the puritanical morality that is reflected in some of our laws. In other words, the critical criminologist contends that in many cases our laws clearly reflect the desires or interests of only a segment of our society.

Fourth, questions are raised regarding the uses of and assumptions about official crime statistics. Traditionally, criminologists have recognized the shortcomings of official statistics and have attempted to obtain additional data on the crime problem through other sources such as victim and self-report studies. In other words, the mainstream criminologist views official statistics on crime as an area that requires more emphasis in terms of developing more accurate methods for collecting these data.

The critical criminologist, however, does not simply view this as a problem in data collection, but instead views the collection and dissemination of official information on the prevalence and incidence of crime as an important theoretical variable in its own right. Thus, for these criminologists, the major focus of concern is the question, "What are the factors that account for the inaccuracies of these statistics?" In other words, the critical criminologist questions the credibility of government statistics because they view the dissemination of this distorted information as part of our overall machinery for social control.

Conflict Perspectives in Criminology

Several criticisms can be leveled against radical criminological arguments. For one thing, contemporary radical criminologists are incorrect in suggesting that early mainstream criminologists were oblivious to the origins of criminal law in social and economic conflicts. Sutherland (in Cohen, Lindesmith, and Schuessler, 1956) sketched the outlines of a "social conflict" perspective on criminal law more than 40 years ago when he observed that:

> [Crime] is part of a process of conflict of which law and punishment are other parts. This process begins in the community before the law is enacted, and continues in the community and in the behavior of particular offenders after punishment is inflicted. This process seems to go somewhat as follows: A certain group of people feel that one of their values—life, property, beauty of landscape, theological doctrine—are endangered by the behavior of others. If the group is politically influential, the value important, and the danger serious, the members of the group secure the enactment of a law and thus win the cooperation of the state in the effort to protect their values. The law is a device of one party in conflict with another party, at least in modern times. Those in the other group do not appreciate so highly this value which the law was designed to protect and do the thing which before was not a crime, but which has been made a crime by the cooperation of the state. This is a continuation of the conflict, which the law has designed to eliminate, but the conflict has become larger in one respect, in that the state is now involved. Punishment is another step in the same conflict. This, also, is a device used by the first group through the agency of the state in the conflict with the second group. This conflict has been described in terms of groups for the reason that almost all crimes do involve either the active participation of more than one person or the passive/active support so that the particular individual who is before the court may be regarded as merely a representative of the group [pp. 103–104].

An earlier statement of the social conflict position regarding the criminal law and its implementation can be found in Thorsten Sellin's (1938) monograph on culture, conflict, and crime, in which he views crime as resulting from the conflicts between either two different cultures (e.g., one group emigrating to another's territory), or the result of conflicts between different subcultural groups in the same society.

More recently, George Vold (1979) advanced the group conflict theory of crime. Vold perceives lawmaking, lawbreaking, and law enforcement as the products of struggle among interest groups in securing and maintaining power. Those who are able to obtain majorities in the legislature are able to control the police and to dictate policies which determine who is likely to be viewed as violating the law. Vold also interprets many kinds of criminal acts as resulting from clashes between groups fighting for political control of society. Groups involved in protest activity aimed at bringing about political reform may engage in ordinary offenses such as murder, sabotage, and the seizure of private property on the grounds that such crimes further the interests and objectives of the reform movement.

McCaghy (1977) has noted that a conflict approach to criminality and deviance has two important virtues: (1) it acknowledges that a relationship exists between deviant behavior and the process of making and enforcing laws; and (2) it recognizes that many acts of rule-breaking are committed in the name of a group or a cause and for purposes other than immediate personal gain or satisfaction (p. 102). In addition, many critics would concede that radical criminologists are correct in asserting that some laws operate to further the interests of those who are wealthy or socially powerful. At the same time, others would prefer to reserve judgment on this question until more research is available on the social sources of crime.

On the other hand, there are some critics who contend that radical criminologists are wrong in their assertions that criminal statutes (homicide, rape) do not enjoy general consensus and that they emerged as a result of the interest-group process or represent the exercise of oppressive power. These critics suggest there are many statutes which enjoy general social consensus. A related argument is that radical criminologists are off the mark in implying that criminal laws develop as the codification of the interests of socially powerful groups only in corporate capitalist society. Instead, so the counter-argument runs, social conflict among classes may be characteristic of all conflicts in industrial societies, with laws arising out of this conflict in all of them (Rock, 1973). It is noteworthy that no extant socialist society can be found which lacks criminal laws and the apparatus for the administration of criminal justice.

None of the problems of radical theory enumerated so far can be considered to be fatal flaws. There is, however, another, larger difficulty with the radical perspective which relates to a common charge by radical theorists that liberal analysis is beclouded by "mystification" and that the radical criminologist's task is to demystify our understanding of crime. Mystification, according to Gibbons (1977), involves the false accounts provided by theories of crime that disguise the part played by the dominant class in producing the conditions which create crime. It is argued that the objective of the radical criminologist is to provide a true account of the nature of our social world in contrast to the deceptive account provided by liberal criminologists. However, what is interesting is the fact that the radical description of the exploitative monolithic power structure of corporate capitalism itself includes a great deal of mystification. In this respect, as Gibbons (1977) notes:

> Radical criminological analyses are replete with claims about the ruling class and its machinations that produce criminality and that have created the criminal justice apparatus in order to deal with those who threaten ruling class interests. These writings present images of a small, malevolent band of corporate managers who make up the ruling class, who are in constant touch with each other, and who are secretly engaged in economic oppression. These corporate heads are

also credited with the creation of such devices as the Omnibus Crime Control bill and Law Enforcement Assistance Administration which is said to directly serve their interests. Many would argue that the radical account of the exercise of power by the ruling class represents vulgar Marxism, i.e., an oversimplified characterization of the real world [p. 208].

Critics of the radical position in criminology question the explanatory adequacy of class conflict to account for a wide range of criminal behavior. McCaghy (1976) states:

> The theory's application is actually limited to explaining legal reactions against behaviors threatening established economic interests. Thus, there is no pretense at explaining such facets of the crime problem as a school janitor sexually molesting a ten-year-old student, parents brutally beating a baby because "it won't stop crying," or two friends trying to stab each other in a dispute over a fifty-cent gambling debt [p. 96].

The strength of the radical approach would appear to lie in its attention to social injustices and the need to correct them; its weakness is its rejection of widely accepted tenets of scientific method, especially those which relate to the empirical approach to discovery. To deny the value of empirical assessments of a perspective, as Shoemaker (1984) observes, is to deny the theoretical process altogether: "One is left having to decide what is acceptable on the subjective grounds of faith and belief" [p. 211].

NON-MARXIST ECONOMIC INTERPRETATIONS

Radical interpretations of crime encompass both explanations of criminality and proposed solutions for the crime problem (Radzinowicz, 1977). By contrast, non-Marxist economic explanations of crime are directed toward describing the extent to which economic factors, along with other variables, contribute to the development of specific patterns of criminal behavior. It is necessary to remember that one can recognize the role of economic considerations in the development of certain types of criminal behavior without subscribing to Marxist political ideology. That is, one does not have to espouse socialism or communism in order to acknowledge the importance of economics in the etiology of some forms of criminal behavior.

Indexes of Crime and Economic Conditions

Examining the relationship between crime and economic conditions is complicated by the lack of exact measures of either of these factors. The major index of crime comprises only those crimes reported to the police. However, as we have indicated, there is a vast disparity between the number of crimes that are reported and those that are committed. This raises the question of whether an actual increase in crime during an economic depression would be accurately reflected in a proportionate increase in the number of crimes reported. There are several reasons for doubting that this would occur. First, an increase in crime may result in people becoming more accustomed to crime, more indifferent toward it, which in turn may bring about greater public apathy and reluctance to report offenses to the police. Also, an increased awareness that adverse economic conditions and poverty are the cause of this increase in crime may result in greater public sympathy and tolerance and may cause victims to be reluctant to report crime to the police. Police efficiency tends to decrease during periods of increasing criminal activity which fosters a feeling that little can be gained from reporting crime, particularly minor violations, to the authorities. These are only a few of the reasons it is difficult, if not impossible, to ascertain the true impact of economic factors on crime.

Selecting an index to measure fluctuations in the economy which can be compared with an index of crime presents at least as many difficulties. While it is feasible to measure the economic situation of a relatively simple agricultural community, it is far more difficult to do so in a society with a complex economic structure. While one industry can serve as the economic barometer of a simple society, measuring economic change in a complex society requires the use of a multiple and diversified index that considers all major industries. The development of a device of this kind is a task that continues to baffle even the most expert economists. Moreover, while this is a difficult problem, an even more formidable problem involves relating these indexes of economic change to trends in crime.

Relationship Between Crime and Economic Conditions

A number of considerations arise in the interpretation of the relationship between crime and economic conditions. First, time considerations are necessary in assessing the impact of economic conditions on crime. It is well to remember that economic changes may not have an immediate influence on the volume of crime, but instead it may take a year or more for the impact of these changes to effect noticeably the volume of crime. For example, if a recession sets in tomorrow, one would not expect that the volume of crime committed would be affected immediately because it would take some time for the effects of this economic decline to be felt. This fact can cause some faulty interpretations of the relationship between crime and economic conditions. In this regard, if crime drops at the beginning of a recession and rises just as we are recovering from it, one possible conclusion is that crime drops during periods of economic decline. However, keeping in mind that there may well be a lag in the effects of economic conditions on crime, a more accurate interpretation of these data may be that the dip in crime volume resulted from previous economic conditions and that the rise in crime toward the end of the recession is a direct result of this economic condition.

Second, it would be unrealistic to expect a direct linear relationship between crime and economic conditions, that is, the crime curve and the economic curve would display the same intensity of change. For example, a 10 percent decline in economic output is unlikely to produce a 10 percent decline in the volume of crime.

Third, it would also be fallacious to assume that crimes committed during periods of economic decline are necessarily "crimes of want" (Radzinowicz, 1977). This is not to suggest that hunger and acute deprivation are not factors in crime occurring during times of economic decline. What is suggested is the connection between deteriorated economic conditions and rises in crime is much more complex. Thus, it may well be that there are a number of other factors that also contribute to crime during times of economic adversity including failure to adapt to changed conditions, rigid habits which have developed during better times, and a latent disposition to crime which is awakened by economic pressure and weaker social ties. For example, an individual may turn to crime rather than accept a job he believes to be below his capabilities and social position. Obviously, this raises issues related to the social and psychological changes that result from variations in economic conditions and how these changes in turn affect criminal behavior. At this point this question remains unanswered and the answer to it may not always be the same.

Fourth, it is naive to assume changes in economic conditions will have a uniform effect on all crime. In fact, we find that fluctuations in economic conditions may result in increases in some types of offenses and in decreases in others.

Fifth, some crimes show increases in both periods of prosperity and depression. This does not imply these offenses are not affected by economic conditions but instead it may mean these crime increases have resulted from different factors. For example, fraud and embezzlement both increase under favorable and unfavorable conditions. During prosperity, increased economic activity results in greater opportunity for these offenses while an expanding level of income may also stimulate the desire to get rich quickly and easily. On the other hand, economic depression has the effect of reducing opportunity which in turn drives some people engaged in commerce and banking to use fraud for purposes of maintaining their current standard of living and professional activity.

Finally, a point that sometimes is overlooked is that there may be considerable variations between countries with different economic conditions and levels of development. Thus, it may well be that economic factors have a greater impact on crime in poorer than in wealthier countries. In order to examine this question the United Nations Secretariat on Social Defense has focused attention on the impact of poverty on crime in the economically underdeveloped countries of Africa and Asia. Mannheim (1965) indicates that this contrast may not be as sharp as we might anticipate. He suggests that a country's total wealth may have less influence on its crime rate than the manner in which the resources of the nation are distributed. In a country in which everyone is poor, there is little motivation to steal; whereas in countries in which there are acute contrasts between the rich and the very poor, there is an awareness among the poor of the availability of goods beyond the scope of their legitimate incomes. This may well explain the reluctance of contemporary Indian criminologists to consider the poverty of their country as a major factor in crime.

Recognizing the many limitations associated with the research relating crime and business conditions is important in interpreting the findings of these studies. This is not to suggest, however, that this research is of little importance; it does provide a perspective on this question. Studies relating to crime and economic conditions both here and abroad date back as far as the turn of the century. Sutherland and Cressey (1978) provide a summary of the conclusions derived from a major segment of the research in this area:

1. During periods of economic depression the general crime rate does not increase significantly.
2. There appears to be a slight yet inconsistent tendency for serious crime to increase during periods of economic depression and to decline in periods of prosperity.
3. Violent property crimes tend to increase during periods of depression; however, nonviolent property crimes such as larceny show an extremely slight but not consistent tendency to rise during periods of depression.
4. Some studies show that drunkenness increases during periods of prosperity, while others indicate that there is no significant change.
5. There is no consistent evidence that crimes against the person are affected by changes in the business cycle.
6. Juvenile delinquency has a tendency to rise during periods of prosperity and to decline in periods of depression.

A study conducted by Brenner (1978) sheds some additional light on this question. Brenner examined the relationships between crime and economic conditions in four major political units—the United States, Canada, England and Wales, and Scotland—from 1900 through 1970. This study is noteworthy because of its attempts to control for many of the factors that throw the results of previous research into question. For example, the reliability and validity of the crime data were increased by drawing the data from a variety of criminal justice sources including the police, criminal courts, and prisons. Crime statistics were not limited to crimes known to the police but also included arrests, crimes brought to trial, conviction, other dispositions, and imprisonment.

Brenner found that there is a strong relationship between increases in crime and declines in employment. His results indicate that:

> In general, the rate of unemployment (or declines in employment and personal income) shows significant and strong relationships to increases in trends of criminal statistical data for all major categories of crime and sources of criminal statistics [1978, p. 562].

Affluence and Relative Deprivation

In addition to economic decline, crime can also be related to economic growth. Explanations may focus on the role of the driving force of prosperity and emphasis on competition and material achievement, or they may be directed toward the ways in which economic growth affects various segments of the population. For example, during periods of intermediate-range economic upswings or long-term economic growth, although there are increases in employment and income levels among our lowest socioeconomic groups, these increases are simply not comparable to those for the general population. In other words, during these periods lower socioeconomic groups actually experience a substantial comparative decline in socioeconomic status (Brenner, 1978). Attention may also be focused on the effects of frustration experienced by those attempting to reach the top. Finally, consideration may be given to the failures of affluent societies, including gaps in the welfare system and untouched pockets of sheer poverty that remain in spite of general progress.

Another method of explaining rising crime in an affluent society is to view it not as an objective consequence of economic need but instead as a result of subjective socioeconomic deprivations and blunted aspirations. Rather than seeking the sources of crime in absolute wealth or poverty or even welfare, this approach looks to relative feelings of discontent or content, satisfaction or dissatisfaction, overstimulation of aspirations, and (the extension of artificial needs) (Radzinowicz, 1977). The major focus of attention is on the sociopsychological implications of economic conditions. This conception is evident in the writing of a number of criminologists. For example, Vold (1958) noted that:

> Poverty is always in part a subjective condition, relative to what others have, rather than any simple objective fact of the presence or absence of a certain amount of property or other measure of wealth. What one man considers poverty, another may view as a level of satisfactory comfort, if not abundance [pp. 173–174].

Criminologists today are more likely to view the frustration resulting from a continued state of, or change in, **relative deprivation** as a causal factor in crime rather than the effects of an immediate decline in material well-being.

Relative deprivation was also noted as a factor contributing to the civil disorders, assassinations, and violence of the 1970s (National Commission on the Causes and Prevention of Violence, 1970; National Advisory Commission on Civil Disorders, 1968). This finding is not unexpected in a culture that places emphasis on achievement and measures it largely in material terms. Our culture leads us to desire goods and services and to feel successful if we obtain them and unsuccessful if we do not. The awareness and desire for products and services are further heightened by our mass communication system. Television more than any other medium graphically displays to ghetto dwellers a variety of products and services that are beyond their reach—a constant reminder that happiness is defined as getting and having things.

This situation is further aggravated by our continued belief that everyone has an equal chance of success and that anyone who fails only has himself or herself to blame. While this may have been true at an earlier period in our national history, today the requirements for upward mobility have changed, including, among other things, educational requirements, which were not the case in the past. Nevertheless, the myth of equal opportunity still exists. The result is that those who fail to succeed experience feelings of frustrations which are further aggravated by rising levels of expectation fueled by unprecedented prosperity, changes in the law, wars on poverty, and a host of other features characteristic of contemporary life. There are a variety of ways of coping with feelings of frustration. Some people drop out entirely from the game and seek escape through the use of drugs and alcohol, mental illness, and even suicide. Others, particularly those whose parents have "succeeded," drop out and experiment with alternative life-styles, including wandering aimlessly, doing drugs, or working at blue-collar jobs, and nonprofitable employment such as handling a newspaper route or yard work. In the inner city, while some employ escapist solutions, others may adopt illegal methods in order to achieve their goals of obtaining more money and higher status among their peers. As the National Advisory Commission on the Causes and Prevention of Violence (1970) suggests:

> To be a young, poor male; to be undereducated and without means of escape from an oppressive environment; to want what society claims is available (but mostly to others); to see around oneself illegitimate and often violent methods being used to achieve material success; and to observe others using these means with impunity—all this is to be burdened with an enormous set of influences that pull many toward crime and delinquency. To also be Negro, Mexican, or Puerto-Rican-American and subject to discrimination and segregation adds considerably to the pull of these other criminogenic forces [p. 31].

Consequently, these young people feel they have no stake in the system and feel they have little to gain by following society's rules and little to lose by not doing so. They feel that the odds against their achieving success through legitimate means are much greater than the odds against their achieving success through crime. Unfortunately, our crime statistics bear out this assumption since their chances of getting caught are rather remote. For the young ghetto male, crime serves as a means of obtaining material objects and violence further serves as a means of validating and maintaining one's masculinity (National Advisory Commission on the Causes and Prevention of Violence, 1970).

Relative deprivation has also been viewed as a major factor in our recent urban riots and incidents of looting and property damage. Davis (1970), after examining rebellions and revolutions both here and abroad, suggests that these insurrections are "most likely to take place when a prolonged period of rising expectations and rising gratifications is followed by a short period of sharp reversal, during which the gap between expectations and gratifications quickly widens and becomes intolerable" (p. 690). He suggests that income differentials when combined with the incidence of violence on the part of police and white citizens raised frustration levels to a point of rebellion. Between 1964 and 1969 there were at least 325 major civil disturbances in our urban ghettos (Reckless, 1973).

Gurr (1970) has put these civil disorders in perspective by examining the conditions associated with strife in other nations. He found that civil strife in this country had the same characteristics as strife in other modern democratic and Western nations. His research demonstrated that civil strife in the United States as well as in other nations was a function of "intense, persistent discontent among groups and a tumultuous history that provides justification enough for violent and collective protests and violent defense" (Graham and Gurr, 1970, p. 572). In this country persistent deprivation is a fact of life for most black Americans, for example. Thus, while there is a small but steadily increasing black middle class, the major proportion of the black population still remains in the ghetto with little hope of escape. This has created a gap between black haves and have-nots which has increased the feelings of deprivation experienced by the latter group. The National Advisory Commission on Civil Disorders (1968) has indicated that the disorders of the 1960s were at least in part a response against being left out and left behind.

This analysis has some general implications for future civil disorders in the United States. Future strife in this country is likely as long as persistent deprivation characterizes a major segment of our population (Gurr, 1970). The New York blackout of 1977 provides a more recent example of a civil disorder that has been largely attributed to these conditions. It is interesting to note that during a similar blackout in New York in 1965 looting was a minor occurrence. (Weather may be viewed as a precipitating factor in the 1977 blackout.) Thus, while the power failure in 1965 occurred on a pleasant, cool evening in November when most people were at home, in 1977 many ghetto residents were on the street seeking relief from the summer's heat wave.) A number of other things had changed in the dozen years between the two blackouts. Unemployment among young ghetto blacks was 20 percent in 1965 as compared with 40 percent in 1977. Further, more blacks had managed to advance to the middle class which only increased the frustrations of those left behind. It is important to recognize that what happened in New York is likely to happen, given some precipitating event, in any large American city with a substantial number of unemployed people.

There is also research to show that crime rates in general are tied to relative deprivation. According to Eberts and Schwirin (1970), the deprivation hypothesis suggests when the upper-income population exceeds the size of the lower-income population, the lower-income group sees itself being more relatively deprived of local economic rewards than in areas in which the populations are of relatively equal size. The resulting frustration is likely to manifest itself in aggressive behavior against other community members. Eberts and Schwirin tested and found empirical support for this hypothesis. Their data indicate that even when controls for basic structural variables are employed, crime rates are highest when one population segment is relatively more economically or occupationally advantaged. Their research also showed that crime rates were at their highest when the low-income population was a discernible local minority and where there was the greatest occupational gap between nonwhites and whites.

The implications of this analysis for crime control are clear. That is, if we expect to achieve lower crime rates, increased consideration must be given to the social structural conditions that produce crime. Thus, crime control attempts which focus on rehabilitation or constraint of individual criminals through institutionalization, and attempts at crime prevention through either strengthening local police forces and/or educating the population to reduce victimization are merely treating the symptoms of social conditions and are not dealing with the underlying causes of antisocial and aggressive behavior.

Crime As a Product of Poverty

In an affluent society it is natural to accept the proposition that abject poverty does not exist. However, in parts of the world where there is abject poverty (i.e., basic needs for food, clothing, and shelter are unmet), it must be considered as an important variable in crime. While the poorest in America and England are certainly better off economically than the majority of the population in underdeveloped countries, there is still evidence that in both England and America there are families that live in

When economic conditions improve, those who are left behind get angrier. People are exposed to television commercials that show everyone enjoying the products of a prosperous society. They are made to feel that enjoyment of consumer goods is a national right, and they bitterly resent a society which seems to deny them the opportunity to acquire these material possessions. Anger shuts out any feelings of guilt they might experience over looting the contents of a store. As one of the two black youths standing outside a stripped bicycle shop near Columbia University said during the 1977 blackout in New York, "We're just out shopping with our parents. This is better than going to Macy's."

A few boasted of their thefts. P. F., a 28-year-old Hispanic in Harlem, sounded like a shipping clerk reading off an invoice list as he told *Time* writer B. J. Phillips: "Well, I got a stereo worth $400, a dining room set that said $600 in the window, and some bedroom furniture, but not a whole suite. I got some tennis shoes, and a few things from the jewelry store, but I got there too late for anything really good. I got it all done in half an hour, that's how quick I was working." He paused to add it all up. "I put the total somewhere between $3200 and $3500." Any remorse? "I've got three kids and I don't have a job. I had the opportunity to rob and I robbed. I'd do it again. I don't feel bad about it."

Source: Based on material reported in Night of terror, *Time*, July 25, 1977, pp. 12–22.

---

conditions that are very close to or at the poverty level. In these cases it is not just a matter of being materially less advantaged than others but of not being able to maintain normal health and development. Research both here and abroad has clearly demonstrated that criminal behavior is related to low economic status and poverty (Radzinowicz, 1977).

Poverty is also associated with certain social conditions that may be of greater significance for crime causation than is economic need (Sutherland and Cressy, 1978). Poverty areas in our modern cities typically involve segregated low-rent districts in which people are invariably exposed to criminal behavior patters. It also characteristically means high unemployment with no future potential for work, and is associated with lost social status, lack of respect, feelings of powerlessness, and the sense of "little to lose." Working parents in these areas are typically away from home most of the time their children are awake and are irritable and fatigued when at home. It also must be noted that approximately 43 percent of this country's poor families are headed by women (Poplin, 1978). This particularly adversely affects the attitudes that male children have toward family responsibilities and work. Typically, a disproportionate number of children in these areas drop out of school at an early age because they see little value in an education. The jobs they obtain are generally low paying, unskilled, not interesting, and offer little chance for economic advancement. Thus, the people living in these areas as well as their children are likely to remain poor. Therefore, since the vast majority of conventional criminal offenders are from poverty areas, it must be considered as a contributing cause to the crime problem.

ECONOMIC MODELS OF CRIMINALITY

The Task Force Report to the President's Crime Commission on the assessment of crime in 1967 marked the first significant attempt to quantify the impact of crime on American society. In the following year, an article by Gary Becker in the *Journal of Political Economy* advanced the thesis that most criminals engage in a rational decision-making process which weighs the costs and benefits associated with given criminal actions. The most important factor in this process, according to Becker, is the opportunity cost of time. The term *opportunity cost* is used by economists to refer to whatever must be sacrificed in order to acquire something else. As Sullivan (1976) points out:

> The opportunity cost of war is peace; of the constraints of marriage, the freedoms of being single; of the earnings in one career, the earnings in another; of choosing legally obtained income, [p. 18].

The opportunity costs of crime can be measured by means of several empirical variables, including age, race, education, unemployment, and average wage rates. Said Becker (1968): "A useful theory of criminal behavior can dispense with special theories of anomie, psychological inadequacies, or inheritance of special traits, and simply extend the economist's usual analysis of choice" (p. 170). Although this thesis has not gone unchallenged, in the years since the publication of Becker's pioneering article, economists have applied the techniques of economic analysis to a steadily widening span of topics ranging from empirical tests of models of criminal behavior derived from economic theories to detailed studies of the operations of the criminal justice system (Orsagh, 1983).

Modeling the Offense Decision

The basic premise of economic theories of crime is that most of the economic principles which underlie the operation of legitimate enterprises must also apply, with certain modifications, to illegitimate activities. This holds true not only for crimes against property, where the motive of criminals is generally economic gain, but also for crimes against the person and consensual, or "victimless," crimes. Common to all of these categories of crime is that the individual's decision to commit or not to commit a crime is an application of the economist's theory of choice. According to Reynolds (1980):

> If the benefits of the illegal action exceed the costs, the crime is committed, and it is not if costs exceed benefits. Offenders are not pictured as 'sick' or 'irrational,' but merely as engaging in activities that yield the most satisfaction, given their available alternatives [p. 34].

Despite the overemphasis that this formulation places on the rationality of the criminal or potential criminal, Reynolds maintains that it does not deny individual differences in emotional stability, certainty, and capacity for careful calculation in making choices among alternatives.

Economic models of criminality postulate that the anticipated benefits and rewards associated with an illegal act may involve both financial and psychological features. Commission of the crime yields either money or goods that can be exchanged for money. In addition to this "paycheck," engaging in an illegal action may produce the kind of thrill that is sometimes referred to as a "criminal high," a compound of pleasure derived from flouting social norms, risk-taking behavior, eluding detection and "getting away with it," and other psychic reinforcements.

Costs can also be reckoned in both monetary and nonmonetary terms. Tullock (1980) makes the intriguing point that the entire penal code is a "price list" with respect to the sanctions imposed for various criminal offenses. Jail and prison time are not only psychologically aversive, but they also subtract from the earnings of crime. Periods of incarceration correspond to "involuntary unemployment" for the offender. On the other hand, jail or prison time provides "free room and board" during periods of confinement.

Heineke (1978) refers to crime decision problems with uncertain consequences in which all "costs" and "benefits" are monetary as a **portfolio approach.** This approach is appropriate if all the consequences of the illegal action can be interpreted in purely financial terms. But Heineke points out that, "although the penalty for unsuccessful [income tax] evasion is almost inevitably a fine, it is doubtful whether the total cost of unsuccessful evasion is a fine, since the convicted evader may experience significant nonmonetary costs in the form of loss of respectability, reputation, etc." (p. 3).

A second approach to modeling the offense decision views the decision as a problem in **time allocation,** which incorporates the psychological costs and benefits associated with criminal activity. The potential criminal calculates:

1. All his practical opportunities of earning legitimate income;
2. The amounts of income offered by these opportunities;
3. The amounts of income offered by various illegal methods;
4. The probability of being arrested if he acts illegally;
5. The probable punishment should he be caught [Sullivan, 1976, p. 19].

Based on these calculations, individuals choose the act or occupation with the highest discounted return. Sullivan notes that criminals must include among their cost calculations the future costs of going to prison if they are apprehended.

These and other economic models of criminality are expressed in mathematical terms. They are then tested by applying them to actual data obtained by an empirical study of a particular area of criminal activity, such as syndicated crime, drug trafficking, or burglary. Analysis of the data leads to confirmation or refutation of the working hypotheses and constitutes the basis for further refinement of the model.

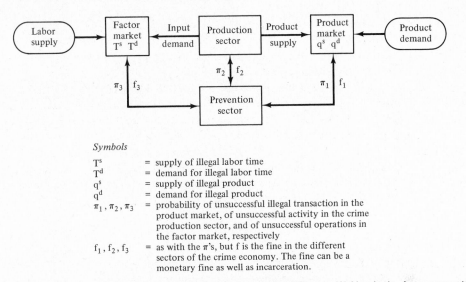

Symbols

T^s	= supply of illegal labor time
T^d	= demand for illegal labor time
q^s	= supply of illegal product
q^d	= demand for illegal product
π_1, π_2, π_3	= probability of unsuccessful illegal transaction in the product market, of unsuccessful activity in the crime production sector, and of unsuccessful operations in the factor market, respectively
f_1, f_2, f_3	= as with the π's, but f is the fine in the different sectors of the crime economy. The fine can be a monetary fine as well as incarceration.

Figure 10.1 Econometric model of the crime industry. (*Source:* W. Vandaele, An econometric model of auto theft in the United States. In J. M. Heineke (ed.), *Economic Models of Criminal Behavior.* Amsterdam: North-Holland, 1978, p. 307. Reproduced by permission of the author and publisher.)

An Econometric Model of Auto Theft The utility and value of the approach described above are illustrated by Vandaele's (1978) theoretical model of motor vehicle theft. Vandaele's model is analogous to an industry supply and demand model: it includes a production sector that produces illegal goods and services, a factor market, and a product market. However, as shown by the design in Figure 10.1, the model also includes a crime prevention sector which has important interactional effects upon the other components of the model.

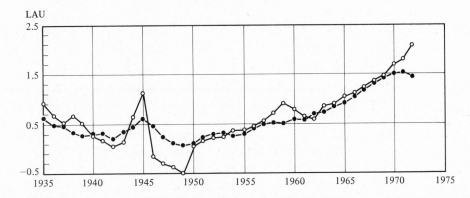

Figure 10.2 Auto theft index simulation output. Symbols: ● Realized, ○ Simulated. (*Source:* W. Vandaele, An econometric model of auto theft in the United States. In J. M. Heineke (ed.), *Economic Models of Criminal Behavior.* Amsterdam: North-Holland, 1978, p. 359. Reproduced by permission of the author and publisher.)

This model was able to accommodate a large number of variables, including the real market value of a stolen car, the per capital number of stolen-car transactions in a given year, the property crime index as measured by official statistical sources, and others. Using these variables, Vandaele carried out a computer simulation study which generated forecasts for the years 1935 to 1972. These curves were then compared with the actual figures for those years. The closeness of fit between the theoretical and empirical curves is depicted in Figure 10.2. In addition to accurately predicting the observed index of motor vehicle theft, the model also appears capable of predicting probability of arrest for this offense. With respect to the implications of the model for policy implementation, Vandaele notes that considerable reduction in the number of stolen vehicles would occur as a consequence of reasonable increases in the probability of arrest or conviction.

SUMMARY

The chapter began with a discussion of crime as a phenomenon related to economic conditions within capitalist societies. Based on the work of Karl Marx and Friedrich Engels, this approach was elaborated by Willem A. Bonger. In addition to providing the first clear and comprehensive application of Marxist principles to the study of crime, Bonger's work is noteworthy for its consideration of the role of learning in crime—an idea that was later enlarged upon by Edwin H. Sutherland—and his identification of specific patterns of criminal behavior, together with the factors attributed to their development.

Radical or critical criminology represents the current designation for approaches which are based on a Marxist theoretical framework. These approaches view crime as resulting from class conflict between the capitalist ruling minority and the working class. Crime, from this perspective, is justified as rebellion by the oppressed proletariat. Law is seen as the means used by the ruling elite to maintain its control; and the criminal justice process is simply the vehicle for accomplishing this aim.

Attention was also given to the importance of various economic factors in crime causation. Initially, we noted some of the factors that need to be considered in interpreting the relationship between crime and economic conditions. It was suggested that economic circumstances are not likely to directly or uniformly affect crime rates; that the economic impact may vary in its effects from one country to another; and that there may be a time lag in the manifestation of economic influences on crime. Research on crime and business conditions indicates that, although economic depressions do not appear to affect crime rates in general, there is some evidence that they affect the rate of violent property offenses.

Relative deprivation was examined in terms of its contribution to recent civil disturbances. Traditional crime control methods will probably have little effect on reducing crime rates that are tied fairly closely to economic conditions. Poverty was discussed in the context of its meaning within an affluent society. The majority of property offenders come from areas in which poverty has an impact on the style of life of community members. People living in these areas are subject to chronic high unemployment rates, and those who are holding down jobs are likely to work in boring, low-income, dead-end positions. The pressures of survival in these circumstances have adverse consequences for family life, especially on child rearing.

The chapter concludes with a discussion of econometric models in the description and prediction of crime. This approach assumes that an individual's decision to commit a crime is based on the same considerations as those which are involved in choosing to engage in legitimate activities. The approach was illustrated by Vandaele's econometric model of auto vehicle theft in the United States. As these models undergo further refinement and elaboration, they will undoubtedly make a significant contribution to future developments in criminological theory.

DISCUSSION QUESTIONS

Find the answers to the following questions in the text.

1. According to Marx and Engels, what was the cause of crime and how was the offender regarded?
2. How did Bonger respond to the question of why individuals engaged in antisocial acts that harm society?
3. How did Bonger explain crime of theft, **crimes of cupidity,** white-collar/economic crimes, sexual crimes, political crimes, and **crimes of vengeance**?
4. According to the radical perspective, what is the cause of crime?
5. Identify and explain the basic tenets of **radical criminology.** What are some of the criticisms of this position?
6. What are some of the reasons we may not see a proportionate increase in crime during an economic depression?
7. What are some of the problems associated with selecting the index of economic conditions?
8. Identify the factors that must be considered in interpreting the relationship between crime and economic conditions.
9. What are the major conclusions of research relating business conditions and crime?
10. Discuss the relationship between crime and **relative deprivation.**
11. How does poverty relate to crime in developed countries such as the United States?
12. What is the basic premise of economic theories of crime?
13. Identify and describe the basic approaches used in construction of economic models of criminality.

TERMS TO IDENTIFY AND REMEMBER

exchange system
crimes of cupidity
crimes of vengeance
radical criminology
class conflict
relative deprivation

object poverty
economic models of crime
cost and benefits of criminal activity
portfolio approach
time allocation

REFERENCES

Becker, G. S. Crime and punishment: An economic approach. *Journal of Political Economy* 76 (1968): 169–217.

Bonger, W. A. *Criminality and Economic Conditions.* Boston: Little, Brown, 1916.

Brenner, H. M. Economic crises and crime. In L. Savitz and N. Johnson (eds.), *Crime in Society.* New York: Wiley, 1978.

Davies, D. C. The J-curve of rising and declining satisfactions as a cause of some great revolutions and a contained rebellion. In H. D. Graham and T. R. Gurr (eds.), *Violence in America: Historical and Comparative Perspectives, A Report to the National Commission on the Causes and Prevention of Violence.* Washington, D.C.: U.S. Government Printing Office, 1969.

Eberts, E., and Schwirian, K. P. Metropolitan crime rates and relative deprivation. In D. G. Glaser (ed.), *Crime in the City.* New York: Harper & Row, 1970.

Engels, F. *The Condition of the Working Class in England in 1844.* London: Allen & Unwin, 1950.

Graham, H. D., and Gurr, T. R. Conclusion. In H. D. Graham and T. R. Gurr (eds.), *Violence in America: Historical and Comparative Perspectives. A Report to the National Commission on the Causes and Prevention of Violence.* Washington, D.C.: U.S. Government Printing Office, 1969.

Gurr, T. R. A comparative study of civil strife. In H. D. Graham and T. R. Gurr (eds.), *The History of Violence in America, A Report to the National Commission on the Causes and Prevention of Violence.* Washington, D.C.: U.S. Government Printing Office, 1969.

Heineke, J. M. (ed.), *Economic Models of Criminal Behavior.* Amsterdam: North-Holland, 1978.

Klein, D., and Kress, J. Any woman's blues: A critical overview of women, crime, and the criminal justice system. *Crime and Social Justice* 5 (1976): 34–46.

McCaghy, C. H. *Deviant Behavior: Crime, Conflict, and Interest Groups.* New York: Macmillan, 1976.

Mannheim, H. *Comparative Criminology.* Boston: Houghton Mifflin, 1965.

Meier, R. F. The new criminology: Continuity in criminological theory. *Journal of Criminal Law and Criminology* 67 (1976): 461–69.

National Commission on the Causes and Prevention of Violence. *To Establish Justice, To Insure Domestic Tranquility.* New York: Bantam Books, 1970.

Orsagh, T. Is there a place for economics in criminology and criminal justice? *Journal of Criminal Justice* 11 (1983): 391–401.

Platt, A. Prospects for a radical criminology. In I. Taylor, P. Walton, and J. Young (eds.), *Critical Criminology.* London: Routledge and Kegan Paul, 1975.

Poplin, D. E. *Social Problems.* Glenview, IL: Scott, Foresman, 1978.

Quinney, R. *Critique of Legal Order.* Boston: Little, Brown, 1974.

Radzinowicz, L. Economic pressures. In L. Radzinowicz and M. E. Wolfgang (eds.), *Crime and Justice: The Criminal in Society.* New York: Basic Books, 1977.

Reckless, W. C. *The Crime Problem.* New York: Appleton-Century-Crofts, 1973.

Report of the National Advisory Commission on Civil Disorders. New York: Bantam Books, 1968.

Reynolds, M. The economics of criminal activity. In R. Andreano and J. J. Siegfried (eds.), *The Economics of Crime.* Cambridge, MA: Schenkman, 1980.

Shoemaker, D. J. *Theories of Delinquency.* New York: Oxford University Press, 1984.

Sullivan, R. F. The economics of crime: An introduction to the literature. In L. J. Kaplan and D. Kessler (eds.), *An Economic Analysis of Crime.* Springfield, IL: Charles C. Thomas, 1976.

Sutherland, E. H., and Cressey, D. R. *Criminology.* Philadelphia: Lippincott, 1978.

Tullock, G. An economic approach to crime. In R. Andreano and J. J. Siegfried (eds.), *The Economics of Crime.* Cambridge, MA: Schenkman, 1980.

Vandaele, W. An econometric model of auto theft in the United States. In J. M. Heineke (ed.), *Economic Models of Criminal Behavior.* Amsterdam: Elsevier North-Holland, 1978.

Vold, G. B. *Theoretical Criminology.* New York: Oxford University Press, 1958.

chapter 11

SOCIOLOGICAL THEORIES OF CRIMINALITY

Sociologists are concerned with the influences of group life on behavior. Explanations for criminal behavior are sought in factors that lie outside the individual and, therefore, are not under his or her direct control. Criminal and delinquent behavior is viewed as resulting from exposure to unfavorable conditions located in the environment.

The major goal of sociological research on crime is to identify social conditions which account for different patterns of crime within society. Sociologists are interested in finding answers to such questions as why the greatest amount of one type of crime—street crime—is found in lower-class communities, while the highest incidence of another kind of crime—economic or white-collar crime—is found among the well-to-do. The sociologist is not especially interested in who commits crimes, but rather in how variations in crime rates are related to such factors as living and growing up male or female, black or white, in a ghetto or in the suburbs, and how these and other factors affect a person's values, opportunities, and views with respect to acceptable means of achieving success in our society.

The various sociological theories that address these kinds of issues are often referred to as structural theories. In this chapter, we shall examine and briefly discuss the major stuctural theories of criminality and attempt to identify some of the strengths and weaknesses of each theory.

SOCIAL PATHOLOGY

Sociologists who studied crime as well as other social problems during the late nineteenth and early twentieth centuries usually formulated their explanations in terms of the **social pathology** position. This approach arose out of the application of the Darwinian ideas about biological phenomena to the study of social institutions and problems. The social Darwinian perspective was rooted in the **organic analogy,** according to which social institutions were conceived as being related to one another in the same manner as are the organs of the body. These are normally healthy but are susceptible to sickness or injury. In its healthy state, a society's social institutions are presumed to be fairly compatible and to function smoothly—like the bodily organs of a healthy individual. Illness, maladjustment, or social pathology (see Figure 11.1) was seen as occurring in a society when one or more of the components disturbed the social equilibrium by clashing with the others because of inability to perform satisfactorily their required functions.

Two factors which were viewed as causing such pathological conditions as alcoholism, prostitution, mental disease, and even unemployment were (1) social change and (2) the inability of certain segments of the population to satisfy their needs and to play their part in the social division of labor. Parmelee (1918) felt that the "criminal class" was composed, at least in part, of individuals unable to adapt to

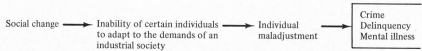

Figure 11.1 Social pathology.

the requirements of society. He included within this group "so-called born criminals," "all feeble-minded criminals," and others who have difficulty adjusting to the existing social order.

Evaluation of the Social Pathology Perspective

Social pathology explanations of criminality were attacked on the grounds that their definitions of pathological conditions are little more than moral condemnations which reflect the predominantly rural backgrounds of their advocates. Conditions such as divorce, prostitution, and premarital sexual relations were so divergent from the circumstances under which these sociologists were raised that they assumed these conditions must be pathological. They were so blinded by their private morality that they failed to recognize that different conditions are not necessarily bad and may even be quite functional in the environment out of which they emerge.

A second major defect ascribed to the social pathology approach was its use of the *organic analogy* (Clinard, 1974). To equate deviance with disease or an unhealthy departure from some universally accepted standard of behavior is to ignore the fact that definitions of what constitutes criminal behavior vary according to time and place—which scarcely makes this phenomenon comparable to such universal afflictions as heart disease or cancer. Obviously, delinquency and criminals behavior are not illnesses in a physiological sense. To call these violations of social norms "disease" is to resort to an extremely dubious kind of comparison. These considerations led to a general repudiation of the social pathology perspective as a valid approach to the understanding of crime and delinquency.

SOCIAL DISORGANIZATION

From the 1920s through the 1940s, the **social disorganization** approach dominated sociological explanation of the causes of crime. The antecedents of this position can be traced to the writings of several early sociologists, including Tönnies, Simmel, and Durkheim, who were all concerned with the transition from rural agricultural society to urban industrial society.

In contrast to social pathology, which relied on a questionable analogy, this approach emphasized the importance of social rules in the maintenance of social organization. It directed attention toward the problems encountered by groups, small geographical areas, and even whole societies when there is a breakdown or disturbance in the rules that guide social behavior. Social organization involves a set of circumstances under which the rules of society maintain the smooth functioning and interrelationship of social institutions; social disorganization occurs when social rules can no longer maintain these conditions. Conditions change and people no longer behave in traditionally expected ways, with the result that social relations are disrupted.

The social disorganization perspective assumed that at some point in the past society was fairly stable—people accepted the rules and played their roles in an expected manner. During this period, basic social institutions such as the family, schools, and the economic system were all functioning to satisfy the needs of individ-

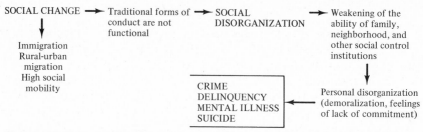

Figure 11.2 Social disorganization.

ual society members and the requirements of society. Simple, rural, agrarian folk societies of the kind found in isolated areas of Quebec, Mexico, and in the Ozarks in the United States were used as models of social organization by disorganization theorists. These simple and smoothly functioning societies are characterized by well-delineated recurring patterns of life—few ambiguities, and few opportunities for personal choice are present and there are mechanisms available for dealing with any difficulties that occur. Tradition and folk knowledge, strong kinship relations, little emphasis on formal institutions and government, team work and high morale, and a relatively homogeneous population are typical of such communities. **Social control** is so effective that serious deviations from conventional standards are extremely rare. Life goals are clearly defined; there is harmony between life expectations and achievement; roles and customs are simple and therefore easily understood and learned. Social control is maintained through customs and informal means. (See Figure 11.2.)

Urbanized western nations like the United States have characteristics that are almost completely opposite from those that are identified with folk societies. These societies—and particularly their urban areas—were therefore seen as disorganized. Disorganization in these areas was attributed to social change, immigration, rural-urban migration, and high mobility. Thomas and Znaniecki (1927) studied the effects of immigration on Polish peasants who came to Chicago. The diruption in the lives of these immigrants caused by the change from a rural, stable, homogeneous folk society to an urban society characterized by anonymity, impersonality, different laws and traditions, and an emphasis on material achievement resulted in increases in the rates of crime and delinquency among this group. No longer bound by old rules, but not yet having internalized the new rules, crimes and other forms of deviance became an alternative method of adjusting to a new environment.

Personal disorganization is interpreted as a consequence or individual manifestation of social disorganization. Crime and delinquency occur when agencies of social control such as the family and the neighborhood are no longer able to restrain individual impulses toward behavior of this kind. Sociologists who adopted the social disorganization position were looking at consequences of the adjustment of the immigrant family as well as those from rural areas in the United States to the urban environment. They found that families faced difficulties in controlling the delinquent behavior of their children. A major part of this difficulty was attributed to a conflict between generations. Parents who had not become assimilated into American (or the

> To better understand the problems faced by immigrants in their transition from a rural to an urban enviroment, the student may consider some of the problems faced by freshmen and their adjustment from high school to college. The college environment is less constraining than the high school environment in that students are not subject to the same pressures to attend classes or to complete their reading assignments, and parental controls are also much looser. Often, students must develop new study habits, the ability to take notes, and sufficient self-direction to attend classes. Students coming from small high schools are also faced with the need to adjust to the relatively impersonal and anonymous environment that is characteristic of most large universities. Some students are unable to make the transition from high school to college and are often forced to drop out. Other students resort to the use of drugs to handle the problems associated with this transition. Still others develop feelings of anxiety and other mental problems which require them to seek counseling. Some students find the problem so insurmountable that they resort to suicide.

new urban) culture held to Old World standards, practices, and habits, while children wishing to become Americanized adopted customs, standards, and mannerisms which they learned in school and in the neighborhood. Consequently, the children developed contempt for their parents; and, without a common basis for understanding, the parents were no longer effectively able to control their behavior. Moreover, the neighborhoods into which these immigrants moved were also viewed as contributing to delinquency and crime. Many of these people came from small villages or small towns, or even sections of major cities, where the adults in the community constituted an effective agency of social control. However, the mobility and heterogenous nature of the slum neighborhoods in which these immigrants initially moved militated against the establishment of strong community control. In communities of this kind, where children are not subject to the control of their elders, although they do not automatically become delinquent, they are much more likely to fall prey to the influences of groups of delinquent children typically found in these areas.

Research

Two methods were employed by the **Chicago School** to assess the validity of their position. The **case study method** was utilized to examine the effects of disorganization on people living in socially disorganized communities (Shaw and McKay, 1972; Thomas and Znaniecki, 1927). The **ecological approach** was employed to identify areas experiencing conditions of social disorganization. Among the latter we may note the detailed study of Park, Burgess, and McKenzie (1925) of the urban pattern of Chicago, which led them to construct the **concentric zone model** as shown in Figure 11.3. According to this schema, the city was divided into five circles or zones. In their investigation of the relationship between delinquency/crime and conditions of social disorganization, Shaw and his colleagues found the highest concentration of

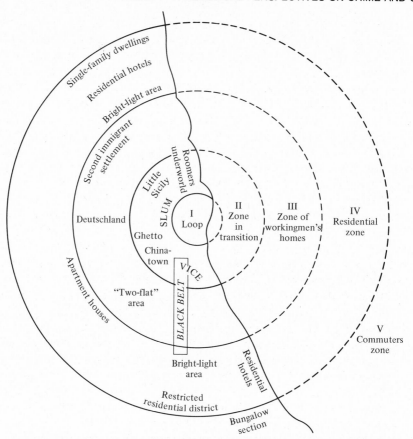

Figure 11.3 Ecological diagram of Chicago. Zone I is the loop business district. Zone II is the business area impinging on the residential section. The outer zone is suburban. The lake front to the east is shown by the wavy line. (*Source:* P. E. Park, E. W. Burgess, and R. D. McKenzie, *The City.* Chicago: University of Chicago Press, 1925, p. 55. Reproduced by permission of the authors and publisher.)

delinquency in Zones 1 and 2. They also discovered that delinquency rates declined in a "**gradient pattern**" from the center of the city outward (from Zone 1 to Zone 5). Associated with high delinquency and crime were high rates of school truancy, infant mortality, and tuberculosis.

Areas of high delinquency and crime exhibited high population mobility, economic dependency (as gauged by a concentration of families on relief), physically deteriorated and condemned buildings, a preponderance of rental units, and a large concentration of foreign-born and black heads of households. These areas retained the highest delinquency rates, regardless of the national or ethnic character of the residents.

The same pattern was found in Philadelphia, Cincinnati, greater Boston, greater Cleveland, and Richmond, Virginia. These studies confirmed the existence of "delinquency areas." They also underscored a relationship between delinquency and the physical structure of the city; that is, delinquency was concentrated in the deteriorated areas, those which lie in close proximity to industry and suffer from other problems including poverty, adult crime, disease, suicide, and family instability (Shaw and McKay, 1972). The fact that delinquency rates remained high in specific areas of Chicago, as well as in other cities, despite the changes in ethnic and racial composition of the population, led Shaw and his associates to conclude that the "delinquency producing factors are inherent in the nature of the community." Shaw believed that the differences in the rates of delinquency in high- versus low-rate communities could be attributed to differences in norms, social values, and attitudes to which children are exposed. Low-rate delinquency areas are characterized by uniform acceptance of conventional values regarding child care, conformity to the law, education, and other related matters. In these areas the family and various informal and formal associations exert pressure on children to keep them engaged in conventional activities, as well as manifesting resistance to behavior that threatens conventional social institutions and values. In contrast, children living in high delinquency areas are exposed to a wide variety of contradictory norms and standards of behavior. While conventional standards remain dominant in these communities, deviant values and traditions represent a powerfully competing style of life. A boy in these communities may be exposed to institutions such as the school and church which espouse conventional values and at the same time also come into contact with groups and institutions that include adult criminal gangs engaged in theft, in the marketing of stolen goods, in quasi-legitimate businesses, and rackets through which partial or complete control of legitimate business is sometimes maintained, which provides support for criminal activities. Thus, in the same community, crime may be defined as acceptable and justified in some groups and as undesirable and improper in others. Youths in these communities may achieve wealth and prestige through either conventional or criminal activities.

Shaw and McKay (1942) also described the process by which delinquent and criminal values are acquired. They suggest these attitudes and habits are acquired to the extent that an individual participates in and becomes identified with groups that engage in criminal and delinquency behavior. They credit Sutherland with labeling this process "differential association." Sutherland's theoretical position will be discussed in Chapter 12.

Evaluation of the Chicago School

As with any approach, the Chicago School is not without critics. Shaw and his colleagues have been accused of overlooking the importance of the fact that police are distributed in different concentrations in various sectors of the city. That is, there is heavier police patrolling of central city areas than suburban communities. Shaw and McKay were also charged with ignoring the impact of differential reporting on crime and delinquency rates. Shaw and McKay were not unaware of these problems. However, they did not feel that these difficulties were sufficient to account for the variations in rates of crime and delinquency.

Several sociologists have questioned the contention by Shaw and McKay that all racial, ethnic, and nationality groups living in similar areas are equally prone to high rates of delinquency and crime (Jonassen, 1949; Robinson, 1936; and Toby,

1950). They have pointed out that the Japanese and Chinese have lived in the most deteriorated areas of some of our large cities and have still been able to maintain effective control of their children so as to keep delinquency and other forms of deviant behavior at a minimum. There is evidence that the rate of delinquency of various ethnic, racial, and nationality groups has varied according to which group is dominant in the area (Robison, 1936). Shaw and McKay's statement that all immigrant and migrant groups "break up" in the first areas of settlement would therefore appear to be of questionable validity.

The pattern of black rates of delinquency requires a further modification of the Shaw and McKay thesis. There is evidence that black rates of delinquency were high when blacks first migrated to an area and experienced the problems attendant on adjustment to an urban industrial environment. However, their rates declined as the population of these areas became predominantly black. What has happened is that while other groups moved out of these areas once they had adjusted to the urban environment, the blacks have remained and over time, as the community became more stable, institutions of social control developed. These findings suggest we cannot conclude that certain ethnic, racial, or nationality groups have high rates of delinquency irrespective of their geographical location, nor can we assert that geographical location is the only factor that determines the crime and delinquency rates of such groups. As Wilks (1967) suggests, the social integration of a particular area appears to be of greater importance in predicting an area's rate of crime and delinquency than simply its geographical location.

Other Ecological Research The work of Bernard Lander (1954) who employed more sophisticated statistical techniques than those of his predecessors, was heralded by some sociologists (e.g., Voss and Peterson, 1971) as the beginning of a new era in ecological studies. Lander applied the Park and Burgess model to the city of Baltimore and computed delinquency rates for each zonal area. He also computed delinquency rates for individual census tracts and found substantial differences. This led him to reject the idea that the location of an area in the city is the determining factor in whether the area will show high or low delinquency rates. He contended that it is the stability of the community, not the specific socioeconomic conditions of an area, which determines whether it will have high delinquency rates. If a community is stable, it will have low delinquency rates, despite the presence of poverty, bad housing, and proximity to the center of the city. On the other hand, delinquency (as well as other forms of deviant behavior) is likely to occur in areas where the group norms are no longer effective in controlling delinquent behavior, that is, where social conditions are present which meet the criteria for **anomie.**

Investigators who have employed **social area analysis** (e.g., Polk, 1967; Quinney, 1964) have demonstrated that urban ecology is far more complex than some of the greatly oversimplified earlier accounts would suggest. To relate crime and delinquency, which are themselves complex phenomena, to such factors as poverty, inferior housing, racial segregation, and lack of family and neighborhood cohesiveness, requires a more sophisticated level of interpretation than is afforded by the concentric zone approach. As Judith Wilks (1967) has noted, "in order to predict and explain an area's crime rate, it is necessary to be aware of the existing social structure, ongoing social processes, the population composition of the area, and the area's position within the larger urban and social complex." Only by viewing area attributes from a perspective of this kind can we (1) "gain an understanding of why the economic, family, and racial composition of an area are associated with offense and offender rates; and (2) understand why the nature of the association between these area characteristics and offense and offender rates vary over time and over different cities" (p. 149).

Despite the criticisms that have been launched against the work of Shaw and McKay, there is no doubt that they have made a major contribution to our understanding of the social conditions that produce delinquency. As Kobrin (1959) suggests, they provided a foundation on which subsequent theories of lower-class delinquency have been built. Short, in his introduction to the revised edition of Shaw and McKay's *Juvenile Delinquency in Urban Areas* (1972), points out that although much has been learned about delinquency in the more than four decades since this book was published, little has happened to alter the picture it presented of the existence and persistence of delinquency areas and their association with the physical structure of the city and other human problems. Indeed, it is extremely rare in the behavioral sciences that such findings continue to be valid for such a long period of time.

Shaw and McKay must be recognized for their development of the **Chicago area projects.** Not satisfied with merely identifying the conditions that produced delinquency, these researchers used their findings to develop delinquency prevention programs in Chicago. These programs have provided a foundation for the development of other programs of prevention for more than 40 years.

FROM SOCIAL DISORGANIZATION TO DIFFERENTIAL SOCIAL ORGANIZATION

The social disorganization approach was abandoned by sociologists for several reasons. First, the concept of social disorganization was criticized as being far too vague and subjective to serve as the basis for examining an entire society. A second objection is that social disorganization presupposes that some previous state of organization has been disrupted—an assumption without foundation. Third, there has also been a tendency among theorists to confuse social change with social disorganization, without any explanation as to why some social changes result in social disorganization while others do not.

A fourth criticism that was leveled against social disorganization theorists echoed earlier objections toward the tendency of the social pathologist to employ analytical concepts in a moralistic or judgmental fashion, that is, behavior considered indicative of social disorganization, like that regarded as symptomatic of social pathology, is thought of as something "bad." Premarital sexual relations, gambling, and drinking are neither bad nor necessarily disruptive to social organization; to imply that they are is a judgmental and value-laden assertion.

A closer look at the areas originally considered disorganized revealed that many, if not most, of them were by no means lacking in social organization. For

Chicago Area Projects

Drawing upon ecological research, case study information, and his experiences as a probation officer, Shaw and his colleagues at the Institute for Juvenile Research developed the Chicago area projects. The first area project was begun in 1932; by 1959 there were projects in 12 Chicago neighborhoods (Kobrin, 1959).

These programs were based on the theory that delinquency in our urban areas was a result of the breakdown of the social control machinery in certain disorganized areas of the city (Zones 1 and 2; see Figure 11.1). This breakdown was presumed to occur as a result of problems faced by immigrants, migrants, and peasants from rural backgrounds in adjusting to a dramatically different set of conditions that are presented by urban industrial areas. This led Shaw to the conclusion that delinquency in these areas could be reduced only if the mechanisms of social control were rebuilt. He felt that this could be most effectively accomplished by mobilizing the residents of these communities to take constructive action toward delinquency. Shaw observed that although delinquency areas might be disorganized, there existed in each of them a core of organized communal life involving religious, economic, and political activities. It was believed that with proper guidance, the leaders of these groups could be taught to organize and administer local youth welfare programs.

The area project neighborhood organizations developed programs that had three basic elements. First, each area project established a recreation program which included, in some instances, summer camping programs. Second, these programs were characterized by campaigns for community improvement, traffic safety, sanitation, physical conservation, and law enforcement. The third facet of the program involved activities specifically directed toward the control and prevention of delinquency. Police and juvenile court personnel were given assistance by project workers in developing plans for the supervision of delinquent youngsters. Boys from the area who were committed to training schools and reformatories were visited by project workers. Further, project workers made contacts with juvenile gangs and worked with them in their own areas. In recent years this has become known as the **detached worker program** and the Chicago area projects, at least in part, can be credited with the development of this method of delinquency prevention. It is important to note that this outreach technique has been found to be one of the few potentially effective methods of reaching gang youngsters who will not participate in any organized recreational activities. Adult parolees were also provided with assistance in adjusting to the community upon their return from prison.

Increased social mobility ➤ Societies characterized by ➤ Alternative and ➤ HIGH RATES
Heightened level of aspiration   differential group organization   inconsistent   OF CRIME
Culture conflict   (multi-group societies)   standards of
Identification of success   conduct (normative
and self-worth with   conflict)
monetary wealth

Figure 11.4 Differential organization.

example, William Foote Whyte—in his classic study of *Street Corner Society* (1943)—demonstrated that although the slum district he studied may have appeared superficially to be disorganized, it actually possessed a well-established and complex organization of its own which was based on a system of personal relations and reciprocal obligations. This organizational structure was not effective in controlling delinquency and dealing with other social problems, but these defects should not be confused with the absence of organization. As Clinard (1974) and other sociologists have suggested, it is quite possible that a variety of life-styles (subcultures) with their different perspectives can actually be an asset to a society by contributing to its integration instead of weakening it and causing social disorganization. It is for these and other reasons that the social disorganization viewpoint has declined in importance in recent decades and been replaced by the concept of differential social organization.

Differential Social Organization

In his original statement of differential association theory, Edwin H. Sutherland attributed systematic criminal behavior to social disorganization. Dissatisfied with this concept, he substituted the notion of **differential social organization** in later revisions of his theory (Sutherland, 1956). Differential social organization was employed to explain why crime rates were differentially distributed in societies, while differential association (which will be discussed in Chapter 12) was used to account for the process or processes by which individuals acquire criminal behavior.

Sutherland contended that differential group organization (see Figure 11.4) is the product of various changes associated with the industrial revolution. These changes include increased mobility, heightened levels of aspiration, the identification of monetary wealth with success and self-worth, culture conflict or normative conflict resulting from the presence of a variety of cultural groups, and an undue stress on individualism. Differential group or social organization means that American society is an amalgam of diverse subcultures. Crime results from the fact that some groups are organized for criminal activities and some are organized *against* such activities. In the most recent statement of the differential social organization position (Sutherland and Cressey, 1978), it is suggested that people in our society may well participate in criminal, noncriminal, and even anticriminal groups simultaneously. As we shall point out in Chapter 12, differential association is offered as an explanation for the reason some individuals adopt criminal life-styles while others do not.

CULTURE CONFLICT

The culture conflict position was an outgrowth of the Chicago School. Rennie (1978) suggests it may also have been indebted to Freudian theories of culture conflict "as a struggle between deeply rooted biological urges that demand expression and culturally created rules that thwart this expression" (p. 133). This position is much more limited in scope than the social disorganization approach; it deals primarily with the problems experienced by people who move from one area to another and subsequently encounter difficulties because of differences in norms between their culture of origin and the new culture.

Sellin (1938) is credited with providing the first systematic discussion of the relationship between culture conflict and crime. He contended that the difference between the criminal and noncriminal is that each is responding to conduct norms of different groups. Conduct norms are rules which reflect the attitudes of a group toward the manner in which a person should behave in a given situation. For every person there is a right and wrong way of behaving in each situation from the standpoint of the group in which he or she is a member. Even in the simplest cultures, people are members of a variety of groups and, as a result, they acquire norms that specify behavior in given situations. Problems develop when a person faces contradictory group expectations.

As a culture becomes more complex, there is a greater likelihood that the number of normative groups which affect a person's behavior will be substantial and in turn this increases the chances that the norms of these groups will fail to agree. Normative conflict occurs when a person is placed in a situation in which the norms that govern his or her responses are inconsistent. That is, the conduct norms of one group may allow that person to act in one way while the norms of another group may permit a completely opposite response.

After making these observations with respect to conduct norms, Sellin went on to examine the concept of culture conflict. Sellin identified two types of culture conflict. **Primary culture conflict** occurs when the norms that condone certain kinds of behavior in one's native culture clash with those of their new culture. For example, Sellin cites a case that occurred in New Jersey in which a Sicilian father killed the 16-year-old seducer of his daughter. The father was completely bewildered when he was arrested, since from his standpoint he had merely been defending the honor of his family in a traditionally Sicilian way. Another example can be found in the newspaper account on the facing page.

Primary culture conflict was also viewed as a factor in the delinquency of the sons and daughters of immigrants. (See Figure 11.5.) These children are usually caught between two cultures. There parents attempt to enforce the standards of their native country; however, the children find that the ways of their parents are unacceptable to the larger community. The shame, emotional tension, and sense of inferiority that stems from this conflict may lead to strife between parents and children, resulting in further tensions which may produce delinquent behavior.

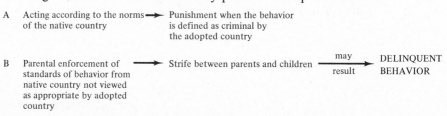

Figure 11.5 Primary culture conflict.

Rejected Albanian Suitor Seized In Shooting Of Father Of Girl 14

The above headline appeared in the *New York Times* on May 27, 1965. The shooting had resulted from a feud that had begun over a year before between the girl's father and the suitor. It seems that the father had finally acceded to his daughter's wishes not to marry the suitor and had informed the young man that he was cancelling a traditional Albanian marriage contract they had entered into. He then returned to the suitor some money and other gifts he had received in consideration of the agreement. However, the suitor had insisted that the marriage contract could not be voided. In Albania, the violation of a pledge is an affair of honor and as a result this has often led to long feuds. In this case, according to neighbors, the father and suitor and his brother had been feuding for about a year. Apparently the brothers finally decided to defend their honor by shooting the father. The two brothers shot the father just after he had emerged from a bus. In addition to seriously wounding the father, they also wounded two bystanders.

Apparently it is not uncommon for Albanians to react in this way. In the same article, the *New York Times* reported that two years earlier an Albanian immigrant had shot and killed another Albanian who had insulted him, and had attempted to cut off the victim's ear before he was seized.

Shoham (1962) examined the role of primary culture conflict in crime and delinquency within the new nation of Israel. For the years 1957 and 1958, delinquency among immigrant youths whose families had come from many different countries in Africa, Asia, Europe, and the Americas was one-third higher than the delinquency rate among the total population. Delinquency rates also differed between oriental Jews and European Jews. Shoham suggests that this difference may be attributed to the problems faced by both the youngster and his or her parents in adjusting to a vastly different culture. The oriental father, no matter how poor he may have been in his country of origin, was the head of his household and held in high esteem. But upon arrival in Israel, he is faced with a different social setup which may make it difficult to maintain his formally high status. "He may be given a job not to his liking and different living conditions may shatter his previous convictions and leave him in a state of confusion in which he cannot exercise proper control over his family" (Shoham, 1966, p. 80). The youngsters, as a result of their contact with the dominant culture, may realize that their father is not the omnipotent patriarch. This image may be further destroyed by such situations as coming home from school and seeing their father sign a document with his inkstained thumb because he cannot write his name. The youngster's own integration is hampered by experiences of discrimination and failure. All of these factors are aspects of culture conflict and "presumably increase the susceptibility of children of immigrant parents to absorb the 'street culture' and to become juvenile delinquents" (Shoham, 1966, p. 81).

Sellin (1938) also identified a so-called **secondary culture conflict**, a by-product of the growth of a society from a uniform, well-integrated type to a diverse and

Complex societies have → Norm violation may result when → Can result in crime or
a variety of social   the behavior required by one   delinquency when the
groups with different   group conflicts with that   norms are in conflict
behavioral expectations   required by another group   with those of the dominant
                                                                  culture

Figure 11.6 Secondary culture conflict.

disintegrated type (see Figure 11.6). The end product of this growth is a culture characterized by a variety of social groups, competitive interests, social anonymity, poorly defined interpersonal relationships, a confusion of norms, and the extensive development of impersonal control agencies whose function is to enforce rules, all of which may not necessarily be supported by the entire community. Conflicts arise within these complex societies as a result of the fact that people are members of a variety of groups, each of which may have its own definitions of appropriate behavior, its own interpretations of social relationships, and its own misunderstandings or ignorance of the social values of other groups. People living in these societies are faced with life situations in which no matter how they act they will violate the norms of one or more of the groups to which they belong. Criminal and delinquent behavior occurs when individuals choose to observe the norms of groups whose value systems are in conflict with those of the dominant culture.

Evaluation of the Culture Conflict Position

Sociologists may have relatively little difficulty identifying the phenomena which support Sellin's viewpoint. Primary culture conflict has been attacked because of the difficulty of determining the specific contribution made by this factor to criminality as distinct from the effects of other variables, such as the move from a rural to an urban environment or from a well-organized to a disorganized society. These factors may have a cumulative effect.

The culture conflict position has also been criticized by those (e.g., Korn and McCorkle, 1961) who disagree with the underlying assumption that criminals are responding to different values and goals. They argue that the culture conflict thesis fails to consider the possibility that individuals and groups who come into conflict may well be pursuing the same goals and may even use similar techniques to achieve them. The conflict arises as a consequence of scarcity of goals. Both the thief and the merchant seek to acquire money and their reasons for wanting to acquire it are likely to be rather similar. The conflict arises when the thief, in pursuit of his "occupation," attempts to deprive the merchant of the money he has acquired in the pursuit of *his* occupation. On the surface, it would appear that the difference is not with respect to goals but instead with regard to the means to achieve them. However, if the thief failed to steal anything of value, no conflict would arise. This being the case, it would be fair to conclude that we are looking at a conflict of interests rather than a conflict of principles.

There is a way to resolve the difference between these two positions. First, Sellin is in no way suggesting that either primary or secondary culture conflict were the *only* elements that produced criminal behavior. It is important to remember that when he advanced this position in 1938 he was trying to provide a systematic discussion of one of the sociological explanations for crime that was prevalent during that period. Second, there is no reason to believe that these two positions are irreconcilable. Granted the thief has as his objective the attainment of the same goal as the merchant, the normative support for the thief's activities may be derived from his membership in a subcultural group which considers his behavior acceptable. There are various instances in which culture conflict may be the dominant element in the causation of crime and delinquency: crimes that occur among newly arrived immigrants, or crimes against the person that are associated with a subculture of violence. The subcultural position, which we shall discuss in the next section, can be considered in some respects an extension of the culture conflict approach.

SUBCULTURAL THEORIES

Before discussing the subcultural perspective, we should try to make clear what is meant by a subculture. As DeFleur, D'Antonio, and DeFleur (1971) define it, "the term *subculture* refers to patterns of norms, beliefs, attitudes, values, and other cultural elements that are shared within particular groups or segments of a society, but that do not normally characterize the society as a whole" (p. 117). Specialized forms of religion or political beliefs, modes of dress, food, and public behavior, even special vocabulary and language patterns, are among the identifying characteristics of various subcultures within a society. People can be born into a subculture, for example, the Sicilian Mafia; they can drift into membership in a subculture, as is typically the case with drug addicts; and people can create subcultures, such as delinquent gangs.

Subcultures serve many functions, which include (1) providing a set of rationalizations and neutralizations for group behavior, especially deviant behavior; (2) facilitating the acquisition of certain goods and services (e.g., drugs) that are necessary for continued deviant behavior; and (3) furnishing the deviant individual with more effective techniques for pursuing deviant behavior. It is important to emphasize that behavior which represents adherence to subcultural norms, although deviant and pathological from the standpoint of general society, is not regarded as deviant and pathological by the members of the subculture: rather, it is considered a normal response to subcultural expectations.

Mannheim (1965) has labeled the theories associated with the subcultural position as "class oriented." Theories identified with this approach, he maintains, are "based on certain characteristic features of the different social classes, on the existing conflicts between the latter and between the subcultures created by them" (p. 499). Dinitz (personal communication) suggests that the subcultural approach to deviance achieved dominance following World War II because many sociologists recognized that the class structure of American society had become rigid, resulting in the emergence of pockets of uniqueness based on educational and occupational differences. Whereas in the past, hard work was the only criterion for success, now success was based on education and occupational background. In other words, the old Horatio Alger myth of the poor boy who worked hard and eventually became an enormous success was no longer valid. Most migrants who came to the city could not succeed because they lacked the necessary educational and occupational background to compete effectively for the better jobs. Unlike their predecessors who were able to work hard and eventually move out of the ghettos, these later arrivals were for the most part unable to improve their economic situation sufficiently to enable them to make such a move. Consequently, we saw the emergence of hardcore slums which gave rise in turn to subcultures. These slums were composed of lower-class whites who were second and third generation slum dwellers, the descendants of immigrants who remained in the slums perhaps because of physical, mental, or other adverse circumstances when their countrymen moved out.

These areas were also inhabited by a disproportionate number of blacks who were relative newcomers to the urban scene. Their low socioeconomic position owed nearly as much to educational and occupational skill deficiences as to racial prejudice and discrimination. Puerto Ricans also lived in these areas, some remaining in them only temporarily before returning to Puerto Rico, while others became permanent residents. Puerto Ricans experienced the same problems as those of other immigrant groups, but their movement up the ladder of social mobility was restrained by educational and occupational requirements. The problems of Mexicans paralleled those of the Puerto Ricans with the addition, for certain segments of this population, of difficulties associated with their illegal entry into the United States.

Whites from the chronically depressed areas of Appalachia have also moved into these areas. Their problems, like those of many blacks who migrated from the South, center upon the necessity for adjusting from a rural to an urban environment. Their low socioeconomic positions results from deficiencies in education and marketable job skills.

In summary, we can see that groups currently living in urban slums are, unlike their predecessors, simply not able to find the means to move out of these areas in the span of a generation. This situation thus facilitates the development of subcultures within these areas. The origins of the subcultural position can be found in the work of Emile Durkheim and Robert K. Merton. Their contributions will be discussed briefly before we deal with the theories advanced by Albert K. Cohen, Richard A. Cloward, Lloyd Ohlin, and Walter B. Miller, which represent the most prominent positions associated with the subcultural perspective.

ANOMIE THEORY: EMILE DURKHEIM

Emile Durkheim (1858–1917), a French sociologist, did not formulate a theory of crime causation, but he is credited with advancing two important postulates concerning crime and deviance. The first is significant because it presented a conception of crime as a normal and functional part of society (Durkheim, 1938). Rejecting the thesis that crime is pathological, Durkheim suggested that *crime is an inevitable aspect of all healthy societies.* It is one of the prices we pay for freedom, which permits innovation—the basis for social progress. However, in order to provide an environment in which the creativity of the inventor is capable of flourishing, we also need to make allowances for the originality of the criminal to be realized. Both the scientist and the criminal are innovators; and in order to furnish an environment in which scientific creativity is encouraged, we must also tolerate a certain amount of *negative innovation,* that is, crime. Durkheim also saw crime as playing a direct role in the evolution of society. Crime not only signifies that social change is possible, but in some cases directly prepares us for these changes. That is, some crimes may reflect a new, though not completely acceptable, type of behavior.

Durkheim's second contribution, the one directly related to the development of the subcultural perspective, was his introduction of the term *anomie,* which he used to refer to *a condition in which the rules governing behavior are not sufficiently clear to permit people to anticipate the actions of others or provide guidelines for their own behavior in specific situations.* "Normlessness" probably best describes the sense in which Durkheim employed the term *anomie.* While he cannot be credited with originating the concept of anomie, for there are indications that it was used in approximately the same sense three centuries earlier, there is no doubt that his resurrection of the term has had an important impact on sociological theories of crime, as the following discussion of the work of Robert K. Merton will make clear.

Robert K. Merton's Contributions to Anomie Theory

Robert K. Merton (1910–19   ), building on the foundations laid by Durkheim, examined the emergence of deviant behavior as a consequence of conditions of anomie. This formulation, which initially appeared in 1938, has been of great importance in the development of the sociology of deviant behavior. When Merton first published his essay in 1938, there was a tendency among sociologists to attribute deviant behavior to a failure of social controls to adequately constrain man's basic biological drives. Granting some role to biological impulses, Merton contended that this still failed to explain why the amount of deviant behavior varies within different social structures (such as social classes) as well as the fact that different patterns and types of deviance are found in different social structures. Merton's (1957) aim was to "discover how some *social structures exert definite pressures on certain persons in society to engage in non-conforming rather than conforming conduct*" (p. 132). It was his contention that if we could identify certain social groups which had fairly high rates of deviant behavior as a result of being subjected to pressures, this nonconforming behavior could not be attributed to distinctive biological tendencies among this group but instead would be best explained by the fact that group members were responding to the social situation in which they found themselves. If this is the case, then nonconforming behavior must be viewed as being as normal as conforming behavior, thus throwing into question the whole contention that deviants are psychologically abnormal.

Merton identifies two characteristics that are common to all social structures: (1) *cultural goals,* which provide the direction for individual behavior; and (2) *socially approved means* or allowable procedures for achieving these goals. However, these regulatory norms do not necessarily represent the most direct or efficient method of achieving these objectives. There are many ways which specific individuals would find far more efficient for securing these desired objectives including among them fraud, theft, and violence, but these methods of achieving the goals are considered outside the realm of accepted behavior. In all cases, the choice of means is limited by regulatory norms. (See Figure 11.7.)

Societies vary over time as well as among themselves regarding the extent to which there is agreement on the goals as well as the socially accepted means of

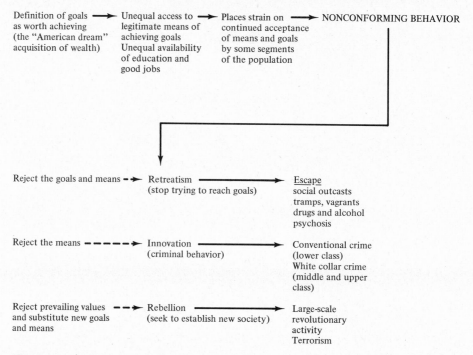

Figure 11.7 Robert K. Merton.

achieving them. As long as all people in a society accept the goals and the socially approved means of obtaining them, there is no deviant behavior. When either the goals or the means for obtaining them are rejected, nonconforming behavior occurs. This lack of concurrence between the means and the goals represents, according to Merton, a state of anomie.

Merton asserts that the amount of deviant behavior in a given society varies in terms of such characteristics as race-ethnic status and social class. This in turn assumes that the differential distribution of deviant behavior within various social groups is paralleled by differential opportunities for members of these groups to achieve societal goals. Groups also develop different modes of adapting to their positions relative to their accessibility to means for achieving societal goals. Not all of those who are subject to pressure to achieve goals and denied access to the means for attaining them become deviant. Merton states that only "those located in places in the social structure which are particularly exposed to such stresses are more likely than others to exhibit deviant behavior" (p. 183). For example, Merton suggests that one alternative which operates to limit deviance is the accessibility to certain groups of alternative goals which are also given prestige by society.

Merton characterizes contemporary American culture as one in which *great emphasis is placed upon certain success goals, without equivalent emphasis being placed on the means employed to achieve them.* Money has come to be viewed as a primary indicator of prestige; however, the means to acquire it are often not subjected to careful scrutiny. Thus, money obtained illegally can be spent just as easily as money

Table 11.1 MERTON'S TYPOLOGY OF MODES OF INDIVIDUAL ADAPTATION

Modes of adaptation	Culture goals[a]	Institutional means
I. Conformity	+	+
II. Innovation	+	−
III. Ritualism	−	+
IV. Retreatism	−	−
V. Rebellion	±	±

[a]Key: + signifies "acceptance," − signifies "rejection," and ± signifies "rejection of prevailing values and substitution of new values."

Source: R. K. Merton, *Social theory and social structure.* New York: Macmillan, 1957; p. 140. Reprinted by permission of the author and publisher.

obtained through legitimate employment for the goods and services that symbolize success—recalling the ancient Latin proverb: *Pecunia non olet* (Money has no odor). The anonymity of the urban environment, along with the pecularities of money, allow wealth, the sources of which may be unknown in a particular community, to serve as a symbol of success at various levels of the social structure. In fact, people are placed in a position where there is constant pressure to acquire just a bit more than one currently has with no end in sight.

Types of Adaptation   Merton has identified five courses of action that people follow with respect to the achievement of social goals. The particular course of action that a person takes may vary as he moves from one social situation to another. These categories therefore represent role behavior in specific types of situations, not specific personality types. Merton is not suggesting that people can be classified according to these five modes of adaptation but rather that they will choose one of these courses of action depending upon the situation and their position in the social structure. In other words, these **modes of adaptation** are viewed by Merton as possible courses of action employed by people in response to pressures to achieve social goals (see Table 11.1).

Conformity.   In a stable society, conformity is the most common form of adaptation. People following this course of action accept the goals as well as the socially approved means of achieving them. If this were not the most common response, the continuity and stability of a society would be severely undermined.

Innovation.   The response of innovation occurs when an individual has accepted the cultural emphasis on a specific goal without also internalizing the institutional rules governing the methods for obtaining them. For example, Merton suggests that in our society there is an undue emphasis on the acquisition of wealth without equal concern being given to the means employed to acquire it.

Merton states that within the upper socioeconomic classes pressures toward innovation may result in a blurring or eradication of the difference between accepted business practices that are consistent with the norms and sharp practices which are beyond the normative limits. These types of criminal innovations were discussed more thoroughly in Chapter 6 dealing with white-collar/economic crimes.

Among the lower classes, pressures toward criminal innovation result from the fact that these people have absorbed the cultural emphasis on monetary success; however, their position in the social structure limits their access to legitimate means for achieving success. Although we espouse an ideology which suggests that everyone has an equal chance for success, those with limited formal education and few economic resources are simply not able to compete effectively. Legitimate channels for acquiring money are not, as our culture leads us to believe, available to all people of equal capability at each level of the class structure. For those in the lower classes whose access to legitimate means for achieving success is limited, the promise for high income and power from organized vice, crime, rackets, and delinquency comes to represent an alluring alternative for achieving success: "In this setting, a cardinal American virtue, 'ambition,' promotes a cardinal American vice, 'deviant behavior' " (Merton, 1957, p. 146). When there is an emphasis on monetary success and a class structure which limits the means for achieving this success, there is a tendency toward these innovative practices.

Pressures for success within the lower classes will produce such notable figures as the Godfather, while the same pressures in the upper classes will produce such scandals as "the great electric company conspiracy," the Equity Funding swindle, the Korean bribery scandals, and Watergate.

Ritualism. Ritualism involves the abandoning or scaling down of the lofty cultural goals of great wealth and rapid social mobility to a point at which one can successfully achieve them. Although people who choose this adaptation reject the cultural requirements to "get ahead in the world" and reduce their aspirations, they continue almost compulsively to abide by institutional norms. Merton recognizes that perhaps this behavior may not be viewed as truly deviant, although it does represent a clear departure from cultural goals which require humans to strive actively for success, preferably using acceptable procedures, and to continue to move onward and upward steadily increasing one's social status.

Merton indicates this type of response is probably most likely found among lower-middle-class Americans. This results from the heavy emphasis placed by lower-middle-class parents on following the moral dictates of society which makes it more difficult for members of this group to engage in deviant behavior. This type of adaptation is characteristic of the person who adopts a philosophy of life that places heavy emphasis on avoiding failure. People who choose this position justify their behavior as follows: "I am playing safe," "I'm not sticking my neck out for anybody," "I am satisfied with what I've got," "If you don't aim too high you are not likely to be disappointed."

Retreatism. People who adapt through retreatism are, according to Merton, "in society but not part of it." These people are not considered true members of society because they fail to share common societal values which are a necessary part of being members of any social group. In this case, the individual rejects both the goals and the means for their achievement. Individuals that choose this adaptation have fully internalized the cultural goals of success as well as the institutional means for pursuing this goal. However, in attempting to attain this goal they find themselves unable to achieve it by legitimate means and they are unable to pursue it through the use of illegitimate means because of internalized prohibitions. Frustrated and handicapped, the individual abandons both the goals and the means and in the process is able to eliminate the conflicts associated with the pursuit of these goals. This escapist reaction includes the adaptive responses of tramps, psychotics, chronic drunkards, vagrants, and drug addicts. These are society's dropouts, who cannot succeed legitimately and refuse to resort to illegitimate means in order to be successful.

Rebellion. Individuals who adapt through rebellion reject both the goals and the means and seek to establish a new or greatly modified social order. This response occurs when the existing social system is regarded as creating the barrier to the satisfaction of legitimate goals. Unlike the other responses which involve adaptations to the existing circumstances, rebellion involves an attempt to establish a new set of goals as well as appropriate means for choosing them. Thus, rather than attempting to work within the system to change inequities, the rebel seeks to destroy the system and establish a new social order. Radical changes of this type have occurred in Cuba and more recently in Iran and Lebanon. The changes in Cuba resulted in the establishment of a Communist-style social order.

The changes in Iran culminated in the overthrow of a traditional monarchy and its replacement by a theocracy or religious government. This fundamentalist Moslem movement has spread throughout the Middle East, resulting in the rise to prominence of such groups as the Shiite minority.

Evaluation of Anomie Theory

Merton (1957) recognized some of the limitations of anomie theory. He acknowledged that the theory largely neglects to consider the role played by sociopsychological processes in determining which adaptation an individual adopts. He is also aware that the theory fails to give consideration to the structural elements which predispose an individual to select one alternative response rather than another.

There is insufficient empirical evidence to support the theory's claim that people in the lower classes are more likely to engage in crime and other forms of deviant behavior than those of other classes. Although official statistics indicate that this is the case, there is considerable evidence to show that members of minority groups and the lower class are more likely to be officially labeled as criminals, delinquents, alcoholics, drug addicts, and mental patients. However, the middle and upper class are involved to a much greater extent in white-collar/economic crimes on which adequate statistical information is not available. There is also evidence to indicate that delinquency, alcoholism, drug addiction, and even mental illness may be as prevalent in the upper and middle classes as they are in the lower classes. In fact, the only difference may be that the resources and opportunities available to the upper and middle classes enable them to better avoid being labeled deviant (Clinard and Meier, 1985).

Many sociologists question Merton's assumption that in modern, complex industrial societies there is a set of universally accepted cultural goals (Clinard, 1964; Lemert, 1967; Thio 1983). In these types of societies people are members of a variety of different groups and as a result consensus on specific goals is likely to vary among different segments of the population. The theory assumes the universal acceptance of monetary goals and the goal of education, but these goals are not equally valued among all segments of the population. Furthermore, the theory's assumption of the universality of illegitimate means is not valid because what constitutes delinquency and crime varies with time and place. For example, (sale) of alcohol in this country was prohibited for over a decade and today there are still jurisdictions in which its sale is unlawful.

Also anomie theory assumes that deviancy is an adaptation to pressures arising from failure to achieve certain goals, whereas actually most deviant behavior is a result of interaction with other deviants who may function as a reference group for the individual (Clinard, 1974). Most individuals do not have an infinite variety of possibilities available to them; they are usually restricted in the types of deviant acts that are open to them by the pressures of the groups to which they belong as well as by their position in the social structure. There is ample evidence to indicate that many deviant acts are expected and/or accepted among certain segments of our population. Drug addiction, homosexuality, prostitution, professional crime, and white-collar crime result from membership in subcultural groups with values that support such types of behavior. Deviance among members of these groups is therefore not the consequence of pressures to achieve success, but rather are results from the fact that a person's reference group considers this behavior acceptable or, in some instances, even regards the behavior as an expected reaction.

Sagarin (1975) suggests that anomie theory sometimes appears to be a "money-is-the-root-of-all-evil" explanation of deviant behavior. There is no doubt that some crimes as well as other forms of deviant behavior are motivated by goals of monetary success. Sagarin indicates that it is not the need for money that primarily motivates people to forge checks, commit acts of bribery, rob, embezzle, steal, burglarize, and swindle. Rather, it is the fact that American culture emphasizes the need to appear successful (represented by high living and the accumulation of wealth) without offering masses of people the opportunities to obtain the unlimited amounts of money they desire except through the employment of illegal methods. The result is crime which is motivated by success goals that involve considerations other than monetary gain. In the case of Watergate, the goal which motivated the break-in as well as the subsequent coverup activities was political success. This was to be achieved even if it was necessary for those involved to commit burglary and fraud. As Sagarin points out, anomie theory which emphasizes "success" offers an almost perfect explanation for the motivation of the primary participants who felt the need to achieve political success at all costs.

This suggests the need, as Merton recognizes, to limit the scope of anomie theory to only certain types of deviant behavior.

It is important to recognize the contributions and value of this theory despite its limitations. Anomie theory must be credited with influencing sociological theories of deviant behavior in general, and crime and delinquency in particular. Prior to 1938, when this theory was first presented, many sociologists tended to view crime and delinquency as resulting from psychological or biological factors. Merton's statement of anomie theory provided an alternative perspective which viewed deviant behavior as resulting from social conditions. More specifically, its influence is apparent in the subcultural theories of delinquency which will be discussed in the remainder of this chapter.

Also, the basic premise of anomie theory, that pressures toward deviation occur when there is a discrepancy between aspirations and the opportunities for achieving them, is valid with some limitation (Thio, 1983).

First, one should not make the assumption, as Merton did, that the pressures toward deviation are any greater in the lower classes than they are in other classes. Instead, it is more accurate to assume that regardless of class, individuals will be predisposed to engage in deviant behavior if they experience a major gap between what they are striving for and the opportunities for realizing their goals. This applies to conventional street crime as well as white-collar/economic crime. Also implicit here is the assumption that anomie theory is limited to explaining *those types* of deviant behavior that result from this gap between aspirations and opportunities for obtaining them. Finally, as we will see, Merton's work provided a foundation for the theories of both Cohen (1955) and Cloward and Ohlin (1960) which are discussed in the next two sections.

DELINQUENCY AND STATUS FRUSTRATION: ALBERT K. COHEN

In 1955, Albert Cohen published *Delinquent Boys,* which sought to explain why a delinquent subculture with a specific content arises and persisits in the working-class neighborhoods of American cities. A delinquent subculture, according to Cohen (1955), is "a way of life that has somehow become traditional among certain groups in American society" (p. 13). The groups he is referring to are boys' gangs, which are found to flourish typically in the impoverished neighborhoods of major American cities. While the members of these groups may grow up either to be law-abiding citizens or graduate to professional or adult forms of criminality, the delinquent traditions in these areas are kept alive by the youngsters who succeed them.

Cohen suggests that a delinquent subculture develops in response to the shared problems of low status that are experienced by youths in working-class neighborhoods as a result of their position in the general social structure. (See Figure 11.8.) Specifically, these problems arise as a result of these boys being evaluated by a "middle-class measuring rod" which places emphasis on traits such as ambition, the possession of skills, and achievement which confirm this; postponement of immediate satisfaction in order to achieve long-range goals; rationality and cultivation of social graces; control of physical aggression and violence; wholesome recreation; and respect for property. The working-class youth is most likely to be confronted with these expectations within the school setting because this is one of the few places where children of all social levels are brought together and compete for status on the basis of middle-class criteria. However, working-class youngsters are at a disadvantage because of their lower social status and their lack of appropriate skills and attitudes to compete with their middle-class peers for recognition by teachers and other adults within the school system.

Cohen outlines three possible responses to the situation, two of which are borrowed from William Foote Whyte's *Street Corner Society* (1943). The first and

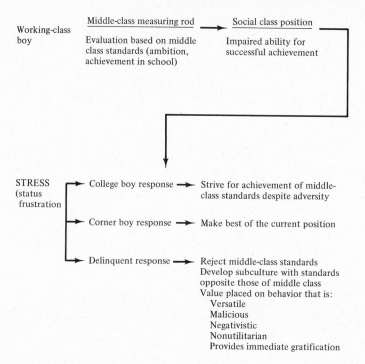

Figure 11.8 Albert K. Cohen.

most common, according to Cohen, is the "stable corner-boy response." Boys who adapt in this way make the best of their current situations and accept the limitations that are imposed on them as a result of their current social positions. On the other hand, those who choose the "college-boy way of life" decide to enter middle-class society.

Working-class boys may choose a third alternative, the delinquent subcultural response, which involves the wholesale and explicit rejection of middle-class standards and the adoption of a completely opposite value system that is exemplified by the following six characteristics.

1. *Non-utilitarian behavior.* This means, for example, that gang delinquents neither want nor need the objects they steal. Instead, they steal for "the hell of it" and/or the status associated with successfully accomplishing the theft.
2. *Malicious behavior.* Delinquent gang members also seem to delight in engaging in activities that cause others discomfort and that defy the norms of the community. They enjoy putting glue or sand in the engine of a person's car, slashing tires, and destroying property in parks, schools, and public transportation. In short, gang delinquents seem to derive pleasure from vandalism.
3. *Negativistic behavior.* The norms that guide gang behavior are in direct opposition to those of respectable middle-class society. If behavior is right or acceptable to middle-class society, it is rejected by gang delinquents and behavior that is opposite becomes respectable and acceptable.

4. *Versatility.* Diversification characterizes the delinquent activities of gang members. Although theft is their primary activity, their stealing involves a variety of objects and victims. These youngsters may steal candy, fruit, clothing, notebooks, newspapers, and cars, while their targets may include homes, stores, schools, as well as old ladies. In addition to stealing, they also engage in other property offenses, vandalism, malicious mischief, trespass, and truancy.

5. *Short-run hedonism.* Gang members have no long-range objectives or aspirations. Instead, behavior is impulsive and based on spur-of-the-moment whims, with the overriding consideration being whether the activities are exciting. Thus, planning for the future, deferred gratification of desires, even the acquisition of skills and knowledge are all totally rejected by gang boys.

6. *Group autonomy.* Delinquent gang members are usually resistant to having any restraints placed on their behavior except those that result from informal pressures within the gang itself. They resist efforts by their parents, teachers, and other adult authority figures to regulate their behavior. Consequently, these youngsters are extremely difficult to reach through conventional means such as schools, recreational centers, and social agencies.

Evaluation of Cohen's Theory

One of the most systematic and detailed critiques of Cohen's approach was done by Kitsuse and Dietrick (1959). First, they questioned Cohen's explanation of how delinquent subculture develops. According to Cohen, working-class boys evaluate themselves in terms of middle-class norms. In their attempts to achieve status on the basis of middle-class standards, they experience severe frustration and anxiety. In order to deal with these anxieties, they develop an alternate system that is the diametric opposite of the one they are rejecting. Psychologists call this process **reaction formation.** But Cohen's own description of the social and cultural conditions of working-class boys provides with its paramount emphasis on peer relationships little basis for the assumption that they internalize middle-class values and are overly concerned with the views of middle-class authority figures. A more plausible interpretation is that these youngsters choose not to strive for status in the middle-class system and resent the presence in their community of people (e.g., teachers) who subscribe to such values and attempt to impose those values upon them.

Second, Kitsuse and Dietrick (1959) have also questioned Cohen's explanation of the content of delinquent subculture. They contend that Cohen's description of delinquent activities as nonutilitarian, malicious, and negativistic does not fit the behavior of contemporary gang delinquents. They claim that among delinquents today there is no absence of calculated, rational, utilitarian behavior. There is also evidence that the kinds of activities which Cohen cites as characteristic of working-class boys are also engaged in by middle-class adolescents. Taken together, these criticisms seriously challenge Cohen's conception of the development and content of the delinquent subculture.

Kitsuse and Dietrick propose an alternative explanation to help clarify Cohen's position on how delinquent subcultures are maintained, once they come into existence. According to Cohen, it is not necessary for the motivational structure which accounts for the emergence of the subculture to also explain its maintenance. Kitsuse and Dietrick suggest that, once established, the subculture can be maintained by participants who engage in gang behavior for a variety of reasons. However, once they start participating in gang activity their behavior leads to rejection by respectable members of the community and to negative sanctions being imposed by schools and the criminal justice system. These juveniles, in turn, respond by rejecting the standards of middle-class society and those that impose them and instead seek status within the delinquent gang. This leads Kitsuse and Dietrick to assert "that the delinquent subculture persists because, once established, it creates for those who participate in it, the very problems which were the basis for emergence" (p. 245).

Cohen and other subcultural theorists have been criticized for failing to recognize that boys engage in delinquent and criminal activity simply because it can be fun and profitable, while being law-abiding is quite dull. This is in marked contrast to Cohen's position that delinquency results from being driven by status problems, blocked opportunities, and other environmental problems. Bordua (1962) also contends that the emphasis placed by Cohen on the nonutilitarian character of group delinquency fails to consider the fact that many of the illegal acts engaged in by these youngsters are quite rational and instrumental in nature. Thus, theft is essentially motivated by the group's desire to maintain its independence from adult authority; delinquents steal in order to acquire food or things which can be sold to buy food and other necessities in order to be able to spend days or weeks away from home. Bordua claimed that Cohen, as well as some other subcultural theorists, placed too much emphasis on class position without giving consideration to other social variables such as family composition and other problems that result from rural migration, immigration, and the disporportionate concentration of multiproblem families in some slum areas. These factors may be as much a source of stress and other problems as class position and hence equally important in delinquency causation.

Cohen's thesis regarding status deprivation was empirically tested by Reiss and Rhodes (1963). They attempted to determine whether lower-class adolescents experienced more status deprivation than middle-class youths, and whether delinquents experienced more status deprivation than nondelinquents. In this study relative status deprivation was measured by asking a sample of Tennessee school children if they thought that most of their fellow students had better clothes and a better house to live in than they did. They found that although lower-class and delinquent kids did seem to experience more status deprivation than other youngsters, the overwhelming majority of adolescents in both groups did not feel that their fellow students had better clothes and housing. More delinquents than nondelinquents indicated they never gave any thought to making status comparisons. Although these data failed to confirm Cohen's hypothesis, there is reason to believe these results would be different if a sample of adolescents from an urban area was used and/or if different measures of status were employed.

Delinquent Subcultures: An Extension of Cohen's Theory

Cohen (in Cohen and Short, 1958) responded to a number of criticisms of his theory, including the contention that there is not a single delinquent subculture but a variety of subcultures. In addition to the *parent-male subculture* that Cohen had originally described in *Delinquent Boys,* which they viewed as possessing certain core characteristics common to many subcultures throughout the country, Cohen and Short identified several other types of delinquent subcultures: a *conflict-oriented subculture,* in which both the individual and gang status are determined by toughness and prowess in intergang "rumbles"; a *drug addict subculture,* in which members direct their energies toward income-producing forms of deviance that support their drug habits; and a *semiprofessional theft subculture,* comprising the membership of a small minority of youths who differentiate themselves from their peers and become heavily committed to rational, planned, systematic stealing.

Cohen and Short sketched a theoretical fifth type of subculture, a *middle-class delinquent subculture,* for which there was much less empirical support than was available for the other subcultures in the typology. They suggested this subculture is likely to be characterized by an emphasis on the deliberate courting of danger and a sophisticated, irresponsible, "playboy" orientation toward activities which are symbolically associated with adults in our society and largely involve sex, liquor, and automobiles (whereas violence, maliciousness, and aggression are apt to be downplayed in middle-class culture).

Cohen and Short recognized the limitations of their typology. Their purpose was to provide a framework which would help to stimulate further research and theorizing in this area. They pointed out that "a fully satisfactory theory of delinquent subcultures must specify the different problems of adjustment to which each of these subcultures is a response, and the ways in which the social structure generates these problems of adjustment and determines the form which the solutions take" (p. 28).

DELINQUENCY AND OPPORTUNITY: RICHARD A. CLOWARD AND LLOYD E. OHLIN

Cloward and Ohlin (1960) claim that differential opportunity theory represents an integration of Merton's and Durkheim's anomie theory with Sutherland's theory of differential association. They contend that anomie theory clearly recognizes that individuals have differential access to legitimate means, although the theory is weak in terms of specifying the individual's position with regard to the availability of illegitimate means. On the other hand, implicit in differential association theory is the idea of variable access to illegitimate means while the significance of differential access to legitimate means is not recognized. Cloward and Ohlin suggest differential opportunity theory unites these two positions by recognizing that individuals have differential access to both legitimate and illegitimate means.

Cloward and Ohlin explain the development of delinquent subcultures in the following manner. They observe that lower-class boys live in a society which generates high social and economic aspirations among lower-class boys and also espouses an ideology of equal opportunity for all, while limiting opportunities for young persons in the lower classes. Deviant behavior among lower-class youths results from the disparity between what they are led to expect and want and what is actually available to them. Cloward and Ohlin summarize their position in the following statement:

> . . . the disparity between what lower class youth are led to want and what is actually available to them is the source of a major problem of adjustment. Adolescents who form delinquent subcultures we suggest have internalized an emphasis upon conventional goals. Faced with limitations on legitimate avenues of access to these goals and unable to revise their aspirations downward, they experience intense frustration; the exploration of nonconformist alternatives may be the result [p. 86].

The authors label the frustration and the adjustment problems experienced by lower-class youth as a result of these discrepancies between aspirations and their chances of fulfillment as **position discontent,** an idea taken from both Durkheim and Cohen. In contrast to Cohen, Cloward and Ohlin suggest that position discontent may not reflect the dissatisfaction of lower-class youths with their present situation as a result of an orientation toward middle-class standards. In their view, while some discontent may result from a wish on the part of lower-class youths to adopt the middle-class way of life, they feel many lower-class youths experience frustration as a result of attempting to achieve a higher position in terms of lower-class rather than middle-class criteria. Position discontent, in the case of these boys, results from their attempt to achieve lower-class success goals.

Cloward and Ohlin maintain that youngsters can resolve the problems resulting from position discontent by developing solitary as well as collective solutions. When individuals attribute their failure to achieve their aspirations to personal deficiencies, they are likely to develop solitary solutions which include alcoholism, drug addiction, and, in extreme cases, mental illness. On the other hand, when individuals view their failure to realize their aspirations as resulting from societal conditions, they are likely to develop collective solutions such as a delinquent subculture. As Cloward and Ohlin point out, a person "who places blame for failure on the unjust organization of the established social order and who finds support from others for withdrawal from legitimacy of official norms may be induced to resort to illegitimate means of achieving success-goals as a stable form of adaptation" (p. 131). The particular collective solution (subculture) that develops in each neighborhood, according to the authors, depends on the opportunities available in the area. They see individuals occupying positions in two opportunity structures—one legitimate, the other illegitimate. The differences in availability of types of illegitimate as well as legitimate opportunities are a function of a person's position within the social structure (see Figure 11.9).

Delinquent Subculture

Cloward and Ohlin (1960) identify three basic types of subculture that develop in specific neighborhoods depending on the availability of illegitimate opportunities in each area.

Criminal Subculture   Criminal subculture develops in lower-class areas characterized by an integration between conventional and criminal value systems. In these

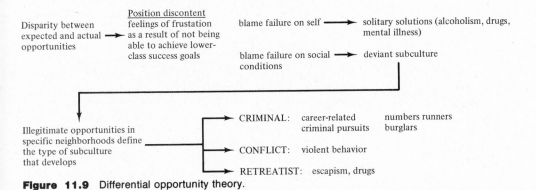

Figure 11.9 Differential opportunity theory.

neighborhoods, one finds an intricate system of relationships between persons engaged in legitimate pursuits, such as lawyers, bondsmen, and junkmen; those engaged in both legitimate and illegitimate pursuits, such as legitimate businessmen that buy stolen property; and those engaged in exclusively illegitimate pursuits, such as criminal fences, conventional criminals and racketeers, and syndicate members. These areas are further characterized by an integration of different age levels of offenders which represents the means by which younger offenders acquire criminal values and skills. Those who are involved in organized crime-related activities use these juveniles as numbers runners and errand boys, while fences may encourage young delinquents to steal and in some cases may even direct their activities by suggesting targets that are the most lucrative and pose the least threat of apprehension. This suggests the operation of an apprentice system which prepares the youngster for a career as an offender by providing opportunities for learning new skills, as well as opportunities for contact with those who are involved in legitimate, semilegitimate, and illegitimate pursuits, all of which are necessary for a successful criminal career. Therefore, the choice of a criminal career in these communities compares with the choice of a conventional career within middle-class communities; that is, it is based on the availability of specific opportunities. The content of the delinquent subculture in these communities represents simply an extension or reflection of the adult criminal subculture that exists in these areas.

Conflict Subculture   Conflict subculture develops in areas that exhibit disorganization resulting from high rates of residential mobility which make efforts to develop community stability almost an impossibility. Pressures for violent behavior among the young result from the fact that these communities can neither provide access to legitimate channels to success goals nor access to stable criminal opportunity systems. Additionally, social controls in these areas are typically weak. This combination of factors, according to Cloward and Ohlin, leads to the emergence of conflict subcultures in these areas. Adolescents in these neighborhoods seize upon violence as a route to status not only because it provides a means of expressing pent-up hostility, anger, and frustration, but also because involvement in violent behavior is not limited by race or social position nor is there a requirement for any special skills or connections. The principal prerequisites for success are capacity to endure pain, and "guts." Status under these circumstances can be acquired as a result of skill in the use of violence, physical strength, and also a willingness to risk injury or death in order to build a "rep." Thus, it is possible for status to be achieved by youngsters who are not overly muscular in physique as well as by those with superior skill and strength.

Retreatist Subculture   The retreatist pattern is likely to be adopted by youngsters who are double failures. These are adolescents who find that legitimate means are not available to them and also find that they cannot achieve status through illegitimate means; that is, they cannot find a place for themselves in either the conflict or criminal subculture. Cloward and Ohlin contend that for those boys who are unable to revise their aspirations downward, the only option open is to "give up the fight" and retreat into a world that does not require them to achieve conventional or subcultural goals. These youngsters orient their activities toward the pursuit of "the kick." Whether in groups or alone, these youngsters are preoccupied with activities that provide them with a "high" including marijuana, alcohol, addicting drugs, unusual sexual experiences, listening to acid rock or any combination of these. While some boys may adopt this pattern during early adolescence, it is more likely that it will be adopted during late adolescence, because at this point illegitimate avenues to high status become more restricted. For example, the conflict orientation becomes less and less acceptable as a youngster becomes older. In late adolescence, the youngster is faced with either assuming criminal or conventional occupational roles. Youngsters without the requisite skills and opportunities to make this transition to adulthood may turn to drugs or alcohol as a means of escape.

Evaluation of Differential Opportunity Theory

Schrag (1970) points out in his critique of differential opportunity theory that Cloward and Ohlin have failed to define such key concepts as *double failure, perception of opportunity, elimination of guilt,* and *denial of legitimacy* in terms that permit them to be tested empirically or related to existing research. Schrag critizes Cloward and Ohlin for their failure to describe clearly and specifically the point at which a collectivity becomes a gang. He questions whether gangs with organizational structures as specialized as the criminal, conflict, and drug subcultures are a widespread, general phenomenon.

Most research (Kobrin et al., 1967; Short and Strodtbeck, 1965; Spergel, 1963, 1967) indicates that juveniles engage in a wide variety of delinquent and nondelinquent activity; that gang behavior is versatile rather than specialized; and that specialization, when it occurs, tends to be limited to cliques that form within gangs. This general pattern of delinquency, which resembles the kind of "parent-delinquent" subculture described by Cohen and Short (1958), has been confirmed by Miller (1976) in his more recent study of gangs in Boston and Philadelphia.

Short and his colleagues (1964, 1965) investigated position discontent and the commitment of gang members to delinquent norms and values. They found that, contrary to Cloward and Ohlin's observations, high educational and occupational aspirations did not appear to pressure boys toward deviance, despite perceived limitations and lack of opportunities for the achievement of these aspirations. For this sample, at least, the data suggested these youths have identified with conventional institutions and values, and it is this stake in conformity that serves to isolate them from delinquent involvement.

Empey (1982) also takes issue with the Cloward and Ohlin position that *frustrated occupational ambition* is a major cause of delinquency. He casts doubt on the validity of Cloward and Ohlin's description of lower-class delinquents as exceedingly goal-oriented, utilitarian, and already convinced that their class position has deprived them of the opportunity for success in the job market. There seems little doubt that this picture is greatly overdrawn. Occupational planning for these boys, particularly in light of the fact that their fathers may not be steadily employed, is frequently vague and uncertain. Like most teenagers, these youths are more concerned with friends, school, and having fun with members of the opposite sex than with giving serious thought to their occupational future.

Bordua (1961, 1962) has criticized Cloward and Ohlin (1960) for their overemphasis on class position as it relates to delinquency causation, to the exclusion of other social attributes that may also be of relevance in explaining delinquency among lower-class boys. He feels that Cloward and Ohlin failed to examine systematically the impact of race, ethnicity, or rural origin; the role of the family and variations in lower-class families; and the concentration of multiproblem families in slum areas. In addition, he believes that Cloward and Ohlin seem to ignore the life histories of their delinquents, which brought them to the point of participation in delinquency. While gang delinquents may well find themselves blocked from whatever occupational opportunities are available, this would seem to be viewed more accurately as resulting from a long history of progressively destroying their own capacities and depriving themselves of opportunity, which may well have its roots in the lower-class family and continue through failure in school and similar events. Bordua is suggesting that participation in gang delinquency may in itself be a factor in depriving a youngster of the opportunity for developing capacities to function effectively in the conventional world. However, Cloward and Ohlin give us the impression that upon reaching adolescence these youngsters suddenly discover their opportunities for achievement have been cut off.

LOWER-CLASS FOCAL CONCERNS: WALTER B. MILLER

Walter B. Miller (1958) offers still another explanation of gang delinquency. Unlike Cohen, and Cloward and Ohlin, Miller's explanation has an empirical basis: his interpretation is based on data collected over a 3-year period on 21 street-corner groups—white and black, male and female, and ranging in age from early to late adolescence. The data sources were varied and included participant observation reports by Miller, social workers' contact reports, and direct tape recordings of both group activities and discussions.

Miller contends that deviance within the lower classes results from adherence by individuals to a distinctive lower-class normative system which is supportive of delinquency and other forms of deviant behavior and is in sharp contrast to that of the middle class. One of the basic features of the lower-class subculture is the female-based household as the primary childrearing unit, typically consisting of one or more adult females and their offspring. This type of family structure results from the practice of "serial monogamy" in which women cohabit with various men for limited periods of time. The result is that each child has the same mother but a different father.

Miller asserts that in lower-class communities the most important social group for both males and females is *the one-sex peer unit* instead of the two-parent family unit. He portrays lower-class society as comprised of a constellation of age-graded, one-sex groups which represent the major reference group and focus of activity for those over 12 or 13 years old. The adolescent street-corner gang represents a variant of this primary lower-class structural form. The delinquent gang, in turn, represents one type of lower-class adolescent group. The street-corner group is important for adolescent males because, in many cases, it represents the most solid and stable primary group to which they have ever belonged. For boys who have grown up in primarily female-based homes, this represents an opportunity for them to learn the basic features of the male role in conjunction with peers who are facing similar types of sex-role identification problems. In order to become an accepted member of a group, as well as to achieve status among his peers, a boy must demonstrate knowledge and adherence to the value qualities of lower-class culture, which Miller labeled **lower-class focal concerns.** (See Figure 11.10.)

Miller identified six major lower-class focal concerns: (1) trouble, (2) toughness, (3) smartness, (4) excitement, (5) fate, and (6) autonomy.

Trouble for men often results from fighting or sexual adventures while drinking; the problems of women result from the disadvantageous consequences of their sexual liaisons. It also includes run-ins with authority, police, and other bureaucratic agencies of middle-class society.

Toughness refers to a concern among lower-class males with manifesting qualities of "masculinity." This includes demonstrating physical prowess through strength and endurance in athletic and conflict situations, conceptualization of women as conquest objects, as well as the absence of traits such as sentimentality which implicate one as "feminine" or "soft."

Smartness involves the capacity to outwit, dupe, or "con" other people, as well as the ability to avoid being "taken" by others, as manifested in card games and other forms of gambling, the mutual exchange of insults, and con schemes. The "smart person" lives by his wits and earns his living through some con scheme or hustle, such as pimping or suckering somebody into some game of chance in which he has an advantage.

Excitement represents a heightened interest in activities that are thrilling, stimulating, and provide a contrast to the dull, routine, and monotonous lower-class

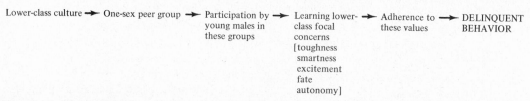

Figure 11.10   Walter B. Miller.

daily existence. Typically, this quest for excitement involves gambling in all forms—dice, cards, playing the numbers, betting on horses—and the prevalent use of alcohol by both sexes. The recurrent practice of "a night on the town" involves drinking, sexual adventuring, and brawling as major components.

Fate reflects a prevailing belief among lower-class members that their lives are subject to forces over which they have relatively little control—the kind of "generalized expectancy" that social learning theorist Julian Rotter (1954, 1972) has related to *external locus of control*. Implicit in this view of events is the conviction that it is futile to make an effort to achieve a goal because, if luck is with you, you will reach the goal without any difficulty and, if luck is against you, no effort on your part will succeed.

Autonomy contains paradoxical elements. On an overt level, autonomy involves resistance to control or domination by others, as expressed in such statements as "No one's gonna push me around," or "I'm gonna tell 'im he can take the job and shove it . . . " (Miller, 1958, p. 12). However, covertly it appears that many lower-class members seek out highly restrictive institutions where stringent controls are exercised over their behavior.

Miller contends that adherence to these focal concerns and participation in lower-class social groupings combine in several ways to produce delinquency and criminality. Those who use the focal concerns to guide their behavior will automatically violate the law. In some instances, this represents a more attractive alternative because it provides a larger and more rapid return for a relatively smaller investment of time and energy. The required response in certain situations encountered in lower-class communities involves the commission of criminal or delinquent acts.

Evaluation of Miller's Theory

Like the other subcultural theories, Miller's positions has not escaped criticism. It has been noted (Bordua, 1961, 1962; Cloward and Ohlin, 1960) that Miller *failed to give sufficient consideration to variations among delinquent groups, as well as to those among lower-class communities*. In this regard, Miller does not account for why some boys engage in theft, others in conflict, and still others in drugs or alcohol. Also, his description of lower-class culture appears to be more relevant to certain areas than to others. The pattern which involves a combination of female-based household and serial monogamy, while applicable to blacks, does not have the same history as other dominant patterns among other lower-class groups.

Cloward and Ohlin (1960) have challenged Miller's position on the grounds that it suggests a "cultural independence" between the lower and middle classes that has probably not existed since the mass immigration of the late nineteenth and early twentieth centuries. Trojanowicz (1978) observes that it is difficult to believe that a distinct lower-class culture can exist today in light of our mass communication system which influences the values and patterns of all classes. There is little doubt that television has shaped some of the ways in which all classes adapt to their environment, whether these responses are legitimate or illegitimate.

Downes (1966) alerts us to another problem with Miller's position. He states that Miller fails to adequately distinguish between lower-class norms in general and delinquent norms in particular. As a result, Miller is forced to imply that the way of life of the lower class is essentially law-violating. Downes contends that this results in a view of the lower-class subculture as a delinquent subculture, if not possibly a delinquent contraculture.

Perhaps the most serious defect in this formulation relates to the questionable independence of certain basic theoretical concepts. Specifically, Miller is criticized for deriving the "focal concerns" from observing lower-class behavior and then using them to explain this same behavior. As Bordua (1961) suggests, there is more than a little danger of tautology in this practice.

A final weakness of Miller's theory is its failure to refute Cohen's contention that the clash between middle-class and lower-class norms is a source of stress among lower-class boys. As Bordua (1961) points out, Miller seems to be implying that the involvement of these boys in lower-class culture is so intense that any contacts with the agents of middle-class dominated institutions, particularly the schools, would have little or no impact. Thus, it is quite possible that lower-class boys have not internalized nor been materially affected by middle-class norms prior to their entrance into school. However, it is extremely unlikely that these boys can spend ten years in a school system which emphasizes middle-class values and rewards behavior that is consistent with these values without being affected in some way. These experiences should either result in their coming to accept these values or becoming more alienated or both. And the consequence of this should be to drive them into deeper involvement in delinquent subcultures.

In spite of all the criticisms leveled against Miller's position, it is important to recognize the real contributions of this formulation. As Schrag (1971) suggests, it provides us with a detailed ethnography of lower-class culture, giving us a perspective on lower-class life as it is experienced by those who inhabit our city slums. Instead of giving us an account of lower-class life from a middle-class view—a quite common practice in research on deviance—it provides us with a perspective on life in these communities from the standpoint of the residents and it serves to fill some of the descriptive gaps found in the statements made by Cohen, and Cloward and Ohlin (Gibbons, 1976).

SUMMARY

This chapter has attempted to trace the development of mainstream sociological approaches to crime and delinquency. The approaches covered in this and the preceding chapter provide a fairly comprehensive perspective on social structural explanations of crime. We began with an examination of the social pathology approach, which was popular at the beginning of this century. Attention was next directed toward the social disorganization approach, which dominated sociological interpretations of the causes of crime and delinquency and significantly influenced research from the 1920s through the 1940s. Even today this theoretical approach continues to make an impression on criminological thought. Discussion was also devoted to case studies and ecological research conducted from the social disorganization perspective, together with later ecological studies which employed a different approach.

Following an examination of the reasons sociologists abandoned the concept of social disorganization and replaced it with the concept of differential social organization, Sellin's systematic exposition of the relationship between culture conflict and crime was presented. Shoham's application of this perspective to crime and delinquency in Israel was briefly considered. The chapter concluded with a critical review of subcultural theories of crime and delinquency. The contributions of Durkheim and Merton to the development of this theoretical position were discussed and attention was given to the work of Cohen, Cloward and Ohlin, and Miller.

Despite the defects of each of these theories, they have called our attention to the importance of the role of social conditions in any explanation of crime and delinquency. Prior to the exposition of these theories, it was thought that people became criminals and delinquents as a result of individual factors—primarily defective physiology. Now it is recognized that social conditions are also important factors in producing crime. Additionally, these theories have called to our attention some of the specific social conditions that cause crime. The difficulty with all of these theories is that they have attempted to take crime, which is a rather complex problem, and explain it by using an extremely limited number of factors. We believe that any explanation of crime that will be of value in the future will have to be more detailed and complex and not focus attention only on social conditions. That is, crime is human behavior and any explanation of human behavior must include physiological, psychological, and social psychological factors, as well as social conditions.

DISCUSSION QUESTIONS

Find the answer to the following questions in the text.

1. What are the major concerns of the sociologist with respect to crime and criminal behavior?
2. Discuss the **organic analogy** and its use by **social pathology** theorists in explaining crime and other forms of deviance.
3. Identify the main tenets of the **social disorganization** approach. How is **personal disorganization** presumed to be related to social disorganization according to this approach?
4. Describe the **concentric zone model** and assess the results of research generated by this approach.
5. Briefly summarize the contributions of Shaw and McKay toward an understanding of crime and delinquency.
6. What are the basic premises of the **culture conflict** approach? Distinguish between **primary and secondary culture conflict.**
7. Define subculture and identify its functions.
8. Discuss the contributions of Durkheim and Merton to **anomie theory.** What do Merton's five types of adaptations seek to describe?
9. How does Cohen attempt to explain delinquency? How does he account for the development of a delinquent subculture?
10. Discuss Cloward and Ohlin's differential opportunity and identify the two approaches that this theory purports to integrate.
11. What are the **focal concerns** of working-class culture as described by Miller? How do they contribute to delinquency?

TERMS TO IDENTIFY AND REMEMBER

social pathology
organic analogy
social disorganization
social control
personal disorganization
case study method
ecological approach
concentric zone model
gradient pattern
status frustration
parent subculture
illegitimate means
Chicago area projects

detached worker program
social area analysis
differential social organization
primary and secondary culture conflict
anomie theory
Chicago School
types of adapation
reaction formation
position discontent
opportunity structures
lower-class focal concerns

REFERENCES

Benedict, M. Review of *Delinquent Boys* by A. K. Cohen. *British Journal of Delinquency* 7 (1956): 323–24.

Bordua, D. J. A critique of sociological interpretations of gang delinquency. *The Annals of the American Academy of Political and Social Sciences* 338 (1961): pp. 120–136.

———. Some comments on theories of gang delinquency. *Sociological Inquiry,* 32, no. 2 (1962): pp.245–60.

Brown, L. *Social Pathlogy.* New York: F. S. Crofts, 1942.

Chilton, R. J. Continuity in delinquency area research: A comparison of studies for Baltimore, Detroit, and Indianapolis. *American Sociological Review* 29 (1964): 71–83.

Clinard, M. B. *Anomie and Deviant Behavior: A Discussion and Critique.* New York: The Free Press, 1964.

Clinard, M. B., and Meier, R. F. *The Sociology of Deviant Behavior.* New York: Holt, Rinehart and Winston, 1985.

Cloward, R. A., and Ohlin, L. E. *Delinquency and Opportunity: A Theory of Delinquent Gangs.* New York: The Free Press, 1960.

Cohen, A. K. Delinquent boys: *The Culture of the Gang.* New York: The Free Press, 1955.

Cohen, A. K., and Short, J. F. Research in delinquent subcultures. *Journal of Social Issues* 14 (1958): 20–37.

DeFleur, M. L., D'Antonio, W. V., and DeFleur, L. B. *Sociology: Man in Society.* Glenview, IL: Scott, Foresman, 1971.

Downes, D. M. *The Delinquent Solution: A Study in Subcultural Theory.* New York: The Free Press, 1966.

Durkheim. E. *The Division of Labor in Society.* New York: The Free Press of Glencoe, 1933.

———. *The Rules of Sociological Method.* S. A. Solovay and J. H. Mueller (trans.); G. E. G. Catlin (ed.). New York: The Free Press, 1938.

———. *Suicide: A Study in Sociology.* J. Spaulding and G. Simpson (trans.); G. Simpson (ed.). New York: The Free Press, 1951.

Empey, L. T. *American Delinquency: Its Meaning and Construction.* Homewood, IL: Dorsey Press, 1982.

Gibbons, D. C. *Delinquency Behavior.* Englewood Cliffs, NJ: Prentice-Hall, 1976. (Originally published 1970.)

Gibbons, D. C., and Jones, J. F. *The Study of Deviance: Perspective and Problems.* Englewood Cliffs, NJ: Prentice-Hall, 1975.

Hartung, F. E. Review of *Delinquent Boys* by A. K. Cohen. *American Sociological Review* 20 (1955): 751–52.

Jonassen, C. T. A re-evaluation and critique of the logic and some methods of Shaw and McKay. *American Sociological Review* 14 (1949): 608–14.

Kavolis, V. Universal criterion of pathology. In E. Rubington and M. S. Weinberg (eds.), *The Study of Social Problems: Five Perspectives.* New York: Oxford University Press, 1977.

Kitsuse, J. I., and Dietrick, D. C. Delinquent boys: A critique. *American Sociological Review* (April 1959): 208–15.

Kobrin, S. The Chicago Area Project–A twenty-five year assessment. *The Annals of the American Academy of Political and Social Science* 322 (1959): 20–29.

———. The formal logical properties of the Shaw-McKay delinquency theory. In H. L. Voss and D. M. Petersen (eds.), *Ecology, Crime and Delinquency.* New York: Appleton-Century-Crofts, 1971.

Kobrin, S., Puntil, J., and Peluso, E. Criteria of status among streetcorner groups. *Journal of Research in Crime and Delinquency* 4 (1967): 98–118.

Korn, R. R., and McCorkle, L. W. *Criminology and Penology.* New York: Holt, Rinehart and Winston, 1961.

Lander, B. *Towards an Understanding of Juvenile Delinquency.* New York: Columbia University Press, 1954.

Lemert, E. M. *Human Deviance, Social Problems, and Social Control.* Englewood Cliffs, NJ: Prentice-Hall, 1967.

Mannheim, H. *Comparative Criminology.* Boston: Houghton Mifflin, 1965.

Merton, R. Social structure and anomie. *American Sociological Review* 3 (1938): 672–82.

———. *Social Theory and Social Structure.* New York: Macmillan, 1957.

Miller, W. B. Lower class culture as a generating milieu of gang delinquency. *Journal of Social Issues* 14, no. 3 (1958): 5–19.

Park, R. E., Burgess, E. W., and McKenzie, R. D. *The City.* Chicago: University of Chicago Press, 1925.

Parmalee, M. *Criminology.* New York: Macmillan, 1918.

Polk, K. Urban social areas and delinquency. *Social Problems* 14 (1967): 320–25.

Reiss, A. J., Jr., and Rhodes, A. L. Status deprivation and delinquent behavior. *Sociological Quarterly* 4 (1963): 135–49.

Rennie, Y. *The Search for Criminal Man.* Lexington, MA: Lexington Books, 1978.

Robinson, S. M. *Can Delinquency Be Measured?* New York: Columbia University Press, 1936.

———. *Juvenile Delinquency: Its Nature and Control.* New York: Henry Holt and Company, 1960.

Sagarin, E. *Deviants and Deviance: An Introduction to the Study of Disvalued People and Behavior.* New York: Praeger, 1975.

Sellin. T. *Culture Conflict and Crime.* New York: Social Science Research Council, 1938.

Schrag, C. *Crime and Justice: American Style.* Rockville, MD: National Institute of Mental Health, 1971.

Shaw, C. R., and McKay, H. D. *Juvenile Delinquency and Urban Areas* (rev. ed.). Chicago and London: University of Chicago Press, 1972. (Originally published 1942.)

Shoham, S. The application of the "culture conflict" hypothesis to the criminality of immigrants in Israel. *Journal of Criminal Law, Criminology, and Police Science* 55 (June 1962): 207–14.

————. *Crime and Social Deviation.* Chicago: Henry Reguery, 1966.

Short, J. F., Jr. Gang delinquency and anomie. In M. Clinard (ed.), *Anomie and Deviant Behavior: A Discussion and Critique.* New York: The Free Press, 1964.

Short, J. F., Jr., and Strodtbeck, F. L. *Group Process and Gang Delinquency.* Chicago and London: University of Chicago Press, 1965.

Sutherland, E. H., and Cressey, D. R. *Principles of Criminology.* Philadelphia: Lippincott, 1955.

————. *Criminology* (10th ed.). Philadelphia: Lippincott, 1978.

Thio, A. *Deviant Behavior.* Boston: Houghton Mifflin, 1983.

Thomas, W. I., and Znaniecki, F. *The Polish Peasant in Europe and America.* New York: Dover, 1958.

Toby, J. Comment on the Jonassen-Shaw and McKay controversy. *American Sociological Review* 15 (1950): 107–108.

Trojanowicz, R. C. *Juvenile Delinquency Concepts and Control.* Englewood Cliffs NJ: Prentice-Hall, 1978.

Voss, H. L., and Petersen, D. M. (eds.). *Ecology, Crime and Delinquency.* New York: Appleton-Century-Crofts, 1971.

Whyte, W. F. *Street Corner Society.* Chicago and London: The University of Chicago Press, 1943.

Wilks, J. A. Ecological correlates of crime and delinquency. In President's Commission on Law Enforcement and Administration of Justice Task Force Report: *Crime and Its Impact—An Assessment.* Washington, D.C.: U.S. Government Printing Office, 1967.

chapter 12

SOCIOPSYCHOLOGICAL THEORIES OF CRIMINALITY

l, theories discussed in the preceding chapter were g situations. These theories sought to explain how iin positions within the society are subjected to s toward criminal behavior. As we have already ist of the people exposed to such pressures do not iile others, who are not subjected to these condi- minal acts. Questions of this kind are of major or *social process,* theories which are dealt with in

icus on the socialization of delinquents and crimi- s generally used to designate the learning experi- s also been employed to refer to learning in adults on of new roles and the encounter with changing intonio, and DeFleur, 1971). The theories covered intion to *the process by which people acquire the and self-conceptions essential to the performance of* the criminal role. These theoretical approaches or perspectives deal not only with the steps associated with the development of criminal careers, but also with situational pressures and circumstances that operate to produce specific deviant acts (Gibbons and Jones, 1975). They recognize that not all crime is the result of progressive in- volvement in deviant behavior but in some instances results from attractions and provocations that are tied to specific situations.

DIFFERENTIAL ASSOCIATION: EDWIN H. SUTHERLAND

Edwin H. Sutherland (1883–1950) is best known for his introduction and develop- ment of the concept of *White-Collar Crime* (1949); for his study of *The Professional Thief* (1937); and for his theory of **differential association** (Sutherland, 1939, 1947). Differential association theory assumes even greater importance when we consider that in the more than three decades since his death, there has been no new major theoretical contribution to the sociological study of adult crime (Gibbons, 1977). In fact, the recent theories discussed in this chapter and the preceding chapter deal primarily with the causes of delinquency.

We have already seen how difficult it is to trace with any precision the many influences that combine to shape the ideas of a theorist, but a few observations on Edwin H. Sutherland's career development may help clarify his indebtedness to some of the leading intellectual figures who were his predecessors or contemporaries. Above all, there was the University of Chicago—the institution that Sutherland at- tended as a graduate student and where he later served as a faculty member from 1929 to 1935. Sutherland is not grouped with others, such as Park, Burgess, Shaw, as a member of the Chicago School, but his work bore the unmistakable imprint of the Chicago sociological tradition.

Sutherland entered the University of Chicago as a graduate student in sociol- ogy in 1906. He was exposed to several teachers, but the person whose ideas appear to have had the greatest impact on Sutherland was William Isaac Thomas. Indeed,

Karl Schuessler (1973), one of Sutherland's protégés, claims that Sutherland's theory of criminal behavior "may be regarded as an adaptation of interactional sociology, as expounded by W. I. Thomas" (p. xi). Schuessler also mentions that Sutherland's empirical research showed the kind of concern for techniques of careful investigation that was the hallmark of the Chicago School of criminology.

We know from Sutherland himself (in Cohen, Lindesmith, and Schuessler, *The Sutherland Papers,* 1956) that he was set on the path that led him toward a career in criminology by E. C. Hayes, head of the Department of Sociology at the University of Illinois who in 1921 asked Sutherland to write a text in criminology for the publishing firm of Lippincott. (Sutherland's interests up to that point had been labor problems.) Although he mentions he had done course work in criminology under Charles R. Henderson, author of *Dependents, Defectives, and Delinquents* (1893), he had found most of the extant materials on criminology so inadequate that he was more or less compelled to ignore textbooks and directly examine the professional literature on crime and delinquency.

When he reached the point where he was ready to begin the task of composing his first major work in criminology, Sutherland states, "I made some effort from the first to apply sociological concepts to criminal behavior, especially Thomas's attitude value and four wishes, but also imitation, isolation, culture-conflict (implicitly rather than explicitly), and a little later Park's and Burgess's four processes" (Schuessler, 1973, p. 14). In this single passage, Sutherland identifies what appear to have been his principal sources of influence. Among this list it is especially important to note the reference to imitation. This clearly indicates the influence of the French sociologist, Gabriel Tarde.

Schafer (1968) calls Sutherland "the most outstanding adherent of Tarde's theories" (p. 240). Tarde, in *La Criminalité Compareé* (1890) did not propose a learning theory, but is generally credited with formulating the proposition that criminal patterns of behavior are a product of interaction with others. It is also worth noting that Vold (1958) refers to Tarde's "law of imitation" as the original theoretical background for criminal ecology, that is, the viewpoint identified with the Chicago School of criminology-discussed in chapter 11. Thus, in absorbing the basic notion from Tarde that people imitate the fashions and customs of others, and that the more contact there is among people, the more imitation takes place, Sutherland would appear to have acquired the fundamental position which he later developed into seven, then nine, postulates covering the acquisition of criminal behavior. Further, his long association with the other leading theorists and researchers of the Chicago School would, in our judgment, seem to place him firmly in this tradition of criminology.

The Development of Differential Association

The theory of differential association evolved over an extended period of time. It is interesting to note (see boxed material on page 336) that Sutherland did not recognize immediately that he actually postulated a theory of crime causation. Sutherland's book *Criminology,* which appeared in its first edition in 1924, provided an overview of the diverse factors (economic, political, physiological, climatic, and oth-

Sutherland was unaware of his progress toward a viewpoint and general hypothesis on criminality until he read a review of the 1934 edition of *Criminology* by a man named Henry McKay. Sutherland points out his surprise when McKay referred to his theory of criminal behavior:

> . . . and I asked him what my theory was. He referred me to pages 51–52 of my book. I looked this up and read
>
>> The hypotheses of this book are as follows: First, any person can be trained to adopt and follow any pattern of behavior which he is able to execute. Second, failure to follow a prescribed pattern of behavior is due to the inconsistencies and lack of harmony in the influences which direct the individual. Third, the conflict of cultures is therefore the fundamental principle in the explanation of crime.

I assure you that I was surprised to learn that I had stated a general hypothesis regarding criminal behavior. . . . I undoubtedly owed much to Wirth's 1931 paper. My thinking was compartmentalized rather than integrated. I wrote one section of the book and forgot it while working on another section. I feel that I am not unique in this respect and that culture is generally compartmentalized rather than integrated in the person and the society. . . . In spite of the statement about hypotheses, if anyone had caught me in my usual frame of mind and asked me what my theory of criminal behavior was, I would have answered, "The multiple-factor theory," and in that theory I would have left the multiple factors co-ordinate and unrelated to each other, I was not aware that I was approaching generalizations of an abstract nature. [15-16]

Source: Reprinted from A. K. Cohen, A. Lindesmith, and K. Schuessler, *The Sutherland Papers*. Bloomington: Indiana University Press, 1956. Reprinted by permission of the authors and publisher.

ers) that had been advanced to explain crime. Although differential association theory was not stated explicitly until 1939, when the third edition of *Criminology* was published, the ideas that formed the basis of this theoretical position are implicit in the criticisms that Sutherland made of theories of criminality in the 1924 edition; and differential association can be seen in embryonic form in the 1934 edition. The theory was stated formally in 1939, and it emerged in its final form in 1947.

In stating the differential association hypothesis, Sutherland's objective was to provide an explanation of crime that was broad enough to account for most criminal behavior. He notes that the available research suggested hundreds of "concrete conditions" associated with criminal behavior. Each of these conditions, however, was only slightly related to other conditions. Being male is a factor most frequently associated with criminal behavior, yet it is obvious that this factor fails to explain a criminal behavior. Sutherland concluded that a "concrete condition cannot be a cause of crime" and that "the only way to get a causal explanation of behavior is by

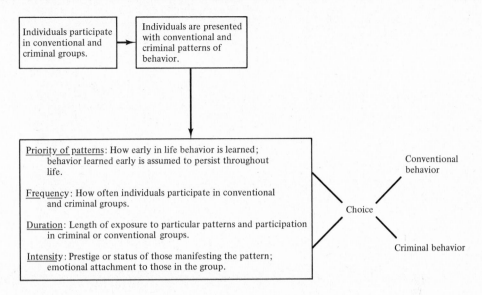

Figure 12.1 Edwin Sutherland's differential association theory.

abstracting from the varying concrete conditions things that are universally associated with crime" (1939, p. 19).

In his search for more abstract conditions to explain behavior, Sutherland drew upon the knowledge he had acquired as a sociologist. He concluded that a theory of criminal behavior should be developed around the processes of learning, interaction, and communication. He acknowledges the influence of Tarde's notion that crime is due to imitation on the development of this position.

In Chapter 11 we noted that Sutherland viewed differential association as emerging within the context of differential social organization, that is, he used the latter concept to account for variations in crime rates, while he employed differential association to explain the process by which individuals become criminals (see Figure 12.1). Sutherland's theory as stated in one of the posthumous editions of his criminology text by his collaborator, Donald R. Cressey, in the nine propositions below (Sutherland and Cressey, 1978, pp. 80–82). The original postulates are given in italics, followed by our explanatory comments.

1. *Criminal behavior is learned.* Criminal behavior, as such, is not inherited. Also, the person who is not trained in crime does not invent criminal behavior.
2. *Criminal behavior is learned in interaction with other persons in a process of communication.* This communication can either be verbal (direct) or symbolic: it includes all "communication of gestures."
3. *The principal part of the learning of criminal behavior occurs within intimate*

personal groups. This statement allows for the influence of the impersonal agencies of communication such as television and the movies, but emphasizes the overwhelming importance of interpersonal relationships on the genesis of criminal behavior.

4. *When criminal behavior is learned, the learning includes (a) techniques of committing the crime, which are sometimes very complicated, sometimes very simple, and (b) the specific direction of motives, drives, rationalizations, and attitudes.* Not only does the learning of criminal behavior involve the way or ways the crime is to be committed, but also why it is to be done.

5. *The specific direction of motives and drives is learned from definitions of the legal codes as favorable or unfavorable.* In some societies, an individual is surrounded by people who invariably regard the laws as rules to be observed, while in others he or she may be surrounded by persons whose definitions (i.e., perceptions) are favorable to violations of the laws. In American society, these definitions are almost always mixed, with the consequence that we have culture conflicts in relation to the legal codes.

6. *A person becomes delinquent because of an excess of definitions favorable to violation of law over definitions unfavorable to violation of law.* This statement represents the differential association principle—the heart of the theory. It refers to both criminal and anticriminal associations and has to do with counteracting forces. When people become criminals, they do so because of contacts with criminal patterns and also because of isolation from anticriminal patterns.

7. *Differential associations may vary in frequency, duration, priority, and intensity.* "Frequency" and "duration" as modalities of associations are obvious and need no explanation. "Priority" is assumed to be important in the sense that either lawful or criminal behavior developed in early childhood may persist throughout life. This tendency, however, has not been adequately demonstrated, and priority seems to be important chiefly through its selective influence. "Intensity" is not precisely defined, but it has to do with such things as the prestige of the source of a criminal or anticriminal pattern and with emotional reactions related to the associations. In a precise description of the criminal behavior of a person, these modalities would be stated in quantitative form and a mathematical ratio reached. A formula in this sense has not been developed and the development of such a formula would be extremely difficult.

8. *The process of learning criminal behavior by association with criminal and anticriminal patterns involves all of the mechanisms that are involved in any other learning.* The learning of criminal behavior is complex and is not restricted to mere imitation. Criminal behavior may differ from noncriminal behavior, but the learning process through which the respective behaviors are acquired is the same.

9. *While criminal behavior is an expression of general needs and values, it is not explained by those needs and values, since noncriminal behavior is an expression of the same needs and values.* Thieves generally steal to secure money, but honest laborers work to secure money. The attempts by many scholars to explain criminal behavior by reference to general drives and values, such as the "happiness principle," striving for social status, the money motive, or frustration, have been and must continue to be futile since they explain lawful behavior as completely as they explain criminal behavior. They are

similar to breathing, which is necessary for any behavior, but which does not differentiate criminal from noncriminal behavior.

Modifications of differential association have been proposed by other criminologists for the purposes of expanding the scope of the theory or to achieve greater precision. DeFleur and Quinney (1966) restated Sutherland's nine postulates, using the language and symbols of set theory. Their formulation of crime causation, based on differential association, asserts that criminal behavior results from the learning of "criminal motivations, attitudes, and techniques" by means of symbolic interaction within close-knit, informal primary groups (DeFleur and Quinney, 1966, p. 14).

Through the concept of **differential identification,** Glaser (1969) has reconceptualized Sutherland's theory in role-taking imagery: "A person pursues criminal behavior to the extent that he identifies himself with real or imaginary persons from whose perspective his criminal behavior seemed acceptable" (p. 525). According to this concept, criminality results not only from membership in criminal or delinquent groups but also from identification with criminal and delinquent roles that are portrayed in the mass media, or as a negative response to anticriminal groups. (See Figure 12.2.)

With television reaching into nearly every home in the country, it is impossible to discount the role of this medium as a source of criminal behavior. Television, as Sagarin (1975) notes, does not tell us to do anything wrong, but it does provide numerous illustrations of criminal behavior, and often supplies detailed accounts of how certain crimes are perpetrated. While criminal offenders on television rarely escape punishment, the object lesson may not prove to be deterrent to those who are either vulnerable to suggestion or desperate. In the trial of 15-year-old Ronnie Zamora, accused of murdering an elderly widow who lived next door, defense attorney Ellis Rubin introduced a plea of not guilty by reason of insanity. He claimed that the defendant was "suffering from and acting under the influence of prolonged, intense, involuntary, subliminal television intoxication" (*Time,* October 10, 1977, p. 87). The jury rejected Rubin's argument and found Zamora guilty of first-degree murder.

Other suggested reformulations of differential association have been addressed to fundamental weaknesses and inadequacies in Sutherland's conceptualization of the learning processes presumed to underlie differntial association. Jeffery (1965),

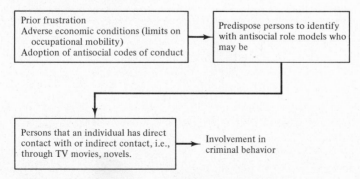

Figure 12.2 Daniel Glaser: differential identification.

Burgess and Akers (1966), and Adams (1973, 1974) have attempted to translate differential association into the conceptual language of modern reinforcement theory, based primarily on the work of psychologist B. F. Skinner. We shall deal with these reformulations in a later chapter.

Evaluation of Differential Association

The theory of differential association has been criticized by Glueck (1966), who contends that the theory fails to organize and integrate the findings of established research. He claims that the theory lacks clarity and adds little to what is already known about the causes of criminal and delinquent behavior.

Glueck also questions the emphasis that Sutherland places on the role of "an excess of definitions favorable to the violation of law over definitions unfavorable to the violation of law" (Sutherland and Cressey, 1978, p. 82) in a person's participation in crime. In the first place, he asserts, nobody has ever really attempted to measure whether the former exceed the latter in the vast majority of delinquents and criminals. This proposition is not likely to be tested because, as Short (1957) points out, it is unlikely that it can be specified in any meaningful quantitative terms. It also ignores several other important considerations. In light of the early onset of delinquency, it is very probable that the frequency, extent, and intensity of conventional school, home, and church influences results in an exposure of these young people to an excess of "definitions unfavorable to the violation of law," even among those who eventually become delinquent and criminal. Secondly, it makes no provision for the fact that individuals will react differently to the same cultural influences as the result of different social experiences, as well as their biological and psychological makeup. Glueck observes that by simply emphasizing the number or ratio of definitions as the controlling factor, differential association suggests that all people react to stimuli in the same way. Following the logic of this position, one would expect that the biggest criminals would be prison guards, professors of criminology, and prison chaplains because they spend a preponderance of their time associating with criminals! To suggest they are not criminals because they define the situation differently from criminals adds little to our understanding of the processes and factors that are critical for the development of criminal behavior. On the other hand, as Glueck points out, the inclusion of the proposition that "differential associations vary in frequency, duration, priority, and intensity" tends to becloud the primary role assigned by this position to an exposure to an overabundance of definitions favorable to criminal behavior. In fact, this latter proposition indicates it is not simply the "differential associations" per se that are crucial in the development of criminal behavior but rather the response of the individual to these associations that appears to make the difference. This response must obviously vary with differences in the biological and psychological structure of individuals exposed to these situations. This being the case, Glueck once again asserts that he feels this position has added little to our knowledge of the dynamics of criminal behavior.

Sutherland himself was aware of many of the limitations of differential association. His own critique of the theory is contained in a paper entitled "The Swan Song of Differential Association," which he wrote in 1944 for circulation among his close associates (Cohen, Lindesmith, and Schuessler, 1956). In this paper he recognizes that differential association is not the only cause of crime and he examines other factors he believes are involved in crime causation, including opportunity, intensity of need, and the role played by "available alternatives."

Cressey conducted a comprehensive review of criticisms of differential association, which he divided into two categories: (1) "literary errors," based on the failure of the reader to understand what Sutherland was attempting to say; and (2) "popular errors," which involved criticisms by criminologists and others regarding the basic claims of the theory (in Sutherland and Cressey, 1978). Two of the more important of these criticisms concerned the failure of differential association to account for the influence of personality variables in the development of definitions favorable to law violation and the difficulty of trying to measure a person's definitions of the law, their sources, and their qualifications.

Cressey provides the following assessment of the current status of differential association:

> . . . it seems safe to conclude that differential association is not a precise statement of the process by which one becomes a criminal. The idea that criminality is a consequence of an excess of intimate associations with criminal behavior patterns is valuable because, for example, it negates assertions that deviation from norms is simply a product of being emotionally insecure or living in a broken home, and then indicates in a general way why only some emotionally insecure persons and only some persons from broken homes commit crimes. Also, it directs attention to the idea that an efficient explanation of individual conduct is consistent with explanations of epidemiology. Yet the statement of the differential association process is not precise enough to stimulate rigorous empirical tests, and it therefore has not been proved or disproved [Sutherland and Cressey, 1978, p. 96].

In differential association, Sutherland made an outstanding contribution to criminological theory. At the time the theory of differential association was advanced, it represented the first concerted effort to provide a theory which incorporated the principal concepts sociologists considered important for explaining crime. As Vold (1979) suggests, the shortcomings of this theory are certainly not a result of the fact that the constellation of variables comprising the differential association approach is any less relevant today than it was fifty years ago. The theory outran the capacity of psychology or social psychology to provide an adequate answer to the question: "Why are there such qualitative selective differences in human association?" There is no doubt that the major value of differential association is that, more than any other theoretical approach, it stimulated and continues to stimulate research and scholarship in the field of criminology.

DELINQUENCY AND DRIFT: DAVID MATZA AND GRESHAM M. SYKES

David Matza, in collaboration with Gresham Sykes (Matza, 1964; Matza and Sykes, 1961; Sykes and Matza, 1957) has formulated a situational social control perspective on delinquency which shares some of the assumptions found in differential association. A major difference between the two theories is that Matza does not construe a youngster's delinquency as the result of participation in, and commitment to, a delinquent group, but instead, construes it as rule-breaking behavior performed by juveniles who are aware that they are violating the law and of the nature of their deeds. This definition is consistent with self-report data on delinquency which show that, although many youngsters engage in delinquency, most of them do not become adult violators. This perspective provides a plausible explanation why most of these juveniles outgrow their delinquency.

The Subculture of Delinquency

Matza suggests that our culture is composed of both conventional and less publicly acknowledged unconventional traditions. These deviant traditions are familiar and tolerated within limits by large segments of the adult population. For instance, a great deal of unconventional behavior is tolerated at conventions and conferences that is not acceptable under normal conditions. Under the cloak of "getting into the spirit of things" and aided by the consumption of alcohol, conventioneers have been known to destroy property, engage in lewd and lascivious behavior, and disturb the peace. One may also see similar types of behavior occurring during house parties and sporting events. The point is that many youngsters are fully aware that these sorts of things are done by adults—and the implications are not lost on most adolescents. Matza and Sykes (1961) identify a cluster of subterranean values that constitute the main features of the subculture which provides the impetus for delinquent behavior:

1. *The search for kicks, which involves an emphasis on activities that are dangerous and require daring.*
2. *A disdain for regular work and a desire for a "big score."*
3. *An emphasis on both physical and verbal aggression as a means of demonstrating toughness and masculinity.*

Middle-class people for the most part limit their pursuit of these values to socially approved situations; delinquents are not quite as discriminating in their choice of situations in which these values are actualized. In a sense, then, delinquency confronts us with an exaggerated and disturbing reflection of our society.

Matza regards the **subculture of delinquency** as "a setting in which the commission of delinquency is common knowledge among a group of juveniles" (Matza, 1964, p. 33). The juveniles who participate in this subculture are influenced by it—some more than others—but they are not constrained by it. Another distinctive feature of the subculture is what Matza calls *"the situation of company,"* which refers to the role played by the youth's peer group in his or her delinquent behavior. Matza contends that delinquent traditions are not formally transmitted to juveniles, but instead are learned, or, more specifically, are *inferred* by these youths from the cues they receive from their peers regarding the acceptability of certain kinds of behavior.

Matza (1964) suggests that adolescents suffer status anxiety as a result of the fact that their adolescent status places them in the position of being neither children nor adults. This creates anxieties among male youths about their masculinity as well as about their standing among their peers. These anxieties lead youths to test their reactions to various types of behavior in order to discover which behaviors are considered manly and which confer status.

Youths never ask directly for peer evaluations of particularly delinquent activities; rather, they derive their assessments from remarks and comments of other anxious youths who themselves are afraid to appear unmanly in the eyes of their peers. If a youth were to ask his peers "Do you think that taking stuff from a local store is a good thing?" their most likely response would be to subject him to ridicule and probably some choice obscenities. Youngsters do not put questions to their peers concerning the appropriateness of delinquency because they know from past experience that their peers would turn these questions around so as to question their masculinity and/or group membership. Expectation of responses such as, "Ain't you one of the boys?" or "Are you really a man?" leads youths to forego the serious exploration of sentiments regarding delinquency on the part of their peers. Consequently, each youngster gets the impression that his peers are committed to delinquency, whereas in reality they are not. Matza calls this set of circumstances **pluralistic ignorance.** As youths become adults and obtain some of the trappings of manhood, such as physical appearance, graduation from high school, a job, marriage, even children, masculine anxiety is reduced because they have in fact secured the status they have been seeking. At this point, Matza claims, most pairs of close friends begin to discuss feelings about delinquency and discover the misunderstandings they shared concerning the appropriateness of this behavior.

Matza suggests that by participating in the delinquent subculture these normally law-abiding youths learn rationalizations which release them from the moral constraints of society and thereby enable them to engage in delinquency. These rationalizations, labeled *techniques of neutralization,* are viewed by Matza as preceding delinquency, thus making the occasional drift into delinquency possible. Five principal techniques of neutralization are identified:

1. *Denial of responsibility,* in which the juvenile refuses to accept personal blame for his actions and attributes them to forces beyond his control (e.g., "I was drunk and out of my head").
2. *Denial of injury,* in which the youth does not deny the act but claims that "nobody got hurt."
3. *Denial of a victim,* in which the damage or injury inflicted was something that the victim had coming to him (e.g., stealing from a "crooked store owner" or beating up a homosexual).
4. *Condemnation of condemners,* which involves a view of authority figures such as teachers, parents, and police officers as hypocrites, deviants in disguise, or motivated by personal spite.
5. *Appeal to higher loyalties,* in which the delinquent rationalizes some of his behavior by placing greater emphasis on the demands of friendship groups, siblings, or gangs than upon loyalty to community or society.

Drift Into Delinquency

Now that we have described the factors that provide the impetus for delinquency, as well as those which free the youngster to engage in this behavior, we turn to an examination of Matza's conception of the interaction process associated with a youth's occasional involvement in delinquency. Matza called this process **drift into delinquency** (see Figure 12.3). This perspective involves a conception of individual behavior that differs from most of the positivistic theories we have discussed, according to which the delinquent or criminal is viewed as something akin to a billiard ball that is pushed or propelled by social conditions outside his control. Thus, the individual is not seen as exercising any choice with respect to his behavior.

Matza's conception of the delinquent falls midway between the positivistic position and the Classical position. He maintains that people fluctuate between choice and constraint: the individual is "neither as free as he feels nor as bound as he fears" (Tompkins, 1962, as cited by Matza, 1964, p. 7). People—delinquents included—are neither wholly free nor completely constrained, but fall somewhere in between. Matza calls his position *soft determinism*. Using this as a point of departure to focus on delinquency, Matza states that most delinquents drift between conventional and delinquent behavior. The delinquent is seen as:

> . . . an actor neither compelled nor committed to deeds, nor freely choosing them; nor different in any simple or fundamental sense from the law abiding, nor the same; conforming to certain traditions in American life while partially unreceptive to other more conventional traditions. . . . The delinquent *transiently* exists in a limbo between convention and crime, responding in turn to the demands of each, flirting now with one, now with the other, postponing commitment, evading decision. Thus, he drifts between criminal and conventional actions [p. 28].

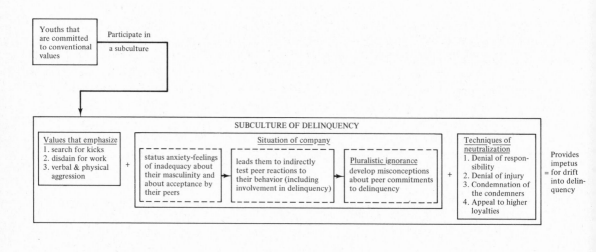

Figure 12.3 David Matza: process of drift into delinquency.

Most delinquents, according to Matza, are essentially drifters and only a few engage in delinquency as a consequence of neurotic impulses or personal commitment to criminal careers—an assertion which is consistent with the fact that most delinquents do not become adult criminal violators. This point is not given sufficient emphasis by those who view delinquency as a commitment to subcultural values. These theorists fail to specify the processes by which juveniles who were once committed or compelled to delinquency cease to be so constrained.

Up to this point, Matza has painted a picture of the delinquent as a youth who occasionally engages in delinquency, belongs to a subculture that provides subterranean values which support involvement in delinquency and provides the youth with rationalizations (techniques of neutralization) which remove the conventional constraints that prevent them from engaging in delinquent behavior, and belongs to a peer group that inadvertently supports the youth's involvement in delinquency. However, none of these factors explains when, how, or why youths decide to engage in acts of delinquency. Matza suggests that *preparation* and *desperation* provide the nerve required by youths for the commission of delinquent acts.

The term **preparation** is used by Matza to refer to the process by which youths learn that it is technically feasible to commit certain delinquent acts. This includes the recognition that they possess the requisite qualities and skills—a moderate amount of strength, speed, agility, dexterity, and cunning—to engage in burglary, shoplifting, and robbery. It also involves managing the fear or apprehension that most youths feel prior to committing acts of delinquency. Subcultural views of the incompetence of law enforcement, along with the belief that their chances of being caught are slim, go a long way toward relieving the apprehensiveness of most youths. They also learn that the juvenile justice system gives the youngster many chances before placing him in an institution.

Feelings of **desperation,** according to Matza, provide the impetus for experimentation with new types of delinquency. He suggests that desperation, rooted in fatalism, serves to neutralize legal barriers against delinquency and enhance a youngster's anxiety about his masculinity and status among his peers. Youths who develop a mood of fatalism feel as though they have no control over their surrounding circumstances and what will happen to them in the future—like puppets whose strings are pulled by forces beyond their control. In order to regain control over their fate, youngsters feel the need to make something dramatic take place. While conventional behavior can serve the same purpose as unconventional behavior, fear of failure in competing in such conventional activities as sports or academics is likely to lead the youth to choose a delinquent act because the chances of success are much greater.

Evaluation of Neutralization Theory

Criticism of neutralization theory has tended to focus on several basic issues: (1) whether delinquents accept more justifications for violations of the law than nondelinquents; (2) whether rationalizations precede or follow the delinquent act; and (3) whether delinquents show a greater commitment to conventional values or to deviant values. Empirical research on all of these issues is inconclusive.

Ball (1966) developed a neutralization inventory and used it to determine whether a sample of delinquents would embrace more justifications for law violations than would nondelinquents. He found that significantly more excuses for a variety of offenses were accepted among institutionalized delinquents than high school students and among youths with numerous self-reported violations as compared to those with relatively few self-reported violations. However, he found in a later study that poor self-concept was more important than neutralization in explaining norm violations (Ball, 1983).

Shoham (1966) and Hirschi (1969) have also questioned Matza's contention that neutralizations precede the delinquent act. Hirschi asserts that the conception of before-the-fact neutralizations is not consistent with reality. It is much more plausible, in his view, to assume that rationalizations follow the delinquent act rather than precede it. He asserts that it is difficult to understand how a boy can subscribe to a belief regarding the acceptability of a delinquent act without having engaged in it. However, Hirschi feels that these considerations do not require that we totally reject the idea that neutralizations play a part in delinquency. On the contrary, he feels that while rationalizations may proceed from the initial acts of delinquency, they may well be the causes of later acts.

Evidence as to whether delinquents are committed to conventional values, as Matza contends, or to deviant values, as subcultural theorists argue, is confusing and contradictory (Austin, 1977; Hindelang, 1980). Cernkovich (1978) found that involvement in delinquency was linked with subterranean values and low commitment to conventional values was associated with frequent and serious delinquencies. It is still an open question at this point whether delinquents are committed to conventional or deviant values.

The research of Schwendinger and Schwendinger (1967) raises some questions regarding the role of neutralization in the dynamics of delinquency. In a novel experiment involving 54 delinquents and nondelinquents, these researchers asked their subjects to play roles as proponents or objectors to the victimization of particular kinds of people. The following represents one of the enactments:

> I want you to act out this story; some teenagers are arguing whether they should beat up an outsider who insulted their club. An outsider is someone outside their circle of friends. Those in favor of beating him up argue with the others about it. The others are finally convinced that the outsider should be beaten up by the entire group [p. 93].

The Schwendingers found that the nondelinquent objectors were concerned with moral issues, while the delinquent objectors were mainly concerned with tactical problems such as the danger of being caught. These results certainly question the assumption of neutralization theory that delinquents feel guilty about their deviant behavior and require justification to neutralize the guilt associated with these acts. They also suggest an alternative explanation for these results might be that while delinquents may have private qualms about the morality of their delinquent behavior, in public they are constrained to espouse deviant attitudes and that it is this public vocabulary which influences their deviant activity. As Hood and Sparks (1970) suggest, this lends some credence to Matza's contention that delinquents misperceive the attitudes of their peers regarding the acceptability of delinquent behavior.

An important criticism is Glaser's (1973) claim that neutralization theory fails to adequately take into consideration the role played by delinquent subculture in reinforcing and transmitting the techniques of neutralization which allow delinquents to remain committed to conventional values and still engage in delinquent behavior without developing feelings of guilt. For example, Reis (1961) found that the delinquent subculture had developed norms which enabled delinquent boys to engage in homosexual prostitution and, at the same time, not be considered homosexual by their peers.

A key point in neutralization theory is the assumption that delinquents harbor feelings of resentment and hostility toward societal authorities, especially representatives of the criminal justice system. Giordano (1976) conducted a comparative survey of attitudes of public school students and youths who had been processed through various stages of the juvenile justice system. She found no significant attitudinal differences between officially adjudicated delinquents and nondelinquent students. Not only did delinquents fail to perceive their treatment as unfair; the further they penetrated the justice system, the more positive were the attitudes they developed. These results raise serious questions about the very foundation on which Matza's theory of drift and neutralization is based.

SOCIAL CONTROL THEORY: TRAVIS HIRSCHI

Most of the theories we have discussed so far take conformity for granted and concentrate on explaining deviance. Hirschi and other **social control** theorists, in contrast, focus their attention on attempting to account for why people *do not* deviate. Delinquency, crime, and other kinds of deviant behavior are exciting, fun, and may represent expedient ways of achieving goals; therefore, people may engage in these acts if they are not restrained from doing so by their ties to the conventional social order. This implies that all people are inherently antisocial, and only the presence of effective social control mechanisms prevents the pervasive occurrence of antisocial behavior. Hirschi's theory seeks to identify the elements of the conventional social order that prevent delinquency.

Hirschi (1969) contends the elements of *attachment, commitment, involvement,* and *belief* are the main factors that tie the individual to conventional society. *Attachment* refers to the strength of a child's bonds to such key persons as teachers, parents, and friends. In this context, norm violations are viewed as acts that are contrary to the wishes and expectations of significant others. Thus, children will only violate norms to the extent that they are indifferent to the wishes and expectations of others, particularly parents and teachers. Parental attachment is considered to be the most important because it is parents who provide the initial socialization and thereby have an extremely important impact on the internalization of norms.

Commitment involves an individual's stake in continuing a particular line of action. People who are committed to conventional forms of conduct such as running a business, going to school, or maintaining a reputation in the community, have invested considerable time, energy, money, and self-esteem in this line of activity. When these people consider engaging in deviant behavior, they must weigh the cost of this deviant behavior in terms of the risks involved in losing the investment they have made in conventional behavior. For example, a person with a business is not likely to risk losing this business by stealing a $10 item that may result in being sent to prison for a period of time. In the case of children, commitment to educational/occupational aspirations and postponement of involvement in adult activities like drinking and smoking are viewed as constraints on delinquency.

Involvement focuses attention on the types of activities that occupy the individual's day, and assumes individuals that engage in conventional activities may be too busy to find time to pursue deviant behavior. However, Hirschi recognizes that it is rather naive to assume that delinquency is prevented simply by juvenile involvement in conventional activities most of the time. In other words, the conception of delinquency as a full-time job is an inaccurate stereotype, because most delinquents only spend a small proportion of their time engaged in deviant activity. Therefore, it is Hirschi's contention that it is involvement in specific activities that parallel attitudinal commitments to conventional success goals that inhibits the commission of delinquent acts. For juveniles, the most important type of involvement is in school-related activities.

Belief refers to a person's sense of obligation to obey the rules of society. There are variations in the degree to which people believe that they should follow the rules of society. The less a person feels that he should obey the rules, the more likely he is to violate them. In the case of delinquents, belief in the rules of society is largely dependent upon their attachment to such authority figures as parents and thereby their concern for the approval of these authority figures.

Hirschi's own research findings have generally supported the elements that he has identified as being causally related to his theory of delinquency (see Figure 12.4). His data indicated that the more a youngster was attached to and identified with his parents, the lower were his chances of delinquency. A child's attachment to his school and teachers was also found to lower the chances of a youngster's involvement in delinquency. Rather than simply identifying this relationship, Hirschi attempted to look at some of the conditions that cause a child's disenchantment with school. His research suggests that the following causal chain produces a lack of attachment to teachers and school: this chain "runs from academic incompetence to poor school performance to disliking of school to rejection of the school's authority to the commission of delinquent acts" (p. 132).

With regard to the dimension of *attachment*—affinity with friends—Hirschi's data revealed two important findings. First, there was a strong tendency among the

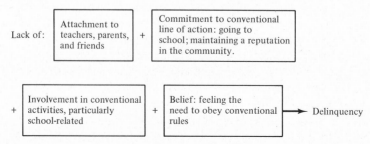

Figure 12.4 Travis Hirschi: social control theory.

juveniles he studied to have friends whose activities and attitudes were congruent with their own. It is unlikely that boys who have a large stake in conformity will have delinquent friends. Secondly, Hirschi asserts that "the idea that delinquents have comparatively warm, intimate relations with each other (or with anyone) is a romantic myth" (p. 159).

In terms of commitment, Hirschi found that youngsters with high educational/occupational aspirations had low rates of delinquency. On the other hand, youngsters who were engaged in adult activities such as drinking, smoking, dating, and use of an automobile, were more likely to commit delinquent acts. In fact, he found that the effect of these activities is cumulative, that is, the more a boy is involved in these adult activities the greater was his involvement in delinquency. By asserting the right to engage in these activities, particularly at an early age, a juvenile rejects his status as a child and concomitantly asserts his claims to adult status. At the same time, he frees himself from the need to be concerned about the expectations of parents and teachers and is therefore more likely to engage in delinquent acts.

Since involvement in conventional activities is to a large degree a consequence of commitment to these activities, it is not surprising that the findings parallel one another. Whereas boys who spent a considerable amount of time doing homework were found to have lower rates of delinquency, those who felt they had nothing to do or reported that they spent a considerable amount of time in cars were considerably more delinquent. Hirschi's hypothesis regarding the relationship between belief and attachment was confirmed. His data showed that boys who were attached to their parents and teachers were likely to feel an obligation to obey the law and to respect police. These same boys were also the ones most likely to have low rates of delinquency. Hirschi concludes that "the beliefs and values that feed delinquency are not peculiar to any social class or [nondelinquent] segment of the population" (p. 230). In other words, his data suggest there are no groups of major proportions in American society that have a configuration of values which positively encourages delinquency or crime.

Evaluation of Social Control Theory

A variety of studies, in addition to Hirschi's own research, provide data that test the various facets of this argument. There is considerable research to show that youths who are attached to their parents have lower rates of involvement in delinquency (Hepburn, 1976; Hindelang, 1973; Jensen, 1972; Jensen and Brownfield, 1983). But Johnson (1979) failed to find evidence to support the contention that parental attachment has direct effects on delinquent behavior. He suggests that either the theory itself or the methods for testing it needs revision.

The notion that delinquency can be deterred merely by occupying a youngster's time by involvement in work-study programs or nonacademic school-related activities received little support from research (Hackler, 1966; Robin, 1969; Schafer, 1969). Johnson (1979) notes that school attachment appears to have the single greatest effect on delinquent associations. Referring to his own research, he identifies the school as the "central arena for the sifting and sorting of adolescent companionships" which have been demonstrated to be important to the involvement in delinquent behavior. According to Johnson, "To the extent that birds of a feather flock together, the level of attachment to school seems to be the central delinquency-relevant 'feathering' criterion" (p. 109).

Research regarding delinquency and peer interaction provides a rather interesting picture of juvenile relationships. There is support for Hirschi's contention that relationships among delinquents are more often characterized by threats and suspiciousness than attachment and, as a result, are extremely fragile in nature (Klein, 1971; Short and Stodtbeck, 1965; Yablonsky, 1962). This certainly questions the popular notion of the juvenile gang as a chohesive unit characterized by warm, intimate relationships. But delinquents do seem to spend a lot of time together and perhaps on a superficial level appear to have commitments to one another. Johnson (1979) suggests delinquent associations produce a difficult-to-measure but important effect on perceptions of risk-taking in the commission of criminal acts: "Having had more exposure to delinquent friends decreases the certainty of getting caught" (p. 111). In short, the picture that emerges of relationships among delinquents is that their interactions are not based so much on considerations of mutual attraction and respect but from the absence of alternative contexts in which they can validate concepts of themselves and find support for their activities. These relationships exist because these juveniles have more to gain than to lose by maintaining them.

Hirschi himself was fully aware of the limitations of his theoretical approach. He acknowledges that his approach underestimated the significance of delinquent peers while at the same time it overstated the importance of participation in conventional activities. These deficiencies Hirschi attributes to his assumption regarding the natural motivation of delinquency which led him to fail to incorporate some notions regarding what delinquency does to the adolescent. Additionally, he recognizes the need to include consideration of the role of self-concept because he feels that it accounts for much juvenile involvement in such activities as drinking, smoking, dating, and driving a car.

Hirschi concludes by stating that while control theory provides some explanations regarding the relationships between these factors in delinquency, much still remains unexplained. However, he is confident that when the relationships between these variables of delinquency are identified, rather than modifying control theory, they will merely supplement it. To some extent, Hirschi's contention has been borne out. Subsequent research has been directed toward expanding social control theory by fusing it with other approaches in order to deal with some of its deficiencies (Conger, 1976; Linden and Hackler, 1973).

CONTAINMENT THEORY: WALTER C. RECKLESS

Walter C. Reckless, who obtained his doctorate at the University of Chicago in 1925, developed containment theory in the early 1960s. Reckless was a student of Robert Park, who sent his students out into the slums of Chicago to learn firsthand some of the difficulties faced by the people in these areas—many of them immigrants or migrants—in adjusting to urban living. This experience profoundly affected Reckless's career as well as his orientation. He became concerned with helping people deal with their problems; and as a result, he spent a considerable part of his career training probation and parole officers. Furthermore, unlike most sociologists of the Chicago School who focused their attention on the social conditions that generated disorganization within these slum areas, Reckless at an early point developed a profound and continuing concern with individual variation within any social context. That is, he became preoccupied with attempting to discover the facts that explain the differential responses of people living under the same circumstances (Reckless, 1943). Reckless wanted to know what factor or factors caused some people to join organized crime syndicates, become involved in delinquent gangs, pursue careers as professional thieves, and engage in illegal business practices while others living under the same social conditions and subjected to the same pressures pursue socially acceptable patterns of behavior. He was critical of sociological theories because they failed to account for the differential response of individuals to social conditions. It was his position that various "self factors" represented the missing element that explained individual variation.

Reckless illustrates his position by looking at the relationship between a person's exposure to the malaria-carrying mosquito and contracting malaria. Not everybody who ventures into the swamps where malaria mosquitoes are spawned and live contracts malaria. Among those who do, some suffer only a light attack, others are very severely affected, and some remain immune. The individual variation in response to malaria is related to an inherited or acquired biological immunity to this disease. While Reckless recognized that an inherited biological immunity to crime was extremely improbable, he felt that the ability of an individual to resist the temptations of involvement in crime is related to the acquisition of certain "self factors." Malaria can also be controlled and prevented by certain factors that are external to the individual, which include exterminating the mosquito, cleaning up the swamp, putting screens on houses, sleeping under mosquito nets, and taking primaquine, an anti-infectant.

Reckless believes that crime and delinquency are controlled in a manner which is analogous to the control and prevention of malaria—by factors within and outside of the individual. Crime and delinquency, in his view, result from a series of external and internal pushes and pulls, as shown in Figure 12.5. On the one hand, the individual is subjected to adverse environmental pressures which include such conditions as poverty, economic insecurity, unemployment, family conflict, lack of opportunities, minority group status, and social inequity, and "pulls," which include such factors as bad companions, a delinquent or criminal subculture, illegitimate opportunity, the

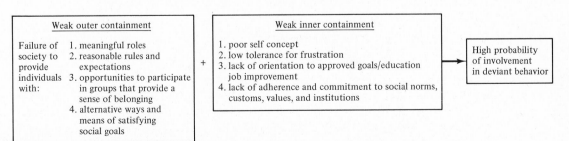

Figure 12.5 Walter Reckless's containment theory.

mass media, deviant groups, etc. On the other hand, individual behavior is also affected by a variety of internal, organic, and psychological "pushes" which include such factors as extreme inner tensions, strong feelings of aggressiveness and hostility, undue restlessness and discontent, extreme rebellion against authority, the need for immediate gratification, strong feelings of inadequacy and inferiority, mental conflicts, compulsions, anxieties, phobias, psychoses, and organic impairments such as brain damage and epilepsy. Reckless posits the existence of two reinforcing structures that act as buffers or insulators against deviancy. These consist of an inner control system (**inner containment**) and an outer control system (**outer containment**).

Outer Containment

The concept of outer containment refers to the ability of society, the state, the tribe, the village, the community, the family, and other nuclear groups to hold the behavior of individuals within the bounds of accepted norms, rules, regulations, laws, expectations, and values. In a modern urban industralized society it involves one or more of the following components: providing the individual with meaningful roles; provision of reasonable limits and responsibilities for individuals, reasonable norms and expectations; fostering of a sense of identity and belonging; and the availability of alternative ways and means of satisfaction when one or more means is closed. In a large society such as ours, these containing elements are primarily provided by the family and other small supportive groups. Reckless argues that the individual who finds a sense of satisfaction, belonging, ego bolstering, and support within a small group is apt to follow the norms of society. He also maintains that external containment may serve as a second line of defense against inner pushes, when the individual's inner containment is weak.

Inner Containment

Inner containment refers to the ability of the individual to direct or steer himself or herself. It is composed of such elements as a favorable self-concept or image; an orientation toward socially approved goals; a high level of frustration tolerance; and adherence, commitment, acceptance, and identification with norms, social customs, values, codes, and institutions. Reckless believes inner containment is of far greater significance in mobile, highly industrial societies because in these settings people spend a good deal of their time away from the family and other supportive groups which can contain them. The result is that they must rely primarily on their own inner strength to function competently.

By subdividing the two containments into strong and weak, we can see more clearly their impact on individual involvement in crime:

1. When a person has strong inner containment and strong outer containment, the chance of his involvement in crime and delinquency is almost nil. This condition is not very prevalent in a mobile, highly industrialized society.
2. When a person has strong inner containment coupled with weak outer containment, there is not much chance of his or her being involved in crime or

delinquency. Although the probability of noninvolvement in crime and delinquency is greater with both strong outer and inner containment, this condition is more characteristic of circumstances within an urban industrialized society.

3. When a person has weak inner containment and external containment is strong, the likelihood of involvement in crime and delinquency is higher than in either of the previous two combinations of containments. However in primitive societies, strong outer containment is sufficient to control deviant behavior because the outer and inner pushes and pulls are not of the same magnitude.

4. When a person has weak inner containment as well as weak outer containment, the chances of being involved in crime and delinquency are maximized. This set of circumstances prevails to some extent in modern urban industrialized societies and also in developing countries in which large segments of their population are emerging from a tribal or semitribal life. This becomes a particular problem among the latter group when they migrate to the city.

Reckless (1967) claims that containment theory is "the best general theory to explain the largest amount of crime and delinquent behavior" (p. 480). He considers this approach a middle-range theory that accounts for the vast majority of crime and delinquency. However, this is not applicable to the small amount of this behavior that results from extreme psychological or organic pushes on the one hand, and atypical social conditions, which include groups or communities that pursue crime as a way of life (e.g., the criminal tribes of India), and abrupt social change such as natural disasters and economic depressions. With the exception of these extreme cases, containment theory is viewed as explaining both crimes against the person and crimes against property. It is also considered to be an approach that can be used equally well by psychologists, psychiatrists, and sociologists as well as practitioners.

Finally, the value of this approach is enhanced because it can be used in developing programs for the treatment of offenders and the prevention of crime and delinquency. The whole spectrum of correctional programs—from prisons to community-based treatment programs—can be oriented toward strengthening the individual's self-concept and reconstructing his or her milieu so as to provide an outer buffer against crime. With respect to prevention, emphasis could be placed on identifying preadolescent youngsters vulnerable to delinquency as a result of living under adverse social conditions and, more importantly, lacking in inner containment. Special programs might be devised for these youngsters which would seek to develop a strong inner buffer that would insulate them against deviancy as well as develop supportive external buffers.

Evaluation of Containment Theory

Containment theory has both virtues and defects. First, it has directed our attention toward the question of why some people who are exposed to adverse environmental conditions become deviant and others do not. Reckless has forced us to grapple with the problem of explaining why most youngsters growing up in slum areas do not become delinquents. This approach provides a framework in which it is possible to examine the interaction of psychological and sociological factors. To its credit is also the fact that it accounts for both criminal and noncriminal behavior by incorporating many of the variables and concepts that other, earlier theoretical approaches have employed. To some extent, Reckless has taken the concepts identified by other theorists as causally related to delinquency and specified their collective impact on crime and delinquency.

This approach also provided a theoretical foundation for the Ohio Youth Project (otherwise known as the "good boy/bad boy studies") and was a stimulus for research by many of Reckless's students and others on the identification of self factors in delinquency. Landis and Scarpitti (in Reckless, 1967) examined the self components of value orientation and awareness of limited opportunity, using two different populations. They found that these components were related to delinquency proneness and delinquency, respectively. Earlier, we noted that Ball (1966) investigated neutralization as a component of self and found a difference between delinquents and nondelinquents in terms of this dimension. He concluded that neutralization as a self factor contributed to norm erosion which, in turn, weakened inner containment and increased the risk of involvement in delinquency. Ball's (1983) later research disclosed that self-concept was a much more important factor in explaining delinquency than either personal neutralization or attributed neutralization for the same group of youngsters in the sixth and ninth grades.

Schwartz and Tangri (1963), using sampling procedures similar to those employed by Reckless and Dinitz in the "good boy/bad boy studies," found differences between the self-conceptions held by these boys, as well as differences in the perceptions of opinions of them by others. Jensen's (1973) research provides some support for the contention that inner containment operates as a buffer against delinquency for youths who are exposed to the same adverse social conditions. His research, which was based on a sample of 4,000 junior and senior high school students in the San Francisco Bay area, yielded results which indicate that self-esteem, a sense of self-control, and an acceptance of conventional morality counted for some immunity to, or variation in, delinquency among youths from similar family situations, similar socioeconomic conditions, and among boys categorized according to the number of friends who were picked up by the police.

Kaplan's (1980) work provides support for containment theory and suggests an interesting connection between self-concept and delinquency. He sees negative self-attitudes as providing the motivation for delinquent behavior. He argues that individuals with insufficient personal resources to cope with their inability to meet conventional group expectations develop negative self-attitudes. To combat these attitudes and enhance their self-concepts, these youths seek membership in deviant groups. Kaplan's own research provides support for this position. He found that some students who reported negative self-feelings and no involvement in deviant behavior at the outset of his research were much more likely to report involvement in deviant behavior at two subsequent test periods than those with good feelings about themselves. Not only do these findings extend containment theory, they also suggest that there is more to delinquent behavior than simply acquiring deviant patterns from one's peers, as is indicated by Sutherland's differential association theory

(Dinitz and Pfau-Vicent, 1982). In some cases, delinquency may be the result of negative experiences in nondeviant groups such as the family, school, or conventional peer group, which result in a poor self-concept. For those with no other resources, delinquency or deviant behavior may represent the only activities that can offset these negative attitudes and enhance self-concept.

The major criticisms of this position relate to its adequacy as a theory. First, Schrag (1971) has quite aptly pointed out that the major criteria for considering any position a theory is that it should be "reduceable to a series of inter-connective propositions from which research hypotheses can be derived" (p. 84). An examination of the Reckless formulation reveals few, if any, testable statements. Another problem with this approach is the way in which its concepts are defined. Instead of providing a clear definition of each concept along with statements that identify observable indications of each of these components, Reckless defines them through the use of illustrations and by identifying the methods by which they control behavior. Certain external conditions are described as "pulls" that draw a person away from conventional patterns of behavior and toward deviant responses. Instead of defining what a "pull" is we are presented with a list of illustrations which include bad companions, prestigious individuals, etc. Moreover, these illustrations are not presented with any statements that give us an indication of how to identify these empirical indicators. How does one recognize a bad companion or, for that matter, a prestigious individual? It is just these kinds of problems that make it difficult to test whether "strong inner containment" actually serves to prevent a person's involvement in crime and delinquency. In the final analysis, despite all its defects, this position must be recognized as making a contribution to our understanding of delinquent and criminal behavior by sensitizing us to the role of certain sociopsychological variables in explaining the differential response of individuals to similar environmental conditions.

SUMMARY

This chapter has reviewed a series of perspectives that examine the process by which people become criminals and delinquents and the differential response factors that explain why some people who are exposed to adverse environmental conditions engage in crime and delinquency and others do not. The chapter began with a discussion of Sutherland's differential association theory which suggested that crime is learned behavior and that learning takes place principally in primary groups. Glaser expanded Sutherland's theory by suggesting learning does not necessarily have to take place in criminal groups but can result from identification with real or imaginary persons. This suggests the need to examine all the factors that affect our choices of the people with whom we identify, that is, role models.

Matza's orientation provided a less deterministic view than differential association in that delinquency was conceived of as emerging out of a process of interaction in which delinquency was one possible option. Most delinquents were viewed as youngsters who were committed to conventional values; however, these youths drifted into delinquency as a result of anxiety over masculinity, peer status, and misunderstandings regarding peer expectations. Guilt over involvement in deliquency was neutralized by a variety of justifications which were provided by the subculture of delinquency. In contrast to other positions we examined, Hirschi's social control theory focused attention on why people do not deviate. It was his contention that juveniles who have a stake in conformity as manifested by attachment to, commitment to, involvement in, and belief in the conventional social order are not likely to engage in delinquent behavior. From his standpoint, deliquency occurs when ties from conventional society are severed.

Reckless's containment theory represented an attempt to provide a perspective that considered both social/cultural factors (outer containment) and internal factors (inner containment) which included sociopsychological factors, psychological factors, and structural factors. Crime and delinquency depended upon the interaction of these two systems. However, in an urban industrial society where outer containment is typically weak, inner containment (i.e., the individual's internal control system), is of far greater significance in insulating a person against involvement in law breaking. In this regard, Reckless and his associates identified several self components—favorable self-concept or image; an orientation toward socially approved goals; a high level of frustration tolerance; and adherence, commitment, acceptance, and identification with the norms, values, codes, institutions, and customs of society—that operated to steer individuals away from involvement in crime and delinquency.

DISCUSSION QUESTIONS

Find the answers to the following questions in the text.
1. What is the principal focus of sociopsychological theories of criminality?
2. Summarize the main arguments of Sutherland's **differential association** theory. What are some of the major criticisms that have been directed toward differential association?
3. Describe **differential identification** as a theoretical approach. How well did this position rectify some of the shortcomings of differential association?
4. Discuss the concept of **drift** and its relevance for understanding delinquent behavior.
5. According to Matza, what was the nature and content of a **"subculture of delinquency"**?
6. Evaluate **neutralization** theory.
7. Briefly describe the main features of **social control theory** and evaluate this approach on the basis of the evidence presented.
8. Discuss **containment theory** with regard to the types of criminal behavior it attempts to explain and its main constructs. How well is containment theory supported by available evidence?

TERMS TO IDENTIFY AND REMEMBER

differential association

subculture of delinquency

pluralistic ignorance

attachment

involvement

soft determinism

outer containment

preparation

differential identification

drift

techniques of neutralization

social control theory

commitment

inner containment

drift into delinquency

desperation

REFERENCES

Austin, R. L. Commitment, neutralization, and delinquency. In T. N. Ferninand (ed.), *Juvenile Delinquency: Little Brother Grows Up.* Beverly Hills, CA: Sage, 1977.

Ball, R. A. An empirical exploration of neutralization theory. *Criminologica* 4 (1966): 22–32.

Breznitz, T. Juvenile delinquents' perception of own and others' commitment to delinquency. *Journal of Research in Crime and Delinquency* 12 (1975): 124–32.

Buffalo, M. D., and Rogers, J. W. Behavioral norms, moral norms, and attachment: Problems of deviance and conformity. *Social Problems* 19 (1971): 101–13.

Cohen, A. K., Lindesmith, A., and Schuessler, K. *The Sutherland Papers.* Bloomington, IN: Indiana University Press, 1956.

Conger, R. D. Social control and social learning models of delinquent behaviors: A synthesis. *Criminology* 14 (1976): 17–40.

Cressey, D. R. The development of a theory: Differential association. *The Pacific Sociological Review* 3 (Fall 1960): 47–54.

DeFleur, M., and Quinney, R. A reformulation of Sutherland's differential association theory and a strategy for empirical verification. *Journal of Research in Crime and Delinquency* 2 (1966): 1–22.

DeFleur M. L., D'Antonio, W. V., and DeFleur, L. B. *Sociology: Man in Society.* Glenview, IL: Scott, Foresman, 1971.

Downes, D. M. *The Delinquent Solution: A Study in Subcultural Theory.* New York: The Free Press, 1966.

Elliott, D. S., and Voss, H. L. *Delinquent and Dropout.* Lexington, MA: Lexington Books, 1974.

Empey, L. T., and Lubeck, S. G. Conformity and deviance in the situation of company. *American Sociological Review* 33 (1968): 761–74.

Erickson, M. L., and Empey, L. T. Class position, peers, and delinquency. *Sociology and Social Research* 49 (April 1965): 268–82.

Gibbons, D. C., and Jones, J. F. *The Study of Deviance: Perspectives and Problems.* Englewood Cliffs, NJ: Prentice-Hall, 1975.

Giordano, P. C. The sense of injustice? An analysis of juveniles' reactions to the justice system. *Criminology* 14 (1976): 93–112.

Glaser, D. Criminality theories and behavioral images. In D. R. Cressey and D. A. Ward (Eds.), *Delinquency, Crime and Social Process.* New York: Harper & Row, 1969.

———. Role models and differential association. In E. Rubington and M. S. Weinberg (eds.), *Deviance: The Interactionist Perspective.* New York: Macmillan, 1973.

Glueck, S. Theory and fact in criminology: A criticism of differential association. *British Journal of Criminology* 19 (1962): 6, 7, 92–98.

Hackler, J. C. Boys, blisters, and behavior—The impact of a work program in an urban central area. *Journal of Research in Crime and Delinquency* 3 (1966): 155–64.

Hepburn, J. R. Casting alternative models of delinquency causation. *Journal of Criminal Law and Criminology* 67 (1976): 450–60.

Hindelang, M. J. The commitment of delinquents to their misdeeds: Do delinquents drift? *Social Problems* 17 (1970): 502–509.

———. Causes of delinquency: A partial replication and extension. *Social Problems* 20 (1973): 471–87.

Hirschi, T. *Causes of Delinquency.* Berkeley, CA: University of California Press, 1969.

Hood, R., and Sparks, R. *Key Issues in Criminology.* New York: World University Library, 1970.

Jensen, G. F. Parents, peers, and delinquents: A test of the differential association hypothesis. *American Journal of Sociology* 78 (1972): 546–49.

Johnson, R. E. *Juvenile Delinquency and Its Origins.* New York: Cambridge University Press, 1979.

Karacki, L., and Toby, J. The uncommitted adolescent: Candidate for gang socialization. *Sociological Inquiry* 32 (1962): 203–15.

Klein, M. W. *Street Gangs and Street Workers.* Englewood Cliffs, NJ: Prentice-Hall, 1971.

Linden, E., and Hackler, J. C. Affective ties and delinquency. *Pacific Sociological Review* 16 (1973): 27–46.

Liska, A. E. *Perspectives on Deviance.* Englewood Cliffs, NJ: Prentice-Hall, 1981.

Matza, D. *Delinquency and Drift.* New York: Wiley, 1964.

Matza, D., and Sykes, G. M. Juvenile delinquency and subterranean values. *American Sociological Review* 26 (1961): 712–19.

Orcutt, J. Self-concept and insulation against delinquency: Some critical notes. *Sociological Quarterly* 2 (Summer 1970): 381–90.

Reckless, W. C. *The Etiology of Delinquent and Criminal Behavior.* New York: Social Science Research Council, 1943.

———. *The Crime Problem.* New York: Appleton-Century-Crofts, 1967.

Reiss, A. J. The social integration of queers and peers. *Social Problems* 9, no. 2 (Fall 1961): 112–19.

Robin, G.D. Anti-poverty program and delinquency. *Journal of Criminal Law, Criminology, and Police Science* 60 (1969): 323–31.

Sagarin, E. *Deviants and Deviance: An Introduction to the Study of Disvalued People and Behavior.* New York: Praeger, 1975.

Schafer, W. E. Participation in interscholastic athletics and delinquency: A preliminary study. *Social Problems* 17, no. 1 (1969): 40–47.

Schrag, C. *Crime and Justice: American Style.* Washington, D.C.: U.S. Government Printing Office, 1971.

Schwartz, M., and Tangri, S. A note on self-concept as an insulator against delinquency. *American Sociological Review* 30 (1963): 922–26.

Schwendinger, H., and Schwendinger, J. Delinquent sterotypes of probable victims. In M. W. Klein and B. G. Myerhoff (eds.), *Juvenile Gangs in Context: Theory, Research, and Action.* Englewood Cliffs, NJ: Prentice-Hall, 1967.

Shoemaker, D. J. *Theories of Delinquency.* New York: Oxford University Press, 1984.

Shoham, S. *Crime and Social Deviation.* Chicago: Henry Reguery, 1966.

Short, J. F. Differential association and delinquency. *Social Problems* 4 (January 1957): 233–239.

Short, J. F., and Strodtbeck, F. L. *Group Process and Gang Delinquency.* Chicago: University of Chicago Press, 1965.

Sutherland, E. H. *Criminology.* Philadelphia: Lippincott, 1924.

———. *The Professional Thief.* Chicago: University of Chicago Press, 1937.

———. *Principles of Criminology* (3rd Ed.). Philadelphia: Lippincott, 1939; 1947.

———. *White Collar Crime.* New York: Dryden Press, 1949.

Sutherland, E. H., and Cressey, D. R. *Criminology* (10th ed.). Philadelphia: Lippincott, 1978.

Sykes, G. M., and Matza, D. Techniques of neutralization: A theory of delinquency. *American Sociological Review* 22 (1957): 664–670.

——— . Juvenile delinquency and subterranean values. *American Sociological Review* 26 (1961): 12–719.

Vold, G. B. *Theoretical Criminology.* New York: Oxford University Press, 1979.

Yablonsky, L. *The Violent Gang.* New York: Macmillan, 1962.

chapter 13

THE LABELING
PERSPECTIVE

The labeling theory or perspective has also been identified as the *social reaction position* and the *interactionist approach*. It has even been identified as *symbolic interactionism* (Kitsuse, 1972). These designations suggest the two major emphases of the labeling perspective. **Social reaction** refers to the importance attributed to the group's reaction to an individual's deviant acts, that is, how formal and informal groups and organizations define individuals as deviants and maintain them in these statuses. The **interactionist approach** refers to the emphasis on the processes involved in the transformation of an individual from a person who commits a deviant act to a person who occupies a deviant status. In fact, the theoretical foundations of the labeling approach can be traced to the perspective toward human behavior in general reflected in the work of George Herbert Mead and Herbert Blumer, and to the use of this perspective by Howard Becker and others to account for deviant behavior.

EARLY PRECURSORS OF LABELING

While the ideas surrounding the labeling perspective were not fully elaborated until it became popular in the 1960s, many of the concepts associated with this approach were expressed long before its formal recognition. An examination of Mead's writings (1917–1918) reveals that he recognized the problems associated with singling out criminal offenders for purposes of prosecution and punishment and then reintegrating them in the community once they are released.

One can also find hints of the labeling approach in the work of some early sociologists. In 1923, W. I. Thomas gave us the now-famous dictum: "If men define situations as real, they are real, they are real in their consequences" (p. 81). This observation suggests people act in ways which reflect their appraisals of situations. These appraisals may be affected by both the objective characteristics of the situation *and* the meaning which the situations holds for them. Once a person has ascribed meaning to a situation, subsequent behavior is largely based on this definition, regardless of its congruence with reality.

Tannenbaum's (1938) remarks on "the dramatization of evil" are often cited as an early statement which provides the rudiments of the labeling position. Identifying as **tagging** what we now call labeling, he describes how community reaction shifts from the definition of an individual's acts as delinquent to *the definition of the person as delinquent*. Once the individual is tagged a delinquent, he is encouraged to become in fact what he is described as being. The result is typically a change in identity as well as movement into a deviant group.

While others hinted at various facets of the labeling approach, Edward Lemert's book *Social Pathology* (1951) is generally considered to contain the first explicit statement of this orientation. Lemert takes as his point of departure the idea that deviance represents one form or variation in a society which unlike others results in social disapproval.

> . . . persons and groups are differentiated in various ways which results in social penalties, rejection, and segregation. These penalties and segregated reactions of society or the community are dynamic factors which increase, decrease, and condition the form which the initial differentiation of deviation takes . . .

> The deviant person is one whose role, status, function, and self-definition are importantly shaped by how much deviation he engages in, by the degree of its social visibility, by the particular exposure he has to the societal reaction, and by the nature and strength of the societal reaction [p. 22–23].

At the heart of Lemert's work is a description of the process by which a person becomes deviant. He recognized that although many people commit deviant acts, most of them do not become deviants. He suggests the terms *primary* and *secondary deviance* to reflect this basic distinction. These terms will be discussed later on in this chapter.

Other later contributors to this position have included Harold Garfinkel (1956), Erving Goffman (1961), Kai Erikson (1962), Aaron Cicourel (1963), Howard Becker (1963), Edwin Schur (1971), and Thomas Scheff (1971).

EMERGENCE OF THE LABELING PERSPECTIVE

Unlike most of the theoretical positions we have examined, the labeling orientation cannot be ascribed to the work of a single person. The themes or viewpoints associated with this position, as we noted above, have been advanced by a variety of people. But it was only in the 1960s that a group of sociologists developed in more or less organized form the theoretical position identified today as labeling. At this point, some sociologists began to shift their attention from a search for the causes of deviant behavior in general to an examination of the dynamics of the process by which people are *defined* as deviant and the consequences of this process for the individual.

The labeling perspective appears to have developed at this time primarily for two reasons. First, there was disenchantment with the study of the causes of delinquency and crime. Criminologists were discouraged by the growing recognition that the current state of knowledge was not sufficiently developed in order to provide the means to construct a "grand theory" which could account for *all* crime.

Second, during the 1960s, there was growing concern over how well—or how poorly—our social institutions were meeting the needs they were supposed to fulfill. Attention was directed toward the schools, economic institutions, and our social control system—the police, courts, and corrections—as well as the family. To some extent this concern was spurred by the civil disturbances that rocked our cities during the mid-1960s. At the same time, sociologists and others began to realize that some of the social organizations which were supposed to help people were actually doing more harm than good. This resulted from the fact that in order for the agencies to assist people they had to label them. It became evident that, in some instances, the consequences of being labeled far outweighed any help or assistance the individual received from the social agencies. Questions were also raised regarding the effectiveness of some of the treatment provided by these agencies. As a result, support was gained for the opinion that it might be better not to try to treat certain groups of people at all. The results of this can be seen in the complementary emphasis on diverting as many people as possible from our mental health and correctional systems. In the area of juvenile justice, for example, stress is laid upon handling juveniles either informally or through programs which do not require that youngsters be adjudicated delinquent.

The labeling perspective provided a framework within which these concerns could be examined from two vantage points. First, studies have focused on the nature, structure, and functions of social control agencies reflecting the social reaction emphasis. We have begun to ask whether there are better ways to organize the various agencies charged with the responsibility of handling deviance so they will better achieve their stated goals. After studying our social control system for a number of years, there is some support for changing the goals of the system to bring them into line with what is considered to be obtainable. Attention has also been directed toward determining at what point in the process the individual became labeled, as well as examining the role played by those who have been labeled by the social control system.

Second, the labeling orientation spurred interest in, and examination of, the dynamics of the process by which the label is applied to the individual and the consequences to the individual from the application of this label. This reflected its roots in symbolic interaction. Who applies the label, the circumstances under which the label is applied, the effects of labeling on the individual, and the development of a deviant subculture were matters of major concern.

The Major Concerns of Labeling

The central thesis of labeling is that deviance and social control involve a process of social definition (Schur, 1971). This leads to concern with three major processes:

1. **Collective rule making,** modification, and enforcement.
2. The **organizations** in society that do the processing.
3. The interaction process by which a deviant act is transformed into a deviant actor.

The following statement by Becker directly reflects the first two concerns and applies to the third.

> . . . *Social groups create deviance by making the rules whose infractions constitute deviance,* and by applying rules to particular people and labeling them as outsiders. From this point of view, deviance is not a quality of the act the person commits, but rather a consequence of the application by others of rules and sanctions to an "offender." The deviant is one to whom that label has been successfully applied; deviant behavior is behavior that people so label [p. 9]. [Italics added]

This in no way suggests that acts such as murder, rape, or burglary would never happen if they were not defined as deviant or criminal. The act of labeling is not construed as *causing* these or any other acts of deviance. On the contrary, this statement indicates that patterns of social reactions materially affect the nature and meaning that is attributed to, as well as the implications and ramifications of, these acts. It is suggested that society determines how people view these acts. Society defines what acts are deviant as well as prescribes how those who engage in this behavior ought to be treated. This has led labeling theorists to be concerned not only with the dynamics of the labeling process but also with the process by which acts come to be prescribed as deviant.

Lemert's (1951, 1967) concepts of primary and secondary deviance provide an orientation to this perspective with special concern to the interpersonal dynamics of the labeling process.

Lemert (1951) has used the term **primary deviance** to refer to deviant behavior that has not materially affected an individual's self-concept, social status or style, or life. Included in this category are (1) those repeatedly arrested for drunkenness, but who are still accepted by their families and employers; (2) drug users who are able to conceal their drug use from those who might take action against them; (3) juveniles who engage in delinquency but have not been arrested and/or adjudicated for their aberrant acts; (4) individuals who temporarily manifest some symptoms associated with mental illness; and (5) adults who engage in occasional criminal acts such as shoplifting. All these behaviors have in common the fact that they are normalized and dealt with as functions of a socially acceptable role by an individual's associates, or the individual restricts his or her involvement to situations which will not result in the imposition of a deviant label. The latter circumstance is illustrated by men who engage in occasional impersonal homosexual relations in public lavatories or with male prostitutes.

Lemert used the term **secondary deviance** to call attention to the importance of social reactions in the etiology of deviance and the responses made by people to the problems created by the social reaction to their deviance. It thus concerns the processes which create, maintain, and amplify a deviant identity. Lemert asserted that this process has consequences for the individual's psychic structure, organization of social rules, and self-attitudes. He described the process as follows:

> . . . (1) *primary deviation;* (2) *social penalties;* (3) *further primary deviation;* (4) *stronger penalties and rejections;* (5) *further deviation,* and perhaps with hostilities and resentment beginning to focus upon those doing the penalizing; (6) crisis reached in the tolerance quotient, expressed in formal action by the community stigmatizing of the deviant; (7) strengthening of the deviant conduct as a reaction to the stigmatizing and penalties; (8) ultimate acceptance of deviant social status and efforts at adjustment on the basis of the associated role [Lemert, 1951, p. 77].

In order to better understand the labeling approach, it is necessary to narrow our focus to the major levels of analysis—rule making, interpersonal relations, and organizational processing—that are characteristics of this perspective. We will first examine certain basic response processes with particular consideration to the level of interpersonal reactions. It is, however, important to note that these processes operate at all levels, as shown in Figure 13.1.

This makes clear a basic premise of this approach: namely, that a deviant status is an *ascribed* status, which means it not only involves deviant acts on the part of an individual, but also involves the reaction of others to these acts (Schur, 1971).

Levels of analysis

Basic response processes	Collective rule-making	Interpersonal reactions	Organizational processing	Outcomes
Stereotyping	Public stereotypes of deviants	Reliance on observed or assumed cues (application of cultural stereotypes in interactions)	Typification in processing "normal cases" (classification partly according to stereotypes)	
Retrospective interpretation	Rule-making that imputes ancillary qualities to the deviator, as in employment policies toward homosexuals	Consideration of actor as having "been that way all along"; review of past for early "cues"	Use of "case record" or "case history"	Individual role engulfment in deviant careers Secondary expansion of deviance "problems" of society
Negotiation	Pressure-group conflict over legal and public definitions	Direct bargaining over labels, as in psychiatric diagnosis	Bargaining between client and organization, as in pleading in criminal court	
Outcomes		Individual role engulfment in deviant careers; secondary expansion of deviance "problems" of society		

Figure 13.1 Basic processes and key levels of analysis. (*Source:* E. M. Schur, *Labeling deviant behavior: Its sociological implications.* New York: Harper & Row, 1971. Reproduced by permission of the author and publisher.)

INTERPERSONAL RELATIONS

This section focuses on the role played by certain social processes in the definition of individuals as deviant and in their own acceptance of a deviant identity.

Retrospective and Current Redefinition of Acts

Once people have been labeled deviant, there is a tendency to reinterpret their past and present behavior in terms of their newly ascribed deviant status. That is, current behavior is examined in order to find evidence that supports the individual's deviant identity. What previously may have been viewed as relatively innocuous or, at the most, unusual behavior is now viewed as deviance or as indicative of deviant behavior: a youngster's harmless prank is now seen as vandalism; sexual advances may now be perceived as aggressive behavior which indicates the individual's willingness to commit rape; a person's inability to obtain a job is now looked upon as suggesting a preference for crime as a means of support.

The individual's past behavior is also reinterpreted in light of his or her deviance. This process is called **biographical reconstruction** or **retrospective reinterpretation** and involves a tendency to reexamine past actions for purposes of identifying acts that show the individual was deviant long before he or she was so labeled. The case of Richard Speck showed how biographical reconstruction also occurs at the public level (Lofland, 1969). The initial material uncovered by the media following Speck's apprehension for the murder of eight student nurses in Chicago showed showed him to be a gentle, intelligent, and sensitive young man, which failed to support his image as a murderer. However, four days after his arrest information was discovered to sustain his current status as a murdered. The facts uncovered included that he was a murder suspect in another case which involved a person he had hated for a long time; had been arrested 36 times; had been incarcerated for 3 years for burglary; and as a youth had been a reckless tough, running around with a leather-jacket gang with a reputation for drunkenness. Schur (1971) notes that retrospective interpretation also tends to occur when social control agencies prepare reports on deviants for purposes of determining an appropriate disposition. These include presentence investigation reports for both adults and juveniles, parole violation reports, and, in the mental health area, case-history reports. These reports can be structured in such a way as to reinforce a definition of the person as deviant and to further justify his or her institutionalization. This is not to suggest the information in these reports is not true, but it is not too difficult to find facts in almost anyone's past history to justify a current label and/or disposition.

Stereotyping and the Self-fulfilling Prophecy

In responding to deviants, people are not likely to adopt a "wait and see" attitude but instead are likely to base their response on preconceptions of deviants and their behavior. In some instances, these preconceptions, or **stereotypes,** are part of early childhood learning, while in other cases they are acquired through the selective portrayal of deviants by newspapers, television, and friends and associates.

Thus, there is a tendency to view deviants not in terms of how they are, but instead in terms of how they are expected to be. For example, once a youngster is labeled a delinquent, teachers, parents, store owners, etc., tend to expect the child to engage in further delinquency. In fact, this youngster is generally the first to be accused when property is missing, damaged, or destroyed. Other parents are likely to forbid their children to play with him for fear that he will influence them to engage in delinquency. In short, the deviant may find it difficult to participate in conventional groups and activities and, consequently, may find that his or her only opportunities lie in involvement in further deviance. Thus, **stereotyping** can serve to set into motion the mechanisms of the **self-fulfilling prophecy.** That is, when people are treated according to popular conceptions of how they are supposed to behave, the result may be that they are given few, if any, other options for alternative behavior.

Role Engulfment

Schur (1971) has used the term **role engulfment** to refer to the sociopsychological impact of labeling on the individual's self-identity. At issue here is the question "When does a person accept a deviant designation?" This is the last step in the process we described earlier as secondary deviance. While the process as we outlined it is a fairly accurate general description, the content of the specific actions and reactions and the period over which they will occur all vary according to the individual, the particular deviation, and the social environment. At the heart of the role engulfment process is the fact that deviance is a *master* or *pivotal status* (Becker, 1963; Lofland, 1969; Schur, 1971). Once a person is identified as a deviant, this status tends to overshadow all other statuses, which makes it difficult for the individual to deny the validity of the deviant label.

Accepting a Deviant Identity   The exact point in time when the individual develops a deviant self-concept varies according to a number of circumstances. It could occur at the point of public recognition, following status degradation ceremonies—formal acts of community censure, such as a criminal trial or a commitment hearing to institutionalize someone who is diagnosed as mentally ill—or at some time during the individual's first institutional experience, or it may even take place after the individual tries unsuccessfully to resume his or her normal roles following the first institutional commitment. For the alcoholic, it may come at the point where a stay in jail or a detoxification center represents an opportunity to receive shelter and some wholesome food. For the juvenile, it may occur at the point of apprehension by the police, although it is far more likely to take place following detention, a juvenile court appearance, or commitment to a training school. While some adults may accept a deviant identity following their experiences with the police and court system, most who have resisted up to this point will find such resistance difficult once they are placed in a maximum- or medium-security prison.

Disavowal of Deviance   Another important dimension of role engulfment is the difficulty experienced by the deviant in **disavowing his or her deviancy** and moving back into the mainstream of social life. The ex-convict, the juvenile released from a training school, the former mental patient, or the drug addict who has successfully completed a treatment program all face problems in convincing people they have changed since their institutionalization. Part of the difficulties encountered by deviants wishing to shake off their prior identities results from the fact that there is no terminal ceremony which marks the removal of the individual's deviant status. As Erikson (1964) observes, the deviant "is ushered into the deviant position by a decisive and often dramatic ceremony, yet is retired from it with hardly a word or public notice and as a result, the deviant often returns home with no proper license to resume a normal life in the community. Nothing has happened to cancel out the stigmas imposed upon him by earlier commitment ceremonies; from a formal point of view, the original verdict or diagnosis is still in effect" (pp. 16–17).

The disavowal of deviance is made additionally difficult because many people are reluctant to believe it is possible for someone to change his or her character; since there is no visible change, people find it hard to accept that any change at all has taken place. The ex-deviant is discouraged in his or her effort to obtain employment even in the most menial occupations. It is this very type of response that prompts deviants to abandon their efforts to participate in conventional groups and activities and to return to deviant associates and activities. If ex-convicts cannot obtain legitimate employment they are left with little alternative but to return to a life of crime in order to support themselves; that is, if they can't find a job they will "do a job" (Potter, 1982). Moreover, for those deviants unable to be accepted by conventional society and for those who did wish to give up their deviant activities, participation in deviant subcultures, as the next section notes, provides a means of insulating them from the demoralization and negative self-concepts that often result from being labeled a deviant.

Subculture Involvement   The involvement of many deviants in deviant groups or subcultures is a direct consequence of their exclusion from conventional groups and activities. Participation in deviant groups and subcultures serves a variety of functions for the deviant, including (1) providing a set of rationalizations and neutralizations for deviant activities that serve to protect the individual from negative attitudes of outsiders; (2) furnishing the deviant with more effective techniques for pursuing deviant behavior and thus providing protection from detection and apprehension; and (3) facilitating the acquisition of contacts, goods, and services that are necessary for the contunuation of deviant behavior. Deviants participate in subcultures because they find that these environments support and encourage their deviant activity. In short, they have "found a home."

From another standpoint, movement into a deviant group can also represent the final step in the individual's acceptance of a deviant identity. For example, juveniles gravitate to delinquent groups because they are excluded from peer groups and also from adult-sponsored activities such as school events, church groups, and Scouts. Delinquents participate in gangs because they provide companionship, support, and acceptance. Gangs also supply members with a system of rationalizations that serves to neutralize and justify their delinquent identities and behavior. In addition, gang participation enables the delinquent to develop more skillful means of carrying on delinquent activities.

Bargaining and Negotiation

The labeling orientation has also made us cognizant of the fact that various forms of bargaining and negotiation may be key elements in the labeling of certain types of deviants. **Negotiation** takes place at various stages in the labeling process and as a result may affect (1) whether a person is labeled, (2) the type of label an individual receives, and (3) the treatment received following detection. To some extent, this rests on the discretionary power available to agents of the system. At every stage of the process, from detection to release, system functionaries have a wide range of discretion. The exercise of this discretion is influenced by factors such as individual characteristics, stereotypes, retrospective interpretation of the individual's past behavior, and also by organizational pressures for low-cost, efficient procedures. Police may ignore an offender's petty violations or recommend that he or she be charged with a lesser offense in exchange for receiving information or assistance in the solution of other cases. Our court system provides a classic illustration of a process that is dependent upon negotiation in order to operate smoothly. The only way the courts can function effectively is to resolve most of their cases through plea bargaining with only a minimum number going to trial.

In conclusion, it is important to note that a variety of factors affect an individual's bargaining position. These include such considerations as (1) social characteristics, that is, individual and family status, race/ethnic status and social class; (2)

circumstances surrounding the incident; (3) public reaction; (4) the offender's value to the agents of the system, for example as an informant; (5) expediency; (6) community tolerance; (7) agency policy; and (8) available resources. This suggests that, once detected, whether a person is labeled a deviant depends to some extent on factors other than the nature and seriousness of the offense.

ORGANIZATIONAL PROCESSING

It should be clear from the foregoing analysis of the basic process involved in the application of deviant labels that the responses of formal organizations are the most critical with respect to whether a person's deviant acts will result in his or her being labeled a deviant. In looking at the role played by organizations in the processing of deviants, attention focuses on certain formal, as well as informal, organizational patterns that influence deviance outcomes (Schur, 1971). The emphasis here is on the agencies involved, roles played by their personnel, and formal and informal processing of people who commit deviant acts.

Organizations play a major role in the selection of those whose deviant acts will result in formal attention. Labeling has alerted us to some of the factors that influence this decision. We have already noted the importance stereotypes play in the reaction of the public to deviants. These also affect the identification of deviants by social control agents. A study of police encounters with juveniles found that a police officer's decision whether to take formal action was dependent on a youth's demeanor, mode of dress, and affiliations, as well as other characteristics (Piliavin and Briar, 1964). Specifically, it has found that more severe dispositions were given to known members of delinquent gangs; blacks; older juveniles; youths with well-oiled hair, soiled denims, and black leather jackets; and boys who were disrespectful to police.

The size of an agency's staff has been found to be related to the volume of people selected (Lofland, 1969). That is, if the number of police at work in a given jurisdiction is increased, there is likely to be an increase in the number of reported crimes. Lofland (1969) has noted that training and specialization also influence selection. Thus, a police department with a specialized juvenile unit comprising trained officers is likely to have higher arrest rates for juveniles than a department lacking such a unit.

In instances where agencies coordinate their activities to form a network, cooperation—or the lack of it—is another factor that influences the selection process. The number and type of deviants identified are likely to be greater when agencies cooperate than when they operate at cross-purposes. The mere identification of an individual as deviant by more than one social agency lends credence to official processing. For example, youths who are identified as troublemakers by the school and subsequently apprehended for delinquent acts are more likely to be referred to the juvenile court for formal action.

Labeling has alerted us to the significance of the informal side of organizational activity (Schur, 1971). With respect to the criminal justice process, one of the most important considerations that forms the basis for the development of informal norms is the discretion allowed functionaries (e.g., police officers, probation officers) in terms of whether or not to take formal action and the type of formal action to be taken. Bittner (1969) found that a patrol officer's decision to take formal action in a skid-row area was determined by such factors as personal knowledge of the community and its residents and informal understandings between officers and community residents, and was characterized by ad hoc decision making that was geared more to the special problems of this type of police work than to formal categories of the law.

In a related way, we have been prompted by this orientation to study the "managers" of the various social control agencies. Goffman's *Asylums* (1961) focused not only on patients but also on the staff of total institutions (e.g., mental hospitals, prisons), providing some valuable insights into the problems they face in handling institutionalized deviants. Skolnick (1966) scrutinized the factors, often conflicting, that influence police behavior. It was his view that the elements of danger and authority, combined with the constant pressure to be efficient, produced a distinctive "working personality" that affects the way police perceive and respond to their environment.

Another consideration in organizational processing of deviants to which labeling alerts us is the ways in which internal and external relations influence an organization's work (Schur, 1971). Unlike private companies who can set their own policies, social control agencies must consider a variety of both public and private organizations and individuals when determining their operating policies. Government units like the legislature, city council, or mayor's office typically provide broad guidelines for the operation of these agencies, or in some instances may even exert direct control or supervision; they certainly exert control by virtue of their funding authority. The old maxim "he who pays the piper decides on the song" is quite applicable. Public agencies must also be responsive to pressures from interest groups, particularly those that have political influence.

In formulating policies, these agencies must consider the views of the public and mass media, as well as agencies that the organization must interact with and private sources of funding and support. Skolnick found, for example, that police departments tended to direct their efforts toward increasing the number of cases cleared in order to raise their clearance rate (ratio of number of cases cleared to number of cases recorded) because this was viewed by police experts, government officials, and the public as a major indicator of efficiency. He discovered that an emphasis on this objective tended to result in the failure to record some reported offenses and in some instances even resulted in fraud and a reversal of the hierarchy of penalties associated with criminal offenses. That is, offenders who could provide detectives with clearances (either due to their participation in yet more undetected offenses or their willingness to admit to offenses they had not committed) may, in some instances, have received sentences that were less severe than offenders who also could not and were originally charged with the same or a less serious offense.

Still another result of the organizational process involves the collection of official data by social control agencies. We have already discussed in detail the problems associated with the collection and tabulation of official statistics on crime. Of relevance here is the role played by these agencies in managing statistics to influence public conceptions of and policies toward deviants. In this regard some organizations may benefit by increased funding from statistics that show crime is increasing dramatically, while for other organizations it may have an adverse effect. Thus, on the one hand, this may justify funding for more patrol officers and equipment while, on the other hand, it may lead to pressure for more punitive treatment of offenders.

In conclusion, while most of these concerns are not new or unique to labeling, this perspective provides a good framework for organization and systematic analysis of these factors.

COLLECTIVE RULE MAKING AND ENFORCEMENT

Finally, labeling has focused attention on the dynamics of the processes associated with rule institution, modification, repeal, and enforcement. It is naive to assume rule enforcement is automatic or inevitable or that rule changes are the result of recognition that modification is necessary in order to bring them into conformity with our basic social values. Becker has alerted us to the fact that rules are not necessarily generated to protect social values.

> People shape values into specific rules and problematic situations. They perceive some area of their existence as troublesome or difficult, requiring action. After considering the various values to which they subscribe, they select one or more of them as relevant to their difficulties and deduce from it a specific rule [p. 131].

Becker is suggesting rules develop only when values become threatened. It should also be noted that instituting a rule to protect one value may result in the violation of another. While there is no question that freedom is a basic value in our society, there are numerous instances of rules that restrict our freedom in order to protect some other values from threat. We have rules that restrict the means by which people can obtain property, as well as the way they can treat other people.

Labeling theorists have also pointed to the role played by interest groups in the passage, modification, and repeal of laws. The idea that rules result from consensus among various segments of the population regarding behavior that is threatening and the appropriate sanctions that should be imposed against those who engage in this behavior is sheer fantasy. This is particularly true of a pluralistic society such as ours. The process typically begins with an individual or group singling out some form of behavior as injurious, troublesome, or harmful to some group in society (e.g., to children, to society at large, or to offenders themselves). The next step is to convince others of the need to prohibit this behavior and concomitantly to institute sanctions against those who engage in it. Temperance leaders lobbied for prohibition by describing alcohol as "demon rum" and maintaining that it made the drinker generally lazy and disinclined to work, caused him to molest women and steal from his friends and family, and led him to entice others to share his vice. In a similar manner, prior to passage of the Marijuana Tax Act in 1934, this drug was portrayed as destroying a person's sanity, causing a person to commit heinous crimes while under the influence, and leading those who were addicts to force their habit on others, particularly small children (Glaser, 1971). Since laws are not passed simply by arousing public opinion, the next step is to marshall support for the prohibition of this behavior among those who have the power to establish rules that define it as deviant. In other words, rule making is a dynamic process affected by such factors as the size of the group that feels threatened by the behavior and its ability to marshall additional support, especially among those with legislative power. All of this is influenced by the extent to which the behavior is perceived as threatening, injurious, or disruptive.

Schur (1971) notes that the impetus for prohibition of, as well as the enforcement of rules against, certain types of behavior may emanate from social control agencies. Both Becker (1963) and Dickenson (1968) have drawn attention to the Federal Bureau of Narcotics and its role in the reinterpretation of the Harrison Narcotics Tax Act and the passage of the Marijuana Tax Act.

Labeling theory shares an interest in the development of social rules with conflict theory. While both see rule making as resulting from group conflict, Marxian conflict theorists see the development of social rules as a means employed by the dominant class to maintain its superiority over the subordinate classes.

CRITIQUE

It is easy to draw the conclusion from the foregoing discussion that the proponents of the labeling perspective subscribe to a common group of ideas and assumptions. This impression must be dispelled before we proceed any further. Far from being a theory or unified perspective, labeling can best be described as an area of concern which has been the focus of attention of a number of writers and researchers. Any effort at assessment must therefore be directed toward the work of a specific author or be based on the evaluator's judgment of what constitutes propositions that are associated with his or her view. For example, Schrag (1971) identified nine basic assumption of labeling. However, not all proponents of this view would consider these propositions central to this position. We will nevertheless attempt to provide an assessment of this position, fully recognizing its limitations.

Labeling Causes Deviance?

To begin with, it is important to dispel the impression that labeling theorists are suggesting that the actual behavior is unimportant in determining deviance because it is the social reaction that creates the deviance. That is, a literal interpretation of the work of some labeling proponents might lead to the conclusion that they are contending deviants are no different behaviorally from nondeviants and the only thing that distinguishes them is the social reaction. This idea is well portrayed by Akers (1973) in the following statement.

> One sometimes gets the impression from reading the literature on labeling that people go about, minding their own business, and then wham—bad society comes along and slaps on them a stigmatized label. Thus forced into the role of deviant, the individual has little choice but to be deviant. The "good" guys become the "bad" guys, and the bad become the good [p. 24].

Thus, it is easy to assume proponents of this view consider factors that lead people to engage in deviant behavior to be irrelevant. While some sociologists with this orientation may come close to espousing this position, the vast majority of people associated with the perspective do not subscribe to such an extreme view. For example, Schur (1971), in discussing this very issue, points out that labeling advocates are not suggesting "that the behavior we call 'homicide,' 'mental illness,' 'homosexuality,' and 'theft' would not occur if it were not defined as 'deviant' " (p.16). Moreover, Lemert, one of the major architects of this position, distinguishes between primary and secondary deviation. It will be recalled that primary deviation focused on the precipitating causes of deviant behavior. In fact, Lemert (1967) saw deviance as resulting from recurring or accidental combinations of cultural, social, psychological, and physiological factors. Most of the confusion arises, however, because proponents of this view have begun their analysis with the social reaction process. This should not be taken to mean they consider causal factors irrelevant. In other words, adherents to this position have simply taken as their major focus the explanation of the amplification and mantenance of deviance, leaving to others the problem of explaining the origin of the behavior. That is, their major concern has been on the processes by which persons and behaviors have come to be perceived, defined, and treated as deviant.

The Role of Social Characteristics in Labeling

Central to the labeling position is the contention that social control agents react to factors other than the individual's behavior in deciding whether to label a person deviant. The research on this question is far from conclusive. It is beyond the scope of the present discussion to review all the studies relevant to this question. We consider it fair, however, to conclude that there is some validity to this proposition, although in the area of crime and delinquency it would appear that offense-related characteristics are more important than other variables (Lemert, 1976; Nettler, 1978; Tittle, 1975; Wellford, 1975; and Paternoster and Iovanni, 1984). However, a review of some recent studies of adult justice suggests that the race of the victim is critical in the decisions by the police and courts regarding the handling of the offender.

Inevitability of the Self-fulfilling Prophecy

An evaluation of this position would not be complete if we failed to assess the validity of the proposition that labeling leads to further deviance, and an altered self-concept and style of life. Critics have attacked labeling theory on the grounds that its proponents view this process as automatic; the critics are correct in questioning this rather deterministic assertion. There is evidence that some types of offenders develop deviant careers without labeling, that others develop careers prior to labeling, and that labeling does not necessarily result in additional deviance or a deviant career. Research shows that marijuana users, most check forgers, and embezzlers pursue careers without labeling ever having taken place. On the other hand, Sutherland (1937) found that bunco artists and pickpockets became career offenders prior to, rather than after, being labeled. At least two studies on shoplifting (Cameron, 1964; Cohn and Stark, 1974) indicate that these offenders seldom repeat the crime, once they have been apprehended.

Tittle (1975) tried to shed some light on whether labeling produces subsequent deviant behavior. He examined 16 longitudinal studies that reported failure rates for inmates on parole and those released from institutions. Despite the fact that some of these offenders were returned for technical violations of parole, it is Tittle's contention that if social reaction does produce subsequent deviance, recidivism rates of ex-offenders should be much greater than chance, that is, greater than 50-50. The studies he examined showed that failure rates ranged from 24 percent to 68 percent with the average being 44 percent.

Studies that have also dealt with the effects of labeling on the subsequent behavior of juveniles provide inconsistent results, as indicated by the summary in Table 13.1. With respect to research on the impact of labeling on a youth's values, commitments, self-image, and social relationships, results are equally inconclusive. Some studies (e.g., Foster, Dinitz, and Reckless, 1972) have found that official encounters with police or courts failed to adversely affect interpersonal relationships. Other studies suggest that labeling may produce negative effects on school performance (Fisher, 1972), self-esteem (Jensen, 1972), and orientation toward further delinquency (Ageton and Elliott, 1974). Still other research (Hepburn, 1977) found that official intervention was not related to either self-satisfaction or delinquent identification.

These findings show the self-fulfilling prophecy is far from inevitable. It would seem that a variety of factors affect whether an individual continues his or her career once labeled, and in fact, labeling would appear to be of little value in understanding the involvement of some people in deviance. Part of the reason this aspect of labeling has been subjected to some criticism is because the critics have failed to recognize

Table 13.1 RESEARCH DEALING WITH THE EFFECTS OF LABELING ON SUBSEQUENT BEHAVIOR OF JUVENILES

Author and date	Subject group	Conclusions
Thornberry, 1971	Male adolescent delinquents	Found no relationship between severity of disposition and subsequent criminality
McEachern, 1968	Male adolescent delinquents	Reported that youths adjudicated delinquent and made wards of the court were involved in less delinquency than those who were dealt with less severely
Meade, 1974	Male adolescent delinquents	Youths who experienced court hearings had higher rates of subsequent detected delinquency than those who were dealt with informally
Haney and Gold, 1973	Male adolescent delinquents	Apprehended youngsters committed more subsequent offenses than did unapprehended matching youngsters

that most of the advocates of this position see labeling as a dynamic process which is affected by a number of social and individual factors. We will address this issue in the following conclusions to this discussion.

CONCLUSIONS

An important source of confusion is the tendency to look at labeling from a deterministic orientation—that labeling provides an explanation both for the origins and the development and persistence of deviance. A close reading of some of the principal proponents of labeling discloses that this approach was never meant to be an all-encompassing position, nor was it intended to suggest that social reactions to deviant behavior automatically propel a person along a path with no exits, resulting in an individual's being bound to become a career deviant (Conover, 1976; Kisuse, 1975; Schur, 1975). As Jensen (1980) notes, there is a need for further research on the differential impact of labels and sanctions for various groups and in different situations or at various points in time. Instead, the aim was to sensitize us to a process that contributes to the amplification and persistence of some forms of deviance. It would be far more useful to look at deviance as a process which follows a variety of paths, one of which is labeling. Viewing labeling as one path must also include the notion that this path has exits. This directs us toward specifying the proportion, conditions, and types of deviance that proceed along this path, exit from it, or follow other paths.

Thorsell and Klemke (1972) discuss the potentialities for differential outcomes of the labeling process. First, they suggest that labeling appears to have different effects depending upon the stage at which it is applied in the person's deviant career. Individuals who undergo labeling at a point when they are first experimenting with crime and delinquency are more likely to end their deviance than to be propelled into a deviant career. Cameron (1964) found that, following apprehension, novice shoplifters usually stopped their activity. She accounted for this on the grounds that novice pilferers did not regard themselves as thieves prior to arrest, and also lacked group support for such a role; hence, being labeled and apprehended resulted in rejection of that role.

Second, Thorsell and Klemke contend that whether the label is ascribed in a confidential or public manner makes a difference with respect to the individual's tendency to continue engaging in deviant behavior. They maintain that labeling which is carried out in a confidential and limited fashion (e.g., in the office of the manager of a department store) differs considerably in impact from that which takes place before a public audience (e.g., in a criminal trial).

It is also noted that even public labeling does not necessarily result in the continuation or intensification of deviant behavior. In an urban industrial society, official labeling ceremonies can be kept secret in some instances, and thus their adverse effect can be minimized.

Third, labeling is more likely to be positive than negative when the deviant is concerned about, and therefore more sensitive to, the way he is viewed by the person doing the labeling. This suggests the need to examine the circumstances surrounding this relationship. On the one hand, deviants involved in groups or subcultures that provide support and justification for their behavior are less likely to be committed to those who ascribe the label of deviant. On the other hand, delinquents, criminals, and other deviants experimenting with various forms of nonconventional behavior may terminate their behavior as the result of an adverse evaluation by people whose views are important to them. For example, juveniles apprehended by the police for delinquent behavior and taken home to their parents (to whom they are committed), may be deterred from further delinquent behavior as a consequence of having been chastised by the parents.

Fourth, whether the label can be easily removed is likely to be an important factor in the stigmatized person's ability to resume conventional roles. In the case of crime, Schwartz and Skolnick (1964) concluded that knowledge of an arrest record, regardless of whether the individual was convicted or acquitted, markedly limited the number of job opportunities for individuals, particularly those in the lower class. It is on this basis that many legal authorities have argued for the expungement of the records of persons who have successfully completed their terms of probation and parole as well as those who are released from correctional institutions.

Fifth, Thorsell and Klemke (1972) state that "the nature of the social reaction which follows or accompanies the application of a label is of central importance in determining whether the outcome of the process will be positive or negative" (p. 400). Thus, the effect of labeling to some extent depends on how the people with whom an individual interacts, particularly those whose friendship, advice, and respect is valued, respond to his or her being identified as deviant. Viewed from this vantage point, the labeling process results in a variety of social responses, ranging from those which are positive, supportive, and sustain existing relationships, to those which are negative, rejecting, and result in the disintegration of conventional relationships. This suggests one reason some juvenile delinquents and adult criminals do not continue antisocial behavior following apprehension and conviction for a crime is that the effects of labeling are neutralized when the offender is able to resume conventional roles as a result of the acceptance he or she receives from family and friends.

Sixth, it is suggested that positive labeling—within reasonable limits—can serve to stimulate the frequency of desirable behavior. This points out the need for us to recognize that positive labels may motivate people to live up to the expectations associated with the label. A study conducted by Rosenthal and Jacobson (1968) illustrates how labeling can be a stimulus to desirable behavior. In this study, teachers were informed that certain students labeled "spurters," based on intelligence tests given at the end of the previous year, could be expected to achieve substantial academic gains during the coming school year. In reality, the "spurters" were chosen at random from a list of students in the school; hence, the ascribed differences between these students and other pupils were completely in the minds of the teachers. At the end of the school year, the "special students" were found to have made significant gains in intellectual development based on IQ test scores as compared with the other children in the school. Moreover, these children were described by their teachers as happier, more interested, more curious, more appealing, better adjusted, more affectionate, and as having a better chance of being successful in later life than the other children. Perhaps we need to give some serious consideration to developing positive labels which can be applied to offenders to produce acceptance, support, and expectations of success.

The Value of the Labeling Perspective

The major contribution of the labeling perspective has been to shift our attention from preoccupation with causal factors in deviance to the processes that affect amplification and persistence of deviant behavior. Labeling can be seen as complementing those criminological theories which seek to account for the origins and development of deviance. The research that has been undertaken in efforts to either challenge or support the labeling perspective has expanded our understanding of deviant behavior and sensitized us to factors that affect the role of rule enforcement and rule change. From a policy standpoint, the labeling perspective has provided much of the impetus for diverting or removing, at the earliest point, as many offenders as possible from the juvenile and criminal justice systems. At this point, as Paternoster and Iovani (1984) suggest, research must move beyond the simple idea that labeling leads to deviance to specify for whom and what conditions sanctions will result in the onset of a deviant career.

SUMMARY

In this chapter, we have examined the labeling perspective, which focuses attention on the significance of the social reaction process for the amplification and stabilization of delinquent careers. It was suggested that the imposition of a deviant label may result in individuals being regarded as deviant and being expected to engage in subsequent deviant behavior; being denied participation in conventional groups and activities; changing their life-styles and redefining their self-concepts; and participating in deviant groups which may provide effective techniques for pursuing, and a set of rationalizations for neutralizing, these normative violations. This perspective recognizes the need to examine the factors which affect rule enforcement, modification, repeal, and enactment. Note was also made of the necessity to examine the agencies that are responsible for the control and treatment of deviance. In some instances, formal treatment of deviant behavior can do more harm than good.

DISCUSSION QUESTIONS

Find the answers to the following questions in the text.
1. What is meant by Thomas's statement that "If men define situations as real, they are real in their consequences"?
2. What are the major concerns of labeling?
3. Distinguish between **primary and secondary deviance.**
4. How does **stereotyping** contribute to the operation of the **self-fulfilling prophecy?**
5. Define **role engulfment.**
6. What problems are experienced by deviants who attempt to " **disavow" their deviancy**?
7. Why do deviants participate in subcultures?

8. What is the role of bargaining and **negotiation** in the labeling of certain types of deviants?

9. Describe the role of organization processing of deviants.

10. Describe the nature of the rule-making process.

11. Discuss the issue of labeling as a cause of deviant behavior.

12. What conclusions can be drawn from an examination of the labeling perspective?

TERMS TO IDENTIFY AND REMEMBER

tagging

secondary deviance

retrospective interpretation

stereotyping

organizational processing

disavowal of deviance

social reaction

primary deviance

biographical reconstruction

self-fulfilling prophecy

role engulfment

collective rule making

negotiation

interactionist approach

REFERENCES

Ageton, S. S., and Elliott, D. S. The effects of legal processing on delinquent orientation. *Social Problems,* 22 (October 1974): 87–100.

Akers, R. Deviant behavior: *A Social Learning Approach.* Belmont, CA: Wadsworth, 1973.

Becker, H. *Outsiders: Studies in the Sociology of Deviance.* New York: The Free Press, 1963.

Cameron, M. O. *The Booster and the Snitch.* New York: The Free Press, 1964.

Cicound, A. V. *The Social Organization of Juvenile Justice.* New York: Wiley, 1968.

Cohen, L. E., and Stark, R. Discriminatory labeling and the five-finger discount. *Journal of Research in Crime and Delinquency,* 11 (January 1974): 25–39.

Conover, P. W. A reassessment of labeling theory: A constructive response to critism. In L. Coser and O. Larsen (eds.), *The Uses of Controversy in Sociology.* New York: The Free Press, 1976.

Dickson, D. T. Bureaucracy and morality: An organizational perspective on a moral crusade. *Social Problems* 16, no. 2 (Fall 1968): 143–156.

Erikson, K. T. Notes on the sociology of deviance. In H. S. Becker (ed.), *The Other Side.* New York: The Free Press, 1964.

Fisher, S. Stigma and deviant careers in schools. *Social Problems,* 20, no. 1 (Summer 1972): 78–83.

Foster, J. D., Dinitz, S., and Reckless, W. C. Perceptions of stigma following public intervention for delinquent behavior. *Social Problems* 20, no. 1 (Fall 1972): 202–209.

Garfinkel, H. Conditions of successful degradation ceremonies. *The American Journal of Sociology* 61 (March 1956): 420–24.

Glaser, D. *Social Deviance.* Chicago: Markham, 1971.

Goffman, E. *Asylums.* Garden City, NY: Doubleday Anchor, 1961.

Gold, M. *Delinquent Behavior in an American City.* Monterey, CA: Brooks/Cole, 1970.

Haney, B., and Gold, M. The juvenile delinquent nobody knows. *Psychology Today* 7, no. 4 (1973): 49–54.

Hepburn, J. R. The impact of police intervention upon juvenile delinquents. *Criminology* (August 1977): 235–262.

Jensen, G. F. Delinquency and adolescent self-concepts: A study of the personal relevance of infraction. *Social Problems,* 20, no. 1 (Summer 1972): 84–103.

————. Parents, peers, and delinquents: A test of the differential association by others. *American Journal of Sociology* 78 (Nov. 1972): 562–75.

————. Inner containment and delinquency. *Journal of Criminal Law and Criminology* 64 (1973): 464–470.

Jensen, G. F., and Erickson, M. L. The social meaning of sanctions. In D. Krohn and L. Akers (eds.), *Crime, Law, and Sanctions.* Beverly Hills, London: Sage, 1978.

Kituse, J. I. Deviance, deviant behaviour, and deviants: Some conceptual problems. In W. J. Filstead (ed.), *An Introduction to Deviance: Readings in the Process of Making Deviants.* Chicago: Markham, 1972.

————. The "new conception of deviance" and its critics. In Walter R. Gove (ed.), *The Labeling of Deviance.* New York: Sage, 1975.

Lemert, E. M. *Social Pathology.* New York: McGraw-Hill, 1951.

————. *Human Deviance, Social Problems, and Social Control.* Englewood Cliffs, NJ: Prentice-Hall, 1967.

————. Response to critics: Feedback and choice. In L. Coser and O. Larsen (eds.), *The Uses of Controversy in Sociology.* New York: The Free Press, 1976.

Lofland, J. *Deviance and Identity.* Englewood Cliffs, NJ: Prentice-Hall, 1969.

Mead, G. H. The psychology of punitive justice. *American Journal of Sociology* (1917–1918): 577–602.

Meade, A. C. The labeling approach to delinquency: State of the theory as function of method. *Social Forces* (September 1974): 83–91.

Nettler, G. N. *Explaining Crime.* New York: McGraw-Hill, 1978.

Parmelee, M. *Criminology.* New York: Macmillan, 1918.

Rosenthal, R., and Jacobson, F. *Pygmalion in the Classroom: Teacher Expectations and Pupil Intellectual Development.* New York: Holt, Rinehart and Winston, 1968.

Scheff, T. *Being Mentally Ill.* Chicago: Aldine, 1966.

Schrag, C. *Crime and Justice: American Style.* Rockville, MD: National Institute of Mental Health, 1971.

Schur, E. M. *Labeling Deviant: Its Sociological Implications.* New York: Harper & Row, 1971.

Schwartz, R., and Skolnick, J. H. Two studies of legal stigma. In H. Becker (ed.), *The Other Side: Perspectives on Deviance.* New York: The Free Press, 1964.

Skolnick, J. H. *Justice Without Trial.* New York: Wiley, 1966.

Sutherland, E. W. *The Professional Thief.* Chicago: University of Chicago Press, 1937.

Tannebaum, F. *Crime and the Community.* New York: Columbia University Press, 1938.

Thomas, W. I. *The Unadjusted Girl.* Boston: Little, Brown, 1923.

Thornberry, T. P. Punishment and crime: The effect of legal dispositions on subsequent criminal behavior. Unpublished Ph.D. dissertation, University of Pennsylvania, 1971.

Thorsell, B. A., and Klemke, L. W. The labeling process: Reinforcement and deterrent. *Law and Society Review* 7 (1972): 372–92.

Tittle, C. R. Labeling and crime: An empirical evaluation. In Walter R. Gove (ed.), *The Labeling of Deviance.* New York: Sage, 1975.

Wellford, C. Labeling theory and criminology: An assessment. *Social Problems* 22, no. 3 (February 1975): 332–45.

Williams, J. R., and Gold, M. From delinquent behavior to official delinquency. *Social Problems* 20, (1972): 209–29.

Wolfgang, M. E., Figlio, R. M., and Sellin, T. *Delinquency in a Birth Cohort.* Chicago: University of Chicago Press, 1972.

chapter 14

PSYCHIATRIC AND PSYCHOLOGICAL THEORIES OF CRIMINALITY

If your household has been looted to your last remaining dime,
By some gentleman recruited from the serried ranks of crime,
Do not think that he was stealing that his pockets he might fill,
But remember he was feeling rather ill. . . .

Men who rob you of your treasures, or who beat you out of spite, Men who think that theft's a pleasure, and that murder's a delight, Men who with their shell games venture to entrap the guileless hick, Should be never named with censure; they are sick.

JAMES J. MONTAGUE (1873–1941)
Who Can Blame Him?

Psychiatry is a branch of medicine; psychology is one of the behavioral sciences. Although ideas pass freely between them, psychiatrists tend to interpret criminality within a *clinical* perspective. Criminal behavior is viewed as a personality disturbance or even a type of mental illness, as the satirical verses above suggest. Thus, dealing with criminality is seen as a task requiring treatment or psychotherapy.

Psychologists, on the other hand, interpret criminality or criminal conduct as a problem in the acquisition or learning of behavior patterns that conform to the same principles as those which govern the learning of any other kinds of behavior, prosocial as well as antisocial. Coping with criminality according to this perspective is mainly a matter of exchanging the factors or variables which help to maintain and reinforce criminal behavior for other variables which provide reinforcement for noncriminal behavior. The laboratory is regarded as a more promising place than the clinic to find potential explanations for criminality.

A bridge between psychiatry and psychology has been supplied by **psychoanalysis,** the body of concepts originally developed by Sigmund Freud and subsequently elaborated and modified by Alfred Adler, Otto Rank, Karen Horney, Erik Erikson, and others. The imaginative terms and ideas used by psychoanalysts to describe the structure and dynamics of personality, its origins and development, its sources of conflict, frustration, and motivation, gave psychiatry and psychology a common conceptual vocabulary for mutual communication. Psychiatrists readily adopted the psychoanalytic theories which bore upon the kinds of maladaptive behavior identified as neurosis, psychosis, and character disorders; psychologists expended considerable effort attempting to reproduce under laboratory conditions such processes as repression ("motivated forgetting") and regression. Most importantly, psychoanalysis provided a theoretical framework for interpreting crime and delinquent behavior in terms of the same processes that were used to explain mental illness. We shall discuss the contributions of psychoanalytic criminology in a later section.

Differences between psychiatrists and psychologists, we must emphasize, are not absolute: some psychiatrists reject the "mental illness" model as a valid basis for interpreting deviant behavior, including criminality; and there is no unanimous endorsement of the learning theory perspective among psychologists. Nevertheless, the distinctions between psychiatry and psychology are extremely important for an understanding of their respective approaches to criminological theory. Unfortunately, the differences are often blurred or ignored in some contemporary accounts.

PSYCHIATRY AND THE CRIMINALITY-AS-MENTAL-ILLNESS APPROACH

Professional practitioners of the medical specialty known as psychiatry have been invested with the responsibility for managing "mental illness." It is extremely difficult to accurately define "mental illness." This term is often used as a ready explanation for any kind of behavior that does not make sense to the observer, reveals no clear or reasonable motivation, or merely disturbs our sensibilities. The following examples illustrate the wide range of behavior that has been diagnosed as "mental illness":

1. In Baltimore, Maryland, a young man entreats the medical staff of a university clinic to perform a surgical operation on him in order to change his gender.
2. In New York, a young man is arrested following an intensive manhunt for a series of slayings of young persons for no apparent reason or motive. The murderer informs the authorities that he was ordered to commit these offenses by the voice of a 6,000-year-old man speaking through a neighbor's dog.
3. In St. Petersburg, Florida, a 55-year-old man is taken by the police to a civil detoxification center after having been found unconscious in a downtown public park from an excess of alcohol consumption. The man's record indicates that he has been picked up 47 times in a similar condition during the previous 5 years.
4. In Buffalo, New York, a nude middle-aged woman is taken into custody by the police after an attendant discovered her washing her clothes in a toilet bowl in the men's room at the Trailways bus depot.
5. In New Orleans, a 19-year-old college student is seen by a psychiatrist because of a compulsion to wash his hands so often in the course of a single day that the skin on his hands is raw, ulcerated, and bleeding.

This list contains only a hint of the scope and diversity of behavior that the "mental health" specialists may encounter, but we must emphasize that each of the examples cited above has been classified at one time or another as "mental illness." It is also apparent from the heterogeneity of these illustrations that "mental health" and "mental illness" do not refer to conditions that can be described with anything approaching the objectivity and precision which characterize the diagnosis of many types of physical illness. As the Rosenhan (1973) study described on page 382 demonstrated in a rather extreme form, psychiatric diagnoses are subject to severe problems of reliability and validity.

According to one viewpoint, "mental illness" can best be understood as a label which represents societal reactions to behavior that deviates from (or in some cases, conforms to) certain normative standards based on cultural values. It is held that the term "mental illness" is loosely and indiscriminately applied to psychosocial problems such as crime, promiscuity, marital infidelity, political fanaticism, general unhappiness and discontent and even to the behavior of those who manage to make themselves disliked.

In contrast to the fairly specific and objective criteria for determining most types of physical disease, the criteria and norms for defining "mental illness" are

Psychodiagnosis and Pseudodiagnosis

Psychologist David Rosenhan of Stanford University conducted a study in which eight normal people (including a psychiatrist, graduate student, painter, housewife, pediatrician, and three psychologists) gained admittance as pseudopatients to twelve public and private mental hospitals at various locations in the United States. Each person contacted a hospital and complained of hearing voices that seemed to say "empty" and "hollow" and "thud." Apart from accompanying indications of being nervous and uneasy during the initial interview, the behavior of the pseudopatients was normal. They gave a fictitious name and occupation to the diagnostician; otherwise all of the life history information they provided was authentic.

Eleven of the twelve admissions received a diagnosis of schizophrenia and one was identified as manic-depressive psychosis. These diagnostic assessments were arrived at primarily on the basis of the reported auditory hallucinations. The pseudopatients spent an average of 19 days per hospitalization, with a range of from 7 to 52 days. During their hospitalization, according to Rosenhan, they received over 2,100 pills. At discharge, the diagnosis was "schizophrenia in remission." In nearly every instance, the first persons to become aware of the true identity of the pseudopatients were the real patients.

If Rosenhan had merely reported that his study had found low validity for psychiatric judgments of mental illness, it is doubtful whether his article would have attracted much attention in professional circles. Instead, by making the very extreme claim that validity of judgments of mental illness is zero, his article was given an extraordinary reception.

Source: D. Rosenhan. On being sane in insane places. *Science* 179 (1973): 250–258.

neither specific nor objective, not are they separable from a multitude of ethical and social considerations implicit in the labeling process. Not surprisingly, therefore, the term "mental disease" is often applied in an indiscriminate way to a collection of social and interpersonal behaviors judged to be deviant according to varying psychological and cultural norms used by people in applying such labels. Understandably the definitions tend to be vague, lacking in uniformity and reliability, and are often remarkably circular. It would seem that the term *mental illness* is actually used in a metaphorical sense to refer to a variety of social and psychological maladjustments and related human problems.

In recent years it has been argued rather convincingly that "mental illness" may be more usefully considered a *social status* than a pathological condition. This contention is based on the claim that the "symptoms of mental illness" are ambiguously defined, widely distributed, and contingent upon social rather than medical interpretations of behavior. According to this formulation, societal reactions to deviant behavior constitute a fundamentally significant variable at every stage in the development of a deviant career. This simple but crucial consideration has not, until relatively recently, been sufficiently stressed in discussions of so-called mental illness.

Criminality as Mental Illness

Given the diversity of behavior that has been labeled "mental illness," it is not surprising to find that a good deal of criminal behavior has been included in this category. Bartol (1980) notes that brutal, senseless killings are almost invariably ascribed to perpetrators who are "sick" or "crazy." Why else would someone rape and butcher a small child? Anyone who commits such a heinous crime—so the argument runs—must obviously be mentally ill.

While psychiatric interpretations are considerably more sophisticated than public reactions to criminal conduct of this kind, psychiatrists still see crime as symptomatic of offenders' maladjustment and an indication of their need for professional help. Halleck (1965), in his historical review of American psychiatry and the criminal, stated that the criminal offender has been a source of interest to the psychiatrist

> . . . because he bears many startling resemblances to those we call mentally ill. When incarcerated (and sometimes before) the offender proved to be a miserable, unhappy person who could be observed to suffer in the same way as the mental patient. Psychoanalytic psychiatry taught us that those psychological mechanisms which produced neurotic suffering were also operant in individuals who demonstrated criminal behavior. These observations fostered psychiatry's hopes of contributing to the understanding and alteration of criminal behavior [pp. 1–2].

In the above passage, Halleck treads a thin line: he does not actually say that criminals *are* mentally ill, only that they bear "startling resemblances" to those who are.

Crime as Adaptation: Halleck   Seymour Halleck views the societal definition of normality as including two directions of adaptation to oppressive stress. One direction requires a passive acceptance of an oppressive situation and an effort to live within the rules of society (conformity). The other direction represents an attempt to change an oppressive situation by acting within the rules or by attempting to change the rules through legally approved individual or group action (activism). An understanding of relevant norms is, therefore, crucial to the issue of defining criminality.

Mental illness cannot be as precisely defined as criminality; there is no single model or definition which has found general agreement among the members of the psychiatric profession. Definitions of mental illness vary because of, among other reasons, cultural biases imposed upon the psychiatrist. Therefore, mental illness, like criminality, is a social definition. In addition, both mental illness and criminality, according to Halleck, are *adaptations to stress:*

> The stresses that lead to mental illness are often the same stresses that lead to crime. . . . While both mental illness behaviors and criminal behaviors provide a

certain degree of mastery over stress, the adaptations themselves often lead to some difficulty with the environment. Mental illness always has a maladaptive quality, and criminality usually has a maladaptive quality. . . .

We have previously noted that mental illness is characterized by the communication of personal suffering, by communication of an inability to control one's behavior, and by society's judgment of unreasonableness of behavior [p. 46].

Criminologists of a nonpsychiatric orientation would be inclined to take issue with Halleck's contention in the preceding passage that criminality "usually has a maladaptive quality." They would be quick to point out for example, that criminal behavior which occurs in an organizational context—corporate offenses, or "crimes in the suites"—incurs lower risks than those involved in street crime and is committed by people who are likely to be indistinguishable in social background and personal characteristics from psychiatrists themselves. At any rate, criminologists would sharply question whether *any* valid claims could be made for something as vague and ill-defined as "criminality" in general.

With regard to the communication of personal suffering, it must be acknowledged that the majority of criminals of nearly all kinds do not convey any evidence of personal suffering that is readily apparent to the observer while in the act or before being caught. The exception to this, of course, is what happens when the offender is apprehended, prosecuted, and convicted. Given such a sequence of events, there is strong likelihood that the criminal will manifest considerable personal anguish.

Inability to control one's behavior raises some very complicated issues. Concepts of free will and determinism are deeply involved in the question of individual self-control. As Menninger (1968) observes:

Free will—to a lawyer—is not a philosophical theory, a religious concept, or scientific hypothesis. It is a given, a basic assumption in legal theory and practice. To the psychiatrist, this position is preposterous; he seeks operational definitions of free and will. On the other hand, the psychiatrist's assumption that motivation and mentation can go on unconsciously is preposterous to lawyers, constituting a veritable self-contradiction in terms [pp. 96–97].

The law operates on the basic premise that most human actions are capable of being interpreted and understood in rational terms. Most criminal behavior, according to this position, can be explained on the basis of goal-seeking behavior which nearly anyone can recognize and comprehend. The law makes provision for exceptions to this rule where the behavior in question does not appear to be related to logical or rational goal attainment, but those exceptions are compelled to meet certain tests before they are admitted as a basis for excluding people from responsibility or accountability for their criminal conduct.

PSYCHOANALYSIS AND CRIMINALITY

The founder of psychoanalysis, Sigmund Freud, had no direct contact with any criminals during his lifetime, and in his extensive writings—24 volumes of *Collected*

Works—there are very few references to crime. Freud did not formulate a theory of criminality; psychoanalysis was intended to be a theoretical system for explaining *all* behavior. Specific applications of psychoanalytic theory were made by Freud's followers or by neo-Freudians (those who had fallen away from orthodoxy in their psychoanalytic doctrines), usually in the form of extended analyses of individual cases.

Much of psychoanalysis has entered into the mainstream, to the extent that terms such as *superego* and *Oedipus complex* have entered into pop art and culture, and even into our everyday language. We speak familiarly of "ego trips," of "Freudian slips," and of psychoanalyzing our friends and relatives. Indeed, so pervasive is the influence of psychoanalysis in our culture and language that it often goes unrecognized as such.

Personality Structure and Dynamics

Freud conceived the development of each individual as dependent upon three principal sets of factors: (1) innate instinctual forces, (2) biologically determined developmental stages, and (3) environmental influences. Although all three sources of influence are important, the central factor in human development, to which Freud applied the term *psychosexual development,* is the sex instinct. As the infant matures, the sex instinct moves from one area of the body to another, causing the occurence of a series of stages, each denoted by the primary *erogenous zone* which constitutes the major area for sexual satisfaction during that phase. According to this schema, psychosexual development can be divided into three periods: infantile sexuality (from birth to approximately five years), latent phase, and puberty. Infantile sexuality can further be divided into the oral, anal, and phallic periods, the latter culminating in the Oedipus complex, the "family romance" in which the child wishes to have intimate relations with the parent of the opposite sex and harbors antagonism toward the parent of the same sex.

Freud postulated that personality is governed by three dynamic systems, to which he gave the names *id, ego,* and *superego.* The *id* consists of instinctual sexual and aggressive drives—the substratum of personality from which all other systems develop. It operates according to the "pleasure principle" by seeking tension reduction through the discharge of impulses. The ego develops as a control system which seeks drive satisfaction through contact with reality. The ego functions to control the impulsiveness of the id in order that drive satisfaction can be obtained, but within the limits imposed on the individual by society. The ego has control over all cognitive and intellectual functions. The superego is the moral element of personality: it represents the totality of internalized demands of parents and of society as a whole.

The most basic means by which the ego can control the id impulses is through the defense of repression. Through repression, the ego forces emerging id impulses to remain unconscious and not function in reality. Since the direct expression of sexual or aggressive impulses is forbidden by social norms, the superego and the id generally operate in opposition to one another. The struggle between the id and superego is often an intense encounter—one of the by-products of such a struggle is anxiety. Anxiety is a warning signal to the ego to take appropriate steps to control emerging impulses from overthrowing the system. Repression, then, provides the ego with its most direct mechanism for anxiety reduction: the sexual or aggressive impulse is forced back into the unconscious, and the delicate balance between the id and super-ego is maintained.

Criminality and the Unconscious

Behavior, as viewed within the psychoanalytic framework, is functional in the sense that it operates to fulfill certain needs or drives and has consequences for other aspects of behavior. But Freud's emphasis on the importance of unconscious factors in mental life adds an element of complexity to the interpretation of behavior. Freud and later psychoanalysts assume that much, if not most, of the behavior exhibited by an individual possesses meaning which lies outside the range of his or her awareness. Thus, the overt or observable behavior of a person must be considered merely the outward or *symbolic expression* of the underlying (i.e., unconscious) drives and impulses of which they are the manifestation.

The immediate and direct implication of this principle for understanding criminal behavior is that a focus upon the criminal action itself (manifest function) defeats any attempt to understand the etiology of the crime. Says Feldman (1969):

> . . . like any other behavior, criminal behavior is a form of self-expression, and what is intended to be expressed in the act of crime is not only unobservable in the act itself, but also may even be beyond the awareness of the criminal actor himself. So, for example, an overt criminal act of stealing may be undertaken for the attainment of purposes which are far removed from, and even contrary to, that of simple illegal aggrandizement; indeed, it may even be, as shall be seen in the sequel, that the criminal, in stealing, seeks not material gain but self-punishment. The etiological basis of a criminal act can, therefore, be understood only in terms of the functions, latent as well as manifest, which the act was intended to accomplish [p. 434].

Although the specific functions of a given criminal act must be sought in the life history of the individual offender, the general etiological formula for psychoanalytic criminology asserts that criminal behavior is an attempt at maintaining psychic balance or restoring psychic balance which has been disrupted. But one encounters difficulties almost immediately with this formula: it is almost the identical explanation for the development of neurosis. What factor or factors, therefore, can be identified which dispose the individuality toward criminality rather than some other form of emotional or mental disorder?

One interpretation which neatly bypasses the whole issue is that criminality is actually a form of neurosis. Unfortunately, empirical data simply fail to support the contention that the criminal is typically a neurotic individual compulsively driven toward self-punishment. On the contrary, criminal offenders appear to put forth every effort and resource to elude capture. Moreover, the empirical evidence we have been able to gather suggests that "neurotic" personality characteristics are distributed within the criminal population in approximately the same proportion as in the noncriminal population.

Equally dubious is the view of the criminal as an antisocial character who seeks immediate gratification, lives entirely in the present, and is unable to withstand tedium and monotony. It is a criminological commonplace that many kinds of criminal behavior require extensive preparation by way of training in specific skills or in systematic planning. Indeed, the areas of professional, syndicated, and white-collar economic crime seem to exemplify the operation of Freud's "reality principle."

In failing to assign appropriate emphasis to the fact that patterned criminality is not the spontaneous creation of the individual offender, psychoanalytic criminology minimizes the crucial importance of social learning. According to Feldman (1969):

> . . . this learning process requires the individual's participation in the formation and maintenance of relationships with others who dispose of the necessary knowledge and put it to use. It is in the context of these relationships that the individual learns his criminality and adopts for himself distinctive criminalistic attitudes and percepts. Presumably, the experiences of such a learning process must have an effect on the personality of the individual undergoing them. Yet, this reciprocating influence of criminal experience on the personality of the criminal appears to have no consideration in psychoanalytic criminology [p. 441].

Once again, we encounter the issue of which comes first in the causal sequence, the personality characteristics or the criminal experience. Psychoanalytic criminology assumes that the personality features produce the involvement in criminal activity, but in the absence of any systematic procedure for verification, this merely begs the question.

In addition to these substantive criticisms, psychoanalytic criminology possesses some serious flaws when judged as a theory on formal grounds. Psychoanalytic constructs tend to be global and all-inclusive in nature and loaded with "surplus meaning"; rarely, if ever, are they anchored in explicit, observable events. Nevertheless, in time such constructs become the "facts" of psychoanalysis upon which even more elaborate and speculative concepts are based.

Most of the research generated by psychoanalytic theory does not seem to be directed toward the subsequent modification of the theory in the light of newly acquired information but rather to demonstrate the essential validity of the basic postulates and assumptions of the theory. Because of the ambiguity and lack of operational specificity of the constructs in the system, no hypothesis derived from psychoanalytic theory can be either clearly confirmed or clearly refuted. For these and other reasons, critics of psychoanalysis have charged that the theory and its proponents do not conform to the widely accepted canons of empirical verification and refutation implicit to the scientific method.

THE SEARCH FOR A "CRIMINAL PERSONALITY"

Instead of pursuing the notion of criminality as mental illness, some psychiatrists and psychologists have tried to determine whether it is possible to identify a "**criminal personality**." They have sought to discover some constellation or cluster of personality traits distinctive to criminal offenders, in general, or to particular categories of offenders. One approach has been to examine the results of personality tests administered to both criminals and noncriminals with the aim of finding significant differences between them. Another approach has looked at the comparative incidence of psychiatrically diagnosed disorders in a criminal population.

Personality Tests and Criminality

Personality test comparisons between delinquent populations and control groups of nondelinquents were reviewed by Schuessler and Cressey (1950). These sociological researchers noted that only 47 (or 42 percent) of the 113 studies they examined were able to differentiate successfully between the two populations.

A later review by Waldo and Dinitz (1967) of the same topic reported significant differences in the predicted directions in 47 of 56 objective tests, 6 of 8 performance tests, and 19 out of 30 projective tests. The most successful instrument employed was the Minnesota Multiphasic Personality Inventory (MMPI), which successfully differentiated between groups in 28 out of 29 studies reviewed. Seventy-six of the 94 studies reviewed by Waldo and Dinitz reported significant differences between populations: 70 of these studies found significant differences in the directions predicted. Waldo and Dinitz caution, however, against uncritical acceptance of these results, especially with regard to the MMPI. They indicate the studies covered in their research show the following shortcomings:

- Failure to control for other variables that might influence crime and delinquency;
- Failure to select random samples of delinquents and nondelinquents;
- Failure to define exactly what is measured by various personality tests;
- Failure to note that differences *within* delinquent and nondelinquent populations are often greater than differences *between* the two groups;
- Failure to specify whether criminal behavior is the result of a certain personality trail or whether the trait is the result of criminal experience [pp. 185–202].

The last point is especially noteworthy. When Tennenbaum (1977) updated the Waldo-Dinitz review of personality studies, he observed that it was impossible to find any significant differences between criminal and noncriminal psychology as revealed by personality tests "because most results are based on tautological argument" (p. 228). Tennenbaum is referring here to the circularity involved in the chicken-egg question: Which came first, the personality trait or the criminal experience? This same observation can be made with regard to the matter of psychiatrically diagnosed disorders among criminal offenders.

Psychiatric Disorders and Criminality

Research on the incidence of psychiatric disorders in an offender population is subject to a great many methodological problems. Earlier reports of an impressionistic type (e.g., Abrahamsen, 1952; Karpman, 1949) stressed the "normal offender" as a myth. In the absence of any reasonable constraints on observation, such assertions are of little or no value. Thus, the contention by Barnes and Teeters (1959) that "the criminal class as a whole (including those not apprehended and arrested as well as those arrested and convicted) is certainly as intelligent and stable, mentally and emotionally, as the general population" (p. 7) is equally difficult to evaluate.

Brodsky (1972) has provided a tabular summary of studies involving psychiatric evaluations of offenders that span a period from 1918 to 1970. As shown by the information reported in Table 14.1 the reported range of psychotic disturbance was narrow, between 1 percent and 2 percent of the population that was assessed. Be-

Table 14.1 STUDIES OF PSYCHIATRIC EVALUATIONS OF OFFENDERS

Source	Population	Diagnosis	Percent
Glueck (1918)	608 Sing Sing prisoners	Psychotic or mentally deteriorated	12.0
		Normal	41.0
		Mentally retarded	28.1
Overholser (1935)	5,000 felons under Briggs law in Mass.	Abnormal	15.0
		Normal	85.0
Bromberg & Thompson (1937)	9,958 offenders before Court of General Session, New York City	Psychotic	1.5
		Psychoneurotic	6.9
		Psychopathic personalities	6.9
		Feebleminded	2.4
		Normal or mild personality defects	82.3
Schilder (1940)	Convicted felons, Court of General Sessions of New York City	Psychotic	1.6
		Neurotic	4.2
		Psychopathic personalities	7.3
		Feebleminded	3.1
		Normal	83.8
Banay (1941)	Sing Sing prisoners	Psychotic	1.0
		Emotionally immature	20.0
		Psychopathic	17.0
		Normal	62.0
Poindexter (1955)	100 problem inmates	Mentally ill	20.0
		Normal	80.0
Schlessinger & Blau (1957)	500 typical prisoners	Character and behavior disorders	85.0
		Normal	15.0
Shands (1958)	1,720 North Carolina felon admissions to Central Prison	Psychotic	3.5
		Personality disorder	55.8
		Psychoneurotic	3.9
		Sociopathic personality	7.0
		Other	5.3
		No psychiatric disorder	4.7
		Transient personality disorder	19.8
Brodsky (1970)	32,511 military prisoners	Character and behavior disorders	77.1
		No psychiatric disease	21.3
		Miscellaneous disorders	1.6

Source: S. Brodsky, *Psychologists in the Criminal Justice System.* (Washington, D.C.: American Psychological Association, 1972). Reproduced by permission of the author and publisher.

cause of the magnitude of the time span involved, meaningful comparisons are difficult to make between studies.

Guze, Goodwin, and Crane (1969) conducted an eight- to nine-year follow-up study of 223 convicted male felons with the expressed aim of determining the prevalence and types of psychiatric disorders in this population. The authors also made an effort to note any possible associations between psychiatric illness, family history, parental home experience, delinquency and criminal history, and school, job, military, and marital histories. They found the principal disorders associated with criminality were sociopathy, alcoholism, and drug dependency. There were no indications that schizophrenia, manic-depressive disorders, organic brain syndromes, neurotic disorders, or homosexuality were encountered more frequently among criminals than in the general male population.

Brodsky (1972) identifies what is undoubtedly the most significant of all limitations on the interpretation of studies of psychiatric disorders in offenders:

> They all deal with groups of persons who have gone through criminal justice proceedings. There may well be reason to believe that this experience swells the magnitude of existing psychological difficulties and perhaps plants new ones where few had taken root [p. 66].

THE CRIMINAL PERSONALITY: YOCHELSON AND SAMENOW

In a book entitled *The Criminal Personality* (1977), Samuel Yochelson and Stanton E. Samenow reported the results of a 15-year project conducted under a federal grant at St. Elizabeth's Hospital in Washington, D.C., involving an intensive study of 255 criminals drawn from a wide variety of backgrounds: rich, poor, white, black, young, old, Christian, Moslem, and Jew. Somewhere between 150,000 and 200,000 contact hours were spent with the subjects and they were given everything from EEG and EKG examinations to finger dexterity tests. In terms of sheer magnitude, the study is probably without precedent in the history of criminological investigation.

Yochelson was a practicing psychoanalyst in Buffalo, New York, who gave up his private practice to pursue his interest in criminality and its determinants. He was joined later in the project by Samenow, a clinical psychologist. Yochelson died in the summer of 1977, about the time the first volume of the projected three-volume series was in press, but Samenow has continued with the project.

During the first 4 years of the project, the data that emerged from the criminal subjects under scrutiny was everything that a psychiatrist with a psychoanalytic orientation could have wished: evidence of Oedipal conflicts, infantile strivings toward omnipotence, childhood traumas, and unconscious drives. Yochelson came to the conclusion, however, that he was being conned by his subjects, who were using their participation in the project as a cover for continued burglaries, rapes, robberies, and other types of criminal enterprise under the protection afforded by the guarantee of privileged communication. The realization of what was going on led Yochelson to an agonizing reappraisal of his professional orientation. Yochelson and Samenow found themselves compelled to dump the entire medical model on the grounds that it proved a hindrance rather than a help in their work. According to the authors:

> Once we had discarded "mental illness" as a factor we began to understand more about a patient's reality. The concept of mental illness had been the greatest barrier to acquiring this knowledge [p. 30].

Yochelson and Samenow turned instead to a probe of thought and action patterns among their criminal subjects. These "reluctant converts" from psychoanalysis subsequently identified 53 thought and action patterns they claim to have found in all of the 255 subjects in the study. These are presented as Loner, Lying, Power Thrust, Anger, Pride, Failure to Assume Obligations, Lack of Time Perspective, and the like. It is interesting to compare these categories with the list of characteristics identified more than 30 years ago by Hervey Cleckley, in *The Mask of Sanity,* as typical of the sociopathic personality. Yochelson and Samenow's descriptions may appear startling to psychiatrists, psychoanalysts, psychologists, or other professionals who have little firsthand contact with criminal offenders, but they are apt to seem quite familiar to those in the criminal justice system who have dealt extensively with criminals.

Furthermore, Yochelson and Samenow reject environmentalism as a valid approach to understanding the criminal:

> . . . the criminal is not a victim of circumstances. He makes choices early in life, regardless of his socioeconomic status, race, or parents' child-rearing practices. A large segment of society has continued to believe that a person becomes a criminal because of environmental influences. Several factors account for the persistence of this conclusion. Parents who have criminal offspring deny that there is something inherent in the individual that surfaces as criminality. They desperately look for a cause and, in the effort to explain, they latch on to some event or series of events in a person's life for which he is not responsible. Many social scientists have promulgated a deterministic view of man and for years have been explaining criminality largely in terms of environmental influences. Government programs have operated on this basis. The media has espoused this attitude. In efforts to eradicate crime, society has tried to do something, rather than nothing. Attacking environmental sources has been considered one positive step. However, these efforts have met with failure for reasons that the reader will understand as he reads this volume. Changing the environment does not change the man. Finally, the criminal is ever ready to present himself as a victim once he is apprehended. He feeds society what he at best only half believes himself. Actually, he knows that circumstances have nothing to do with his violations, but he uses that rhetoric if he thinks it will lead others to view him more sympathetically [p. 249].

The Yochelson-Samenow study has been criticized for its methodological crudity: there are no control groups, little or no attempt at quantification, no pretense to having followed a research design that lends itself to tests of statistical significance, numerous contradictions in the descriptions, and little reliance on objectivity throughout the work. The most serious shortcoming of the study—and the one that makes it all but impossible to repose any confidence in its conclusions—is the idiosyncratic use by the authors of the term *criminal:*

> It is essential for the reader to understand that we do not use "criminal" in a legal sense. Our emphasis is on *thinking processes* that the irresponsible but non-arrestable person, the petty thief, and the "professional" criminal all manifest, but to different degrees and with different consequences. A person who lies frequently may be cut of the same mental fabric as the arrestable criminal [p.253].

As Humpty Dumpty once advised Alice with regard to making words mean a variety of things, it is merely a question of who is to be the master. It is at least possible to conclude that Yochelson and Samenow have not resolved the question of whether it is possible to identify a "criminal personality," however they choose to define it.

LEARNING THEORY AND CRIMINALITY

Common sense affirms the belief that aggressiveness can be taught to those for whom aggression is not a feature of their normal behavior. From time immemorial, this belief has guided and structured the kind of basic military training a recruit receives. In addition to close-order drill, the use and maintenance of weapons and other types of military equipment, and military etiquette, the rookie is exposed to a kind of indoctrination intended to inculcate aggressiveness. Paul Bäumer, the protagonist of Eric Maria Remarque's classic novel *All Quiet on the Western Front* (1929), reminisces about the training he received as a new recruit in the German army in World War I:

> We were trained in the army for ten weeks and in this time more profoundly influenced than by ten years of school. . . . At first astonished, then embittered, and finally indifferent, we recognized that what matters is not the mind but the boot brush, not intelligence but the system, not freedom but drill. . . . We became hard, suspicious, pitiless, vicious, tough—and that was good; for these attributes had been entirely lacking in us. Had we gone into the trenches without this period of training most of us would certainly have gone mad. Only thus were we prepared for what awaited us . . . [pp. 20–25].

One world war later, novelist John Masters—in *Bugles and a Tiger* (1962)—had remarkably similar reflections to make about the training he had experienced as a cadet in the Royal Military College at Sandhurst, England, during the early 1930s.

It is one thing to assert that a given response or pattern of behavior is learned; it is quite a different matter to be able to describe with precision and in detail how such behavior is acquired, maintained, or changed. Yet significant advances toward accomplishing the latter objectives have been made by psychologists over more than a century of systematic and painstaking research. On the basis of this voluminous body of carefully garnered facts, learning theorists have formulated the following principles:

1. The association between a stimulus and a response is strengthened each time the response is followed by reinforcement. This is *acquisition*.
2. The association is weakened each time the response occurs and is *not* fol-

lowed by reinforcement. This is *extinction.* Disuse alone does not lead to extinction.

3. A response to a given stimulus may be seen to recur after complete extinction when the stimulus is presented again. This phenomenon is known as *spontaneous recovery.*

4. Once a specific stimulus-response habit has been acquired, another stimulus which is similar in some way to the original stimulus can also elicit the learned response. This is *stimulus generalization.*

5. Responses that occurred just prior to the reinforced, learned response will also be strengthened, those nearest in time being strengthened more than those further away. This is the *gradient of reinforcement.*

6. Responses near to the point of occurrence of the reinforcement tend to occur before their original time in the response sequence and crowd out earlier, useless behaviors. This is the development of *anticipatory responses.*

7. Drives can act as cues and elicit specific learned responses, or act as responses and be elicited by certain cues, and strengthened by reinforcement [list adapted from Suinn, 1970].

Much of the experimentation within the laboratory and in other settings from which the principles listed above were derived has been conducted by behavioral scientists identified with the work of B. F. Skinner, the founder of *operant learning theory.* The two major tenets of operant learning may be stated as follows: (1) behavior is affected by its consequences, and (2) anything which increases the probability of occurrence of behavior is a reinforcer. If jumping through a hoop to the command "Jump!" secures the dog a tasty biscuit, then the biscuit acts as a reinforcer to increase the probability that the dog will jump on command. Thus, the behavior (jumping) is affected by its consequences (reinforcement). One of the most impressive accomplishments of the operant learning approach has been its demonstrable capacity to attain control over a steadily widening range of behavior. These achievements helped contribute to the attempts on the part of several authors (Adams, 1971, 1973; Burgess and Akers, 1966; Jeffery, 1965) to update the work of Edwin H. Sutherland by translating differential association into the conceptual language of operant learning theory. As we noted in our discussion of Sutherland's work in an earlier chapter, in the form in which it was originally stated, differential association remained largely untested. Criminological investigators were unable to operationalize such mentalistic constructs as "attitudes" and "motives."

Differential Reinforcement

Jeffery   C. R. Jeffery (1965), a sociologist who studied under Sutherland, suggests that criminal or delinquent behavior is acquired through a process of **differential reinforcement.** Simply stated, a person is more likely to repeat behavior which results in positive consequences (reward or removal of an aversive stimulus) than behavior culminating in negative conditioners (punishment or removal of a positive stimulus) or ending in neutral consequences. Criminal behavior, like any other behavior, is maintained by its consequences. Thus, theft may result in the positive reinforcement elicited by the stolen item; murder and assault can produce positive reinforcement through biochemical change; or, in the case of addiction, taking drugs can remove the aversive conditions of withdrawal.

According to Jeffery, differential reinforcement theory makes several important assumptions:

1. The reinforcing quality of differential stimuli differs for different actors depending on the past conditioning history of each.
2. Some individuals have been reinforced for criminal behavior whereas other individuals have not been.
3. Some individuals have been punished for criminal behavior whereas other individuals have not been.
4. An individual will be intermittently reinforced and/or punished for criminal behavior, that is, he will not be reinforced every time he commits a criminal act [1965, pp. 295–96].

In other words, no two people are identical; everyone has a different history of conditioning. In a given situation involving individuals with identical families, backgrounds, and association where only one steals is explained by the fact that behavior is dependent upon:

1. the reinforcing quality of the stolen item;
2. past stealing responses which have been reinforced; and
3. past stealing responses which have been punished.

These three characteristics will differ between any pair of individuals despite any similarities in backgrounds or associations. Hence, Jeffery invokes the term *differential* reinforcement because different conditioning histories exist for different individuals. Differential association theory cannot account for this phenomenon. Thus, through Jeffery's application of reinforcement contingencies, a serious weakness of Sutherland's original theory is eliminated.

Of primary importance in Sutherland's theory is the proposition that social reinforcement is the mainstay of criminal behavior. More simply, other people serve as reinforcement either through verbal adulation or active confederation in the behavior. People also serve as discriminative stimuli which provide valuable information to the individual on the potential for reward or punishment. For example, it is highly unlikely that delinquent behavior will occur in the presence of a uniformed police officer. The officer indicates that the potential for reward is highly limited and that criminal behavior will, in all likelihood, result in punishment. Conversely, a juvenile in the presence of his peers is more likely to misbehave, as the potential for the rewards of social acceptance and praise is quite high. The behavior patterns of the typical juvenile gang demonstrate this phenomenon. People also can act as aversive stimuli through reprimanding, arresting, or even shooting the offender. All of these behaviors represent Sutherland's concept of "attitudes" favorable or unfavorable to the criminal behavior.

Jeffery questions the sole importance of social reinforcement, pointing out that some criminal behavior is reinforcing in itself. For example, stolen goods serve as positive reinforcement whether or not anyone other than the thief is aware of the fact that he stole them. Thus, Jeffery demonstrates a model of criminal behavior which minimizes the importance of social reinforcement. Adams (1974) reported an empirical study which compared the effects of social and nonsocial reinforcers on the acquisition of misbehavior. Results supported the conclusion that once criminal behavior has been acquired, it may be maintained by nonsocial reinforcers with social factors involved to only a minor extent.

Burgess and Akers   Robert Burgess and Ronald Akers (1966) presented a complete reformulation of Sutherland's differential association theory. They applied the principles of operant learning as outlined by Jeffery and verified their propiety through the presentation of experimental evidence. They reformed Sutherland's original nine proposals into a seven-statement presentation, incorporating modern learning theory into the original concepts.

Reed Adams (1973) conducted a detailed analysis of the Burgess and Akers reformulation of differential association (see Table 14.2). He contrasts their propositions with Sutherland's original statements and emphasizes that the former are not theoretical formulations in the same sense with which theory is comprehended in sociology. Rather, these propositions should be regarded as empirical generalizations which have been arrived at through the inductive processes of experimental research. He recommends abandoning speculations about intangibles and simply focusing on the consequences of behavior:

> It will be found that some consequences are followed by changes, while others are not. It is a simple matter to deal solely with those consequences having an observable impact on behavior and disregarding the remainder. By so doing, we increase the likelihood that the relationships we consider are the important ones [1973, p. 467].

Differential association is thereby transformed from a vague series of largely descriptive statements to a theory that can be empirically tested and confirmed.

Social Learning Theory: Bandura

Albert Bandura of Stanford University is an experimental psychologist whose distinguished contributions to social learning theory have included a lengthy series of imaginative and carefully executed studies of the variables affecting the acquisition and maintenance of aggression—behavior that results in personal injury or in destruction of property (Bandura, 1976). His theory of how aggressive behavior is learned emphasizes both **observational learning** and **direct experience.**

Observational Learning   We are obviously affected by what we see others doing in the world around us. By observing the actions of others, a person may form ideas of how to perform deviant acts. Bandura points out that one can learn general strategies which provide guides for action beyond those associated with a particular model.

Table 14.2   PROPOSITIONS REGARDING CRIMINAL BEHAVIOR

Sutherland	Burgess-Akers	This presentation
I. Criminal behavior is learned. VIII. The process of learning criminal behavior by association with criminal and anticriminal patterns involves all of the mechanisms that are involved in any other learning.	I. Criminal behavior is learned according to the principles of operant conditioning.	I. Criminal behavior is learned according to the principles of operant conditioning.
II. Criminal behavior is learned in interaction with other persons in a process of communication.	II. Criminal behavior is learned both in nonsocial situations that are reinforcing or discriminative and through that social interaction in which the behavior of other persons is reinforcing or discriminative for criminal behavior.	**Differentiation Association** II. Criminal behavior is learned both in nonsocial situations that are reinforcing or discrimnative and through that social interaction in which the behavior of other persons is reinforcing or discriminative for criminal behavior.
III. The principal part of the learning of criminal behavior occurs within intimate personal groups.	III. The principal part of the learning of criminal behavior occurs in those groups which comprise the individual's major source of reinforcements.	III. The principal part of the learning of criminal behavior occurs in those groups which comprise the individual's major source of reinforcements.
IV. When criminal behavior is learned, the learning includes techniques of committing the crime, which are sometimes very complicated, sometimes very simple, and the specific direction of motives, drives, rationalizations, and attitudes.	IV. The learning of criminal behavior, including specific techniques, attitudes, and avoidance procedures, is a function of the effective and available reinforcers, and the existing reinforcement contingencies.	IV. The learning of criminal behavior, including its frequency, specific techniques, stimulus, and response chains; and avoidance procedures, is a function of the reinforcers and punishers, the existing reinforcement and punishment contingencies, and the S°s controlling such behavior.
V. The specific direction of motives and drives is learned from definition of the legal codes as favorable or unfavorable.	V. The specific class of behaviors which are learned and their frequency of occurrences are a function of the reinforcers which are effective and available, and the rules and norms by which these reinforcers are applied.	Subsumed under IV.
VI. A person becomes delinquent because of an excess of definitions favorable to violation of law over defintions unfavorable to violations of law.	VI. Criminal behavior is a function of norms which are discriminative for criminal behavior, the learning of which takes place when such behavior is more highly reinforced than noncriminal behavior.	**Social Problems** V. Criminal behavior occurs in situations where the stimuli have greater S° strength for crimnal than for noncriminal behavior and is learned when the balance of reinforcers and punishments favors such behavior more than noncriminal behavior.

396

Table 14.2   (*Continued*)

Sutherland	Burgess-Akers	This presentation
VII. Differential associations may vary in frequency, duration, priority, and intensity.	VII. The strength of criminal behavior is a direct function of the amount, frequency, and probability of its reinforcement.	VI. The strength of the criminal learning is a direct function of the amount, frequency, and probability of its reinforcement and punishment, and the condition of its state variables.
IX. While criminal behavior is an expression of general needs and values, it is not explained by those general needs and values since noncriminal behavior is an expression of the same needs and values.	Omit	Omit

Source: L. R. Adams, Differential association and learning principles revisited. *Social Problems* 20 (1973): 460. Reproduced by permission of the author and publisher.

The observer must be able to pick out the essentials of a model's behavior and remember them. Says Bandura (1971):

> When an observer witnesses a model exhibit a sequence of responses the observer acquires, through contiguous association of the sensory events, perceptual and symbolic responses possessing cue properties that are capable of eliciting, at some time after a demonstration, overt responses corresponding to those that had been modeled [p. 14].

Social learning theory also distinguishes between acquisition of a behavior and the actual carrying out of that behavior.

> Mere exposure to modeling stimuli does not provide sufficient conditions for imitative or observational learning. Factors other than mere contiguity of sensory stimulation undoubtedly influence imitative response acquisition. Degree of imitative learning depends on attention-directing variables, rate, amount and complexity of stimuli. Frequently, recently and serial order effects associative interference [p. 122].

Bandura identifies three major sources of social learning models: the family, the subculture, and symbolic modeling.

Familial influences   Aggressive behavior can be modeled and reinforced by aggressive behavior of family members. Seeing parents fight provides a model. The parents' words are just as significant as their actions, and their attitudes can be the source for the general strategy mentioned earlier. Children who are victims of parental abuse can imitate the same actions in their interactions with peers and later in child-rearing practices when they become parents themselves. Parents who enforce discipline by coercive methods may impose passivity within the home but reward aggressive behavior on the part of their children within the community.

Subcultural influences   In some subcultural settings, aggressiveness is a highly valued attribute. Status is gained in neighborhood gangs through fighting prowess. And there are occupational or career roles which place a premium on aggressiveness as a basic requirement, for example, salespeople, professional athletes, or combat soldiers.

Symbolic modeling   In the most widely publicized phase of Bandura's work, groups of children were exposed to adult models who either exhibited aggressive or nonaggressive behavior toward a large Bobo doll. The children were then subjected to a mildly frustrating experience, then a record was made of their reactions. Children who had been exposed to the aggressive model showed a greater number of imitative aggressive responses than did the children who were exposed to the nonaggressive model. These same results occurred when children were exposed to the aggressive and nonaggressive models by means of television. In view of the amount of time spent by the average child in front of the television set, the implications of these experimental findings were quickly recognized. Davidson (1977) reports on the impact of one television character, "the Fonze":

> By January 1976, letters were coming in from parents, educators, and psychologists from all over the country. "Billy would never eat vegetables until he hear Fonzie say that eating vegetables is cool. Now I can't give him enough peas, carrots, and beans," wrote one mother. "I'm a guidance counselor working with an autistic child," another letter began. "Last week I scored a great breakthrough when I got her to say her first polysyllable word. The word was Fonzarelli. It was then I discovered that Robin watches Fonzie every week. It's the only show that can hold her attention for a half hour." And third: "I've been having a lot of trouble with my 14 year old son, Eric, and I couldn't get his respect and obedience until I told him I was the Fonzie of my neighborhood back in 1951. That impressed him more than the fact that I won the Silver Star in the Marines in Korea" [p. 98].

Direct Experience   It is not enough for there to be a model to follow; the child must enact what he or she has seen and experience the consequences. If the child does not suffer any punishment for a deviant act, or is, in fact, rewarded in some way, then the activity is reinforced.

Aggressive behavior, once viewed, cannot always be imitated immediately. A karate *kata,* for example, may be observed closely but has so many individual moves that only through lengthy and repetitious practice can they be integrated into the individual's repertory.

Motivators of Aggressive Behavior   Bandura notes that models serve a variety of functions. A model may fulfill a *discriminative function* when the model's acts in the past have been rewarded or reinforced. For example, the model speeds down the highway and gets to work early without being pulled over for a ticket, thus encouraging others to exceed the speed limit. When the acts of the model tend to eliminate or help to avoid adverse consequences, they serve a *disinhibitory function.* The aggressive or hostile behavior of the model may produce emotional arousal in the observer. And models may serve to provide a *stimulus-enhancing function* by directing attention to actions or implements involved in aggressive behavior. An example which combines the last two functions was an incident in Boston in which a group of boys had watched a television show depicting the sadistic murder of an elderly derelict by a gang of juveniles who doused him with gasoline and set him afire. When the program ended, the youthful television fans did an instant replay of the murder using a victim from their own community. Moreover, a short time later, the publicity of this incident on television resulted in a repeat performance in Miami.

Aversive treatment   Frustration engendered by mistreatment can be the push which motivates aggressive behavior. If counterattacks forestall abuse, then a person may engage in physical aggression to avoid physical mistreatment. This may lead in time to the initiation of aggressive behavior for purposes of securing other advantages. Verbal threats and insults may cause a person to resort to physical assaults in order to avoid future verbal threats.

Incentive inducements   While aversive treatment may push someone into aggressive acts, the anticipation of positive consequences provides the *pull* of expected reward. Tangible rewards, or **incentive inducements,** are the most obvious form of external reinforcement. Bandura (1976) refers to a study by Patterson (1967) which showed that aggressive behavior in children actually produced rewards for them 80 percent of the time. The narcotics addict's "high" is usually cited as the main incentive for the commission of crimes that help to fuel his habit.

Directive motivators   Two other motivators mentioned by Bandura are instructional and delusional control. In instructional control, people are conditioned (or socialized) to obey orders; and their subsequent actions, even when these take on aspects of sadistic cruelty, are more readily understood as a function of social conditions than of inherently monstrous qualities. Says Bandura (1973):

> A series of controversial experiments conducted by Milgram show how demands of legitimate authorities can be powerful instigators of inhumane aggressive actions. Ordinarily sensible people will respond in a cruel and callous manner when told to do so by a seemingly legitimate authority in an organization of an unknown character as well as in a university situation of high integrity. People can also be induced to perform cruel acts by the collective pressure exerted by peers. It requires appropriate social inducements rather than monstrous people to produce cruel actions [p. 176].

The Milgram findings make it slightly easier for us to understand the Nazi crimes against humanity or the more recent My Lai massacre.

The second concept, in which psychotic individuals exhibit delusions—false beliefs or systems of false beliefs which are maintained in the face of contradictory evidence and which lead to distorted perceptions of objects, events, and people—subject them to a form of bizarre symbolic control. Delusional beliefs are often defended vigorously by the person despite logical absurdity or proof to the contrary.

They may result in only harmless eccentricity or they can lead to homicidal aggression. For example, the perpetrator of the "Son of Sam" murders in New York during 1977, for example, told the authorities that his actions were in compliance with some supernatural mandate; and two women on opposite sides of the country murdered their children in the delusional belief that they were possessed.

Vicarious Reinforcement and Vicarious Punishment   "Vicarious reinforcement is indicated when observers increase behavior for which they have seen others reinforced. In the process of vicarious punishment, observed negative consequences reduce the tendency to behave in similar or related ways" (Bandura, 1977, pp. 118–19). In light of Bandura's studies, our entire criminal justice system can be thought of as an inducement to crime. A clear example of **vicarious reinforcement** occurs when people see reports in the media every day of the "benefits" of criminal acts and subsequent nonpunishment.

Often people who are guilty of various driving violations are sent to classes featuring movies which contain detailed coverage of horrifying accidents. The showing of such movies to traffic violators would be a form of **vicarious punishment**.

LEARNING THEORY AND BEHAVIOR MODIFICATION

Applications of learning theory to the **behavior modification** of criminals are generally referred to as **contingency management** programs. A contingency, as Lillyquist (1980) notes, "is something that may or may not occur; the management aspect involves increasing the chances that it *will* occur" (p. 232). In the case of contingency management in a correctional setting, the aim is to increase the probability of occurrence of certain kinds of desired behaviors by reinforcing those behaviors when they do occur. Participation in an educational or vocational training program, saving money, reduced aggression, and employment interview skills are some of the kinds of behavior that have been dealt with in contingency management programs (Brankmann et al., 1975). Reinforcers can include anything from verbal praise ("Good job," "That's fine," "You're really getting a handle on this") to obtaining release from prison. Tangible reinforcers such as candy, soft drinks, cigarettes, and snacks may be augmented by access to desired activities such as watching television, making phone calls, and extra visits from family members.

Token Economies

If something which has no reinforcing value of its own is associated with a reinforcer, it will tend to acquire reinforcing properties. We call this a secondary reinforcer. A $20 bill has no intrinsic reinforcing qualities, but it acquires value as a medium of exchange. This principle of secondary reinforcement underlies the establishment of a **token economy**. A token is a secondary reinforcer which, like money, can be exchanged for goods or services according to a standard scale. In addition to the obvious advantages of ease and convenience, the principal benefit of using tokens is that it encourages stability and continuity of behavior. According to Lillyquist (1980):

A person in a social learning program that uses television watching and soda sipping as reinforcers is not always desirous of these rewards because appetites for all things wax and wane. But desirable behavior can be maintained if it can be made contingent on the presentation of a token that promises future reinforcement when the person is more in the mood for it [pp. 232–33].

Token economies seemed particularly well suited to the institutional setting, where the management of behavioral contingencies presents considerably fewer problems than in a free-response environment. In fact, the earliest token economy programs were established in mental hospitals and institutions for the mentally retarded.

Aversive Conditioning of Deviant Sexual Behavior

Aversive conditioning consists of reducing or eliminating certain patterns of behavior by associating them with unpleasant or noxious stimuli. Variations of this method have been used to alter an individual's sexual behavior by teaching him to dislike and avoid stimuli which *he* regards as sources of abnormal sexual excitation. That is, the individual himself must consider his behavior deviant and be willing to cooperate in its elimination, otherwise the aversive conditioning will not work—it will be considered punishment.

Nausea-inducing drugs received considerable use in early studies. These drugs were usually given by injection to induce vomiting while the individual carried out the undesirable behavior. This procedure, which was unpleasant and often traumatic, was designed to condition the sexual deviate to feel nausea whenever he subsequently tried to carry out the undesirable behavior. Electric shock replaced drugs as a source of aversive stimuli. In the boxed example on page 402, the shock was administered to the subject, a male transvestite, through the soles of his feet. Later experiments with aversive conditioning of deviant sexual behavior made use of techniques which applied electrical shock directly to the genital organs.

Criticisms of Behavior Modification

Science fiction is replete with stories of a nightmarish future in which people are depersonalized and dehumanized: Ayn Rand's *Anthem,* about a world grown so collectivized that the very concept of self has been lost and has to be rediscovered; Aldous Huxley's *Brave New World,* with its test-tube genetics and mind-altering drugs; and George Orwell's *1984,* with Newspeak and thought crime and the omnipresent eye of Big Brother forever watching. Such a future may have seemed already upon us when the magazine *Psychology Today* published an article in 1970 in which an author named James McConnell made the following claim:

I believe the day has come when we can combine sensory deprivation with drugs, hypnosis, and astute manipulation of reward and punishment to gain almost absolute control over an individual's behavior. . . . We have the techniques now to do it. . . . I forsee the day when we could convert the worst criminal into a decent respectable citizen in a matter of a few months—or perhaps even less time than that [p. 4].

The electric grid was made from a 4 feet by 3 feet rubber mat with a corrugated upper aspect. Tinned copper wire, one-tenth of an inch thick, was stapled lengthwise in the grooves of this mat at approximately half-inch intervals. . . . A manually operated G.P.O. type generator . . . produced a current of approximately 100 volts a.c. when resistance of 10,000 ohms an upwards were introduced on to the grid surface. Two rapid turns of the generator handle were sufficient to give a sharp and unpleasant electric shock to the feet and ankles of the person standing on the grid. . . . Treatment sessions were administered every half-hour, each session consisting of 5 trials with one minute's rest between each trial. A total of 400 trials was given over 6 days (average 65 to 75 per day). . . . The patient utilized his own clothing, which was not interfered with in any way, except that slits were cut into the feet of his nylon hose to enable a metal conductor to be inserted into the soles of his black court shoes. He commenced dressing up at the beginning of each trial and continued until he received a signal to undress irrespective of the number of garments he was wearing at the time. This signal was either a shock from the grid or the sound of the buzzer which was introduced at random into half the 400 trials. The shock or buzzer recurred at regular intervals until he had completely undressed.

Source: J. C. Barker, Behavior therapy for transvestism: A comparison of pharmacological and electrical aversion techniques. *British Journal of Psychiatry* 111 (1965): 271. Reproduced by permission of the author and publisher.

Two years later, Schwitzgebel (1972) reported on the use of Anectine (succinylcholine chloride), which produces subjective sensations of suffocation, in experiments on aversive conditioning of alcoholics in California. The kind of program in which this approach is used was singled out by Jessica Mitford (1974) in her influential book *Kind and Usual Punishment* as an example of outrages perpetrated in the name of correctional treatment.

Other criticisms of behavior modification have included excessive claims for successful results, the use of inmates as guinea pigs, and the establishment of behavior modification programs as a thinly disguised means of furthering various institutional objectives at the expense of the inmates. In 1974, the Law Enforcement Assistance Administration withdrew federal support from any and all programs using "behavior modification." This ban has never been lifted.

In addition to spirited attacks from their critics, proponents of behavior modification have also experienced a noticeable waning in the enthusiasm that made zealots out of many of the earlier behavior modifiers. The approaches used have also gained in sophistication and humaneness. As Lazarus (1977) observes, "behavior therapists do not deny consciousness . . . do not treat people like Pavlovian dogs . . . and are not ignorant of the part played by mutual trust and other relationship factors among our treatment variables" (p. 553). Nevertheless, institutional authorities have dropped the term "behavior" from their program designations for defensive purposes, knowing that it has acquired many of the characteristics of an aversive conditioning stimulus.

SUMMARY

Distinctions were made among psychiatry, psychoanalysis, and psychology in terms of their approaches to the explanation of criminality. As medical practitioners, psychiatrists tend to view crime as a syndrome or category of mental illness that is susceptible to some of the methods of treatment used with other forms of mental illness. Psychoanalysis, whose theories originated with Sigmund Freud, interprets criminality as the acting out of unconscious impulses or conflicts and the criminal as an individual fixated at some more primitive level of socialization. Psychologists see criminality as behavior acquired in the same way as any other learned pattern, that is, through reinforcement. The reduction or elimination of criminal behavior therefore becomes a problem in changing the reinforcers which help maintain such behavior.

The psychiatric approach has fostered two lines of inquiry: (1) the search for a "criminal personality"; and (2) the assessment of psychiatric disorders in offender populations. Both of these areas of research have failed to provide the kind of results that offer confirmation for the theories on which they are based. Neither clinical observation nor psychological tests have managed to identify any cluster of personality traits distinctive to the criminal. With the exception of alcoholism, drug addiction, and sociopathy or psychopathy—dubious terms at best which are often defined with reference to the same criminal behavior they are supposed to explain—psychiatric disorders appear to occur with about the same frequency in criminal and noncriminal populations.

Learning approaches to criminality, which have developed chiefly from laboratory studies of both infrahuman and human subjects, have provided some of the clearest theoretical accounts of how criminal behavior may be acquired, maintained, and changed. Attempts to modify criminal behavior by means of various approaches, ranging from contingency management in token economies to aversive conditioning of sexually deviant behavior, have generated intense opposition to **"psychotechnology."** Outrage over certain projects which seemed to reduce human beings to the level of animal subjects led to the withdrawal in 1974 of federal support from any projects involving "behavior modification." Current programs have dropped the language of psychotechnology and are inclined to show a great deal of restraint in their claims and methods.

DISCUSSION QUESTIONS

Find the answers to the following questions in the text.
1. Distinguish between psychiatry and psychology in terms of their respective approaches to the explanation of criminality.
2. What are the principal criticisms of the "criminality-as-mental illness" concept?
3. Discuss the implications of David Rosenhan's study of being "sane in insane places." Who were the first people in the various institutions to become aware of the true identity of the pseudopatients?
4. How do psychoanalysts explain criminal behavior? What are some of the major criticisms of the psychoanalytic approach to criminality?

5. Summarize the results of research on the **"criminal personality"** and indicate what the authors have identified as the basic dilemma confronting investigations in this area and in the assessment of psychiatric disorders among criminals.
6. Distinguish between social and nonsocial reinforcers. What is the importance of this distinction with regard to criminal behavior?
7. In what way or ways has the reformulation of differential association in the conceptual language of **differential reinforcement** improved on Sutherland's original theory?
8. How does Bandura's work on **symbolic modeling** and **vicarious reinforcement** help enlarge our understanding of how complex patterns of criminal behavior can be learned?
9. Identify some of the sources of concern for the misuses and potential abuses of **psychotechnology.**

TERMS TO IDENTIFY AND REMEMBER

psychiatry

psychosexual development

contingency management

token economy

vicarious reinforcement

aversive treatment

observational learning

incentive inducements

direct experience

psychoanalysis

"criminal personality"

differential reinforcement

psychotechnology

vicarious punishment

behavior modification

symbolic modeling

directive motivators

REFERENCES

Abrahamsen, D. *Who Are the Guilty?* New York: Rinehart, 1952.

Adams, R. Differential association and learning principles revisited. *Social Problems* 20 (1973): 458–70.

———. The adequacy of differential reinforcement theory. *Journal of Research in Crime and Delinquency* 11 (1974): 1–8.

Bandura, A. *Psychological Modeling.* Chicago: Aldine-Atherton, 1971.

———. *Aggression: A Social Learning Analysis.* Englewood Cliffs, NJ: Prentice-Hall, 1973.

———. *A Social Learning Theory.* Englewood Cliffs, NJ: Prentice-Hall, 1977.

Barker, J. C. Behaviour therapy for transvestites: A comparison of pharmacological and electrical aversion techniques. *British Journal of Psychiatry* 111 (1965): 268–76.

Barnes, H. E., and Teeters, N. K. *New Horizons in Criminology.* Englewood Cliffs, NJ: Prentice-Hall, 1959.

Braukmann, C., Fixen, D., Phillips, E., and Wolf, M. Behavioral approaches to treatment in the crime and delinquency field. *Criminology* 13 (1975): 299–331.

Brodsky, S. *Psychologists in the Criminal Justice System.* Washington, D.C.: American Psychological Association, 1972.

Burgess, R. L., and Akers, R. A. A differential association-reinforcement theory of criminal behavior. *Social Problems* 14 (1966): 128–47.

Cleckley, H. *The Mask of Sanity.* St. Louis: Mosby, 1970.

Davidson, B. The Fonzie phenomenon. *Family Circle* 60 (1977): 94–98.

Feldman, D. Psychoanalysis and crime. In D. R. Cressey and D. Ward (eds.), *Delinquency, Crime, and Social Process.* New York: Harper & Row, 1969.

Guze, S. B., Goodwin, D. W., and Crane, J. B. Criminality and psychiatric disorders. *Archives of General Psychiatry* 20 (1969): 583–91.

Halleck, S. L. American psychiatry and the criminal: A historical review. *American Journal of Psychiatry* 121 (1965): 1–21.

———. *Psychiatry and the Dilemmas of Crime.* New York: Hoeber-Harper, 1967.

Jeffery, C. R. Criminal behavior and learning theory. *Journal of Criminal Law, Criminology, and Police Science* 56 (1965): 294–300.

Karpman, B. Criminality, insanity, and the law. *Journal of Criminal Law and Criminology* 39 (1949): 584–605.

Lazarus, A. Has behavior therapy outlived its usefulness? *American Psychologist* 32 (1977): 550–54.

Lillyquist, M. J. *Understanding and Changing Criminal Behavior.* Englewood Cliffs, NJ: Prentice-Hall, 1980.

McConnell, J. Stimulus/Response: Criminals can be brainwashed—now. *Psychology Today* 3 (1970): 14–18, 74.

Masters, J. *Bugles and a Tiger.* London: New English Library, 1962.

Menninger, K. *The Crime of Punishment.* New York: Viking Press, 1968.

Mitford, J. *Kind and Usual Punishment: The Prison Business.* New York: Random House, 1974.

Remarque, E. M. *All Quiet on the Western Front.* Boston: Little, Brown, 1929.

Rosenhan, D. On being sane in insane places. *Science* 179 (1973): 250–258.

Schuessler, K. F., and Cressey, D. R. Personality characteristics of criminals. *American Journal of Sociology* 55 (1950): 476–84.

Slater, E., and Roth, M. *Clinical Psychiatry.* London: Balliere, Tindall, and Cassell, 1969.

Tennenbaum, D. J. Personality and criminality: A summary and implications of the literature. *Journal of Criminal Justice* 5 (1977): 225–35.

Waldo, G. P., and Dinitz, S. Personality attributes of the criminal: An analysis of research studies. *Journal of Research in Crime and Delinquency* 4 (1967): 185–201.

Yochelson, S., and Samenow, S. E. *The Criminal Personality, Vol. I: A Profile for Change.* New York: Jason Aaronson, 1977.

chapter 15

BIOLOGICAL THEORIES OF CRIMINALITY

If criminality could be tied conclusively to some abnormal condition of the body, crime might someday be eliminated by medication, surgery, or eugenics. Thus, today, whenever a new mind-altering drug, surgical technique, medical intervention, or genetic discovery is introduced to the public, there is a predictable rush to speculate on the prospects that the answer to the crime problem may be here at last.

In the early 1970s, for example, many researchers thought aggressive male sexuality was causally linked to the XYY chromosome defect. Criminologists, however, especially those with a sociological orientation, were skeptical about the link; criminality, deviance, and various kinds of disapproved behavior have often been "explained" by defective biology. And in many cases, the defects have been attributed to racial or ethnic inferiority. So far, however, research has failed to demonstrate that a significant percentage of convicted rapists are XYY males.

In 1851, in a lecture to the Louisiana Medical Association ("The Diseases and Physical Peculiarities of the Negro Race"), Dr. Samuel A. Cartwright argued, based on "incontrovertible scientific evidence," that the "slothful negro" was biologically destined for slavery. Describing a myriad of disorders, diseases, and abnormalities peculiar to "indolent Negroes"—conditions that produced the "debasement of mind" that made the native peoples of Africa incapable of caring for themselves—Cartwright concluded that slavery was a just and humane institution. Two of the "diseases" he identified would be referred to today as behavior disorders. According to Chorover (1973):

> Cartwright insisted that slaves who ran away from their masters were not willfully disobedient. On the contrary, they were suffering from a disease of the mind. He named this disease *drapetomania* (from the ancient Greek words *drapetes* for runaway, and *mania* for madness) and suggested that the best remedy is to treat all "Negroes with firmness and kindness, and they are easily governed."

> But sometimes the treatment fails, Cartwright said, because of another disease also "peculiar to Negroes." This one he named *dysaesthesia aethiopis,* or "behetude of mind and obtuse sensibility of body." He described it as one of the more prevalent "maladies of the Negro race" and expressed wonder that it had escaped the attention of his medical colleagues for so long. Afflicted individuals, he said, tended to engage in much mischief, to slight their work, to abuse tools and break them and generally to raise disturbances. Most remarkably, he saw the disease as being accompanied by an "obviously pathological" change in the functioning of the nervous system: an apparent insensibility to "pain when being punished." The treatment Cartwright prescribed included anointing the entire body with oil and, "slapping the oil in with a broad leather strap," and then putting "the patient to some hard kind of work in the open air and sunshine" [p. 44].

Before dismissing Cartwright's views as hopelessly antiquated racist claptrap, it must be pointed out that he spoke as an eminent physician and a highly respected member of the medical community. Nor is his report a "quaint relic of bygone days." More than a century later, we find an echo of Cartwright's views in a letter which appeared in the *Journal of the American Medical Association* not long after the Detroit riots of 1967. This letter, which was written by William Sweet, Chief of Neuro-surgical Services at Massachusetts General Hospital, Vernon Mark, Chief of Neurosurgical Services of Boston City Hospital, and Frank Ervin, then a psychiatrist at Massachusetts General Hospital, asserted the social causes of urban rioting were well known but raised the possibility of "the more subtle role of other possible factors, including brain dysfunction in the rioters who engaged in arson, sniping, and physical assault." They distinguished between the majority of peaceful, law-abiding slum dwellers and the minority of violent slum dwellers, who might have been react-ing on the basis of lesions in the brain.

This theme was pursued in much greater detail in a book published three years later by Mark and Ervin, entitled *Violence and the Brain.* The authors directed atten-tion to a condition called the **episodic dyscontrol syndrome,** a condition characterized by paroxysmal, seizure-like outbursts during which the individual may lose contact with the environment and commit acts of violence, including spouse and child beat-ing and sexual assaults. The relevance of the dyscontrol syndrome rests on an anal-ogy between this condition and classical temporal lobe epilepsy. Mark and Ervin speculated that the cause of dyscontrol syndrome is "limbic brain disease." The limbic system is a complex area of the brain which plays an important but as yet not too well understood role in a variety of basic functions: sleeping and wakefulness, eating, sexual behavior, emotional arousal, and aggression.

Mark and Ervin acknowledged that, in the absence of any direct diagnostic tests for "limbic brain disease," they were forced to rely on two indirect methods of diagnosis: first, to see whether the violent person has any symptoms of recognizable brain disease, and second, if that fails, to compare their behavior with that of people known to have this type of disease. On the basis of such shaky and imperfect diag-noses, Mark and Ervin were prepared to carry out surgery on people identified as having "poor control of violent impulses."

Nassi and Abramowitz (1976) and Chorover (1973) have taken Mark and Ervin to task for the numerous weaknesses and shortcomings in their work. Chorover calls their book a promotional treatise:

> It explicitly seeks to justify as "therapeutic" the destruction of brain tissue in people who exhibit allegedly unprovoked, uncontrollable, and unreasonable fits of violent behavior. They do not seriously consider the possibility that the causes of such behavior may lie elsewhere than within the brain of the individuals com-mitting the violence. And they do not give clear and complete accounts of the symptoms that justify the use of radical physical treatments such as injections of various drugs, surgery on the limbic system, and electrical stimulation of the brain with implanted electrodes. Nor do they provide a critical assessment of a number of disastrous outcomes from their "therapeutic interventions" [p. 48].

In the light of such criticisms, it is interesting to find Gene Stephens, a profes-sor of criminal justice at the University of South Carolina, suggesting that "genetic engineering could eliminate the offensive traits from future generations" (p. 51). Writing about crime in the year 2000 in the pages of *The Futurist* magazine, Stephens comments:

Microsurgery of DNA in humans may also be a possibility . . . and in the twenty-first century, gene insertion, deletion and correction surgery should be part of standard medical practice. Scientists may be able chemically to influence memory (and specific memories), intelligence, pain, pleasure, perception, and other aspects of human consciousness. . . . Computers, communications devices, and new forms of transportation may well have led to a more integrated, perhaps more controlled, society by the year 2000—the kind of society in which the use of medical technologies to control behavior would not seem particularly unusual [1981, pp. 49-50].

Civil libertarians are apt to be distressed by such discussions. The disturbing feature of the above approach is the bland acceptance of the proposition that the only problem is finding the right technique for eliminating unacceptable or objectionable behavior—or people. This recalls an earlier claim that criminal behavior is the direct result of the impact of the environment on low-grade human organisms, and that characteristic patterns of crime are committed by people of various races and nationalities. And what is Hooton's conclusion? "The elimination of crime can be effected only by the extirpation of the physically, mentally, and moral unfit or by their complete segregation in a socially asceptive environment" (p. 13). As we noted earlier, these sentiments were uttered in 1939. But the author was not a Nazi working for "extirpation" as part of Hitler's "Final Solution" in Europe; he was an American anthropologist named Ernest Hooton.

A great deal of biological research on criminal behavior in the not too distant past was seriously flawed by "extravagant claims, meager empirical evidence, naiveté, gross inadequacy" and stated or implied doctrines of racial or ethnic inferiority of the kind noted above (Allen, 1970, p. 2). This "disreputable history," in Allen's judgment, compels criminologists to approach the topic of biological factors and criminality with extreme caution.

Biocriminology has pursued three broad lines of inquiry. The first of these, which we dealt with in our discussion of the historical background of criminological theory, was the morphological or anthropological approach. This approach began with Lombroso and was continued by such investigators as Hooton, Sheldon, and the Gluecks. The second line of inquiry was concerned with genetics and criminality. Beginning with Taymen's studies of criminal families (Dugdale, 1895) and Goddard's (1912) work on heredity and feeblemindedness, genetic research in criminality has continued up to the present. Among the contemporary studies of importance can be noted the research on the XYY chromosome anomaly in the 1960s and 1970s and the investigations of Mednick and Christiansen (1977) in Denmark and those of Dalgaard and Kringlen (1976) in Norway. The third line of biocriminological inquiry has been directed toward the possible involvement of a broad range of physiological factors in criminal behavior. Brain waves, sex hormones, skin conductance, uric acid, brain damage, and aspects of nutrition and diet are only a few of the many factors that have engaged the attention of researchers.

One point that needs to be clarified before proceeding with our discussion of biocriminology involves the matter of inherited versus acquired characteristics. Some accounts tend to leave the reader with the mistaken impression that everyone who conducts research on biological factors and criminality assumes that such factors are

---

Predicting Crime

Should a criminal be jailed because of crimes he *might* commit in the future?

This controversial idea, called selective incapacitation, has as its goal prevention, not punishment or even rehabilitation. If John Smith is likely to commit 15 muggings, avoiding them may be worth the cost of imprisoning him.

Science, some feel, faces the major challenge of providing a way to determine how many crimes John Smith is likely to commit. Judges now make that determination by instinct and the person's record. Peter Greenwood, of Rand Corporation, on the other hand, suggests two types of research. One develops statistical profiles of many criminals' arrest histories. The other uses "self-reports" in which convicts anonymously provide data on their own criminal activities. Greenwood believes such research can lead to a reliable estimate of the number of crimes John Smith might commit annually.

American Civil Liberties Union lawyer David Landau disagrees. "Almost all social-science studies show that you cannot predict future criminality with any accuracy," he warns. "There's also a constitutional objection. You're talking about punishing people for crimes they haven't committed."

Although he has certain reservations, Alfred Blumstein, who was the chairman of a National Academy of Sciences panel on deterrence, counters with a comparison. The idea of imposing a stiff jail sentence or even the death penalty as a deterrent to other would-be criminals is now widely accepted. Yet, he says, this amounts to punishing the criminal for *other people's* future crimes. And nobody knows how well it works. "In many respects," says Blumstein, "I feel more comfortable with the idea of putting people in jail for their own future crimes than for other people's crimes."

Most people would probably agree.

Source R. Coniff, 21st century crime-stoppers. *Science Digest* 90 (1982): p. 62. Reproduced by permission of the author and publisher.

---

genetically based. It should be emphasized that one can conduct biocriminological research without taking a hard and fast position on the issue of "nature versus nature." It is probably safe to say that most of the people working in this field regard the issue of heredity and environment as one that remains to be resolved by further research.

The following discussion is not intended to provide a detailed critical review of biocriminological research and theory; rather, its objective is to acquaint the reader with a few of the topics that have engaged the attention of contemporary researchers and theorists. Regardless of the position one takes on the controversial issues raised by biological studies of criminality, it is our contention that criminologists and students of criminology cannot ignore this field of inquiry. We shall be in a much better position to weigh the claims and evidence from biocriminological research if we possess some understanding of how such evidence was obtained.

GENETICS AND CRIMINALITY

Do people become criminals because they are "born that way" or do they commit crimes because of influences from the environment in which they were raised? Are criminal tendencies a matter of "doing what comes naturally" or can anyone become a criminal if exposed to the right set of environmental circumstances? To ask the question in this way is to raise one of the oldest issues in the social and behavioral sciences: nature versus nurture.

Maxwell Anderson's play adaptation of novelist William March's *The Bad Seed* tells the fateful tale of a little girl named Rhoda Penmark, whose grandmother was the infamous murderess, Bessie Denker. Rhoda's mother, Christine, is a kind and loving parent, but she is haunted by the fear that she may have transmitted Bessie's "bad seed" to Rhoda. Through a chilling sequence of killings, Rhoda is disclosed to the audience as a monster in human guise. In desperation, Christine gives Rhoda a lethal dose of poison and takes her own life—but Rhoda survives. As the final curtain descends, Rhoda's grief-striken father consoles himself by wrapping the malignant child in his arms. No one in the audience, however, believes they have heard the last of Rhoda.

March's answer to the nature-nurture question, at least in Rhoda's case, is nature. That is, Rhoda inherited her homicidal tendencies from her grandmother, the murderess. But scientists are not artists; in their attempts to untangle the skein of causation, they are required to carry out painstaking studies in order to verify what the artist concludes on the basis of sheer intuition. If we ask, therefore, how scientists could try to measure the relative contributions of heredity and environment to Rhoda's inclinations toward homicide, a good place to start would be with a brief examination of the methods they might use to investigate this question.

Methods of Genetic Investigation

Human genetic research has relied on three investigative procedures: (1) family history or pedigree studies, (2) adoption studies, and (3) twin studies. For obvious reasons, the selective breeding procedures which furnish the geneticist with valuable information about animal subjects are out of the question with humans, although it should be noted that some abortive attempts in this direction were made by the Nazis during the 12 years of Adolf Hitler's "Thousand Year Reich."

The **family history or pedigree approach** to the inheritance of criminal behavior predispositions was the first method used by virtue of its obviousness: if one looks into the "roots" of an individual who engages in criminal behavior, it should be possible to determine how frequently the same or similar kinds of crimes have been committed in previous generations of that individual's family.

Certain criticisms are attached to this method of study. Criminality is usually regarded as a disgrace to the family in which it occurs. Hence, many families will go to extreme lengths to conceal the present or past occurrence of such behavior among their members. This leaves the investigator almost completely dependent upon official records whose reliability and accuracy are likely to suffer in direct proportion to the amount of time that has elapsed since they were originally complied.

Do Criminals Have "Roots"? The Infamous Jukes and Kallikaks

Studies of the famed lineages of the Juke family by Richard Dugdale in the nineteenth century and the Kallikak family in the early twentieth century by Henry H. Goddard supported the claim that some individuals were "born criminals" and that "bad genes" could be passed from generation to generation. Although Dugdale did not invent the Jukes, he often used his imagination when the facts failed to bolster his theory of the hereditary causes of crime. When information about individuals was difficult to obtain, Dugdale resorted to the characterizations such as "supposed to have attempted rape," "reputed sheep stealer but never caught," and "hardened character."

Goddard studied the descendants of two clans of the Kallikak family. Although both clans descended from the same Revolutionary War soldier, Martin Kallikak, the "bad" Kallikaks were attributed to the soldier's union with a feebleminded girl. There is little evidence that these families committed actual crime. In fact, Goddard found only three official cases of crime. All of the supposedly "good" Kallikaks descended from the soldier's marriage with a Quaker woman. Since none of the good Kallikaks seem to have inherited any "bad genes," something rather strange must have occurred in the lineage, for we know that a certain number of the good offspring should have shown some "degenerate" traits.

Source: Alberta J. Nassi and Stephen I. Abramowitz. From phrenology to psychosurgery and back again: Biological studies of criminality. *American Journal of Orthopsychiatry* 46 (1976): pp. 595–960. Reproduced by permission of the authors and publisher.

There is the additional problem that changing social and cultural norms during the past century make any comparisons that are not limited to major felony offenses (such as homicide, robbery, forcible rape, and armed robbery) of extremely questionable validity.

Adoption studies involve comparisons between adoptees and their biological versus adoptive parents on some attribute or characteristic. Some of the earliest studies of intelligence, for example, showed closer links in IQ between adoptees and biological parents than between adoptees and their adoptive parents. Hutchings and Mednick (1977) investigated the outcomes of 1,145 adoptions of male children in Denmark and found that those whose biological fathers were criminals were more than twice as likely to become criminals themselves than were the children of noncriminals, even though they had never had any contact with their natural parents.

Another major method of investigation is the **twin study.** Although it demands a considerable contribution of time, effort, and expense, the twin study is favored by many researchers as a much more reliable method than the family history. Inasmuch as **monozygotic (MZ) twins** (those who develop from a single fertilized ovum) represent the closest approximation to identical heredity that is available to the scientist, they are a valuable source of information on the contribution of genetic factors to behavioral variation. In the extremely rare cases of identical twins reared apart, a further source of information is supplied which could not be obtained through the controlled procedures of laboratory research.

The twin study is not without its drawbacks. Although a given pair of MZ twins might appear to possess identical genetic endowments, Burt (1966) cautions that one twin may have resulted from the less developed half of the embryo. Therefore, that twin may be smaller and weaker than the other. Monozygoticity, in short, does not guarantee absolutely identical inheritance.

Criminality in Twins   Attempts to isolate hereditary factors in crime have used comparisons between identical (MZ) and fraternal **(dizygotic, DZ) twins.** If MZ twins are genetically identical and DZ twins are genetically dissimilar, then it is postulated that MZ twins ought to show greater behavioral resemblances than should DZ twins. Thus, if criminal tendencies are inherited, one would predict a high rate of **concordance** (association of crime in both twins) among MZ twins and a low rate of concordance in DZ twins.

Christiansen (1977 *a*) summarized the results of adult twin studies that go back as far as Lange's 1929 investigation. As shown in Table 15.1, concordance is about twice as high as discordance in monozygotic twins. These findings suggest, at first glance, that genetic factors exert a decisive influence in predispositions toward criminality. However, as Nassi and Abramowitz (1976) point out, these studies are flawed by a number of methodological errors that cast serious doubts on this conclusion. In addition to the small size of the samples used in the studies, differentiation between MZ and DZ twins was handled by means of external observation—which makes it

Table 15.1   SUMMARY OF TWIN-CRIMINALITY STUDIES

	Monozygotic		Dizygotic[a]	
	Number of pairs	Pairwise concordance percent	Number of pairs	Pairwise concordance percent
Lange (1929)	13	76.9	17	11.8
Legras (1932)	4	100.0	5	0.0
Rosanoff et al. (1941)				
Adult criminality	45	77.8	27	22.2
Juvenile delinquency	41	97.6	26	80.8
Stumpfl (1936)[b]	18	64.5	19	36.8
Kranz (1936)	39	65.6	48	53.5
Borgstrom (1939)	4	75.0	5	40.0
Yoshimasu (1962)[c]	28	60.6	18	11.1
Dalgaard and Kringlen (1976)[d]	31	25.8	54	14.9

Source: S. A. Mednick and K. O. Christiansen, *Biosocial Bases of Criminal Behavior* (New York: Gardner Press, 1977). Reproduced by permission of the authors and publisher.
[a] Tienari's results are not entered in this table because he has no group of dizygotic pairs.
[b] A monozygotic concordant pair is found in both Stumpfl's and Kranz's samples.
[c] The figures from Yashimasu (1962) stem from two investigations in 1941 and 1947.
[d] Crime in the strict sense.

impossible to determine with sufficient accuracy whether the twins of similar appearance were, in fact, monozygotic twins. All of the studies suffer from the deficiency that environmental factors were not controlled. Since MZ twins are more likely to be exposed to a similar social environment than are DZ twins, the discrepancy in results could be accounted for on the basis of the greater similarity of environment in identical twins.

Christiansen (1977 b) claims to have dealt effectively with the methodological problems, including small sample size, that marred previous twin research. In a study of 7,172 Danish twins, he found a 35 percent concordance for criminality in identical (MZ) twins, as compared with a concordance rate of only 13 percent in fraternal (DZ) twins.

Male Agressiveness and the XYY Syndrome   While aggressive and violent behavior in and of itself does not constitute criminality, it increases the likelihood that an individual so predisposed would experience difficulty in normal socialization, thereby reinforcing the development of antisocial or criminal behavior patterns as a means of adaptation. Genetic studies that have sought to relate aggressive male behavior to hereditary factors have focused on the condition known as the **XYY syndrome or chromosomal anomaly.** Public interest in this genetic anomaly was aroused in 1968 when a Frenchman named Daniel Hugon was brought to trial in Paris on the charge of murdering a prostitute. Later Hugon was given a thorough physical examination after he had attempted to commit suicide. Clinical tests revealed he was an XYY male, that is, one of those presumably rare individuals born with an extra Y (male) chromosome instead of the normal complement of only one X (female) and one Y chromosome. Hugon was given a reduced sentence as a result of this disclosure.

The pioneer study which attempted to relate the XYY anomaly to criminality was conducted by Dr. Patricia Jacobs (1965) and her colleagues at a prison hospital in Edinburgh, Scotland. The subjects of this research were 197 inmates, all with "violent or criminal tendencies." Seven men were identified as XYY males—a frequency of 3.5 percent of the prison population. Although no precise figures were available for the comparative incidence of this condition within the general male population of comparable age, the investigators believed that the presence of as many as seven XYY males in the prison population was a highly significant finding.

Criminologists have been extremely interested in the XYY syndrome because of the provocative possibility of linkage between the XYY chromosomal anomaly and aggressive behavior. This possibility continued to sustain interest in the XYY syndrome through a lengthy series of studies that reported contradictory findings. However, when most, if not all, of the principal methodological objections to previous research were met and overcome in a study by Witkin and his coworkers (1977) of the XYY syndrome in Danish subjects the results failed to confirm the presence of unusually aggressive behavior among men with this genetic anomaly. As the authors stated: "Because such men do not appear to contribute particularly to society's problem with aggressive crimes, their identification would not serve to ameliorate this problem" (p. 187). Nevertheless, some geneticists insist that the question of possible linkage between chromosomal abnormalities and aggressive behavior is still not settled.

THE BIOCHEMICAL APPROACH

In 1968, Linus Pauling—twice the recipient of the Nobel prize in chemistry—coined the term **orthomolecular psychiatry.** He suggested that mental illness and behavior disorders are caused mostly by abnormal reaction rates in the body which result from constitutional defects, faulty diet, and abnormal concentrations of essential elements. Pauling recommended that treatment of behavior disorders include the establishment of an optimal chemical state for the brain and nervous system. He attracted national interest in his vigorous advocacy of massive doses of vitamin C as a remedy for the common cold.

Orthomolecular views are reflected in the perspective that has been termed the **biochemical approach** (Hippchen, 1978; Hoffer, 1978). Adherents of this approach maintain that various kinds of delinquent and criminal behavior are not psychosocial reactions, but rather, are indications of metabolic or biochemical imbalances. That is, an adolescent youth may engage in violent behavior not because he is the unfortunate victim of maternal rejection or a broken home but because he is suffering from faulty diet, inadequate nutrition, or the presence in his body of some toxic substance such as mercury which adversely affects his general health and functioning.

As a case in point, the argument has been made that hyperactivity in youngsters, a syndrome characterized by restlessness, distractability, excessive physical activity, and aggressive behavior, is often regarded as antisocial or delinquent behavior. Hyperactivity, it has been suggested, is principally caused by nutritional deficiencies and a low level of blood sugar (hypoglycemia). Both of these conditions may be systematically related to the types of "junk food" that youngsters in this country consume in large quantities and which are loaded with the processed sugar, starches, and toxic additives that produce orthomolecular imbalances. As Thornton, James, and Doerner (1982) observe:

> Children who are hyperactive often become labeled as problem cases by parents and teachers. Unable to concentrate and learn, these youth can grow into adulthood lacking a wide variety of knowledge and skills. Thus, they are prime candidates for truancy and dropping out of school, activities conducive to delinquent behavior [p. 82.]

Steven Schoenthaler (1985), Coordinator of Criminal Justice at California State College (Stanislaus), has spent several years conducting diet-behavior studies on more than 5,000 confined juveniles in ten juvenile detention facilities located in Alabama, California, and Virginia. Each juvenile facility has been recording any serious incidents which resulted in formal disciplinary action being taken by the institution. Neither the juveniles themselves nor the staff members whose responsibility it was to report disciplinary problems was informed of the study.

In nine of the institutions the primary goal was to reduce sugar consumption by replacing foods and beverages with products that contained less sucrose. Soft drinks were replaced with fruit juices; candy and "junk food" snacks were replaced with fresh fruits, vegetables, nuts, and popcorn; and high sugar-content breakfast cereals were replaced with more nutritious cereals. After the diets were changed, all ten of the institutions reported a significant decline in the number of serious incidents, ranging from a low of 21 percent to a high of 54 percent. Schoenthaler (1985) plans to continue his studies in educational, adult correctional, and mental health facilities, in addition to doing further research in juvenile institutions.

Critique

Most criminologists would agree with the basic premise of the biochemical approach that nutritional and biochemical factors influence behavior. It is much less certain, however, to what extent and in what specific ways such factors are involved in deliquent and criminal behavior. Schoenthaler, for example, points out that the improvement in behavior his study noted among institutionalized delinquents might have been caused by the increase in nutritious fruits, vegetables, and grains, rather than the reduction in high sugar "junk food." Another possibility is that food additives in the high-sugared products may be the real culprits.

Arguments by adherents of the biochemical approach that low blood sugar levels and various kinds of biochemical imbalances are mainly responsible for causing such crimes as rape, robbery, arson, assault, and homicide, or that nearly all convicted murderers are suffering from vitamin deficiencies or hypoglycemia (Hippchen, 1978) must be considered hypotheses that await confirmation or refutation through controlled research of the kind that Steven Schoenthaler has initiated.

LEARNING DISABILITIES AND DELIQUENCY

The term **learning disability** is defined as an impairment in sensory or motor functioning which leads to deviant classroom performance and is the product of some abnormal physical condition (Holzman, 1979; Valetutti, 1975). While several forms of learning disability are thought to exist, the three major types presently identified are **dyslexia, aphasia,** and **hyperkinesis.** Dyslexia is a "disorder in children who, despite conventional classroom experience, fail to attain the language skills of reading, writing, and spelling commensurate with their intellectual abilities" (Critchley, 1972, p. 11). Aphasia includes both visual and auditory deficiencies, which can produce problems in communicating verbally or understanding the speech of others. Hyperkinesis is often equated with hyperactivity, "a long term childhood pattern characterized by excessive restlessness and inattentiveness" (Safer and Allen, 1976, p. 5).

Critique

The causes of dyslexia, aphasia, and hyperkinesis are not well understood. There seems to be a good deal of agreement that eventually research will disclose an organic or neurological basis for learning disabilities (Cott, 1978; Holzman, 1979; Kelly, 1979; Murray, 1976). Whether or not these disorders are rooted in organic pathology, there are some basic issues involved in any attempt to relate learning disabilities to delinquency or crime.

As Shoemaker (1984) points out, one possible explanation for the linkage between learning disabilities and delinquency is the possibility that such disorders "affect cognitive development and processes of understanding, which, in turn, render one less appreciative of social rules and sanctions" (p. 30). Another possible explanation is that learning disabilities produce poor academic achievement, resulting in the development of negative attitudes toward the disabled juvenile from family members, peers, and school officials. The combination of poor grades and negative attitudes can lead to feelings of rejection on the part of the juvenile and a tendency to seek associations with peers who are trying to cope with school failure through truancy and other forms of maladaptive behavior. According to this view, the organically based learning disability is only one of a number of possible preconditions of delinquency. The more proximate cause of delinquency, Shoemaker observes, is the combination of school failure, social rejection, and association with "bad" companions.

At any rate, evidence linking learning disabilities and delinquency is limited. As Murray (1976) notes, although some researchers maintain that over 90 percent of delinquents have some kind of learning disability, these assertions are based on subjective and uncritical assessments. Studies are flawed by small sample sizes, conflicting definitions of delinquency, and inconsistencies in measurement of learning disabilities. Murray's conclusion that research has not yet demonstrated a causal connection between learning disabilities and delinquency is buttressed by the reported findings of Keilitz, Zaremba, and Broder (1982) that disabled juveniles commit the same kinds and amount of delinquency as other youngsters.

EPILEPSY AND CRIMINALITY

An alleged relationship between epilepsy and violent behavior has long been one of the popular myths that relate criminality to mental illness. Epileptic reactions—the "falling sickness" of classical reference—constitute a group of heterogenous, complex, and controversial disorders characterized by the recurrence of convulsive attacks or seizures. Batchelor (1969) feels that it is more accurate to speak of the epilepsies as symptoms rather than disorders: "The essential feature is not the convulsive seizure or the disturbance of consciousness, but the episodic sudden disturbance of function in the central nervous system" (p. 420). Experimental studies involving brain stimulation have shown that some kinds of seizures which closely resemble epileptic attacks can be elicited by electrical means.

The epilepsies have been known from antiquity, and behavior pathologists are fond of compiling lists of world-famous figures who have been afflicted. With Alexander of Macedon, Julius Caesar, and Napoleon heading this parade, the student might wonder whether epilepsy and visions of world conquest go hand in hand. However, there are enough gifted artists, writers, and musicians in the tally—Maupassant, Van Gogh, and Byron, for instance—to indicate the democratic nature of the affliction.

The major types of epilepsy are grand mal, petit mal, Jacksonian, and psychomotor epilepsy. Grand mal, the most common and dramatic of the epileptic reactions, features severe motor convulsions and an interruption or loss of consciousness. Petit mal, which is rare in adults over 21, represents a fleeting disruption of consciousness and may go unrecognized for a long time. Jacksonian seizures tend to resemble grand mal attacks in most major respects. The Jacksonian attack begins with a spasmodic muscular contraction in an arm or leg and usually extends to involve the whole side of the body where it originated.

Psychomotor epilepsy (or "psychic equivalents") also represents a disruption of consciousness but the elileptic often manages to carry out some fairly complicated patterns of behavior. Among such patterns—according to standard views—are violence and aggression, up to and including mass murder (Suinn, 1970). It is almost traditional in discussions of epilepsy and violence to cite the case of the Flemish painter Vincent Van Gogh who sliced off one of his own ears with a razor, carefully packed it in cotton, and presented it to a prostitute in a provincial French bordello whose favors he had enjoyed. Van Gogh is believed to have carried out this act of self-mutilation during one of his psychomotor *fugues.*

On examination, the murderous reputation of the psychomotor epileptic turns out to be largely folklore. For example, Turner and Merlis (1962) reported that only 5 out of 337 epileptics whose case records they examined had carried out antisocial behavior during their seizures. Rodin (1973) found no instances of aggressive or violent behavior in 57 patients with psychomotor epilepsy who were photographed during seizures and only 34 instances of aggressive actions in 700 case histories he examined.

PHYSIOLOGICAL FACTORS AND THE ANTISOCIAL PERSONALITY

Since the introduction of the concept of psychopathy more than a century ago, the diagnosis of psychopath, sociopath, or antisocial personality has been applied with much higher frequency to criminal offenders than to the general population (Frances, 1980; Hare, 1981). As reported by Sutherland and Cressey (1978), wide variations in the diagnostic rate from one setting to another were attributed to the shortcomings and limitations of the American Psychiatric Association's *Diagnostic and Statistical Manual of Mental Disorders* (1968). In this edition, known as DSM-II, the diagnosis of personality disorder is made primarily on the basis of inferred personality traits rather than specific behavioral criteria:

> They [antisocial personalities] are incapable of significant loyalty to individuals, groups, or social values. They are grossly selfish, callous, irresponsible, impulsive and unable to feel guilt or to learn from experience and punishment. Frustration tolerance is low. They tend to blame others or offer plausible rationalizations for their behavior [p. 43].

It is instructive to compare this passage with the list of descriptive criteria of those with personality disorders provided by psychiatrist Hervey Cleckley (1964) in his famous book, *The Mask of Sanity*:

1. Superficial charm and intelligence.
2. Absence of delusions and other signs of irrational thinking.
3. Absence of "nervousness" or neurotic manifestations.
4. Unreliability.

5. Untruthfulness and insincerity.
6. Lack of remorse or shame.
7. Antisocial behavior without apparent compunction.
8. Poor judgment and failure to learn from experience.
9. Pathological egocentricity and incapacity for love.
10. General poverty in major affective relations.
11. Specific loss of insight.
12. Unresponsiveness in general interpersonal relations.
13. Fantastic and uninviting behavior with drink and sometimes without.
14. Suicide threats rarely carried out.
15. Sex life impersonal, trivial, and poorly integrated.
16. Failure to follow any life plan.

The antisocial personality, said Cleckley (1970), "mimics the human personality but is unable to *feel*" (pp. 355–356). A number of the characteristics cited by Cleckley as typical of the psychopath or sociopath are captured in the boxed material on page 420.

The author of the above report noted that Donald did not perceive anything wrong with his behavior. He suffered no guilt or remorse for having manipulated others for his own selfish purposes, thus causing them grief and injury. Punishment that he received from time to time did nothing to lessen his self-confidence or diminish his egotism. In the long run, Hare observed, his behavior is self-defeating, but Donald considers it to be "practical and possessed of good sense" (1970, p. 4).

Clinical descriptions of the antisocial personality have emphasized certain behavioral characteristics as typical of this personality configuration. Impulsivity, callousness, lack of remorse, inability to withstand tedium and monotony, and lack of capacity for love and affection are the features cited most frequently. Considerable research has been devoted to investigating whether these behavioral characteristics might be linked to certain physiological abnormalities. Biocriminologists have studied brain waves, chemical levels in the blood, skin conductance, heart and pulse rates, and a number of other processes in individuals identified as antisocial personalities.

Brain-Wave Studies

The **electroencephalograph (EEG)** is an instrument which picks up electrical activity in brain cells by means of electrodes attached to the scalp and records this activity in oscillating patterns called *brain waves* by a machine connected to the electrodes. EEG studies have been used to investigate criminals since the early 1940s (Mednick and Volavka, 1980). Over the years, research has indicated a rather high incidence of brain-wave abnormalities among antisocial personalities, especially in slow-wave activity in the temporal lobe of the brain. Hare (1970) suggested that such anomalies might be a reflection of abnormal functioning of inhibitory mechanisms in the central nervous system and that "this malfunction makes it difficult to learn to inhibit behavior that is likely to lead to punishment" (pp. 33–34). This is an important point to which we shall return later.

Mednick (1981) conducted a longitudinal study of 265 youngsters drawn from

Antisocial Personality: A Profile

Donald S., 30 years old, has just completed a three-year prison term for fraud, bigamy, false pretenses, and escaping lawful custody. The circumstances leading up to these offenses are interesting and consistent with his past behavior. With less than a month left to serve on an earlier 18-month term for fraud, he faked illness and escaped from the prison hospital. During the ten months of freedom that followed he engaged in a variety of illegal enterprises; the activity that resulted in his recapture was typical of his method of operation. By passing himself off as the "field executive" of an international philanthropic foundation, he was able to enlist the aid of several religious organizations in a fund-raising campaign. The campaign moved slowly at first, and in an attempt to speed things up, he arranged an interview with the local TV station. His performance during the interview was so impressive that funds started to pour in. However, unfortunately for Donald, the interview was also carried on a national news network. He was recognized and quickly arrested. During the ensuing trial it became evident that he experienced no sense of wrongdoing for his activities. He maintained, for example, that his passionate plea for funds "primed the pump"—that is, induced people to give to other charities as well as to the one he professed to represent. At the same time, he stated that most donations to charity are made by those who feel guilty about something and who therefore deserve to be bilked. This ability to rationalize his behavior and his lack of self-criticism were also evident in his attempts to solicit aid from the very people he had misled. Perhaps it is a tribute to his persuasiveness that a number of individuals actually did come to his support. During his three-year prison term, Donald spent much time searching for legal loopholes and writing to outside authorities, including local lawyers, the Prime Minister of Canada, and a Canadian representative to the United Nations. In each case he verbally attacked them for representing the authority and injustice responsible for his predicament. At the same time he requested them to intercede on his behalf and in the name of the justice they professed to represent. . . .

By all accounts, Donald was considered a willful and difficult child. When his desire for candy or toys was frustrated he would begin with a show of affection, and if this failed he would throw a temper tantrum; the latter was seldom necessary because his angelic appearance and artful ways usually got him what he wanted. Similar tactics were used to avoid punishment for his numerous misdeeds. At first he would attempt to cover up with an elaborate facade of lies, often shifting the blame to his brothers. If this did not work, he would give a convincing display of remorse and contrition. When punishment was unavoidable he would become sullenly defiant, regarding it as an unjustifiable tax on his pleasures.

Although he was obviously very intelligent, his school years were academically undistinguished. He was restless, easily bored, and frequently truant. His behavior in the presence of the teacher or some other authority was usually quite good, but when he was on his own he generally got himself or others into trouble. Although he was often suspected of being the culprit, he was adept at talking his way out of difficulty. . . .

His sexual experiences were frequent, casual, and callous. When he was 22 he married a 41-year-old woman whom he had met in a bar. Several other marriages followed, all bigamous. In each case the pattern was the same: he would marry someone on impulse, let her support him for several months, and then leave. One marriage was particularly interesting. After being charged with fraud Donald was sent to a psychiatric institution for a period of observation. While there he came to the attention of a female member of the professional staff. His charm, physical attractiveness, and convincing promises to reform led her to intervene on his behalf. He was given a suspended sentence and they were married a week later. At first things went reasonably well, but when she refused to pay some of his gambling debts he forged her name to a check and left. He was soon caught and given an 18-month prison term. As mentioned earlier, he escaped with less than a month left to serve.

Source: R. D. Hare, *Psychopathy: Theory and Research.* New York: Wiley, 1970, pp. 1–4.

a Danish birth cohort. Seventy-two children with schizophrenic parents were matched with 72 children of "psychopathic fathers or character disorder mothers" for which psychiatric hospitalization records were available. The control subjects (n = 121) were children whose parents had never been hospitalized. All of the subjects were given an exhaustive assessment that included psychological, neurological, and social-familial measures.

EEG results significantly discriminated delinquents from nondelinquents, although the findings did not support the hypothesis that delinquents exhibit a developmental lag. The fact that the measures were taken well before the individuals exhibited delinquent behavior and are therefore *predictive* led Mednick (1979) to suggest the possibility that the EEG could conceivably find future use as part of a test battery to help in the prevention of delinquency.

Skin Conductance Studies

When people are upset, anxious, fearful, or otherwise emotionally aroused, their palms perspire. This perspiration increases the electrical **conductivity of the skin,** which yields a measure of the galvanic skin response (GSR). Individuals with high levels of emotional arousal tend to show significantly higher levels of GSR reactivity than those who exhibit relatively low levels of anxiety, fear, or anger.

An early study by Lykken (1957) indicated that psychopathic offenders showed a combination of lower arousal as measured by the GSR and significantly lower anxiety scores on questionnaires. Lykken concluded that psychopathic individuals had fewer inhibitions about committing antisocial behavior because they experience little anxiety over their actions. Subsequent research has consistently affirmed this kind of finding on skin conductance measures with criminals, especially violent offenders (Hare, 1970; Lippert, 1965).

Cardiac Lability Studies

In 1949, Funkenstein, a psychiatrist, and his colleagues identified a condition called **cardiac lability** which referred to a consistently exaggerated response of the heart and blood circulatory or cardiovascular system in a study involving chronically antisocial individuals. Fifteen psychopaths who were characterized as "hostile recidivists" were selected from among referrals to the Boston Psychopathic Hospital. All of the subjects in this group had committed crimes of violence and all of them claimed to be "nervous," although they exhibited no overt signs of anxiety.

Each individual was injected intravenously with a substance called epinephrine which produces a rise in heart rate and blood pressure in normal subjects. The antisocial subjects exhibited significantly higher increases than those observed in normal and noncriminal (psychotic and neurotic) control subjects. These findings were later confirmed in a study by Schachter and Latane (1964).

In 1970, a research team at Ohio State University (Lindner et al., 1970) carried out a carefully controlled and detailed investigation with antisocial offenders drawn from consecutively admitted prisoners at the Ohio State Penitentiary. The 43 subjects selected for the study were administered either an injection of epinephrine or a placebo according to the familiar "double blind" procedure for experiments involving drugs. Following the administration of the drug, subjects were given the task of solving a maze while avoiding a mild electrical shock for incorrect responses.

The researchers were rather puzzled when their results failed to show significant differences in heart rate and skin conductance measures between the psychopaths and nonpsychopathic controls. These findings led them to question whether the psychopathic group was really homogeneous, that is, composed of identical psychopathic individuals. After an extensive examination of the backgrounds of these individuals, the investigators concluded they were, in fact, dealing with two different groups, which they identified as " simple" and "hostile" psychopaths, respectively. Simple psychopaths were older, from larger, intact families, better educated, higher in the socioeconomic scale, and a greater percentage were married. Records also indicated that they had more previous arrests, more prior convictions and incarcerations for longer periods of time, and twice as many parole violations as the hostile psychopaths. The latter group showed a higher percentage of crimes against the person than the simple psychopaths.

On the physiological measures, simple psychopaths showed a consistently higher rate of cardiac lability than the hostile psychopaths. The simple psychopath appeared to be an individual who requires more intense and varied experiences to stimulate him to a normal degree. Also, he tended to respond to emotionally provocative situations in an all-or-none, "switched on–switched off" fashion. That is, he either does not respond at all to what many people would regard as a provocative stimulus and then reacts impulsively or explosively to a situation which seems only slightly more provocative or higher in stimulation. To a minor insult he might not respond at all; to a somewhat more offensive remark, he might react by committing assault or even murder.

One possible interpretation of these findings is that the exaggerated autonomic responses of the simple psychopath and his characteristic pattern of impulsive overt behavior may be in turn related to a simple biological defect in the sympathetic nervous system. The exact nature of this defect is a matter of conjecture; but whatever its specific identity, it would appear to operate in such a way as to block or obstruct the transmission of certain nervous impulses into both the organs of the body and the central nervous system and brain.

Drug Treatment of the Simple Psychopath   The results of the previous research suggested to the Ohio State University investigator that the simple psychopath mimics in several ways, behaviorally and possibly organically, the untreated hyperactive child. Inasmuch as hyperactivity in children has lent itself to effective treatment by drugs which produce arousal, there was reason to believe simple psychopaths might also respond to chemotherapy by means of arousal drugs. Accordingly, an experimental drug treatment program was begun in 1972 at Chillicothe Correctional Institute in which 41 subjects were rotated on a drug stimulating agent (imipramine) and placebo. Twenty-two men completed the six-month program, including nine simple psychopaths, all of whom had spent a minimum of 30 percent of their adult lives in prison. Seven of these nine had records of escape attempts.

The improvement in behavior of the simple psychopaths as a result of drug-induced arousal was obvious not only to the researchers but also to institutional staff members and other inmates as well. A number of these men were given jobs of greater trust and reduced custody; two of the nine on medication were permitted outside the prison. According to Goldman et al. (1974):

> . . . the great achievement of this program was neither in the organic symptom changes, the behavioral ratings, nor in subject cooperation but rather in the self-reported positive changes in each subject's psychological status. They reported themselves to be more energetic, less anxious, having more restful sleep, better appetite, less impulsivity, decreased irritability and above all else, a markedly increased feeling of well-being [p. 70].

These results suggest the possibility that for the small number of individuals who exhibit the characteristics identified with the simple psychopath, there may be considerable promise in a program that combines parole and closely supervised medication. The authors rightly emphasize the serious moral, ethical, and legal implications of such a decision and acknowledge that the criminal justice system will "have to surround the treatment of this severe behavioral disorder with every possible legal safeguard to prevent encroachment on the civil liberties of this population" (p. 72).

TOWARD A BIOSOCIAL THEORY OF CRIMINALITY

Mednick (1977) has stated that none of the research which has been reported thus far has provided conclusive evidence of genetic over environmental factors in the genesis of criminality:

> Given the nature of the genetic and environmental facts, it is still an appropriate a priori hypothesis that *heredity and environment always interact in a dynamic*

fashion to bring about and shape criminal behavior, and that both the mutual interaction and the mutual strength of the two factors form a continuous dimension for all persons and situations (p. 88).

He makes the further point that criminality can only be studied meaningfully from a genetic perspective if it is closely associated with a "well-defined somatic or psychological state."

Has biocriminological research identified any such somatic or psychological states? In Mednick's judgment, the evidence from nearly thirty years of investigation indicates that autonomic nervous system deviance has been demonstrated to reliably differentiate the antisocial individual. Lykken (1957) reported abnormally diminished autonomic nervous system (ANS) reactivity and slow recovery in psychopathic offenders, as measured by the GSR. Skin conductance measures afford a convenient peripheral indication of ANS activity.

In 1967, Hare reported that psychopathic inmates at a maximum security prison were sluggish ANS responders. Ten years later, he found that those who had committed additional serious crimes exhibited the slowest recovery rates (Hare, 1978). Thus, abnormally diminished ANS reactivity and slow recovery had predictive validity in forecasting serious criminality.

Further research by Bell et al. (1977) has demonstrated the heritability of ANS reactivity in a study of electrodermal responses of children with criminal and noncriminal fathers.

Mednick has attempted to formulate a theory which explains how ANS deviance may help to account for some types of crime and some percentage of criminals. His approach seeks to understand the possible interaction of biological and social factors in the socialization process and assumes that:

1. Law-abiding behavior must be learned.
2. The learning of such behavior involves certain environmental conditions and individual abilities.
3. Lack of any of these conditions might be responsible for some forms of antisocial behavior.

An essential part of socialization involves learning to inhibit antisocial or asocial behavior such as aggression. Typically this occurs when the commission of aggressive behavior is followed by punishment. The child learns to avoid further punishment by suppressing or inhibiting the disapproved behavior. Fear reduction is a powerful, naturally occurring reinforcement in this passive avoidance learning sequence. That is, the individual both avoids punishment and reduces fear by *learning not to do something* for which he or she was previously punished.

According to this approach, four conditions must be present in order for the child to learn effectively to inhibit antisocial behavior:

1. A censuring agent (typically the family or peers).
2. An adequate fear response.
3. The ability to learn the fear response in anticipation of an asocial act.
4. Fast dissipation of fear to quickly reinforce the inhibiting response.

TERMS TO IDENTIFY AND REMEMBER

family history (pedigree) approach

adoption study

monozygotic (MZ) twins

hyperactivity

electroencephalogram (EEG)

cardiac liability

biochemical approach

aphasia

hyperkinesis

XYY chromosomal anomaly

twin study

concordance

dizygotic (DZ) twins

episodic dyscontrol syndrome

dyslexia

skin conductance

learning disability

simple and hostile psychopaths

orthomolecular psychiatry

REFERENCES

Allen, H. E. A biosocial model of antisocial behavior. Paper presented at the Ohio Valley Sociological Association meeting, Akron, OH, May 1, 1970.

Batchelor, I. R. C. *Henderson and Gillespie's Textbook of Psychiatry.* London: Oxford University Press, 1969.

Bell, B., Mednick, S. A., Gottesman, I. I., and Sergeant, J. Electrodermal parameters in young normal male twins. In S. A. Mednick and K. O. Christiansen (eds.), *Biosocial Bases of Criminal Behavior.* New York: Gardner Press, 1977.

Bonnet, P., and Pfeiffer, C. C. Biochemical diagnosis of delinquent behavior. In L. J. Hippchen (ed.), *Ecologic-Biochemical Approaches to Treatment of Delinquents and Criminals.* New York: Van Nostrand Reinhold, 1978.

Burt, C. The genetic determination of differences in intelligence: A study of monozygotic twins reared together and apart. *British Journal of Psychology* 57 (1966): 137–153.

Chorover, S. L. Big Brother and psychotechnology. *Psychology Today* 7 (1973): 43–54.

Christiansen, K. O. A review of studies of criminality among twins. In S. A. Mednick and K. O. Christiansen (eds.), *Biosocial Bases of Criminal Behavior.* New York: Gardner Press, 1977a.

———. A preliminary study of criminality among twins. In S. A. Mednick and K. O. Christiansen (eds.), *Biosocial Bases of Criminal Behavior.* New York: Gardner Press, 1977b.

Cortes, J. B., and Gatti, F. M. *Delinquency and Crime.* New York: Seminar Press, 1972.

Cott, A. The etiology of learning disabilities. In L. J. Hippchen (ed.), *Ecologic-Biochemical Approaches to Treatment of Delinquents and Criminals.* New York: Van Nostrand Reinhold, 1978.

Currie, S. Clinical course and prognosis of temporal lobe epilepsy. *Brain* 94 (1971): 173–190.

Dalgaard, O. S., and Kringlen, E. A Norwegian twin study of criminality. *British Journal of Criminology* 16 (1976): 213–232.

Dugdale, R. L. *The Jukes: A Study in Crime, Pauperism, Disease, and Heredity.* New York: Putnam, 1895.

Funkenstein, D. H., Greenblatt, M., and Solomon, H. C. Psychophysiological study of mentally ill patients. Part I: The status of the peripheral a.n.s. as determined by the reaction to epinephrine and mecholyl. *American Journal of Psychiatry* 106 (1949): 16–28.

Goddard, H. H. *The Kallikak Family: A Study in the Heredity of Feeblemindedness.* New York: Macmillan, 1912.

Goldman, H., Dinitz, S., Lindner, L., Foster, T., and Allen, H. E. *A Designed Treatment Program of Sociopathy by Means of Drugs: A Summary Report.* Columbus, OH: Program for the Study of Crime and Delinquency, 1974.

Gunn, J., and Fenton, G. Epilepsy, automatism and crime. *Lancet* 1 (1971): 1173–76.

Hare, R. D. *Psychopathy: Theory and Research.* New York: Wiley, 1970.

Hare, R. D., and Schalling, D. (eds.), *Psychopathic Behaviour.* New York: Wiley, 1978.

Hippchen, L. J. The need for a new approach to the delinquent-criminal problem. In L. J. Hippchen (ed.), *Ecologic-Biochemical Approaches to Treatment of Delinquents and Criminals.* New York: Van Nostrand Reinhold, 1978.

Hoffer, A. Some theoretical principles basic to orthomolecular psychiatric treatment. In L. J. Hippchen (ed.), *Ecologic-Biochemical Approaches to Treatment of Delinquents and Criminals.* New York: Van Nostrand Reinhold, 1978.

Holzman, H. R. Learning disabilities and juvenile delinquency: Biological and sociological theories. In C. R. Jeffery (ed.), *Biology and Crime.* Beverly Hills, CA: Sage, 1979.

Hutchings, B., and Mednick, S. A. Criminality in adoptees and their adoptive and biological parents: A pilot study. In S. A. Mednick and K. O. Christiansen (eds.), *Biosocial Bases of Criminal Behavior.* New York: Gardner Press, 1977.

Jacobs, P. A., Brunton, M., and Melville, M. M. Aggressive behavior, mental subnormality and the XYY male. *Nature* 208 (1965): 1351.

Jeffery, C. R. *Crime Control Through Environmental Design.* Beverly Hills, CA: Sage Publications, 1977.

———. (ed.), *Biology and Crime.* Beverly Hills, CA: Sage, 1979.

Keilitz, I., Zaremba, B. A., and Broder, P. K. Learning disabilities and juvenile delinquency. In L. D. Savitz and N. Johnson (eds.), *Contemporary Criminology.* New York: Wiley, 1982.

Kelly, H. E. Biosociology and crime. In C. R. Jeffery (ed.), *Biology and Crime.* Beverly Hills, CA: Sage, 1979.

Lindner, L., Goldman, H., Dinitz, S., and Allen, H. E. An antisocial personality with cardiac lability. *Archives of General Psychiatry* 23 (1970): 260–267.

Lippert, W. W. The electrodermal system of the psychopath. Unpublished Ph.D. dissertation, University of Cincinnati, 1965.

Mark, V., and Ervin, F. *Violence and the Brain.* New York: Harper & Row, 1970.

Mazur, A., and Robertson, L. S. *Biology and Social Behavior.* New York: The Free Press, 1972.

Mednick, S. A. Biosocial factors and primary prevention of antisocial behavior. In S. A. Mednick and S. G. Shoham (eds.), *New Paths in Criminology: Interdisciplinary and Intercultural Explorations.* Lexington, MA: Lexington Books, 1979.

Mednick, S. A., and Volavka, J. Biology and crime. In N. Morris and M. Tonry (eds.), *Crime and Justice: An Annual Review of Research.* Chicago: University of Chicago Press, 1980.

Mednick, S. A., Volavka, J., Gabrielli, W. F., and Itil, T. M. EEG as a predictor of antisocial behavior. *Criminology* 19 (1981): 219–229.

Monroe, R. *Episodic Behavioral Disorder: A Psychodynamic and Neurological Analysis.* Cambridge, MA: Harvard University Press, 1970.

Montagu, A. Chromosomes and crime. *Psychology Today* 2 (1968): 43–49.

Morrison, H. L. The asocial child: A destiny of sociopath? In W. H. Reid (ed.), *The Psychopath.* New York: Brunner/Mazel, 1978.

Murray, C. A. *The Link Between Learning Disabilities and Juvenile Delinquency.* Washington, D.C.: U.S. Government Printing Office, 1976.

Nassi, A., and Abramowitz, S. I. From phrenology to psychosurgery and back again: Biological studies of criminality. *American Journal of Orthopsychiatry* 46 (1976): 591–607.

Philpott, W. H. Ecological aspects of antisocial behavior. In L. J. Hippchen (ed.), *Ecologic-Biochemical Approaches to Treatment of Delinquents and Criminals.* New York: Van Nostrand Reinhold, 1978.

Rodin, E. Psychomotor epilepsy and aggressive behavior. *Archives of General Psychiatry* 28 (1973): 210–213.

Safer, D., and Allen, R. *Hyperactive Children.* Baltimore, MD: Univeristy Park Press, 1976.

Satterfield, J. H. The hyperactive child syndrome: A precursor of adult psychopathy? In R. D. Hare and D. Schalling (eds.), *Psychopathic Behavior.* New York: Wiley, 1978.

Schachter, S., and Latane, B. Crime, cognition, and the autonomic nervous system. In D. Levine (ed.), *Nebraska Symposium on Motivation.* Lincoln: University of Nebraska Press, 1964.

Schauss, A. *Diet, Crime, and Delinquency.* Berkeley, CA: Parker House, 1981

Schlapp, M. G., and Smith, E. H. *The New Criminology.* New York: Boni and Liveright, 1928.

Schoenthaler, S. Personal communication, Jan. 1975.

Shah, S. A., and Roth, L. H. Biological and physiological factors in criminality. In D. Glaser (ed.), *Handbook of Criminology.* Chicago: Rand McNally, 1974.

Shoemaker, D. J. *Theories of Delinquency.* New York: Oxford University Press, 1984.

Slavin, S. H. Information processing defects in delinquents. In L. J. Hippchen (ed.), *Ecologic-Biochemical Approaches to Treatment of Delinquents and Criminals.* New York: Van Nostrand Reinhold, 1978.

Stephens, G. Crime in the year 2000. *The Futurist* 25 (1981): 48–52.

Suinn, R. M. *Fundamentals of Behavior Pathology.* New York: Wiley, 1970.

Thornton, W. E., James, J. A., and Doerner, W. G. *Delinquency and Justice.* Glenview, IL: Scott, Foresman, 1982.

Turner, W. J., and Merlis, S. Clinical correlations between electroencephalography and antisocial behavior. *Medical Times* 90 (1962): 505–511.

Valetutti, P. The teacher's role in the diagnosis and management of students with medical problems. In R. Haslam and P. Valetutti (eds.), *Medical Problems in the Classroom.* Baltimore, MD: University Park Press, 1975.

Vetter, H. J., and Wright, J. *Introduction to Criminology.* Springfield, IL: Charles C. Thomas, 1974.

Ware, E. M. Some effects of nicotinic and ascorbic acids on the behavior of institutionalized delinquents. In L. J. Hippchen (ed.), *Ecologic-Biochemical Approaches to Treatment of Delinquents and Criminals.* New York: Van Nostrand Reinhold, 1978.

Wilson, E. O. *Sociobiology.* Cambridge, MA: Harvard University Press, 1975.

———. Foreword. In D. P. Barash, *Sociobiology.* New York: Elsevier, 1977.

Witkin, H. A., Mednick, S. A., Schulsinger, F., Bakkestrom, D. R., Christiansen, K. O., Goodenough, D. R., Hirschhorn, K., Lundstein, C., Owen, D. R., Philip, J., Rubin, D. B., and Stocking, M. Criminality, aggression and intelligence among XYY and XXY men. In S. A. Mednick and K. O. Christiansen (eds.), *Biosocial Bases of Criminal Behavior.* New York: Gardner Press, 1977.

Wunderlich, R. C. Neuroallergy as a contributing factor to social misfits: Diagnosis and treatment. In L. J. Hippchen (ed.), *Ecologic-Biochemical Approaches to Treatment of Delinquents and Criminals.* New York: Van Nostrand Reinhold, 1978.

Yaryura-Tobias, J. A. Biological research on violent behaivor. In L. J. Hippchen (ed.), *Ecologic-Biochemical Approaches to Treatment of Delingents and Criminals.* New York: Van Nostrand Reinhold, 1978.

FOUR

THE ADMINISTRATION OF JUSTICE

People tend to view American society and its criminal justice system as reacting to a "crime problem." In many ways this is correct. But it is also correct to say that society and various criminal justice agencies create "crime problems." They do so in terms of their exercise of discretion in determining when, how, and against whom to make and enforce laws. Thus, our crime situation is not merely an occurrence; it is, at least in part, a product of organizational activity.

Discretion is a fundamental element in the operation of the criminal justice system and process: where agents are free to choose among alternatives in making decisions, we speak of their exercising choice; when that choice is not open to review, we speak of the choice as discretionary. Many individuals and agencies—for example, police, prosecutors, judges, juries, parole boards, correctional officials—are involved directly or indirectly with discretionary decisions, but review of decisions other than those of the judiciary is infrequent, and considerable disparity can result. A decision by the police whether to arrest and, if arrest, what charges to file has an impact on the criminal process, including a possible sentence. Prosecutors determine specific charges to place against offenders. The charge, in turn, often dictates a different sentence if the accused is convicted. Judges exercise discretion in sentencing and correctional officials may have wide latitude in decisions involving the conditional release of offenders from confinement.

The principal role and responsibility of the police is to maintain peace and public order within a carefully established framework of individual liberties, that is, in a manner consistent with the freedoms secured by the U.S. Constitution. That responsibility is shared by other elements of society, beginning with each individual and spreading to each institution and each level of government—local, state, and federal. However, because crime is an immediate threat to our respective communities, the police have a highly visible and perhaps even primary role in controlling the threat and fear of crime.

The preservation of peace and order is more complex than simply preventing crimes, making arrests for violations of the law, recovering stolen property, and providing assistance in the prosecution of those accused of crimes. The police only spend something on the order of 10 to 15 percent of their time enforcing the law. The most substantial portion of their time goes toward providing less glamorous services that are, nevertheless, essential to maintaining public order and well-being.

Law enforcement is faced today with many critical problems and issues, including the proper use of discretion, the assimilation of minority members and women, the impact of job-related stress on police officers, police use of deadly force, and the professionalization of policing.

During the past two decades it has been recognized that the period from arrest to trial (or acceptance of a guilty plea) is perhaps the most crucial phase in the criminal process. This pretrial period is the time when many important decisions are made about what will happen to the defendant. If the grand jury proceeding or preliminary hearing results in sufficient evidence to charge the individual with a crime (i.e., a finding of "probable cause"), the defendant is arraigned and given the opportunity to enter a plea to the charges. He is informed of his constitutional rights, particularly as to representation by counsel, and may be placed in confinement, freed on bail, or released on his own recognizance.

The two critical issues which arise during the pretrial period both involve discretion. The first of these is pretrial release. A defendant who is detained in jail suffers adverse consequences from the experience, but his individual plight has to be weighed against the possibility that his release will result in further danger to society. The second issue is plea negotiation. Since the criminal justice system lacks the resources to try every person accused of a crime, the practice of plea negotiation—despite its critics and detractors—is seen as an essential element in the administrative disposition of a large percentage of cases. Compared with the total volume of cases entering the criminal justice system, relatively few cases are disposed of by trial. Nevertheless, the criminal trial is an indispensable feature of our system. The accused is brought to trial under a presumption of innocence; it is the task of the prosecution to prove beyond a reasonable doubt that the defendant is guilty of the crime with which he or she is charged.

Sentencing is perhaps the most important phase of the criminal process, for it is in this stage that the disposition of the criminal offender is decided. In earlier periods, offenders were subject to retaliation and physical abuse as a punishment for wrongdoing. The contemporary criminal justice system is still punitive in its orientation, but the punishment is justified on several utilitarian grounds, including deterrence and incapacitation. In recent years, support has grown for the position that retribution ("the law of just deserts") is an appropriate objective of sentencing. Traditional dispositions include fines, probation, and imprisonment, with probation being the most common choice.

Jails are the intake point of our entire criminal justice system and are the most prevalent type of correctional institution. They are primarily a function of local government, and they are as diverse in size, physical condition, and efficiency as the units of government that operate them. The three types of jails are pretrial detention facilities for persons awaiting trial, sentenced facilities for persons serving sentences, and combination facilities for pretrial detainees and some convicted persons. Jails in the United States are quite old and are frequently in need of extensive repair. In addition, many are offensive to the eye and nose because of noxious odors, dirty lavatories, dirty floors, stained walls, and vermin. In many places, juveniles are held in adult jails and are exposed to the threat of physical and sexual abuse from older inmates. Jail suicide is estimated to claim one thousand lives each year.

The social, political, and racial forces within America's largest and most dangerous prisons have changed dramatically in the past two decades. The inmate social system and codes of conduct described by criminologists in the 1960s are no longer accurate. A new type of inmate has entered prisons in large numbers since the 1960s, and many political changes have occurred in society since that time.

One of the most significant changes in prison life has been the emergence of gangs. These gangs are generally divided among blacks, whites, and Chicanos. Black gangs emerged in the 1950s as an outgrowth of the civil rights and black movements outside of prisons. White gangs developed largely as a result of violence directed against them by black and Chicano gangs. Chicano gangs were an extension of street gangs operating in the cities and towns of California and Texas; hostilities that existed between these groups on the streets carried over into prison. At one point, the attacks and counterattacks between gangs in California prisons were so frequent that authorities segregated gangs by assigning them to different prisons.

Community-based correctional programs are viewed as alternatives to imprisonment: they are situated in local communities; they are usually smaller in size; they include day programs that have no residential requirements; and they allow for greater contact and interaction between the community and the "outmates" participating in these programs.

The backbone of community corrections is probation, the assignment of offenders to community supervision as an alternative to incarceration in a jail or prison. Supervision is carried out by probation officers who often combine probation and parole functions. These officers are responsible for securing compliance by their clients to the conditions of their probation or parole and with assisting their establishment of a law-abiding style of life. The role conflict between the supervisory and therapeutic or counseling functions of the probation officer is a major source of job-related stress for many officers.

Parole is the administrative process by means of which imprisoned offenders are released under community supervision before the expiration of their maximum sentences. The release is decided by an administrative body known as a parole board, and it is the board that makes the final decision to return to prison the parolee who has committed a new crime or violated the conditions of parole.

Parole decision making has, in the past, been susceptible to many subjective biases. In an attempt to rectify this situation, parole decision-making guidelines have been adopted in a number of correctional systems. Many research studies have been carried out using recidivism as the dependent variable, and these studies show that a number of background characteristics of offenders are related to the probability of success on parole. The evidence that specific institutional arrangements and treatment modalities can significantly affect success rates is less convincing.

No area in corrections is in a greater state of flux than parole and other forms of conditional release. Some correctional practititioners, scholars, and political figures favor abolishing parole; others point to conditional release as the safety valve for the nation's overcrowded and volatile prisons. The controversy has continued since the 1870s, when Zebulon R. Brockway introduced the indeterminate sentence and parole at Elmira Reformatory. It seems likely the debate will continue, because the real issue is not parole or conditional release, but basic philosophies and principles that underlie our societal response to crime and punishment.

chapter 16

THE CRIMINAL JUSTICE SYSTEM

COMPONENTS OF THE CRIMINAL JUSTICE SYSTEM

CRIMINAL PROCEDURE

CRIME CONTROL VERSUS DUE PROCESS

SUMMARY

DISCUSSION QUESTIONS

TERMS TO IDENTIFY AND REMEMBER

REFERENCES

As fear of crime has intensified in the United States, so has the debate over the ways by which crime might be decreased or even prevented. The agents of the **criminal justice system**—law enforcement, prosecution, courts, and corrections—are the principal actors in the fight against crime. The police are responsible for detecting and apprehending people who violate the criminal laws; prosecutors decide whether the circumstances warrant initiating prosecution by filing formal charges against suspects; the courts decide guilt or innocence and impose sentence upon those who are convicted or plead guilty; and the correctional component of the criminal justice system is charged with the responsibility for carrying out the sentence of the court.

When described in this fashion, the administration of justice sounds neat, orderly, and systematic. Unfortunately, it is none of these things—least of all systematic. Until recently, it was something of a standing joke among criminal justice practitioners and criminologists to refer to the "criminal justice nonsystem." Investigative reporters and television documentaries have introduced the public to some of the idiosyncrasies of "justice American-style," and such characterizations are no longer a private matter.

The comedian Lenny Bruce once observed that, "In the Halls of Justice, all of the justice is in the halls." The quip summons up a picture of lawyers and clients huddled in discussion in the drafty corridors of some mildewed county courthouse as they haggle over the details of a bargained plea. Bruce was not trying to be funny: his comment was based on his own first-hand experiences with the criminal justice system as a frequent violator of public order statutes and the drug laws. But the remark is not without accuracy as a rough description of how the administration of justice operates in the United States.

Part of the difficulty lies with the use of the term *criminal justice system.* This expression is a convenient abstraction with no counterpart in reality. The American criminal justice system is not a single system but a hodgepodge of separate systems, subsystems, institutions, and procedures. Throughout the tens of thousands of towns, cities, counties, and states in the United States, and in the federal government as well, there are different types of criminal justice systems. While they may appear similar in that they all apprehend, prosecute, convict, and try to correct lawbreakers, no two systems are exactly alike and very few are linked together in any comprehensive manner.

Among criminal justice professionals there is a widely held view that coping with crime and its consequences is (or ought to be) everyone's business. Unfortunately, many public agencies and private citizens refuse even to acknowledge that they have any responsibility for trying to reduce crime. Moreover, the effectiveness of the criminal justice system is lessened by intramural conflicts among the police, courts, and correctional agencies. In addition, many courts, law enforcement agencies, and correctional facilities have few or no working relationships with the various private and public organizations that might provide valuable services for their clients. Even worse, however, is the fact that most agencies have no clear policies for obtaining such assistance, even if there is awareness of its availability.

The term *system* connotes an orderly arrangement of parts according to some plan or design. The basic notion involved is that relationships among parts or components in a system are deliberate rather than haphazard. Further, it strongly implies the arrangement exists to achieve some goal or purpose. A major characteristic of systems in their operating aspects is that anything which affects one part can potentially affect other parts, as well as the entire system in its total functioning. These features are incorporated in the *linear process model* (see Figure 16.1), an orderly progression of events from input to output. Coffey, Eldefonso, and Hartinger (1974), who developed this model, have described the system in this manner: "The input is what the system deals with; the process is *how* the system deals with the input; and the output is the *results* of the process . . ." (p. 9). If we apply this model to the criminal justice system, input refers to selected law violations (i.e., reported crimes); process refers to the activities of the police, courts, and corrections; and output includes the results (i.e., success or failure) obtained from the process.

The major difficulty with this model, in our judgment, is that by directing attention to the administration of justice as a system, the model diverts attention from the real way the administration of justice occurs in thousands of daily transactions: namely, through the operation of **discretion** and **accommodation.** Discretion refers to the range of options available to those who are charged with the responsibility and authority to carry out the various tasks assigned by the laws of the municipal, county, state, or federal governments. As we shall try to show, from the police officer who can choose between issuing a warning or a citation, to the parole board members who can decide whether to release an offender from prison next week, next month, or next year, practitioners in all components of the criminal justice system are armed with discretionary powers. Needless to say, these powers are susceptible to influences of many types and are often misused or abused, but they are regarded as an indispensable requirement of the criminal justice system.

Accommodation is a term that covers the interactions between practitioners in the criminal justice system by means of which the vast bulk of daily business is conducted in the administration of justice. These interactions take place within the context of a bureaucracy whose members occupy various work roles and positions. In addition to whatever goals and objectives the system may set with regard to equity and justice, there are other—often competing—goals and objectives that are related to job performance and efficiency. Thus, police departments are interested in "clearing cases" through arrests of suspected offenders; prosecutors are concerned with a backlog of cases; judges complain about crowded dockets; and correctional authorities are distressed by jail and prison overcrowding. Consequently, many decisions are made through "give-and-take" discussions which appear to be considerably less than just and equitable to the accused person, however satisfactory they may seem to the achievement of administrative efficiency. We shall take a closer look at some of the

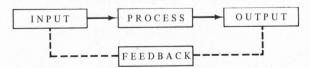

Figure 16.1 Linear process model. (*Source:* A. Coffey, E. Eldefonso, and W. Hartinger, *An Introduction to the Criminal Justice System and Process.* Englewood Cliffs, N.J.: Prentice-Hall, 1974, p. 9. Reproduced by permission of the authors and publisher.)

conflicts between these objectives when we discuss the due-process and crime-control models.

It is practically impossible to exaggerate the importance of discretion and accommodation as the key to understanding the criminal justice system and process in the United States. The use of machine models and analogies tends to leave many people with the feeling that there is some "right way" for justice to be administered, while any deviation from this prescribed path is tantamount to a miscarriage of justice. Even the nature of the interaction between criminal justice practitioners is subject to distortion and misinterpretation. For example, while carrying out a study of inmates on Florida's death row, one of the authors asked prisoners whether they believed they had received a fair trial. With rare exceptions the answer was "no," which, under the circumstances, was perfectly predictable. But when asked why they felt that their trial had been unfair, inmate after inmate replied in roughly the same way: in recesses during the trial they had seen their attorney (who was usually a public defender or court-appointed lawyer) talking in a friendly way and joking or laughing with members of the staff of the prosecutor (Lewis et al. 1979).

The administration of justice is not a series of abstract operations or processes which takes place according to some blueprint or computer program; it is a series of human interactions. Defense attorneys negotiate with assistant prosecutors to reduce charges against defendants; judges confer with probation officers over details in a presentence report, trying to determine whether the ends of justice are better served by putting offenders in jail or prison or letting them go free. The objectives are balanced between what is needed and required for the well-being of the offender and for the welfare and protection of society. The tool is compromise through accommodation.

COMPONENTS OF THE CRIMINAL JUSTICE SYSTEM

Law Enforcement

To both criminals and law-abiding citizens, the police represent the most visible part of the criminal justice system. They are the entry point for the failures of other agencies in society that deal in human services, as well as the failures of the other components or subsystems of the criminal justice system. Because the police are the *only* part of the criminal justice system that is in direct daily contact with both offenders and the public, their duties and responsibilities are more distinctive than those of other service agencies. Furthermore, law enforcement policies—to a considerable extent—are created by police officers themselves. Kaplan (1973) observes:

> A criminal code, in practice, is not a set of specific instructions to policemen but a more or less rough map of the territory in which policemen work. How an individual policeman moves around that territory depends largely on his personal discretion [p. 74].

Police officers make the principal determination in each instance of whether or not the criminal process is begun.

The highly discretionary character of police work contrasts with the widespread public view that "the police enforce the criminal laws and preserve peace mechanically, simply by arresting anyone who has deviated from legislative norms of acceptable behavior" (President's Commission on Law Enforcement and Administration of Justice, 1967*b*, p. 120). In reality, the police do not possess the resources to enforce all criminal laws equally, and, if they had such capabilities, the other components of the criminal justice system would be unable to cope with the number of violators entering the system as a result of such rigid enforcement policies.

Police are faced with the necessity of enforcing many laws dealing with areas of public order and moral conduct—laws which are often extremely controversial, unpopular, ambiguous, or unenforceable, or which affect the everyday activities of law-abiding citizens, even though they were meant only to apply to activities of certain kinds of criminals. Gambling and sex are examples of just such activities regulated by law.

Finally, police officers are responsible for considering the foreseeable consequences of an arrest. As the *Task Force Report: The Police* (President's Commission on Law Enforcement and Administration of justice, 1967*b*) states, "in light of these inherent limitations, individual police officers must, of necessity, be given considerable latitude in exercising their arrest power. As a result, no task committed to individual judgment is more complex or delicate. A mistake in judgment can precipitate a riot or, on the other hand, culminate in subsequent criminal activity by a person who was erroneously released by an officer" (p. 120). An unjustified arrest can seriously, perhaps permanently, affect the future course of a person's life. With today's critical attitudes toward law enforcement, an officer's decision to act can have a long-range negative effect on his or her future, as well. The importance of the power to arrest and the need for rational exercise of this power cannot be overstated.

Police are called upon to make instant, legally correct decisions under stress, and often without advice, that will hold up under hours of scrutiny and legal research by a defense lawyer. Further, police are often required to settle domestic fights, help deliver babies, and perform a vast variety of tasks which do not directly involve criminal activity. They also are called upon to prevent crime, a task which above all requires an intuitive sense for suspicious conduct and an understanding of human behavior; in short, they must be "streetwise." As Dr. Ruth Levy (*Task Force Report: The Police*, 1967*b*) has stated:

> Reviewing the tasks we expect of our law enforcement officers, it is my impression that their complexity is perhaps greater than that of any other profession. On the other hand, we expect our law enforcement officer to possess the nurturing, caretaking, sympathetic, empathizing, gentle characteristics of a physician, nurse, social worker, etc., as he deals with school traffic, acute illness and injury, suicidal threats, missing persons, etc. On the other hand, we expect him to command respect, demonstrate courage, control hostile impulses, and meet great physical hazards. . . . He is to control crowds, prevent riots, apprehend criminals, and chase after speeding vehicles. I can think of no other profession which constantly demands such seemingly opposite characteristics [p. 121].

Traditionally, the two principal missions of the police have been maintenance of order and enforcement of the law. With the increasing complexity of society, numerous and varied demands have been put upon the police because of their unique authority. The National Advisory Commission on Criminal Justice Standards and Goals (1973) recognized the following to be among the many functions which police agencies perform:

- Prevention of criminal activity
- Detection of criminal activity
- Apprehension of criminal offenders
- Participation in court proceedings
- Protection of constitutional guarantees
- Assistance to those who cannot care for themselves or who are in danger of physical harm
- Control of traffic
- Resolution of day-to-day conflicts among family, friends, and neighbors
- Promotion and preservation of civil order

These functions represent core elements in the contemporary police role. As we shall see, there is a great deal of controversy regarding the emphasis that ought to be placed on each of these functions.

It has been estimated that law enforcement duties require only about 10 percent of the police officer's time and energy; the remaining 90 percent encompasses what might be called **social service functions.** One may frequently hear police officers complain that there seems to be a contest among police departments to see who can undertake the largest number and most unusual kinds of non-law-enforcement projects. One police administrator (Clark, 1968) recommended police departments move from deliquency prevention and family crisis intervention programs to various forms of offender *treatment,* such as detoxification units, week-enders, and halfway house programs, which are currently, at least, the responsibility of the correctional subsystem of the criminal justice program. The situation is reminiscent of one confronting Raymond Chandler's fictional detective, Bernie Ohls, in the novel *The Long Goodbye* (1954). The novel's hero, a private investigator named Philip Marlowe, asks Ohls and his fellow detective, "You two characters been seeing any psychiatrists lately?"

> "Jesus," Ohls said, "hadn't you heard? We got them in our hair all the time these days. We've got two of them on the staff. This ain't police business any more. It's getting to be a branch of the medical racket. They're in and out of jail, the courts, and the interrogation rooms. They write reports fifteen pages long on why some punk of a juvenile held up a liquor store or raped a schoolgirl or peddled tea to the senior class. Ten years from now guys like Hernandez and me will be doing Rorschach tests and word associations instead of chin-ups and target practice. When we go out on a case we'll carry little black bags with portable lie detectors and bottles of truth serum. Too bad we didn't grab the four hard monkeys that poured it on Big Willie Magoon. We might have been able to unmaladjust them and make them love their mothers" [p. 286].

Much of the confusion about the role of the police officer, from the viewpoint of both the public and officers themselves, stems from confusion of the terms "law enforcement" and "crime prevention." These are both the designated duties of today's police officers, but despite their apparent similarity, they are not one and the same. The concept of a police force evolved from the need for an agency of government to enforce the law. As a matter of administrative convenience, the police force has also been charged with the task of preventing crime. The presence of a police officer may, of course, operate as a deterrent to some crimes; what the officer does beyond that point is left to his or her discretion.

Prosecution

Under our system of criminal law, a crime is defined as a public injury, that is an offense against "the people." This definition embodies the notion that the community as a whole is injured whenever harm is done to one of its members. Consequently, the right to take action against a criminal offense is delegated to the state, acting as the representative of the people. In accordance with this principle, prosecution as a public function has become a distinctive feature of American criminal justice.

Some states have created the office of public prosecutor by provisions of the state constitution; others have established the office by legislative enactment. These officials are known by a variety of titles: district attorney, prosecuting attorney, state attorney, county attorney, county solicitor, and commonwealth attorney are among the more popular designations. Regardless of differences in title, however, the duties and responsibilities of the public prosecutor are similar from one jurisdiction to another.

The office of public prosecutor is invested with broad and plenary powers. These are necessary in order for the prosecutor to carry out a wide range of functions pertaining to the administration of justice. Prosecutors can decide whether or not to prosecute a particular case; they have discretionary authority to grant immunity to an individual who wishes to turn state's evidence; they can make the choice of submitting a case to the grand jury for indictment or they can bypass the grand jury altogether by using a bill of information; they are empowered to bargain with the defense concerning the nature of the final plea, which generally means accepting a plea of guilty to a lesser charge in exchange for a recommendation of leniency; and they are responsible for organizing and presenting evidence in court and are influential with regard to the disposition of cases by suggesting appropriate penalties to the judge and jury. In summary, as Puttkammer (1953) phrases it, "There are no important limitations on the prosecuting attorney's power to terminate a case" [p. 192].

Prosecutors' effectiveness is usually measured by the number of convictions they can obtain while in office. Since their political careers depend in large part on their success in securing convictions, it is not surprising to find that they may dismiss or bargain away those cases which show little promise of conviction. In cases where they see no possibility of winning a conviction, prosecutors may negotiate for community supervision without prosecution ("deferred prosecution"). The public is seldom concerned about how prosecutors secure their convictions, only that they get them.

The decision to charge an offender is made after the police have made the arrest and presented their information to the prosecuting attorney. Except in those few police departments having legal advisors on call 24 hours a day, the prosecutor is the first *legally trained* individual to examine the facts. It is his or her job to decide whether to charge the suspect or dismiss ("no paper") the case. (A " **no paper" action** means the prosecutor has decided there is insufficient probability of a conviction and therefore no reason to file any information.)

A legal decision to proceed with prosecution depends on all of the "elements"[1] of the alleged crime being present: a narrowly defined unlawful act must have occurred, with the presence of criminal intent. The "intent" must apply to the specific unlawful act or the case is on shaky legal grounds. Many crimes for which an offender was arrested have a number of "lesser included offenses" contained within their definition. A good prosecutor can relate intent and the unlawful acts suitably, assuring a stronger case for conviction. If the prosecutor thinks there is a possibility of the defendant pleading guilty to a lesser charge (and accepting a lesser penalty), he or she may bargain for a reduced charge; however, if the defendant will not accept the lesser charge, the case may be dropped because of the unlikelihood of conviction. In addition to wasting state money, a trial without a conviction may also hurt the prosecutor's chances for reelection or advancement.

Aside from the "legal sufficiency" issue, a complaint also will be considered by the prosecutor from the extralegal standpoint. Often the most important of these extralegal considerations are matters of equity and office policy. Age, sex, race, social status, prior convictions, and other factors are not matters related to guilt or innocence, but they obviously are taken into account in the decision to charge. For instance, policies may be established to divert all first offenders or all persons under 18 years old to nonjudicial programs or, on the other hand, a very tough position may be taken on certain offenses that may result in charges in almost all of these cases and processing through the courts.

The prosecuting attorney's initial screening of suspects is a critically important stage in the criminal justice system; however, although more statistics are becoming available on this decision process, it is still an area that has undergone relatively little investigation. As early as 1933, Baker wrote:

> How much more significant would it be to have figures on the situations arising behind closed doors in the prosecutor's office! Court statistics are enlightening to such an extent that it is now almost commonplace to designate the prosecutor as the most powerful official in local government. If we had some means of checking the decisions of the prosecutor when the question "to prosecute or not to prosecute" arises, such figures would go much further to substantiate such a statement [p. 771].

Fifty years later, we are still seeking information that will help clarify this crucially important decision-making process.

---

[1]The *elements* of a crime refers to specific and precise statutory conditions of fact that must exist for a crime to have taken place. For instance it must be *dark* for "burglary in the night season" to take place.

Courts

The criminal court is the core of the American judicial system. The courts are highly organized, deeply venerated, and rigidly circumscribed by law and tradition. The entire criminal justice system is dependent upon, and responsible to, the court in its role as interpreter of the law. The police are guided and restricted by decisions of the court; prosecutors must weigh the legal and extralegal issues of cases before them in terms of the court which will try them; and the correctional system depends on the court for its workload. The formal processes that take place in the courtroom are not merely symbolic but are often vital for the protection of both the accused individual and society.

The structure and operations of the courts in the United States are more complex than any other judicial system in the Western world. Some of this complexity exists because the founding fathers adopted a federal form of government, with powers constitutionally divided between two levels of authority. This action necessitated some arrangement for the handling of cases arising under two distinct sets of laws: those of the national government and those of the individual states. To solve this problem, two separate and complete court systems, with trial courts and appellate courts, were established to operate side by side. Each state was free to fashion its judicial apparatus as it saw fit. As a result, we now have over one hundred district and appellate courts which comprise the federal court system, as well as the individual judicial systems of the fifty states, each with its own organization, personnel, and rules of procedure. Constitutionally, the parallel structures of national and state court systems are independent and equal in their respective spheres of authority.

The authority of a court, as established by the legal limits within which it is empowered to handle cases, is its **jurisdiction.** Kerper (1972) identifies the following courts in terms of their various jurisdictions:

- **Trial courts** A court that has authority to try a case is a trial court. This court impanels a jury, hears the evidence and arguments of counsel, receives the verdict, and sentences the defendant. Such a court has *original jurisdiction* of a case.
- **Appellate courts** A court that reviews cases which have originally been tried in a trial court is called an appeals court or an appellate court, and is said to have *appellate jurisdiction.*
- **Courts of record** A court of record's decisions are reviewed *on the record.* This means an appellate court does not hear the testimony of witnesses and the arguments of counsel over again. Instead, it reads the written transcript (or record) of what went on in the trial and bases its findings and decision on the record [p. 210].

All courts which try felony cases and most which try serious misdemeanor cases (those which carry possible jail sentences) keep records of court activity in a case; "court of record" is an expression used to distinguish them from *courts of limited jurisdiction,* that is, courts such as magistrate or justice of the peace courts which do not hold jury trials or handle appeals.

Original jurisdiction means that a court is authorized to try cases; general jurisdiction signifies that it can hold jury trials, hear the arguments of counsel, examine evidence, listen to testimony from witnesses, and so on; appellate jurisdiction indicates that a court has the authority to hear a defendant's appeal to set aside a conviction. Courts with original jurisdiction seldom have appellate jurisdiction and never with regard to a case they have tried. Cases can be appealed to *intermediate appellate courts* in a state, but the highest tribunal to which a case can be appealed is the **court of last resort**—the state equivalent of a supreme court.

It is fairly common practice to refer to "lower" as **inferior courts** and "higher" as **superior courts.** Included among the former are courts of limited jurisdiction; the latter comprises the appellate courts, especially courts of last resort. The status of trial courts (courts of general jurisdiction) in this hierarchical schema is equivocal: sometimes they are included among the lower courts and sometimes they are placed among the higher courts. It helps to remember that such distinctions are largely the result of custom and usage—a reflection of the prestige accorded to the various courts by members of the legal profession.

The Federal Court System

The United States Supreme Court is the only federal court specifically mandated by the Constitution. Other federal courts are established by legislative action. Article III, Section I of the Constitution states that "the judicial power of the United States shall be vested in one Supreme Court, and in such inferior courts as the Congress may from time to time ordain and establish."

The federal court system is arranged in hierarchical fashion, with the district courts at the base, the courts of appeals at the intermediate level, and the Supreme Court at the apex. Also a part of the federal judiciary are the United States magistrates, formerly called United States commissioners, and a variety of specialized courts that are rather closely circumscribed in their jurisdictional scope. Among these are the United States Court of Military Appeals, United States Court of Claims, United States Custom Court, United States Court of Customs and Patent Appeals, and Tax Court of the United States. The titles of these courts define fairly well their specialized functions.

The United States Supreme Court

The United States Supreme Court, often referred to simply as "the Court," consists of nine judges who are called "justices." These justices are appointed by the president, but their appointment is subject to confirmation by the Senate. The president also appoints one member of the Court to act as chief justice. His or her role is essentially that of chairperson of the Court; the chief justice has no formal powers of coercion over the other justices, although he or she may act administratively to apportion caseloads or direct the writing of a judicial decision.

Justices hold their tenure for "life or good behavior," as provided by the Constitution. A justice can only be removed by voluntary retirement or impeachment.

The Constitution also denies to the Congress the authority to reduce the salaries of the justices.

The working term of the Court is variable. Although statutory law requires that the term begin each year on the first Monday of October, it does not set a closing date. Thus, the Court continues in session for as long as it has business to transact. The workload has been steadily increasing with the expansion of the federal and state judiciaries. Although the Supreme Court gets most of its cases on appeal from these courts, the number of justices on the Court has not changed to meet the growing volume of judicial transactions. Each term, approximately three thousand cases are handled in the Court.

The appellate jurisdiction of the Supreme Court comprises the overwhelming bulk of its business. It reviews cases coming from lower federal courts and from state tribunals when issues pertaining to the Constitution or laws of the United States are involved. The Court has almost absolute power to control its agenda and this enables it to be highly selective and to assume jurisdiction only in those cases which raise the issue it currently wishes to consider. Over half of the requests come from the losing parties in the United States courts of appeals, and most of the remainder of cases are from disappointed litigants in the state tribunals of last resort.

Only at the level of the Supreme Court is there a bridge between the federal and state judicial structures. No path of appeal exists from a state court to any federal tribunal at lower levels in the hierarchy. If the Supreme Court grants *certiorari* (accepts jurisdiction), it will scrutinize the constitutional issue at stake and either sustain the state tribunal's finding or reverse the decision and release the appellant who has been fortunate enough to have had his or her appeal accepted. The Supreme Court reverses its state counterparts in about two-thirds of the cases it hears, partly as a result of the careful screening by the Court for cases which have "rightness," the specific issues which the Court wishes to address.

The Lower Federal Courts[2]

United States Courts of Appeals   The United States courts of appeals were established in 1891 to lighten the Supreme Court's growing burden of cases appealed from the federal district courts. Until 1984, the United States courts of appeals were known as circuit courts of appeals. They are characterized as *intermediate appellate courts* because they stand between the federal district courts, the United States Magistrates, and the specialized federal courts, on the one hand, and the Supreme Court on the other hand. They have the principal responsibility of reviewing judicial decisions reached in the lower courts.

There are 11 United States courts of appeals (including one for the District of Columbia), each with jurisdiction over a particular geographical section of the country—a so-called judicial circuit. The number of judges in each court of appeals ranges from three to nine. At least two judges must sit in a case, but normally

---

[2] Federal courts other than the Supreme Court are often referred to collectively as "lower federal courts."

decisions are made by a panel of three. The composition of these subgroups varies from case to case, with the presiding judge in each court making the assignments. On occasion, when disagreement arises among the members on an important point of law, the matter may be decided by the full court in what is called an *en banc decision,* for which all of the judges of the tribunal are sitting at the same time. Judges of the courts of appeals, like the Supreme Court Justices, hold their appointments for "life or good behavior."

United States District Courts   The 93 United States district courts are trial courts in the federal system. They are tribunals of original jurisdiction or first instance. It is here that the vast majority of noncriminal (civil) suits arising under national law are initiated and terminated: actions on patent rights, postal problems, copyright violations, bankruptcy, and so forth. Here also crimes committed against the federal government (i.e., those which involve conduct prohibited by Congress and which are punishable by the federal government) are tried. Each state contains no less than one district court (some having multiple divisions); sixteen states have two tribunals, eight contain three, and New York and Texas have four. Every district has at least one judge, depending on the workload, and some districts (e.g., the Southern District of New York) have as many as 24. A single judge conducts the trials in these lower tribunals except in cases involving the constitutionality of national and state statutes. Three judges must preside in trials of the latter type.

State and Local Courts

The complexity and variety of jurisdictions, functions, and titles of state and local courts defeat any attempt at making universally applicable generalizations. Although there are structural parallels between state court systems and the federal judicial system, as diagrammed in Figure 16.2, hierarchical arrangement in any given state may include two, three, four, or even more levels of courts. To confound matters even further, many persons in the criminal justice system often forget that the nomenclature for various courts is rather arbitrary. Consequently, they tend to increase confusion when they refer to courts by their titles rather than their jurisdictions or functions.

Court of Last Resort   Each state has an appellate tribunal which serves as the court of last resort. Titles are variable: in New York, Kentucky, and Maryland, the court of last resort is known as the court of appeals. In other states it is called the supreme court of appeals, supreme court of errors, court of criminal appeals, or supreme judicial court. Whatever the title, the court of last resort is the final authority on cases involving issues of state law.

Presided over by three to nine judges (usually there are seven), courts of last resort relate to the lower state courts in much the same way the United States Supreme Court relates to the lower federal courts. As the highest judicial body of the sovereign states, these tribunals have discretionary power to choose the cases they will hear. For this purpose, the **writ of** *certiorari,* a writ of review issued by the court

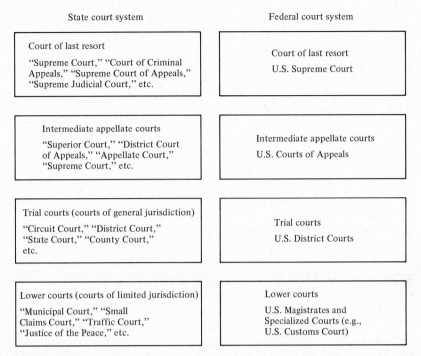

Figure 16.2 Parallels between the state court system and the federal court system.

commanding a lower court to "send up the record" of a case for consideration, is used in the same way it is used by the Supreme Court.

Intermediate Appellate Court   In addition to courts of last resort, 20 of the most heavily populated states have an intermediate level of appellate courts corresponding to the United States courts of appeals. As in the federal system, these intermediate courts provide relief for the overburdened state supreme courts and serve as courts of last resort for the majority of appeals received from the courts of original jurisdiction. New York became the first state to create a system of appellate courts shortly before the turn of the century.

Once again, a confusing variety of court designations is encountered: superior court, appellate court, and supreme court are some of the names given to intermediate appellate courts. In some states, courts of appeal may have original as well as appellate jurisdiction; in others, jurisdiction may be restricted to particular kinds of cases. Some states assign the defendant the right to appeal, regardless of whether or not the court wants to hear the case.

Trial Courts (Courts of General and Original Jurisdiction)   Trial courts are also known as courts of general or original jurisdiction. They are the primary courts having original jurisdiction in most serious criminal cases; they are the lowest courts of record at the state level. They can be referred to as district, circuit, or superior courts, or courts of common pleas, and there are numerous structural variations from state to state. Some systems provide for separate criminal and civil divisions; a few retain equity or chancery tribunals; and others have special probate and domestic relations courts. Regardless of how they are constituted, the judicial bodies on this level handle the bulk of major litigation under state law. All important civil litigation originates here, and persons accused of criminal offenses, other than petty crimes, are tried in these courts. These tribunals also serve as appellate units for cases instituted in the courts of limited jurisdiction. However, because they try such cases *de novo* (as though they had not previously been heard), further appeal normally lies with a higher court.

Lower Courts (Courts of Limited and Special Jurisdiction)   At the bottom of the hierarchy are the lower courts, of which there are 12,636 in the United States, according to the *National Survey of Court Organization 1971,* published by the Law Enforcement Assistance Administration (1972). These numerous minor tribunals of local character are identified by titles such as justice of the peace, magistrate, municipal, police, and small claims courts. These courts have various duties and varying degrees of limited jurisdiction. They are not courts of record; consequently, appeals from these courts are usually for a completely new trial before the next tier of courts within the state system.

   The jurisdiction of justices of the peace and the other lesser court functionaries is confined to minor infractions of the law, such as disorderly conduct, vagrancy, traffic violations, and civil suits involving small sums of money. In some states, justices of the peace and magistrates also conduct preliminary hearings in criminal matters to determine whether accused individuals should be bound over for trial in a higher tribunal. Historically, the American experience with these lesser organs of the system has not been very reassuring. They have been widely regarded as the weakest link in the administration of justice, although in recent years various reforms have been instituted under pressure from bar associations and civic groups. It was common practice in the past, and still is in some areas, for laymen having no formal legal training and with little judicial aptitude to preside over these courts. Considering this background, the comment of one justice of the peace about defendants brought before him is hardly surprising: "I don't ever remember having one who *wasn't* guilty. If the sheriff picks up a man for violating the law, he's guilty or he wouldn't bring him in here. Anyway, I don't get anything out of it if they aren't guilty" (Banks, 1961, p. 188). The following extract from the *Task Force Report: The Courts* (1967a) by the President's Commission on Law Enforcement and Administration of Justice conveys something of the atmosphere which characterizes the functioning of the lower courts:

> An observer in the lower criminal courts ordinarily sees a trial bearing little resemblance to those carried out under traditional notions of due process. There is usually no court reporter unless the defendant can afford to pay one. One result is an informality in the proceedings which would not be tolerated in a felony trial. Rules of evidence are largely ignored. Speed is the watchword. . . . Traditional safeguards honored in felony cases lose their meaning in such proceedings; yet there is still the possibility of lengthy imprisonment or heavy fine.

> In some cities trials are conducted without counsel for either side; the case is prosecuted by a police officer and defended by the accused himself. . . . Short jail sentences of one, two, or three months are commonly imposed on an assembly line basis . . . [pp. 31–33].

An offender who is subjected to a process of the kind described above is not likely to emerge from it with any beneficial changes. He returns to the streets to begin the cycle again in all its futility.

Corrections

Corrections represents those agencies of social control which attempt to change, neutralize, or eliminate the deviant behavior of adult criminals and juvenile delinquents. In theory, the correctional component of the criminal justice system begins to function with social and legal authority following the adjudication of guilt of an adult offender in the criminal courts, or when its services are invoked by the juvenile court authorities in the case of a minor charged with the commission of a delinquent act. In practice, the correctional function may be initiated informally prior to formal assumption of responsibility following court action. For instance, most police departments have officers on their staffs who specialize in work with juveniles and youthful offenders, and departments of social welfare provide protective services for children and adolescents with behavior problems. Such agencies may become involved with youngsters even before a referral is made to the juvenile court; in some cases, they manage to keep the juvenile out of court entirely.

Included in corrections are jails and lockups, prisons, detention centers for juveniles, probation and parole programs, and community-based treatment centers of various kinds. The corrections system is plagued by an overlapping of jurisdictions, contradictory philosophies, and a welter of organizational structures that are fragmented and isolated in terms of the functions they perform and the responsibilities they try to meet. Corrections has grown piecemeal, sometimes out of experience, sometimes out of sheer necessity, and sometimes out of folly.

If the correctional component of the criminal justice system is the least visible part of the system in its daily operations, then correctional institutions have the lowest visibility of all correctional facilities. Many prisons, particularly the older institutions, are located in isolated, thinly-populated, rural areas. Visits by community leaders, politicians, or judges who may routinely sentence offenders to confinement in these places are a rarity. In many instances the remoteness and difficulty of access of the prison impose real hardships on the families of prisoners and severely curtail the chances for relatives to remain in close touch during the convict's period of incarceration. All too often the public only becomes aware of correctional institutions when they become the subject of a news report because of a riot, prison break, guard or inmate slaying, or some other kind of dramatic event.

Escapes from prisons or jails produce public outcries for the tightening of security. To meet these demands, correctional authorities tend to over-supervise, overlock, and overcount their charges. The result is institutionalization, both for the prisoners and their keepers. The prison *routine* becomes the most important aspect of prison administration, and any variation from the concept of strict and unbending custody and discipline is viewed with skepticism.

The civil rights conflicts which the free world tries to escape by retreating from urban ghettos to segregated suburbs are magnified in the total correctional institution. The prisoner's instincts for self-preservation in this tense atmosphere are embodied in inmate defense groups and assassination squads. Bottled-up anger and frustration can explode in gang rape and intensified racial conflict between inmates and in prisoner-guard relations.

Corrections is unfairly taxed with problems that are overwhelmingly concentrated within a single component of the total correctional enterprise; namely, the prisons. Despite the large numbers of offenders who are dealt with by facilities and programs that either provide alternatives to incarceration, such as diversion or probation, and conditional release from imprisonment, such as parole and work release, discussion of correctional failures is concentrated almost exclusively on the problems that plague the prisons. Corrections, in turn, inherits most of the recalcitrant, intractable, and essentially incorrigible offenders who are not disposed of elsewhere in the criminal justice system. The criminal justice system, in turn, falls heir eventually to nearly every unsolved social problem in our society—which can be seen in daily transactions involving the mentally retarded, emotionally disturbed, actively psychotic, hopelessly incompetent, and ferally unsocialized individuals who make up a significant portion of the criminal justice system's clientele. Former Georgia Governor Lester Maddox, with what could fairly be described as Pickwickian humor, observed that the major problem facing Georgia's prisons was that they needed a better class of inmate. With a perfectly straight face—and equal justification—the same could be said for both the criminal justice system in general and corrections in particular.

A growing number of criminologists and other social scientists believe that even the most treatment-oriented correctional institutions, employing the most detailed rehabilitation programs, cannot live up to their manifest goals of resocializing offenders. Maintaining institutional routines and handling everyday problems—in short, "running the show"—tend to supersede the efforts of rehabilitation programs, especially when there are conflicts between them. Security measures which have to be taken because of the mandate given to these organizations are another obstacle to the achievement of rehabilitation goals. Thus, the experience of incarceration results, more often than not, in changes that are the exact opposite of those of resocialization and reformation. As Morris (1974) notes:

> . . . prison may be no more than an irrelevant interlude in a career of crime. . . . It may well be that the true function of the prison is no more than symbolic, a statement that even if penal treatments neither reform or deter, at least society has expressed its disapproval of crime [p. 83].

These considerations, plus the continually mounting costs of incarcerating prisoners who, in many instances, do not need to be kept in prison, have given urgency to the search for alternatives to confinement. Community-based correctional programs are conducted outside the prison walls, are located in or near population centers, and make use of locally available resources and services. They include such programs and facilities as in the following list.

Probation is a court action which permits the convicted offender to retain his freedom in the community, subject to court control and the supervision and guidance of a probation officer. Probation sustains the offender's ability to continue working and to protect his family's welfare, while avoiding the stigma and possible damaging effects of imprisonment.

Parole is a procedure by which prisoners are selected for release and then a service by which they are provided with the controls, assistance, and guidance they need as they serve the remainder of their sentences within the free community.

Halfway houses are small, homelike residential facilities located in the community for offenders who need more control than probation or other types of community supervision can provide. Halfway houses are also used for gradual readjustment to community life for those who have come out of institutions. Halfway house programs usually offer supervised living and counseling services, and draw upon the community for education, training, jobs, and recreation to aid in the rehabilitation process.

Under the alternative of **work release,** the offender is confined in an institution only at night or on weekends, but is permitted to pursue his or her normal life the remainder of the time. Such a program makes possible a greater degree of community supervision, but avoids total disruption of family life and employment.

Prerelease centers are supervised programs designed to ease the transition from total confinement to freedom by involving people from the community who come to the prison to provide information in areas of vital interest to the inmate who is about to be released. Subjects covered include such topics as employment, finances, family life, community services, and legal sources.

Community corrections has often been touted as "the wave of the future" in corrections. Community correctional administrators are apt to take a more sober and restrained view of the assets and limitations of community-based programs and approaches. As Kaye Harris, formerly of the National Council on Crime and Delinquency, observed: "If community corrections can reduce the severity of sentences, reduce the harm done by imprisonment, make services available to those who are otherwise denied them or reduce the huge capital outlays for new prisons, then we can say that community corrections is a successful strategy" (Blackmore, 1981, p. 17).

Juvenile Justice

The juvenile justice system evolved as an attempt to deal constructively with the problems of dependent, neglected, and delinquent youngsters within an informal and nonadversarial setting. The juvenile court operated as a blend of social casework agency and criminal court; procedural informality often resulted in the denial of rights to juveniles which are guaranteed to adults under the U.S. Constitution. Finally, in a series of important decisions, the U.S. Supreme Court undertook to extend due process and equal protection rights to juveniles.

A strong effort is made to divert as many youths as possible from the juvenile justice system. Once a juvenile has been adjudicated delinquent, a variety of post-adjudication alternatives are available to the court. Both residential and nonresidential programs are available which provide a variety of services. Despite efforts to place as many delinquents as possible in community-based correctional programs, the training school continues to handle most adjudicated delinquents. Release from training school may allow the youngster to remain in the community under supervision in an "aftercare" status, which roughly corresponds to parole for adult offenders.

Large cities in the United States may be experiencing a resurgence of gang violence. Juveniles participating in such activities belong, in many cases, to the category of "life-style violent juveniles," who have been born and reared in a subculture which reinforces exploitative aggression. Dealing with such individuals has thus far proven to be beyond the capabilities of the juvenile justice system. Indications are that many juveniles who have committed violent crimes are shuttled in and out of the system until they reach the age when they become the responsibility of the adult criminal courts.

CRIMINAL PROCEDURE

The U.S. Constitution is the most authoritative source of criminal procedure in our country. Americans are introduced as schoolchildren to the first ten amendments to the Constitution, known collectively as the Bill of Rights. They are instructed that the Bill of Rights provides certain safeguards to American citizens that are covered by such ringing phrases as "due process" and "equal protection under the law." They are less likely to be familiar with the historical fact that not until the passage of the Fourteenth Amendment in 1868 were these safeguards for the rights of the person accused of a crime made applicable to state courts. Prior to the Fourteenth Amendment, the Bill of Rights directly applied only to proceedings which took place in federal courts.

The Fourteenth Amendment

The Fourteenth Amendment to the U.S. Constitution declares, in part, "No State shall make or enforce any law which shall abridge the privileges of immunities of citizens of the United States, nor shall any State deprive any person of life, liberty, or property, without due process of law; nor deny any person within its jurisdiction the equal protection of the law . . ." Together with the Thirteenth and Fifteenth amendments, which were passed in the immediate post–Civil War period, the Fourteenth Amendment extended citizenship to former slaves and guaranteed them the same protections of law that the Constitution provided for other citizens. But the "due process" and "equal protection" phrases of the Fourteenth Amendment did not find their immediate application in the civil rights area. Until the turn of the century and for some time afterward, state courts and the U.S. Supreme Court employed these features of the Fourteenth Amendment primarily in order to protect business corporations from government regulation.

In 1884, in the case of *Hurtado* v. *California,* the Supreme Court rejected the **"shorthand doctrine,"** that is, making a blanket application of the Bill of Rights provisions binding on the states. The subsequent judicial history of the Fourteenth Amendment involved a continuing dialogue or debate within the U.S. Supreme Court between proponents of a piecemeal application of the due process and equal protection provisions and those justices who supported a variety of viewpoints which inclined toward total incorporation.

During the period 1961–1969—a period frequently referred to as the **due process revolution**—the U.S. Supreme Court took an activist role, becoming, quite literally, givers of the law rather than interpreters of it. The Warren court's activist role in the piecemeal extension of the provisions of the Bill of Rights, via the due process clause of the Fourteenth Amendment, to criminal proceedings in the respective states may have been a policy decision, as Swanson and Territo (1983) point out. Normally the Supreme Court will write opinions in about 115 cases during any particular term. During the 1938–1939 term, for example, only five cases appear under the heading of criminal law. Three decades later, during the height of the due process revolution, about one-quarter of each term's decisions related to criminal law.

Among the key decisions in the due process revolution were *Mapp* v. *Ohio, Gideon* v. *Wainwright, Escobedo* v. *Illinois,* and *Miranda* v. *Arizona.* These cases focused on the two vitally important areas of search and seizure and the right to counsel. They constitute, collectively, a watershed period in the administration of criminal justice in the United States.

The Fourth Amendment: Search and Seizure

The Fourth Amendment to the Constitution guarantees people the right "to be secure in their persons, houses, papers, and effects, against unreasonable searches and seizures." It was not until 1914, however, that the Supreme Court, in the case of *Weeks* v. *United States,* established the so-called **Exclusionary Rule** to govern the operation of the federal courts. According to the Exclusionary Rule, evidence obtained as a result of an unreasonable or illegal search is not admissible in a federal criminal prosecution.

The Exclusionary Rule curbed, but did not eliminate, abuses of the Fourth Amendment. Evidence obtained illegally by state law enforcement officers continued to find its way into federal prosecutions on the grounds that no federal official had participated in the violation of the defendant's rights. This type of federal-state search-and-seizure practice became known as the **"silver platter" doctrine,** a name which originated in Justice Frankfurter's decision in *Lustig* v. *United States* (1949). According to Justice Frankfurter, "the crux of that doctrine is that a search is a search by a federal official if he had a hand in it; it is not a search by a federal official if evidence secured by state authorities is turned over to the federal authorities on a silver platter" (pp. 78–79). The Supreme Court condemned this practice with regard to criminal investigations in the case of *Elkins* v. *United States* (1960). Writing for the majority, Justice Stewart held that the "silver platter" doctrine constituted an "inducement to subterfuge and evasion" (p. 222).

In the case of *Mapp* v. *Ohio* (1961), the Exclusionary Rule was extended to the state courts. This represented a reversal of the 1949 decision in *Wolf* v. *Colorado,* which permitted the states to establish their own procedural safeguards against unreasonable searches. The Court held in *Mapp* v. *Ohio* that

> . . . all evidence obtained by searches and seizures in violation of the Constitution is, by that same authority, inadmissible in a state court. Since the Fourth Amendment's right of privacy has been declared enforceable against the States through the Due Process clause of the Fourteenth Amendment, it is enforceable against them by the same sanction of exclusion as is used against the Federal Government . . . [p. 1691].

An even broader extension of the Exclusionary Rule is the doctrine known as the "fruit of the poisonous tree," which prohibits the admission of evidence obtained *as a result* of an "illegal or initially 'tainted' admission, confession, or search" (Kerper, 1972, p. 316). Let us assume, as an example of this doctrine, that the police have employed coercive methods to extract from a suspect a confession that names a second party as an accomplice in the illegal sale of narcotics. The police carry out a search of the residence occupied by the second party, on the basis of a properly executed search warrant, and confiscate a quantity of heroin. The fact that the search was authorized by legal warrant does not validate the admission of the heroin as evidence, because the police came by the information that led to the search and seizure in an unauthorized or "tainted" manner.

Many law enforcement officials have long maintained that the chief purpose of the Exclusionary Rule is the suppression of police "misconduct" that involves disregard of the Fourth Amendment. While no one would defend the proposition that police officers should be free to disregard the U.S. Constitution in pursuit of a conviction, the Exclusionary Rule—it is argued—also punishes mistakes made in good faith by honest, conscientious police officers. Such mistakes might include the wrong address on an affidavit, the wrong address on a warrant, or an incomplete description of the premises to be searched.

Until the 1984 term of the U.S. Supreme Court of Appeals, the leading good faith case was *U.S.* v. *Williams,* decided by the U.S. Court of Appeals, Fifth Circuit, on July 31, 1980. Joan Williams, the defendant, had been found guilty in an Ohio federal court of possession of heroin. While the conviction was being appealed, Williams was released on the condition that she remain in Ohio. The agent who had arrested her in Ohio was patrolling Atlanta International Airport and recognized Williams as she walked off a nonstop flight from Los Angeles.

The agent, Paul Markonni, arrested her for "jumping bail." He took her to the airport police office, searched her, and found a packet of heroin in her coat pocket. Williams had checked a couple of pieces of luggage from Los Angeles through Atlanta to Lexington, Kentucky. Markonni found the luggage, secured it in the airport police office, and the following day was granted a warrant to search it. The luggage contained large quantities of heroin.

What did agent Markonni do that might call for suppressing evidence of the heroin seized from Williams? It turns out that "bail jumping," though certainly a crime, is not considered a crime of urgency that can be acted on without specific direction from a judge. Therefore, Markonni had made an unauthorized arrest of Williams when she walked off the plane. Because the arrest was unauthorized, the subsequent searches were not legally valid.

Markonni thought he was authorized to make an arrest for bail jumping. He was mistaken, but was acting reasonably, because bail jumping is, after all, a crime. The Court of Appeals held that "evidence is not to be suppressed under the exclusionary rule where it is discovered by officers in the course of actions that are taken in good faith and in the reasonable, maybe mistaken, belief that they are authorized." And so the evidence was ruled admissible.

In completing its work for the 1984 term, the Supreme Court made a ruling on the good faith exception to the Exclusionary Rule which allowed for the admission of some illegally obtained evidence in criminal trials. Although the decision was less sweeping than some had predicted, the Court held 6 to 3 that when judges issue warrants which are later ruled defective, the evidence gathered by the police may still be used at trial in most cases. In 1981, Alberto Leon was one of several people indicted on drug conspiracy charges in California after police searches of their homes and cars had turned up a large quantity of drugs. A judge had issued the warrant, even though it was based on outdated information supplied by an informant of uncertain reliability. Two federal courts later threw out much of the key evidence because the warrant had been issued without a showing of probable cause that a crime had been committed.

A second case before the Court was the classical kind of legal horror story that leads critics to rail against the consequences of the Exclusionary Rule. A Boston detective investigating a woman's brutal murder had good reason to suspect her boyfriend, Osborne Sheppard. Unable to find the proper warrant form, the officer tried unsuccessfully to alter a form normally used in drug cases. A judge okayed the form and Sheppard was convicted. But because of this technical imperfection, the highest court in Massachusetts declared the search illegal and threw out the incriminating evidence, including bloodstained clothing, that had been found in the suspect's home. The Supreme Court accepted the lower courts' determinations that both warrants were defective, but ruled that the police had acted in the good faith belief that the searches they made were lawful. Mr. Justice White argued that the principal justification for the Exclusionary Rule is to deter police misconduct. But when police have obtained what they reasonably think to be a valid warrant, there is no police illegality and, therefore, nothing to deter. Penalizing the officer for the error of the magistrate, rather than his or her own mistake, in White's opinion cannot logically contribute to the deterrence of Fourth Amendment violations by the law enforcement agents.

Civil libertarians believe that good faith exceptions to the Exclusionary Rule will result in wholesale police abuses. Americans for Effective Law Enforcement (AELE) offers an opposing view:

> Visions of police harassment of innocent persons in their homes at 3:00 am, however dramatic, are not in issue. The "real" issue is the good faith mistake of a professionally trained officer, or an unnoticed minor error, or the retroactive

effect of an overturned court precedent, or even a 3-to-2 decision that a particular law or procedure is "unconstitutional." Defense attorneys, who sometimes constitute the largest group of state legislators, have a vested interest in perpetuating the status quo.

The real goal of criminal justice should be the encouragement of professional law enforcement and to obtain convictions of the guilty. A search for technicalities does not further that end. The good faith exception, however, encourages police professionalism and still punishes intentional misconduct or an indifferent attitude to the rights of society. Good faith legislation is the modification of a rigid rule that in no way affects its principal purpose [*Impact*, p. 3].

The AELE believes that most of the problems raised by opponents of the good faith exception can be resolved by statutes that give the courts as much direction and as little discretion as possible.

The Fifth Amendment: Self-incrimination

Among the provisions of the Fifth Amendment is the right of protection against self-incrimination: "No person . . . shall be compelled in any criminal case to be a witness against himself. . . ." This right goes to the very heart of the adversary system of criminal justice, because it implies the state must prove the guilt of the accused. It has its greatest relevance to the matter of interrogation and how confessions are elicited from suspects. The Supreme Court ruled in *Brown* v. *Mississippi* (1936) that confessions secured by physical abuse were inadmissible in state courts. In the cases of *Escobedo* v. *Illinois* (1964) and *Miranda* v. *Arizona* (1966), the Court added that suspects must be notified of their rights against self-incrimination and of representation by counsel during an interrogation in order to secure the validity of confessions.

In March of 1963, Ernesto Miranda had been arrested for kidnapping and rape. After being identified by the victim, he was questioned by police for several hours and signed a confession which included a statement that the confession had been made voluntarily. Over the objections of Miranda's attorney, the confession was admitted into evidence and Miranda was found guilty. The Supreme Court of Arizona affirmed the conviction and held that Miranda's constitutional rights had not been violated in obtaining the conviction because, following the earlier *Escobedo* ruling, Miranda had not specifically requested counsel. The U.S. Supreme Court, in reversing the decision, attempted to clarify its intent in the *Escobedo* case by spelling out specific guidelines to be followed by police before they interrogate persons in custody and attempt to use their statements as evidence. The guidelines require that after a person is taken into custody for an offense and prior to any questioning by law enforcement officers, if there is intent to use a suspect's statements in court, he must first be advised of certain rights. These guidelines, as they have been incorporated into the **"Miranda warning,"** have become familiar to many Americans by their frequent reiteration on crime and police shows on television. A copy of the Miranda warning, which we have reproduced from a card carried by urban law enforcement officers, is shown in Figure 16.3.

The Miranda story had a violent ending. On Saturday night, January 13, 1976, Ernesto Miranda became involved in a fight over a card game in a skid-row bar in

MIRANDA WARNING

1. You have the right to remain silent.
2. Anything you say can and will be used against you in a court of law.
3. You have the right to talk to a lawyer and have him present with you while you are being questioned.
4. If you cannot afford to hire a lawyer, one will be appointed to represent you before any questioning, if you wish.
5. You can decide at any time to exercise these rights and not answer any questions or make any statements.

WAIVER

After the warning and in order to secure a waiver, the following questions should be asked and an affirmative reply secured to each question.

1. Do you understand each of these rights I have explained to you?
2. Having these rights in mind, do you wish to talk to us now?

Figure 16.3 Contents of a typical Miranda warning card issued to police officers by local prosecutors.

Phoenix, Arizona. He was stabbed twice by one of the card players—an illegal alien from Mexico named Fernando Zamora Rodriguez—and was dead on arrival at the hospital. One assumes that the police officer who later arrested Rodriguez remembered to read him his Miranda rights!

The Sixth Amendment: Right to Counsel

No prison is without its share of "jailhouse lawyers," men who have become familiar with the law from first-hand experience. In the days when the right to an attorney was not available in court, much less behind the walls, these jailhouse lawyers were helpful in putting cases together for appellate review. With time on their hands and great personal interest in their cases, these men paved the way for the prisoners of today. Perhaps the most famous appeal was made by Clarence Earl Gideon, an indigent prisoner in Florida State Prison at Raiford. He is described by journalist Anthony Lewis in *Gideon's Trumpet* (1966):

> Gideon was a fifty-one-year old white man who had been in and out of prisons much of his life. He had served time for four previous felonies, and he bore the physical marks of a destitute life: a wrinkled, prematurely aged face, a voice and hands that trembled, a frail body, white hair. He had never been a professional criminal or a man of violence; he just could not seem to settle down to work, and so he had made his way by gambling and occasional thefts. Those who had known him, even the men who had arrested him and those who were now his jailers, considered Gideon a perfectly harmless human being, rather likeable, but one tossed aside by life. Anyone meeting him for the first time would be likely to regard him as the most wretched of men.
>
> And yet a flame still burned in Clarence Earl Gideon. He had not given up caring about life or freedom; he had not lost his sense of injustice. Right now he had a

passionate—some thought almost irrational—feeling of having been wronged by the State of Florida, and he had the determination to try to do something about it [pp. 5–6].

His petition, submitted to the United States Supreme Court, was done as a pauper under a special federal statute. This statute makes great allowances for those unable to afford the expense of counsel and administrative technicalities. As an example, the number of typewritten copies of a petition that are normally required is 40; Gideon submitted one, handwritten in pencil on lined yellow sheets. Although Gideon did not have counsel in 1961, when he stood trial for the crime of breaking into a pool hall, he surely *did* have counsel before the Supreme Court when his petition was heard in the 1962–1963 terms. Abe Fortas, one of Washington's most successful lawyers and who later was to become a U.S. Supreme Court justice, was appointed as Gideon's attorney for this case. The decision of the Court was unanimous and their position was stated in *Gideon* v. *Wainwright* (1963):

> In deciding as it did—that "appointment of counsel is not a fundamental right, essential to a fair trial"—the Court in *Betts* made an abrupt break with its own well-considered precedents. In returning to these old precedents, sounder we believe than the new, we but restore constitutional principles established to achieve a fair system of justice. Not only these precedents but also reason and reflection require us to recognize that in our adversary system of criminal justice, any person haled into court, who is too poor to hire a lawyer, cannot be assured a fair trial unless counsel is provided for him [p. 796].

As if to emphasize the Court's finding, when Gideon was finally retried with counsel, he was acquitted. The right to counsel has since moved rapidly in both directions along the criminal justice continuum. In decision after decision, the Supreme Court has ruled in favor of the right to counsel at a "critical stage" in the defendant's case. This "critical stage" has been extended from initial police contact to the preparation of a brief for appeal and even to assistance in having transcripts of the trial prepared. The right to counsel has moved into the prison as well as in the courtroom. A milestone case was decided in the 1967–1968 terms in *Mempa* v. *Rhay* (1968) in which the right to counsel was extended to state probation revocation hearings, previously considered essentially an administrative action. The Court held that the application of a deferred sentence was a "critical point" in the proceeding.

Conclusion: The Rule of Law

During the past several decades, the U.S. Supreme Court has made more changes in criminal procedure than had been made by the Court in the nearly two hundred years of its previous existence. Critics of the Court have objected that these changes have resulted in the "coddling of criminals" and reflect a permissiveness that is detrimental to the rights of law-abiding citizens. The Supreme Court has not created any new rights for criminals: what it has done is *moved toward equalizing the rights of rich and poor suspects.* The major consequence of the "due process revolution" has been to extend to the poor, the illiterate, and the ignorant some of those rights which have long been known and enjoyed by the middle-class or upper-class defendant. But this is a revolution that remains unfinished. Although the Court may have equalized rights on paper, many barriers still effectively bar the poor from the full benefits of due process and equal protection under the law.

CRIME CONTROL VERSUS DUE PROCESS

The conflicts that exist among the various components of the criminal justice system involve much more than mere differences of professional opinion over procedural matters in the administration of justice. In the view of a leading authority in criminal law (Packer, 1968), the real source of intramural conflict lies in two competing systems of values. Packer suggests these value systems give rise to quite different conceptualizations of the criminal process—conceptualizations which he identifies as the **crime-control model** and the **due-process model.** The crime-control model, according to Packer, is "based on the proposition that the repression of criminal conduct is by far the most important function to be performed by the criminal process" (p. 158). Anything that promotes the efficient operation of this "people processing" approach is seen as contributing to the maintenance of public order and individual freedom of law-abiding citizens. Conversely, anything which detracts from technical efficiency is viewed as a potential threat to the security of individuals and society. For example, court decisions that restrict the use of wiretaps and other forms of electronic surveillance, that guarantee the accused person right to counsel at the beginning of the criminal process, or that place curbs on the admissibility of illegally obtained evidence are criticized as hampering law enforcement agencies in their efforts to protect society.

Implicit in the crime-control model is the assumption that the screening performed by police and prosecutors separates a substantial majority of innocent individuals from those who are probably guilty of criminal offenses. Thus, it is the presumption of guilt which makes it possible for the system to rapidly process large numbers of people, with more than 90 percent pleading guilty. Reduced to its essentials, this model provides an administrative fact-finding process which results in either exoneration of the suspect or the entry of a guilty plea.

The goals of the crime-control model are sought, for the most part, in punishment of offenders. Two theories which attempt to provide a rationale for punishment are *retribution* and *utilitarianism* (Grupp, 1971). Retributive theory holds that a person who violates the law deserves to be punished. This position is also known as the doctrine of "just deserts," that is, criminals who are punished are only getting what is coming to them.

As we noted earlier, the theory of *utilitarianism* argues that punishment can only be justified to the extent that it accomplishes some useful and worthwhile purpose: to discourage people from law-violating behavior (deterrence), to curb the opportunities for offenders to commit further crimes (incapacitation), or to encourage offenders to "turn over a new leaf" and seek to change themselves in a prosocial direction (rehabilitation). Utilitarian theory poses thorny problems for the administration of justice. Reliable and valid empirical support for deterrence is difficult or impossible to demonstrate for most areas of criminal activity; and for many people, there are powerful moral, philosophical, and pragmatic objections to policies which are based on incapacitation. The argument that punishment and rehabilitation are compatible is an extremely interesting one, but it is beyond the scope of the present discussion.

If the image conveyed by the crime-control model is that of an assembly line, the due-process model—as Packer observes—looks very much like an obstacle course:

> Each of its successive stages is designed to present formidable impediments to carrying the accused any further along in the process. Its ideology is not the converse of that underlying the Crime Control Model. It does not rest on the idea that it is not socially desirable to repress crime, although critics of its application have been known to claim so. Its ideology is composed of a complex of ideas, some of them based on judgments about the efficacy of crime control devices, others having to do with quite different considerations. The ideology of due process is far more deeply impressed on the formal structure of the law than is the ideology of crime control . . . [p. 163].

Due process, which is deeply rooted in English common law, asserts that defendants must receive formal notification of the charges placed against them. They must be given the opportunity to confront their accusers and witnesses, to present evidence in their own defense, and to have this proof assessed by an impartial jury of their peers under the guidance of a judge who is also impartial. In addition, they have the right to be represented by counsel.

The due-process model rejects punishment as an appropriate goal of the criminal justice system. Instead, the model seeks the rehabilitation of the offender. Not only must individuals be protected against the power of the state; they must also be given access to the resources of society—resources which they have been denied—in order to accomplish the tasks of rehabilitation. Punishment and rehabilitation are seen as incompatible.

As a result of the above considerations, the criminal justice system at times may seen unwieldly and inefficient in its operation. Yet, it is this very lack of efficiency that expresses an abiding American value. As stated in *The Challenge of Crime in a Free Society* (President's Commission on Law Enforcement and Administration of Justice, 1967c):

> Unquestionably adherence to due process complicates, and in many instances handicaps, the work of the courts. They could be more efficient—in the sense that the likelihood and speed of conviction would be greater—if the constitutional requirements of due process were not so demanding. But the law rightly values due process over efficient process. And by permitting the accused to challenge its fairness and legality at every stage of his prosecution, the system provides the occasion for the law to develop in accordance with changes in society and society's ideals [p. 125].

This system may allow the guilty to go unpunished in some cases, but it safeguards other defendants in cases of questionable merit.

SUMMARY

The formal functioning of the criminal justice system, described in this chapter, begins with the broad discretionary powers to the police and proceeds through the initiation of prosecution, the courts, and corrections. Emphasis is placed upon the importance of discretion and accommodation—the give-and-take interaction among practitioners in the criminal justice system—in the daily transactions which make up the administration of justice. Problems faced by the correctional system have led to the increasing use of alternatives to confinement, wherever possible, for nonviolent offenders. The concluding portion of the chapter is devoted to a description and discussion of the competing philosophies or value systems, summarized in the crime-control model and the due-process model, as one of the principal sources of intramural conflict within the criminal justice system.

DISCUSSION QUESTIONS

Find the answers to the following questions in the text.

1. Discuss the concepts of **discretion** and **accommodation.** Why are they important for understanding the operation of the **criminal justice system**?
2. Identify some of the aspects of the police officer's job that are characterized as **social service functions.** How do these tasks and responsibilities compare with the conventional view of the police function as maintenance of law and order and crime prevention?
3. Why is the prosecutor such an influential figure in the criminal justice system and process?
4. Discuss parallels in the structure and operations of the federal and state judicial systems.
5. What are the principal areas of **jurisdiction** of the U.S. Supreme Court? How does the Court obtain its cases?
6. Identify some of the community correctional programs that are available as alternatives to imprisonment.
7. What are the provisions of the Fourteenth Amendment which contributed so significantly to the **due-process revolution**?
8. What is the **Exclusionary Rule**? What is considered a "good faith exception" to the Exclusionary Rule?
9. Of what significance was the U.S. Supreme Court's decision in *Gideon* v. *Wainwright*?
10. Distinguish between the **crime-control model** and **due-process model.** How do these models help us understand conflicts within the criminal justice system?

TERMS TO IDENTIFY AND REMEMBER

accommodation	discretion
criminal justice system	social service functions
"no paper" action	trial court
court of record	appellate court
court of last resort	jurisdiction
inferior courts	superior courts
en banc decision	*certiorari*
probation	parole
halfway house	work release
prerelease center	"shorthand doctrine"
due-process revolution	"silver platter" doctrine
Exclusionary Rule	Miranda warning
crime-control model	due-process model

REFERENCES

Americans for Effective Law Enforcement. *Impact* (July 1982), 1–4.

Baker, N. The prosecutor: Initiator of prosecution. *Journal of Criminal Law, Criminology, and Police Science* 23 (1933): 771–780.

Banks, L. The crisis in the courts. *Fortune* 64 (1961): 186–189.

Blackmore, J. Does community corrections work? From the experts, a resounding "Maybe." *Corrections Magazine* 7 (1981): 15–18, 21–27.

Brown v. *Missisippi,* 297 U.S. 278, 56 S.Ct. 461, 80 L. Ed. 682 (1936).

Chandler, R. *The Long Goodbye.* Boston: Houghton Mifflin, 1954.

Clark, B. Is law enforcement headed in the right direction? *Police* 12 (1968): 31–34.

Coffey, A., Eldefonso, E., and Hartinger, W. *Introduction to the Criminal Justice System and Process.* Englewood Cliffs, NJ: Prentice-Hall, 1974.

Elkins v. *United States,* 364 U.S. 206, 80 S.Ct. 1437, 4 L. Ed. 2d 1669 (1960).

Escobedo v. *Illinois,* 375 U.S. 902, 84 S.Ct. 203, 11 L. Ed. 2d 143 (1964).

Gideon v. *Wainwright,* 372 U.S. 335, 83 S.Ct. 792, 9 L. Ed. 2d 799 (1963).

Grupp, S. (d.), *Theories of Punishment.* Bloomington: University of Indiana Press, 1971.

Hurtado v. *California,* 110 U.S. 516, 4 S.Ct. 111, 4 S.Ct. 292, 28 L. Ed. 232 (1884).

Kaplan, J. *Criminal Justice: Introductory Cases and Materials.* Mineola, NY: Foundation Press, 1973.

Kerper, H. B. *Introduction to the Criminal Justice System.* St. Paul, MN: West Publishing Company, 1972.

Law Enforcement Assistance Administration. *National Survey of Court Organization 1970.* Washington, D.C.: U.S. Government Printing Office, 1971.

Lewis, A. *Gideon's Trumpet.* New York: Random House, 1964.

Lewis, P., and People, K. *The Supreme Court and the Criminal Process—Cases and Comments.* Philadelphia: W. B. Saunders, 1978.

Lewis, P. W., Mannle, H. W., Allen, H. E., and Vetter, H. J. A post-*Furman* profile of Florida's condemned—A question of discrimination in terms of the race of the victim and a comment on *Spinkellink* v. *Wainwright. Stetson Law Review* 9 (1979): 1–45.

Lustig v. *United States,* 338 U.S. 74, 69 S.Ct. 1372, 93 L. Ed. 1819 (1949).

Mapp v. *Ohio,* 367 U.S. 643, 81 S.Ct. 1684, 6 L. Ed. 2d 1081 (1961).

Mempa v. *Rhay,* 389 U.S. 128, 88 S.Ct. 254, 19 L. Ed. 2d 336 (1967).

Miranda v. *Arizona,* 384 U.S. 436, 86 S.Ct. 1602, 16 L. Ed. 2d 694 (1966).

Morris, N. *The Future of Imprisonment.* Chicago: University of Chicago Press, 1974.

National Advisory Commission on Criminal Justice Standards and Goals. *Courts.* Washington, D.C.: U.S. Government Printing Office, 1973.

Packer, H. *The Limits of the Criminal Sanction,* Palo Alto, CA: Standard University Press, 1968.

President's Commission on Law Enforcement and Administration of Justice. *Task Force Report: The Courts.* Washington, D.C.: U.S. Government Printing Office, 1967*a.*

———. *Task Force Report: The Police.* Washington, D.C.: U.S. Government Printing Office, 1967*b.*

———. *The Challenge of Crime in a Free Society.* Washington, D.C.: U.S. Government Printing Office, 1967*c.*

Puttkammer, E. *Administration of Criminal Law.* Chicago: University of Chicago Press, 1959.

Swanson, C. R., and Territo, L. *Police Administration.* New York: Macmillan, 1983.

U.S. v. *Williams,* 622 F. 2d 830 (5th Cir. 1980).

Weeks. v. *United States,* 232 U.S. 383, 34 S.Ct. 341, 58 L. Ed. 652 (1914).

Wolf v. *Colorado,* 338 U.S. 25, 69 S.Ct. 1359, 93 L. Ed. 1782 (1949).

chapter **17**

LAW ENFORCEMENT

Many criminologists regard law enforcement as an important and challenging area for systematic study. They are interested in the complex and variegated tasks of law enforcement, ranging from the traditional responsibilities for crime control and crime prevention to the delivery of human services to the victims of man-made or natural disasters. Criminologists are concerned with the organization and administration of law enforcement at local, state, and federal levels, a major institutional complex in our society with hundreds of thousands of persons in its employ. The rules, laws, and constitutional safeguards which have been designed to protect citizens against the arbitrary use of police authority in situations involving search and seizure, interrogation, and self-incrimination, and their operation are a major focus of criminological research. Finally, criminologists are interested in the people who pursue careers in the field of law enforcement—in their recruitment, selection, training, job performance, attitudes, and values.

POLICE ROLES AND RESPONSIBILITIES

"Police work" is a phrase that conjures up an image of dramatic confrontation between a police officer and a lawbreaker, with victory going to the party with the stronger arm, faster gun, or craftier wit. While there are plenty of high-tension incidents in law enforcement—more than one hundred police officers are killed each year in the line of duty in this country—the majority of situations to which police officers respond are not *criminal* situations, that is, those which call for arrest and the possibility of prosecution, trial, and punishment. Rather, many of these situations involve public nuisances the community wants stopped: the blaring radio or television set in the middle of the night; the barking dog; the intoxicated revelers at a party in the neighborhood. In addition, there are other situations that involve people who need help whether they want it or not: runaway boys or girls looking for a place to "crash"; helpless drunks sleeping in doorways on a subzero night in midwinter; someone high on cocaine looking for a little excitement in a dangerous neighborhood. Still other situations may be threatening although they involve lawful conduct: a sidewalk orator exercising the right of free speech in the midst of a hostile crowd or a late-night gathering of youths on a street corner. Any of these situations could lead to a serious breach of public order or the commission of a crime. A great deal of police work consists of seeing to it that matters do not proceed to this extreme.

It is obvious from the above examples that policing necessitates intimate personal involvement with the problems and lives of citizens of all kinds. This is the consequence of **"calling the cops,"** an idiom which Bittner (1970) identifies as referring to one of the principal methods employed by many people, particularly those who live in large cities, to cope with a variety of difficulties.

> Many puzzling aspects of police work fall into place when one ceases to look at it as principally concerned with law enforcement and crime control, and only incidentally and often incongruously concerned with an infinite variety of other matters. It makes much more sense to say that the police are nothing else than *a mechanism for the distribution of situationally justified force in society* . . . whether it involves protection against an undesired imposition, caring for those

who cannot care for themselves, attempting to solve a crime, helping to save a life, abating a nuisance, or settling an explosive dispute, police intervention means above all making use of the capacity and authority to overpower resistance to an attempted solution in the native habitat of the problem [pp. 38–44]. (Italics added.)

In Bittner's view, the question, What are police officers supposed to do? cannot be distinguished meaningfully from the question, What kinds of situations require remedies that are nonnegotiably coercible? According to Bittner:

✳ By "non-negotiably coercible" we mean that when a deputized police officer decides that force is necessary, then, within the boundaries of this situation, he is not accountable to anyone, nor is he required to brook the arguments or opposition of anyone who might object to it. We set this forth not as a legal but as a practical rule [p. 42].

The implications of this situation for the self-image or conceptualization of the conventional police force are rather considerable. The police are compelled to justify activities that do not directly involve crime fighting by linking them in some way to law enforcement or by "defining them as nuisance demands for service." To the extent that this view is widely held by police officers, two unfortunate consequences can be discerned. One is a tendency for the excessive use or threatened use of arrest powers in a wide variety of problem situations where there is no real intention of initiating prosecution. This "quasi-legal" procedure, in Bittner's view, is not the result of errors in judgment concerning the applicability of penal sanctions; rather it represents "deliberate pretense resorted to because more appropriate methods of handling problems have not been developed." Second, and more important, the conviction that crime control is the only worthwhile and significant activity for a police officer—as contrasted with the myriad of other duties that occupy the time and attention of uniformed patrol officers—has seriously adverse effects on morale. Bittner points out that no one who takes pride in his or her work can derive any satisfaction from performing tasks on a daily basis that are derided by fellow workers. In addition, "the low evaluation of these duties leads to neglecting the development of skill and knowledge that are required to discharge them properly and efficiently" (p. 43).

The police have traditionally based their operational policies on the goals of (1) eliminating or substantially reducing crime and (2) apprehending all perpetrators of crimes. Elliott and Sardino (1970) question whether crime prevention is a realistic objective for the police, particularly in view of the limitations on the police to act against crime. Even in theory, crime deterrence is a responsibility that the police share with the entire criminal justice system; the police are specifically responsible for only the initial stage of the process, that is, arrest. The police have no control over the subsequent actions of the prosecutor or the courts.

In contrast, Elliott and Sardino see apprehension of the criminal offender as a realistic goal for the police: "Within certain legal limitations, no element of society can interfere with the police's attempts to realize this goal, and the degree of realization of this goal depends only upon the efforts of the police themselves" (p. 4). If police effectiveness is defined operationally in terms of the objective of arresting all perpetrators of crime, then its measurement becomes a fairly straightforward matter: it is the difference between the number of crimes reported and known to the police and the number of crimes cleared by arrest. As this difference approaches zero, police action approaches the ideal.

If we return to the question, What do the police do? it will be seen that Bittner supplies an answer which differs considerably from that provided by Elliott and Sardino. Police work, as Bittner sees it, is inherently committed to a tremendously variegated range of activities and tasks by the unique nature of the responsibilities assigned to the police as the mechanism in our society for the "distribution of situationally justifiable force." Elliott and Sardino, on the other hand, analyze the police task with reference to the respective goals of crime prevention and the apprehension of criminal offenders. They question the legitimacy of the former objective and offer some cogent reasons for their contention that clearing crimes through arrest is the more appropriate goal for the conventional police force.

It is noteworthy that one of the seven basic objectives identified by the President's Commission in its *Task Force Report: The Police* (1967) was to immediately develop and apply all available police agency, community, and other criminal justice resources to apprehend criminal offenders. Despite this priority, it is rather obvious that the police are going to continue to be called upon to carry out a great many tasks which fall outside the range of either crime prevention or apprehension of criminal offenders. If police officers are to evolve into professional specialists in crime fighting, as some authorities have argued they should, we are left with the question of who shall assume the responsibility for discharging the duties currently demanded of the police. In the meantime, police officers are given a good deal of discretionary authority and power in the performance of their jobs.

THE STRUCTURE OF AMERICAN LAW ENFORCEMENT

A national manpower survey carried out in 1978 by the Law Enforcement Assistance Administration indicated that nearly 600,000 people were employed in police service, 80 percent of them as sworn officers, by more than 40,000 agencies (LEAA, *Manpower Survey,* 1978). About 50 of these agencies are operated by the federal government, the states account for about 200 more, and the remainder are distributed among the countries, cities, and townships at the local level of government. With few exceptions, each local government, regardless of how small or poor it may be, insists upon its own police department. Thus, the most striking characteristics of American law enforcement are its decentralization and fragmentation.

Federal Law Enforcement

The United States is one of the few major countries that does not have a national police force. The reasons for this are largely historical. Concern for the arbitrary exercise of police power by Parliament or the Crown was one of the principal motives which led the founding fathers to place close constraints upon the enforcement powers of the new federal government; thus there is no single federal agency responsible for the enforcement of federal laws. Responsibility for the enforcement of federal laws is shared among approximately 50 agencies.

When Congress creates a law enforcement agency, congressional legislation establishes the specific authority and jurisdiction of that agency. The Federal Bureau of Investigation (FBI), for example, has authority to deal with about 180 federal crimes. Its jurisdiction is limited to the United States and its possessions, including Puerto Rico, Guam, and the Virgin Islands.

Questions of jurisdiction tend to raise confusion: homicide provides an illustration of this point. Murder is not a federal offense, but is usually the responsibility of the state or local police authority which has jurisdiction. But if the same offense is committed on federally owned property, either at home or abroad, legislation specifically provides that its investigation falls within the jurisdiction of the FBI.

The Federal Bureau of Investigation, Federal Drug Enforcement Administration, and the Secret Service (which investigates criminal offenses involving the counterfeiting of American currency and protects the president, among other duties) are perhaps the most visible law enforcement agencies at the federal level. Surprisingly, these three agencies perform less than 1 percent of federal law enforcement duties. Other federal law enforcement agencies and related investigative functions are performed by the following agencies or organizations:

The Department of Justice

Immigration and Naturalization Service: Border Patrol

United States Marshall: Civil Rights

Federal Drug Enforcement Administration

Federal Bureau of Investigation (FBI)

The Department of the Treasury

Bureau of Customs

Internal Revenue Service (IRS)

Secret Service

Treasury Guard Force

White House Police Force

Bureau of Alcohol, Firearms, and Tobacco Tax

The Department of Defense

Office of Special Intelligence (OSI), United States Air Force

Office of Naval Intelligence (ONI), United States Navy

Criminal Investigation Division (CID), United States Army

The Post Office Department

Bureau of Postal Inspection

The Department Of Transportation

United States Coast Guard

Law enforcement units are also maintained within the departments of state; interior; labor; agriculture; commerce; and health, education, and welfare. Moreover, law enforcement units have been established within the following independent agencies of the federal government:

Atomic Energy Commission (AEC)

Civil Aeronautics Board (CAB)

Federal Communication Commission (FCC)

Interstate Commerce Commission

United States Civil Service Commission

State Law Enforcement

Unlike the federal government, many states maintain law enforcement agencies which have **general police powers,** that is, the authority and responsibility of enforcing *all* state laws anywhere within the geographical boundaries of the state. State law enforcement agencies may be specifically provided for in the state constitution but more generally are established by state legislative action. They are usually designated by such titles as "state police," "state highway patrol," or "department of public safety." These and similar titles can be misleading because they fail to convey the fact that an agency designated "state highway patrol," for example, may still possess general police powers.

Some state agencies may be given **restricted police powers.** The California Highway Patrol, for instance, is restricted in its operations to dealing with the enforcement of state traffic laws, the investigation and prevention of accidents, and general highway safety. Other states may provide more than one state law enforcement agency with restricted police powers. Florida's State Highway Patrol deals with traffic and minor criminal offenses, while the Florida Department of Law Enforcement is responsible for investigative and enforcement duties with respect to the more serious offenses.

Administrative bureaus in state government which have regulatory control over such diverse activities as the sale of alcoholic beverages, public utilities, fishing and hunting, insurance, environmental protection, and agriculture also maintain law enforcement agencies. Although these agencies are specialized in function and limited in the scope of their enforcement activities, their combined efforts comprise a significant part of the total law enforcement process in the United States.

Local Law Enforcement

Law enforcement at the local level is generally labeled urban, suburban, or rural. Such terminology more accurately portrays the characteristics of the population being served than the formal structure of government within which it is established, maintained, and regulated. It is more precise to characterize the various local law enforcement agencies as either *county* or *municipal* (city, town, borough, village, township), as determined by their charter or origin and not by demographic characteristics.

County law enforcement, which accounts for approximately 3,000 of the 40,000 agencies in the United States, is of two main types: the county sheriff and the county police. Typically the sheriff is the principal law enforcement officer of the county and his position is established by the authority of the state constitution. The sheriff is usually an elected official who may or may not possess the qualifications considered essential for the performance of the complex duties required by his or her office. Deputy sheriffs are appointed by and serve at the discretion of the sheriff, which helps account for the wide range of qualitative variation in deputies. At one extreme is the stereotyped figure of the slow-witted brother-in-law who holds his job as deputy through the indulgence of the sheriff and a little gentle persuasion from the family. At the other end of the continuum is the Los Angeles County Sheriff's deputies, who are among the best-trained and most highly respected law enforcement officers in the country, or the Multnomah County deputies in Oregon, the first such agency to require a bachelor's degree for all sworn officers.

There is great organizational and functional diversity among the hundreds of sheriffs' departments in the United States. In some states, the county sheriff is primarily an officer of the court and criminal investigation or traffic enforcement is the responsibility of state or other local agencies. In other states, particularly those in the South and West, the sheriff and his deputies are involved in both traffic and criminal duties. The sheriff's staff may range in size from one—the sheriff himself or herself—to several hundreds, including cililian personnel as well as sworn deputies. Similarly, there is a wide range of technical proficiency and expertise among sheriffs' departments. Some sheriffs and their deputies may be poorly trained and possess little in the way of equipment, while others may boast fleets of patrol vehicles, lavishly equipped crime laboratories, and even airplanes or helicopters.

County police are not to be confused with the county sheriff and deputies. County police are found in many areas of the country where city and county governments have been merged (e.g., Jacksonville, Florida). They are headed by a police chief who is usually an administrator appointed from within the department, and who is accountable to a county commissioner, prosecutor, manager, or director of public safety.

DELIVERY OF POLICE SERVICES

The organizational chart depicted in Figure 17.1 shows the structure of a municipal police department for a medium-sized city. The distribution of manpower in a department with this organizational structure might be approximately as follows:

Administration 8%

Operations 85%

Services 7%

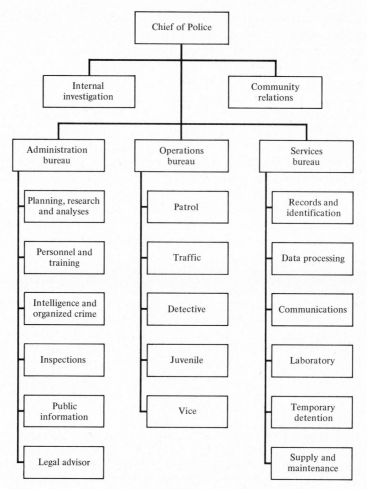

Figure 17.1 Organizational structure of a municipal police department for a medium-sized city.

The personnel strength assigned to Operations would tend to show the following breakdown:

Patrol 55%

Traffic 12%

Investigation 15%

These figures, of course, are extremely flexible and will vary from agency to agency as a consequence of many factors.

Patrol Bureau

Patrol is the deployment of police officers within a given community to provide day-to-day services and to deter and prevent the commission of criminal offenses. The organizational pattern depicted in Figure 17.1 reflects the expressed conviction of police administrators that the day-to-day job of the patrol officer is probably the most important of all the various functions performed by the police. The National Advisory Commission on Criminal Justice Standards and Goals (1973) refers to the patrol officer as "the community's first line of defense against crime" (p. 111). The bases for this contention are not hard to find: nearly half of all arrests are made within two hours of the commission of the crime and 36 percent are made within one hour. The Commission recommended that "ways be found of getting persons with investigative experience to crime scenes with the greatest possible rapidity—before crimes, in police terms, are cold" (p. 248). In the view of the National Advisory Commission, one way to achieve this objective would be to assign broad responsibilities for investigative functions to the patrol officer.

The first assignment for almost all police officers graduating from the police academy is in the **patrol bureau.** This assignment—for better or worse—is the foundation on which all other police experiences will be formed. Skolnick (1966), in commenting on the similarity of experiences among American police officers, has stated:

> The policeman's working personality is most highly developed in his constabulary role of the man on the beat. For analytical purposes that role is sometimes regarded as an enforcement specialty, but in the general discussion of the policemen as they comport themselves while working, the uniformed cop is seen as the foundation for the policeman's working personality. There is a sound organizational basis for making this assumption. The police, unlike the military, draw no caste distinction in socialization even though their order of rank title approximates the military. Thus one cannot join a local police department as, for instance, a lieutenant, as a West point graduate joins the Army. Every officer must serve an apprenticeship as a patrolman. This feature of police organizations means that the constabulary role is the primary one for all police officers and that whatever the special requirements of roles in law enforcement specialties they are carried out with a common background of constabulary experience [pp. 43–44].

The rookie officer is usually assigned to work directly with a senior patrol officer, who bears the designation of "field training officer," "coach," or some similar title. These senior officers are carefully selected in most instances to "break in" rookies, and are often extremely influential in the professional development of the new officers who are placed under their tutelage. The amount of time that rookie and senior officers spend working together is a function of the policies of the organization, the pace at which the new officer masters certain basic skills, and the needs of the organization.

Patrol Bureau: Backbone or Manpower Tool?　Although most chief administrators in law enforcement almost routinely espouse the position that the patrol bureau is the "backbone" of the agency, they proceed systematically to transfer the best and brightest officers from that bureau to other assignments, such as the detective bureau, vice squad, or training academy. This practice, which is common to many police departments, creates some rather severe personnel problems. If continued with any degree of regularity, it guarantees that the "backbone" of the police department will be composed primarily of inexperienced officers and those who are average, at best, or even below average in terms of their ability and motivation.

Why would a police administrator employ a policy that depletes the department's primary operating unit of its finest people? There are at least a couple of answers to this question. First, the chief administrator may not really believe the patrol bureau is as important as most police administration experts suggest that it is. Second, the chief may not believe the patrol bureau is sufficiently stimulating, rewarding, or challenging to keep the best, brightest, and most able officers satisfied and therefore feels compelled to provide them with higher status and more challenging positions. This is done to keep such officers from resigning or becoming so dissatisfied and bored with their patrol assignment that they become focal sources of discontent within the unit. A chief of police who clings to such beliefs has probably instituted policies which do indeed make an assignment to the patrol bureau one that is unchallenging and of low status. For instance, if a police chief believes that patrol officers should have no responsibility for handling the investigation of even the most routine criminal offenses, but rather that all segments of an investigation should be conducted by a detective, then the chief has eliminated one of the most interesting and challenging functions of police work, namely, criminal investigation.

The Kansas City Preventive Patrol Experiment   Police patrol strategies, as Kelling et al. (1974) have noted, have generally been based on two "unproven but widely accepted hypotheses: first, that visible police presence prevents crime by deterring potential offenders; second, that the public's fear of crime is diminished by such police presence" (p. 42).

From October 1, 1972, to September 30, 1973, the Kansas City Police Department, with the support of the Police Foundation, sought to test whether routine patrol had any measurable impact upon crime or upon the public's sense of security. A "beat" is a limited area of geographical responsibility which is ordinarily patrolled by marked vehicles operated by one or two uniformed officers. As depicted in Figure 17.2 a total of 15 beats, representing a 32-square-mile area with a 1970 resident population of 148,395, was involved. Beats were designated as being reactive, proactive, or control. Reactive beats did not receive preventive patrol; officers entered the area only upon citizens' requests for service. When not responding to calls, reactive units patrolled the boundaries of their beats or adjacent proactive beats. In proactive beats the amount of routine preventive patrol was intensified some two to three times its usual level. The normal amount of patrolling was conducted in control beats. The evaluation of the experiment was as follows:

1. The amount of reported crime between reactive, control, and proactive beats showed that only one significant statistical variation—"other sex crimes," which excludes rape while including such offenses as exhibitionism and molestation—was higher in reactive than control areas. However, the judgment of the project evaluators was that the statistical significance was probably a random occurrence.
2. As crime is considerably underreported, a victimization study was conducted to determine if fluctuations could be detected in levels of crime

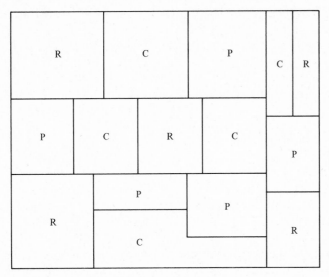

P Proactive   C Control   R Reactive

Figure 17.2 Schematic representation of the 15-beat experimental area. (*Source:* G. L. Kelling et al., *The Kansas City Patrol Experiment*. Washington, D.C.: Police Foundation, 1974, p. 9. Reproduced by permission of the authors and publisher.)

which were not officially reported to the police; no statistically significant differences were found between the three types of areas.

3. Crimes that citizens and businessmen said they reported to the police showed statistically significant differences between reactive, control, and proactive beats in only 5 of 48 comparisons, and these differences showed no consistent pattern. In two instances the change was greater in control beats, twice it was greater in the proactive beats, and only once was it greater in reactive beats.

4. There were no statistically significant differences in arrests between the three types of beats.

5. Citizens fear of crime was not significantly altered by changes in the level of routine preventive patrol.

6. Variations in the level of patrolling did not significantly alter the security measure taken by citizens or businesses.

7. Little correlation was found to exist between level of patrol and citizens and business persons' attitudes toward the policing.

8. The amount of time taken by police in answering calls was not significantly altered by variations in the level of routine preventive patrol.

9. There was no significant effect upon the incidence of traffic accidents due to differing levels of service.

The interpretations and findings of the Kansas City Preventive Patrol study are highly controversial and there is no agreement on them.

Upon learning the results of the study, some local government leaders felt that further increases in police manpower were not warranted and that decreases might be justified. Such persons failed to consider that just because the prevailing method of preventing crime—routine preventive patrol—was not effective, it did not follow that no strategy of prevention would work. The findings do suggest that administrators can divert a significant number of manhours from routine patrol to other policing approaches without the risk of producing an intolerable crime rate and with the genuine possibility of actually lowering the crime rate.

Traffic Bureau

Traffic is the most all-pervasive problem confronting the police agency. Every person who drives and every vehicle on the street is part of the problem. Obviously the responsibility for congestion control, traffic law enforcement, and accident prevention cannot be fixed on any single unit; traffic duty must be shared to some degree by every uniformed member of the force. The degree to which the patrol officer may be held accountable for traffic duties is dictated by the extent of the traffic problem itself.

In cities where traffic constitutes a significant problem it may be necessary to assign specific duties to a **traffic bureau.** This ensures a concentration of police efforts not possible when traffic duties are dispersed throughout the organization. The existence of traffic specialists does not relieve patrol officers of all responsibility for the traffic problem; however, it does free them to discharge their traffic responsibilities in relation to their other duties.

As in the case of other areas of police activity, police departments vary in their traffic organizational structuring. The traffic bureau generally includes traffic control, accident investigation, and traffic law enforcement functions. A safety division primarily concerned with traffic safety education may also be a part of the traffic bureau. The traffic bureau shares its traffic-related responsibilities with the patrol bureau, relieving the patrol officer of traffic duties that tend to be time consuming or immobilizing. The traffic bureau provides the initiative and guidance for the traffic program of the department. These programs are largely concentrated in specific areas of traffic need, and implemented by traffic specialists (Caldwell, 1972, p. 48).

Detective Bureau

Three common stereotypes influence the public's perceptions of investigative effectiveness. First is the media image, which many detectives would claim for themselves: resourceful, streetwise cops who always "get their man." Next is the historical stereotype, the image held by oldtimers on the force of the detective's contributions to law and order. Finally, there is the critical stereotype, which recent studies have tended to develop. Some combination of these alternative stereotypes provides the basis for current investigative policies in most police department **detective bureaus** today (Greenwood and Petersilia, 1975).

The media image, which is especially pervasive in widely viewed television series, depicts the detective as a clever, imaginative, aggressive individual who occasionally treads a thin line between legality and illegality in tracking down crafty criminals. Detectives and their sidekicks roam the entire city for days or weeks trying to break a single case, which is ultimately solved by the sheer deductive powers of investigators. This is the image that many detectives prefer. They would probably concede that criminals are rarely as crafty or diabolical as those portrayed in the media, but may not quarrel with the media characterization of their own capabilities.

Some current investigative practices appear to be mainly a means to preserve a medialike image or to give victims the kind of services they except largely because of that image. That is, fingerprint dusting, mug shot showing, or questioning witnesses are often done without any hope of developing leads, but simply for public relations.

The stereotyped images held by older police administrators are influenced by the special status detectives held in earlier times (Smith, 1960). Not too many years ago various forms of illicit activity such as vice, gambling, prostitution, and speakeasies were much more openly tolerated by city governments than they are today. The existence of these illegal, but accepted, enterprises created problems for the city police. How could they keep such institutions under control without driving them completely out of business? The police dealings with these institutions were frequently carried on by detectives. The detectives ensured that the businesses were run in a somewhat orderly fashion and that "undesirables" who attempted to take part were driven out. By this delicate handling of a troublesome situation the detectives often won the favor of the business leaders and politicans connected with these activities. Such political connections made the detective a person of respect and influence.

A more critical stereotype of investigative effectiveness can be gleaned from a number of studies which attempt to analyze how detectives go about their work. One of the earliest critics of detection practices and detectives was Raymond Fosdick (1921). After visiting police departments in all the major cities of the United States, he criticized detectives for:

- Lack of civil service standards in selection
- Lack of training
- Poor coordination with patrol operations
- Lack of effective supervision
- Lack of ordinary "business systems" for handling their administrative work

In some departments, these criticisms are just as appropriate. Recent analysts have argued that:

- Police agencies do not routinely collect and summarize data that can be used to determine the effectiveness of investigation activities. Clearance and arrest statistics in particular are unsuitable because they fail to distinguish outputs of investigative effects from those of other units in the department. Clearance data alone are also extremely unreliable indicators of police performance because of their subjective nature.
- The solution rate of crimes assigned to detectives appears insensitive to the number assigned, implying that detectives can accurately predict which cases can be solved and work on only those, or that the cases solve themselves.
- A high proportion of cases are closed when a patrol officer makes an arrest at the scene of the crime.

- Investigators make scant use of physical evidence such as fingerprints , tool-
marks, and the like.

Uncomplimentary views are also being espoused by a number of progressive
police chiefs who have seen reforms and new initiatives take hold in every other area
of policing, but find their detectives the last bastion of the status quo. In their
departments, an appointment to the detective bureau is no longer viewed as the best
path to promotion. In some departments (e.g., the Los Angeles Police Department),
an independent detective bureau no longer exists. Investigators are now assigned
directly to a local operations commander.

Many of these chiefs are quite candidly critical of the old freewheeling detective
style of operation. They see their detectives as simply trying to preserve the freedom
and perquisites of their jobs without making any efforts to adapt to the rapidly
shifting community and legal climate in which they must work.

The Rand Criminal Investigation Study   In 1973, the Rand Corporation was
awarded a grant by the National Institute of Law Enforcement and Criminal Justice
to undertake a nationwide study of the criminal investigation practices of major
metropolitan police agencies. The purposes of the **Rand criminal investigation study**
were to describe how police investigations were organized and managed and to assess
the contribution of various investigation activities to overall police effectiveness.
Prior to the Rand study, police investigators had not been subject to the type of
analytic scrutiny which was being focused on other types of police activity. Most
police administrators knew little about the effectiveness or day-to-day activities of
their investigative units and even less about the practices of other departments
(Greenwood, 1979).

The Rand study concentrated on the investigation of Index offenses—serious
crimes against unwilling victims—as opposed to vice, narcotics, gambling, or traffic
offenses. Information on current practices was obtained by a national survey of all
municipal or county police agencies that employed more than 150 officers or that
served jurisdictions with a 1970 population in excess of 100,000. Interviews and
observations were conducted in more than 25 departments selected to represent
different investigative styles. Data on investigation outcomes were obtained from the
Uniform Crime Reports tapes maintained by the FBI; samples of completed cases,
which were coded for the purpose of this study; and internal evaluations or statistics
compiled by individual departments. Data on the allocation of investigation efforts
were obtained from a computerized workload file maintained by the Kansas City
Police Department.

The national survey and *UCR* data were combined for the purposes of analyzing relationships between departmental characteristics and apprehension effectiveness. The special case samples were analyzed to determine how specific cases were
actually solved. On the basis of this study, a number of policy recommendations were
made.

First, the study suggested that postarrest investigation activities be coordinated
more directly with prosecutors by either assigning investigators to their offices or by
allowing them to exert more guidance over the policies and practices which they

follow. This move was expected to result in a higher percentage of prosecutable cases.

Secondly, it was suggested that patrol officers be given a larger role in conducting preliminary investigations, both to provide an adequate basis for case screening and to eliminate the need for redundant efforts by an investigator. It appears that most cases can be closed on the basis of the preliminary investigation and that patrol officers can be trained to conduct them adequately. This expanded role for patrol officers is also consistent with other moves toward geographic decentralization and patrol officer job enrichment.

The study recommended that additional resources be devoted to processing latent prints and that improved systems be developed for organizing and searching latent print files.

Finally, in conducting followup investigations for those cases which a department elected to pursue, it recommended they distinguish between those cases which involved only routine clerical processing and those involving the need for special investigation or legal skills. The former could be handled by lower-level clerical personnel while the latter could be assigned to a major offense bureau for careful monitoring and continuous evaluation.

Following its release, the Rand study was given extremely wide coverage in the popular media and was the subject of heated controversy within the police profession. Many police officials, especially those who had not come up through the detective ranks, were sympathetic to the study in that it supported their own impressions of how investigators functioned. Some went so far as to criticize the report for "telling us what we already knew." A number of police chiefs were hostile to the report because it was being used by other city officials as an excuse to cut police budgets. Others refused to accept the findings because of the limited number of departments from which some of the principal findings were drawn.

Although there have not been any major attempts to replicate or extend the findings of the Rand study, there have been several reports published which contain findings that are consistent with it. Bloch and Weidman's (1976) analysis of the Rochester, New York, police department's investigation practices and Greenberg's (1977) efforts to develop a felony investigation decision model both resulted in findings supportive of the notion that the preliminary investigation conducted by patrol officers produces the majority of arrests and can provide adequate information for screening out unsolvable cases. A report by the Vera Institute (1977) on felony arrest dispositions in New York City supplied evidence that a substantial portion of felony arrests for street crimes involves offenders who are known to their victims. A report by Forst (1978) on the disposition of felony arrests in Washington, D.C., demonstrates the importance of physical evidence and multiple witnesses in securing convictions for felony street crimes.

Geographical and Team Policing

In the years prior to World War II, patrol officers in the urban areas typically discharged their responsibilities by "walking a beat." The foot patrol concept was largely abandoned by the 1950s for a variety of reasons: chronic shortages of sworn officers; the inability of officers on foot to respond quickly to emergencies; rapid expansion of city boundaries; and the belief that on-foot patrol officers might be susceptible to corruption if they became too familiar with the local residents. Thus, the familiar cop on the beat was replaced by the unfamiliar uniformed stranger in a patrol car.

More recently, police departments have recognized the need to develop programs based on the stable assignment of patrol officers to particular communities without sacrificing the speed of response and flexibility provided by the patrol car. The guiding concept in such programs is **geographical policing,** according to which police agencies require patrol officers assigned to a given neighborhood or community to meet regularly with local residents to discuss crime problems that are of mutual concern and to formulate possible cooperative efforts toward their solution. Geographical policing is based on the notion that (1) an officer assigned to a particular area who is given primary responsibility for reducing crime in that area can be more effective than an officer who is assigned by random and given no specific responsibility for crime reduction and (2) community support, obtained through long-term assignment of individual officers, is essential for successful police work.

Team policing incorporates and extends the basic development strategy of geographical policing. The term itself and the concept originated in Aberdeen, Scotland, during the years immediately following World War II in a project designed to counteract boredom and low morale among individual officers patroling quiet areas. Patrol teams of five and ten men, in cars and afoot, were detailed to specific locations within the city characterized by a high concentration of crimes or calls for service. As the workload varied they were moved to different areas.

Another approach called "unit beat policing" was developed in 1966 in the town of Accrington, County of Coventry, England. The purpose of the Coventry approach was to overcome manpower shortages by maximizing effective utilization of available resources. Under this approach, constables were assigned to teams based in a specific area. They operated individually but supplied information to a collator about their particular location. The collator processed incoming reports and provided for the exchange of information among the other members of the team. Thus, fewer constables were effectively able to cover a larger patrol area.

The President's Commission on Law Enforcement and Administration of Justice (1967) made the following recommendation:

> Police departments should commence experimentation with a team policing concept that envisions those officers with patrol and investigative duties combining under unified command with flexible assignments to deal with the crime problem in a defined sector [p. 118].

In fact, a certain amount of experimentation with various forms of team policing had already taken place by the time the Commission's Task Force on Police made its report. For example, the Aberdeen system had been tried and abandoned by 1963 in Tucson, Arizona, and also in a number of other American cities. Sherman, Milton, and Kelly (1973) reported the results of an extensive study of team policing in seven cities: Los Angeles, Detroit, New York, Syracuse, Dayton, Holyoke, and Richmond,

California. These authors noted that team policing had failed or reached only partial success for a variety of reasons:

1. The departments' middle management, seeing team policing as a threat to their power, subverted and, in some cases, actively sabotaged the plans.
2. The dispatching technology did not permit the patrols to remain in their neighborhoods, despite the stated intentions of adjusting that technology to the pilot projects.
3. The patrols never received a sufficiently clear definition of how their behavior and role should differ from that of a regular patrol; at the same time, they were considered an elite group by their peers who often resented not having been chosen for the project [pp. 107-108].

Nevertheless, the National Advisory Commission on Criminal Justice Standards and Goals (1973) believed that the experience of cities which had implemented various team policing approaches indicated that these programs had a significant potential for crime control. The commission recommended the approach it called *total team policing*, which it defined as follows:

1. Combining all line operations of patrol, traffic, and investigation into a single group under common supervision;
2. Forming teams with a mixture of patrolmen, investigators, and specialists in such areas as juvenile delinquency and drug abuse;
3. Permanently assigning teams to geographic areas; and
4. Charging the teams with total responsibility for all police services within their respective areas [p. 114].

Family Crisis Intervention

One of the most dangerous tasks a patrol officer is called upon to perform is dealing with family disturbances. In 1982, for example, 13 percent of all police officers killed in the line of duty were slain while answering disturbance complaints; and 27 percent of the assaults on policemen occurred in the same setting.

For the participants in such quarrels, the hazards are even greater. Approximately 25 percent of all murders reported in 1982 took place between family members, 7.1 percent occurred during a "lovers' quarrel," and 41.2 percent as a consequence of other arguments. By far the largest majority of aggravated assault cases involve family members, relatives, friends, neighbors, or acquaintances.

A pioneering study by Morton Bard (1970) demonstrated that training of police officers in the management of interpersonal conflict could improve their handling of domestic disturbances. In addition, research strongly suggested that the skillful performance of **family crisis intervention** was regarded by the community as a valuable service.

Bard (1973) notes that the special circumstances of police work place the police officer in a strategic position to intervene in crisis situations. Among the wide variety of crisis events that the policeman is likely to encounter, Bard lists the following:

1. *Crime victimization.* The victims of crimes, particularly those against the person, experience extraordinary stress reactions. A policeman trained in crisis intervention techniques can have the dual effect of helping the victim in stress while at the same time eliciting information necessary for the successful investigation of the crime.

2. *Natural disaster.* In this category are included such events as fire, flood, explosion, earthquake, tornado, etc. The suddenness and impact of the event leads to a "disaster syndrome." The dimensions of this syndrome and specific techniques for combating it are essential knowledge for the police who must restore order after such an event.

3. *Notification.* A frequent police activity with little recognition by laymen, this involves informing the family or next of kin of the death or injury of a family member. In this circumstance, the police officer himself both causes the crisis and can act as an agent in its resolution.

4. *Accident.* Ranging from vehicular homicides to falling objects, these events differ somewhat from the "disaster syndrome" in that the chaos is personal and exists in an otherwise ordered and intact environment.

5. *Psychotic reactions.* These reactions have profound effects upon others, particularly family members.

6. *Suicides and attempted suicides.* As with psychotic reactions, these occurrences profoundly affect others. Skillful intervention by police may offer significant preventive opportunities [p. 3].

Bard stresses the "unique potentials for crisis intervention in the police service delivery system." This is the positive dimension of what Bittner (1970), whom we quoted earlier, refers to as the "distribution of situationally justifiable force." It is this outreach capacity of the law enforcement subsystem, which is incapable of realization by other members of the "helping professions," that permits the achievement of immediacy in time and place on the part of the policeofficer's efforts. Bard states that: "If there is a commitment to prevention in mental health, then there must be a challenge to develop means for utilizing the immediacy and authority of the police system" (p. 3).

COORDINATION WITH OTHER CRIMINAL JUSTICE SUBSYSTEMS

The police are the most advantageously situated of all subsystems of the criminal justice system to observe the direct, tangible effects of crime upon the victim and the potential disruption of order. But it is rare for the police to be consulted formally by other criminal justice agencies facing decisions on such important matters as diversion, screening, plea bargaining, and so on. A survey cited by the National Advisory Commission (1973) of more than 3,400 criminal justice practitioners showed that 2,274, or 66 percent, agreed that it was undesirable for the prosecutor to engage in plea negotiations without consulting the arresting officer. Nevertheless, 2,393 (70 percent) indicated that this was the probable course of action followed by the majority of prosecutors in most cases.

We have emphasized that no component of the criminal justice system operates independently of the other elements of the system, and that no subsystem fulfills its obligations and responsibilities solely by realizing its own immediate objectives. Admittedly, a deliberate effort is called for on the part of the police, prosecutor, the courts, and corrections to communicate and cooperate with one another, because of the legal and administrative tangles which presently block easy access from one agency to another. But some steps already have been taken to facilitate coordination between the police and other criminal justice agencies.

Case Preparation Unit

Cooperation between the office of the prosecutor and the police is essential to the development of evidence necessary to obtain the conviction of arrested persons. The Detroit Police Department has experimented with the establishment of a special **case preparation unit** to relieve precinct investigators from spending excessive periods of time in court or on court-related activities. It was found that the unit saved the department nearly 900 manhours per month in investigative and patrol measures. More important, the case preparation improved both the quality of the evidentiary materials presented and the working relationship between the police, the prosecutor, and the courts. The National Advisory Commission (1973) was led to recommend that police departments in other metropolitan areas make use of case preparation specialists to insure that all evidence that may lead to the conviction or acquittal of defendants is systematically prepared and presented for review by the prosecutor.

Major Violators and Case Follow-up

The sequential processing of defendants through the criminal justice system encourages personnel at every stage to assume that their functions have ended once the defendant has been moved along to the next phase. Thus, many police officers tend to assume that, except for appearances as witnesses, their responsibilities are over when a criminal complaint has been issued. Some police agencies, however, have perceived a need to take a more active role in the disposition of criminal cases involving serious violations.

Programs have been undertaken in New York and Washington, D.C., to concentrate police attention on "major violators," individuals suspected of being responsible for a large number of crimes in a given area. By focusing upon such persons, police departments—in coordination with prosecutors and the courts—have been able to spotlight prosecution efforts on criminal offenders who might otherwise escape special attention on crowded court dockets. Prosecutors in these two cities have generally agreed to assign priority handling to cases involving major violators and to exempt such offenders from plea bargaining.

The National Advisory Commission (1973) was sufficiently impressed with the major violator programs in New York and Washington, D.C., to make the following recommendations:

Every police agency in cooperation with local courts, prosecutors, and corrections agencies should provide for the adequate followup of criminal cases.

Police agencies should identify major violators and should follow the progress of these individuals through the criminal justice system. Police agencies should review all major criminal cases that prosecutors refuse to prosecute or later cause to be dismissed in order that administrative action may be taken to correct any police actions that may have weakened the case. The review procedure should also serve to inform the prosecuting office of deficiencies that the police feel the prosecution has made in the case in order that the prosecutor may correct those inconsistencies [p. 134].

JOB STRESS AND POLICE PERSONNEL

The stress imposed by the physical hazards of policing is well known. Few occupations require an employee to face the kinds of dangerous situations that a police officer may encounter as part of his or her daily routine. Television police shows have familiarized viewers with the risks involved in "hot pursuits," stop-and-search situations, and answering domestic disturbance calls. These are among the more obvious dangers police officers face when attempting to protect society from the lawbreaker. They constitute a "unique type of stress placed on the police by the physically dangerous and often violent nature of their employment, and, more importantly, by their conceptualization of this hazard" (Lewis, 1973, p. 488). The constant exposure of police officers to physical danger, as Lewis points out, leads to a "conflict of hazard and instinct, continually reinforced by the observation of incidents of bleeding, injury, and death over an extended period of time" (p. 480).

Police officers themselves are inclined to rate the physical hazards of policing as less stressful than other aspects of the job. Organizational stress which results from the administrative and professional requirements of the job is seen as a more serious problem than the "danger-stress" situation by many officers. When Kroes and his associates (1974) surveyed 100 Cincinnati police officers regarding their perceptions of job-related stress, the officers ranked the four principal sources of stress they associated with work in this order:

1. The courts: lack of consideration in scheduling court appearances by officers; leniency toward criminals.
2. Police administration: policies and procedures; lack of rapport and support.
3. Equipment: disrepair and shortages.
4. Community relations: public apathy and nonsupport; negative image of police officers.

While crisis situations of the kind which creats danger-stress were recognized as important, most officers felt they could deal effectively with "danger-stressors" if they were not required to cope with the additional pressures created by **organizational stressors.**

Among organizational stressors are irregular duty hours (shifts), departmental management policies, and competition for advancement. Law enforcement agencies are typically structured according to a paramilitary hierarchy which tends to be rigidly stratified and unresponsive to individual needs and problems. Excessive paperwork, red tape, lack of participation in decision-making processes that directly concern him or her, antiquated promotional policies, and disciplinary regulations that require the police officer to maintain significantly higher personal and moral standards than are expected of civilians—these are some of the stress factors that police officers identify as endemic to law enforcement organizational structures.

In the stress-filled working environment of the police officer, peer group identification serves an important defensive function. Reiser (1974) has noted that peer group support bolsters the individual officer's confidence and self-esteem, allowing him or her to tolerate higher levels of anger, hostility, and abuse from external sources. Reiser uses the term **John Wayne syndrome** to refer to a commonly occurring reaction to stress by police officers, marked by emotional withdrawal, cynicism, overseriousness, coldness, authoritarian attitudes, "tunnel vision," and the development of rigid, dichotomous thinking, according to which everything is either good or bad, and the world is divided into decent people and "assholes." As long as peer group supports are intact, camaraderie and esprit de corps dominate. But if the peer support group is disrupted by promotion, transfer, death, or other reasons, the result is apt to be depression, alienation, and lowered morale, and friendships and family relations are severely affected.

Stress also affects us physically, emotionally, and interpersonally. Its immediate physical effects are increased heartbeat, perspiration, increased breathing rate, inhibition of the digestive processes, dilated pupils, and a number of other physical adjustments made by the body in reaction to stress. More prolonged exposure to stress results in a lowering of resistance, which increases susceptibility to infectious diseases. As Hans Selyé (1974) points out, this protracted state of readiness may lead to various "diseases of adaptation"—cardiovascular and kidney ailments, rheumatism and arthritis, ulcers, and allergic diseases—all of which are interpreted as symptomatic of the body's efforts at coping with the consequences of stress.

Emotional reactions to stress include confusion, anxiety, fear, anger, cynicism, and even hysteria. An interpersonal reaction to stress is one which directly inhibits a person's ability to communicate effectively with others. One who is interpersonally affected by stress may vacillate from one extreme of irrational emotional outbursts to the other extreme of remaining completely silent. Some end results of continued exposure to high-stress situations, if left untreated, are alcoholism, divorce, and even suicide. The prevalence of these stress syndromes among police officers has been reported by study after study in the professional literature. The "drinking cop" (Dishlacoff, 1975) is a familiar figure, and suicide rates for police officers have been pegged at six times the rate for the general population (Siegal, 1978). Marital discord, family problems, and high divorce rates among police officers have been identified by other investigators of job-related stress in policing and its consequences (Danish and Brodsky, 1970).

Stress Intervention and Management

Law enforcement executives have responded to the problem of job-related stress in policing by instituting programs aimed at stress inoculation and management. Large agencies such as the Los Angeles County Sheriffs Department and the New York Police Department have developed comprehensive programs which range all the way from physical fitness training to family orientation and counseling. These programs are carried on primarily with personnel attached to the Psychological Services Unit of the agency itself. Smaller departments such as Florida's Fort Lauderdale–Hollywood Police Department have contracted with private consulting firms for the delivery of stress training and counseling services.

The many suggestions made for reducing stress or learning to cope with it include the following methods, techniques, and programs [International Association of Chiefs of Police (IACP), 1978, p. 3]:

- More efficient preemployment screening to weed out those who cannot cope with a high-stress job.
- Increased practical training for police personnel on stress, including the simulation of high-stress situations.
- A more supportive attitude by police executives toward the stress-related problems of patrol officers.
- A mandatory alcoholic rehabilitation program.
- Immediate consultation with officers involved in traumatic events such as justifiable homicides.
- Complete false-arrest and liability insurance to relieve officers of having to second-guess their decisions.
- The provision of departmental psychological services to police officers and their families.

All the methods listed call for a firm commitment from both the individual and the agency or department. In this controversial area, one thing is certain; namely, efforts toward increasing an officer's effectiveness in coping with stress are less successful in the absence of close cooperation between the individual officer and the department.

POLICE USE OF DEADLY FORCE

No aspect of policing elicits more passionate concern or more divided opinion than the use of **deadly force.** Many community groups and minority organizations believe police killings of civilians are excessive and often unjustifiable. Police agencies, on the other hand, are sometimes apprehensive and angry about the unprovoked assault on patrol officers (Wilson, 1980, p. 16).

No one would argue that police officers have the right to use deadly force if necessary to protect themselves or the life of some innocent person. However, in many states the law and individual police policies allow their officer discretion that goes far beyond the simple edicts of self-defense or defense of others. Many states and police agencies still model their laws and departmental policies after the old English common law, which allows a police officer to use deadly force to apprehend someone reasonably believed to have committed a felony. The rationale for this formula is grounded in the fact that until the early 1800s in both the United States and England, virtually all felonies were punishable by death. A felon was someone who, by his or her act, had forfeited the right to life (Milton et al., p. 39).

Although many states still retain the common law rule or some variant of it, lawmakers increasingly have questioned the rule as a basis for authorizing the use of deadly force and have significantly modified that rule in some jurisdictions. While some have codified the common law rule, many others have enacted stricter statutes. The statutes vary in terms of degree of knowledge an officer must have to justify killing a suspected felon. Some require a "felony in fact"; others call for "reasonable belief." Some limit the kinds of felonies that will justify the use of deadly force; others distinguish between an arrestee and an escapee. The modern trend, however, has been toward the adoption of both statutes and department policies which strongly control and narrowly define the circumstances under which deadly force may be used by a police officer.

In 1962 the American Law Institute proposed a model penal code that included the following section on policy for use of deadly force in law enforcement.

The use of deadly force is not justifiable under this section unless:

1. the arrest is for a felony and
2. the person effecting the arrest is authorized to act as a peace officer or is assisting a person whom he believes to be authorized to act as a peace officer;
3. the actor believes the force employed creates substantial risk of injury to innocent persons; and
4. the actor believes that: the crime for which the arrest is made involves conduct including the use or threatened use of deadly force; or there is substantial risk that the person to be arrested will cause death or serious bodily harm if apprehension is delayed [pp. 3–7].

In 1968 the University of Wisconsin Institute of Government Affairs published a model deadly force policy, the basis of which is as follows:

Deadly force can be used only as a last resort and then only:

When an officer reasonably believes that he or others are threatened by death or great bodily harm; or to make a legal arrest for a felony which normally causes or threatens death or serious bodily harm to the officer or others or which involves the breaking and entering of a building, and the officer reasonably believes that the arrest cannot be made, or custody cannot otherwise be maintained or regained.

An officer may use deadly force in self defense only as a last resort and only if he reasonably believes that such force is necessary to prevent death or great bodily harm.

An officer is privileged to defend a third person from real or apparent unlawful interference by another under the same condition and at the same means applicable to the privilege of self defense [Sec. 800].

The FBI's policy on the use of firearms and/or force directs that:

1. special agents can use firearms only in defense of themselves or others wherein it reasonably appears that they are in danger of death or grievous bodily harm;

2. special agents will use force as necessary to expeditiously make an arrest but no force in excess of that which is actually required;

3. special agents may draw a firearm to the ready when making an arrest if it appears reasonably or likely under the specific circumstances that they might be confronted with existing deadly force;

4. special agents may not fire a warning shot to stop a fleeing person or for any other purpose [Fyfe, 1979].

These types of recommendations which restrict police discretion in the use of deadly force are becoming more common in law enforcement agencies. For example, it is apparent from the research findings and reports of the Police Foundation (Milton et al., 1977) and the International Association of Chiefs of Police (Matulia, 1982) that these influential organizations support the present trend in many large cities to limit the use of deadly force to situations involving self-defense, defense of others, and the apprehension of suspects in violent or potentially lethal felonies.

Legal, Political, and Social Implications of Deadly Force

Quite apart from the humanitarian reasons for the control of police use of deadly force, there are legal, political, and social considerations as well. Presidential commissions established for the purpose of studying the causes of urban riots have pointed out how frequently the event which triggers an outburst of violence is an incident in which a young male member of a minority community is shot by a police officer (Koerner, 1968). On other occasions, such occurrences may produce less explosive but equally harmful results.

Mention must also be made of financial liability in deadly force situations. Deaths resulting from police actions have often resulted in substantial judgments against financially hard-pressed cities. In other instances, individual police officers have been held responsible for injuries sustained by persons they have shot.

In the final analysis, it would appear that the incentive to restrict the police use of deadly force far outweighs the arguments anyone might present in keeping them broad and ill-defined. It is quite likely that by the end of the 1980s many departments which now adhere to the common law rule will move toward the use of much more restrictive policies, in great part to avoid some of the unfavorable consequences of police shootings we just discussed.

PROFESSIONALISM AND THE POLICE

The solution to whatever ails law enforcement has consistently been sought in the "professionalization" of policing, and the term *professional* has acquired almost mystical properties in the law enforcement community. If police officers wish to commend a fellow officer's performance, they are likely to praise it for being professional. A well-organized, smoothly functioning police department is complimented for its professionalism. Conversely, behavior unbecoming of a police officer is put down in the harshest terms for being unprofessional.

Over Million Dollar Judgment Given Youth Shot in Store Being Looted During 1967 Detroit Riot.

A six-member Wayne County Circuit Court jury awarded a judgment of $875,000 plus over $150,000 in back interest to a young black high school student who was shot during the Detroit riot of 1967. The youth, then 13, alleged he was shot after entering a closed five-and-dime store to warn others "that the police were coming." The decision is unusual because the boy was unable to identify the officers who came to the scene "brandishing rifles," according to his testimony. Detroit police denied any knowledge of the shooting there and stated they had not themselves fired any shots in the vicinity. Attorneys for Albert Wilson, now 18, said the verdict against the City of Detroit is the largest ever awarded in Michigan for an injury to one person.

Wilson and two other witnesses testified that before the shooting they saw Detroit policemen, carrying rifles, arrive at the scene. The plaintiff stated that he was crouching behind a partition and looking through a small space when he saw a police officer aim at him. He "saw a flash, heard a pop and felt a slug hit him before he fell unconscious." A bullet entered the boy's left side, destroyed a kidney, left him paralyzed below the waist and confined to a wheelchair.

The policeman who allegedly fired the shot was never identified and the bullet that struck Wilson was determined to be 30 caliber, but was so badly damaged that ballistics tests could not be made. City attorneys denied that a Detroit policeman was guilty and contended that Wilson was not wounded in the store.

The original suit asked for $750,000 in damages, but Wilson's attorney, in his closing statement, requested that the sum be increased "to a reasonable amount, not to exceed $1.7 million." In addition to the tax free $875,000, Wilson is to be paid six percent annual interest on that amount from the time the suit was filed in April, 1969.

Source. AELE Law Enforcement Legal Liability Reporter, Sample Issue, p. 5.

Officer Held Liable for Shooting 17-year-old.

A police officer was ordered to pay $45,000 to a 17-year-old youth he shot as the youth was escaping through the window of a house he was burglarizing. The youth was not armed at the time, but guns had been observed at the scene. The jury found that the shooting was justified, but the officer was found negligent for violating a regulation that prohibits firing at a suspect unless the officer believes that life is in danger. The jury also found that the youth had suffered $74,000 in damages, but this was reduced to $45,000 because he was 40% contributorily negligent.

Source: AELE Law Enforcement Legal Liability Reporter, Feb. 1979, p. 9.

There seems little doubt that at least part of the preoccupation with profession-alization among police officers and administrators is the direct result of experiences within the criminal justice system in which they cannot help but contrast the defer-ence and high salaries accorded the representatives of various professions with their own perceived position near the bottom of the occupational status totem pole. They encounter members of the legal profession in their roles as prosecutors, defense counsels, and judges; physicians and psychiatrists; expert witnesses from a diversity of specialties and disciplines, usually with earned doctorates or other advanced de-grees; and police officers almost inevitably come up on the short end of any compari-sons based on prestige and income.

Formal education has been the traditional path to both self-improvement and increase in the status of a particular line of work. With the passage of the Omnibus Crime Bill in 1968, public funds were made available to police personnel to pursue a college degree program at federal expense—or with at least partial federal subsidiza-tion. Many officers and administrators took advantage of such financial assistance, with the result that today's law enforcement personnel are much better educated, on the average, than they were prior to the availability of federal funding.

The Rationale for Collegiate Standards

Do college graduates make better police officers than those who lack a college educa-tion? This is a deceptively simple question. What kinds of specific criteria are in-volved in defining "better"—higher arrest rates, fewer citizen complaints, faster promotion? For instance, in a police department with extremely low productivity in terms of arrest rates, clearance rates, and the like, one might very well expect that the infusion of officers with a collegiate background would lead to increased productiv-ity, as measured by these standards. If this were definitively one of the goals of recruiting collegiate officers, and the behavior of the officers was directed to these ends, then certainly higher arrest and clearance rates would indicate the success of the imposition of higher educational requirements. On the other hand, however, arrest and clearance rates are often highly inflated and, in fact, counterproductive. That is, arrests are made in many situations which would lend themselves to an alternative solution; arrests are made with insufficient evidence; or crimes are re-ported cleared upon dubious criteria. If this situation is attributed to the competence of agency personnel, and it often can be, then the infusion of collegiate officers might very will result in a reduction of arrests and clearance rates, although reductions in these rates are usually thought of as indicating poorer performance.

Similarly, one might expect the crime rate to go up or down depending upon the perceived ability of officers to establish community rapport and affect extent of reporting, and thus expect rates to rise in some instances and fall in others. In short, determining the success of any police program, including higher personnel standards, is an extremely complex task. The appropriateness of a particular productivity mea-sure is dependent upon individual agency and situational characteristics. Hence, efforts at establishing the credibility of higher educational standards for the police are plagued by the lack of agreement about what constitutes "good" performance from "bad" performance.

For example, in some police departments reward systems are based primarily upon the ability to make arrests, while in other police agencies notoriety may be obtained by either becoming involved in a gun battle or making a "big bust." A college education contributes little to one's ability to perform either of these endeavors more effectively than anyone else. On the other hand, the proper referral of a criminal offender in need of psychiatric care either goes unrecognized or may even be negatively rewarded. The following two similar situations involving officers from the same police department illustrate this point.

In the first case, two officers were fired upon by a man with a handgun, but did not return the fire. Instead they implored him to throw the gun down, then chased him into a house and seized him just as he was reaching for a loaded shotgun. Command personnel were present immediately after the occurrence, but no commendation or verbal compliment ensued. The incident the following month involved another mental subject, this time armed with a rifle. The subject fired the rifle, then began approaching the police car. When he would not halt, he was shot and killed by the responding officers. In the second incident both officers received letters of commendation from the chief of police for bravery in the line of duty. The point is not that the officers in the second incident did not deserve the letter; they held their fire for as long as they thought was reasonable. However, it is important to note that similar action was not taken in the first incident. Thus it appears that the system, at least in some police departments, is geared to reward those who are involved in spectacular shootings and arrests.

Determining Enhanced Productivity

The problem of determining enhanced productivity is complicated by inappropriate expectations. What we have unfortunately failed to recognize in both police training and educational programming is that some of the specific tasks of patrol officers can only be learned adequately through experience. The police role involves knowledge of dozens of formulas, dozens of forms, and scores of "ways of doing things." No amount of formal instruction given in the classroom will, for instance, prevent a police recruit from being "had" a few times by con artists on the street. Some sociologists have observed that there is a significant body of knowledge in the police service characterized by the term *street wisdom.* It is unfortunate that far too many administrators, and even a number of educators, have looked to formal educational programs to enhance a student's ability to apply and use street wisdom; it simply will not happen. As a matter of fact, we might even expect certain deficiencies in this regard on the part of middle-class college graduates. One aspect of street wisdom is knowledge of the value systems, jargon, and the like of lower socioeconomic classes, and middle-class college graduates would not normally be expected to possess such knowledge. However, experience would soon remedy that deficiency.

Another serious methodological problem plaguing efforts to justify higher educational standards for the police is establishing precisely what level of improved performance justifies the imposition of higher standards. That is to say, it is not merely enough to establish that collegiate police officers do perform more adequately, however defined, than noncollegiate officers. It must be established that the increase in productivity justifies the increased expense resulting from the higher salaries frequently associated with higher education. Such a determination would be difficult enough to make if police productivity was easily measured, or the goals of the police service universally agreed upon by those in the field. However, this is not the case.

The problem of determining "significant" productivity differences is compounded by the fact that the nature of the police patrol officers task is too often quite limited in scope. If we conceive of the task as merely writing traffic tickets and shining a spotlight in windows to ascertain whether they are broken, or arresting drunks, then certainly arguments for higher educational standards are weak. However, if the task is made what it ought to be, then any standard less than a bachelor degree is inappropriate.

SUMMARY

Police roles and responsibilities are numerous and complex, ranging from the apprehension of offenders to intervening in domestic disturbances. Law enforcement tasks are carried out at the local, state, and federal levels, and the principal characteristics of policing in the United States are fragmentation and decentralization. Enforcement of federal laws is shared among agencies that include the Federal Bureau of Investigation and the Secret Service. At the state level, law enforcement agencies may be given general or restricted police powers, that is, authority to enforce all state laws within the geographical boundaries of the state or authority to enforce certain statutes, such as those which cover traffic and highway safety. Law enforcement at the local level is usually designated either municipal or county. The former is likely to be a police department headed by a chief who is an appointed public official; the latter is a sheriff's department headed by an elected official who may have both civil and criminal law responsibilities. Police and sheriff's departments in large metropolitan areas show many more similarities than differences in organization, training, and functions.

The largest of the police operations bureaus and the one to which almost all new police officers are assigned is the patrol bureau. It forms the base upon which all future police experiences are built. When first assigned to the patrol bureau, the rookie officer typically works under the direct tutelage of a senior officer before being permitted to work alone. The patrol bureau, for better or worse, regularly serves as a manpower pool for the other more specialized and prestigious assignments. The residual effect of this practice is a disproportionate number of officers who are either relatively inexperienced or are not considered to be among the best and brightest officers. This tendency is reinforced by the desire of many patrol officers to be transferred to other bureaus because of the difficulties associated with the environment of the patrol officer's work and the clientele served.

Team policing in the patrol bureau was begun as a way to reduce the isolation of the police from the community and to induce the support of citizens in their efforts to reduce crime. The results of the Kansas City patrol experiment raised serious questions about the value of marked patrol units in reducing crime and their value in reducing the public's fear of crime. The controversy caused by these findings has not yet ended within the law enforcement community.

Discussion was devoted to the activities of the traffic bureau and the detective bureau. Traffic officers have an obligation to engage in the selective enforcement of traffic violations and not to write tickets arbitrarily merely to meet a quota or to keep their sergeants happy. What detectives do in their attempts to solve crimes is a crucially important part of policing. The most comprehensive study ever undertaken to analyze the day-to-day effectiveness of detectives was done by the Rand Corporation. The study concluded by recommending closer postarrest cooperation between the police and prosecutor's office, giving patrol officers greater responsibility in conducting preliminary investigations and improving the system to differentiate between cases that need only clerical processing and those that require high-level investigative or legal skills.

Among the issues that rank high in contemporary policing, job-related stress and police use of deadly force have received a great deal of attention in the professional literature. Law enforcement officials have instituted programs aimed at stress intervention and management, which range from physical fitness training to family orientation and counseling. With regard to the second issue, the use of deadly force by an officer can create serious problems for the individual police officer, the department, citizens, and the community at large. It would appear that the present trend of many police departments to restrict the use of deadly force by their officers will continue well into the 1980s and beyond. These restrictions generally prohibit the use of deadly force except in those situations where the officer's life or the life of some innocent person is threatened.

Police leaders believe that moving toward professionalization of the police would eventually allow them to enjoy the prestige, respect, and high earnings that are normally commanded by professionals in other areas of specialization. Linked to this pursuit of professionalization is higher education and degree programs. The acquisition of the baccalaureate degree, or even graduate degrees, is no guarantee to greater job productivity or a reduction in crime rates. Much of what police officers do involves delivering social services, resolving conflicts, and maintaining order. It may be that the greatest benefits police and citizens will derive from the professionalization of the police is not so much improvements in their technical skills as improvements in their human relations skills.

DISCUSSION QUESTIONS

Find the answers to the following questions in the text.

1. What is the meaning of Bittner's characterization of the police as a "mechanism for the distribution of situationally justified force in society"? How does this characterization help us to understand police roles and responsibilities in a democratic society?
2. Discuss the contention of the authors that the most striking characteristics of American law enforcement are its decentralization and fragmentation.
3. Distinguish between **general** and **restricted police powers** as they pertain to state law enforcement agencies.

4. What are the major distinctions between county and municipal law enforcement?
5. Briefly describe the organizational structure of a municipal police department for a medium-sized city. How are personnel and resources allotted to the **patrol, traffic,** and **detective bureaus**?
6. What policy recommendations were made on the basis of the **Rand criminal investigation study**?
7. How does **team policing** differ from conventional approaches to police patrol?
8. What is **family crisis intervention** and how does it operate?
9. Identify the principal features of policing which make it one of the most stressful of all occupations. What measures can be taken at the individual and departmental levels to aid police personnel in coping more effectively with job-related stress?
10. What trends now exist in law enforcement regarding departmental policies which govern the use of **deadly force**?
11. Discuss the role of higher education in police professionalism.

TERMS TO IDENTIFY AND REMEMBER

"calling the cops"
restricted police powers
family crisis intervention
patrol bureau
detective bureau
"working personality"
team policing
John Wayne syndrome
geographical policing

general police powers
case preparation unit
county police
traffic bureau
Rand criminal investigation
   study
organizational stressors
deadly force

REFERENCES

American Law Institute Model Penal Code. Proposed Official Draft 3–07, 1962.

Bard, M. Alternative to traditional law enforcement. In E. F. Korten (ed.), *Psychology and the Problems of Society.* Washington, D.C.: American Psychological Association, 1970.

Bard, M. *Family Crisis Intervention: From Concept to Implementation.* Washington, D.C.: U.S. Department of Justice, 1973.

Bittner, E. *The Function of the Police in a Modern Society.* Chevy Chase, MD: National Institute of Mental Health, 1970.

Bloch, P., and Weidman, D. *Managing Criminal Investigations: Prescriptive Package.* Washington, D.C.: U.S. Government Printing Office, 1975.

Caldwell, H. *Basic Law Enforcement.* Pacific Palisades, CA: Goodyear, 1972.

Danish, S. J., and Brodsky, S. L. Training of policemen in emotional control and awareness. *American Psychologist* 25 (1970): 368–369.

Dishlacoff, L. The drinking cop. *Police Chief* 43 (1976): 34–36, 39.

Elliott, J. F., and Sardino, T. J. *Crime Control Team.* Springfield, IL: Charles C. Thomas, 1971.

Forst, B. *What Happens After Arrest?* Washington, D.C.: U.S. Government Printing Office, 1978.

Fosdick, R. *American Police Systems.* New York: Century, 1921.

Fyfe, J. J. Deadly force. *FBI Law Enforcement Bulletin* 48 (1979): 7–9.

Greenberg, B., et al. *Felony Investigation Decision Model: An Analysis of Investigative Elements of Information.* Washington, D.C.: U.S. Government Printing Office, 1977.

Greenwood, P. W. *The Rand Criminal Investigation Study: Its Findings and Impacts To Date.* Santa Monica, CA: Rand Paper Service, 1979.

Greenwood, P. W., and Petersilia, J. *The Criminal Investigation Process, Vol. I: Summary and Policy Implications.* Santa Monica, CA: Rand Corporation, 1975.

Kelling, G. L., Pate, T., Dieckman, D., and Brown, C. E. *The Kansas City Preventive Patrol Experiment.* Washington, D.C.: The Police Foundation, 1974.

Koerner, O. *Report of the National Commission on Civil Disorders.* New York: Bantam Books, 1968.

Kroes, W. H. *Society's Victim—The Policeman.* Springfield, IL: Charles C. Thomas, 1976.

Lewis, R. W. Toward an understanding of police anomie. *Journal of Police Science and Administration* 1 (1973): 484–90.

Matulia, K. J. *A Balance of Forces.* Gaithersburg, MD: International Association of Chiefs of Police, 1982.

Milton, K., Halleck, J. W., Lardner, J., and Abrecht, G. L. *Police Use of Deadly Force.* Washington, D.C.: The Police Foundation, 1977.

National Advisory Commission on Criminal Justice Standards and Goals. *Police.* Washington, D.C.: U.S. Government Printing Office, 1973.

President's Commission on Law Enforcement and Administration of Justice. *Task Force Report: The Police.* Washington, D.C.: U.S. Government Printing Office, 1967.

Selyé, H. *Stress Without Distress.* Philadelphia: Lippincott, 1974.

Sherman, L. W., Milton, C. H., and Kelly, T. V. *Team Policing.* Washington, D.C.: The Police Foundation, 1973.

Skolnick, J. *Justice Without Trial.* New York: Wiley, 1966.

Smith, B. *Police Systems in the United States.* New York: Harper & Row, 1960.

U.S. Department of Justice, Law Enforcement Assistance Administration. *Manpower Survey of the Criminal Justice System: Executive Summary.* Washington, D.C.: U.S. Government Printing Office, 1978.

Vera Institute of Justice. *Felony Arrests: Their Prosecution and Disposition in New York City's Courts.* New York: Vera Institute of Justice, 1977.

chapter 18

THE JUDICIAL PROCESS

However important the criminal trial by jury may be for the purposes of the novelist or dramatist, it occupies a relatively minor position in the administration of justice in the United States. In any given year, less than 10 percent of those who are apprehended as suspects in serious crimes are processed through the formal steps of a criminal trial. Thus, much of the criminal process is administrative rather than judicial. That is, the process is accomplished through negotiation rather than adversarial proceedings.

The fact that this administrative model is inconsistent with the traditional model of litigated criminal prosecution should not be viewed as a cause for alarm. Given the enormous number of cases that require handling, particularly in large metropolitan areas, the resources of the criminal justice system would be strained beyond the breaking point if a substantial percentage of these cases could not be dropped or carried to some negotiated conclusion. The administration of justice would not be merely slowed down; it would come to a complete halt.

In addition, the facts in many criminal cases are not in dispute; suspects either clearly did or did not commit the offenses with which they are charged. If the facts are beyond dispute, then there is no need for a criminal trial, which is an expensive, time-consuming, and laborious procedure for weighing, sifting, and evaluating disputed facts.

During the time between arrest and trial or plea—the pretrial period—most of the important decisions are made which affect the disposition of the case and the fate of the accused. Defendants may be released from custody pending trial by posting bond or by release on their own recognizance (ROR), that is, the promise to appear at a later date to stand trial. If they are unable to post bail, they may face the prospect of remaining in detention until the case is tried—a period of weeks or even months. Attorneys for defendants may engage in negotiations with the prosecutor during this period in an effort to secure a reduced charge or other advantages for their clients. Both bail bond and the practice of plea bargaining are topics of fierce debate and continuing controversy within the criminal justice system.

INITIATION OF PROSECUTION ✓

The process of bringing a criminal offender to justice is put into motion by an arrest. The term *arrest* refers to the apprehension or detention of a person so that he or she will be made available to answer for an alleged crime. An arrest on a criminal charge can be made upon the issuance of a **warrant.** However, a warrant is not absolutely necessary. In fact, in the majority of situations, arrests are usually made without a warrant. A valid warrant may be executed against the individual named in the warrant by any law enforcement agent or private citizen to whom the warrant is directed.

Prosecution for a misdemeanor is usually initiated by the issuance of a **complaint**; prosecution for a felony offense is begun by **information** or by **grand jury indictment.**

Misdemeanors

While the public imagination and interest are captured by trials involving bizarre crimes or show business celebrities, the vast majority of criminal justice transactions occur within the lower courts and typically consist of misdemeanor offenses carrying sentences of less than one year in the county jail or relatively small fines. In these misdemeanor cases, prosecution is usually initiated upon the complaint of a victim of, or witness to, the crime. Often it is the arresting officer who is the complaining witness. Suspects are brought before a magistrate's court or justice of the peace. Magistrates have *summary* jurisdiction, that is, they are empowered to determine guilt or innocence and can impose minor sentences for petty offenses. In many states, the accused can request a jury trial. In the case of more serious crimes, the magistrate holds a preliminary hearing to determine whether sufficient evidence has been presented to justify holding the suspect for further action.

Felony Offenses

Some felony offenses are settled by dismissal or by entrance of a guilty plea at some early stage in the criminal justice process. (See Figure 18.1.) Those cases which are not settled in this manner progress through a series of stages, beginning with the initial appearance of the accused person before the court.

Initial Appearance   Most states have a statutory requirement that suspects must be brought before a judge within a reasonable period of time following arrest. At this **initial appearance** or **presentment,** suspects are given formal notice of the charges against them, are informed of their right to counsel, and are provided with a court-appointed attorney or public defender if they are too poor to afford the services of a lawyer. At this time, depending on the nature of the offense with which they are charged, they may be given an opportunity to obtain release pending trial.

Pretrial Release   Suspects may be afforded **pretrial release** by two methods: (1) posting **bail**; and (2) **release on recognizance (ROR).** Bail is a legal procedure for securing temporary liberty following arrest through a written promise to appear in court as required. In support of this promise, it may be necessary to provide cash bail, post a surety bond, or supply evidence of an equity in real property, together with the written assurance of another person or persons. Release on recognizance also involves a written promise to appear in court, subject to various conditions, but dispenses with cash or other forms of surety.

When the accused lacks financial resources, the bail system adds a discriminatory element to the administration of justice. Indigent (poor) defendants are unable to pay for the investigation necessary to present their case adequately, especially when incarceration pending trial interrupts their normal earnings. The appearance in court of the defendant under guard may have an adverse effect on the jury. Even when convicted, the bailed defendant has the advantage of showing evidence of steady employment and good conduct while awaiting trial.

Release on one's own recognizance has become a widely accepted alternative to the bail system as a means of securing pretrial release for defendants with ties to family and community, a stable work history, and other screening criteria. The pioneering efforts of the Vera Institute of Justice in New York City demonstrated that

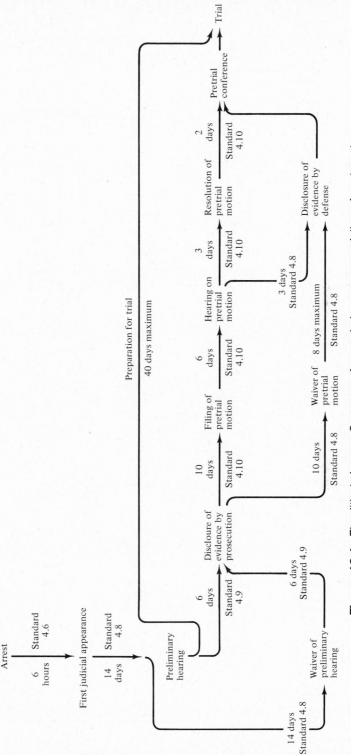

Figure 18.1 The litigated case: Summary of commission recommendations for steps to achieve trial in a felony case within 60 days of arrest. (*Source:* National Advisory Commission on Criminal Justice Standards and Goals. *Courts.* Washington, D.C.: U.S. Government Printing Office, 1973, pp. xx–xxi.)

defendants who were able to meet such criteria had a better record of court appearances than those who were released on bond (Thomas, 1976).

Despite the success of ROR programs, some judges are reluctant to release accused persons on their own recognizance. For these judges, a number of states have followed an approach known as the Illinois Ten Percent Deposit Plan. According to this system, defendants pay 10 percent of the bonding fee directly to the court instead of to a commercial bail bondsman. Upon completion of the case, the money is refunded to the defendant minus a service fee of only 1 percent. The most immediate result of this approach, as Thomas (1976) observes, was to put bail bondsmen out of business in the state of Illinois.

Crime on Bail: The Preventive Detention Issue   One of the continuing impediments to bail reform is the fear that individuals charged with serious crimes, especially crimes against the person, would be free to commit further crimes if released on bail or upon recognizance. It was this kind of fear that led the Congress to pass a bill authorizing preventive detention in the District of Columbia—where crime had been depicted by the news media as being "out of control"—for a period of up to 60 days without bond for defendants charged with crimes of violence and "dangerous" crimes.

The team of Bases and McDonald (1974) conducted a study of this D.C. preventive detention law. They reported that, during its first ten months of operation, it resulted in the detention of only 10 of 6,000 felony defendants. At present, when jails throughout the country are under pressure from federal consent decrees to reduce the problems of overcrowding, we are not likely to see much advocacy for an expansion of preventive detention legislation.

Preliminary Hearing   The purpose of the **preliminary hearing** is to weigh the evidence against suspects. The state is required to show **probable cause** to hold the accused person for trial. The expression **probable cause** has the distinct flavor of legal cant, because it is highly **improbable** that a prosecutor would initiate judicial proceedings unless the available evidence against the accused pointed to the probability of conviction. Nevertheless, the legal view persists that the preliminary hearing is beneficial to the suspect.

The state seeks to reveal only enough of its evidence against the accused to support its contention that further prosecution is warranted. If the defendants are fortunate enough to be represented by an alert and experienced counsel, they may be able to extract some definite advantages from the preliminary hearing, particularly in discovery of the strength of the case presented by the state. Some jurisdictions still fail to provide free counsel for indigent defendants at this early stage of the judicial process and most unrepresented defendants are not equipped to take full advantage of the preliminary hearing; hence, the preliminary hearing tends to be weighted heavily on the side of the prosecution. For these and other reasons, the preliminary hearing has been critized as a moribund procedure that is little more than a dress rehearsal for the prosecution's case.

Indictment or Information   People in the United States cannot be required to stand trial on a felony charge unless or until they have been formally accused through an indictment by the grand jury or an information filed by the prosecutor. The purpose of both the indictment and information is the same: to determine whether there is sufficient evidence against the accused to warrant further action by the state. The use of one method or the other is largely a matter of historical developments. The Fifth Amendment to the U.S. Constitution specifies that "no person shall be held to answer for a capital or otherwise infamous charge unless on a presentment or indictment of a grand jury." Grand juries originated in England, where they were intended to prevent hasty, oppressive, and arbitrary convictions, and were also designed to spare defendants the difficulty and expense of a criminal trial before establishing the likelihood that they had committed the crime with which they were charged. The grand jury does not seek to determine guilt or innocence; rather, it duplicates in many respects the function of the preliminary hearing, the major difference being that the defendant has no legal right to be present at the grand jury deliberations. Therefore, the decision on whether or not to indict is made solely on the evidence presented by the prosecuting attorney.

If the grand jury is convinced by the prosecutor's evidence, a **true bill** of indictment will be returned, indicating probable cause to proceed to trial. If, on the other hand, the grand jury has not been persuaded by the prosecution's evidence, it can "ignore" the charges by returning a "no bill" finding, in which case the prosecutor may charge the defendant with a lesser offense. In the overwhelming majority of indictment presentations, the grand jury tends to follow the inclination of the prosecutor. Most states require a preliminary hearing prior to charging in felony offenses. Grand jury indictments are a statutory requirement in 20 states and the federal courts.

In jurisdictions which do not use the grand jury, prosecutors may return an information—a legal document which is a formal accusation against the accused person—based on the available evidence. Even after a preliminary hearing has found probable cause for proceeding against the suspect, prosecutors may ask for a *nolle prosequi,* which signifies there will be no further action by the state. A "nol pross," as it is known informally, is usually regarded as an acknowledgment that the prosecutor's case has collapsed (perhaps a crucial piece of evidence was lost or stolen, or a key witness died or disappeared before making a deposition). A nol pross may also be requested if it is determined that a defendant is not guilty. For whatever reason, the prosecutor decides not to go any further with the prosecution.

Arraignment   **Arraignment** refers to the process of bringing an accused person before the court to answer an indictment or for information. The term has acquired the informal meaning of any appearance before a magistrate or before the trial court to enter a plea. More precisely, arraignment should be restricted in meaning to the appearance of the accused person in a felony case before the magistrate who has the power to receive the defendant's plea. Arraignment usually takes place in the court where the case will be tried. Thus, the defendant would appear before a different magistrate than the one who had been handling his or her case in a lower court.

The prosecutor formally reads in open court the bill of indictment, which specifies the charges brought against the accused by the state. The defendant is informed again of constitutional right to counsel. If the defendant is indigent and has not already had counsel assigned, counsel will be appointed at this time.

The defendant may enter a plea of guilty or not guilty. In some states other options may be available: "not guilty by reason of insanity," "former jeopardy," and *nolo contendere* ("no contest") are some of the possible alternatives. The plea of *nolo contendere* in a criminal proceeding is generally regarded as the same as a guilty plea, although in some states it means simply that the defendant does not understand the charges brought against him or her. The chief advantage of a *nolo contendere* plea is that it may spare the defendant from certain civil penalties that might follow a plea of guilty. Another option of the defendant is standing mute, in which case the court will automatically enter a plea of guilty in many jurisdictions.

In order for the plea of guilty to be accepted by the court, certain conditions must be met. The plea must be entered voluntarily and the defendant must be aware of and understand the implications of his plea. A guilty plea is considered equivalent to a verdict of guilty. The court may deliver sentence at this time or set a future date for sentencing.

PLEA BARGAINING

Prosecutors are also concerned with convictions. Since many major crimes subsume the elements of lesser crimes (e.g., murder also includes aggravated assault), prosecutors with shaky cases may accept guilty pleas to "lesser included offenses" and save the time and money of a risky trial for the major crime. Prosecutors may also offer various incentives to accused persons in efforts to elicit information from them regarding other offenders known to them or to induce defendants to give testimony which will help the prosecution's case. This process of negotiation is widely and informally known as **plea bargaining.** One such incentive is the offer to accept a *plea of guilty to a lesser charge*; another is immunity from further prosecution on the incidental charge. Thus, a number of misdemeanors begin as felony charges: drunken driving may be reduced to "reckless driving," or statutory rape may be reduced to "contributing to the delinquency of a minor." Prosecutors may also bargain for a plea of guilty in return for a *reduction in sentence.*

There are many reasons plea negotiation finds defenders among criminal justice personnel and legal authorities: society's need to dispose of criminal charges without incurring the expense of a trial; a defendant's willingness to plead guilty; the administrative burden imposed by the number of trials that would have to be conducted if plea negotiation were not permitted; the probability of an enhanced opportunity for rehabilitation on the part of the offender after an agreed-upon disposition; and the chance to individualize punishment, which can lessen the bitterness felt by many defendants after trial.

While the state has obvious reasons to use plea negotiation, so does the defendant. For someone who is guilty, a negotiated plea may prevent a long stay in jail awaiting trial, the notoriety and stigma of a criminal trial, and, most important, enhance the chance for a minimum sentence.

Factors Affecting Plea Bargaining

The following variables have been identified as those likely to exert the most significant influence on the determination of a guilty plea or trial case disposition: (1)

caseload pressures on the prosecutor; (2) strength or weakness of the prosecution's case; (3) type of defense attorney (court-appointed, public defender, or private counsel); (4) personal characteristics of the defendant (age, sex, race, prior record, bail status); and (5) the type of crime with which the defendant is charged. Mather (1979) conducted an empirical study of the case disposition process in Los Angeles County Superior Court in an effort to determine how these factors affected the dynamics of plea bargaining.

Mather found that the two factors which appeared to have the greatest influence on case disposition were: (1) the *seriousness* of the case, as measured by the likelihood of the defendant receiving a severe sentence; and (2) the *strength* of the prosecution case, based on the amount and type of available evidence. Mather stresses the *unimportance* of caseload pressure as a source of influence upon plea negotiation in the Los Angeles criminal courts; and notes that this finding is consistent with studies reported by Eisenstein and Jacob (1977), Freeley (1975), Heumann (1975), Levin (1977), and Rosett and Cressey (1976). She also noted that the type of attorney—whether counsel was a public defender or a private lawyer—did not appear to be a source of difference in the decision to plea bargain or stand trial. Lehtinen and Smith (1974) analyzed felony dispositions in Los Angeles and found only marginal differences in sentences. They suggested that "it does not really matter in the actual results whether convicted offenders are represented by public defenders or private attorneys" (p. 17).

The practice of plea negotiation or plea bargaining has been attacked and defended by a wide variety of legal and criminal justice authorities. The National Advisory Commission on Criminal Justice Standards and Goals (1973) referred to it as a "notorious" practice and strongly recommended that it be completely abolished by the year 1978. The Commission's recommendation was not followed, however, and plea bargaining still continues today. The U.S. Supreme Court, on the other hand—in *Santobello* v. *New York*, (1971)—held that plea negotiation is a legitimate means of securing a guilty plea from a criminal defendant. At any rate, guilty pleas are the mainstay of the criminal justice system, and experienced offenders soon become adept in the techniques of plea negotiation of plea bargaining ("copping a plea").

PRETRIAL MOTIONS

It is fairly common practice for defense attorneys to move for a dismissal of the charges against their clients, even before a plea has been entered. The general strategy is to attack the information or indictment, claiming improprieties in the organization or methods of the grand jury. Other possible grounds for a motion to dismiss might include prior jeopardy and the statute of limitations.

A more effective pretrial motion is one requesting the state to reveal information or evidence that the prosecution has gathered against the defendant. This is called a motion for a **bill of particulars.** If some or all of the evidence was obtained illegally—as has been the case in a number of prosecutions involving drugs—there are good prospects for the case to be thrown out.

If the counsel for the defense believes that the defendant cannot get a fair trial in the place where the crime was committed because of adverse pretrial publicity, counsel may move for a **change of venue.** Despite the attention paid to media coverage of criminal trials, particularly those with sensationalistic aspects, this motion is made rather infrequently. Equally infrequent is a motion for a separate trial in cases involving co-defendants.

The Sixth Amendment guarantees a defendant's rights to a trial before an impartial jury. Unless the defendant waives a jury trial, the trial in a felony case and in many serious misdemeanor offenses will be before a jury. In some states, the defendant must file a request for a jury trial at the time he enters his plea or at some time specified before the beginning of the court term at which a jury will be impaneled. Failure to file a request for a jury trial constitutes a waiver of the right to a jury trial. In other states, an express waiver of jury trial is mandatory.

THE CRIMINAL TRIAL

Criminal trials in the United States conform to the following outline (Wells and Weston, 1977):

1. Jury selection, impaneling, and administration of oath
2. Opening by both sides (statements, facts only)
3. The state's case
4. The defense case
5. Rebuttal (state)
6. Surrebuttal (defense)
7. Closing by both sides (argument)
8. Charge to the jury (instructions of law)
9. Verdict
10. Judgment

Selection of the Jury

The jury in a criminal trial is chosen by a complex and often time-consuming process. Since the prosecution and the defense both rely upon the jurors for a favorable decision, the factors involved in their selection are a matter of extreme concern to both parties in the adversary proceeding.

Eligible voters or taxpayers comprise the list from which a group of potential jurors, called the jury panel or *venire,* is selected. These are people who meet the qualifications set by statute for jury duty in the geographical area corresponding to the jurisdiction of the court. A group of **veniremen** (sometimes called the **array)** is summoned from the panel of jurors to appear in a given case. The *voir dire* (usually translated by the phrase "to speak the truth") is a procedure by which potential jurors are examined as a group and individually with regard to their eligibility to serve as members of a trial jury. They are questioned about their knowledge of the case and whether such knowledge might affect their ability to hear the evidence impartially. They are asked about their acquaintance with the participants in the trial (the defendant, judge, attorneys, and witnesses) as a possible source of bias in their judgment of the evidence. And they are asked whether they have already formed an opinion of the facts or issues involved in the case. If the answer to any of these questions is yes, the panel member may be dismissed "for cause" by the judge. The prosecution and the defense have an unlimited number of challenges for cause and the widest latitude for questioning. They may query prospective jurors on almost any matter that bears on their ability or willingness to reach an impartial decision in the case. In addition, the judge may exercise the option to examine the jurors.

Each side now has a specified number of **peremptory challenges.** These are requests to the court for the exclusion of a prospective juror for which no reasons need to be given. The prosecutor may decide that he or she does not want a woman under 45 or a man over 50 on the jury; or the defense attorney may feel uneasy about a potential juror on the basis of his or her facial expression, clothing, or demeanor. Whatever the reason or reasons, neither the prosecutor nor the defense counsel is required to justify them—or even state them—to the court.

Scientific Jury Selection During the 1970s, the topic of **scientific jury selection** became something of a "minimovement" (Ellison and Buckhout, 1981). But once the glare of publicity had dimmed, skepticism about its alleged successes and concern for ethical issues tended to divert professional attention to technical details. One of the factors that tended to limit enthusiasm for scientific methods of jury selection is their cost. Expenses in the Joan Little case topped $300,000.

Scientific jury selection refers to the application of tools and techniques which have long been familiar in social science research—questionnaires, interviews, attitude scales, public opinion surveys, and careful sampling procedures—to the detailed examination of relevant information concerning prospective jurors. The data obtained from field research are analyzed in an effort to identify key variables that may affect the jury decision-making processes.

Critics of scientific jury selection have charged that it represents "sophisticated jury tampering, seeks to identify jurors who are not simply impartial but partial to the defendant, replaces trial by jury with 'trial by social scientists,' and discriminates against the ordinary defendant who cannot even afford the cost of a lawyer, let alone that of consultants and surveys" (Robin, 1980, p. 276). Proponents of scientific jury selection claim that it provides the means for detecting covert biases among prospective jurors that would not be uncovered during the *voir dire* examination and thus contributes toward implementing constitutional rights to a fair trial by an impartial jury. Indications are that scientific jury selection may spell the difference between conviction and acquittal in cases where the evidence presented in the trial is less important than are the attitudes and personalities of the jurors.

Jury Size There is nothing in the U.S. Constitution which expressly mandates that a criminal trial jury shall consist of "twelve good men and true." The significance of the figure 12 has been attributed to the Twelve Apostles, the Twelve Tribes of Israel, and the Twelve Patriarchs, but all of this lies in the realm of conjecture. About all we can say with certainty is that the jury of 12 persons in the United States continued a tradition whose origins are lost in antiquity (Klein, 1977).

While few states have altered the right of a person accused of a serious crime to demand a trial by a jury of 12 persons, a number of states have amended their constitutions to permit variations in civil cases and in criminal cases involving misde-

Scientific Jury Selection: The Joan Little Case

On August 27, 1974, a young black woman named Joan Little who was being held in Beaufort County Jail, North Carolina, pending appeal on a conviction for burglary, killed a 62-year-old white jailor and escaped. A little over a week later, she surrendered to the state police and was subsequently indicted for first-degree murder. Her defense was that the jailor had forced her to have oral sex with him by threatening her with an ice pick. According to her account, he dropped the ice pick in the heat of passion, whereupon she grabbed it and used it as a weapon to defend herself.

Psychologists conducted a public opinion survey among the residents of two dozen counties in the Beaufort area in order to determine their attitudes toward race and justice. Results indicated that racial prejudice among the predominantly white inhabitants of this conservative Southern community had already decided the case against Joan Little. A change of venue was granted and the trial was subsequently held in Raleigh, the state capital, in Wake County.

The researchers constructed a psychological profile of the kind of juror who would most likely be sympathetic to the defendant. They also came up with a series of questions for the defense attorneys to use in spotting prejudiced jurors and exercising challenges to remove them from the array. Nearly 150 veniremen were examined over a ten-day period before the jury was finally impaneled. The trial jury finally selected included six blacks and six whites. Prior to retiring to deliberate their verdict, the members of the jury were informed by the judge that the charge of first-degree murder was reduced to second-degree murder and manslaughter because the prosecution had failed to prove premeditation.

On August 15, 1975, after 78 hours of deliberation, the jury returned a verdict of not guilty. The circumstantial evidence in the case failed to convince the "scientifically" selected jury of Joan Little's guilt "beyond a reasonable doubt." Chief counsel for the defense credited scientific methods of jury selection for the acquittal.

meanors. Six-person juries were introduced into the federal court system in 1971. A year earlier, in *Williams* v. *Florida* (1970), the U.S. Supreme Court upheld the right of state courts to try individuals charged with serious felony offenses by juries of 6 persons. The Court maintained that, as long as the unanimity requirement is maintained, a 6-person jury is as reliable a fact-finding body, can exercise as much commonsense judgment, and ensure the same shared responsibility and community participation in the determination of guilt or innocence as a 12-person jury.

Opening Statements

After the jury is impaneled, the trial opens with a reading of the indictment or information. Then the prosecution presents its **opening statement.** (The order in which the defense and prosecution present their cases may vary from state to state, but it follows a legally established procedure. Generally, the prosecution goes first.) The prosecutor, in his or her address to the jury, explains the charge, describes the crime the defendant is alleged to have committed, and draws a general picture of what the state intends to prove "beyond a reasonable doubt." The purpose of the opening statement is to provide the members of the jury, who lack familiarity with legal matters and criminal investigation procedures, with an outline of the major objectives of the prosecution's case, the evidence it plans to present, the witnesses it intends to summon, and what it will seek to prove through the testimony of these witnesses. The rationale for this opening statement is to make it easier for the jurors to grasp the meaning and significance of the various pieces of evidence and testimony, and to help them avoid becoming confused by the complexities of the case.

When the prosecution has concluded its opening statement, the defense has the option to follow with its opening statement or to defer its presentation until later in the case. The usual procedure is for the defense counsel to describe how he plans to expose the weaknesses or inadequacies of the prosecution's case and to demonstrate to the jury his client's innocence. In *no* state is the defense *compelled* to make an opening statement.

The Case for the State

After the opening statements have been concluded, the prosecution calls its first witness. The witness takes an oath or affirmation to tell the truth. The prosecutor then begins the presentation of evidence by *direct examination* of the witness. This is a question-and-answer procedure designed to elicit information from the witness about the case. The only questions that can be put to the witness are those of the prosecutor, the defense counsel, and the judge. Although some states allow jurors to ask questions of the witness through the judge, this is not a prevalent practice.

On a good many occasions, the prosecutor's first witness is the arresting officer. Direct examination would tend to take the following form:

> PROSECUTOR: Sergeant Brown, you are a detective in the Blank County Sheriff's Office?
>
> WITNESS: Yes, ma'am.
>
> PROSECUTOR: On the night of January 15, 1985, were you directed to investigate a homicide reported at 10:00 PM?
>
> WITNESS: Yes, I was.
>
> PROSECUTOR: Please describe your investigation.

The witness would proceed to provide the details of the investigation as it was conducted.

When the prosecutor has finished with the witness, the defense attorney has the option to conduct a **cross-examination** of his testimony. Cross-examination is a procedure designed to test the witnesses' powers of observation and recollection, their truthfulness, and their possible bias against the cross-examiner's side. On cross-examination, witnesses can be asked only about things to which they testified on direct examination, but the cross-examiner is permitted to ask **leading questions,** that is, questions suggestive of answers. A skillful cross-examiner attempts to get witnesses confused, flustered, angry, or frightened, and cause them to lose their composure and self-control. The objective of the defense attorney is to impeach the witness, that is, to discredit the witness's testimony.

Upon completion of cross-examination, the prosecutor may conduct a *redirect examination* to clarify some point or issue raised during the cross-examination. The defense counsel may then carry out a *recross-examination.* These examinations are restricted to matters dealt with in the immediately preceding examination.

Subsequent witnesses are called by the prosecution, and the procedure outlined above is followed with each of them. The prosecution presents all of its witnesses before any witnesses are called by the defense. After the last witness for the prosecution has completed his or her testimony, the prosecution rests its case.

Motions for Dismissal or Directed Verdict

At the conclusion of the prosecution's case, the defense attorney asks—almost as a matter of routine—for the jury to be sent out of the courtroom while he or she moves for a dismissal of the case or a **directed verdict** of innocence from the judge on one or several possible grounds:

1. The prosecution failed to show a crime was committed.
2. The prosecution failed to show the defendant had anything to do with the commission of the crime.
3. The prosecution failed to demonstrate the guilt of the defendant beyond a reasonable doubt.

In practice, such motions are rarely granted; a prosecutor will not take a case to trial if he is not convinced of his ability to prove the guilt of the defendant beyond a reasonable doubt. If the state has failed to meet the burden of proof, the judge may grant the motion and acquit the defendant. If the motion is denied, the defense proceeds with its case.

The Case for the Defense

The format for the presentation of the case for the defense is similar to that of the prosecution. The defense counsel calls witnesses and directly examines them, then turns them over to the prosecutor for cross-examination. We must emphasize several important procedural considerations with regard to the defense:

1. The defendant is not required by law to present witnesses; he can base his defense entirely on the evidence and testimony presented by the state.
2. The defendant is not required to give personal testimony, regardless of whether or not he calls witnesses. His refusal to take the stand cannot be called to the attention of the jury by either the prosecutor or the judge. If he *does* choose to take the witness stand, he faces the same hazards of cross-examination as any other witness.
3. The defense counsel is not obligated to prove the innocence of his client, but merely to show that the state has failed to prove his guilt.

When the testimony of the last defense witness has been completed, and all of the evidence has been introduced, the defense counsel will rest his or her case.

Rebuttal and Surrebuttal

At the conclusion of the defense case, the prosecutor is given an opportunity for rebuttal. That is, he or she may summon additional witnesses for the purpose of buttressing the case, which may have been weakened by the evidence and testimony presented by the defense. Testimony offered in rebuttal must be limited to specific matters covered in the defense's case. In addition, if the prosecutor chooses to conduct a rebuttal, the defense may summon surrebutal witnesses to bolster its case.

Closing Arguments

Closing arguments, or **summations,** provide the defense counsel and the prosecutor with an opportunity to summarize the evidence and testimony and attempt to persuade the jury to accept their interpretation of its meaning and significance.

Charging the Jury

When all of the evidence has been presented and both sides have rested their cases, it is the responsibility of the judge to instruct the jury. Deciding the facts, as we have already noted, is the prerogative of the jury, but the court must instruct the members of the jury in those aspects of the law which are applicable to the case. For example, if the defense is based on insanity, the judge is required to explain to the jurors how insanity is determined in that particular state. Both the prosecutor and defense counsel are given the opportunity to submit the instructions they wish to be given to the jurors. These instructions incorporate the theories of the respective attorneys as to the interpretation of the facts of the case.

Judges select from instructions suggested by the attorneys, or they may prepare instructions of their own. These instructions are read to the jury in open court. In addition to any instructions relating to specific issues or testimony in the case, they traditionally cover the following areas:

1. The definition of the crime with which the defendant is charged.
2. The presumption of the defendant's innocence.
3. The fact that the burden of proof is on the prosecution.
4. That if, after consideration of all the evidence, there remains reasonable doubt as to the defendant's guilt, the defendant must be acquitted.
5. Procedures for electing a foreman and returning a verdict.
6. Possible verdicts they may render. "Guilty" and "not guilty" are the usual alternatives in a criminal case, although the jury may be given the option of deciding on the *degree of the offense* in a particular case (e.g., "murder in the first degree" or "murder in the second degree").

Jury Deliberations

At this point in the trial, the jurors retire to the jury room to begin their deliberations in an effort to arrive at a verdict. Members of the jury are restricted from communicating with anyone except the bailiff or the judge during their deliberations; once deliberations have begun, most jurisdictions require the jurors to be sequestered in a hotel or motel and denied access to newspapers and television accounts of the trial.

A unanimous verdict of the jury in criminal cases has been a basic requirement of common law since the fourteenth century. The U.S. Supreme Court has upheld this requirement in both the nineteenth and twentieth centuries, and most states have endorsed this position in their jury trial provisions. In *Johnson* v. *Louisiana* (1972), however, the Court held that Louisiana's use of 9 to 3 verdicts in major criminal cases was constitutional; and in *Apodaca* v. *Oregon* (1972), the Court decided that Oregon's 10 to 2 verdict in serious criminal cases did not violate the U.S. Constitution. More recently, the Court dealt with the issue of less than unanimous verdicts in cases involving juries with fewer than 12 persons. In *Burch* v. *Louisiana* (1979) the Court held that a 5 to 1 vote for conviction failed to satisfy the minimum constitutional requirements.

If the jury finds itself hopelessly deadlocked after prolonged deliberations, it may be returned to the courtroom where the judge will instruct the members to be sent back to the jury room for a final effort to arrive at a verdict. Usually the judge sets some specific time period for this to be done. If all reasonable methods are exhausted without reaching unanimity, resulting in a "hung jury," the judge dismisses the jury, declares a mistrial, and schedules a retrial of the case with a new jury. A mistrial places the defendant in the same position as if no trial had occurred, and proceedings may be reinstated against the defendant. If the verdict is "not guilty," the defendant is discharged.

SENTENCING

Sentencing has been regarded, with justification, as the most important phase of the criminal process, for it is in this stage that decisions are made affecting the disposition of the criminal offender. In earlier periods, offenders were subjected to retaliation and physical abuse in order to punish wrongdoing. The contemporary criminal justice system is still punitive in its orientation, although punishment is justified on a number of utilitarian grounds, including deterrence and incapacitation. In recent years, there has been an increase in the number of supporters of the position that retribution (the doctrine of "just deserts") is an appropriate objective of sentencing.

Sentencing Alternatives

If sentences were intended merely to mete out punishment to the criminal offender, the task of judges would be much simpler and less controversial. But sentencing—at least in modern times—has also been viewed as the cornerstone of rehabilitative efforts. These broadly divergent objectives constitute part of the dilemma faced by many judges: Is it possible simultaneously to punish *and* rehabilitate an offender?

Apart from the many additional problems that plague the sentencing process, this punishment-rehabilitation dilemma is a major source of difficulty and controversy in the administration of justice.

In many jurisdictions, decisions concerning where and how accused people may spend years of their lives are made by a judge whose discretion is virtually unchecked or unguided by criteria, procedural constraints, or further review. Often a sentence is meted out with no information before the judge except the offender's name and the crime of which he or she is guilty. The reliability and accuracy of information provided to the court by presentence investigation reports often goes unchallenged. The laws in many states concerning selection of sentence alternatives are chaotic. In some states, mandatory "flat time" sentences allow the court no discretion, whereas, in other states, the judge has full discretion as to the nature and extent of the sentence to be imposed. Disparity of sentences has been cited as one of the major causes of unrest leading to violence in prisons.

The types of sentences usually given to offenders include (in ascending order of severity) (1) fines, (2) community service, (3) split sentences and shock probation, (4) probation, (5) incarceration, and (6) the death penalty.

Fines are an economic penalty that requires the offender to pay a specific sum of money within the limits set by law. Fines are often imposed in addition to probation or as an alternative to imprisonment. Many of the laws that govern the imposition of fines are currently undergoing revision. These revisions often provide for more flexible means of ensuring equality in the imposition of fines, "day fines" geared to the offender's daily wage, payment of fines on an installment plan, and a restriction on confinement to situations that amount to intentional refusal to pay.

Community service is a penalty that requires an offender to provide a specific number of hours of public-service work, such as collecting trash or providing assistance for people who are confined to their homes by age or illness. By 1979, nearly one-third of the states had authorized community service work orders. Community service is often imposed as a specific condition of probation.

Restitution is a requirement that the offender provide financial remuneration for the losses incurred by the victim. Nearly all states have statutory provisions for the collection and disbursement of restitution. In 1982, a federal restitution law was enacted.

Split sentences and shock probation are penalties that require the convicted person to serve a period of confinement in a local, state, or federal facility (the "shock"), followed by a period of probation. This kind of penalty attempts to combine the use of community supervision with a brief taste of what it is like to serve time in jail or prison.

Probation is the sentencing of an offender to community supervision by a probation agency, often as a result of suspending a sentence to incarceration. Such supervision normally entails the provision of specific rules of conduct while in the community. If these rules are violated, a judge may impose a sentence of confinement. Probation is the most widely used sentencing alternative in the United States. State or local governments operate more than 2,000 probation agencies which provide supervision for more than 1.5 million adults and juveniles on probation.

Incarceration is a penalty that imposes confinement of a convicted criminal in a state or federal prison. Criminals convicted of a felony offense may be incarcerated in a state or federal prison; misdemeanants are confined in a local jail. As of 1982, more than 4,300 correctional facilities were maintained by local, state, or federal governments. On a given day in 1982, approximately 412,000 persons were confined in state and federal prisons and approximately half that number were confined in local jails.

The ultimate sanction that a court can impose is the death penalty. Most death penalty sentences are for murder. Depending on the state, an offender can be executed by means of electrocution, lethal gas, hanging, lethal injection, or firing squad. By the summer of 1984, the death-row population in the United States had passed 1,300.

Sentencing Strategies

States use primarily three strategies for sentencing: (1) indeterminate sentences, (2) determinate sentences, and (3) mandatory prison sentences.

Indeterminate sentences usually provide a maximum and a minimum term, either of which may be reduced by "good time" (time credits gained by inmates for good conduct or special achievement) or by a decision of the parole authorities. The maximum sentence may be set as a range (e.g., 5 to 10 years) rather than a specific number of years.

Determinate sentences customarily provide a fixed term that may be reduced by good time or parole. Judicial discretion may be available to grant probation or suspend the sentence. Sentencing laws generally provide a maximum (or a range) for sentence duration. Determinate systems are usually based on a definite length for a sentence that can be increased or decreased for aggravating or mitigating factors or on guidelines that define sentence lengths, deviations from which must be justified by sentencing judges.

√ **Mandatory sentences** are defined by law and must be given on conviction; the judge is not permitted to grant probation or to suspend the sentence. Crimes for which mandatory sentences have been established include murder, rape, robbery, and repeated violations of drug laws.

Many states may have a predominant orientation toward one strategy (e.g., indeterminate sentencing) and require another strategy (e.g., mandatory sentencing) for particular offenses. The strategies utilized by states are constantly evolving, thus complicating overall classification. As of September 1981, some states that required mandatory prison sentences for certain offenses used a predominantly indeterminate strategy, while others used a determinate strategy.

Sentencing Disparities

Do offenders who commit similar crimes under comparable circumstances generally receive similar sentences? Judges in the same jurisdictions, administering the same laws, and disposing of offenders to the same correctional institutions often show wide variations in their sentencing policies, as reflected in the use of such terms as "softy," "hanging judge," or "Maximum John"—the nickname given to federal judge

John Sirica of Watergate fame. These impressions tend to be confirmed by systematic research (Patridge and Eldridge, 1974; Diamond and Aeisel, 1975; Diamond, 1981). In fact, disparities in sentencing are viewed as one of the most serious shortcomings in our system of criminal justice.

Disparities in sentencing among judges may be ascribed to a number of factors: the conflicting goals of criminal justice; the fact that judges are a product of different backgrounds and have different social values; the administrative pressures on the judge; and the influence of community values on the system. Each of these factors structures to some extent the judge's exercise of discretion in sentencing offenders. In addition, it may be suggested that a judge's perception of these factors is dependent on his or her own attitudes toward the law, toward a particular crime, or toward a type of offender. Gaylin (1974) relates an amusing but instructive anecdote:

> A visitor to a Texas court was amazed to hear the judge impose a suspended sentence where a man had pleaded guilty to manslaughter. A few minutes later the same judge sentenced a man who pleaded guilty to stealing a horse and gave him life imprisonment. When the judge was asked by the visitor about the disparity of the two sentences, he replied, "Well, down here there is some men that need killin,' but there ain't no horses that need stealin' " [p. 8].

Sentencing Reforms

Attempts to rectify the sentencing process and to introduce greater uniformity and fairness have tended to follow several lines of recommended improvement. One of these involves legislative overhaul of the criminal statutes. Another approach is the establishment of sentencing guidelines for trial court judges. A third approach seeks to organize sentencing councils or institutes which afford an opportunity for judges to meet and discuss the factors that influence them in their sentencing decisions, with the goal of developing sentencing norms for similar offenses and offenders within a given jurisdiction. Finally, reform efforts have been directed toward the appellate review of sentencing in those jurisdictions where sentences have not been subjected to such review in the past.

APPEAL AND POSTCONVICTION REMEDIES

Only a few decades ago, very few criminal cases were appealed. Since *Gideon* v. *Wainwright* (1963), however, the picture has undergone dramatic change. Securing the right to counsel for all defendants, which stemmed from that historic decision, opened floodgates in appellate courts across the country. Collateral attack, or the filing of an appeal in the federal court system while the state case is still undecided— a procedure which was almost unknown prior to the 1960s—is now almost routine in many state courts. The result of this overloading of the review system has been an unprecedented increase in caseloads for judges. It has also created extended periods of litigation, often over a protracted period of time, eroding public belief in the finality of conviction for a criminal offense. The review procedure can result in as many as eleven steps in some state systems, and it is not unusual for a defendant to explore at least four or five of these. The major steps, according to the National Advisory Commission (1973), are:

1. New trial motion filed in court where conviction was imposed
2. Appeal to state intermediate appellate court (in states where there is no intermediate appellate court this step would not be available)
3. Appeal to state supreme court
4. Petition to U.S. Supreme Court to review state court decision on appeal
5. Postconviction proceeding in state trial court
6. Appeal of postconviction proceeding to state intermediate appellate court
7. Appeal to state supreme court
8. Petition to U.S. Supreme Court to review state court decision on appeal from postconviction proceeding
9. Habeas corpus petition in federal district court
10. Appeal to U.S. Court of Appeals
11. Petition to U.S. Supreme Court to review court of appeals decision on habeas corpus petition [p. 113].

It is easy to see why the review process can take so long, especially when some steps may be utilized several times in a single appeal, with review also taking place consecutively in more than one court system. Thus, due process may be a long and complicated procedure, and when appeal is part of the scheme it can become a drawn-out, seemingly endless cycle.

The spate of appellate decisions in favor of the incarcerated offender that took place in the 1960s has had diverse effects on the criminal justice system. On the positive side, the appeals have extended the protections of the Fourth, Fifth, Sixth, and Eighth amendments to incarcerated offenders through a series of appeals that used the "due process" and "equal protection" clauses of the Fourteenth Amendment as a wedge. These rights have been affirmed in may cases because of the existing pattern of gross abuses. The success of these appeals, and some of the possibilities gained from them, have encouraged more and more defendants to follow the appeal route. The result has been an appeal rate of as much as 90 percent in some jurisdictions, where less than one out of ten had been appealed in previous years.

Postconviction Remedies

Few states in the past have permitted the appellate review of sentences. At present, slightly more than half of the states allow for the merits of a sentence to be reviewed upon appeal. According to Kratcoski and Walker (1978), review has not been available in many jurisdictions because of fears of increased litigation, concern that appellate judges are less qualified than trial judges to determine appropriate sentences, and the belief that sentencing is a matter of judicial discretion and not a matter of law. On the other hand, the American Bar Association (1968) Committee on Minimum Standards for Criminal Justice maintains that "judicial review should be available for all sentences imposed in cases where provision is made for review of the convictions" (p. 7).

Sentencing review constitutes one of a number of **postconviction remedies**: "procedural devices available to a person who, after conviction and sentence, wants to vacate or reduce the sentences imposed, invalidate his pleas of guilty, or set aside his conviction" (Popper, 1978, p. 1). As an illustration, an individual who was not represented by counsel at trial but had not waived his right of representation might claim that his sentence or plea was defective and seek redress by some postconviction proceeding.

Popper notes that petitions filed in U.S. District Courts (including civil rights cases) by state and federal prisoners rose from 2,177 in 1960 to 19,307 in 1975. This "explosion" represented an increase of nearly 800 percent. Said Popper:

> As impressive as these figures are, they do not even reflect the number of prisoner petitions filed in state courts. It is this burgeoning post-conviction activity which, in past, accounts for pleas by court administrators, judges, and some communities to put a lid to litigation by cutting back on the chances for post-conviction relief [p. 4].

In its assessment of the appellate process, the National Advisory Commission on Criminal Justice Standards and Goals (1973) questioned whether any lasting benefits would result from efforts to speed up the existing review apparatus. Instead, it recommended a restructuring of the entire process of review:

> . . . there should be a single, unified review proceeding in which all arguable defects in the trial proceeding can be examined and settled finally, subject only to narrowly defined exceptional circumstances where there are compelling reasons to provide for a further review [p. 113].

This single unified review would amalgamate into one proceeding all of the issues that are presently litigated on the basis of motions for new trials, direct appeals, and postconviction proceedings. Thus, the new trial motion would be abolished and the traditional distinction between direct appeal and collateral attack would be abandoned. The self-evident merits of this proposal, unfortunately, have not resulted thus far in the establishment of a unified review. A number of states have instituted sentencing review by means of special panels of trial judges who meet to examine the propriety of sentences in individual cases. After reviewing the case, the panel may decide to decrease or increase the original sentence. In eight other states, appeals for the review of sentences can be brought to a regular appellate court.

SUMMARY

During the past two decades, it has been recognized that the period from arrest to trial (or acceptance of a guilty plea) is perhaps the most crucial phase in the criminal process. It is during this pretrial period that many important decisions are made about what will happen to the defendant. If the grand jury proceeding or preliminary hearing results in sufficient evidence to charge the individual with a crime (i.e., a finding of "probable cause"), the defendant is arraigned and given the opportunity to enter a plea to the charges. He is informed of his constitutional rights, particularly with respect to representation by counsel, and may be placed in confinement, freed on bail, or released on his own recognizance.

The two critical issues which arise during the pretrial period both involve discretion. The first of these is pretrial release. A defendant who is detained in jail suffers adverse consequences from the experience, but his individual plight has to be weighed against the possibility that his release will result in further danger to society. The second issue is plea negotiation. Since the criminal justice system lacks the resources to try every person accused of a crime, the practice of plea negotiation—despite its critics and detractors—is seen as an essential element in the administrative disposition of a large number of cases.

Compared with the total volume of cases entering the criminal justice system, relatively few cases are disposed of by trial. Nevertheless, the criminal trial is an indispensable feature of our system. The accused is brought to trial under a presumption of innocence; it is the task of the prosecution to prove beyond a reasonable doubt that the defendant is guilty of the crime with which he or she is charged.

The adversary concept of criminal justice is most clearly exhibited in the trial. The prosecutor uses the authority and resources of the state to gather enough evidence to convince the court and the jury of the guilt of the defendant. The defense counsel attacks the weaknesses of the prosecution's case, seeks to impeach the testimony of state witnesses, questions the validity and reliability of the prosecution's evidence, and is alert to any tactics of the opposing counsel that violate the constitutional rights of the defendant.

An extremely important aspect of the trial is the selection of people to serve on the jury. Jurors are chosen by a procedure called *voir dire,* which assigns the prosecution and defense a number of challenges for cause (stated reasons why a particular person is unfit to serve as a juror) and peremptory challenges (for which no reasons need be given). In recent years, there have been some noteworthy attempts to use the methods of the social scientist to pick jurors who would be inclined to favor the defendant. The process of scientific jury selection has been attacked as "jury stacking" as well as defended as a guarantor of fairness. Whatever its defects or merits, however, the expenses involved in its use will probably keep it from becoming a routine procedure in criminal trials.

Trials are governed by rules and procedures that have evolved over many years and are enforced by the judge who acts as an arbiter or referee. The order of a criminal trial may vary somewhat from one jurisdiction to another, but it generally conforms to a standard pattern. After a reading of the formal charges against the defendant, the prosecution presents it case by introducing evidence and witnesses whose testimony is subject to cross-examination by the defense. At the conclusion of the prosecution's case, the defense presents it case, including evidence and testimony, and may call on the defendant to testify on his or her own behalf. Following closing statements by both sides, the judge instructs the jury on points of law, and the jury is then sequestered until it reaches a verdict or finds itself hopelessly deadlocked.

Sentencing is perhaps the most important phase of the criminal process, for it is in this stage that the disposition of the offender is decided. In earlier periods, offenders were subject to retaliation and physical abuse as punishment for wrong-doing. The contemporary criminal justice system is still punitive in its orientation, but the punishment is justified on several utilitarian grounds, including deterrence and incapacitation. In recent years, support has grown for the position that retribu-tion ("the law of just deserts") is an appropriate objective sentencing. Traditional dispositions include fines, probation, and imprisonment, with probation being the most common choice.

One of the most significant features of the sentencing process is its tripartite structure involving the legislature, a judge, and correctional agencies. The actions of each of these parties affect the type and length of sentence imposed on the offender. Thus, the system often results in sentence disparities, with courts seeking to fit the sentence to the individual offender rather than to the crime. To make dispositions more uniform, some states now allow appellate review of sentences and use sentenc-ing councils and institutes.

DISCUSSION QUESTIONS

Find the answers to the following questions in the text.

1. How is prosecution initiated in misdemeanor cases? How is prosecution initiated in felony offenses?
2. Are there any advantages for the defendant in the **preliminary hearing**? What are the advantages for the prosecutor in the preliminary hearing?
3. List the major functions and responsibilities of the grand jury.
4. Of what value is **plea bargaining** to the defendant? What are the advantages of plea bargaining for the prosecutor?
5. Discuss the principal factors affecting plea bargaining. How significant were these factors in the research findings reported by Lynn Mather?
6. Briefly describe the process involved in jury selection and identify some of the issues raised by **scientific jury selection.**
7. What do opposing counsels seek to accomplish in their **opening statements**? Which one goes first?
8. Distinguish between **direct examination** and **cross-examination.** What limitations are im-posed on cross-examination?
9. Indicate the principal matters covered by the judge in to the jury.
10. Why is sentencing such an important phase of the criminal process?
11. What is the distinction between an **indeterminate sentence** and a **determine sentence**?
12. How did the National Advisory Commission on Criminal Justice Standards and Goals propose to reform the appellate process?

TERMS TO IDENTIFY AND REMEMBER

arrest
warrant
initial appearance
complaint
information
grand jury indictment

presentment
true bill
nolo contendere
bill of particulars
voir dire
opening statement

cross-examination
summation
determinate sentence
direct examination
pretrial release
release on recognizance (ROR)
bail
preliminary hearing
probable cause
arraignment

plea bargaining
change of venue
array (veniremen)
peremptory challenge
leading question
scientific jury selection
motion for directed verdict
indeterminate sentence
mandatory sentence
postconviction remedies

REFERENCES

American Bar Association. *Standards Relating to Sentencing Alternatives and Procedures.* New York: Institute of Judicial Administration, 1968.

Apodaca v. *Oregon,* 406 U.S. 404. 92 S.Ct. 1628, 32 L. Ed. 2d 184 (1972).

Bases, N. C., and McDonald, W. F. *Preventive Detention in the District of Columbia: The First Ten Months.* New York: Vera Institute of Justice, 1974.

Burch v. *Louisiana,* 441 U.S. 130, 99 S.Ct. 1623, 60 L. Ed. 2d 96 (1979).

Diamond, S. S. Exploring sources of trial disparity. In B. D. Sales (ed.), *The Trial Process.* New York: Plenum Press, 1981.

Diamond, S. S., and Zeisel, H. Sentencing councils: A study of sentence disparity and its reduction. *University of Chicago Law Review* 43 (1975): 109–149.

Eisenstein, J., and Jacob, H. *Felony Justice: An Organizational Analysis of Criminal Courts.* Boston: Little, Brown, 1977.

Ellison, K. W., and Buckhout, R. *Psychology and Criminal Justice.* New York: Harper & Row, 1981.

Feeley, M. The effects of a heavy caseload. Paper delivered at the Annual Meeting of the American Political Science Association, San Francisco, September 2–5, 1975.

Gaylin, W. *Partial Justice.* New York: Vintage Books, 1974,

Gideon v. *Wainwright,* 372 U.S. 335, 83 S.Ct. 792, 9 L. Ed. 2d 143 (1963).

Heumann, M. *Plea Bargaining.* Chicago: University of Chicago Press, 1978.

Johnson v. *Louisiana,* 409 U.S. 1085, 93 S.Ct. 691, 34 L. Ed. 2d 672 (1972).

Klein, F. J. *Federal and State Court Systems—A Guide.* Cambridge, MA: Ballinger, 1977.

Kratcoski, P. C., and Walker, D. B. *Criminal Justice in America: Process and Issues.* Glenview, IL: Scott, Foresman, 1978.

Lehtinen, M., and Smith, G. W. The relative effectiveness of public defenders and private attorneys: A comparison. *Legal Aid Briefcase* 34 (1974): 12–20.

Levin, M. A. *Urban Politics and the Criminal Courts.* Chicago: University of Chicago Press, 1977.

Mather, L. M. *Plea Bargaining or Trial?* Lexington, MA: Lexington Books, 1979.

National Advisory Commission on Criminal Justice Standards and Goals. *Courts.* Washington, D.C.: U.S. Government Printing Office, 1973.

Patridge, A., and Eldridge, W. *The Second Circuit Sentencing Study: A Report to the Judge of the Second Circuit.* Washington, D.C.: U.S. Government Printing Office, 1974.

Popper, R. *Post-Conviction Remedies.* St. Paul, MN: West, 1978.

Robin, G. D. *Introduction to the Criminal Justice System.* New York: Harper & Row, 1980.

Rosett, A. I., and Cressey, D. R. *Justice by Consent: Plea Bargains in the American Courthouse.* Philadelphia: Lippincott, 1976.

Santobello v. *New York* 404 U.S. 257 (1971).

Thomas, W. H. *Bail Reform in America.* Berkeley: University of California Press, 1976.

Williams v. *Florida,* 399 U.S. 78, 90 S.Ct. 1893, 26 L. Ed. 2d 446 (1970).

chapter **19**

CORRECTIONS

Corrections has come to stand for a broad variety of systematic efforts directed toward punishing criminals, changing offender behavior, protecting society from criminal acts, and compensating victims of crime (Snarr and Wolford, 1985). As society's primary formal response to the problems raised by the disposition of criminals, correctional activities range from the detention and imprisonment of offenders to the search for alternatives to incarceration that seek to provide assistance, support, and supervision of offenders within the community. Inevitably, such widely divergent activities and goals involve differences in philosophies, approaches, and techniques that often conflict with, or even contradict, one another.

CONFINEMENT: DETENTION AND IMPRISONMENT

Confinement is one of society's responses to offenders at various stages of the criminal justice system and process. Persons accused of crimes may be placed in a detention facility. Such facilities are designated as jails or lockups and are operated by the city or county. An individual who has been convicted of, or pled guilty to, a criminal charge may be sentenced to imprisonment in a county, state, or federal institution, depending on the nature of the offense. Facilities of this kind are generally designated correctional institutions.

Detention: Jails and Lockups

Colonists brought to the new world the concept of the jail as an instrument of confinement, coercion, and correction of those who broke the law or were merely nuisances. In the early nineteenth century, the American innovation of the state penitentiary made punitive confinement the principal response to criminal acts and removed the serious offender from the local jail. Gradually, with the building of insane asylums, orphanages, and hospitals, the jail ceased to be the repository of some social casualties. But it continued to house the town's minor offenders along with the poor and the vagrant, all crowded together without regard to sex, age, and history, typically in squalor and misery. Jails became residual facilities into which were shunted the more vexing and unpalatable social problems of each locality. Thus, "the poor, the sick, the morally deviant, and the merely unaesthetic, in addition to the true criminal—all [ended] in jail" (Mattick and Aikman, 1969, p. 14).

Jails are primarily a responsibility of local government. Approximately 85 percent of our jails are county-operated, although large cities operate their own facilities. Some cities and counties have a separate department of corrections (separate, that is, from the state), but such arrangements are in the minority. Although larger urban areas have built some facilities for special groups of offenders, in most parts of the country a single local institution today retains the dual purposes of custodial confinement and misdemeanant punishment. The most conspicuous additions to the jail have been the homeless, public drunks, and the mentally disturbed. Ever since the states began emptying their mental hospitals by releasing patients for community-based treatment, the jails have become a repository for a growing number of mentally ill persons (Swanson and Territo, 1984).

Types of Jails

Three types of jails can be identified:

1. The **pretrial detention facility,** used solely to confine those who are awaiting trial.
2. The **sentenced offender facility,** where those who have been convicted serve their sentences. Usually the inmates in these facilities are misdemeanants, although in a few states offenders convicted of minor felonies may serve short terms in jail instead of in prison.
3. The **combined jail facility,** which houses both pretrial and detainees and some convicted offenders, usually misdemeanants. The combined facility is the most common type of jail in the United States at the present time.

Physical Condition of Jails

A jail census by the U.S. Department of Justice (1975) indicated that most of the institutions surveyed had no provisions for exercise or recreation. Educational facilities were supplied in only about 10 percent of the jails, and medical facilities were provided in only half of the jails in the census. One out of four of the institutions located in the cities had no arrangements for visitation. About one quarter of the cells within the jails in the census had been in use more than 50 years and some were over a century old.

Most jails are fairly uniform in their physical arrangements. The basic design is one which permits a trade-off between the smallest possible staff and the most secure confinement for inmates. There is usually a large central cagelike structure called the **"bullpen."** This is used for the majority of the nonviolent prisoners and the drunks. The bullpen is also often referred to as the "tank" because of its extensive use for drunks. Larger jails may contain several bullpens and a separate drunk tank. The central area is usually surrounded by rows of cells facing inward toward the bullpens. Like caged animals, the amount of contact is often reduced by passing food into the bullpens and cells through slots in the doors. The result is a minimization of personal contact between inmates and staff. While this avoidance of contact is generally maintained in the interests of security, it exacerbates the trend toward extreme impersonality that is characteristic of many jails.

Sanitary facilities are another major problem in many of the old and crumbling jails. The age and manner of construction used in the old structures add to the problem of maintenance and modernization. Even in those equipped with adequate plumbing and sanitary facilities, the violence and frustration of the inmates are often vented on these objects. The lack of privacy and the personal degradation associated with the open use of sanitary facilities add to the resentment and acting-out against the already limited equipment.

Many jails visited by the National Jail Census did not have any functioning flush toilets. The use of buckets and other expedients is still a prevailing practice in many of the jails in America. Although toilets are a problem, the need for showers and washroom facilities is even more critical. The large percentage of drunks and others who are placed in the "tank," some filthy with their own vomit and excrement, are often left in that condition due to a lack of adequate cleanup facilities. By 1983, a later jail census reported that some improvements had been made, especially in larger, urban jails, but many small, rural jails and lockups continued to suffer from overcrowding and lack of adequate sanitation facilities (Bureau of Justice Statistics Bulletin, 1984).

Juveniles in Jails

The Office of Juvenile Justice and Delinquency Prevention (OJJDP) (1980) estimates that 500,000 juveniles a year are held for varying periods of time in adult jails and lockups in the United States and suggests that this half-million figure may be "grossly understated." Although federal legislation requires that juveniles be separated by "sight and sound" from adult offenders, in many states and communities adults and juveniles are confined together in the same facilities. In some places, "sight and sound separation" has resulted in juveniles being placed in solitary confinement for long periods.

According to the OJJDP report, the majority of juveniles in jails are confined for property or minor offenses. Eighteen percent are in jail for acts such as running away from home or being "incorrigible"—status offenses which would not be crimes if committed by adults. Moreover, many runaways are not seeking thrills or adventure, but are fleeing emotional, physical, or sexual abuse at home. Homosexual rape, beatings and injuries, and jail suicides are the most grievous and predictable consequences of confining juveniles with adult offenders.

Judges and law enforcement officials often deplore jailing juveniles, but justify their actions on the grounds that juvenile detention facilities are unavailable or overcrowded. This claim is disputed by the OJJDP report (1980), which contends that even where detention centers are readily available and existing legislation prohibits the jailing of juveniles, children are still placed in jails. A Children's Defense Fund project (1976) discovered that several thousand juveniles were confined in adult jails every year in a Texas county which had a large juvenile detention center. It seems clear that where the jailing of children is permitted legally or through lack of enforcement of statutory prohibitions, jails will be used to hold juveniles.

IMPRISONMENT: AN HISTORICAL PERSPECTIVE

Imprisonment as the primary means of enforcing the laws, mores, and customs of a society is a relatively modern practice. In earlier times, restitution, exile, and a variety of methods of corporal and capital punishment, many of them unspeakably barbarous, were used. Confinement was used only for purposes of detention (National Advisory Commission on Criminal Justice Standards and Goals, *Corrections,* 1973).

The colonists who came to North America brought with them the harsh penal codes and practices of their homelands. It was in Pennsylvania, founded by William Penn, that initial attempts were made to find alternatives to the brutality of British penal practice. Penn knew well the nature of confinement because he had spent six months in Newgate Prison, London, for his religious convictions.

√In the **Great Law of Pennsylvania,** enacted in 1682, Penn made provisions to eliminate to a large extent the stocks, pillories, branding iron, and gallows. The Great Law directed " . . . that every county within the province of Pennsylvania and territories thereunto belonging shall . . . build or cause to be built in the most convenient place in each respective county a sufficient house for restraint, labor, and punishment of all such persons as shall be thereunto commited by laws."

In time William Penn's jails, like those in other parts of the New World up to and including the present, became places where the untried, the mentally ill, the promiscuous, the debtor, and myriad petty offenders were confined indiscriminately.

In 1787, when the Constitutional Convention was meeting in Philadelphia and men were thinking of institutions based on the concept of the dignity of man, the Philadelphia Society for Alleviating the Miseries of Public Prisons was organized. The society believed the sole end of punishment was to prevent crime and that punishment should not destroy the offender. The society, many of whose members were influential citizens, worked hard to create a new penology in Pennsylvania, a penology which to a large degree eliminated capital and corporal punishment as the principal sanctions for major crimes. The penitentiary was invented as a substitute for these punishments.

In the first three decades of the nineteenth century, citizens of New York, Pennsylvania, New Jersey, Massachusetts, and Connecticut were busy planning and building monumental penitentiaries. These were not cheap installations built from the crumbs of the public treasury. In fact, the Eastern State Penitentiary in Philadelphia was the most expensive public building constructed in the New World up to that time. States were extremely proud of these physical plants. Moreover, they saw in them an almost utopian ideal: they were to become stabilizers of society; they were to become laboratories committed to the improvement of all mankind (Rothman, 1980).

When these new penitentiaries were being planned and constructed, practitioners and theorists held three factors to be the primary contributors to criminal behavior. The first was environment. Report after report on offenders pointed out the harmful effects of family, home, and other aspects of environment on the offender's behavior. The second factor usually cited was the offender's lack of aptitude and work skills. This quality led to indolence and a life of crime. The third cause was seen as the felon's ignorance of right and wrong because he or she had not been taught the Scriptures.

The social planners of the first quarter of the nineteenth century designed prison architecture and programs to create an experience for the offender in which (1) there would be no injurious influences, (2) the offender would learn the value of labor and work skills, and (3) the offender would have the opportunity to learn about the Scriptures and accept from them the principles of right and wrong that would then guide him or her.

Various states pursued this triad of purposes in one of two basic methods. The **Pennsylvania system** was based on solitary confinement, accompanied by bench labor within the prisoner's cell. There, the offender was denied all contact with the outside world except that provided by the Scriptures, religious tracts, and visits from specially selected, exemplary citizens. The prison was designed painstakingly to make this kind of solitary experience possible. The walls between cells were thick, and the cells themselves were large, each equipped with plumbing and running water. In the cell there were a work bench and tools. In addition, each cell had its own small walled area for solitary exercise. The institution was designed magnificently for its three purposes: elimination of external influences; provision of work; and opportunity for penitence, introspection, and acquisition of religious knowledge (Barnes, 1976).

New York's **Auburn system** pursued the same three goals by a different method. Like the Pennsylvania system, it isolated the offender from the world outside and permitted him or her virtually no external contact. However, it provided small cells in which the convicts were confined only on the Sabbath and during nonworking hours. During working hours inmates labored in factorylike shops. The contaminating effect of the congregate work situation was eliminated by a rule of silence. Inmates were prohibited from communicating in any way with other inmates or the jailers.

The relative merits of these two systems were debated vigorously for half a century. The Auburn system ultimately prevailed in the United States, because it was less expensive and because it lent itself more easily to production methods of the industrial revolution.

The Reformatory Movement

The **reformatory movement** originated in efforts to resolve the struggle between supporters of the Pennsylvania system and the Auburn system. In its reliance on vocational training, indeterminate sentencing, and parole, it drew heavily on the contributions of Captain **Alexander Maconochie** of the Royal Navy and Sir **Walter Crofton.**

When Maconochie was appointed in 1840 as administrator of Norfolk Island, a penal colony off the coast of Australia, he eliminated the old flat-time sentence system and replaced it with a "mark system," under which convicts were able to earn credit toward their release for good conduct, hard work, and study. The more rapidly the offender earned the "good marks" he needed, the sooner he was released. As Maconochie declared, "When a man keeps the key of his own prison, he is soon persuaded to fit it to the lock." Under Maconochie's plan, an offender moved through degrees of freedom, from strict custody to liberty. He was finally released on a "ticket-of-leave."

Sir Walter Crofton, head of the Irish prison system, added refinements to the ticket-of-leave system Maconochie had devised. He agreed with Maconochie that the purpose of prison was to rehabilitate, and his prisoners moved through his system under an indeterminate sentence, from solitary confinement to conditional leave under supervision. Crofton created the position of "Inspector of Released Prisoners" whose function was to protect the community by checking on his charges and further to assist the offender in his readjustment to society. Barnes and Teeters (1959) note that this represents the first extensive employment of what later was called parole.

Reformers during the post–Civil War period lobbied for the adoption in our prison system of the methods pioneered by Maconochie and Crofton. The ideas of these reformers were enunciated in a declaration of principles at a meeting in 1870 by an organization which became the American Correctional Association. The declaration advocated "reformation as opposed to the adoption of punishment, progressive classification of prisoners based on the mark system, the indeterminate sentence, and cultivation of the inmate's self-respect" (Barnes and Teeters, 1959). These progressive and humane methods were intended to apply to all offenders, but reformers were only successful in having them applied to young first offenders in a new kind of institution called a reformatory.

The first reformatory was opened in 1877 in Elmira, New York, and remained under the direction of Zebulon R. Brockway for the next two decades. Despite his reliance on corporal punishment as a means of enforcing discipline, Brockway made a determined effort to invoke the spirit and methods of the 1870 ACA declaration. Judges were to send to this institution first-time felons between the ages of 16 and 30 years who were, in their opinion, capable of reformation (Rothman, 1980). These offenders were given a modified indeterminate sentence whereby they could be released within a year under community supervision if they progressed through a grade system that awarded marks for completing work and school assignments and for good behavior. Brockway's approach emphasized physical fitness, close-order military drill, educational programs ranging from basic literacy to college curricula, and vocational training in more than 30 skilled trades.

While Elmira, under Brockway, at least made an effort to carry out in penal practice the ideas of the 1870 declaration, other reformatories proved less successful. Most prison administrators, and perhaps the rest of the country as well, were not ready to accept the notion of a prison system based on other than punitive considerations. The reformatory movement helped to crystallize progressive correctional thought, but it was not until the 1950s that real efforts were made to establish institutions which sought to accomplish the rehabilitation of offenders.

The Big House

For the first century after the development of the penitentiary, most prisons in the United States were built to reflect an ultimate value: security. Their principal features were high walls, towers which housed armed guards, cagelike cells, and a bare minimum of recreation space. They resembled fortresses; their purpose was to keep prisoners in and the public out.

These institutions supplied the physical backdrop for a period of American penal history that is best enshrined perhaps in vintage James Cagney movies. Many people appear to have developed their ideas of what prison life is like in contemporary institutions from the atmosphere depicted in such movies, including the more recent film *Alcatraz*. Despite the fact that these institutions have all but disappeared, their influence is still apparent today. This was the type of prison called the **"big house."**

Although many institutions permitted inmates to decorate their sparse, cramped quarters, the big house was generally a harsh, depressing world of concrete and steel where prisoners were subjected to the chilling cold of winter, the heat and stench of summer, and an unnerving level of constant noise. Short of the death penalty, which during this period was imposed and carried out on a more or less regular basis (there were 891 executions in the United States between 1935 and 1939), the big house represented the state's most extreme form of punishment. It is not surprising, therefore, that the big house was a place characterized by routine, monotony, and a sense of isolation, which was accentuated by the location of these institutions in the remotest areas of the state.

Social World of Inmates   The world of the inmate included several subcultures, a variety of adaptations to prison life, and a status system. Central to the inmate world was a **convict code**—a prison variation of the thieves' code. The principal tenet of this code was "Thou shalt not snitch." For thieves in prison, this came to mean, "Do not rat on another prisoner" and "Do your own time." Thieves following this code were expected to maintain dignity and respect, help each other, leave most other inmates alone, and not display any weakness.

The inmate status system was based on prestige, privilege, and power. At the top of the hierarchy were the **"right guys,"** who were given this title because they could always be depended on to do the right thing according to the inmate code (Korn and McCorkle, 1959). Their high prestige as thieves, along with their tendency to cooperate with one another and a demeanor of toughness and coolness, further enhanced their position. The "merchants," "politicians," and "gamblers" were also close to the top of the stack because of the influence and control they wielded over scarce prison luxuries, commodities, and resources such as cigarettes, "hooch" (alcohol), coffee, and job or cell assignments.

Next in line were the prison toughs, who displayed a constant, open, and deepseated attitude of hostility toward guards, prison officials, most other prisoners, and conventional society. The prison middle class, which encompassed the majority of inmates, was comprised mostly of lower- and working-class men with little or no criminal skill and, consequently, no respect, and "square johns," who were usually accidental offenders.

The lowest stratum included prison "queens" who were openly homosexual and manifested effeminate characteristics in dress and manner; "punks," young inmates who had been coerced into providing sexual favors as a consequence of the threatened or actual use of force; "rats," inmates who had acted as informants to the staff; and "rapos," who were serving time for sexual offenses and were repulsive as a group to most other inmates.

At the absolute bottom of the heap were the **"dingbats,"** who were crazy but harmless and as a rule were ignored and excluded from informal inmate activities.

Prison Programs   Programs for breaking the monotony of the prison routine and improving the skills of inmates were extremely limited in the big house. By 1929, most state and federal institutions were restricted by "state use" legislation, which only allowed prisons to turn out products for use by other state or federal agencies (Barnes and Teeters, 1959). This kind of legislation effectively eliminated most prison industries. If it had not been for the phenomenal development of the automobile during the 1920s, which resulted in a growing demand for license plates, many state prisons would have had no industry at all. While this activity provided a service for the state, it did little for the inmate, apart from breaking the monotony. Where outside of prison could an ex-convict find a job making license plates?

A large percentage of the men in these institutions were employed in jobs that were a part of institutional maintenance: cleaning up cellblocks, working in the kitchen, or doing routine upkeep on buildings. Due to lack of meaningful work, institutional maintenance teams often had two to ten times more men on a crew than a job demanded. Also, a small number of inmates were employed as clerks to manage the institutional records and paperwork. Some prisoners occupied their time by making handicrafts that were sold in prison shops, but in all too many institutions most of the men were completely idle.

The big house was not noted for its contributions to inmates' self-improvement. Some institutions, like San Quentin, had fairly comprehensive educational programs, but most prisons were quite backward in providing inmates with constructive educational opportunities (Barnes and Teeters, 1959). All too often, classroom instruction was limited to primary education courses, that is, instruction in basic literacy. Although many of these institutions had civilian education directors, the bulk of instruction was provided by inmate teachers: hence, the quality of instruction was not very impressive. Moreover, not all of the inmates who wished to participate in these programs could do so, since space was limited. Those who desired more advanced education could avail themselves in some instances of correspondence courses. Prisons fared even worse with regard to vocational training. Formal offerings were very meager and only a small percentage of the prison population could participate in these programs (Rothman, 1980).

In reflecting on the changes that took place during the big-house era (1900–1950), it seems fair to conclude that this period was characterized by gradual movement toward less brutality and punishment and more humane routines. One need only remember that at the beginning of this era, the silent system was in effect, inmates could be flogged for violations of prison rules, and it was not unusual for some inmates to spend more than two-thirds of their sentences in their cells. It was during this period that the stage was set for an emerging conflict between treatment and custody orientations. In the later period of the correctional institution, these two competing philosophies surfaced in the guise of competing branches of the prison structure.

The Correctional Institution

As we noted, the blueprint for the **correctional institution** had been drawn as early as 1870, at the National Prison Association meeting, but it was not until after World War II that these institutions replaced the big house in many states. Correctional institutions which were constructed during this period differed in appearance, organization, prisoner population, and inmate social worlds from the big houses. Most importantly, they differed in terms of their impact on offenders. By the 1950s, these institutions had come to dominate the prison system—if not in actual numbers, at least in the direction that most penologists felt the system ought to follow.

The Correctional Orientation   The emergence of the correctional institution heralded the onset of a new era, in which the orientation of prisons was to be changed from punishment to rehabilitation. This change required a philosophy based to the fullest extent on individual treatment, even in maximum security facilities.

All aspects of the institutional setting were intended to support the major objective of changing offenders and providing them with an opportunity to "make it" in conventional society. Institutions were charged with the responsibility of providing academic, vocational, and work programs consistent with the needs and interests of offenders; and the latter two programs were to be directed toward helping offenders acquire the kinds of skills which would enable them to obtain meaningful jobs upon release. Individual and group psychotherapy and counseling were to be offered to inmates under the supervision of psychiatrists, psychologists, and trained counselors. Institutions were to have adequate resources, competent staffs, physical plants in good condition, and the equipment needed to achieve rehabilitative goals. There was a great deal of variation in the extent to which these criteria were met by correctional institutions. Some merely changed the name on the sign over the entrance to the prison; others made real efforts to introduce correctional programs.

Institutions which developed correctional programs usually lacked the financial resources to hire professionals and, therefore, were dependent on nonprofessional staff members with no training in psychology or social work. The success of these programs, which relied heavily on group counseling techniques and approaches, was adversely affected by a number of factors. Not only were staff members inexperienced, they also failed to receive appropriate training and supervision during their tenure as counselors. Although participation in these groups was "voluntary," many inmates felt compelled to attend group sessions because treatment staff and parole board members led them to believe they would not be given favorable consideration for parole unless they participated (Irwin, 1980).

The Decline and Fall of the Rehabilitative Approach   The notion that prisons could be transformed into hospitals capable of curing offenders, though laudable, was simply unrealistic. Our understanding of criminality and its causes lagged far behind our capacity to fashion diagnostic instruments and treatment programs necessary for changing criminal behavior. Also, it was doubtful that inmates could be sufficiently motivated to take advantage of programs aimed at "curing" criminality, even if such programs had been available. Even under ideal conditions, the correctional institution was doomed to an early demise.

Numerous prisoners participated in rehabilitation programs, either voluntarily or because they believed that parole was contingent upon their involvement. If a large enough percentage of prisoners had been able to be reintegrated into society following their release, this would have provided support for rehabilitative programs. It is difficult, however, to maintain the illusion that rehabilitation is effective when those who have participated in such programs return to prison in large numbers. As convicts became disillusioned with rehabilitation, they began to blame their criminality on their life circumstances rather than on individual problems.

It is worth noting that the emphasis of the rehabilitation perspective on the improvement of one's abilities inadvertently contributed to the development of a prison intelligentsia which began to examine critically not only the prison system itself, but also the society that had produced it. This group became a potent force in encouraging the rejection of the rehabilitative approach among prisoners. However, inmate disillusionment was not the only factor which shattered the fragile peace of the correctional institution and hastened the demise of rehabilitation. Changes in the ethnic/racial composition of the prison population, along with the politicization of inmates—the prisoner revolution—and the administrative reaction to these changes in the prison environment, all contributed in various ways to the decline and fall of the correctional institution and set the stage for the problems faced by the contemporary prison.

THE CONTEMPORARY PRISON

During the 1970s, problems in many prisons reached crisis levels because of events that were the result of both external and internal influences. Crime rates began to rise rapidly, not only in urban areas but also in the suburbs, which previously had not experienced much crime. People who had fled the city to avoid the crime problem now discovered that their communities were no longer safe havens. As the decade progressed, it became extremely rare for anyone not to be acquainted with at least one person who had been a victim of a violent crime.

Fear of victimization and anger toward criminals resulted in public outrage over the criminal justice system and a new hard line toward the treatment of criminals. No longer concerned with rehabilitation, the public now sees the criminal justice system functioning to incapacitate and punish offenders. In response to this sense of outrage, many trial judges have been imposing longer sentences. Some states have totally eliminated parole and in others it is not granted as frequently. Since 1977, a total of 37 states have enacted mandatory sentencing laws for certain categories of offenses that deny judges any flexibility in either shortening or suspending sentences for these offenses.

The result of all this has been an almost perpendicular increase in the prison population, which rose from approximately 230,000 in 1974 to a record high of close to 500,000 by the middle of 1985 (*New York Times,* Sept. 16, 1985). This record growth has caused severe problems of overcrowding, with state prisons on the average operating at 10 percent over capacity. Overcrowding has strained the already overburdened resources of prisons and placed not only inmates but also guards and administrators under undue stress because both staff members and prisoners are exposed to the frustration, tension, and frequent explosive reactions that result from overcrowded conditions and limited resources (Fox, 1982).

Not only has the inmate population increased, it has also become more populated by blacks. Blacks are disproportionately incarcerated: in 1978, blacks accounted for 45.7 percent of the males imprisoned and only 5.4 percent of the general population (Christianson, 1981). Extensive research has shown that racial discrimination in the criminal justice system is a significant factor in the racial imbalance in our prisons.

Divisiveness is the primary characteristic of the contemporary prison environment. Inmates are divided by extreme hatred, distrust, and ethnic/racial as well as criminal orientations. Blacks now comprise nearly 50 percent of the prison population; and in some parts of the country, Chicanos and Puerto Ricans constitute a significant minority of inmates in correctional institutions. A variety of criminal types—pimps, bikers, "dopefiends," street gang members—compete for power and respect.

To survive in an environment divided by racial hatred between blacks and whites, most prisoners have come to distrust any inmate with whom they are not familiar. For their own protection, inmates have restricted their interaction to small cliques of friends and other social groups such as gangs which include members of their own ethnic/racial group. Other characteristics that determine the groups and cliques with which inmates associate include proximity based on cell or work assignments; shared preprison experiences, such as serving time in another prison or hailing from the same town or city; shared prison interests; and similar criminal orientations (Irwin, 1980).

Ethnic/Racial Relations

The most potent source of friction and division in our contemporary prisons is the hate and distrust that exist between white and black prisoners. One of the clearest manifestations of black rage is homosexual assaults of blacks upon whites, wherein white inmates suffer extreme humiliation as a consequence of losing their "manhood." (Carroll, 1977). The motivations behind these assaults involve not only longstanding black oppression, but also prison conditions and the inmates' membership in the black-male-offender subculture (Carroll, 1977; Lockwood, 1980). The prison provides black inmates with an opportunity to vent their rage against individuals who are viewed to be representatives of their oppressors. In addition, prison further increases their sense of rage because in these institutions black inmates are contained and surrounded by highly visible reminders of white oppression—subject to the control of predominantly white custodial staff—and are prevented from validating their masculinity through heterosexual contact. The following quotation from an interview with a black inmate illustrates these feelings:

> It's getting even I guess . . . You guys (whites) been cuttin' our balls off ever since we been in this country. Punkin whites is just one way of getting even.
>
> To the general way of thinking it's 'cause we're confined and we got hard rocks. But it ain't it at all. It's a way for the black man to get back at the white man. It's one way he can assert his manhood. Anything white, even a defenseless punk, is part of what the black man hates. It's part of what he's had to fight all his life just to survive, just to have a hole to sleep in and some garbage to eat. . . . It's a new ego thing. He can show he's a man by making a white guy into a girl [Carroll, 1977, p. 422].

It is all too easy to misconstrue this analysis to suggest that black culture represents an important element in the motivation behind prison sexual aggression. If racial animosity alone were the only element behind sexual aggression then we would naturally expect to find the same victim/offender/ethnic relationship on the street as we would find in prison, which is not the case. Thus, it is not black culture that is the basis of prison sexual aggression but instead the criminal-male-youthful-black subculture of violence (Lockwood, 1980).

Whether or not white prisoners are prejudiced or extremely racially hostile when they enter the prison, they tend to become so after they have experienced the hate, hostility, and violence directed against them by black inmates. Fox's (1982) study of attitudes of inmates at four men's and one women's institutions helps illuminate the issue of racism within the prisons. His data suggest that other racial minorities in prison have greater concerns about racism than whites. However, he notes that whites express more concern about racial conflict and violence particularly when they consider themselves as the target of a "pay-back."

Whites' prejudice and hate as well as their fear of blacks are further increased when they are not organized to resist black inmates. Whether blacks are in the majority or represent as little as 22 percent of the population, their high degree of solidarity puts them in a much better position to achieve their objectives and to protect their own members from attack (Carroll, 1974; 1977). Even in institutions where white groups are formed in response to racial animosities, they are likely to involve a much smaller number of whites—in some cases as little as 10 percent or 15 percent of the population—and this greatly reduces their ability to provide effective protection (Jacobs, 1977). In the absence of solidarity and/or membership in a strong group or clique, white inmates are much more vulnerable to physical as well as sexual assault since there is little fear of organized retaliation.

Another factor that further increases racial tensions within the institution is the perception by black inmates of staff bias and identification with white inmates. Carroll (1974) indicates that one of the factors contributing to black solidarity is the fear on the part of blacks of the alliance between white prisoners and staff. Although, as the New York State Commission on Attica (1972) noted, racism among correctional officers may be no greater than that which is present in society at large, its effects are more intense within the institution because there is no place where inmates can go to escape racially based staff confrontations.

The Inmate Social System: Making It in Prison   The inmate social system has also been affected by changes in the prison system and the characteristics of the prison population. The "right guy," who was a product of the thief subculture and dominated the inmate world during the big-house era, was unable to retain his position in the correctional institution as a result of the diminishing number of thieves who entered prisons during this period. The escalation of violence and the emergence of gangs in many prisons has all but eliminated the right guy as a potent force in the inmate environment. Convict leaders/elders in the more violent prisons found they were unable to keep low-rider gang members in a subordinate status or otherwise control them (Irwin, 1980). Other traditional prison roles (e.g., "square johns" and "politicians") may also be disappearing in the violent prisons, to be replaced by such new roles as gang leader, lieutenant, and soldier (Gibbs, 1974).

The "wise guy," "hog," or "bad dude" is now the most respected convict figure and dominates the inmate world in the violent prisons. This new convict identity places primary emphasis on toughness, which is manifested by an individual's ability to take care of himself in the prison world—a place where predators attack with little or no provocation and the weak are victimized. These convicts will kill to protect themselves. They give their allegiance to a strong group of other inmates, usually of their own racial or ethnic background, and openly manifest their opposition to the prison administration, even if this means harsh punishment. They control the prison economic system, as well as any activities such as demonstrations and prison representative organizations which involve the entire inmate population. In order to survive in this environment, most inmates must adopt the convict role and, with rare exceptions, develop some type of affiliation with a powerful racial gang or clique (Irwin, 1980).

"Independents" represent a second category of inmates who are able to circulate freely within the violent prison. Some of these inmates maintain loose friendships with one or more major gangs and this gives them immunity from gang attack. A small number of tough independents can move freely because they have emerged the victors in many prison assaults. Other inmates whose independence is tolerated include those politically oriented convicts who pursue prisoners' rights objectives or inmates such as "dingbats" who provide a source of comic relief for other prisoners.

Larger and more violent prisons also have other groups such as the Muslims and cliques of "syndicate-organized crime-men" and their friends who are able to exist free from attachment to the more violent factions within the prison. Irwin (1980) indicates that the presence and prominence of these groups in an institution may act as a stabilizing force that inhibits the complete takeover of the inmate world by violent cliques and gangs.

Prisons have always contained a certain number of violence-prone individuals, including "state-raised youths" who had spent substantial portions of their childhood and adolescence in juvenile reform schools, and "fuck-ups"—lower-class and working-class criminals who had little respect for older offenders and "regular convicts." These individuals constantly posed a threat to the stability of the prison. However, if they went too far, older prison regulars would use force to bring them back into line (Irwin, 1980). The "baby boom" of the 1950s, 1960s, and 1970s swelled the youthful population of the ghettos, and this in turn resulted in a bulge in the juvenile institutional population. The adult institutions began to receive increasing numbers of these openly aggressive, young, criminally unskilled, urban toughs as they "aged out" of the juvenile justice system. As their numbers grew, the ability of the more stable elements of the prison community to control these inmates faltered. The impact of the arrival of these young hoodlums in the prison system varied from state to state, depending on their backgrounds and the nature of the correctional systems they entered. Drawing on their street savvy, as well as their training-school experience, these inmates formed racial/ethnic cliques based on previous outside friendship, similar criminal orientation, and/or work or cell assignment. In some cases, these cliques were tied into supergangs, which have resulted from the incarceration of large numbers of individuals who were affiliated with a particular gang on the street.

Inmates derive many benefits from joining gangs, particularly in institutions where they dominate the prison world (Jacobs, 1974; Porter, 1982). Gangs provide their members with protection from physical and sexual assault as well as from being the victims of extortion or theft. "Independents" and members of the other gangs know that if a gang member is attacked, his comrades will retaliate. In addition, gangs also have private stores and provide new inmates and those without outside resources with candy, cigarettes, pies, canned food, canned meat, and other things that make prison life more tolerable. Gang members, unlike independents, are not expected to pay back these debts of two for one, or 100 percent interest. Gangs also serve as a source of information for their members. By getting their members assigned to strategic jobs in the prison, including positions as clerks in the administration building, runners, and house help, the gang can provide its members with valuable information on decisions made on them by the administration and the parole board. Gang affiliation also provides a member with an opportunity to operate within the prison economy. Although gangs do not necessarily control all the illicit activities in institutions in which they are dominant, it appears that illicit activities do not operate in these institutions without at least the tacit approval of gang leaders. Therefore, an affiliated inmate who wishes to operate in the prison economy can easily establish connections and can muscle in on independents who are not paying off to one of the other gangs. The gang arranges for visitors and even people to correspond with members who have no outside family or other contacts. Released members in gangs with outside affiliates can expect to receive assistance when they return to their communities. Some gangs have education programs which teach members how to read and write.

However, for many gang members, the primary function of these groups is to provide them with psychological support. That is, the gang provides its members with a feeling of belonging, a source of identification, and an air of importance. For the inmate who is a product of an unstable family, and who has a poor self-concept, the gang allows him to feel like a man and to be part of a family which he never had.

Withdrawal Rather than become associated with a gang or get caught up in the combative inmate world, many inmates in the more violent prisons choose a more circumscribed way of life. They minimize their forays into public areas and avoid involvement in the activities of the convict world (Irwin, 1980; Sheehan, 1978). In this way, they avoid the need to respond violently to an off-color remark or a threatened attack by aggressive inmates. Although these prisoners do not completely withdraw from the prison world, they attempt to avoid potentially dangerous situations. They only maintain close contact with a few individuals, including friends they know from the outside or inmates they have met in the cellblock and with whom they share interests or work assignments.

"Convicts" tend to disrespect and usually ignore those who withdraw from the prison world, even older thieves and others who formerly held high status within the inmate social structure. Inmates who choose to cope with the prison world in this way may have to show deference when they accidentally come into contract with "convicts." By behaving in this way, however, they reduce the risk of robbery or assault. This strategy is not effective for young and effeminate prisoners because their characteristics make them prime candidates to be pursued by aggressive, homosexually oriented convicts to force them into sexual liaisons or rape. For these inmates, the only safe haven in the prison may well be transfer to a protective segregation unit.

ALTERNATIVES TO CONFINEMENT

Offenders sent away to prison return, sooner or later, to free society. Due to the fact that so many freed criminals revert to crime, society has continually sought alternatives to confinement. In recent years the emphasis has been on involving offenders in programs and facilities based within the community. Such programs allow society to provide offenders with only the amount of supervision they require.

Because crime has its roots within the community, it is reasonable to expect the community to assume some responsibility for dealing with offenders. This approach also tends to minimize the problem of reintegration. That is, it is much easier to reintegrate someone who has been allowed to remain in the community under supervision than someone who has been sent away to prison.

Probation and parole are the two methods most often used to replace imprisonment with community supervision. More than half of all the persons convicted of felonies each year are placed on probation. However, the number of prisoners released on parole is currently declining because of dissatisfaction with selection procedures and skepticism about the effectiveness of parole. Strictly speaking, parole is not an alternative to incarceration in the same sense as probation; it is a form of conditional release for someone already serving a prison term.

Probation

Probation has been called "the least visible, least studied, most diffuse and most underfunded part of the criminal processing apparatus" (Krajick, 1980, p. 7). Yet probation is the sanction that a criminal court is most apt to impose on offenders. Between 60 and 80 percent of sentences meted out by the courts involve probation; and, on any given day, there are about one million people on probation in the United States (U.S. Department of Justice, 1982). Some jurisdictions practice "postcard probation," in which clients report their activities once or twice a month by sending in preaddressed postcards. This kind of probation ends when clients lose or misplace their cards.

Probation is intended as a combination of treatment and punishment. An offender serving time on probation is also supposed to be treated in the context of community-based supervision. Ideally, probationers receive counseling and guidance to aid them in adjusting to free society. But probation is also punitive, because restrictions are placed on the probationer. Many authorities deny the punitive aspects of probation and insist that their policies are entirely rehabilitative.

Both liberal and conservative critics of the criminal justice system agree that placing an offender on probation without making use of community resources and services is equal to doing nothing. Such actions are neither treatment nor punishment. As a criminal court judge observed: "The offender continues with his life style . . . If he is a wealthy doctor, he continues with his practice; if he is an unemployed youth, he continues to be unemployed. Probation is a meaningless ritual; it is a sop to the conscience of the court" (Krajick, 1980, p. 7).

John Augustus: Father of Probation A nineteenth century Boston shoemaker named **John Augustus** is regarded as the "father of probation." Augustus spent a good deal of his leisure time in the courts and was distressed by the fact that common drunks were forced to remain in jail because they had no money to pay their fines (Augustus, 1852). A humane and sympathetic man, Augustus convinced the authorities to allow him to pay offenders' fines; after their release, he provided them with friendly counsel and supervision. Between 1841 and 1859, he bailed out more than two thousand persons. He was sharply criticized for his "strange" ideas.

John Augustus's efforts encouraged his home state of Massachusetts to pass the first probation statute in 1878. Five more states followed suit before the turn of the century. Probation was established as a legitimate alternative to penal confinement and was given great impetus by the creation of the first juvenile court in 1899. The need to provide supervision for youths in trouble and to keep them out of adult prisons provided strong motivation toward the development of probation in the United States.

Conditions of Probation   Even though probation usually is managed by the courts and parole by an executive department of government, the general and specific conditions are similar for both. The conditions are customarily established jointly by the legislature, the court, and the probation and parole commission. Some regulations (e.g., requirements to report regularly to one's probation or parole officer, not to leave the state without the court's permission, and to pay court costs) are fixed by statute and affect all persons on probation and parole. These general conditions make no allowance for discretion by the trial court or the probation and parole commission. Unique conditions may be imposed in certain individual cases. For example, probationers or parolees may be required to stay home or leave home, support their parents, get a steady job during the day, make restitution to their crime victims, or regularly attend church.

Conditions of probation and parole have often been challenged because of their vagueness, overgenerality, interference with an individual's constitutional rights, or lack of relationship to the underlying offense. For instance, the condition that a probationer "live honorably" was found to be impermissibly vague [*Norris* v. *State,* 383 So.2d 691 (Fla. App. 1980)]. Conditions may be imposed which are impossible for performance: ordering an alcoholic to stop drinking or a drug addict to refrain from the use of drugs constitutes the imposition of unlawful "impossible" conditions [*Sweeney* v. *United States,* 353 F. 2d 10 (7th Cir. 1965)]. On the other hand, requiring a person to obtain treatment or to submit to reasonable tests in order to determine progress would tend to be upheld by the courts.

Intensive Supervision   **Intensive supervision** programs have been developed as an alternative or supplement to traditional probation. They are primarily intended to relieve prison overcrowding at an acceptable cost, although they are also broadly designed to meet other needs of offenders.

An example of extensive supervised custody in the community is Florida's Community Control Program, which opened on October 1, 1983, as a result of the passage of the Correctional Reform Act of 1983 by the Florida State Legislature. Its objectives were to: (1) help reduce prison overcrowding; (2) provide safe, punishment-oriented community alternatives to imprisonment; (3) divert offenders from prisons and county jails; (4) provide weekend as well as weekday surveillance and supervision; (5) provide public work programs for community controlees; (6) limit community control caseloads to 20 cases per officer; and (7) impose and enforce noninstitutional sanctions and house arrest.

Under the Community Control Program, nearly two thousand offenders have become "outmates" who live in their own neighborhoods, in their own homes, with their own families. The program is directed toward first-time felons convicted of nonviolent crimes carrying a maximum sentence of two years.

Outmates can expect at least 28 unexpected visits per month at any time during the day or night from the community control (CC) officers. A daily log listing activities, hour by hour, must be filled out by the offender. Community service work is required and prisoners often must make financial restitution to their crime victims. They are also expected to pay up to $50 per month to the Department of Corrections for their supervision. At the direction of CC officers, outmates must participate in self-help programs, ranging from Alcoholics Anonymous to psychological counseling. On demand, they must submit to breathalyzer, urinalysis, and blood tests. CC officers are responsible for knowing what their charges are doing at all times.

From the outset, representatives from probation and parole, the police, the courts, and the general public have been receptive to community control because the program emphasizes punitive sanctions, accountability and responsibility, and small caseloads to insure credibility and public safety. Since much of community control work has been a pioneering effort, a wide range of techniques and procedures has evolved. Only experienced probation and parole officers have been used as staff, and they have been given opportunities for extensive training. Additional pay incentives are needed, however, to continue to attract high-caliber, experienced professionals vital to the success of the program.

In a review of evaluations of intensive supervision programs in the United States, Travis (1984) found the failure rates of regular and intensive supervision programs were similar. He noted, however, that new offenses and technical violations can mask the success of intensive supervision programs in reducing new offense behavior. It should also be emphasized that comparable or slightly higher violation rates can be considered a "success" in situations where intensive supervision programs serve a higher-risk population than is handled in a traditional probation program.

Presentence Investigation (PSI) and Report   Probation is a method of individualization and is predicated on the proper selection of offenders. To determine which offenders will make promising candidates for probation, sentencing judges rely heavily on thorough, carefully prepared presentence reports. According to Killinger, Kerper, and Cromwell (1976), "The ultimate merit of probation as a correctional tool is dependent to a very large extent upon the nature and quality of the presentence report" (p. 68). Although the information secured for this report is primarily intended to aid in the assessment of factors that bear importantly on successful community adjustment in lieu of incarceration, the **presentence investigation (PSI)** report can be used at almost every stage in the criminal justice system and process: (1) by the courts in deciding the appropriate sentence; (2) by the prison classification team in assigning custody level and treatment; (3) by the parole board in determining when the offender is ready to be returned to the community; (4) by probation and parole officers as they aid the offender in readjusting to the demands of free society; and (5) by correctional researchers as they try to identify the characteristics most closely associated with success on probation (Carter and Wilkins, 1976).

There are wide variations in the scope and depth of information contained in the PSI report. The probation officer who prepares the report has considerable latitude in what to include in the report, but certain facts that are pertinent to the case are usually covered: a description of the offense, including statements of co-defendants; the defendant's own version of the offense and prior criminal record; family and marital history; description of the neighborhood in which the defendant was reared; and facts regarding the defendant's education, religion, interest, mental and physical health records, employment history, and military service record. Probation officers may choose to include other optional data such as "attitudes of defendant toward arresting officers" and amount of bail bond posted, if they feel that such information adds substantially to the report. Judges in many jurisdictions ask for recommendations from probation officers with respect to sentencing alternatives, or recommendations concerning a treatment plan if the defendant is placed on probation.

Shock Probation   Twenty years ago, the state of Ohio introduced a program of **shock probation**—a procedure which allowed the courts to impose a sentence consisting of a brief period of incarceration followed by probation. The rationale for this program was to impress offenders with the seriousness of their crimes by giving them "a taste of the bars" (Parisi, 1981), yet releasing them from confinement under supervision in the community before they have begun to become "prisonized." *Shock probation,* as Reid (1981) points out, is a misnomer for this procedure because probation is traditionally and technically an alternative to incarceration, whereas conditional release following a period of imprisonment constitutes parole. At any rate, the term *shock probation* has proven fairly durable. Ironically, as shock probation underwent an eclipse in Ohio, it was discovered by a number of other states, where it was viewed as a possible aid in reducing prison overcrowding. Vito (1984) examined an extensive body of research on shock probation and concluded that if use is made of this approach, it should be reserved for selected offenders who are poor risks for regular probation.

Probation in Retrospect   Probation has sometimes been viewed as the bright hope for corrections. It is generally conceded, however, that the full potential of this alternative to confinement cannot be attained without some effort to resolve two major issues: (1) development of an effective system for determining which offenders should receive probation and (2) provision of support and services to probationers in the community which would allow them to live independently in a socially acceptable way.

Since 1972, the U.S. Parole Commission has used an actuarial instrument as an aid in assessing parole diagnosis in conjunction with explicit decision guidelines (Hoffman, 1983). These guidelines use a two-dimensional matrix to establish a range of time (in months) to be served for various combinations of offenses, ranked in order of severity, and offender characteristics. We shall examine this instrument in our discussion of parole prognosis in the following section. Corresponding applications of prediction methods in probation are currently within reach and await only testing and large-scale research (Albanese et al., 1981).

With regard to the second issue, probation services need major improvements in organization, staffing, and funding. The National Advisory Commission on Criminal Justice Standards and Goals (1973) officially endorsed probation as the recommended disposition for offenders, preferably without adjudication of guilt. It also recommended that probation, which started as a volunteer activity, seek volunteers to serve in all capacities in probation. The persuasive arguments favoring probation over imprisonment underline reduced stigma, community support, and other benefits to the offender. But if probation is to be strengthened as a realistic and effective alternative to incarceration, decisions to shift money and resources to community based projects are a fundamental requirement.

Parole

All offenders except those who are executed or committed to prison for "life certain" terms must eventually be released. How well they fare once they are returned to society—whether they are successfully reintegrated or commit further offenses that lead them back into prison—is subject to many complex factors, one of which is the sheer length of time a person has spent in prison. Reid (1981) cites the case of Ralph Lobaugh, who was released in 1977 after spending 30 years in prison in Indiana:

> The freedom for which he had fought during 14 years, however, was too much for him. After two months, Lobaugh decided he could not cope with life outside the walls and went back to prison. According to Harold G. Roddy, director of the work-release program in Indiana, Lobaugh "just wanted to live in a cell again and be with his old friends" [p. 282].

The Lobaugh case may be extreme, but the problems of readjustment to a free society for a released prisoner are anything but unusual or atypical.

Parole is the traditional means by which the majority of incarcerated prisoners are released each year from correctional institutions. Parole is the conditional release, under supervision, of an offender from a correctional institute after he has served a portion of his sentence. The word is taken from the French and is used in the sense of *parole d' honneur* ("word of honor"). The concept has its roots in military history, referring to the practice of releasing a captured soldier on his "parole," that is, on his word of honor that he would not again take up arms against his captors. Similarly, the inmate is released to free society on his word or honor that he will not again become an enemy of society. Parole differs from probation because it implies the offender has "served time." Administratively, parole is a function of the executive branch of government, while probation is a judicial act of the court. Selection, supervision, regulations, revocation, and release procedures are similar, and the two kinds of conditional release often become confusing to the public.

Prisoners have always been released on the arrival of their "mandatory release date"; that is, sentences normally have a termination date. In inmate jargon, this is referred to as serving "flat time" or "day-to-day." Parole is a conditional release. Inmates who appear to be making genuine progress toward rehabilitation are selected to serve a final portion of their sentences, under some form of supervision, in the community.

The Selection Process in Parole   Prisoners seeking release on parole must follow a procedure of recommendation and review that is intended to determine their readiness for this option. The general practice of most parole boards is to assign cases to individual board members and let them review the cases in detail, after which they make recommendations to the full board when it meets. In most cases, the recommendation of the individual board member is accepted, but sometimes the assembled board will request more details and will ask the prisoner to appear. Some states send individual members of the board to the institutions to interview the inmate and the institutional staff; others convene the entire board at the individual institutions on a regular schedule. If inmates fail to meet whatever criteria the board uses, their sentences are continued and they are **"flopped."** In the case where parole is granted, the inmate is prepared for turnover to the adult parole authority for a period of supervision determined by the parole board. A major problem in making parole decisions often lies in the boards' disregard of offenders' rights to know the criteria they are expected to achieve and the reasons they were flopped.

Four inmates of the Indiana State Penitentiary have described how parole candidates resent at least three aspects of the parole decision process. First, the tendency of parole boards is to place great emphasis on the candidate's prior record:

> What is so frustrating to men who keep getting rejected for parole because of "past record" is that there is obviously nothing that the individual can do about it. It cannot be changed, it cannot be expunged. It therefore generates a feeling of helplessness and frustration, especially in men who take seriously what they are told about rehabilitation and perfect institutional records. These men cannot understand the rationale behind parole denials based on past records if the major goal of the correctional system is rehabilitation and if they have tried to take advantage of every rehabilitation program offered by the institution. The men know that merely serving another two or five years is not going to further the "rehabilitation" process [Griswold et al., 1970].

The second source of resentment comes from the attitude of parole boards that their principal responsibility is to protect society and that the rehabilitation of the offender is secondary. With this as their guide, parole boards are reluctant to release offenders who are considered poor risks, preferring to let them serve day-for-day and later return to the community without supervision. This practice undoubtedly reduces the recidivism rate for persons on parole and enhances the public image of parole boards. Its impact on the overall recidivism rate, however, should be the paramount consideration. The issue is whether keeping poor parole risks in prison for a longer period of time makes them better parole risks. The answer for some is yes. The passage of time, more than anything in the dehumanizing prison atmosphere, seems to mature a few inmates. But for the most, the longer offenders are subjected to the criminogenic environment of a penitentiary, the more likely they are to absorb the values, techniques, and rationalizations of the criminal subculture.

Lastly, inmates are convinced that parole boards are more responsive to public opinion and political pressures than to the factual situation and record of the individual applicant. This feeling on the part of prisoners only adds to their cynicism toward the entire parole process.

Conditions for Parole   Many earlier parole procedures imposed unreasonable restrictions on the released offender. Too often the rules for parole were simply a convenient pretext for returning the parolee to prison, which was done if the parolee created even the slightest fuss for the parole officer. Today, the rules that a parolee is expected to follow are much more reasonable and realistic.

As recently as 20 years ago, it was not uncommon for the conditions of parole to include such rules as one which required the parolee to "only associate with persons of good reputation." Conforming to that sort of requirement would be next to impossible for an offender whose family members may have included persons with criminal records. Rules of this type gave the parole officer great discretionary power over the parolee. Offenders knew that their parole could be revoked for a technical violation of the conditions at almost any time the parole officer desired. This situation does not create a relationship which is conducive to reform and respect for the law. The parolee's attitude was often one of "If I'm going to get busted for a technical violation, I might as well do something *really* wrong." The simpler nonrestrictive rules shown on page 540 were aimed at eliminating this kind of rationalization by the parolee.

Enhancing parole prediction   Parole boards are constantly engaged in a type of activity most people associate with tea leaves and crystal balls: namely, predicting the future. The decision to release or not to release an inmate involves an action based on the parole board members' appraisal of the individual's likelihood of either lawful or criminal future behavior. In study after study, the main criteria affecting this prediction have been (1) the seriousness of the crime for which the offender was convicted, (2) the individual's criminal record, and (3) the prospects of success on parole for the individual, as viewed by the members of the parole board.

In an effort to increase the objectivity—and consequently the reliability and validity—of parole prediction, statistical tables have been devised by parole boards to augment the subjective aspects of the decision-making process. One of the best known of these approaches is called the **Salient Factor Scale**. It was developed through research by the Federal Parole Commission. The Salient Factor Scale relates uniform amounts of prison time served to severity of crime and level of risk. Data were obtained from ratings made by parole commissioners; base-sentence ranges shown in Figure 19.1 were established for each of seven categories of offense by computing the average amount of time that inmates had served for these crimes.

No one has suggested that prediction tables, however accurate they may prove to be in field operations, are likely to take the place of parole boards. For one thing, there is little likelihood that parole boards are going to relinquish their authority in

Statement of Parole Agreement

The Members of the Parole Board have agreed that you have earned the opportunity of parole and eventually a final release from your present conviction. The Parole Board is therefore ordering a Parole Release in your case.

Parole Status has a two-fold meaning: One is a trust status in which the Parole Board accepts your word you will do your best to abide by the Conditions of Parole that are set down in your case; the other, by State law, means the Adult Parole Authority has the legal duty to enforce the Conditions of Parole even to the extent of arrest and return to the institution should that become necessary.

The following Conditions of Parole are in effect in your Parole Release:

1. Upon release from the institution, report as instructed to your Parole Officer (or any other person designated) and thereafter report as often as directed.
2. Secure written permission of the Adult Parole Authority before leaving the [said] State.
3. Obey all municipal ordinances, state and federal laws, and at all times conduct yourself as a responsible law-abiding citizen.
4. Never purchase, own, possess, use or have under your control, a deadly weapon or firearm.
5. Follow all instructions given you by your Parole Officer or other officials of the Adult Parole Authority.
6. If you feel any of the Conditions, or instructions, are causing problems, you may request a meeting with your parole officer's supervisor. The request stating your reasons for the conference should be in writing when possible.
7. Special Conditions: (as determined).

I have read, or have had read to me, the foregoing Conditions of my Parole. I fully understand them and I agree to observe and abide by my Parole Conditions.

Witness _____ Parole Candidate _____

Date _____

---

the parole decision-making process to any instrument, however well recommended it may be on the basis of scientific research. A more realistic alternative is Glaser's (1964) suggestion that actuarial tables augment and complement the more subjective aspects of parole board deliberations and provide a valuable check on the potential effects of bias or prejudice.

Legal Issues Affecting Probation and Parole   The decision to grant probation or parole is highly discretionary; the probationer or parolee has relatively few legal

Offense severity (some crimes eliminated or summarized)	Salient factor score (parole prognosis)			
	Very good	Good	Fair	Poor
LOW: possession of a small amount of marijuana; simple theft under $1,000	6–10 months	8–12 months	10–14 months	12–18 months
LOW/MODERATE: income tax evasion less than $10,000; immigration law violations; embezzlement, fraud, forgery under $1,000	8–12 months	12–16 months	16–20 months	20–28 months
MODERATE: bribery; possession of 50 lbs. or less of marijuana, with intent to sell; illegal firearms; income tax evasion $10,000 to $50,000; nonviolent property offenses $1,000 to $19,999; auto theft, not for resale	12–16 months	16–20 months	20–24 months	24–32 months
HIGH: counterfeiting; marijuana possession with intent to sell, 50 to 1,000 lbs; auto theft, for resale; nonviolent property offenses, $20,000 to $100,000	16–20 months	20–26 months	26–34 months	34–44 months
VERY HIGH: robbery; breaking and entering bank or post office; extortion; marijuana possession with intent to sell, over 2,000 lbs; hard drugs possession with intent to sell, not more than $100,000; nonviolent property offenses over $100,000 but not exceeding $500,000	26–36 months	36–48 months	48–60 months	60–72 months
GREATEST I: explosive detonation; multiple robbery; aggravated felony (weapon fired — no serious injury); hard drugs, over $100,000; forcible rape	40–55 months	55–70 months	70–85 months	85–110 months
GREATEST II: aircraft hijacking espionage; kidnapping; homicide	Greater than above. No specific ranges because of limited number and extreme variation in cases			

Figure 19.1 Federal parole guidelines: The Salient Factor Scale. (*Source:* K. Krajick. Parole: Discretion is out, guidelines are in. *Corrections Magazine* 4 (1978): 46. Reproduced by permission of the author and publisher.)

rights. But once probation or parole has been granted, the candidate receives a form of conditional liberty which bears important consequences with regard to both supervision within the community and any decision to revoke this freedom. One of the most significant developments in this area is the constitutional basis for the revocation process.

In the landmark case of *Morrissey* v. *Brewer* (1971), the U.S. Supreme Court held that although a prisoner does not have a constitutional right to parole, once paroled he cannot be deprived of his freedom by means that are inconsistent with due process. The elements of due process the Court identified as required by parole revocation were:

1. Written notice of the alleged violations of parole.
2. Disclosure to the parolee of the evidence of violation.

3. Opportunity to be heard in person and to present evidence as well as summon witnesses.
4. Right to confront and cross-examine adverse witnesses unless good cause can be shown for not allowing this confrontation.
5. Right to judgment by a detached and neutral hearing body.
6. Written statement of reasons for revoking parole as well as of the evidence used in arriving at that decision.

The term revocation, as Cohen (1983) points out, at times refers to the act of imprisonment or reimprisonment, and at other times to the process of establishing that a violation has occurred. Cohen suggests that revocation may be best viewed as a process resembling a "cameo trial at which facts are alleged and proven to show a violation; that is, that the supervisee was at 'fault' by committing a new crime or violating a condition of his release" (p. 1244).

The Beleaguered Status of Parole   The attack on parole has come from a variety of diverse sources, ranging from the American Friends Service Committee to the director of the U.S. Bureau of Prisons, Norman Carlson. More than a decade ago, the following indictment of parole was delivered by Citizens' Inquiry on Parole and Criminal Justice, Inc. (1974):

> Parole is a tragic failure. Conspiring with other elements of the criminal justice system—unnecessary pre-trial detention, over-long sentences, oppressive conditions—it renders American treatment of those who break society's rules irrational and arbitrary [p. 38].

A couple of years later, the state of California abolished indeterminate sentencing on a broad scale; along with the abolition of the indeterminate sentence, it also abolished the Adult Authority or parole board. In July 1977, the state that had pioneered the use of indeterminate sentencing made uniform determinate sentencing a fundamental part of its correctional practice and philosophy.

Is the replacement of indeterminate sentencing with mandatory flat-time sentencing an opening or closing of Pandora's Box? Not enough time has passed to permit an informed answer to this question; in the meantime, other states have followed California's lead in abolishing indeterminate sentencing. It seems rather unlikely that parole will be abandoned altogether as a form of conditional release from confinement. Even sharp critics of parole such as von Hirsch and Hanrahan (1979) have argued for the retention, at least for some time, of the parole board as a safety net. In addition, as Singer (1979) observes, the movement toward reducing sentence disparities by means of guidelines and sentencing institutes or councils has helped defuse a good deal of the animosity prisoners have felt toward the parole system. But continuing public clamor for tougher laws and stricter law enforcement makes it abundantly clear that parole will be subjected to very close constraints for the foreseeable future.

Other Forms of Conditional Release

Work Release   The pioneering reform efforts of Crofton in Ireland during the nineteenth century were an attempt to provide prisoners with the chance to work within the community for a period of time prior to their release. This idea has been revived in recent years: the **work-release** program has become an important adjunct to institutional programs. Under work-release arrangements, offenders are allowed to work at jobs in the community and still receive the benefit of certain programs and services available at an institution.

The origin of work-release legislation is a 1913 Wisconsin statute which allowed misdemeanants to continue to work at their jobs while serving short sentences in jail. North Carolina applied the principles of the Wisconsin statute to felony offenders in 1957, under limited conditions; Michigan and Maryland soon followed suit with similar acts. In 1965, Congress passed the Federal Prisoner Rehabilitation Act, which provided for work release, furloughs, and community treatment centers for federal prisoners. Many states followed suit.

Work-release programs are not really alternatives to incarceration in an "either/or" sense. They do provide a chance for the offender to test his work skills and control over his own behavior in the community, and allow him to spend the major part of the day away from the total institution. However, because the inmate is still required to return to the institution, the work-release program is referred to here as only a partial alternative to incarceration.

Work release has benefits other than allowing the inmate to be outside the prison or jail walls for a period of time each day. The income derived from the work can be used in a number of ways. If he has a family, the earnings can be used to keep them off welfare rolls or to augment the assistance they might be receiving. He may reimburse the victim for his loss, or he may be able to acquire a nest egg for the time when he will be released. One of the major benefits, however, is that private citizens will see that an offender can work in the community without creating problems for himself or for others. His association with fellow workers enjoying more stable lives in freedom may also give the offender support and guidance which he cannot gain inside the institution walls. In the American tradition, the ability to produce a day's work is highly valued and tends to instill a feeling of self-worth in many offenders in work-release programs.

Study Release   The **study-release** program is a correctional alternative that possesses many of the same features as the work-release concept. Study-release programs are a rather recent innovation in corrections; prior to 1960, the only state that reported a study-release program in operation was Connecticut. At present, 41 states have study-release programs of some kind, most of them open to both male and female participants (Shichor and Allen, 1977). The range of educational services offered by these programs is extremely broad, from vocational training and basic adult skills training to college-level education. Variables involved in the screening of offenders for study release are comparable to those employed in work-release programs: current offense, length of time served, custody grade, educational needs, attitudes of the offender toward the institution and program, etc. Since educational attainments are a significant employment consideration in our achievement-oriented society, programs that seek to increase the marketability of the offender by raising the level of his or her job-related skills have a good deal of plausibility as alternatives to imprisonment. We are not in a position, however, to make more than cautious statements about the value of such programs because we are still awaiting reliable and valid information on the evaluation of study-release programs.

Furloughs   Another form of partial incarceration is the **furlough.** Work- and study-release programs and furloughs extend the limits of confinement by allowing unsupervised absences from the prison. Furloughs and home visits have been used for many years on an informal basis. The death of a family member or some other type of crisis situation has been the most common reason for granting a furlough. As states have passed legislation making furloughs a legal tool of corrections, they have come to be used for a variety of purposes. Furloughs are usually granted for a home visit during holiday periods. Furloughs have also been used during the period just prior to release in order to ease the transition from confinement to freedom. It seems probable that furlough practices will gain further exploration and support as correctional administrators acquire further experience in their use.

Graduated Release   An offender who has served a long sentence in a total institutional setting may suffer "culture shock" when suddenly returned to the community from which he or she came. Just as astronauts must reenter the atmosphere in a series of steps, so too the offender needs to reenter society in gradual stages. This system, referred to as a **graduated-release** program, is intended to ease the pressures of culture shock experienced by institutionalized offenders. Some concepts designed to reduce the adverse effects of reentry are presently being practiced; others must wait until there is a true correctional continuum in operation. Any preparation for release is better than none, but preparation that includes nonincarcerated periods is even more effective.

The periods immediately preceding and following the release of an offender are especially crucial to his or her adjustment to society. Despite the bravado of their statements to the media, most ex-offenders know they will have serious problems in trying to reestablish a life for themselves outside the institution. Their fears and apprehensions build as they approach the time for release.

Some inmates become "jackrabbits" and run away in fear of release shortly before they are due to be freed. These deliberate offenses allow them to return to the total dependency afforded them in the institution. Recognition of this phenomenon has caused many thoughtful correctional administrators to establish prerelease–postrelease programs aimed at assisting the ex-offender through this critical period. Topics covered in such programs include how to get a driver's license, how to open a savings account, credit buying, how to fill out an employment application, sex and family adjustment, and so on.

The Sam Houston Institute of Contemporary Corrections provides some pointers on the establishment of prerelease and graduated-release programs:

1. Pre-release preparation should begin as early as possible in the sentence and inmates should know in advance the purpose and intention of the program.

2. Reliance must be placed on a sound program and not upon the use of special privileges as an enticement to participate.

3. The program should be organized with realistic goals in mind and should be part of the total treatment process.

4. The counseling program should be geared toward dealing with the immediate problems of adjustment rather than with underlying personality problems.

5. Participants should be carefully selected by the staff on an individual basis rather than according to predetermined arbitrary standards.

6. Employee-employer rather than custodian-inmate relationships should exist between the staff and the inmates.

7. Every effort should be made to enlist the support and participation of the community, and family contact should be encouraged.

8. Whenever possible, work release should be included.

The center itself should be minimum security and should encourage personal responsibility. If pre-release programs are to be made a part of the treatment process, there should be some provision for determining their effectiveness [Frank, 1973, pp. 228–29].

Graduated-release and prerelease programs are not "either/or" alternatives to incarceration, but they do recognize the destructive and dependency-producing effects of imprisonment.

SUMMARY

Confinement, as we noted at the beginning of this chapter, involves both detention and imprisonment. Jails, lockups, and juvenile facilities are intended to provide short-term detention for individuals awaiting adjudication, those serving sentences of less than one year, and prisoners awaiting transfer to state or federal prisons. For reasons which we discussed in the text, conditions in these facilities are usually much worse than conditions in state institutions: inadequate, unsanity, and antiquated physical plants, together with poorly trained staffs, contribute to making the jails a national disgrace. One glaring symptom of this deplorable state of affairs is the prevalence of avoidable suicide in jails and detention facilities.

The use of imprisonment as a societal response to criminals superseded the use of techniques that included corporal punishment, capital punishment, and transportation. Early models for the prison were provided by the Pennsylvania system, which stressed solitary confinement and penitence, and the Auburn system, which emphasized the corrective value of congregate work under a strict rule of silence. The latter system became the principal model for prisons in the United States and vestiges of its influences could be seen well into the twentieth century.

During the first half of the twentieth century, the big house was the primary type of penal institution in this country. This facility incorporated the concept of banishment (i.e., prisons were fortresses located in remote areas from which escape was nearly impossible). The regimen within the institution was rigid, mobility was strictly curtailed, and idleness and monotony were the daily diet of the inmate. There was a sharply defined social structure among convicts which functioned to keep the big house relatively tranquil. Guards were untrained, poorly paid, and generally from the lowest stratum of society. The major prison programs were related to institutional maintenance; some educational opportunities were provided and there were limited prison industry programs (e.g., making license plates).

The transition from the big house to the correctional institution occurred during the post–World War II period and reflected a spirit of optimism regarding the ability of corrections to "rehabilitate" offenders. This move toward rehabilitation mirrored a change from a punitive philosophy and orientation toward prisoners to an approach which emphasized diagnosis and treatment. In accordance with this philosophy, some new institutions were built while others changed their terminology to conform to the new trend. The major facets of the correctional programs included classification, treatment, and indeterminate sentencing. Use of these strategies involved endemic problems which ultimately resulted in the demise of the rehabilitative ideology. This demise was hastened by changes that took place in the character of the prison population.

In sketching the transition from the correctional institution to the contemporary prison, two major factors appear to have been most significant. One is the change in the ethnic/racial composition of the inmate population; the second was emergence of the prisoner movement and accompanying politicization of inmates. These factors, along with a number of external conditions, have helped make the contemporary prison an increasingly dangerous and unmanageable place. If nothing of consequence occurs to introduce certain essential changes in this situation, it seems probable that the contemporary prison will continue to exist in a climate of instability and tension, punctuated by explosive outburts of violence.

Community-based correctional programs are viewed as alternatives to imprisonment: they are situated in local communities; they are usually smaller in size; they include day programs that have no residential requirements; and they allow for greater contact and interaction between the community and the "outmates" participating in these programs.

The backbone of community corrections is probation, the assignment of offenders to community supervision as an alternative to incarceration in a jail or prison. Supervision is carried out by probation officers who often combine probation and parole functions. These officers are responsible for securing compliance by their clients to the conditions of their probation or parole and for assisting them to establish a law-abiding style of life. The role conflict between the supervisory and therapeutic or counseling functions of the probation officer is a major source of job-related stress for many officers.

Probationers who fail to conform to the conditions of their probation are subject to revocation. This is most likely to happen when a serious crime has been committed, but it may also occur when a probationer commits a number of petty offenses or acts which constitute technical violations of probation conditions. Until the early 1970s, community supervision was considered a privilege that was capable of being revoked at any time on the whim of the granting authority. Since the U.S. Supreme Court decisions in *Morrissey* v. *Brewer* and *Gagnon* v. *Scarpelli,* probation operations—including revocation proceedings—have increasingly been subject to due process requirements.

Due to lack of research, it is difficult to draw definitive conclusions about the effectiveness of probation. Data indicate that direct costs are far less than those of imprisonment. Results concerning recidivism are inconclusive due mainly to wide variations in definition and measurement.

Parole is the administrative process by means of which imprisoned offenders are released under community supervision before the expiration of their maximum sentences. The release is decided by an administrative body known as a parole board, and it is the board that makes the final decision to return to prison the parolee who has committed a new crime or violated the conditions of parole.

Parole decision making has, in the past, been subjected to many subjective biases. In an attempt to rectify this situation, parole decision-making guidelines have been adopted in a number of correctional systems. Many research studies, using recidivism as the dependent variable, have shown that a number of background characteristics of offenders are related to the probability of success on parole. The evidence that specific institutional arrangements and treatment modalities can significantly affect success rates is less convincing.

No area in corrections is in a greater state of flux than parole and other forms of conditional release. Some correctional practioners, scholars, and political figures favor abolishing parole; other point to conditional release as the safety valve for the nation's overcrowded and volatile prison system. The controversy has continued since the 1970s, when Zebulon R. Brockway introduced the indeterminate sentence and parole at Elmira Reformatory. It seems likely that the debate will continue, because the real issue is not parole or conditional release, but basic philosophies and principles that underlie our societal response to crime and punishment.

DISCUSSION QUESTIONS

Find the answers to the following questions in the text.

1. What are the three types of jails identified in the text? Which of the three is the most common type in use today?
2. Distinguish between the **Pennsylvania system** and the **Auburn system.** Which of these two approaches to prison organization ultimately prevailed in the United States?
3. Briefly summarize the contributions of **Maconochie, Crofton,** and **Brockway** to the **reformatory movement.**
4. What were the main characteristics of prisons during the **"big house"** era? How did the big house differ from the **correctional institution** which replaced it?
5. Discuss some of the reasons for the decline and fall of the correctional institution.
6. Identify some of the conditions within the contemporary prison which are conducive to high rates of institutional violence.
7. What is meant by the contention that **probation** is a combination of punishment and treatment? Can such a combination be expected to work?
8. How does **intensive supervision** differ from regular probation?

9. Identify some of the major uses that are made of the **presentence investigation (PSI)** report.
10. What is the underlying rationale for the procedure known as **shock probation**?
11. Discuss some of the more important issues involved in the **parole** selection process.
12. Discuss the significance of the case of *Morrissey* v. *Brewer* for parole revocation.
13. What are the main arguments for abolishing parole? Do you think we are better off with or without a parole system?

TERMS TO IDENTIFY AND REMEMBER

pretrial detention facility
combined jail facility
Great Law of Pennsylvania
Auburn system
Alexander Maconochie
Zebulon R. Brockway
"right guys"
convict code
probation
intensive supervision
shock probation
"flopped"
Morrissey v. *Brewer* study release
sentenced offender facility
"bullpen"

Pennsylvania system
reformatory movement
Walter Crofton
"big house"
"dingbats"
correctional institution
"independents"
John Augustus
presentence investigation (PSI)
parole
Salient Factor Scale
work release
furlough
graduated release

REFERENCES

Abadinsky, H. *Probation and Parole: Theory and Practice.* Englewood Cliffs, NJ: Prentice-Hall, 1982.

Albanese, J., Fiore, B. A., Powell, J. H., and Storti, J. R. *Is Probation Working?* Washington, D.C.: University Press of America, 1981.

Allen, H. E., Carlson, E. W., and Parks, E. C. *Critical Issues in Adult Probation.* Washington, D.C.: U.S. Government Printing Office, 1979.

American Bar Association Project on Standards for Criminal Justice. *Standards Relating to Probation.* New York: Institute of Judicial Administration, 1970.

Anderson, K., Branegan, J., and Constable, A. What are prisons for? No longer rehabilitation but to punish—and lock the worst away. *Time,* Sept. 13, 1983, pp. 38–41.

Augustus, J. *A Report of the Labors of John Augustus, For the Last Ten Years, in Aid of the Unfortunate.* Boston: Wright and Hasty, 1852.

Barnes, H. E. *The Story of Punishment.* Montclair, NJ: Smith Patterson, 1976.

Barnes, H. E., and Teeters, N. K. *New Horizons in Criminology.* Englewood Cliffs, NJ: Prentice-Hall, 1959.

Berkman, R. *Opening the Gates; The Rise of the Prisoners' Movement.* Lexington, MA: Lexington Books, 1979.

Bingaman, J. *Report of the Attorney General on the February 2 and 3, 1980 Riot at the Penitentiary of New Mexico. Part I: The Penitentiary, The Riot, The Aftermath.* State of New Mexico, Office of the Attorney General, June 1980.

Brown, R. J. Living room inmates. *Tampa Tribune,* May 6, 1984, pp. 1-A, 6-A.

Bureau of Justice Statistics Bulletin. *The 1983 Jail Census.* Washington, D.C.: U.S. Department of Justice, November 1984.

California Department of Youth Authority. *An Evaluation of Seven Selected Probation Subsidy Programs.* Sacramento: California Youth Authority, 1977.

Carney, L. B. *Probation and Parole: Legal and Social Dimensions.* New York: McGraw-Hill, 1977.

Carroll, L. *Hacks, Blacks, and Cons: Race Relations in a Maximum Security Prison.* Lexington, MA: Lexington Books, 1974.

———. Humanitarian reform and biracial sexual assault in a maximum security prison. *Urban Life* 5 (1977): 417–437.

Carter, R. M., and Wilkins, L. T. (eds.), *Probation and Parole: Selected Readings.* New York: Wiley, 1976.

Charlé, S. Suicide in the cellblocks. *Corrections Magazine* 7 (1981): 6–16.

Children's Defense Fund. *Children in Adult Jails.* Washington, D.C.: Children's Defense Fund, 1976.

Christianson, S. Our black prisons. *Crime and Delinquency* 27 (1981): 364–735.

Citizens' Inquiry on Parole and Criminal Justice, Incorporated. *Prison Without Walls: Report on New York Parole.* New York: Praeger, 1975.

Clear, T. R., and O'Leary, V. *Controlling the Offender in the Community.* Lexington, MA: Lexington Books, 1983.

Clemmer, D. *The Prison Community.* New York: Holt, Rinehart and Winston, 1958.

Cohen, F. Probation and parole. 2. Procedural protection. In S. Kadish (ed.), *Encyclopedia of Crime and Justice.* New York: The Free Press, 1983.

Conrad, J. P. Where there's hope there's life: Beyond the justice model. Paper presented at the Justice Model Seminar, University of St. Louis, Oct. 20–21, 1977.

———. *Advanced Materials for Management Training for Prison Discipline.* Columbus, OH: Academy for Contemporary Problems, 1980.

———. The redefinition of probation: Drastic proposals to solve an urgent problem. In P. D. McAnany, D. Thomson, and D. Fogel (eds.), *Probation and Justice: Reconsideration of Mission.* Cambridge, MA: Oelgeschlager, Gunn, and Hain, 1984.

De Beaumont, G., and de Tocqueville, A. *On the Penitentiary System of the United States and its Application in France.* Carbondale, IL: Southern Illinois University Press, 1964.

DiCerbo, E. C. When should probation be revoked? *Federal Probation* 30 (1966): 11–17.

Dressler, D. *Practice and Theory of Probation and Parole.* New York: Columbia University Press, 1969.

Epstein, R., *The Legal Aspects of Contract Parole.* Resource Document 08, American Correctional Association, 1976.

Esparza, R. Attempted and committed suicides in county jails. In B. L. Danto (ed.), *Jail House Blues.* Orchard Lake, MI: Epic, 1973.

Evrard, F. H. *Successful Parole.* Springfield, IL: Charles C. Thomas, 1971.

Fawcett, J., and Marrs, B. Suicide at the County Jail. In B. L. Danto (ed.), *Jail House Blues.* Orchard Lake, MI: Epic, 1973.

Fielding, N. *Probation Practice: Client Support Under Social Control.* Brookfield, VT: Gower, 1984.

Florida Probation and Parole Services. *Preliminary Report on Community Control.* Tallahassee: Florida Department of Corrections, 1984.

Fox, J. G. *Organizational and Racial Conflict in Maximum Security Prisons.* Lexington, MA: Lexington Books, 1982.

Frank, B. Graduated release. In B. Frank (ed.), *Contemporary Corrections.* Reston, VA: Reston Publishing Company, 1973.

Gettinger, S. Separating the cop from the counselor. *Corrections Magazine* 7 (1981): 34–38.

Glaser, D. *The Effectiveness of a Prison and Parole System.* Indianapolis: Bobbs-Merrill, 1964.

Gottfredson, D. M. Probation and parole. 3. Release and revocation. In S. Kadish (ed.), *Encyclopedia of Crime and Justice.* New York: The Free Press, 1983.

Gottfredson, D. M., Wilkins, L. T., and Hoffman, P. B. *Guidelines for Probation and Sentencing.* Lexington, MA: Lexington Books, 1978.

Henningsen, R. J. *Probation and Parole.* New York: Harcourt Brace Jovanovich, 1981.

Hoffman, P. B. "Screening for risk": A revised salient factor score. *Journal of Criminal Justice* 6 (1983): 539–547.

Hussey, F. A., and Duffee, D. E. *Probation, Parole, and Community Field Services: Policy, Structure, and Process.* New York: Harper & Row, 1980.

Irwin, J. *Prisons in Turmoil.* Boston: Little, Brown, 1980.

Jacobs, J. Street gangs behind bars. *Social Problems* 21 (1974): 395–409.

———. *Stateville: The Penitentiary in Mass Society.* Chicago: University of Chicago Press, 1977.

Joint Commission on Correctional Manpower and Training. *Corrections 1968: A Climate for Change.* Washington, D.C.: U.S. Government Printing Office, 1968.

———. *Perspectives on Correctional Manpower and Training.* Washington, D.C.: U.S. Government Printing Office, 1970.

Keve, P. W. *Corrections.* New York: Wiley, 1981.

Killinger, G. G., and Cromwell, P. F. (eds.), *Corrections in the Community: Alternatives to Imprisonment.* St. Paul, MN: West, 1978.

Killinger, G. G., Kerper, H. B., and Cromwell, P. F. *Probation and Parole in the Criminal Justice System.* St. Paul, MN: West, 1976.

Korn, R. K., and McCorkle, L. W. *Criminology and Penology.* New York: Holt, Rinehart and Winston, 1959.

Krajick, K. Probation: The original community program. *Corrections Magazine* 6 (1980): 7–13.

Lemert, E. M., and Dill, F. *Offenders in the Community: The Probation Subsidy Program in California.* Lexington, MA: Lexington Books, 1978.

Lockwood, D. *Prison Sexual Violence.* New York: Elsevier, 1980.

Macnaughton-Smith, P. N. M. *Permission to be Slightly Free.* Toronto: Center of Criminology, University of Toronto, 1976.

Mannheim, H., and Wilkins, L. T. *Prediction Methods in Relation to Borstal Training.* London: HM Stationery Office, 1955.

Mattick, H. W., and Aikman, A. The cloacal region of American corrections. In *Annals of the American Academy of Political and Social Science,* 1969, p. 381.

Montgomery, R., and Dillingham, S. *Probation and Parole in Practice.* Cincinnati: Pilgrimage Press, 1983.

Morris, N. *The Future of Imprisonment.* Chicago: University of Chicago Press, 1974.

Morrissey v. *Brewer,* 408 U.S. 471 (1971).

Murchek, P. Probation without adjudication. *Proceedings of the 18th Annual Southern Conference on Corrections.* Tallahassee, Florida, 1973.

National Advisory Commission on Criminal Justice Standards and Goals. *Corrections.* Washington, D.C.: U.S. Government Printing Office, 1973.

National Commission on the Causes and Prevention of Violence. *Final Report.* Washington, D.C.: U.S. Government Printing Office, 1970.

National Commission on Law Observance and Enforcement. *Report on Penal Institutions, Probation, and Parole.* Washington, D.C.: U.S. Government Printing Office, 1931.

National Council on Crime and Delinquency. *Annulment of a Conviction of Crime: A Model Act.* Paramus, NJ: National Council on Crime and Delinquency, 1962.

National Council on Crime and Delinquency, Research Center West. National Probation Reports Feasibility Study on *NPR Aggregate Probation Data Inquiry: Probation in the U.S.: 1979.* San Francisco: National Council on Crime and Delinquency, 1981.

New York State Commission on Attica. *Attica.* New York: Bantam Books, 1972.

New York Times, Nation's prison population growing more quickly. September 16, 1985, p. 12.

Norland, S., and Mann, P. J. Being troublesome: Women on probation. *Criminal Justice and Behavior* 11 (1984): 115–135.

Office of Juvenile Justice and Delinquency Prevention. *Removing Children from Adult Jails: A Guide to Action.* Urbana-Champaign, IL: Community Research Forum, 1980.

Ohio House Bill 511, 1974.

Ohlin, L. E., Miller, A. D., and Coates, R. B. *Juvenile Correctional Reform in Massachusetts: A Preliminary Report of the Center for Criminal Justice of Harvard Law School.* Washington, D.C.: U.S. Government Printing Office, 1977.

Parisi, N. A taste of the bars. *Journal of Criminal Law and Criminology* 72 (1981): 1109–1123.

Pisciotta, A. W. Scientific reform: The new 'penology' at Elmira, 1876–1900. *Crime and Delinquency* 29 (1983): 613–630.

Piven, H., and Alcabes, A. *The Crisis of Qualified Manpower for Criminal Justice: An Analytic Assessment with Guidelines for New Policy.* Washington, D.C.: U.S. Government Printing Office, 1969.

Porter, B. California prison gangs: The price of control. *Corrections Magazine* 8 (1982): 6–9.

Porter, E. M. Criteria for parole selection. *Proceedings of the American Correctional Association,* New York, 1958.

Reid, S. T. *The Correctional System: An Introduction.* New York: Holt, Rinehart and Winston, 1981.

Robison, J., Wilkins, L. T., and Carter, R. M. *The San Francisco Project: A Study of Federal Probation and Parole.* Berkeley: University of California School of Criminology, 1969.

Rothman, D. J. *Conscience and Convenience: The Asylum and its Alternatives in Progressive America.* Boston: Little, Brown, 1980.

Roundtree, G. A., Edwards, D. W., and Parker, J. B. A study of the personal characteristics of probationers as related to recidivism. *Journal of Offender Counseling, Services, and Rehabilitation* 8 (1984): 53–61.

Sacks, H. R., and Logan, C. H. *Does Parole Make a Difference?* Storrs: University of Connecticut School of Law Press, 1979.

Schmidt, J. *Demystifying Probation.* Lexington, MA: Lexington Books, 1977.

Scudder, K. J. The opposition to probation with a jail sentence. *Federal Probation* 23 (1959): 12–17.

Sellin, T. *Slavery and the Penal System.* New York: Elsevier, 1976.

Sigler, R. T., and McGraw, B. Adult probation and parole officers: Influence of their weapons, role perceptions and role conflict. *Criminal Justice Review* 9 (1984): 28–32.

Silberman, C. E. *Criminal Violence, Criminal Justice.* New York: Random House, 1978.

Singer, R. G. *Just Deserts: Sentencing Based on Equality and Desert.* Cambridge, MA: Ballinger, 1979.

Smith, A., and Berlin, L. *Introduction to Probation and Parole.* St. Paul, MN: West, 1979.

Smykla, J. O. *Community-Based Corrections: Principles and Practices.* New York: Macmillan, 1981.

Snarr, R. W., and Wolford, B. I. *Introduction to Corrections.* Dubuque, IA: William C. Brown, 1985.

Stanley, D. T. *Prisoners Among Us: The Problem of Parole.* Washington, D.C.: Brookings Institute, 1976.

State of Ohio, Department of Rehabilitation and Corrections, Adult Parole Authority. *Statement of Parole Agreement (APA-271).* Columbus: State of Ohio, 1973.

Swanson, C. R. *Jail Overview.* Athens: University of Georgia Institute of Government, 1983.

Swanson, C. R., and Territo, L. Planning and implementing change in jails. In C. R. Swanson (ed.), *Jail Management.* Athens: University of Georgia Institute of Government, 1983.

Sweeney v. *United States,* 353 F. 2d 10 (7th Cir. 1965).

Tarlton v. *Clark,* 441 F. 2d 384, 385 (5th Cir. 1971), cert. denied, 403 U.S. 934 (1971).

Travis, L. F. Intensive supervision in probation and parole. *Corrections Today* 46 (1984): 34, 36, 38, 40.

Trester, H. B. *Supervision of the Offender.* Englewood Cliffs, NJ: Prentice-Hall, 1981.

Turner, O. L. An opinion on probation without adjudication. *Proceedings of the 18th Annual Southern Conference on Corrections,* Tallahassee, Florida, 1973.

U.S. Department of Justice. *Census of Jails and Survey of Jail Inmates, 1974.* Washington, D.C.: U.S. Government Printing Office, 1975.

———. *Probationers in the United States.* Washington, D.C.: U.S. Government Printing Office, 1982.

———. *Prisoners at Midyear 1983: Bureau of Justice Statistics Bulletin, October 1983.* Washington, D.C.: U.S. Government Printing Office, 1983.

———. *Profile of Jail Inmates.* Washington, D.C.: U.S. Government Printing Office, 1983.

Vito, G. F. Developments in shock probation: A review of research findings and policy implications. *Federal Probation* 48 (1984): 22–27.

Von Hirsch, A., and Hanrahan, K. J. *The Question of Parole: Retention, Reform, or Abolition?* Cambridge, MA: Ballinger, 1979.

Wright, K. N., Clear, T. R., and Dickson, P. Universal applicability of probation risk-assessment instruments: A critique. *Criminology* 22 (1984): 113–34.

EPILOGUE

Is crime at an all-time high in the United States at the present time? Will crime rates increase as the end of the century approaches? Can any major changes in the nature of crime be expected between now and the year 2000? Criminologists share a common interest with criminal justice authorities in exploring the factors that affect trends in criminal activity, including responses to crime and criminals among significant sectors of society.

CRIME TRENDS: PAST AND FUTURE

We can identify a number of factors that helped to produce increases in crime during the 1960–1980 period: (1) shifts in the distribution of age groups within the population; (2) migration of rural Americans to urban areas; (3) expansion of the drug consumer population; (4) changes in retail merchandise display methods and security arrangements; (5) frustrations of members of minority groups; and (6) changes in the nature of routine activities within our society.

Past Trends in Crime

Age Group Changes in Population Changes in the composition and distribution of the U.S. population help account for some of the changes we have seen in crime trends over the past twenty-five years. More than 50 percent of those arrested in 1979 were under 25 years of age. Any increase in the relative number of young people in the population can be expected to produce an increase in reported crime. Children born during the post–World War II "baby boom" became teenagers and young adults during the 1960s and 1970s; this increase in the ranks of the high crime-risk component of the population was reflected in the steep increases in crime rates that were registered between 1960 and 1980.

A decline in the number of young adults was expected to produce a substantial drop in the crime rate by the early 1980s. However, this prediction failed to take into account the fact that while the baby boom in general was coming to an end, the still high birthrate in the inner city, where much of the crime problem is concentrated, kept the crime rates from declining as anticipated. A drop in the number of ghetto youths is not expected until the late 1980s. Therefore, while crime rates may show minor decreases in the immediate future, it seems doubtful whether we can anticipate a major drop in crime rates until sometime in the next decade.

Fox predicts that by the 1990s the children of the baby boom generation will swell the ranks of the youthful population and produce another surge in violent crime. Also, as the baby boom generation moves out of the high-risk population for conventional crimes, Fox anticipates an increase in economic/white-collar crimes such as embezzlement, fraud, and computer theft (*Tampa Tribune,* 1983).

Urban Migration   A decline in the proportion of people living in small towns and rural areas, which have traditionally exhibited lower crime rates than the cities, together with a steady growth in urban populations have contributed to increases in crime. The anonymity which characterizes urban living helps foster criminal activity for a variety of reasons. There is not only greater tolerance for deviant behavior in the city, but also much less likelihood that the victims of crime will be able to recognize their assailants. In addition, cities provide a much greater range and number of targets for criminal opportunity. Thus, growth in the urban population affects the rates of reported crime.

Table E.1   **THE RISE IN DRUG USE IN THE UNITED STATES 1972–1982**

| | Percentage Who Have Ever Used the Drug | | | | | |
| | Youths aged 12–17 | | Young adults aged 18–25 | | Older adults aged 26 and older | |
Drug	1972	1982	1972	1982	1972	1982
Marijuana	14%	27%	48%	64%	7%	23%
Hallucinogens	5	7	17	21	1	6
Cocaine	2	5	9	28	2	9
Heroin	1	†	5	1	†	1
Stimulants**	4	7	12	18	3	6
Sedatives**	3	6	10	19	2	5
Tranquilizers	3	5	7	15	5	4
Alcohol	54*	65	82*	95	73*	88
Cigarettes	52*	50	69*	77	65*	79

†less than ½ of 1%
*Figures not available for 1972. Figures from 1974.
**Nonmedical use
Source: National Institute on Drug Abuse. *The National Household Survey on Drug Abuse.* Washington, D.C.: National Institute on Drug Abuse, 1983. Reproduced by permission of the National Institute on Drug Abuse.

Expansion of the Drug Consumer Population   Between 1972 and 1982, drug use among children (aged 12 to 17 years) and young adults (aged 18 to 25 years) increased at a rate that led to the use of such characterizations as "epidemic." Marijuana, cocaine, heroin, stimulants, sedatives, tranquilizers, and hallucinogenic substances like "angel dust" were consumed in increasing quantities and helped spawn a multibillion dollar illegal industry (Ubell, 1984). This rise in drug use in the United States was documented by the national household survey conducted by the National Institute on Drug Abuse (1983), as shown in Table E.1. Increases in drug consumption occurred in all three of the age groups sampled and in nearly every category of drug. Can this trend be halted?

An even more ominous development in the area of nonmedical drug use has been introduced during the past several years by the advent of so-called designer drugs (see box on page 556). Because of the increasing sophistication of "kitchen chemists," they are able to produce incredibly powerful drugs that do not require importation, are inexpensive to produce, and are beyond the reach of law enforcement agencies.

Changes in Business and Security Practices   Post–World War II changes in the pattern of retail business operations contributed significantly to increases in property crimes such as shoplifting and employee theft. Most retail stores had been accustomed to keeping merchandise in enclosed display cases, behind counters, and on shelves. Today, practically all retail merchandise is displayed on open counters. Moreover, the individually owned retail establishment has been replaced by the chain supermarket, department store, or discount house. Instead of an owner-manager, there is a salaried employee-manager; and there has been a drastic reduction in the number of salespersons. In some stores, the only salespeople one sees are behind the cash register.

Changes in security practices, interior design, and location have made some businesses much more vulnerable to crime victimization. For example, the rise in bank robberies during the past twenty years has been attributed to the proliferation of small, poorly protected branch banks in the suburbs—the kind that are sometimes referred to in banking circles as "mom and pop" banks. At present, there appears to be a reversal of this trend, especially in rapidly growing sections of the country such as the Sun Belt, where larger banking institutions are acquiring smaller banks through mergers and outright purchase.

Minority Group Frustration   Minority group frustration has also been identified as contributing to increases in crime during the 1960–1980 period. Minority group members have been led to believe by our culture that everyone has an equal opportunity to succeed. However, while this may have been the case for the immigrant in the early part of this century, today's educational requirements serve as impediments to employment at average- or above-average-paying jobs. Thus, for some people, crime has represented the only means possible to get a "piece of the action."

Changes in Routine Activities   Changes in the nature of our routine activities have also been linked to changing patterns of criminality. These changes affect our vulner-

"Designer Drugs"

Fentanyl, a synthetic narcotic, was imported to the United States in 1968, trademarked "Sublimaze," as a surgical anesthetic. Its usefulness is unquestionable—it has since become the surgical anesthetic of choice, now used in approximately 70% of major surgeries in this country. Over the last several years, fentanyl has appeared on the illicit drug market as a heroin substitute, and has been a central drug in the high-tech "Designer Drug" phenomenon.

The name "designer drug" was coined by Dr. Gary Henderson, Ph.D., of the University of California, Davis, School of Medicine. The term denotes those controlled drugs which have been chemically altered into legality without losing the original drug's major effects. Because the legal system requires the government to identify the exact chemical structure and name of each drug to be controlled, illicit chemists can simply design a chemical variation on the original so that the new drug, or analog, is taken beyond the immediate reach of the law. By the time the federal Drug Enforcement Administration has administratively controlled the analog, another analog has been designed.

Fentanyl, in recent years, has been widely distributed within California's heroin user community as high-grade "China White" heroin. Because it need not be imported and is relatively inexpensive to synthesize, in comparison with the production costs for heroin, stable supplies of fentanyl are more easily maintained, at lower cost and at a higher profit. Long-time organic (derived from the opium poppy) heroin users are said to be able to distinguish between organic heroin and the synthetic fentanyl substitute, and to prefer the original. Nevertheless, the market for fentanyl has flourished.

When law enforcement "heat" directed against China White sales began to threaten seriously the supplies and illicit profits, the suppliers simply went into analog production, giving birth to the designer drug era. Knowing they had a good thing going financially, chemists and suppliers of fentanyl decided they would rather switch than fight. Alpha-methyl fentanyl, 3-methyl fentanyl, and the possibility of synthesizing hundreds of different fentanyl analogs became realities. Law enforcement agencies are hamstrung, and it comes as no surprise that those involved in illicit drug supply and distribution networks are exploiting the situation.

The scare factor in using one of the fentanyls is that there is a wide variation in potency among the analogs, ranging to thousands of times more potent than morphine. An effective dose of the more potent fentanyls is measured in micrograms. Since an ordinary postage stamp weighs about 60,000 micrograms, the potential for overdose is readily apparent.

On the street, drug users are the guinea pigs. There are no quality controls, no standards, no procedures to remove contaminants. To date, over 57 deaths have been associated with fentanyl use, all but a few in California. Some of those who have died did so with the needle still stuck in their arms.

Source: From information supplied to the President's Commission on Organized Crime in Miami, Florida, by Robert J. Roberton, Chief of the Division of Drug Programs, Department of Alcohol and Drug Programs of the State of California, February 21, 1985.

ability to victimization. The risk of burglary has increased substantially as a result of a rise in the number of unattended households during this period. Several factors have contributed to an increase in the period of time that homes are left unattended. Increases in the number of women in the labor force and attending college have resulted in homes being left vacant during the day. Between 1960 and 1970, the number of daylight burglaries increased more than 300 percent (U.S. Department of Justice, 1971, 1976). Opportunities for both daytime and nighttime burglary rose during this period as a result of increases in the rates of out-of-town travel. There is no doubt that an increase in the amount of time in which houses and apartments are left unattended has produced a rise in the volume of residential burglary, regardless of the hour of the day or night.

Future Crime Trends

As we consider the potential impact of variables that may affect crime trends between the present and the end of the century, we might try to identify those factors which might lead to a decrease in certain categories of crime and those which could lead to either no substantial change or an increase in some types of criminal activity.

Decreasing Crime Rates   As business and industry move to counter the vulnerabilities created by changes in interior design, location, merchandising display, and security practices, we might anticipate a drop in larceny-theft statistics. Shoplifting and employee pilferage are especially responsive to crime control and prevention efforts. Also, growing sophistication in computer programming and monitoring can be expected to have considerable influence on such crimes as embezzlement and fraud which are closely linked to electronic data processing and computer operations.

Recently there has been a strong trend in our society to remove the criminal sanctions associated with certain types of antisocial behavior. Not too long ago, we began to reclassify certain types of behaviors that were previously dealt with by the criminal justice system. By default, as a consequence of the lack of any alternative programs and as an effort to use the law to enforce the morality of particular segments of society, both alcoholism and drug addition have come to be treated as mental health problems in recent years; and it seems rather probable that we will also change our approach to the handling of marijuana use. Currently, in most jurisdictions, marijuana is classified as a "controlled substance," which makes its users liable for criminal prosecution. There is some indication that, at the very least, marijuana use will be decriminalized in a variety of jurisdictions. At present, almost every state has reduced the simple possession of this drug to a misdemeanor and eleven states have adopted decriminalization legislation. There seems little doubt that decriminalization legislation will be passed in more states in the future.

Some experts believe that marijuana may well assume a status similar to that which alcohol and tobacco have at present. This new status is likely to be influenced by a variety of factors which include broader middle-class use paralleled by an increasing intolerance of its classification as a crime; scant evidence of any serious adverse effects; a recognition that our resources may be more effectively spent on efforts to control hard drugs which create more problems; a concern with improving public faith in and support for the criminal justice system; and finally, recognition that the extensive use of marijuana could represent a profitable source of public revenue. If marijuana assumes a regulated legal status, this may also reduce the number of users who experiment with harder drugs. That is, if marijuana is available under the same conditions as alcohol, users would not be forced to obtain their supplies from pushers who also sell harder drugs. There is no doubt that some marijuana users become hard drug users as a result of their associations with people selling a variety of drugs.

Another strong trend in our society is the removal of criminal sanctions from a variety of behaviors which have previously been regarded as sex crimes. This trend has been occasioned by a greater openness and greater tolerance for individual preferences in sexual activities. In effect, a substantial segment of the population has become increasingly unwilling to consider a variety of sexual behaviors as justification for the use of criminal sanctions simply because they are not consistent with orthodox Judeo-Christian morality. Thus, the trend is toward taking the position that acts between consenting adults in private should not be subject to criminal sanctions. In this regard, most states no longer have fornication laws and many do not have general statutes that outlaw "unnatural acts." Homosexual behavior between consenting adults in private will undoubtedly be included in this process of decriminalization.

There is also every likelihood that our greater tolerance of individual preferences in sexuality will result in a completely different approach to commercial sex. Once prostitution is taken out of the moral realm it is likely to be legalized and subjected to regulation. This trend may be further influenced by public health considerations relating to the control of venereal disease which is now reported to be skyrocketing, efforts to control teenage prostitution, and a desire in many large cities to reduce the public nuisance associated with open sexual solicitation. Regulation would also enable us to control those prostitutes who are in the business as a result of drug addiction. In recent years, we have also taken a far more liberalized view of pornography. This trend is likely to continue in the future with regulation being limited to pornography involving children and violence.

Gambling is another offense that is likely to achieve regulated status in the near future. New Jersey is currently experimenting with casino gambling and there are groups in New York and Florida that also want to increase the attraction of their hotels by opening casinos. Two factors that are likely to increase the acceptance of regulated gambling are an increasing lack of support for the maintenance of current gambling laws in order to support certain moral traditions, as well as a search for new sources of tax revenue. Plans are already available for state operated off-track betting, sports betting, and even a numbers operation. There is no doubt that as the moral support for gambling laws wanes, we will increasingly see state regulated gambling. We have already noted the close relationship between gambling and loansharking. It is quite possible that when gambling becomes a regulated industry this will adversely affect loansharking activities.

Increasing Crime Rates   On the debit side of the ledger we must note several factors that seem conducive to *increases* in future crime. Offsetting the declining birthrate, we are witnessing the continuing effects of illegal immigration on the composition of our urban population. The U.S. Immigration and Naturalization Service estimates that approximately 800,000 illegal immigrants enter the United States each year and are added to the populations of large cities. For example, Los Angeles has more than one million illegal immigrants living within its city limits. All available figures indicate that illegal aliens quickly become involved in narcotics trafficking, street gang activities, property theft, and organized crime.

Minority frustrations have contributed greatly to the crime problem over the past several decades and there are few grounds for optimism that the conditions which have produced these frustrations are susceptible to improvement in the near future. It is much more likely that educational requirements for jobs will increase as we move toward a more technologically oriented style of life, thus further narrowing the opportunities open to the poor for meaningful and rewarding employment.

There is every reason to believe that we will experience increases in the frequency and variety of female crimes. Although the increases in reported crime rates for women have been more dramatic than their absolute numbers would warrant, the social changes that are taking place within our society can scarcely fail to have an impact on the crime statistics in the future. Although they may be somewhat slower in coming than we have been led to expect, increases in female involvement in economic/white collar crimes would seem to be the inevitable consequence of expanded occupational and professional opportunities for women. But it seems likely that female crime will be registered primarily in the larceny-theft statistics. Crime trends, like the society whose characteristics they reflect, will continue to show the effects of male domination.

Several current trends suggest that in the future we will see the emergence of certain new offenses. Over the last decade we have seen a major change in the methods employed for recording and transmitting information. The use of the computer and electronic data communications equipment have replaced traditional communications and tangible record-keeping systems. Today all but the smallest businesses and government agencies employ computers to transfer, exchange, and keep records of money, securities, titles, and money substitutes such as credit cards, checking accounts, letters of credit, and money orders, and as a means for maintaining control of inventories. Criminals have also recognized the vast potential for employing this new technology to their own advantage. Computers and telecommunication systems have been manipulated for purposes of embezzling money, stealing cargo, concealing the theft of inventories, falsification, and insurance fraud.

Computers have also provided us with the capability to acquire and record substantial amounts of information about people. There is growing concern that this information may be misused. If controls are not instituted, we are likely to see the emergence of a new category of crime involving the dissemination, retention, or utilization of misinformation. This offense is likely to include the manipulation of information about medical histories, debt payments, educational training, delinquent and criminal histories, as well as the accumulation of dossiers of information in data banks from a variety of sources on individuals.

Technological advances in reproduction techniques have recently spawned another new area of crime. Xerox machines and other comparable copying devices have made it easy to make reproductions of books, manuscripts, journals, and, in fact, any kind of printed material, with obvious consequences for the whole publishing industry. This is an area that is extremely difficult, if not impossible, to control. Moreover, our reproduction capabilities are likely to increase in the future, making it even easier for people to reproduce materials without the permission of authors and publishers. At this point it is extremely difficult to say whether an illegal industry will evolve that competes with legitimate publishers by selling reproductions of original materials at lower prices. We already have a minor, though significant, criminal industry that illegally reproduces and markets records and tapes. More recently we have seen the development of an industry that provides illegally reproduced tapes of movies, television shows, and the like. With improved technology there is no doubt that the illicit reproduction industry will increase in the future.

Some criminologists have suggested that we will see in the future an increase in the perpetration of offenses for purely "recreational" purposes. Sykes (1978) observes that some people may engage in crime as a form of sport to relieve the boredom of a routinized and bureaucratic society. Currently, a segment of juvenile crime is motivated by efforts to find activities that are fun and adventuresome. There is every reason to believe that adults will also find these activities equally rewarding. If this does occur, we are likely to see increases in a broad spectrum of offenses ranging from vandalism to white-collar crimes. While this will probably involve property damage, there is no doubt that some injuries to persons will also occur. This type of crime will be very difficult to prevent because the people perpetrating it may have as their only objective the desire to overcome obstacles to the successful commission of the offense.

RESPONSE TO FUTURE CRIME

After careful consideration of the influence of various factors we have identified above on past and current rates of crime, we see little or no basis for anticipating any sudden rise or drop in crime rates within the foreseeable future. A major consideration in any attempt to forecast the reactions of the criminal justice system to future crime trends is public indignation toward the crime problem and current public demands for the criminal justice system to "do something" about crime and criminals. We see nothing on the horizon that supports any belief that such demands are likely to decrease, possibly until the end of the century or beyond.

Prediction, as John Conrad (1981) has observed, is a risky business, at best. Perhaps we can reduce some of the hazards by restricting the focus of our predictions to the three areas which, in our judgment, seem most sensitive to contemporary ideological influences: (1) official responses to the plight and rights of crime victims; (2) citizen and community involvement in crime prevention; and (3) the disposition of criminal offenders, that is, corrections.

The Victims of Crime

Crime victims can hardly be blamed for feeling that the American system of criminal justice has totally neglected them in what appears to be an exaggerated concern for the rights of offenders. Not only do victims suffer financial losses; they are often forced to pay for the treatment of their injuries, while the criminal receives free medical attention. Public funds take care of the prosecution, and if the criminal has no money, also pays for the defense. The victim usually has to handle the costs of the crime without public assistance. Victims may be threatened with reprisals by defendants who have been freed on bail or on their own recognizance. They can be intimidated by domineering defense attorneys and forced to take off valuable days from work in order to appear as witnesses in hearings that are postponed again and again. Rarely are they given any notification of scheduled court dates and no one bothers to keep them posted about the results of plea bargaining. Months may pass before they are able to recover stolen property which is being held as evidence.

The report of the President's Task Force on Victims of Crime (1983) made a series of proposals which, if implemented, could begin to redress these longstanding inequities. Recommendations range from training those who deal with victims to be more courteous and sensitive, to modifying the Exclusionary Rule and abolishing parole. The Task Force urges state and federal legislation to require that victim impact statements be presented to the court before sentencing, that victims and witnesses be protected from intimidation, and that victims of sexual assault not be compelled to pay for physical examinations and for the medical kits that are used to collect evidence.

The task force comes out strongly for federal funding for state victim compensation programs. "It is simply unfair that victims should have to liquidate their assets, mortgage their homes or sacrifice their health or education or that of their children while the offender escapes responsibility for the financial hardship he has imposed" (p. 79). Thirty-six states now have at least token funds for victims, but almost all are inadequately financed; some have too little money or state officials try to keep it a secret. Hospitals should be required to give emergency treatment to crime victims without regard to their ability to pay, then collect from state compensation funds, the task force recommends. It says judges should order offenders to make restitution to victims whenever possible, even when the offender is sent to prison, and then make sure payments are made. Judges also should give as much weight to the interests of victims as to defendants in ruling on continuances. There should be more referral and counseling services for victims, involving not only social agencies but the mental health community and ministry, the report says. Prosecutors should make sure victims are informed about the progress of the case. Victims should get police protection if necessary in instances of harassment.

The task force also makes several highly controversial proposals: that bail be denied to persons judged to be clearly dangerous; that parole be abolished (because it undercuts the courts and is unfair to victims and because parole boards lack accountability); and that the Exclusionary Rule regarding evidence be done away with ["It does not work, severely compromises the truth-finding process, imposes an intolerable burden on the system and prevents the court from doing justice" (p. 28)].

Finally, the task force proposes an amendment to the Constitution that would add the following to the Sixth Amendment: "The victim in every criminal prosecution shall have the right to be present and to be heard at all critical stages of judicial proceedings" (p. 114).

Serious objections are being raised to several of the recommendations that go beyond cosmetic changes in the way victims are treated. But it will take more than courtesy and sensitivity to correct the criminal justice system's excessive concern for offenders and its lack of fairness for the victims that society has failed to protect.

Concern for the crime victim within the criminal justice system and the agencies of local, state, and federal government has been paralleled by a revival of interest in crime victims among criminologists. Although contributions have been made by criminologists to what, as Edelhertz and Geis (1974) point out, has been "gracelessly dubbed" the field of *victimology*—the systematic study of criminal-victim relationships—over a period of more than two centuries, the crime victim has never occupied a position of prominence in the field of criminology. Recently, attention has been directed toward various groups within our society that are especially prone to victimization by criminal offenders (e.g., the elderly, children, and the poor).

Citizen and Community Involvement in Crime Prevention

Among the adverse consequences of the persisting serious crime problem is the encouragement it offers toward the development of a fortress or siege mentality among our citizens. There is an understandable yearning on the part of many people to dig a hole and pull it in after them. The traditional maxim that a person's home is his or her castle is no longer a mere figure of speech: all that is lacking these days in a growing number of residences is a moat, drawbridge, and portcullis. But unless people are prepared to take refuge for the rest of their days in a concrete bunker or steel vault, there are rapidly diminishing returns to an investment in even the most sophisticated alarm equipment and security hardware.

One alternative to the siege mentality is to study the martial arts and invest in firearms. It has been estimated that Americans already own enough weapons—handguns, rifles, shotguns—to arm every man, woman, and child in the country. Feelings of impatience toward the glacial pace of criminal justice, lack of confidence in the ability of police to provide protection, and rising anger toward criminals provide indications that people in high-crime areas are becoming increasingly aggressive in their efforts to cope with crime in their communities. Unfortunately, as the 1984 case of Bernhard Goetz, the "Subway Vigilante," demonstrates, this form of structured action against violence is a form of treatment that is as severe as the condition it seeks to cure.

There is another kind of structured action against violence that may prove to be a more satisfactory alternative to violence—one that may both help to reduce the risk of further violence and improve the prospects of lowering the crime rate in the future. This is the approach to crime prevention and control that calls for increased citizen involvement at the group and community levels in cooperation with the agencies and personnel of the criminal justice system.

Modern crime prevention concepts were not formally adopted in the United States until the 1960s, when the National Crime Prevention Institute was founded with joint funding from the U.S. Department of Justice, the Law Enforcement Assistance Administration, the Kentucky Crime Commission, and the University of Louisville. Since that time, other crime prevention centers have been established, and many police departments now have units created specifically to address the issues of crime prevention and to set up liaisons with citizen groups.

Citizen involvement in crime prevention is not only desirable, but also necessary. Citizen efforts should be aimed at the infrastructure of crime—toward problems such as unemployment, poor education, and lack of recreational activities.

Citizens can take many actions to supplement and strengthen the various components of the criminal justice system. For example, they can institute neighborhood security activities, citizen patrols, and crime reporting programs. They can work with the courts as volunteers in probation, as court watchers (monitoring the performances of judges and prosecutors), as volunteers in intervention programs to divert defendants from the criminal justice system at a point between arrest and trial (thus reducing case loads), and as volunteer counselors for delinquent youths and their parents. In corrections, citizens can volunteer medical and legal aid to inmates; inspect and survey jails, prisons, and juvenile institutions; counsel and listen to inmates and serve as intermediaries between them and their families; and provide job training programs for inmates (through business associations).

Until recently, law enforcement and criminal justice efforts to mobilize citizen participation in crime prevention programs have met with apathy and disinterest. Whisenand (1977) tells of the California police departments that rented the Los Angeles Coliseum in anticipation of the vast crowds they expected to turn out in response to a carefully designed and widely advertised crime prevention program they were sponsoring. A total of 300 people showed up. It is this sort of reaction that led two law enforcement officials to refer to citizen involvement in criminal justice as a "crumbling cornerstone" (Heinrich and Appel, 1980). But crime prevention may be an idea whose time has finally come.

The Future of Corrections

The crisis facing corrections in the 1980s is a result of both internal and external forces that will continue to have an impact for at least the remainder of this decade. Prison populations will continue to grow because of longer prison sentences and an increase in the number of offenders sentenced to institutions. Recent changes in sentencing practices and laws including mandatory prison terms for violent crimes (43 states have such laws), habitual offender laws (in effect in 30 states), and determinate/presumptive sentencing (in effect in 26 states) have resulted in longer prison terms. In the immediate future there is little likelihood of a change in sentencing practices to reduce prison terms and, in fact, if public outrage with criminals continues, there is every likelihood that legislatures will change sentencing statutes to impose even longer prison terms.

Growth in the number of males in the prison-prone age group, 20- to 29-year-olds, as a consequence of the steady maturing of the baby boom generation is another factor that has accounted for the recent increase in prison populations. Given that this age group has not yet peaked, even if we continue to incarcerate these offenders at current rates, the continued growth of this group will drive the prison population upward during the 1980s. As we noted earlier, there appears to be few prospects for any substantial decrease in this population before the 1990s. This situation is likely to be further aggravated by the increasing severity of sentences delivered by judges in response to growing pressure for toughness in handling criminals, as well as legislatures responding to similar pressures by changing the sentencing structure to require longer sentences for certain offenses. The net effect will be the growth of prison populations through the 1990s and into the twenty-first century.

The prison system will continue to be subject to close scrutiny by the courts to insure compliance with Eighth Amendment protections against cruel and unusual punishment. At this point, due to the record growth of prison populations during the late 1970s, most states are under some court order or involved in litigation as a consequence of existing unconstitutional conditions in their prison systems. As of February 1983:

> The courts had declared unconstitutional the entire prison systems of Alabama, Florida, Mississippi, Oklahoma, Rhode Island, Tennessee, Texas, and all male penal facilities in Michigan.
>
> One or more facilities in 21 states was operating under a court order or consent decree as a result of inmate crowding and/or the conditions of confinement.
>
> Seven states were involved in litigation relating to crowding and/or the conditions of release.
>
> In eight states courts had appointed receivers or masters to operate the corrections system or facilities, had ordered emergency release of inmates as a result of crowding, or had ordered the closing of specific institutions. (U.S. Department of Justice, 1983, p. 80).

In order to meet court mandated changes as of July 1983, it was estimated that prison building projects totalling nearly two billion dollars were currently in progress in at least 39 states (Bureau of Justice Statistics, October 1983). While this new construction may well meet current conditions of overcrowding, it is doubtful whether these new facilities will be able to handle the constantly increasing prison population. It seems probable that, at least throughout the 1980s, facilities will be built as the need arises or as courts require; thus, overcrowding is a problem that may persist during this period.

Another major problem that is facing the criminal justice system in general and which has a major impact on our corrections system involves the justifications advanced for punishing offenders. These rationales, which include rehabilitation, deterrence, incapacitation, and retribution, have been used not only to justify certain types of sentences but have also come to be viewed as the objectives of the corrections system. The inability of the corrections system to achieve most of these objectives has caused people to term the system a failure. Earlier we suggested that corrections is in no position to rehabilitate offenders because our knowledge of the cause of criminal behavior as well as the appropriate types of treatment is simply not sufficient to accomplish this objective. Second, as Conrad (1982) notes, no one has provided conclusive proof that punishing criminals has any material effect on the number of crimes committed. Criminals, like many others in our society, play the odds which, unfortunately, at this point are in their favor. For people who are inclined to commit crimes, chances are that they will get away with it even if they are unfortunate enough to be arrested. Punishment for purposes of incapacitation, even on a selective basis, involves technical as well as legal problems. The errors associated with existing prediction models are far beyond the limits of either justice or cost effectiveness. Selective incapacitation assumes that we have the ability to predict with reasonable accuracy people who will engage in further criminal activity. Unfortunately, if we were to use existing instruments as a means of selectively incapacitating serious offenders, we would be unnecessarily incarcerating over 50 percent of those who were selected. Not only would a policy of this kind raise legal as well as moral questions, but it could conceivably double and triple prison populations, resulting in construction and maintenance costs that would no doubt cause tax revolts in many states (Blackmore and Welsh, 1983).

Clearly, the criminal justice system is not in a position to achieve the objectives of rehabilitation, deterrence, and incapacitation, which leaves us with the goal of retribution. While some people may deplore the idea of retribution as the appropriate goal of the criminal justice process, we would like to suggest some reasons for accepting this view. For centuries, we have responded to crime by subjecting the offender to some form of sanction because this conveys the idea that people who commit crime must pay for their actions. It is further believed that in order to insure the integrity of the law, sanctions must not only exist but also be applied. At this point, consequences set limits on what may or may not be done in our society. It is argued that if laws lack sanctions there is no reason for law-abiding citizens to obey the law because they see that those who violate these rules are not punished. In fact, the current pressure on the criminal justice system to a large extent results from public perceptions that not only are we failing to apprehend enough offenders but also that those who are apprehended are not punished severely enough. Since the 1970s, public opinion polls have regularly reported that more than three-quarters of our citizens think the courts are not dealing harshly enough with criminals (Flanagan and McLeod, 1983). It is obvious the public believes that whatever else the courts are doing they are not imposing harsh enough sentences on convicted felons. These same polls indicate that two-thirds of the public favor the death penalty for persons convicted of murder and more than one-third favor it for those convicted of rape. This suggests public support for retribution as a primary objective of the criminal justice process.

Second, retribution provides an objective that the criminal justice system can accomplish. That is, the purpose of the criminal justice system will be to "administer the consequences of law violations" (Conrad, 1981). It is further expected that these consequences will be graded according to society's perception of the seriousness of crimes which, of course, will change from generation to generation. If we adopt this position, the criminal justice process—and specifically the corrections system—will no longer be held responsible for "reforming offenders so that they will commit no further offenses." This goal is impossible to attain because we lack the means to change the behavior of all offenders. In addition, it would require some basic social changes which are beyond the purview of the criminal justice system. While it is reasonable to expect that the criminal justice system can punish those who fail to abide by society's legal standards, it is unreasonable to expect that the criminal justice process can deal with the multiplicity of problems faced by society's "losers" who end up as clients of the system.

Finally, by accepting retribution as the objective of the criminal justice process and by following the model of sentencing in which proportionality is observed, we are also able to realize the objectives of incapacitation and deterrence without making them explicit (Conrad, 1981). A ten-year sentence for armed robbery will not only incapacitate an offender for this period of time, but it will also announce to the public that robbery is something that is not acceptable. Moreover, this position permits us temporarily to restrain offenders and thereby prevent them from committing crimes for a certain period of time without having to deal with the many problems associated with predicting future criminality.

In discussing the future of corrections, Conrad (1981a, 1983) identifies several trends, some of which are reversible, but which, if they continue, will produce even more unmanageable prison conditions than those of today. First, maximum security prisons which currently contain a substantial proportion of violent men will become more dangerous as this proportion grows and as we begin to feel the impact of the longer sentences served by these offenders. Current levels of violence involve not only assaults by prisoners upon prisoners, which in recent years has become more common, but also assaults by prisoners on their keepers which in the past was a rare occurrence, but will increase as the proportion of violent offenders grows. Reformers have argued that prisons should be used exclusively for violent offenders and in many institutions today we are approaching that aim; there is little doubt that if this trend continues most states will have at least one institution that exclusively houses violent offenders. Heavily urban states may have more than one prison of this kind. The only problem is that our old techniques of prison management are not adequate to deal with these kinds of institutions.

Second, while the courts will require that states provide funds for new prisons to house the growing prison population, there is no requirement that these institutions provide any kind of programming. Legislatures are under pressure from the public to reduce taxes, and thus they are not likely to be generous in authorizing funds for new prison programs and enlarged staffs to operate them. Prisons may well have to continue to cope with a predominantly idle population, hoping that a combination of television, a liberal visiting program, weightlifting, and lots of yard time will keep our captives peaceful. While to some members of the public this may seem more than the average prisoner deserves, it makes the very difficult task of controlling a violent population nearly impossible. Moreover, it is an almost foolproof prescription for failure when these offenders are released.

Third, economic pressures and changes in technology will increasingly reduce the need for unskilled labor in our society. This, along with opposition by employers and labor, will provide few incentives for businesses to open plants within our prison walls. Thus, there is little hope that privately operated prison industries will decrease the idleness in our prisons.

Fourth, not only will staff be difficult to recruit, but it will also be hard to retrain existing staff to deal with increasing levels of violence in a lawful manner. Demands by guard unions for procedures that protect correctional personnel, especially line officers, are being placed ahead of all other considerations in the negotiation of work rules. These demands are often translated into less contact between line officers and inmates. Unfortunately, a strategy of this kind not only fails to reduce danger but will actually increase it because it limits the opportunity for the types of contacts that are necessary to gather from inmates information that is vital to the development of an effective control strategy.

Fifth, more drugs will be brought into the prisons as the outside population becomes more tolerant of recreational drug use. Although some may argue convincingly for less restrictions on the use of drugs in the free community, drugs in the prison present major control problems because of their distribution through the prison economic system, which is dominated by internal gangs. Consequently, the increased use of drugs will increase the dominance of existing gangs and will probably result in the formation of new groups or gangs in institutions where heretofore they have not existed. Economic incentives and lack of control will provide unscrupulous correctional personnel with the motivation to collaborate with prison gangs for the purpose of bringing drugs and other contraband into the prison. Occasionally, corrupt personnel will be caught and subjected to severe punishment to deter others; but low salaries, high monetary rewards, and a network of cooperating personnel will override any risk of apprehension. In fact, it is quite possible that if old, established personnel are found to be trafficking in contraband, they will not be punished at all and their behavior may well be excused by the "good ole boy" network resulting from personal problems and/or economic pressure.

The future picture of our corrections system, if we continue to drift without making any policy changes, is indeed grim. Gangs and violent cliques will increasingly dominate not only the inmate world but the inside of the prison as well, while staff will control the perimeter. Murders, suicides, and riots such as the one that occurred in New Mexico will occur much more regularly and the prison will become a barren and hopeless warehouse for society's losers. Fortunately, this grim picture is alterable. While we recognize and agree with the idea that correctional policy should follow public demands that criminals be punished, we believe that punishment should be carried out in a civilized manner with strict limits placed on the conditions under which the offender is restrained. In this context, punishment comes to be defined as the restraint of the offender under humane conditions. In the course of several papers, Conrad (1977, 1980, 1981) and Dinitz (1980) have offered a prescription for the achievement of this objective. They argue that prisons must be lawful, safe, industrious, and provide the offender with reasonable care and personal dignity.

Prisons must provide inmates with decent and clean housing, sufficient clothing, adequate diets, and medical care that is designed to meet routine and emergency care needs. In addition, the maintenance and enhancement of personal dignity is also an important feature in assisting offenders to become conventional members of society. Inmates typically come from areas of our cities where self-respect is hard to come by and more likely than not have had numerous experiences with government agents, such as unemployment personnel, where they have been treated without any concern for their personal dignity. The inmate's sense of worth has been further damaged by the degradations of confinement. It should be the responsibility of staff members to restore and enhance the inmate's self-worth rather than damage it further. This requires careful staff screening and training. All too often correctional officers have felt the need to humiliate and denigrate offenders in order to deal with their own problems of status inadequacy. Where possible, these correctional officers must be trained to deal with their problems or be removed from direct contact with inmates. Adequate selection and training procedures will handle this situation with respect to new recruits. Inmates must also recognize that they share some responsibility in ensuring the maintenance of self-respect and interactions within the prisons.

While it is convenient for the community to blame the crime problem on those who perpetrate these offenses and on the criminal justice system that is responsible for the control and prevention of this problem, this type of deception will do little to ameliorate the problem. The only hope that we have of reducing the crime problem is to provide inmates with an environment in which they come to recognize that there are alternatives to a life of crime. Inhumane prisons and rejection of inmates upon release is a sure formula for failure. On the other hand, prisons that are lawful, safe, industrious, hopeful, and assure the inmate's personal dignity have a good chance of releasing offenders who will at least make an effort toward becoming conventional members of society.

REFERENCES

Allen, H. E., and Latessa, E. J. Corrections in America: 2000 AD. *Journal of Contemporary Criminal Justice* 1 (1980): 1–3.

Blackmore, J., and Welsh, J. Selective incapacitation: Sentencing according to risk. *Crime and Delinquency* 29 (1983): 504–528.

Conrad, J. P. Ending the drift and returning to duty: Two scenarios for the future of corrections. Paper presented at the Annual Meeting of the Congress of Corrections, Miami Beach, Florida, August 17, 1981(*a*).

———. It is very hard to predict, especially the future. In. D. Ward, and K. Schoen (eds.), *Confinement in Maximum Custody: New Last Resort Prisons in the United States and Western Europe.* Lexington, MA: Lexington Books, 1981(*b*).

———. *Justice and Consequences.* Lexington, MA: Lexington Books, 1981(*c*).

———. Can corrections be rehabilitated? *Federal Probation* 46 (1982): 3–8.

———. The hard lessons of the grim past. Paper presented at the Annual Meeting of the American Society of Criminology, Denver, Colorado, November 9–12, 1983.

Dinitz, S. Are safe and humane prisons possible? The John Vincent Barry Memorial Lecture, University of Melbourne, Australia, October 8, 1980.

Flanagan, T. J., and McLeod, M. (eds.), *Sourcebook of Criminal Justice Statistics 1982.* Washington, D.C.: U.S. Government Printing Office, 1983.

Heinrich, W. C., and Appel, S. W. Citizen involvement in criminal justice—A crumbling cornerstone. *FBI Law Enforcement Bulletin* 49 (1980): 17–19.

National Institute on Drug Abuse. *The National Household Survey on Drug Abuse, 1982.* Washington, D.C.: National Institute on Drug Abuse, 1982.

President's Task Force on Victims of Crime. *Final Report, December 1982.* Washington, D.C.: U.S. Government Printing Office, 1983.

Ubell, E. How you can help turn off the drug abuse. *Parade,* March 4, 1984, pp. 13–15.

U.S. Department of Justice, Federal Bureau of Investigation. *Uniform Crime Reports—1970.* Washington, D.C.: U.S. Government Printing Office, 1971.

———. *Uniform Crime Reports—1975.* Washington, D.C.: U.S. Government Printing Office, 1976.

U.S. Department of Justice, Bureau of Justice Statistics. *Report to the Nation on Crime and Justice: The Data.* Washington, D.C.: U.S. Government Printing Office, 1983.

Whisenand, P. M. *Crime Prevention.* Boston, MA: Holbrook, 1977.

GLOSSARY

Actus reus The conduct that constitutes a specific crime.

Addictive drinker A person distinguished as a "true alcoholic" from the problem drinker by the loss of control over drinking, the appearance of blackouts, solitary drinking, and the tendency to drink until he or she passes out.

Adversary system A system of criminal justice characterized by the testing of propositions by argument and proof.

Aggravated assault Unlawful attack by one person upon another for the purpose of inflicting severe or aggravated bodily injury.

Agri-crime (agricultural crime) Designation for crimes that occur in a rural, agricultural setting, including thefts of farm equipment, livestock, and chemical products such as fertilizer and pesticides.

Anomie A state of normlessness in society which may be caused by decreased homogeneity and is conducive to crime and other deviant behavior.

Appellate court A court that reviews cases that have been tried in a trial court. Except in special cases in which original jurisdiction is conferred, an appellate court is not a trial court or a court of first instance.

Arraignment The event that formally initiates the trial process. The first official occasion in which the accused is given an opportunity to establish his or her identity and enter a plea in response to the accusation. Arraignment takes place in the court in which the case is to be tried.

Array (veniremen) The whole body of potential jurors summoned to court as they are arranged or ranked on the panel.

Arrest The taking of a person into legal custody for the purpose of holding or detaining him or her to answer to a court of law for an offense with which he or she has been charged.

Arson The willful and malicious setting of fires.

Assigned counsel system System in which members of the local bar association are appointed to serve as counsel for indigent defendants for little or no compensation.

Atavism   From the Latin *atavus,* meaning "ancestor." Term that implies certain "born criminals" are an evolutionary throwback to an earlier, more primitive human form.

Bail   A system of posting a bond to ensure a defendant will appear at trial, while allowing him or her to remain free until that time.

Bailiff   An officer of the court whose principal duty is to maintain the security and decorum of the court. The bailiff is responsible for keeping an eye on defendants delivered to the court and for assuring the legality of actions involving witnesses and jurors. He or she summons witnesses when it is their turn to testify, and sees that witnesses and jurors do not discuss cases when they are so restricted. The bailiff is also responsible for maintaining the secrecy of jury deliberations and for arranging for food and lodging for the jury.

Behavior modification   The systematic application of learning principles to the change, reduction, or elimination of targeted behavior.

Bill of particulars   A form of discovery in which the prosecution sets forth the place, manner, and means of the commission of the crime as alleged in the complaint or indictment.

Biographical reconstruction (retrospective reinterpretation)   After an individual has been labeled a deviant, his or her past actions are reexamined for purposes of showing that the individual was deviant before being labeled.

Birth cohort analysis   Research that, over a period of time, examines a group consisting of all individuals born in a given year.

Buffer   A person who occupies this role position in a syndicated La Cosa Nostra (LCN) crime family operates as an administrative assistant to the *capo* (boss) and may act, as circumstances require, in the capacity of messenger, driver, bodyguard, or go-between in various transactions.

Burglary   Unlawful entry of a structure to commit a felony or theft.

Call girl   A top-ranked prostitute who commands the highest prices for dispensing sexual favors; so called because she screens her clientele by means of a telephone referral service.

***Capo* (boss)**   Highest ranking figure in an LCN syndicated crime family.

Cartographic school   An approach to criminological explanation which examined population data to determine the influence of social conditions and geographical factors such as climate, location, and topography on criminal behavior.

Case load   The number of cases being defended or prosecuted by an attorney at a given time.

Case study   Intensive, detailed analysis of a single individual, using life-history data, social background information, and other relevant sources of data.

Certiorari   Latin for "to be informed of, to be made certain in regard to." *Certiorari* is a writ of review or inquiry directed by a superior court to an inferior court, asking that the record of the case be sent up for review. This method of obtaining a review of a case is used by the U.S. Supreme Court.

Challenge for cause   An attempt by the prosecutor or defense counsel to exclude a prospective juror during the *voir dire* examination by pointing out to the court why the person in question is unfit to serve or would not be impartial.

Change of venue   Moving a trial to a jurisdiction other than the one in which the crime was committed to guarantee a fair trial for the accused.

Chicago Area Projects   Continuing programs developed in the 1930s in high delinquency areas of the city aimed at mobilizing residents of those communities to take constructive action toward reducing or eliminating causes of delinquent behavior.

Chop shop   Garages that strip stolen cars of usable parts for sale to auto repair shops.

Circumstantial evidence   All evidence of an indirect nature; circumstances from which the court or jury may infer a principal fact in a case.

Clearance rate   Solution rate (percent) of crimes reported to the police.

Clearing the books Efforts by police to improve clearance rates by getting people already charged with a crime to confess to other crimes they have not committed.

Collateral attack A challenge against the legality of confinement as opposed to an appeal based on the merits of the conviction. A writ of federal habeas corpus is the principal method used by state prisoners seeking review of their convictions.

Combination facility A facility that houses pretrial detainees and some convicted persons, usually misdemeanants; the most common type of jail.

Common law The body of legal fact and theory that developed in England over a period of centuries and became uniform throughout the country as judges followed precedents (previous court decisions) in handling new, but similar, cases. Distinguished from *code law,* which seeks to lay down legal principles in the form of statutes.

Common-law rule (on use of deadly force) Policy by which police officers are allowed to use deadly force to apprehend someone reasonably believed to have committed a felony.

Compensation Action taken by the state to restore some or all of the losses sustained by a crime victim.

Competency In the law of evidence, the presence of those characteristics that render a witness legally fit and qualified to give testimony.

Complaint A charge stated before a magistrate of jurisdiction that a person named has committed a specified criminal offense.

Composition The sum of money paid by the aggressor to the victim (or the victim's family if the victim dies) as satisfaction for wrong or personal injury.

Consensual crime Illegal acts in which the parties willingly participate in a transaction involving the sale or gift of desired goods or services (e.g., gambling or prostitution).

Consigliere **(counselor)** Figure in a syndicated LCN crime family who functions as an elder statesman and provides advice and counsel to the *capo* (boss).

Contingency-management program Treatment in which desirable behavior is reinforced by reward.

Contraband Anything possessed by an inmate in violation of institutional rules and regulations.

Contract parole (mutual agreement programming) System in which the parole board, correctional department, and inmate agree to a three-way contract in which the prisoner assumes responsibility for his or her own rehabilitation program, with the goal of obtaining parole release on a specific date.

Count A method of accounting for all prisoners to be sure that none has escaped, usually conducted on a regular basis.

Court of first instance A court to which a case must originally be brought; usually a trial court.

Court of general jurisdiction The largest jurisdiction a court of first instance can have in a given political unit (i.e., state, federal, district, circuit, county).

Court of intermediate appeal A court of appeals established in several states to lessen the workload of the highest reviewing tribunal. Ultimate review can still be held in the highest court by that court's permission or, in limited cases, as a matter of right.

Court of last resort A court from which there is no appeal to a higher court in the same jurisdiction.

Court of record A court that is required to keep a record of its proceedings and that has the authority to fine or imprison convicted offenders.

Crime data manipulation Falsification of crime data submitted to the FBI *Uniform Crime Reports* by state and local police.

Crime Index The FBI, in its annual *Uniform Crime Reports,* uses eight categories of crime (murder and nonnegligent manslaughter, forcible rape, robbery, aggravated assault, arson, burglary, larceny-theft, and motor vehicle theft) to measure trends and distribution of criminality in the United States.

Crime rate Number of Index crimes committed per 100,000 inhabitants.

Crimes of cupidity Term used by criminologist Willem A. Bonger to refer to crimes committed in a capitalist country that are motivated by a desire for wealth and luxury.

Crimes of vengeance Bonger's term for crimes in capitalist society generated by an economic system characterized by strife and competition.

Criminal enterprise A group of offenders organized to provide illegal goods or services (e.g., illicit drugs) on a regular basis.

Criminal homicide The willful, nonnegligent killing of one human being by another.

Criminalistics A branch of forensic science that deals with the study of physical evidence related to crime.

Criminal justice system The complex of institutions and agencies responsible for controlling crime. The system includes the police, the prosecution, the courts, and corrections.

Criminal personality A hypothetical constellation or cluster of traits and characteristics that distinguishes criminals from noncriminals.

Crisis intervention Techniques for the management of interpersonal conflict and the resolution of hostility and potential violence.

Cross-examination The questioning of a witness in a trial or deposition by the party opposed to the one that produced the witness.

Defendant A person charged with a crime.

Defense attorneys Attorneys retained or appointed to defend individuals charged with committing criminal offenses.

Delinquent A juvenile who violates the criminal law or commits a status offense.

Determinate sentence A fixed term of imprisonment set by the legislature; the offender is required to serve the entire sentence, with no possibility of parole.

Deterrence A justification for punishment based on the idea that crime can be discouraged or prevented by instilling in potential criminals a fear of punishing consequences. Punished offenders, it is hoped, will serve as examples to deter potential criminals from antisocial conduct.

Direct examination The first interrogation or examination of a witness by the party for whose benefit he or she is summoned.

Directed verdict An instruction by the judge to the jury to return a specific verdict.

Direct evidence Proof of facts by witnesses who witnessed acts or heard words spoken, as distinct from circumstantial evidence.

District attorney, state attorney Common titles for the position of prosecutor.

Diversion The removal of an offender from the criminal justice system by channeling him or her into a social casework, mental health, or other type of agency. The term has also been used to describe the handling of juveniles in a system separate from the adult criminal justice system and the sentencing of offenders to community-based correctional facilities rather than to prison.

Due process The legal concept which summarizes the many and diverse protections guaranteed an accused person by the U.S. Constitution and state constitutions. Due process insures that every person will receive the benefits of general law. Due process is codified in the Fourteenth Amendment to the U.S. Constitution, which provides that no state shall "deprive any person of life, liberty, or property without due process of law."

Economic crime Illegal acts committed by nonphysical means and by concealment or guile to obtain money or property, to avoid the payment or loss of money or property, or to obtain business or personal advantage (see also white-collar crime).

Electronic data processing (EDP) crimes Crimes in which the computer is used in perpetrating the offense (e.g., embezzlement) or those which involve the theft of computer time, services, or confidential data.

Electroencephalograph (EEG) An instrument that picks up electrical activity in brain cells by electrodes attached to the scalp. Activity is recorded in oscillating patterns called brain waves by a machine connected to the electrodes. The visual recording that results is called an electroencephalogram.

En banc **decision** Judicial decision rendered by the whole court with all members sitting as a body.

Epilepsy A group of nervous disorders characterized by recurring attacks of motor, sensory, or psychic disturbances, sometimes accompanied by convulsive movements and loss of consciousness.

Ethnic succession A concept asserting that each group of immigrants to the United States used organized (syndicated) crime to acquire wealth and power before gaining a foothold in legitimate business.

Exclusionary rule A rule which prohibits the admission in a court of law of any evidence obtained in violation of the constitutional rights of the accused.

Expert witness A person who testifies in relation to some scientific, technical, or professional matter (i.e., persons qualified to speak authoritatively by reason of their special training, skill, or familiarity with a subject).

FBI *Uniform Crime Reports* Annual reports distributed by the FBI and based upon crime data provided by state and local police.

Felony A criminal offense punishable by death or by incarceration in a state prison for one year or longer.

Felony-murder doctrine An accidental killing committed while perpetrating a felony which may make that killing a murder.

Fence A criminal receiver of stolen goods.

Field training officer A senior patrol officer selected to "break in" rookie officers. Also known as a "coach."

Follow-up (latent) investigation The portion of an investigation following the preliminary investigation.

Forcible rape The carnal knowledge of a person, forcibly and against her or his will.

Forensic science That part of science applied to answering legal questions.

Frisks Individual "pat searches" of inmates in which officers run their hands along the outside of the inmate's clothing to detect concealed contraband.

Fugue A pathological amnesic condition during which an individual is apparently conscious of his or her actions; upon a return to normal, however, the sufferer has no recollection of those actions.

Furlough Temporary leave of absence given to an inmate housed in an institution; usually consists of a brief visit to the home or the community.

Galvanic skin response (GSR) The GSR is a component of the polygraph, or "lie detector," apparatus. The apparatus measures minute changes in electropotential on the surface of the skin to provide an index of emotional responses such as anxiety.

Good samaritan doctrine The concept that a person who sees another person in imminent and serious peril through the negligence of another cannot be charged with contributory negligence (as a matter of law) by risking his or her own life or serious injury in attempting to effect a rescue (provided the attempt is not recklessly or rashly made).

Grand jury A jury of inquiry whose duties are to receive complaints in criminal cases, to hear the evidence produced by the state, and to indict in situations where a trial is warranted.

Great Law of Pennsylvania Law enacted in 1682 that largely eliminated the use of stocks, pillories, branding irons, and gallows.

Habeas corpus   Latin for "you have the body." A writ of habeas corpus orders a person who is holding another person in confinement to produce the person being detained.

Hacks (or screws)   Derogatory terms used by inmates to refer to correctional officers.

Halfway house   A community correctional facility that provides a residence for convicted offenders who do not require the secure custody of a prison; also a transitional setting for prisoners being released from a correctional institution.

Hearsay   Secondhand evidence of which the witness lacks personal knowledge; the witness merely repeats something that someone else said.

Impeachment of witness   An attack on the credibility of a witness by the testimony of other witnesses.

Incapacitation   A theory of punishment and a goal of sentencing, generally implemented by imprisoning an offender to prevent him or her from committing further crimes.

Indecent exposure   Expressed impulse to expose the male genitals to an unsuspecting female as a final form of sexual gratification.

Indeterminate sentence   An indefinite sentence of "not less than" and "not more than" a certain number of years. The exact term to be served is determined by parole authorities within the minimum and maximum limits set by the court or by statute.

Indictment   An accusation in writing found and presented by a grand jury, charging that a person named therein has committed some act or has been guilty of some omission which, by law, is a crime.

Indigent   A person who cannot afford legal counsel.

Inferior court   In the federal system, all courts created under Article III, Section 1, of the U.S. Constitution, except the U.S. Supreme Court; in the state systems, all courts of limited original jurisdiction.

Information   An accusation against a person for an alleged criminal offense. An information differs from an indictment in that it is presented by a competent public officer rather than by a grand jury.

Initial appearance   Suspects must be brought before a judge within a reasonable period of time following arrest and given formal notice of charges against them, informed of their right to counsel, and provided with an attorney if they are too poor to hire one.

Intensive supervision   Program which supplements traditional probation and provides for close surveillance of offenders within the community; participants are restricted in their movements and activities, and are subject to unannounced visits from surveillance officers at any hour of the day or night.

Inventory shrinkage   A term which is widely used in business and industrial security circles to refer to losses incurred by employee theft.

Jurisdiction   The lawful right to exercise official authority, whether executive, judicial, or legislative; for police, it refers to the geographical boundaries of power; for courts, it refers to the power to hear and decide cases.

Juvenile   A person subject to the jurisdiction of the juvenile court based on an age limit imposed by statute. Jurisdiction is based on the age of the juvenile at the time the misconduct occurred; thus, a person 20 years of age would be tried in a juvenile court for a crime committed when he or she was 17 years old.

La Cosa Nostra ("this thing of ours")   This term, which originated in the revelations of a syndicated crime figure named Joe Valachi, refers to Italian-Sicilian dominated organized crime families; it is used in the abbreviation LCN by the Department of Justice as a convenient shorthand expression for any Italian crime syndicate.

Larceny   Theft of property without force or fear.

Leading question   A question that suggests to the witness the desired answer. Leading questions are prohibited in direct examination.

Legal aid Legal assistance paid for by the state and made available at little or no cost to defendants unable to afford an attorney.

Legal malpractice Civil action taken against an attorney, usually for some serious failure in the attorney-client relationship (e.g., dishonesty, incompetence, or other acts of misconduct).

Lex talionis (**"talion law"**) The "law of equivalent retaliation," which asserts that an injured party is entitled to no more than "an eye for an eye." The aggrieved party is entitled to appropriate retaliation in kind or measure.

Lotteries Contests in which tokens are distributed or sold, the winning token or tokens being secretly predetermined or ultimately selected in a chance drawing.

Mala in se Latin for "evil in itself." Refers to crimes that are considered intrinsically wrong, regardless of existing legal sanctions (e.g., murder, rape, robbery).

Mala prohibita Refers to acts that are wrong because they are prohibited by law (i.e., declared wrong by legislative action); examples would include traffic violations and sale of liquor on Sunday.

Mandatory sentence Fixed prison term set by legislature for particular crimes; sentence *must* be carried out by judge, with no range of discretion.

Master fence A top-ranking fence who operates as a broker or arranger for the sale and distribution of expensive stolen merchandise.

Material evidence Evidence that is relevant and bears upon the substantial issues in dispute.

Maxi-maxi prisons Facilities characterized by high perimeter security, high internal security, and operating regulations that curtail movement and maximize control; inmates include persistent property offenders, troublesome inmates, and individuals considered to be dangerous because of the nature of their offenses.

Maximum-security prisons Facilities geared to the fullest possible supervision, control, and surveillance of inmates; usually surrounded by a masonry wall or double fence with gun towers, electronic sensors, and bright lighting.

Medium-security correctional centers Facilities in which the most intensive correctional or rehabilitation efforts are conducted. The primary consideration is security, however, and many centers have the same features as maximum-security facilities (i.e., gun towers, masonry walls, and electronic sensors).

Mens rea The "guilty mind" or criminal intent required for an accused person to be held responsible for criminal actions; the state of mind at the time a crime occurs.

Mental illness A wide range of complicated emotional disorders that may involve physical, mental, or behavioral disturbances.

Merchant (or peddler) An inmate who exploits fellow prisoners by manipulation and trickery and who typically sells or trades goods in short supply.

Minimum-security correctional centers Range from large drug rehabilitation centers to small farms, road, and forestry campuses in rural America; inmates are considered nonviolent and low risk for escape.

Miranda warning Police officers are required to inform suspects under arrest of their constitutional rights to remain silent, to be represented by counsel, and to be provided with a lawyer if they cannot afford one.

Misdemeanor A less serious crime punishable by a fine or by a period of incarceration of up to one year in a city or county jail.

Motor vehicle theft Theft or attempted theft of a vehicle for nontemporary use.

"No paper" action A prosecutor dismisses a case after deciding there is insufficient probability of a conviction and therefore no need to file an information.

Nolle prosequi Latin for "I refuse to prosecute." Refers to the discretionary authority of the state prosecutor to refuse to file a charge against an accused person, even though the evidence might support such a charge.

Nolo contendere   Latin for "I will not contest it." A plea in a criminal action that has the same legal effect as a plea of guilty with respect to all proceedings on the indictment on which the defendant may be sentenced. A plea of *nolo contendere,* however, may spare the defendant from certain civil penalties that might follow a plea of guilty.

Occasional property offender   Has a criminal record consisting of a single offense or a few property offenses; commits crimes which show little sophistication or planning; and crime is a minor part of offender's life-style.

Ombudsman   An official or semiofficial office to which people may come with grievances against the government. The ombudsman stands between the citizen and government and represents the citizen.

Opening statement   In an opening statement to the jury at the start of a trial, the lawyers for each side explain the version of the facts best supporting their side of the case, how these facts will be proved, and how they think the law applies to the case.

Ordinary career criminal   Crime represents a major part of the life-style of this offender; he or she typically progresses from petty to more serious offenses, and makes all or most of his or her living from crimes that include burglary, larceny, and robbery.

Organized crime   A business that provides illegal, but desired, goods and services for the noncriminal public.

Orthomolecular psychiatry   Doctrine based on the belief that various kinds of deviant behavior, including delinquent and criminal activity, are systematically related to abnormal reaction rates in the body as a result of constitutional defects, faulty diet, and abnormal concentrations of essential elements.

Parens patriae   Latin for "father of his country"; a doctrine specifying that the juvenile court treat youngsters as if it were a "kind and loving parent."

Parole   Supervision of an offender in the community before expiration of his or her sentence. If parole conditions are violated, parole may be revoked and the offender may be returned to the institution for the remainder of the sentence.

Part two offenses (FBI *Uniform Crime Reports)*   Comprises 21 categories of crime that range from curfew and loitering law violations to fraud, embezzlement, and forgery. These offense categories, together with the eight Crime Index offenses, make up the crimes known to the police reported annually in the FBI *Uniform Crime Reports.*

Participant-observer   An investigator gathers data on a phenomenon by studying it in its natural setting (e.g., a criminologist lives with a group of professional robbers in order to study the social factors affecting participation in armed robbery).

Patrol bureau   Component or division of a police department which deploys uniformed officers within the community to provide daily services and help prevent crimes.

Penal sanction   Criminal statutes must not only give citizens warning of what behavior to avoid, but must also give an indication of the penalties incurred by the commission of such acts in violation of the criminal law.

Pennsylvania system   A corrections system (begun ca. 1830) based on solitary confinement with bench labor in each inmate's cell.

Peremptory challenge   A challenge the prosecutor or defense counsel may use to reject prospective jurors without stating a cause for the rejection.

Pigeon drop   A con game in which one of two confederates approaches a prospective victim claiming to have found a lost wallet or purse containing money, offers to split the contents if the victim will deposit "earnest money" with the second confederate; following a switch, the two con operators disappear, leaving the victim with an envelope containing worthless scraps of paper.

Plea bargaining   The interaction of the prosecutor, defense counsel, and judge in negotiating a final charge and sentence without resorting to trial.

Political crime   Illegal acts against the government (e.g., treason, sedition, rebellion) or illegal acts committed by agents of government against individuals, groups, or the general public.

Polydrug user   Nonmedical drug user who regularly consumes drugs such as amphetamines or barbiturates in combination with heroin, cocaine, or alcohol.

Positivist School (of criminology)   An approach to criminology which denied that people are individually responsible for their criminal acts and sought the explanation for criminal behavior in biological, psychological, and social factors that affected the individual.

Power of discretion   The legal power inherent in the position of the prosecutor to decide whether or not to initiate criminal prosecution.

Preliminary hearing   Hearing in which the accused is advised of his or her constitutional rights and in which the judge determines if there is probable cause to bind the defendant over to an appropriate court for trial.

Preliminary investigation   The investigation generally performed by the first police officer on the scene of a crime. Includes caring for any injured person, apprehending the criminal if he or she is still in the immediate area, protecting the crime scene, and establishing communications with the police dispatcher to broadcast descriptions of wanted persons.

Presentence investigation   An investigation by a probation officer or court-appointed social worker into an offender's background and prospects for rehabilitation. This investigation produces a report and recommendations which are considered by a judge in a presentence hearing.

Presumptive sentencing   A method for determining punishment in which the legislature sets a standard sentence in the statute but the judge may vary that sentence if the case has aggravating or mitigating circumstances.

Pretrial motion   Motion made by the defense counsel to suppress the introduction at trial of incriminating evidence, alleging that the evidence was acquired illegally. Pretrial motions are often made to suppress evidence obtained by police in violation of the Fourth or Fifth Amendments.

Pretrial release   An individual charged with a crime may be released from custody while awaiting trial either on bail or on his or her own recognizance, that is, a written promise to appear for trial.

Primary deviance   Deviant behavior that has not materially affected a person's self-concept and social status.

Proactive beat   An area regularly patrolled by the police. Patrols are dispatched before citizens call for help.

Probable cause   Probable cause exists where the facts and circumstances would warrant a person of reasonable caution to believe that an offense was or is being committed.

Probation   A form of sentencing that allows the offender to remain free in the community under supervision and subject to conditions set by the court; violation of these conditions may lead to revocation.

Procedural law   Laws which fix the duties, establish rights and responsibilities among and for persons, are substantive laws; those which prescribe the manner in which such rights and responsibilities may be exercised and enforced in a court of law are procedural laws.

Professional criminal   Term applied to a small group of criminals who have the most highly developed criminal careers and the highest status and skill level among criminals.

Proscription   Statement of behavior that is forbidden (e.g., murder, rape, treason) and discouraged by the application of negative sanctions (punishment).

Prosecutor   An attorney (usually elected) in public office who presents the state's case against individuals charged with crimes against the state.

Public defender system   A publicly funded system with a staff of full-time attorneys available to defend indigent persons accused by the state of committing crimes.

Public-order offense   An illegal act in which the offender engages in behavior that is not markedly different from conventional behavior (e.g., gambling or public intoxication) and which differs from many other crimes only to the extent that it usually involves only the offender (see also *consensual crime* and *victimless crime*).

Quota system   A system requiring officers to write a specified number of traffic tickets in a given time period.

Radical criminology   An approach to crime based on the assumption that criminal law reflects the power of elite groups in society and is manifested by the use of the criminal justice system to maintain control of the production and distribution of wealth.

Rat (or squealer)   An inmate who betrays a fellow prisoner.

Reactive beat   An area that is not patrolled until a request comes in for police service.

Rebuttal   The introduction of rebutting evidence; arguments showing that statements of witnesses are not true; the stage of the trial at which rebutting evidence may be introduced.

Reception and classification centers   Facilities (usually maximum security) where most new prisoners are sent for observation, testing, interviewing, and eventual assignment to a state prison.

Recidivist   From the French *recidiver* ("to repeat"); a recidivist is an individual who shows commitment to criminality by repeated arrests and convictions.

Red-light district   In an earlier period of our history, referred to a section of a town or city where houses of prostitution were located and identified by a red light over the entrance.

Reformatory movement   A movement in American penology during the nineteenth and early twentieth centuries which emphasized vocational training, indeterminate sentencing, and the use of parole.

Rehabilitation   A rationale for the reformation of offenders based on the premise that human behavior is the result of antecedent causes that may be identified and controlled by objective analysis. The focus is on treatment of the offender, not punishment.

Reintegration   A philosophy of punishment that focuses on returning the offender to the community with restored education, employment, and family ties.

Release on recognizance (ROR)   The release of a defendant, by permission of the court, which permits the defendant to be at liberty upon his or her own agreement and without furnishing sureties for appearance at a pending trial.

Restitution   The repayment by a criminal, in money or services, of losses suffered by the victim or society as a result of the criminal's offense.

Retribution   A theory of punishment that maintains that an offender should be punished for the crimes he or she commits because he or she deserves the punishment.

Reverse discrimination   Within the context of police work, reverse discrimination involves allegations by white male officers that departmental affirmative action policies discriminate against them in assignments and promotions.

Right guy   An inmate loyal to fellow inmates who keeps his promises, minds his own business, does not discuss his own business, defends himself, and doesn't look for trouble.

Robbery   Theft or attempted theft by use of force, violence, or by putting the victim in fear.

Saturday night special   An inexpensive handgun, usually a .22 caliber revolver.

Secondary deviance   The probable result of the imposition of a deviant label; that an individual will be regarded as a deviant, will participate in deviant activities and groups, and will adopt a deviant self-identity.

Selective traffic enforcement   The direction of enforcement efforts to areas experiencing the most traffic accidents. Such areas are monitored closely during peak accident periods.

Self-report studies   Attempts to measure delinquency or crime by interviewing a cross section of the population about their involvement as offenders in delinquent or criminal behavior.

Sentenced offender facility   A facility where convicted persons serve their sentences.

Serial murderer   A murderer who kills a number of people over a period of time, usually in more than one location.

Sex offenders   Persons arrested for indecent exposure, window peeping, child molestation, and rape.

Shakedown   A thorough search of a jail or prison for contraband.

Shock parole (probation)   System in which an offender is imprisoned for a brief period of time (to acquaint him or her with the rigors of incarceration), after which he or she is released under community supervision.

Social control theory   An explanation of criminal behavior which focuses on the control mechanisms, techniques, and strategies for regulating human behavior and argues that deviance occurs when social controls are weakened or break down, resulting in lack of motivation to conform to social norms.

Social pathology   A criminological approach based on the organic analogy, according to which social institutions were seen as related to one another in the same way as organs of the body; crime, therefore, was viewed as a symptom of disturbance or illness within society.

Sottocapo **(underboss)**   The underboss in an LCN syndicated crime family occupies a position comparable to that of a vice-president who relays orders and instructions from the boss.

Special prisoners   Jail prisoners who require special care and attention; generally includes alcoholics, diabetics, epileptics, the mentally ill, suicidal persons, drug addicts, and sex offenders.

Stare decisis   Latin for "let the decision stand." Means that court decisions on points of law are binding on future cases that are essentially the same (i.e., those future cases in which the totality of circumstances does not vary from the original case).

Status offense   The violation of a statute that applies only to juveniles and that has no counterpart in the adult criminal code (e.g., truancy, running away from home, "incorrigibility").

Statutory rape   Unlawful sexual intercourse with a female under the age of consent (16, 17, or 18 years of age, depending on the state) with or without her consent.

Streetwalker   Prostitute who makes contacts by soliciting customers on the street.

Street wisdom   Knowledge gained primarily from working the streets as a law enforcement officer.

Strict liability offense   Established by statute which imposes criminal sanction for an unlawful act without requiring a showing of criminal intent.

Study release   Correctional program which allows for the conditional release of the offender from confinement in order to pursue a course of instruction in an educational or vocational training program, but may require return to confinement overnight and on weekends.

Summation   Each lawyer's presentation of a review of the evidence at the close of the trial.

Superior court   A court of general original jurisdiction in the first instance and which exercises a control or supervision over a system of lower courts, either by appeal, error, or *certiorari*.

Tagging Term used by one of the early precursors (Tannenbaum) of the labeling perspective to describe how community reactions shift from the definition of a person's acts as deviant to the definition of the person himself or herself as deviant.

Team policing A system that combines all line functions (patrol, traffic, and investigation) into a single unit comprised of teams under common supervision.

Token economy A method of reinforcement often used in institutional settings. People are rewarded for constructive social behavior with tokens that can be exchanged for desired objects or activities.

Torch Term used in law enforcement circles to refer to a professional arsonist.

Traffic bureau Division or component of a police department which handles traffic control, accident investigation, and traffic law enforcement.

Trial court Generic term for courts where civil actions or criminal proceedings are first commenced at the state level (variously called municipal, circuit, district, or county courts).

True bill In criminal practice, the endorsement made by a grand jury upon a bill of indictment when they find it sufficient evidence to warrant a criminal charge.

Twin study Research study in which an attempt is made to control for heredity by examining developments in identical (monozygotic) twins separated shortly following birth and reared apart.

Venture A group of criminals who come together for a brief period in order to perpetrate a single offense.

Verdict The formal finding or decision made by a jury, reported to the court, and accepted by the court.

Victimless crime Illegal acts between consenting adults (e.g., prostitution, gambling) that are presumed not to cause any direct harm, loss, or injury to anyone and in which there is no "victim" in the ordinary sense (as there is in robbery or burglary) (see also *white-collar crime*).

Victimology A growing body of fact and theory reflecting the systematic study of crime victims, their relationship with criminals, and programs intended for victim assistance and reparation.

Victim precipitation The direct, immediate, and positive contribution of the victim to an occurrence of a crime. The term is used primarily to refer to crimes against the person (homicide, rape, and assault).

Violent predator A category of individual identified in research on criminal careers comprising individuals with a lengthy history of commitment to state juvenile institutions, unstable work histories, costly and intensive drug use, and a predisposition toward the use of violence in the commission of crimes.

Voir dire French for "to speak the truth." Refers to the examination of prospective jurors by the prosecutor, defense attorney, and (sometimes) the court to determine their fitness to serve as jurors in a trial and to eliminate persons who would not be impartial. Also refers to the questioning of a witness to ascertain potential bias or, in the case of an expert witness, to determine qualifications and competence.

Voyeurism ("peeping") Type of sexual deviation in which sexual gratification is obtained by observing a nude person or some part of the nude person's body without consent of the person involved.

Waiver of prosecution A desire on the part of a crime victim to have the state not prosecute the assailant.

Warrant A legal document, issued by a court, that authorizes specific acts by law enforcement officers (e.g., the arrest of a person named in the warrant or the search of a specific place).

White-collar crime Originally used to designate offenses committed by "a person of respectability and high social status in the course of his occupation" (Sutherland, 1949). The term is now being replaced by more specific titles—economic crime, occupational crime, and corporate crime (see also *economic crime*).

Wolf (or fag) An inmate unable to endure prolonged deprivation of heterosexual relationships who consequently enters into homosexual activity. The wolf plays the active role and the fag the passive role.

Work release Conditional release from prison to work in the community. Persons on work release may reside at a facility within the community or they may commute from the prison to their work site.

XXY syndrome A chromosomal abnormality in males (the presence of an extra Y chromosome) that was once thought to be related to sexually aggressive behavior.

Youth corrections centers Facilities designed to house youthful offenders (ages 16 to 30 years); built to provide medium to minimum security.

NAME INDEX

SUBJECT INDEX

587